ASPEN PUBLISHERS

Rigos Bar Review Series™

Uniform Multistate Essay Exam (MEE) Review
(Course 5328)

Wolters Kluwer

Law & Business

AUSTIN   BOSTON   CHICAGO   NEW YORK   THE NETHERLANDS

James J. Rigos
230 Skinner Building
1326 Fifth Avenue
Seattle, WA 98101
Telephone: (206) 624-0716
Fax: (206) 624-0731
rigos@rigos.net

To contact Aspen Publishers' Customer Care, e-mail customer.care@
aspenpublishers.com, call 1-800-234-1660, fax 1-800-901-9075,
or mail correspondence to:

Aspen Publishers
Attn: Order Department
PO Box 990
Frederick, MD 21705

Printed in the United States of America.

1 2 3 4 5 6 7 8 9 0

ISBN 978-07355-8970-4

This book is intended as a general review of a legal subject. It is not intended as
a source for advice for the solution of legal matters or problems. For advice on
legal matters, the reader should consult an attorney.

Magic Memory Outlines® is a registered trademark owned by Rigos Professional
Education Programs, Ltd.

About Wolters Kluwer Law & Business

Wolters Kluwer Law & Business is a leading provider of research information and workflow solutions in key specialty areas. The strengths of the individual brands of Aspen Publishers, CCH, Kluwer Law International and Loislaw are aligned within Wolters Kluwer Law & Business to provide comprehensive, in-depth solutions and expert-authored content for the legal, professional and education markets.

CCH was founded in 1913 and has served more than four generations of business professionals and their clients. The CCH products in the Wolters Kluwer Law & Business group are highly regarded electronic and print resources for legal, securities, antitrust and trade regulation, government contracting, banking, pension, payroll, employment and labor, and healthcare reimbursement and compliance professionals.

Aspen Publishers is a leading information provider for attorneys, business professionals and law students. Written by preeminent authorities, Aspen products offer analytical and practical information in a range of specialty practice areas from securities law and intellectual property to mergers and acquisitions and pension/benefits. Aspen's trusted legal education resources provide professors and students with high-quality, up-to-date and effective resources for successful instruction and study in all areas of the law.

Kluwer Law International supplies the global business community with comprehensive English-language international legal information. Legal practitioners, corporate counsel and business executives around the world rely on the Kluwer Law International journals, loose-leafs, books and electronic products for authoritative information in many areas of international legal practice.

Loislaw is a premier provider of digitized legal content to small law firm practitioners of various specializations. Loislaw provides attorneys with the ability to quickly and efficiently find the necessary legal information they need, when and where they need it, by facilitating access to primary law as well as state-specific law, records, forms and treatises.

Wolters Kluwer Law & Business, a unit of Wolters Kluwer, is headquartered in New York and Riverwoods, Illinois. Wolters Kluwer is a leading multinational publisher and information services company.

Welcome

Welcome to the Rigos Bar Review Series Multistate Essay Exam (MEE) self-study review course. This comprehensive review course is all you need to pass the United States MEE administered by the National Conference of Bar Examiners (NCBE) offered in a growing number of jurisdictions. Please begin by carefully reading the introductory portion of this text. It contains valuable information about the MEE exam and provides insights into the subjective essay questions. The orientation also serves as your planning session and roadmap for successfully passing the MEE.

Editorial Direction

James J. Rigos is an Attorney-CPA and a graduate of Boston University Law School. He is Editor-in-Chief of the creating team of this Bar Review Series. He has written and lectured for professional associations and bar and CPA exam review programs for more than 30 years. Over 100,000 students have used the Rigos courses to pass their professional entrance exams. He is active in and for many years has served as a national Director of the American Association of Attorney-CPAs. He has also created a series of CLE and CPE courses focusing on professional ethics.

Acknowledgments

This work product was substantially enriched because of the robust encouragement and editorial involvement of many thoughtful individuals. Laura Colberg, Matt Conrad, Tracy Duany, Lisa Goldoftas, Leah Golshani, Steve Johnson, Gina Lowe, Laura McCabe, Carolyn Plant, Aaron Rocke, Joanna Roth, Tom Smith, Kevin Stemp, Jason Stonefeld, Sidney Tribe, and Tracy Wood made significant drafting contributions. Law school Professors Janet Ainsworth, Jim Bond, Mark Chinen, David DeWolf, Sam Donaldson, Christian Halliburton, Gregory Hicks, Tom Lininger, John Parry, Chris Rigos, and Karl Tegland made important suggestions on substantive improvements and reviewed the Rigos Bar Review Series textbooks. A special thanks to our past students for their many suggestions of substantive improvement and creative new learning aids. Their recommendations and successes are a part of every page of this Rigos Bar Review Series. The direction and guidance of Steve Errick's Boston editorial team (especially Megan Ablondi, Melody Davies, Barbara Lasoff, Carol McGeehan, and Dana Wilson) from Aspen Publishers brought this all to fruition.

RIGOS BAR REVIEW SERIES

AFFILIATED WITH ASPEN PUBLISHERS – EMANUEL LAW OUTLINES

UNIFORM MULTISTATE ESSAY EXAM (MEE) REVIEW

SECOND EDITION

Table of Contents

Chapter	Subject	Page
	Introduction and Success on the MEE	1
1	Business Associations	1-25
2	Conflict of Laws	2-125
3	Family Law	3-163
4	Federal Civil Procedure	4-199
5	Trusts, Wills, and Estates	5-265
6	UCC Article 3 – Commercial Paper	6-323
7	UCC Article 9 – Secured Transactions	7-369
8	ABA Professional Responsibility Rules	8-415
9	Common Law Contracts and UCC Sales	9-481
10	Torts	10-505
11	Real Property and Future Interests	11-529
12	Evidence	12-553
13	Constitutional Law	13-573
14	Criminal Law and Procedure	14-595
15	Acronyms and Mnemonics	15-621
	Index	643
	User Survey and Critique	659

PRACTICE MAKES PERFECT

DESIRE MORE HANDS-ON GUIDANCE IN PERFECTING YOUR BAR ESSAY SKILLS?

Rigos Bar Review offers an extra online Essay Grading service. Our answer approach and recommended presentation format is based upon the traditional NCBE 30-minute, 5 or 6-issue, medium-depth in analysis question which is the most frequent format followed. If your state differs substantially, we try to customize our essay writing program to your individual state essay characteristics. This includes the tradeoff between the number of issues and depth of analysis. The Rigos grading program includes:

- Start with 2 questions tailored after the NCBE's Uniform Essay Exam to assess our helpfulness and benefits. If helpful, try 5 additional questions or a full 14 all subject coverage. We focus on the 30-minute usual 4 to 6 issue NCBE style of essay questions containing the typical number of issues and required depth of analysis.

- Submit your answer electronically to our grading team who are recent Rigos students who performed well in our Essay review program.

- We will grade your essay work product, provide a detailed grading guide / pointer sheet summary and preferable model sample answer. Included in our guidance are specific tips and suggestions for your answers.

- Our advice covers how you can improve both your substantive answer and presentation skills.

- You may correct and resubmit your improved answer for a second review. By incorporating our suggestions, you learn from your mistakes. This is the technique that turns a good answer into a great answer, and provides you with your own self-created model for pre-exam review.

- Telephone and/or email one-on-one student / grader-tutor discussion sessions may be scheduled after you have completed five essay questions. At this point, we will have sufficient information to further focus on improving your individual essay writing style and analytical skills.

Register at http://www.rigos.net/new/Essaygrading.asp.

PRACTICE MAKES PERFECT AND RIGOS MAKES PRACTICE EASY

Uniform Multistate Essay Exam (MEE) Review
(Course 5328)

RIGOS BAR REVIEW SERIES

UNIFORM MULTISTATE ESSAY EXAM (MEE) REVIEW

INTRODUCTION AND SUCCESS ON THE MEE

Table of Contents

I. **OVERVIEW** 3
    A. Welcome and Introduction ....
    B. Positive Mental Attitude ....
    C. Learning Material ....

II. **ESSAY PORTION OF NCBE UNIFORM BAR EXAMINATION** 3
    A. MEE Structure..
        1. Essays Only..
        2. Substantive Portion ....
        3. Purpose of the MEE...
        4. Topics ....
        5. Testing Distribution ....
        6. Instructions..
    B. About the Exam Questions ....
        1. NCBE Committee..
        2. Combination Questions ....
        3. Identifying Broad Topic Areas..
        4. Issues to be Discussed ....
    C. Grading Process ....
        1. Grading by Local Board of Law / Bar Examiners..
        2. Qualitative Factors ....
        3. Requirement Format ....
        4. Scoring ....
            a. Issue Weight ....
            b. Low Score ....
            c. High Score ....
        5. Grades Submitted Timely ....
        6. Candidate Notification...

III. **YOUR PERSONAL PREPARATION PROGRAM** 6
    A. Organized Approach...
        1. Preview..
        2. Learning Session..
        3. Create Your Magic Memory Outlines ....
        4. Work Through Questions and Answers..
        5. Practice Makes Perfect ....
    B. Necessary Time Commitment ....
    C. Computers v. Handwriting..
        1. Usual Procedure..
        2. Laptop Advantage...
        3. Laptop Disadvantage ....
        4. Practice in Your Chosen Format..
        5. Handwriting and Correcting..
    D. A Few Study Tips ....
        1. 180 Minute Time Blocks ....
        2. Buddy System...
        3. Alternate Study Topics ....
        4. Your Own Study Place ....
        5. Review Personal and Professional Commitments ....

    E. Motivational and Inspirational Tools ....

    F. A Sound Mind in a Sound Body ....

IV.   **EXAM DAYS' PROCEDURES**   **8**

    A. Be Punctual...

       1. Transportation ....

       2. Check In...

    B. Exam Procedures ....

V.   **ESSAY WRITING STRATEGIES**   **9**

    A. Overview..

       1. Language as a Tool ....

       2. Bar Exam Focus ....

       3. Objective...

       4. Clear, Concise, and Vigorous Writing..

    B. Watch Time and Answer Length ....

       1. Question Set...

       2. Time Allocation Strategy ....

       3. Keep Writing Until the End ....

       4. The Fine Art of Punting ....

VI.   **ANSWERING THE QUESTION**   **14**

    A. Overall Organization and Presentation ....

       1. Same Coverage as Grading Guide..

       2. Develop a Standard Writing System ....

       3. State the Obvious ....

       4. Use a Modified IRAC Presentation Format ....

       5. Avoid a Mere "Brain Dump"...

       6. Use a Logical Sequence ....

       7. Technique to Fill Up Pages ....

    B. Powerful 6-Step Approach to Analyzing and Writing an Exam Question.....................

       1. Determine Your Answer Sequence ....

       2. Identify the Requirements and Spot the Issues ....

          a. Focus on the Call...

          b. Read and Study the Facts..

       3. Plan Answer Organization ....

          a. Essay Planning and Outlining...

          b. Organize Your Approach to Follow the Facts ....

          c. Chronological Order ....

          d. Scrutinize Details...

       4. Analyze Elements of Each Cause of Action ....

          a. Required Elements to Make P's Prima Facie Case....................................

          b. Possible Defenses...

          c. Rebuttal Argument...

          d. Short Conclusion to Issue ....

          e. Counterclaims ....

       5. Answer the Question ....

       6. Final review of Question and Your Answer...

VII.   **RIGOS BAR REVIEW SERIES WRITING PROGRAM DOs AND DON'Ts**   **19**

VIII. **MEE SUBJECT DISTRIBUTION HISTORY**   **22**

IX.   **STUDENT PREPARATION PLANNING SCHEDULE AND**
          WEEKLY AND HOURLY TIME ALLOCATION   **23**

RIGOS BAR REVIEW SERIES

UNIFORM MULTISTATE ESSAY EXAM (MEE) REVIEW

INTRODUCTION AND SUCCESS ON THE MEE

I. OVERVIEW: PREPARING FOR AND TAKING THE MEE EXAM

A. Welcome and Introduction

Welcome to Rigos Bar Review Series. The Rigos program contains everything you need to pass the Multistate Essay Exam at the first sitting. We offer both live classes and self-study programs. The information in this preface will be very useful to the success of your preparation.

B. Positive Mental Attitude

What the mind can conceive, hard work can achieve. You must believe you can and will pass the bar exam and become a successful attorney. Rigos has over 100,000 professional alumni, so your objective of passing the exam is attainable. Exam confidence is the result of a well-organized and well-executed "seamless process" review program. Our program will prepare you to pass your bar exam.

C. Learning Material

Most jurisdictions require essays to evaluate a candidate's competency to practice law.

1. Format: The text is written in a lecture format, and may either be used in a review class structure or organized self-study format. Magic Memory Outlines® should be used to create individualized summary outlines. See details *infra*.

2. Practice Writing Essays: You should stop at the end of every chapter and practice writing essay answers. Essay answer creation will reinforce the text and test your knowledge and understanding of the subject. Following each chapter, we present a selection of realistic NCBE style subject essay questions and passing answers prepared by our editors. We also provide state-specific volumes for those states that test subjects beyond the NCBE. You should write all of the questions to gain practice and reinforce the legal concepts tested. Correct your omissions and mistakes with a red pencil to highlight items you need to review again prior to the exam.

II. ESSAY PORTION OF NCBE UNIFORM BAR EXAMINATION

A. MEE Structure

1. Essays Only: All jurisdictions test a bar candidate's written communication skills. A state Board of Law / Bar Examiners may prepare their own essays and grading guides, or subscribe to the multistate essay service of the National Conference of Bar Examiners (NCBE). Many states do both. The NCBE offers nine questions twice a year composed of a fact pattern three to five paragraphs long followed by two to four single-sentence questions. The actual exam is administered and graded by the local State Board of Law / Bar Examiners. There are no multiple-choice or other objective questions in this MEE section, only subjective essays.

2. Substantive Portion: You will have three hours to answer six questions on the MEE, so the average time per question is thirty (30) minutes. You must decide the order in which you will answer the questions. Answer booklets are provided. Answer only one question in each answer booklet.

3. Purpose of the MEE: The examiners have carefully crafted each exam essay question to assess your ability to (a) identify legal issues raised by a hypothetical fact pattern; (b) separate relevant material from irrelevant; (c) present a well-reasoned analysis of relevant issues in a clear, concise, and well-organized way, and (d) demonstrate your understanding of the fundamental legal principles relevant to solving the issues in the fact pattern.

4. Topics: There are ten NCBE subjects: agency and partnership, commercial paper, conflicts of law, corporations and LLC, decedents' estate, family law, federal civil procedure, sales, secured transactions, and trusts and future interests. The Rigos text covers all of the necessary subject matter of these subjects. Questions may include issues from more than one area of law. The NCBE has recently began to offer essays covering the six MBE topics. The Rigos Bar Review Series – MBE Third Edition volumes should be used as text in conjunction with the subject's practice essay questions contained in this MEE volume. This book also covers Professional Responsibility, which is tested in many states by essays as well as in the MPRE during law school.

5. Testing Distribution: Every chapter of this guide begins with the subject frequency distribution for the last 19 MEE exams available, an opening argument, and list of most frequently tested primary issues.

6. Instructions: Your exam instructions may differ, but each question packet on the 2009 exams instructed the following:

"Do not break the seal on this booklet until you are told to begin. Each question is designed to be answered in 30 minutes. There will be no break once the formal testing session begins. You may answer the questions in any order you wish. Do not answer more than one question in each answer booklet. If you make a mistake or wish to revise your answer, simply draw a line through the material you wish to delete. If you are using a laptop computer to answer the questions, your jurisdiction will provide you with specific instructions to follow. Read each fact situation very carefully and do not assume facts that are not given in the question. Do not assume that each question covers only a single area of the law; some of the questions may cover more than one of the areas you are responsible for knowing. Demonstrate your ability to reason and analyze. Each of your answers should show an understanding of the facts, a recognition of the issues included, a knowledge of the applicable principles of law, and the reasoning by which you arrive at your conclusion. The value of your answer depends not as much upon your conclusions as upon the presence and quality of the elements mentioned above. Clarity and conciseness are important, but make your answer complete. Do not volunteer irrelevant or immaterial information. Your jurisdiction may instruct you to answer MEE questions according to the law of the jurisdiction. Absent such an instruction, you should answer the questions by applying fundamental legal principles rather than local case or local statutory law."

B. About the Exam Questions

1. NCBE Committees: The NCBE has committees that cover each of the above subjects. Each committee handles all aspects of writing the subjective essay question and related grading guide-pointer sheets preparation. Nine questions are created and distributed. The individual state decides how many and which questions to use on a particular exam. Since 2007, the MEE has been expanded to include three essays covering the six MBE subjects.

2. Combination Questions: Crossover questions are possible and not infrequent. Frequent combinations include conflict of laws-civil procedure, family law-jointly owned property, decedents' estates-trusts, and agency-partnership. A lawyer's professional responsibility may be combined with other subjects.

3. Identifying Broad Topic Areas: Essay questions are not labeled by topic, but merely by numbers. You will learn from taking practice exams that you must always read the call of the question to confirm in which forest you'll be identifying the trees. For example, a Criminal Law question may contain aspects that resemble a Criminal Procedure, Evidence, or even a Torts question.

4. Issues to be Discussed: The question's author must detail the most significant key issues fairly raised by the facts and requirements. This is formalized in a key word answer pointer sheet of the law ("grading guide") that is expected to be demonstrated in competent answers. Every sentence in the facts usually raises an issue; there are no red herrings.

a. Not Subtle: This requirement ensures that the issues are usually straight forward (relative to law school) with very few hidden tricks and little subtlety.

b. Objective: An equal depth and degree of difficulty of the issues to be rewarded is intended to ensure fairness in the grading process.

c. Relative Weight: Every question usually counts the same. This suggests a balanced approach and the necessity to achieve a defensive score on every question.

d. Quality Control: A seasoned NCBE review panel critically edits every word of each new question to eliminate possible ambiguity and misinterpretation. The testing standard is the knowledge level required of a new associate in a law firm.

C. Grading Process

1. Grading by Local Board of Law / Bar Examiners: Some states hire full-time graders while others rely on volunteers. In most jurisdictions, graders read the first 50 answers to gain a thorough knowledge and establish answer grading standards. This occurs before the actual grading begins. The grader is directed to read every word of your essay. The grader accomplishes a consistent, even grading level by going back and occasionally reviewing the best and worst answers. Graders read many essays a day, so your objective is to make your discussion interesting and easy for the grader to award the maximum points.

2. Qualitative Factors: Grammar, syntax, and legibility do count a little. While outlines may be accepted in some jurisdictions, most essay graders do react favorably to full articulate sentences.

3. Requirement Format: Some instructions are outcome oriented such as "who will prevail?" More frequently, the call of the question has specific directed multiple sub-parts requiring sharply focused answers. Aim for a 5 or 6 paragraph answer per question.

4. Scoring: The NCBE provides the jurisdiction with a pointer sheet and grading guide. In many states, graders are allowed to award points for other issues and/or local law.

a. Issue Weight: Half point grading increments are usual. Three to five of the issues are given double weight which requires expanded analysis and argument.

b. Low Score: In many jurisdictions the graders have to justify a score of 4 or under with a narrative description of the candidate's inadequacy. Thus there are few very low scores given if a thorough display of relevant vocabulary is demonstrated in a complete answer.

c. High Scores: There are very few 10s or 9.5 scores awarded, however. The average score is probably between 7 and 8. To pass the MEE portion usually requires an average score of 7 on each question or 42 out of 60 points.

5. Grades Submitted Timely: Graders must submit grades to the local Board of Law/Bar Examiners on a timely basis, within the deadline set by the particular jurisdiction.

6. Candidate Notification: Most jurisdictions send the grades to candidates approximately 2 to 3 months after the exam. Your score is often not revealed if you pass. Failing scores usually allow the candidates to request that their actual answers be returned accompanied by the state's model answers. Most states do supply model answers.

III. YOUR PERSONAL PREPARATION PROGRAM

A. <u>Organized Approach</u>

Your preparation program must be well-organized to maximize the efficacy and efficiency of your effort. You must cover all parts of the exam – MBE, MPT, and the essays the MEE and/or your local Board of Law / Bar Examiners require – in an organized paced program. Use the overall preparation planning and weekly calendar on page 23 and 24 to organize and schedule your study time. You must master every subject. Study defensively by spending more time on your weak areas.

1. Preview: Prior to your learning session, get acquainted with the major topics, their subparts and vocabularies. Become familiar with your Magic Memory Outlines®, topic distribution charts, and primary issues statements that are frequently tested.

2. Learning Session: This may be live, over the internet, or on your own in intense reading sessions. Concentrate on both the legal issues presented and the sequencing of the rules.

3. Create Your Magic Memory Outlines®: Create your own Magic Memory Outlines® with our Word software templates. Be concise: your outline should be a summary that captures the essence of the black letter law and Rigos Tips. Well-crafted outlines, once memorized, will serve as your primary substantive knowledge base.

4. Work Through Questions and Answers: Merely learning the law is not enough without practicing writing answers to essay questions. Our editors present a variety of NCBE-style questions and answers covering the 14 MEE tested subjects. Consider adding ours or a local writing program to provide more questions and detailed improvement suggestions.

a. Fact Focus: Every sentence in the facts is usually written to raise one or more issues. Missing issues is the major reason candidates do poorly on the MEE. Analyze the fact clusters carefully and appreciate the issue-by-issue consequences of each significant fact.

b. Examples: In a contracts question, "A and B agree" raises potential issues of offer, acceptance, statute of frauds, and whether the contract is unilateral or bilateral. Similarly, "Seller delivers non-conforming goods" raises issues of perfect tender, breach of warranty, buyer may accept none, some, or all, "cover" remedy, and incidental and consequential damages.

c. **Practice Fact – Issue Spotting:** It helps to analyze examiners' favorite fact patterns that raise important legal issues. The topic distribution charts and primary issue lists under each subject focus on the most important law the facts raise. Try creating your own exam fact scenarios containing frequently tested clusters of facts.

5. Practice Makes Perfect: Practice as many essay questions as you can. Check your answers, but take style and format into account. Consider rewriting poor answers and subscribing to the optional Rigos essay assistance program. Learning from your mistakes will develop your knowledge and confidence.

B. Necessary Time Commitment

To pass, candidates must realize that a significant time commitment is necessary.

1. Quantitative Measures: Most successful first-time bar candidates' learning and studying effort is 400 to 600 hours for all sections of the bar exam. Candidates who have been away from academia for long periods or whose grades were not so strong will find more time is required. Please do not underestimate the effort required to pass this exam.

2. Serious, Focused Program: Superficial or spotty knowledge is not adequate and your analysis must be focused. As a result, one must be ready to commit to a serious, focused, structured review program. Prepare defensively. Start early to spread the required time over a longer period. Use our Weekly Planning Sheet to get organized. If there is any question whether you can devote the necessary time, we recommend you postpone preparation until you can make it a priority. Do it right the first time. The bar exam is not a challenge to be undertaken lightly.

C. Computers v. Handwriting

In most jurisdictions, you may either handwrite or type your answers on your laptop using approved software. It has often been said that typed answers make a good answer seem better and a bad answer seem worse. Still, it is your choice.

1. Usual Procedure: Typically, you must download the Board of Law / Bar Examiners approved exam edition of the software even if you used the same or similar testing software in law school. The software will disable all other programs on your laptop while you are using it. More information is available at your Board of Law / Bar Examiners and you should inquire early. Laptop users are usually placed in a separate room from hand writers.

2. Laptop Advantage: Usually more words can be written in less time leaving more time to think and organize. Note the character limitation imposed by your local jurisdiction. Spell check is not available on most approved software, but cut and paste usually is. This allows you to rearrange issues to where they more logically belong. Typed answers are easier to read, if your typing is accurate. Also, typing may be physically more comfortable.

3. Laptop Disadvantage: Computers can malfunction and power may fail. The Examiners will typically disclaim any responsibility. Mistakes and spelling errors are more apparent when typing. If you elect to type, be sure to bring along some pens just in case.

4. Practice in Your Chosen Format: You should choose the method that will be the most comfortable and least distracting to you. All things being equal, typing seems preferable, especially if you typed your exams in law school. If you are uncomfortable with typing or don't have a dependable laptop to practice with and use in the exam, you may elect to handwrite. If you are going to use a laptop for the exam, use this method for all of your practice answers.

5. Handwriting and Correcting: If you hand write, get an easy-flowing black ink pen and don't press hard. Some jurisdictions provide mandatory writing instruments. If not, find your favorite smooth-writing large barrel black ink pen. The ink should flow easily. White-out strips are preferable to liquid White-out or crossing out words. Avoid strain on your fingers, hand, shoulders, and neck muscles by pausing to stretch between questions.

D. A Few Study Tips

1. 180-Minute Time Blocks: Study in 3-hour time blocks to get used to intense concentration for this full time period without a break. This is the required time block the MBE sessions and usually for the MEE sessions. You may need to work up to this length.

2. Buddy System: If you used a study group in law school, you may want to consider cross-critiquing your buddy's essay answers. Two people is often best, beyond four people is cumbersome. All members of the group must create their own Magic Memory Outlines®.

3. Alternate Study Topics: By varying the subjects of study, most students find they can concentrate for longer periods of time.

4. Your Own Study Place: Some candidates find that concentration and efficiency are improved by a new study place. Turn off your phone. Use a bright light and a firm chair.

5. Review Personal and Professional Commitments: The most precious commodity a serious candidate has is time. Review and prioritize your commitments, and do not volunteer for new assignments. Defer optional professional and social activities. Short-term sacrifices will lead to long-term benefits. Tell your friends that between now and the exam, they will see less of you while you prepare for the exam.

E. Motivational and Inspirational Tools

You must approach your review with enthusiasm, persistence, sincerity, determination, and self-discipline. This exam is your stepping stone to professional recognition.

F. A Sound Mind in a Sound Body

Take care of your body and your health. Get plenty of sleep so you can concentrate at your highest level. Three square meals a day will keep your energy level high; avoid junk food and get regular exercise. Moderation is the rule during the review program.

IV. EXAM DAYS' PROCEDURES

A. Be Punctual

Plan to arrive at the exam site significantly before the scheduled starting time.

1. Transportation: Consider staying at a hotel near the exam location. Avoid hurrying or arriving late because it is disconcerting and may adversely affect your composure.

2. Check in: When you check in at the registrar's desk, you will be assigned a seat and confidential candidate number. If your assignment is in an uncomfortable location, you may usually ask the proctors to re-assign you before the exam begins.

B. Exam Procedures

1. Relax and Contemplate: Consciously try to relax; use deep, slow breathing. Don't listen to the pre-exam chatter of the other candidates. It is too late to add anything to your knowledge; this distraction will only confuse and drain you. If their nervousness is bothering you, take a little walk. Make a commitment to yourself not to leave any exam set early.

2. Follow Instructions: Listen closely to the proctors' instructions. Do not open the question booklet covers or write notes on any paper until told to begin. Read carefully the announcement schedule and all instructions on each question set.

3. Confidence and Poise: Approach the exams with confidence and poise. Don't get discouraged or leave early. You are there to pass.

4. Preserve Your Mental Energy: Get a full night's sleep. Take at least one short stretch break per exam set. Fight to focus on your writing style and memory power.

5. Focus on the Task: During the exam, the only thing that matters is your superior essay answering performance. Personal problems must be left outside the exam room. Don't day dream or allow your thoughts to wonder. Stay focused.

6. Time Management: You must manage your time to get through all the essays. You need to write enough to get at least a defensive score on every answer.

7. Go the Distance: Do not leave early. Fight to the end of every exam session. The difference between a pass and a fail is often only a few extra points. You never know for sure when you have crossed the finish line, so keep writing and improving your answers until the proctor says "time."

8. Breaks: Restroom breaks are on your own time and break your concentration. Avoid drinking too much coffee right before the start of the exam set.

V. ESSAY WRITING STRATEGIES

A. Overview

1. Language as a Tool: Language is an art as well as a tool in the task of writing an essay exam answer. For the MEE, it is a communication tool stripped down to its essential function of conveying focused written legal knowledge. Because of time and character limitations, relevant black letter law must be expressed economically. Use a direct and simple writing style with a vigorous approach, concise wording, and clarity in word choice.

2. Bar Exam Focus: As in law school, scoring points on the bar exam results from being able to spot the issues and developing a well-crafted legal analysis. The bar essay exam is not the place to show off your vocabulary or flowery prose. Demonstrate your compelling understanding and analysis of black letter law using correct and focused legal terminology. Word choice and clarity are critical because they promote readability.

3. Objective: Strive for a passing grade on every question. Remember that essay graders are production oriented and grade hundreds of answers. They are not casual readers. The grader's first impression is important, and a system of headings and subheadings help. If you are consistently methodical and organized, the grader will find it easy to give you maximum credit and keep their grading time to a minimum. Simple, step-by-step organization is the key to clear and concise writing. Follow three important structural rules:

a. One Issue per Paragraph: Every paragraph should clearly discuss a major issue of the subject. Present it in a logical, coherent sequence with a short introduction. You may underline for emphasis, but do not overuse this technique.

b. Short Sentences and Key Ideas: Each sentence should be short and arranged to support the key idea or issue in the paragraph. Cramming multiple rules into one sentence usually dilutes the overall issue scoring impact.

c. Brevity: Maximize working words and minimize glue words that add little to your writing (discussed further *infra*). If you type and there is a character limit, insert only one space after periods and other punctuation, and don't put in extra spaces before you hit "enter" to go to a new paragraph.

4. Clear, Concise, and Vigorous Writing: In addition to being methodical, aim to be clear, concise, and vigorous when writing your exam. Vigorous writing is interesting and fun to read. Clear writing ensures you get the maximum score your substance warrants. Your answer must analyze a lot of legal rules and your writing should be exciting, full of action, and a pleasure to read. A few grammatical principles will help.

a. Subject-Verb-Object Sentence Order: The Subject of the sentence (noun) is who or what does the action (Verb) to the Object. Example: *The attorney filed the complaint.* Here, the *attorney* is the subject who did the action, *filed* is the action (verb), to the object that received the action, *complaint.*

b. Concrete Nouns: Use definite, discrete wording for nouns to promote straightforward and clear sentences. Use concrete nouns and avoid protracted, abstract subject modifiers. Compare:

> *Draft:*   *The brief addressed the court of appeals decision-making process.*
> *Rewrite:*   *The brief addressed the decision-making process at the court of appeals.*

c. Strong Verbs: Verbs show what the subject is doing to the object. Strong verbs make your writing snap, crackle, and pop. They give vitality and force to a sentence. Use precise, vivid, and action-filled verbs. Avoid weak verbs such as "is/are," "was/were," "do," and "make." Many graders read for verbs when they first skim the essay answer. Strong verbs grab a grader's attention. In the examples below, the verb *prepared* became the derivative noun, *preparation*, and the verb *authorized* became the derivative noun *authorization*. By converting these nouns back to verbs, we create shorter and stronger sentences:

> *Draft:*   *Preparation of the bar exam student was dedicated.*
> *Rewrite:*   *The bar exam student prepared with dedication.*

> *Draft:*   *Authorization to change venue was granted by the trial court.*
> *Rewrite:*   *The trial court authorized the change of venue.*

Course 5328. Copyright by Rigos Bar Review Series – MEE.

d. Use Active Voice: With the active voice, the subject does the action. This gives the sentence life and vitality. The passive voice reverses the "Subject-Verb-Object" word order and usually is longer, because it adds a "to be" verb. When you see "am," "was," "were," or "is going to" before a verb, the sentence usually uses the passive voice. Weaker sentences convert verbs to adjectives or derivative nouns (e.g., the verb is "prepare"; the derivative noun is "preparation"). In the following sentences, compare verb use, directness, and economy.

> *Draft:*   *The claim was dismissed due to lack of jurisdiction by the court.*
> *Rewrite:*   *The court dismissed the claim for lack of jurisdiction.*

> *Draft:*   *It was held by the court that the defendant was liable for breaching the contract.*
> *Rewrite:*   *The court held the defendant breached the contract.*

> *Draft:*   *The drafting of the brief was done in an efficient manner by the attorney.*
> *Rewrite:*   *The attorney efficiently drafted the brief.*

e. Modifiers: Keep the clarity of your Subject-Verb-Object pattern and avoid confusing sentences. Necessary modifiers or modifying phrases should go next to the word or words they modify. Put subject modifiers in front of the subject and away from the verb. Verb modifiers may weaken the emphasis of a strong verb. If used, place them directly in front of the verb they modify. Also place object modifiers after the object. Placing modifiers in the wrong place can change the meaning of your sentence. Compare the meanings of these sentences:

> *Meaning 1:*   *The parties **almost** settled their entire case.*
> *Meaning 2:*   *The parties settled **almost** their entire case.*

> *Meaning 1:*   *The merchant shipped the goods the client ordered with **reasonable care**.*
> *Meaning 2:*   *The merchant used **reasonable care** shipping the goods the client ordered.*

f. Avoid Common Usage Mistakes: Some grammatical errors are legendary and immediately brand the writer as a lightweight. While all graders have their own personal list, the following are often included:

- **affect / effect:** "Affect" is a verb. "Effect" is a noun.
- **cite / site / sight:** "Cite" is to a quotation or reference; "site" is a location (including an internet site); "sight" is vision.
- **farther / further:** "Farther" refers to distance. "Further" refers to depth / detail.
- **i.e. / e.g.:** "I.e." is an explanation, definition, or clarification of what has just been said. "E.g." means "for example" and may be followed by an open-ended list or specific illustrations.
- **imply / infer:** Writers "imply." Readers, such as exam graders, "infer."
- **its / it's:** "Its" is a possessive pronoun just like "ours / hers / his." When "it's" has an apostrophe, it is always a contraction of "it is" (just as "don't" is a contraction of "do not"). If you're not sure which to use, just replace "it's" with "it is." If it's nonsensical, ditch the apostrophe.
- **judgment:** Do not write "judg<u>e</u>ment" with an "e." Laypersons use the "e"; lawyers do not.

- **lien / not lean:** A lien is an encumbrance on property. "Lean" is what you do against the wall.
- **Parol Evidence Rule:** NOT "parol_e_" unless you have been in prison.
- **principal / principle:** "Principal" of an agent or dollar amount. "Principle" of law, truth, or philosophy.
- **seisin / not season:** Title is of seisin, not a time of year.
- **seasonably / not seasonally:** "Seasonably" is used to mean "timely"; "seasonally" means relating to the time of year or season (e.g., winter or spring).
- **then / than:** "Then" refers to time ("now and then"). "Than" is a comparison term ("better than nothing").
- **there / their / they're:** "There" is location ("over there"); "their" is possessive ("their books"); "they're is the contraction for "they are."
- **which / that:** "Which" usually is preceded by a comma and is followed by a non-essential clause. "That" is not preceded by a comma and is followed by an essential clause. Compare:
  —*Mitch wore a green sweater, which his father had given him.*
  —*Mitch wore the green sweater that was worn by the arsonist.*

g. Avoid Repetition: Even if you mean to be thorough, avoid repetition. You only get one point for the issue and it looks like padding if you repeat words or phrases. Here are two tips. First, if you need to repeat a list, state it once. For example, if the facts state there are multiple wills, each of which requires listing the required elements, write the list initially and then later simply refer back to the analysis "*supra*." Note any significant applications or differences. Second, if you have extra time and want to address the same issue, try to vary the wording and depth of analysis so repetition is less obvious.

h. Avoid Verbose Word Clusters: Avoid archaic legal language that uses multiple words to express the meaning of one. So-called "glue or wobbley words" add unnecessary length, slow things down, and do not develop substance, but do use up your limited space or character count. Some writers use glue words to add bulk to their writing or imply they are discussing very intellectual concepts. This indulgence is not helpful on bar essay answers which favors concise writing. Look for unnecessary prepositions, relative pronouns, and throat-clearers such as "it would appear to be the case that."

<u>Avoid These</u>	<u>Substitute These</u>
aforementioned	*supra* or above
along the line of	like
at that point in time	then
at the present time	now
based on the fact that	because
be of the opinion that	believe, argue
despite the fact that	although
for the purpose of	to
for the reason that	because, since
from the point of view of	from, for
here to follow	*infra* or below
in a number of cases	some, often, frequently
in a position to	can, may
in a satisfactory manner	satisfactorily

in accordance with	by, under, because
in advance of	before, preceding
in any case	regardless
in as much as	since, because
in connection with	with, about, concerning
in favor of	for
in many instances/cases	often
in my opinion/view	it seems
in order to	to
in our present circumstances	presently, now
in regard to	about, concerning
in spite of the fact that	although
in terms of	of, concerning
in the instant case of	concerning, here
in the event of	if
in the nature of	like
is indicative of	indicates
it is often the case that	frequently
on a few occasions	occasionally
on the basis of	by, because
on the ground that	since, because
owing to the fact that	since, because
the said party	Plaintiff/Defendant or P/D
with a view to (toward)	to
with reference to	about, concerning
with regard to	about, concerning
with respect to	on, about, concerning
with the result that	so that, resulting in
without regard to	regardless

B. Watch Time and Answer Length

On each set of the essay exam, you will be given 30 minute questions.

1. Question Set: It is up to you to monitor your time. Three hours divided by six questions gives you 30 minutes per question. After two questions, make sure you have not exceeded 65 minutes. Check your time after each question.

2. Time Allocation Strategy: Consider spending more time on the difficult questions. At the end of each question, check your time. Do not leave the worst question to the last. If you run short of time, you may be unable to write a full answer for the last question.

3. Keep Writing Until the End: Very short answers send the message to the grader that your knowledge is skimpy. The more you write, the more issues you are likely to cover. Be creative.

4. The Fine Art of Punting: If you feel that you are "done" but you still have time, consider using the "fine art of punting." Take a step back and look for overall areas you may have missed or may supplement. As an example, students sometimes "complete" a contracts question without discussing remedies. Skim the fact pattern and think about the six classic questions below:

a. What: Acronym applies? Theory of recovery? Rights of parties? Defenses? Elements? Definition? Effect? Consequence? Legal procedure?

b. Why: Important? Useful? Purpose of act or procedure? Suitable?

c. When: Appropriate timing? Relevant date? To apply a particular legal procedure or test? Statute of limitations? Laches?

d. How: Method to accomplish? How much are the damages? How is the rule applied?

e. Where: Applicable? Appropriate? Source?

f. Who: Participants? Stakeholders? Interested/affected parties? Legal roles or capacities?

5. Out of Time? If you find yourself unable to finish an answer, do not write "out of time" or similar words admitting a time management deficiency. This could make the grader think you are unorganized, unprepared, and unworthy of a decent score. Instead, simply outline the rest of what you would have written.

VI.   ANSWERING THE QUESTION

A. Overall Organization and Presentation

Make it easy for the grader to award you the maximum credit your answer deserves. Simple, step-by-step organization is the key to a clear and concise writing style. Every paragraph should clearly discuss and analyze a major issue. Your paragraphs should be presented in a logical sequence. Use the active voice Subject-Verb-Object order in each sentence. Here are some other strategies and tips:

1. Same Coverage as Grading Guide: Usually, the examiner's facts and grading guides-pointer sheets are presented in chronological order and cover all possible issues that may be given credit. Compare your essay answers with our grading guide outline of the point-by-point scoring issues. Carefully examine the grading guide, and strive to cover the same content as that guide. No candidate is expected to cover every issue in the "perfect" essay grading guide. Just aim high to ensure that you'll achieve at least a defensive score.

2. Develop a Standard Writing System: Develop a writing method that can be applied consistently to any fact pattern in any subject. It is not enough to know the substantive law; you also need to know how to organize and convey the law to the grader within the time allotted and in the best presentation style possible.

3. State the Obvious: Good answer analysis states the obvious. You can't get points for what you don't write down. Emphasis is on concise, but comprehensive statements of the relevant black letter law, issue recognition, and application of the controlling rule. In some questions there may not be enough time to fully argue both sides of all the issues.

4. Use a Modified IRAC Presentation Format: This sequential approach will keep your issues clear and succinct and allow you to keep a forward issue-to-issue momentum through the question. A successful strategy is as follows:

a. Opening Argument and Primary Issues: Start your answer with an opening argument containing a statement of the controlling legal principle. An example is: "Will and probate law governs the disposition of assets upon death" or "A lawyer's duty of loyalty…" A partial listing of standard openings for each subject area can be found in every chapter after the prior exam question distribution chart.

b. Flag Issues: Each subject-issue paragraph of your answer should start with one word or a short phrase identifying the issue to be discussed in that paragraph. This could be one word, a phrase, or a short question. Underlining or using bold type for the issue helps the reader. For example, at the beginning of a paragraph discussing the enforceability of an oral contract, the flag could be "Statute of Frauds Application."

c. State the Issue / Rule: This is the most important step and cannot be too cursory, simplistic, or conclusory. Rather than "a contract requires an offer," state "Offer – A valid contract requires an offer that includes a manifestation of present intent to be bound, certainty and definitiveness of terms, and communication to the offeree creating a power of acceptance. Here…" This defines the rule and creates an issue to be analyzed.

d. State the "Analysis": The analysis should be concise, yet comprehensive. State as much of the law as you can reasonably put into your analysis. This discussion should relate to the events in the fact pattern that support both sides of the argument.

e. Conclusion: If you reach a conclusion, specify why the facts support the application of the controlling law. For example, in a fact pattern where an offer was not properly accepted, the "AC" portion would be, "Here, no contract was formed because Smith's offer was not accepted by Brown."

5. Avoid a Mere "Brain Dump": Do not discuss everything you know about a topic. Discuss only the issues actually raised by the facts. The writer arranges the facts to raise legal issues. Failure to realize the significance of a significant fact is the major reason candidates miss an issue or only argue one side of the controversy.

6. Use a Logical Sequence: Make it easy for the graders to give you points. The sequencing of your discussion is important because it conveys the impression of a well organized candidate. Usually the chronology of factual events is the best structure and sequence.

7. Technique to Fill Up Pages: If allowed, skipping a line between paragraphs gives the grader visual relief and allows added thoughts later. This is especially important if you do not type and you write small or slowly.

B. Powerful 6-Step Approach to Analyzing and Answering Essay Questions

To ensure a defensive score on every question, we recommend the below described essay writing approach.

1. Determine Your Answer Sequence: Some candidates just take each essay as it comes. Others find it is psychologically beneficial to quickly plan the entire six question set. Quickly read both the first couple of sentences and the requirements which usually are contained in numbered questions at the end of the fact pattern. This will identify the topics to be addressed in your six answers during the 3-hour period. Do not spend more than 5 minutes on this analysis. Still, it will allow you to plan the sequence of the essay battles ahead.

a. Easiest First: Begin by writing what for you appears to be the easiest question. If you are more confident about a topic, you are likely to finish under or within the time allocated for that question. Take advantage of the opportunity to build momentum and score easy points, since every point counts. Try to finish in less than 30 minutes so you have extra time for the hardest question.

b. Hardest Second: Do the most difficult essay question second or third. Complete these in the middle of the set while your momentum and confidence are strong. Spend extra time on these questions. Give them full coverage to ensure a defensive score.

c. Final Question: The middle-degree difficulty questions should be done last. Stay on schedule. Don't cut your time too short to complete the last question.

2. Identify the Requirements and Spot the Issues: The call of the question defines the playing field and triggers point-scoring issues in the fact pattern.

a. Focus on the Call: The call invariably is at the end of the fact pattern. Read and circle the call before you read the facts and focus on that as you approach the subject. The two predominant requirement styles are general outcome specific, such as "discuss all issues and defenses," or "which party will most likely win at trial," and legal issue specific, such as "will A's defense prevail?" or "will Creditor be able to pierce the corporate veil?" In the latter form the NCBE may pose up to three sub-questions. Become familiar with the subject's usual form and wording and focus your attention on anything out of the ordinary.

b. Read and Study the Facts: Don't just jump in – pay attention to the factual details and events so your answer is focused on the relevant law and accurate. Look for familiar recurring facts you learned in the review course. Most substantive legal subjects have patterns in the question facts leading to the issue requirements. Read intensely and analyze the fact pattern events carefully.

(1) Circle Parties' Names: Circle the name of each party at least the first time they appear as you read the fact pattern. This will help you organize the facts and designate the P and D in your answer. Note any examiners' clues as to gender, as this will help to identify parties.

(2) Spot Detailed Issues: Underline or box the fact and/or event raising the issues and note them in the margin or on the blank sheets provided. Be alert for trigger wording including seemingly meaningless detail about a person or thing; the detail is there for a purpose. This is usually a coding indicating a classification important to your analysis, such as merchant, statute of limitations, or holder in due course.

(3) Read Carefully: Ask yourself, "What issue(s) did the writer intend the facts and events in this sentence to raise?" You may miss a required issue if you do not recognize that significant facts were intended to provide you with an analytical opportunity. Failure to spot issues is the most frequent reason applicants fail the bar exam.

(4) Example: Here is an MEE type of exam essay question with the key contracts issues raised by the underlined facts shown in the right margin. This issue spotting recording could also be done on the blank sheets provided with the exam question set. You need to practice during your review program to build this skill.

Course 5328. Copyright by Rigos Bar Review Series – MEE.

FACTS	LEGAL ISSUES
Neptune is an upscale seafood restaurant that opened in a convenient downtown location six months ago. It has become well known for the quality of its food and service. It has several dishes featuring salmon that are particularly popular with patrons.	Common law v. UCC
Neptune entered into a valid written contract with Seafood Uptown Providers (SUP) under which SUP agreed to supply Neptune with $1,000 per week of fresh Pacific salmon at $4.00 per pound for the next year.	2 merchants Quantity can be calculated – 250 lbs.
Three months after the making of the contract, a large widely publicized oil spill occurred in Pacific coast waters. The spill greatly reduced the catch of salmon. Salmon began selling on the open market for at least $5.00 per pound. SUP then told Neptune that it would supply salmon only at a price of $6.00 per pound. Neptune refused to pay more than the contract price. In fact, SUP has found a new customer willing to pay $6.00 per pound, and is now selling its entire supply (about 450 pounds of salmon per week) to that customer.	Excusable nonperformance Modification sought Anticipatory repudiation
Neptune, faced with the prospect of having to obtain salmon for its daily restaurant menu and also for special events that it caters, found a supplier willing to meet about one-half of Neptune's weekly requirement for salmon at $5.00 per pound. With further effort, Neptune might have filled a portion of the remaining weekly requirement for salmon at $6.00 per pound, but was uncertain to what extent salmon would continue to be obtainable and how high the market price might go. Neptune decided instead to reduce its menu offerings of salmon and to cancel several catering contracts.	Cover damages Mitigation – Price increase after breach
Within a month after reducing its menu offerings of salmon, Neptune experienced a 25% decline in its restaurant business from the previous month. It also had a 75% decline in new bookings for catering jobs. Neptune still has the immediate and long-term problem of how to obtain a reliable source of salmon, and wants to sue SUP. What rights and remedies does Neptune have against SUP? Discuss. What damages, if any, might Neptune recover? Discuss. What defenses, if any, should SUP assert? Discuss.	Certainty of damages – too speculative? Specific performance Duty of reasonableness in requirement contract Call of Question – rights and remedies, damages, and defenses

3. Plan Answer Organization: After you have spotted the few major issues, quickly plan how to best present your organized answer. Spend enough time in this planning phase, especially when you are practicing, to become confident that your overall organization ties the major issues together in an attractive sequence.

a. Essay Planning and Outlining: Planning and outlining is important and should flow through your mind as you read through the question. Think about how best to develop your answer around the issues you have spotted. This may help you get through a tough issue or topical area. Go through your Magic Memory Outlines® in your mind.

b. Organize Your Approach to Follow the Facts: If the facts are very complicated, consider creating a brief factual chart of the individuals, transactions, events chronology, or other interactions.

c. Chronological Order: It is usually best to use a straight time-line sequence when discussing the issues. This usually follows the facts, which are almost always presented in chronological order.

d. Scrutinize Details: Be alert for seemingly meaningless factual detail about a person or thing. There are no red herrings, so the detail is there for a purpose. This is usually a coding indicating a classification (e.g., merchant or statute of limitations). This kind of classification is almost always important to your analysis.

4. Analyze Elements of Each Cause of Action: A "party-to-party" analysis establishes the adversarial relationship between the parties and the relevant theories of law. All possible causes of action should be discussed, even if they likely would fail at trial. After you organize the issues, analyze them using a P v. D advocacy legal framework. The following approach often works well:

a. Required Elements to Make P's Prima Facie Case: Every cause of action deserves at least one paragraph – and perhaps more if quite important. Focus your discussion on the prima facie elements P must demonstrate to survive summary judgment or judgment as a matter of law (directed verdict). Do not make this too cursory; most of the points lie here.

b. Possible Defenses: Consider whether a plausible privilege or defense can eliminate, reduce, or mitigate the elements necessary to establish a P's prima facie case.

c. Rebuttal Argument: If the facts suggest the P has a reasonable rebuttal to the defense, address it.

d. Short Conclusion to Issue: If you have time and the issue is of large import, finish the analysis with a short conclusion. The conclusion may contain a transition to the next discussion issue. In your conclusion, reflect the call of the question and the factual reason why and how it applies. Example: "Arnold will be deemed to have made a valid offer because . . . . This raises the issue of Betty's acceptance timeliness." The next paragraph would then explore the issues of contract acceptance.

e. Counterclaims: After P's claim is fully analyzed, turn to D's counterclaims. Use the same approach discussed *supra* focusing on the required prima facie elements, defenses, and rebuttal.

5. Answer the Question: You must spot the issues in the facts and write about them clearly, concisely, and engagingly. Organization and presentation are pivotal to show the grader you know and understand the law.

a. Paragraph Structure: Most answers have five or six medium sized paragraphs.

(1) At Least One Paragraph for Each Issue: A good general rule is to write at least one paragraph for every major issue in every viable claim and any defenses. Spend more effort and length on the more important or complex issues. The issue distribution charts in each chapter are your best indication of the relative importance of the issues.

(2) Identify Issues at Start of Paragraph: State and underline the issue at the beginning of the paragraph in a word or a short phrase.

b. Maximize Readability: Make it easy for the grader to award you points. Choose the clear, concrete word over the abstract or convoluted. Use standard legal terminology to express your meaning. Select the familiar word rather than the one that will send the grader running for a dictionary. The familiar word will best convey the correct meaning and speed your discussion and reader comprehension. Mushy wordiness distracts from the sharpness of your legal analysis.

c. Be Concise: A stream of consciousness writing is neither efficient nor effective on the bar exam. Use short sentences (generally no more than 25 words) and avoid glue words, wordiness, and excessive use of semicolons or commas.

6. Final Review of Question and Your Answer: Manage your time so you can re-read the question and review your answer.

a. Question Yourself: Did you answer the specific required call of the question? Do you see anything new in the facts? Did you miss an issue? If so, can you abbreviate words or delete some previous discussion to free up some more space? Are there spelling errors? How will the grader regard the organization of your answer? Does the end of your answer leave the grader on an up-note?

b. Remember Why Graders Mark Down: As you ask yourself the above questions, remember the three justifications graders give for awarding a low score. First, the answer is poorly organized; second, some important issues were not identified and analyzed; and third, the analysis was not responsive to the specific inquiries, particularly on the most important issues. Avoid these three deficiencies and your essay answers should receive a passing score.

VII. RIGOS BAR REVIEW SERIES ESSAY WRITING PROGRAM DOs AND DON'Ts

A. 10 Dos

1. Do Read Carefully: Read the question through at least twice before you begin to write. Circle the parties' names as you read. Keep characters (genders and names) and events clear to eliminate any confusion in your answer. Diagram the facts, if complicated. A chronological approach is usually best.

2. Do Note Topic Area and Call of Question: Determine the subject category from the first few sentences and the "call of the question" in the requirements.

3. Do Have an Opening Statement: Begin with a comprehensive opening argument.

4. Do Use "Visual Aids": Indent, underline, or capitalize to draw attention to the issue you are going to discuss next. Use one or two words, a phrase at most. Do not use a colored highlighter in your answer, as the grader receives only a photocopy of your essay.

5. Do Use Modified IRAC: For each issue, name the issue, state the rule of law, and combine your analysis and conclusion in a single statement (IR/AC as opposed to full I/R/A/C).

6. Do Watch For Crossover Subjects: Many MEE questions combine more than one substantive topic. A candidate misses the crossover subjects at his or her peril.

7. Do Apply Law Without Repeating: As you state a list of elements (e.g., the requirements of a negotiable instrument – NUTSS), apply each element to the facts the first time through your analysis. If you apply the same principle of law again (say the maker issues a second check or note), simply refer back to the elements and focus on the differences. This way you say it only once and provide detailed analysis in less space.

8. Do Make Sure You've Answered the Question Asked. Refer back frequently to the call of the question in the requirements and address each issue requested or fairly raised.

9. Do Pace Yourself: Time management is important. Spend more time on your weak subjects and answer those questions in the middle of the MEE set. You must achieve a defensive score on every question.

10. Do Use the Formal Legal Vocabulary: For example, write "meretricious relationship" rather than "living together." Use "burglary," not "robbery" to describe a break-in when no persons are present. Fine distinctions show your precise understanding of the law.

B. 10 Don'ts

1. Don't Instantly Start Writing: Let the facts and applicable legal issues of the question sink in, gather your thoughts, organize your approach, and then begin.

2. Don't Outline Extensively Before Writing: Rely on your recall of your Magic Memory Outlines®. Begin writing once your thoughts are organized.

3. Don't Brain Dump: Keep your analysis clear and specific. Focus on answering the call of the question; don't just throw in anything you think of in the general subject area. With the exception of a few crucial issues, discussing non-issues earns no points.

4. Don't Simply Repeat Facts: Don't repeat facts from the pattern without simultaneous analysis. The grader has read dozens or hundreds of answers, and does not need you to tell him the facts. Compare:

"Betty failed to respond within 20 days. Charles made a default motion. Failure to respond was a default. Charles' motion was proper."

Rewrite: "Here, Betty's failure to respond timely within 20 days resulted in a default, and Charles' motion was proper."

5. Don't Stray From the Topic: Don't stray into other areas of law unless it's clearly an overlapping question. If a side issue merits mention, do not spend more than a sentence on it. Once you identify the area of law, focus your discussion. Don't get sidetracked.

6. Don't Use Bald Abbreviations: Don't use abbreviations unless you have defined the full term, e.g., "holder in due course" (HDC) or "purchase money security interest" (PMSI).

7. Don't Repeat: You only get one point per issue. It looks like padding if you repeat words or phrases. If you need to repeat a list (for analysis of the five NUTSS elements of a negotiable instrument), list the elements initially and then simply refer back (using "supra"), noting any differences. If an issue merits further discussion, vary the wording to mask repetition.

8. Don't Stop Writing: Fill at least two-thirds of the space. The more you write, the more issues you are likely to cover. If your writing is small, skip a line between paragraphs.

9. Don't Drink Too Much Fluid: Restroom breaks are on your own time. More than a short stretch will take away from your writing time and/or break your concentration.

10. Don't Leave Any Exam Session Early: Never surrender and leave points behind. You never know for sure when you have crossed the passing line. Re-read your answers thoroughly and underline key points if you have extra time.

VII. CONCLUSION

The essay portion of the bar exam is passable the first time. The Rigos Bar Review Series "seamless process" preparation program works well for candidates committed to success and willing to work hard. There is simply no shortcut to planning and following a thorough preparation program. Plan to spend a significant amount of time preparing.

As discussed above, you will likely not pass if all you do is learn the text. Understanding and memorization is necessary, but to pass, you need to be able to communicate this knowledge to the grader. Writing style and presentation skills are improved by doing. You must practice analyzing, organizing, and writing out essay and performance answers.

Use the overall preparation schedule on page 23 and Daily-Weekly planning chart on page 24. The recommended 15 week – 600 hour schedule allows you to break your effort into manageable modules. If helpful, incorporate the planning into your electronic calendar. Date your completion date of each learning module on your schedule on page 23. Leave time at the end for the practice final exam sessions and a review of the review. Go over your prior Magic Memory Outlines® at least weekly while you master the next subjects. Mark your mistakes as you go along for the final review.

While your main emphasis here should be on improving your writing skills, do not forget the MBE multiple-choice questions. Use the "Make Your Own Exam" software drills to continue practicing the MBE subjects when you have a few minutes to switch style of questions. Plan for success, and stay on schedule!

After you get your results, please take the time to fill out the evaluation at the end of this book. It will help us improve our course for the students who will follow you, and we may publish your thoughts and ideas. Good luck on the bar exam and in your legal career.

James J. Rigos
Editor-in-Chief
Rigos Bar Review Series

RIGOS BAR REVIEW SERIES
UNIFORM MEE SUBJECT FREQUENCY DISTRIBUTION OF NCBE ESSAYS

SUBJECT	2/09	7/08	2/08	7/07	2/07	7/06	2/06	7/05	2/05	7/04	2/04	7/03	2/03	7/02	2/02	7/01	2/01	7/00	2/00	7/99	2/99
Agency & Partnerships	–	–		–	–	–	–		–	–	–	–	–	–	–	–	–		–	–	–
Corporations & LLCs	–		–			–	–	–	–	–		–	–		–		–	–	–	–	–
Conflict of Laws	–	–		–	–	–				–			–	–					–	–	–
Family Law	–	–	–	–	–	–	–	=	–	–	–	–	–	–	–	–	–	–	–	–	–
Federal Civil Procedure	–	–	–	–	–	–	–												–	–	–
UCC Art. 3 - Comm. Paper	–	–	–	–	–	–		–	–	–	–		–	–	–			–	–	–	–
UCC Art. 9 - Secure Trans.	–	–	–	–	–	–	–	–	–	–	–	–				–	–	–	–	–	–
Trusts, Wills, & Estates	–	–	=	–	=	–	=	=	–	=	=	–	=	=	–	=	=	–	–	–	–
Contracts & UCC Sales		–		–									–					–			
Constitutional Law		–		–																	
Criminal Law & Crim. Pro.			–																		
Evidence	–		–																		
Real Property	–	–		–																	
Torts	–	–	–																		

RIGOS BAR REVIEW SERIES

OVERALL 15-WEEK PREPARATION PLANNING SCHEDULE

For _____, Candidate

The Rigos bar "seamless process" preparation program contemplates a 600 hour integrated review effort. Our paced schedule is best spread over an extended preparation period of a 15-week time period. Complete each weekly learning schedule and enter the date.

Week 15. _____ Get organized by registering with your bar admission board and reviewing the Introduction section of the Rigos MBE, MEE, and MPT texts. Review and become familiar with all our subjects tested in your state including any local topics.

Week 14. _____ Use Weekly Planning Sheet to learn, prepare Rigos MMO, and work through all Contracts, Chapter 1, MBE multiple-choice questions and MEE essays.

Week 13. _____ Use Weekly Planning Sheet to learn, prepare Rigos MMO, and work through all Torts, Chapter 2, MBE multiple-choice questions and MEE essays.

Week 12. _____ Use Weekly Planning Sheet to learn, prepare Rigos MMO, and work through all Property, Chapter 3, MBE multiple-choice questions and MEE essays.

Week 11. _____ Use Weekly Planning Sheet to learn, prepare Rigos MMO, and work through all Evidence, Chapter 4, MBE multiple-choice questions and MEE essays.

Week 10. _____ Use Weekly Planning Sheet to learn, prepare Rigos MMO, and work through all Constitution Law, Chapter 5, MBE multiple-choice questions and MEE essays.

Week 9. _____ Use Weekly Planning Sheet to learn, prepare Rigos MMO, and work through all Criminal Law and Procedure, Chapter 6, MBE multiple-choice questions and MEE essays.

Week 8. _____ Use Weekly Planning Sheet to learn, prepare Rigos MMO, and work through all Business Associations MEE essay questions.

Week 7. _____ Use Weekly Planning Sheet to learn, prepare Rigos MMO, and work through all Conflicts of Law and Family Law MEE essay questions.

Week 6. _____ Use Weekly Planning Sheet to learn, prepare Rigos MMO, and work through all Civil Procedure and Trust, Wills, and Estates MEE essay questions.

Week 5. _____ Use Weekly Planning Sheet to learn, prepare Rigos MMO, and work through all Commercial Paper and Secured Transactions MEE essay questions.

Week 4. _____ Use Weekly Planning Sheet to learn PR and work related essays.

Week 3. _____ Use Weekly Planning Sheet to learn and complete Performance tasks.

Week 2. _____ Review Contracts, Torts, Property, Evidence, and the MEE subjects covered in week 8 and 7.

Week 1. _____ Review Constitutional Law, Criminal Law and Procedure, and the MEE subjects covered in week 6, 5, and 4.

Saturday – take and score both MBE practice exams and review the rationales to the missed questions.
Sunday – write a few essays and performance questions and review answers from all the subjects.
Monday – review all essay and performance questions in the program, focusing on the law and fact clusters used to raise issues, especially those subjects in which your scores were low.
Tuesday evening – Review all MBE questions you missed during the MBE review program.

RIGOS BAR REVIEW SERIES

MBE, MEE, and MPT SECTIONS

WEEKLY AND DAILY PLANNING SHEET

WEEK: From Monday _____ **to Sunday** _____.

THE BAR EXAM IS _____ **WEEKS AWAY**

WEEKLY OBJECTIVES:

	Subject Studied	Do Learning Questions	Prepare MMO	Memorize MMO and Acronyms	Do Chapter Questions
Mon					
Tues					
Wed					
Thurs					
Friday					
Sat/ Sun					

DAILY SCHEDULE BY HOUR

Time	Monday	Tuesday	Wednesday	Thursday	Friday	Saturday	Sunday
6-7:00am							
7-8:00							
8-9:00							
9-10:00							
10-11:00							
11-12:00							
12-1:00pm							
1-2:00							
2-3:00							
3-4:00							
4-5:00							
5-6:00							
6-7:00							
7-8:00							
8-9:00							
9-10:00							
10-11:00							

CHAPTER 1

BUSINESS ASSOCIATIONS

CHAPTER 1

PART A

AGENCY

RIGOS BAR REVIEW SERIES

UNIFORM MULTISTATE ESSAY EXAM (MEE) REVIEW

CHAPTER 1

BUSINESS ASSOCIATIONS

AGENCY

Table of Contents

A.	Sub-Topic Exam Issue Distribution		Text 1-31
B.	Opening Argument and Primary Issues		Text 1-33
C.	Text		Text 1-35
	I.	Introduction: Business Entities Generally	Text 1-35
	II.	Creation of Agency	Text 1-36
	III.	Liability to Third Parties	Text 1-38
	IV.	Agent's Duties	Text 1-40
	V.	Principal's Duties	Text 1-41
	VI.	Agency Termination	Text 1-41
D.	Magic Memory Outlines®		Magic Memory Outlines 1-43
E.	Agency Essay Questions		Questions 1-113
F.	Agency Essay Answers		Answers 1-117
G.	Agency Index		Index 1-47
H.	Acronyms		Acronyms 15-623

RIGOS BAR REVIEW SERIES
MEE SUB-TOPIC FREQUENCY DISTRIBUTION

AGENCY

	2/09	7/08	2/08	7/07	2/07	7/06	2/06	7/05	2/05	7/04	2/04	7/03	2/03	7/02	2/02	7/01
Opening Argument (df. "Agency," etc.)	/						/		/	/			/	/		//
Agency-Principal Contract Relationship	/						/		/	/			/	/		//
Express (Actual) Authority	//								/	/				/		//
Statute of Frauds	/												/			
Implied (Inherent) Authority									/							
Apparent Authority	//								/	/		/	/			/
Ratification																
Liability of Agent							/								/	//
Fiduciary Duties							/								/	//
Taking Opportunity of Principal																
Interference w/Contract																
Principal Tort Liability	/								/	/		/	/			/
Negligent Hiring							/									

	2/09	7/08	2/08	7/07	2/07	7/06	2/06	7/05	2/05	7/04	2/04	7/03	2/03	7/02	2/02	7/01
Negligent Supervision							/									
Contract Liability	/								/	/		/				/
Identified Principal	/									/						/
Tort Liability							/			/			/			//
Agent Liable for Own																
Respondeat Superior							/									
Course & Scope of Employment							/			/			/			/
Frolic of One's Own							/									
Employee v. Independent Contractor							/			/			/			/
Intentional Torts																
Termination of Agency	/												/			/
Death of Agent / principal																/

OPENING ARGUMENT AND PRIMARY ISSUES

BUSINESS ASSOCIATIONS

There are a few thoughts that should usually be stated at the beginning of every answer. These will score you easy points and let the grader know you are in the right topic area.

Most essays should have an "opening argument": a brief, broad statement that shows you understand the broad significance of a legal topic. The opening argument also suggests to the grader that she is about to read a thoughtful and well-organized essay.

Many subjects also have "primary issues" that can be discussed up front or integrated into the essay answer. IMPORTANT: Do not merely regurgitate these statements on the exam without addressing the issues actually raised by the facts, or you will not pass.

AGENCY

- **Agency Opening Argument:** Agency is the fiduciary relationship created when a person ("agent") consents to act on the behalf of a principal in affecting legal relationships with third parties.

- **Sample Primary Issue Statements:**

  - Express authority is conferred upon the agent through affirmative appointment by the principal.

  - The Statute of Frauds applies to a principal-agent contract requiring a writing if the subject is land, over one year to completion, or an applicable state statute requires a writing.

  - An agent has apparent authority to act on behalf of a principal when a third party reasonably believes the agent is so authorized, and the belief is based upon the principal's conduct.

  - If a third party is aware the principal has placed restrictions on the agent, no recovery is allowed for activities exceeding the restriction.

  - An undisclosed principal may enforce an agent's contracts with a third party unless this would cause a material change in performance, or the third party would not have knowingly contracted with the undisclosed principal.

  - Independent contractors do not impute liability to a principal unless the duties involve an unreasonable risk of harm to the public.

  - An agent owes her principal the fiduciary duties of honest dealings, obedience, undivided loyalty and trust.

  - An agent is not personally liable in contract to a third party unless the principal was undisclosed or the agent is acting on their own account.

- Agents are always liable for their own torts. "Respondeat superior" creates vicarious liability of the principal for torts committed by the agent in the course and scope of the agency.

- To terminate an agent's apparent authority, there must be actual notice given to customers and constructive notice by publication to third parties without prior dealings.

CHAPTER 1

BUSINESS ASSOCIATIONS

AGENCY

I.   INTRODUCTION: BUSINESS ENTITES GENERALLY

The law of Agency is covered in this chapter, along with the business entities Partnership, Corporations, and Limited Liability Companies (LLC). Agency and Partnership are combined on the NCBE Content Specification Outlines. The two subjects may be tested alone but are frequently combined.

A. All Business Entities Using an Assumed Name Must be Registered

All business entities (including General Partnerships, Corporations, LLCs, charities, and solo entrepreneurships) using an "assumed name" must register with the Office of the Secretary of State. Registration for truly-named businesses is optional.

1. Assumed Names: An "assumed name" is any name used to identify a business other than a person's own real and true name. This includes words or phrases that suggest additional owners, e.g., "Company," "& Company," "& Daughters," "& Associates."

2. Requirements: Registration applications must include all **NAB** information:

a. Names: The name of the assumed business and the real and true names of the people intending to carry on or transact the business, and their representatives.

b. Addresses of the business, the people intending to carry on the business, and their representatives.

c. Business Activity conducted by the applicant entity.

B. Registration Status

1. Refusal and Revocation: The Secretary of State may reject an application if an assumed business name is not distinguishable from another active registered or reserved business name, or from the name of a person. Any fraudulent representation by an applicant or intentional creation of a confusion of identity is cause for rejection or revocation by the State.

2. Cancellation: The Secretary of State may cancel registration if the only registrant of an assumed business name is a domestic corporation that has been dissolved, or is a foreign corporation whose authority to transact business has been revoked.

3. Amendments – Within 60 Days: Generally, an application to amend a registration of an assumed business name must be delivered to the Secretary of State within 60 days after the following:

a. Changes in the Identity, Names or Addresses: A change in the identity of persons carrying on, conducting or transacting a registered business, or a change in the identity of their legal representative must be reported.

b. Changes in Location: The registrant begins to transact business under the assumed business name in a county / counties different from those stated in the original application for registration, or the address of the principal place of business is changed.

II. CREATION OF AGENCY

Agency is a consensual relationship wherein an agent agrees to and/or acts on a principal's behalf in affecting legal relationships with third parties. The exam usually covers an agent's power to bind the principal to third parties in contract and/or tort, and reciprocal duties between principals and agents. It is important to understand: 1) how agency relationships are created; 2) when a principal assumes liability for the torts and contracts of an agent; 3) the duties principals and agents owe to one another; and 4) how agency relationships are terminated.

> **MEE Tip:** Most agency issues involve potential liability of the principal to a third party. Such liability requires demonstrating that an agency exists, which requires identification of the type of agency authority, or express / implied ratification by the principal of an agent's acts.

A. Express Authority

Express authority to bind the principal is conferred upon the agent through actual affirmative appointment by the principal. Examples include a power of attorney or an employment contract. The principal may also specifically authorize the agent to deal with third parties.

1. General or Special Agency: The appointment scope could be either a general agency or a special agency limited to a single transaction or area of responsibility.

2. Statute of Frauds: The statute of frauds may prohibit oral appointment of agents.

a. Land or Related: A writing is required if the subject of the agency is an agreement to purchase land or a real estate agent or broker selling or buying for compensation.

b. Over One Year: A contract for an agency period expressly ending on a date over one year from the agreement date must be written in most states.

c. At-Will Contract: An agency of indefinite duration, but terminable upon notice, may be oral because termination may be within a year.

d. Sales Representative: In most states, a contract between a principal and a sales agent must be in writing and set forth the compensation method. A provision in such a contract specifying that the venue in any litigation must be outside the state is usually void.

3. Factor: A factor is a commercial agent with possession of goods and authority to sell them as if her own. This gives her the power to transfer all ownership rights to a retail buyer.

4. Del Credere Agent: A del credere agent personally guarantees his customers will pay the principal. Sales agents representing multiple product lines often extend this assurance to the principal.

5. Express Authority Limitations: If a third party is aware the principal has placed restrictions on the agent, no recovery is allowed beyond the restriction. Under some circumstances, a third party may have a duty to investigate if the agent had authority to affect the transaction.

B. Implied or Inherent Authority

Implied authority may arise from express authority or from the status of the agent. Ask whether the act / contract was "necessary or usual in carrying out functions which were expressly authorized." Inherent authority may also flow from the relationship, as with one spouse's ability to bind the community.

1. Business Manager: A business manager has implied authority to make all day-to-day business decisions in the best interest of the enterprise (but not to sell assets in a bulk sale).

2. Salesperson: Salespeople with express authority to sell goods have implied authority to make the usual sales representations and warranties. Some cases suggest this may be nullified by an "integration" clause in the contract.

3. Delivery Person: An agent with express authority to deliver goods has implied authority to receive payment – the buyer is thus protected, even if the agent does not remit payment to the principal.

4. Purchase Agent: Express appointment to purchase implies authority to disburse the principal's funds (the principal cannot demand the third party repay the funds).

> **MEE Tip:** A common fact pattern involves an agent who receives funds from a customer and does not remit them to her principal.

C. Apparent or Ostensible Authority

Apparent or ostensible authority may also create liability to the principal.

1. Implied Authority Lacking: If there is no actual or implied authority, but the principal's actions would lead an ordinarily prudent person to reasonably believe the agent has authority, the principal may be liable.

2. Exam Facts: Look for a principal who has actual knowledge that an otherwise unauthorized agent is dealing on his behalf with relying third parties.

D. Estoppel

Estoppel authority is similar to apparent authority, but is applicable when the principal's inaction or lack of full disclosure causes a third party to reasonably conclude that an agent had authority to deal. If the principal "clothed the agent with the trappings of authority" and fails in some way to correct this error, the principal is estopped from denying liability.

E. Ratification

A principal is not normally bound by unauthorized contracts. Ratification cures the lack of express, implied, or apparent authority, and relates back to the original contract date.

1. Representation Necessary: The agent must have represented to the third party that she was acting for the benefit of the principal.

2. Express or Implied: A principal can expressly ratify a contract, or may do so implicitly by receiving the benefits of the agent's contract. To ratify, a principal must have knowledge of all material facts concerning the contract, and must ratify the entire contract.

3. In Existence at Contract Date: The principal must have been in existence at the contract date, and a third party may withdraw or rescind prior to ratification. Once the principal ratifies a contract he or she cannot withdraw ratification to the third party's detriment.

F. Necessity

Necessity may create an agency in an emergency situation, such as a family member contracting for medical assistance, hospital aid, or other necessities.

> **MEE Tip:** More than one type of agency authority might exist in one question.

G. Miscellaneous

1. Capacity:

a. Infant Agent: An infant can be an agent and thus bind an adult principal to third parties, even though the infant agent could avoid the agency contract with the principal.

b. Infant Principal: An infant principal can avoid her agent's contract, unless the agency was created to secure necessities, e.g., food, clothing, shelter, education, medical care.

c. Nondisclosure of Principal's Incapacity: An agent who does not disclose a principal's incapacity will be potentially liable in contract on the to third parties.

2. Business Entities: Corporations act exclusively through agents. All general partners are agents for the partnership principal. Where a business entity is still in the formation stage, a promoter-agent may avoid liability if the third party agrees to look to the future entity for performance. The burden is on the promoter to show intent to effectuate a novation upon formation.

> **MBE Tip:** Agency questions may combine authority with the parol evidence rule and warranty exclusions. The principal may be defending against an unauthorized or expressly disclaimed false promise by a salesperson. Or, the principal seller may argue that evidence of the salesman's representations may not be introduced because the contract was "integrated" under the parol evidence rule. However, "usage of trade" evidence may establish apparent authority.

III. LIABILITY TO THIRD PARTIES

A. Contract Liability

1. Liability of the Principal: Liability for contracts entered into by an agent is imputed to the principal if the agent had express, implied, or apparent authority, or if the contract was later ratified.

2. Liability of the Agent:

a. When an Agent is not Liable: An agent is not personally liable on a third-party contract if she fully discloses that she is acting as an agent, and identifies her principal.

b. When an Agent is Liable: An agent is personally liable on the contract if her principal was undisclosed, partially undisclosed, or lacked capacity. The agent may incur personal liability if she misrepresents the scope of her authority, represented that she was dealing for her own account, or guaranteed performance of the contract (creating del credere agency).

3. Undisclosed, Partially Disclosed, and Disclosed Principals: A principal is undisclosed when an agent does not reveal that he is acting on behalf of a principal. A principal is partially disclosed when an agent discloses that he is acting on behalf of an unidentified principal. A principal is fully disclosed when an agent represents to the third party that he is acting on behalf of an identified particular principal. If a principal is undisclosed, apparent authority is impossible, as apparent authority usually requires some affirmative action by the principal that leads a third party to reasonably believe that an agency relationship exists.

a. Liability of Agent and Undisclosed or Partially Disclosed Principal: Both the agent and the undisclosed or partially disclosed principal are liable to third parties. While a third party may enforce rights against both, there is a limit of one recovery.

b. Enforcement Power of an Undisclosed Principal: An undisclosed principal can enforce a contract against a third party. This rule usually applies even if the third party would not have contracted if they knew the identity of the principal since they could have insisted upon a non-assignment provision. The agent may not intentionally conceal the principal's identity with knowledge that the identity is material to the third party. If sued by an undisclosed principal, a third party may use any defense it would have had against the agent if the agent was the principal.

B. Tort Liability

1. Liability of the Principal: Tort liability to the principal is called "respondeat superior" (let the superior respond) and may apply even if the act was unauthorized or prohibited by the principal.

a. Employment Nexus: The principal is liable if the agent's act creating the tort was within the course and scope of the agency or employment. The scope of employment includes acts intended to benefit or further the employer's business. The issue is often whether the deviation / detour from "the normal course and scope" was so extreme that there was no "nexus" to the principal's business and thus the agent was "on a frolic and detour of his own."

b. Independent Contractors: A principal is not generally liable for the torts of independent contractors. Independent contractors are agents assigned with a task who are not subject to the principal's control or supervision as to the means, manner, or detail of how the work must be done. A real estate agent is a good example of an independent contractor.

(1) Characteristics: Independent contractors may work for more than one principal, have their own tools, set their own hours, and may be paid on a piece-work basis.

(2) Non-Delegable Activities: Use of an independent contractor will not insulate the principal if the work involves an unreasonable risk of harm to the public. A principal may not delegate liability resulting from dangerous activities, or the duty of care owed to the public. For example, if a developer hires an explosives contractor to perform dynamite blasting, public policy allows injured parties to sue the developer, even though the tortfeasor was an independent company.

c. Negligent Selection or Appointment: The principal may also be liable for negligence in the selection of the agent, (e.g., history of violence and failure to check references). After gaining knowledge, negligent retention of the agent is possible. Lack of proper supervision may also create liability. If an agent is negligent in selecting a sub-agent, the negligence may be imputed to the principal if it is customary for such agents to hire sub-agents.

2. Liability of the Agent: Agents are always liable to third parties for their own torts.

MEE Tip: If a third party suffers tortious injury caused by an agent, the agent is always liable, but there is no principal liability if the agent substantially deviated / detoured from the course and scope of her employment and had not reentered it at the time of the tort.

C. Criminal Liability

Criminal liability is not imputed to the principal unless she participated in the crime.

IV. AGENT'S DUTIES

A. Fiduciary Duties

Many agents are deemed to be fiduciaries to the principal, with a duty of good faith.

1. Basic Standard – HOLT: An agent's fiduciary responsibilities include duties of honest dealing, obedience, loyalty, and trust.

2. Full Disclosure: An agent has the responsibility of full disclosure to the principal.

3. Conflict of Interest: An agent cannot deal for his own account, take a secret profit or advantage, or commingle funds. Representing competing principals is only possible where there is full disclosure and informed consent obtained from both principals.

4. Delegation of Duties: An agent cannot usually delegate agency duties without permission of the principal, unless authority to sub-delegate is actually authorized or clearly implied. Both the agent and sub-agent have potential liability.

B. Standard of Care

An agent must exercise reasonable care in the performance of his duties.

1. Obey Instructions: The agent must obey all reasonable orders and is liable to the principal for damages caused by breach.

2. Inform Principal: The agent must keep the principal informed of all relevant facts. Thus an agent's knowledge is imputed to the principal if the information at issue is within the agent's authority to acquire.

3. Gratuitous Agent: A gratuitous agent is not obliged to perform, but if she begins, she cannot be negligent.

C. Exceeding Express Authority

An agent who exceeds the limitations of express authority is liable to a third party for breach of warranty of authority. Such an agent is also liable to the principal. Damages are third party claims minus any benefit to the principal.

D. Shop Rights

The "shop rights" doctrine allows both the principal and the agent a non-exclusive right to use an invention or improvement created in the employer's workplace. However, if the employee was hired to perform as an inventor, the principal has an exclusive right to the results.

V. PRINCIPAL'S DUTIES

A. Reimbursement and Indemnification

1. Reimburse Business Expenses: The principal must reimburse the agent for business-related expenses.

2. Indemnify for Liability: The principal must indemnify the agent for liability flowing from duties performed under the principal's direction.

B. Safe Work Place

An employer must furnish his employees with a reasonably safe work place.

C. Compensation

Unless agreed to the contrary, an agent is entitled to reasonable compensation for authorized services performed.

D. Assumption of Risk Abolished

A principal is liable for employees' personal injuries suffered in performance of work duties. In most states, assumption of risk is no longer a valid defense.

E. Fellow Servant Rule

Workers' Compensation normally covers work-related injuries, even if caused by another employee. The "fellow servant" who caused the injury must be a part of management, or the act authorized by management, for the employer to be liable to the employee.

VI. AGENCY TERMINATION

A. Voluntary

1. Completion, Agreement, or Breach: Voluntary termination can occur by agreement, with completion of the job or expiration of a specified (or reasonable) time period. Breach of contract may also terminate agency.

2. Revocation or Renunciation: Termination may be by revocation of authority by the principal or a renunciation by the agent; this usually requires reasonable notice to the other party. Such termination is effective because an agency agreement is a personal service contract. Courts will not generally order specific performance. Except for a gratuitous agent who has not begun performance, termination may result in a suit for breach of contract.

3. At-Will Employee: Absent a contract, an employee may be terminated without cause by the employer. The reason for the "at-will" termination cannot violate public policy or be a retaliatory discharge for reporting law violations.

B. Involuntary – ISIS

The contract law doctrine of "excusable nonperformance" may allow involuntary termination of agency

1. Incapacity or Death of the Principal: Death of a principal is frequently tested and can cross-over into estates and probate. A principal's death terminates an agency, except as to third persons who relied on written authority and have no notice of the principal's demise. An agency created in a durable power of attorney may survive the principal's incapacity.

2. Source of Agency Supply Destroyed: An agent for sale of an apple orchard is involuntarily discharged if a winter flood from an adjoining river destroys the land.

3. Illegality of Agency Agreement: Subsequent legislation may allow termination. An agent selling alcoholic beverages is terminated if Congress reinstates prohibition.

4. Subject Matter of Agency Destroyed: An agent for the sale of an apple orchard harvest is involuntarily discharged if a winter freeze destroys the crop.

C. Agency Coupled with an Interest

Written agency, coupled with an interest in the agency property, is irrevocable. For example, if a principal gives a mortgage to a bank which includes the right to act as her agent and sell her property on default of her mortgage, she cannot revoke the agency without paying the debt. The agent has an interest in the property which is the subject of the agency.

D. Notice to Creditors or Customers

To avoid future liability from third parties, a principal must terminate both express and apparent authority of the agent in future dealing with third parties.

> **MBE Tip:** Authority termination notice to third parties is a popular topic.

1. Actual Notice to Past Customers: This requires actual notice of the agency termination to past customers and third parties who have had previous dealings with the agent acting on behalf of this principal.

2. Constructive Notice to Third Parties: Constructive notice through publication in a local newspaper or trade journal may suffice for all others. Constructive notice is adequate to terminate apparent authority with prospective parties who have not had previous dealings with the agent.

> **MEE Tip:** Agency issues arise in torts and contracts as well as business association questions.

Magic Memory Outlines®

I. INTRODUCTION: BUSINESS ENTITES GENERALLY

   A. Business Using an Assumed Name Must Be Registered ....

      1. Assumed Names ....

      2. Requirements – **NAB** ....

         a. **N**ames ....

         b. **A**ddresses ....

         c. **B**usiness Activity ....

   B. Registration Status ....

      1. Refusal and Revocation ....

      2. Cancellation ....

      3. Amendments – Within 60 Days ....

         a. Changes in Identity, Names, or Addresses ....

         b. Changes in Location ....

II. CREATION OF AGENCY

   A. Express Authority ....

      1. General or Special Agency ....

      2. Statute of Frauds ....

         a. Land or Related ....

         b. Over One Year ....

         c. At Will Contract ....

         d. Sales Representative ....

      3. Factor ....

      4. Del Credere Agent ....

      5. Express Authority Limitations ....

   B. Implied or Inherent Authority ....

      1. Business Manager ....

      2. Salesperson ....

      3. Delivery Person ....

    4. Purchase Agent ....

C. Apparent or Ostensible Authority ....

    1. Implied Authority Lacking ....

    2. Exam Facts ....

D. Estoppel ....

E. Ratification ....

    1. Representation Necessary ....

    2. Express or Implied ....

    3. In Existence at Contract Date ....

F. Necessity ....

G. Miscellaneous ....

    1. Capacity ....

        a. Infant Agent ....

        b. Infant Principal ....

        c. Nondisclosure of Principal's Incapacity...

    2. Business Entities ....

III. LIABILITY TO THIRD PARTIES

A. Contract Liability ....

    1. Liability of the Principal ....

    2. Liability of the Agent ....

        a. When an Agent is not Liable ....

        b. When an Agent is Liable ....

    3. Undisclosed, Partially Disclosed, and Disclosed Principals ....

        a. Liability of Agent and Undisclosed or Partially Disclosed Principal...............

        b. Enforcement Power of an Undisclosed or Partially Disclosed Principal ....

B. Tort Liability ....

    1. Liability of the Principal ....

        a. Employment Nexus...

        b. Independent Contractors ....

            (1) Characteristics...

            (2) Non-Delegable Activities ....

        c. Negligence Selection or Appointment ....

    2. Liability of the Agent ....

C. Criminal Liability ....

IV. AGENT'S DUTIES

A. Fiduciary Duties ....

    1. Basic Standard – **HOLT** ....

    2. Full Disclosure ....

    3. Conflict of Interest...

    4. Delegation of Duties...

B. Standard of Care...

    1. Obey Instructions...

    2. Inform Principal..

    3. Gratuitous Agent...

C. Exceeding Express Authority ....

D. Shop Rights ....

V. PRINCIPAL'S DUTIES

A. Reimbursement and Indemnification ....

    1. Reimburse Business Expenses ....

    2. Indemnify for Liability ....

B. Safe Work Place...

C. Compensation...

D. Assumption of Risk Abolished...

E. Fellow Servant Rule...

VI. TERMINATION

A. Voluntary..

    1. Completion, Agreement, or Breach ....

    2. Revocation or Renunciation ....

    3. At-Will Employee...

B. Involuntary – **ISIS** ....

    1. **I**ncapacity or Death of Principal ....

    2. **S**ource of Agency Supply Destroyed ....

    3. **I**llegality of Agency Agreement..

    4. **S**ubject Matter of Agency Destroyed ....

C. Agency Coupled with an Interest ....

D. Notice to Creditors or Customers ....

    1. Actual Notice to Past Customers...

    2. Constructive Notice to Third Parties...

CHAPTER 1

BUSINESS ASSOCIATIONS

Agency Index

Actual Customer Notice .... T 1-42

Agent's Breach of Warranty
of Authority .... T 1-41

Agency Coupled with an
Interest .... T 1-42

Agency Termination .... T 1-41

Agent Liability .... T 1-39

Agent's Duties .... T 1-40

Apparent Authority .... T 1-37, 42

Assumption of Risk .... T 1-41

At Will Contract .... T 1-36

At-Will Employee .... T 1-42

Breach of Fiduciary Duty .... T 1-40

Business Entities .... T 1-38

Business Manager .... T 1-37

Capacity .... T 1-38

Compensation .... T 1-41

Conflict of Interest .... T 1-40

Constructive Notice .... T 1-42

Contract Liability .... T 1-38

Creation of Agency .... T 1-36

Criminal Liability .... T 1-40

Dangerous Activity Delegation .... T 1-39

Death of Principal .... T 1-42

Definition .... T 1-35

Del Credere Agent .... T 1-36

Delegation of Duties .... T 1-40

Deliveryperson .... T 1-37

Disclosed Principal .... T 1-39

Employment Nexus .... T 1-39

Estoppel Authority .... T 1-37

Exceeding Express Authority .... T 1-41

Express Authority .... T 1-36

Express Authority Limitations ..... T 1-36

Factor .... T 1-36

Fellow Servant Rule .... T 1-41

Fiduciary Duties .... T 1-40

Frolic and Detour .... T 1-39

Full Disclosure .... T 1-40

General Agency .... T 1-36

Gratuitous Agent .... T 1-40

Illegality of Agency .... T 1-42

Implied Authority .... T 1-37

Implied Authority Lacking .... T 1-37

Incapacity of Agent .... T 1-38

Incapacity of Principal .... T 1-42

Indemnification .... T 1-41

Independent Contractors .... T 1-39

Infant Agent .... T 1-38

Infant Principal .... T 1-38

Inform Principal .... T 1-40

Inherent Authority .... T 1-37

Involuntary Termination .... T 1-42

Land or Related .... T 1-36

Liability of the Agent .... T 1-40

Liability of the Principal .... T 1-38, 39

Liability to Third Parties .... T 1-38

Necessity .... T 1-38

Negligent Selection or
Appointment .... T 1-40

Non-Delegable Activities .... T 1-39

Nondisclosure of Principal's
Incapacity .... T 1-38

Notice to Creditors or
Customers .... T 1-42

Oral Appointment .... T 1-36

Ostensible Authority .... T 1-37

Partially Disclosed Principal .... T 1-39

Past Customers .... T 1-42

Principal's Duties .... T 1-41

Prior Issue Distribution .... T 1-13

Purchase Agent .... T 1-37

Ratification .... T 1-37

Real Estate .... T 1-36

Registration Alteration .... T 1-35

Registration Cancellation .... T 1-35

Registration Requirements .... T 1-35

Registration Status .... T 1-35

Reimbursement .... T 1-41

Renunciation of Agency .... T 1-41

Revocation .... T 1-41

Safe Work Place .... T 1-41

Sales Representative .... T 1-36

Salesperson .... T 1-37

Shop Rights Doctrine .... T 1-41

Source of Agency Supply
Destroyed .... T 1-42

Special Agency .... T 1-36

Standard of Care .... T 1-40

Statute of Frauds .... T 1-36

Subject Matter of Agency
   Destroyed ....T 1-42
Termination....................................T 1-41
Tort Liability ....T 1-39
Undisclosed Principal ....T 1-39
Voluntary Termination..................T 1-41
Work Place Safety.........................T 1-41

CHAPTER 1

PART B

PARTNERSHIPS

RIGOS BAR REVIEW SERIES

UNIFORM MULTISTATE ESSAY EXAM (MEE) REVIEW

CHAPTER 1

BUSINESS ASSOCIATIONS

PARTNERSHIPS

Table of Contents

A.   Sub-Topic Exam Issue Distribution.. Text 1-53

B.   Opening Argument and Primary Issues... Text 1-55

C.   Text .... Text 1-57

    I.   Partnership Introduction.. Text 1-57

    II.   Partnership Entity Organization .... Text 1-57

    III.   Partnership Property Rights... Text 1-59

    IV.   Partnership Rights and Relationships.. Text 1-60

    V.   Partnership Liability to Third Parties .... Text 1-61

    VI.   Partnership Dissociation... Text 1-63

    VII.   Partnership Dissolution and Windup.. Text 1-64

    VIII.   Partnership Conversion and Mergers .... Text 1-65

    IX.   Limited Partnerships .... Text 1-65

    X.   Limited Liability Partnership .... Text 1-68

D.   Magic Memory Outlines® .... Magic Memory Outlines 1-69

E.   Partnership Essay Questions...Questions 1-113

F.   Partnership Essay Answers .... Answers 1-117

G.   Partnership Index... Index 1-73

H.   Acronyms .... Acronyms 15-623

RIGOS BAR REVIEW SERIES
MEE SUB-TOPIC FREQUENCY DISTRIBUTION

PARTNERSHIP

	2/09	7/08	2/08	7/07	2/07	7/06	2/06	7/05	2/05	7/04	2/04	7/03	2/03	7/02	2/02	7/01	2/01
Opening Argument		/			/	/					/	/					/
Definition		/			/	/					/	/			/		/
Formation		/				/											
Implied						/											
Sharing Profits						/											
Property Rights of a Partner		/													/		
Partners' Ownership Interest		//													/		
Attachment by Judgment Creditors		//															
Relations of Partners to One Another		/				/					/	/					/
Profit and Loss		/				/					/	/					/
Management Rules		/									/	/			/		/
Right to Books & Records		/													/		
Liability to Third Parties						/					/						/
Agency Rules		/				/					/						/
Authority		/															
Termination																	/

	2/09	7/08	2/08	7/07	2/07	7/06	2/06	7/05	2/05	7/04	2/04	7/03	2/03	7/02	2/02	7/01	2/01
Within Scope of Partnership		/				/					/	/					/
Contracts with Third Parties						/					/	/					
Dissociation		/									/						/
Dissolution		/									/						/
Winding Up		/									/						/
Triggered if Partner Leaves											/						
Notice to Third Parties																	/
Limited Partnerships					//						/						
Rights of Limited Partners					//												
Requests for Information					//												
Obligations and Liabilities of Limited Partners					/												
Control Rule					//												

OPENING ARGUMENT AND PRIMARY ISSUES

BUSINESS ASSOCIATIONS

There are a few thoughts that should usually be stated at the beginning of every answer. These will score you easy points and let the grader know you are in the right topic area.

Most essays should have an "opening argument": a brief, broad statement that shows you understand the broad significance of a legal topic. The opening argument also suggests to the grader that she is about to read a thoughtful and well-organized essay.

Many subjects also have "primary issues" that can be discussed up front or integrated into the essay answer. IMPORTANT: Do not merely regurgitate these statements on the exam without addressing the issues actually raised by the facts, or you will not pass.

<u>PARTNERSHIP</u>

- **Partnership Opening Argument:** A partnership is an association to carry on and manage as co-owners a business for profit. Express intent to form a partnership is not required.

- **Sample Primary Issue Statements:**

  - To create a partnership, parties must intentionally act, but they do not need to realize they are forming a partnership or describe it as a partnership.

  - No written agreement or filing is usually required to form a partnership.

  - Partners have unlimited joint and several liability for all partnership debts.

  - Sharing of profits is presumptive evidence of partnership status.

  - Unless otherwise agreed, all partners share partnership profit and losses equally.

  - The apparent or inherent authority of a partner in carrying out the ordinary course of partnership business binds the partnership in contract.

  - Partnership tort vicarious liability may be present if the partner was acting in the ordinary scope and course of the partnership business.

  - A conveyance of a partner's ownership interest without permission no longer terminates the entity, but merely transfers the right to receive profits and losses, not participation in management.

  - Partnership creditors may attach property held in an individual partner's name if partnership assets were used for the acquisition.

- All partners are fiduciaries with a duty of loyalty including the requirement to exercise due care, operate in good faith and fair dealing, not compete or take partnership opportunities, and account to the partnership for any benefit received.

- Dissociation of a partner occurs upon withdrawal, expulsion, death, or incapacity.

LIMITED PARTNERSHIP

- **Limited Partnership Opening Argument:** A limited partnership (LP) is created by state statute.

- **Sample Primary Issue Statements:**

  - A written LP certificate must be filed centrally at the Secretary of State's office.

  - A general partner has a fiduciary duty of loyalty and care to the partnership entity and limited partners.

  - A limited partner's liability is limited to their contributed capital unless they participate in management or allow their name to be used in the partnership trade name.

I. PARTNERSHIP INTRODUCTION

A. RUPA In General

This section covers provisions of the 1997 ALI's Revised Uniform Partnership Act (RUPA), as amended. Partners may negotiate terms that override the RUPA default provisions. However, no provision may eliminate a partner's duty of good faith, fair dealings, and loyalty. Similarly, a partner's access to partnership records and financial statements may not be unreasonably restricted by the partnership agreement. Third-party rights cannot be restricted.

B. Definition

A general partnership is an association of two or more persons who intend to carry on and manage as co-owners a business for profit.

> **MEE Tip:** Always begin your essay answer with this definition.

1. Types of Partnerships: A partnership may be 1) for a definite term; 2) for a particular undertaking (i.e., a joint venture); or 3) at will (the default rule) with no time limit.

2. Co-Owner Requirement: The "co-owner" requirement distinguishes a partnership from an agency relationship where the agent receives a share of the business profits.

3. No Presumption: A joint tenancy, tenancy in common, tenancy by the entireties, joint property or community property does not of itself establish a partnership.

4. Share of Profits: Receipt of a share of profits of a business is presumptive evidence of partnership status (and so potential personal liability). Profits do not include sharing gross receipts, distributions for wages, proceeds of a sale, rents, or principal or interest on a loan.

5. Capital and Profit: All partners have the same percentage interest in capital, profit and loss allocations, and distributions unless agreed to the contrary. [RUPA § 202]

II. PARTNERSHIP ENTITY ORGANIZATION

A. Requirements

There are no filing requirements for a general partnership, parties must intentionally act in such a way as to create a partnership. However, it is not necessary that the parties realize they are forming a partnership or describe their business as a partnership.

1. Statement of Partnership Authority: A written partnership agreement is not usually required. However, a partnership may file a written Statement of Partnership Authority which contains the partnership name, the address of the chief executive office, and usually an in-state office. It may list partners' names and designate authority to transfer real property; this designation is conclusive against buyers in most jurisdictions.

2. Statement of Denial: A person named as a partner may file a statement of denial of the authority or status of a partner. This imputes constructive notice to third parties. Filing is effective for five years.

3. Fictitious Name: A partnership operating under a fictitious name other than the true partners' names must usually register with the Department of Licensing in the state.

4. Non-Waivable Provisions: No partnership agreement may restrict the individual partner's access to financial statements, right to inspect books or records, eliminate the obligation of good faith and fair dealings between partners, or restrict the rights of third parties.

B. Capacity

Common law rules apply to capacity. Infants may disaffirm their partnership interest, but cannot withdraw contributed capital to the detriment of creditors. Corporations, LLCs, and other partnerships may be a partner in most states. Either spouse can be a partner in a non-realty partnership without the other's consent.

C. Formation Methods

1. Express:

a. Statute of Frauds: An express partnership agreement must be written if the term is specified as over one year. If the partnership is "at will," an oral agreement is allowed. A few jurisdictions require a writing if the purpose of the partnership is to purchase real property.

b. Contributions: There are no restrictions on what can be contributed in return for a partnership interest; services or promissory notes qualify.

c. Equal Capital Accounts: Under the RUPA, after capital contributions, all partners own the same percentage of equity capital interest and share profits equally.

2. Implied:

a. Sharing Profits: Partnership may be implied by the owners sharing net profits (not gross returns). This is prima facie evidence which establishes a rebuttable presumption of joint and several liability. The burden of proof shifts to the alleged partner to show he was not a partner, but rather an employee, independent contractor, or creditor.

b. Other Situations: Depending upon the facts and circumstances, partnership liability may also extend for situations involving sharing in management, contribution to capital, or other activity that strongly indicates a partnership.

3. Estoppel: A person who represents himself by word or conduct as a partner, or knowingly allows his name to be used in the partnership's tradename, may become a partner by

estoppel. This protects third parties who have extended credit on the faith of such representation. If the representation was made in a public manner, this protection may be extended to creditors who did not actually receive the communication. [§308]

> **MEE Tip:** Look for a transaction with a third party who wants to go against the other partners under a joint and several liability theory. Was there sufficient intent demonstrated to indicate that a partnership was formed so the owners are jointly and severally liable?

III. PARTNERSHIP PROPERTY RIGHTS

A. Definition

Partners have property rights in their ownership interest in the partnership as an entity and the right to participate in management.

1. Entity Ownership: Partnership property is not owned by the partners individually, but rather the partnership as an entity. [§ 501]

2. Presumptions: Property acquired with partnership assets is partnership property even if not held in the partnership name. Conversely, property acquired in the partners' individual names is presumed to be separate, even if used for partnership purposes. [§203 and 204] Both these presumptions are rebuttable. Other factors to be considered include whether improvements to the property were made by the partnership.

> **MEE Tip:** Look for a partnership creditor attempting to go against property held in the name of one or more of the individual partners. Were partnership assets used for the acquisition or did the partnership pay for property improvements?

B. Partners' Ownership Interest

The partner's ownership interest in the partnership is his share of profits and losses and right to receive distributions. This is to be treated as personal property. [§ 502]

1. Common Law: A conveyance of partnership ownership interest under the common law dissolved the partnership.

2. Modern Conveyance: Under the RUPA, a conveyance merely entitles the assignee to receive their transferor's share of profits and losses. The transferee has no right to participate in management or administration of the partnership, unless all the other general partners agree. In addition, the transferee cannot inspect the partnership books or require any information or account of partnership transactions. These rights remain with the transferor partner. [§ 503]

> **MEE Tip:** Many exam questions involve on partner conveying his ownership interest to a third party.

C. Charging Orders

A judgment creditor of an individual partner can request a court order charging the interest of the partner for the unsatisfied amount of the judgment. Any distribution, share of profits, or money due the debtor partner is thereafter paid directly to the judgment creditor. A receiver may be appointed to liquidate the debtor partner's ownership interest.

IV. PARTNERSHIP RIGHTS AND RELATIONSHIPS

A. Fiduciaries

All partners are fiduciaries with both a duty of loyalty and a duty of care in their dealings with one another and the partnership.

1. General Standards:

a. Loyalty: A partner's duty of loyalty to both the partnership and the other partners has three **CAP** aspects.

(1) Competition: To refrain from competing with the partnership before the partnership is dissolved. This non-competition duty terminates upon disassociation.

(2) Adverse Interests: To refrain from dealing with the partnership as a party or on behalf of a party that has an interest adverse to the partnership.

(3) Partnership Benefits and Property: To account to the partnership and hold as trustee for it any property, or benefit derived by the partner in the conduct and winding up of the partnership business or derived from a use by the partner of partnership property. This includes the misappropriation of a partnership opportunity.

b. Care: Partners cannot engage in grossly negligent or reckless conduct, intentional misconduct, or a knowing violation of law.

c. Good Faith and Fair Dealing: In addition to the duties of loyalty and care, each partner has an obligation of good faith and fair dealing with respect to the partnership.

d. Partnership Transactions: The RUPA authorizes partners to lend money to and transact other business with the partnership subject to other applicable law.

2. Liability of Partner: A partnership may bring an action against a partner for a breach of the partnership agreement or a duty that causes harm to the partnership. [§ 404]

MEE Tip: Breach of fiduciary duty, competing with the partnership, or taking a partnership opportunity are frequently tested on the bar exam.

B. Profit and Loss Sharing

Each partner shares equally in profits, losses, and liabilities, unless special allocations are agreed upon. Profit sharing ratios are applicable to loss allocations unless otherwise agreed. No partner is entitled to compensation for partnership activities, except for "winding up" activities (dissolving the partnership) or for extraordinary efforts under the common law. The partnership shall reimburse and indemnify all the partners for expenditures and personal obligations incurred in the ordinary and proper conduct of its business. [§ 401]

C. Management Rule

1. Majority Rule: All partners have equal rights in day-to-day management. Ordinary partnership decisions are to be determined by the majority vote of the general partners.

2. Unanimous Approval: Admission and expulsion of general partners, as well as changing the partnership agreement, requires unanimous approval of all partners.

3. Outside Ordinary Course: Decisions "outside the ordinary course" of the partnership business may increase all partners' legal exposure and therefore require unanimous approval of the partners. [§ 150(10)] The UPA previously included in this category confessing judgment against the partnership, submitting a claim for arbitration, an assignment for the benefit of creditors, or any act which would make it impossible to carry on the partnership business, such as a bulk sale of assets or a sale of the business's goodwill. What is now important enough to be "outside the ordinary course" of business is left to the court to decide. [§ 401]

> **MEE Tip:** Prior law listed five extraordinary acts that required unanimous consent before the partnership was bound. The court now makes this decision.

D. Right to Books and Records

Books and records are to be kept at the chief executive office of the partnership. Each partner shall have access to and a right to inspect and copy relevant documents during ordinary business hours in a reasonable manner. Prior notice is required and a reasonable copying charge may be imposed. All partners are also entitled to an annual accounting. [§ 403]

E. Information

A partnership must render true and full information about its business and affairs to all partners. A partner may demand access to any other reasonable, proper information.

> **MEE Tip:** Denying access to partnership financial statements and records and failure to render information are frequent claims asserted by minority partners.

F. Action by Partnership and Partners

A partnership may maintain an action against a partner for breach of contract or violation of duty. A partner may bring suit for legal or equitable relief against the partnership or another partner without causing a dissolution. Courts are available to resolve internal disputes as the partnership continues in operation. [§ 405]

V. PARTNERSHIP LIABILITY TO THIRD PARTIES

A. General Liability

All partners are personally liable for all partnership debts. The partnership is bound by admissions of any partner and charged with knowledge or notice communicated to any partner by a third party source. [§§ 101(5) and (6)] However, § 125 provides that an entering partner is liable only to the extent of his contribution for partnership obligations incurred prior to his admission.

B. Agency Rules

Every partner is an agent for the partnership principal. [§ 301]

1. Contract Liability:

a. Ordinary Course: The apparent or inherent authority of a partner in carrying out the ordinary course of the partnership business binds the partnership in contract.

b. Not in Ordinary Course: A partnership is not liable for acts where express, implied, or apparent authority is missing, such as a law firm partner buying an apartment building. There is also no partnership liability if the third party knew or had received notice that the acting partner lacked authority. A partner's act that is not apparently in the ordinary course and scope of the partnership business requires actual authority to bind the partnership.

2. Tort Liability: Tort vicarious liability may be present if the partner was acting in the ordinary scope and course of the partnership business. [§ 305]

> **MEE Tip:** Partnership questions always include agency issues. Partners enter into contracts or damage a third party. Was there sufficient (usually apparent) authority to bind the partnership?

C. Joint and Several Liability

All partners are jointly and severally liable for partnership obligations to third parties, both contracts and torts committed in the ordinary course of business. [§ 306 and 307]

> **MEE Tip:** Joint and several liability is heavily tested and must be discussed in every answer. Partners' liability is one of the reasons why LP, LLP, and LLC entities are so popular today.

D. Conveyance of Partnership Property

1. Property Held in Partnership's Name: Any partner may convey title to partnership property held in the partnership's name. If the conveyance violated the partnership agreement or lacked authority, the partnership may recover if the third party grantee knew of the lack of authority. Recovery is not allowed if the grantee re-conveyed the property to a subsequent transferee without knowledge the original conveyance was unauthorized.

2. Property Held in Individual Partner's Name: Conveyance of partnership property by a partner in his own name transfers only that partner's equitable interest. A transfer limited to equitable interest also applies if the property is held in the name of both the partnership and some or all of the individual partners.

3. Real Property Transfer: The RUPA includes real and personal property in the above transfer rules. The partnership may specify in its filed Statement of Partnership Authority which partners are authorized to transfer partnership real property. Such an authorization is binding constructive notice upon transferees of the real property. An unauthorized conveyance may be recovered by the partnership. [§ 302]

VI. PARTNERSHIP DISSOCIATION

> **MEE Tip:** Look for partners leaving the partnership – voluntarily, through expulsion, or death.

A partner may become dissociated from a partnership. If so, the dissociated partner should be paid the value of her ownership interest. If there were only two partners, dissolution and winding up is necessary. [§ 601 and 602]

A. Dissociation Events

1. Express Will: A partner may withdraw at any time. This power is not a legal right if it violates the partnership agreement, e.g., leaving before the end of the specified term.

2. Expulsion:

a. By Partners: The other partners, by unanimous vote, may expel a partner with or without cause if this power is contained in the partnership agreement. Otherwise, expulsion is allowed only for limited reasons, such as transferal of ownership interest without approval, wrongful conduct, or materially breaking the partnership agreement.

b. Judicial: A court may expel a partner who engages in misconduct relating to the partnership business.

3. Insolvency: A petition for bankruptcy, assignment of essential assets to creditors, a court order charging the partner's interest, or appointment of a bankruptcy trustee will all qualify, unless vacated or stayed within 90 days.

4. Death of Partner: Dissociation is automatic upon a partner's death or incapacity.

B. Wrongful Dissociation

Withdrawal in violation of the partnership agreement may create damages in favor of the other partners or the partnership. Dissociation by a partner is not wrongful if made within ninety days of another partner's dissociation or pursuant to a judicial determination.

C. Dissociation Effect

Dissociation does not necessarily terminate the partnership, as under prior law. However, if a partner of a partnership-at-will dissociates, the partnership will dissolve. The dissociated partners lose their right to participate in management and conduct of the partnership business. The partner's duties of loyalty and care survive only for matters arising out of and events occurring before the partner's dissociation.

D. Purchase of Dissociated Interest

If the entity is not dissolved, the partnership shall purchase the dissociated partner's ownership interest.

1. Price: The buyout price is the pro-rata share of the partnership net assets (assets minus liabilities) on a going concern basis or asset liquidation basis. This price calculation may be specified in the partnership agreement or otherwise agreed on. Damages for wrongful dissociation may be offset against the buyout price.

2. Non-Agreement: If the parties cannot agree on a buyout price within 120 days, the partnership shall tender in cash to the dissociating partner its estimate of buyout price. This must include an explanation of the proposed buyout price and current financial statements. The dissociating partner then has 120 days to initiate a legal action, or one year if the partnership failed to tender payment or an offer to pay. [§ 701]

E. Dissociating Partner's Ongoing Liability

1. Authority Terminates: A partner loses actual authority to bind the partnership upon dissociation but this does not necessarily cancel lingering apparent authority to third parties.

2. Two-Year Window: A third party who reasonably believed that the dissociated partner was still a partner may go against the partnership within two years of dissociation. [§ 702]

3. Statement of Dissociation: The ongoing partnership or dissociating partner may file a statement of dissociation with the office of the Secretary of State. 90 days after filing, all persons are deemed to have constructive notice. [§ 704]

4. Prior Obligations: Dissociation does not discharge any liability for obligations incurred before dissociation. The partnership shall indemnify a dissociated partner for future-created liabilities, but this does not extinguish a third party's rights. [§ 703]

5. Partner's Name: Continued use of the dissociated partner's name by the partnership does not necessarily make the dissociated partner liable. [§ 705]

MEE Tip: Dissociation is fairly new to the Revised Act and should be discussed in your answer.

VII. PARTNERSHIP DISSOLUTION AND WINDUP

A. Events Causing Dissolution

Dissolution will occur if at least half of the remaining partners so decide. The partnership is automatically dissolved and its business must be wound up.

1. Partnership Agreement: The agreement may specify a terminating event or the stated partnership term may expire causing termination.

2. Illegality: An event making the business unlawful causes dissolution.

3. Judicial Determination: A court may order dissolution upon a showing of economic frustration, a partner's conduct making business continuation impractical, or a showing that it is equitable to wind up the partnership business. [§ 801]

B. Partnership Continues After Dissolution

1. Purpose: After dissolution, a partnership continues only for the purpose of winding up the business, after which it is terminated.

2. Participation: A partner who has not wrongfully dissociated may participate in winding up. Judicial supervision of winding up is possible.

3. Liability: A partnership is only bound by appropriate winding-up action by a partner, unless a third party to a transaction did not have notice of dissolution. A partner who creates liability by an unauthorized act is liable to the partnership for any damages. [§ 802]

4. Statement of Dissolution: A partner may file a statement that the partnership has dissolved and is winding up its business. This cancels a filed statement of partnership authority and limits agency apparent authority. Constructive notice to third parties is effective 90 days later.

C. Liquidation Distribution Priority – CPU

Dissolution requires "winding up" and liquidation of assets. Profits or losses from asset liquidation are credited or charged to the partners' accounts. Partnership debts are paid, and a final distribution made to the partners. Each class shares pro rata in **CPU** distribution priority:

- <u>C</u>reditors, including, to the extent permitted by law, partners who are creditors,
- <u>P</u>artners for capital account contributions, and finally,
- <u>U</u>ndistributed profits to partners.

D. Settlement and Contribution Right

If distribution results in partnership insolvency, partners may be assessed a required contribution. The allocation of an insolvent partner's share may turn obligations between partners and the partnership into liabilities between the partners personally. Any partner or creditor may enforce the contribution right. If a partner pays more than his equal share, he has a right of contribution. [§ 807]

VIII. PARTNERSHIP CONVERSIONS AND MERGERS

The RUPA covers the conversion of a partnership to a limited partnership, and mergers of two or more partnerships. Conversion or merger must be approved by the partners. Dissenters have appraisal rights to receive the fair value of their partnership interest. After conversion, the partnership must file a certificate of limited partnership.

IX. LIMITED PARTNERSHIPS

A. Requirements

Limited partnerships (LPs) are based on the Revised Uniform Limited Partnership Act (RULPA) in most jurisdictions. This statute adds certain requirements to general partnership rules. An LP combines characteristics of a partnership and a corporation. Matters not covered by the RULPA are controlled by the general partnership statute (RUPA).

> **MEE Tip:** In many jurisdictions, LLCs and LLPs have made traditional LPs obsolete. But LPs may still appear on the MEE.

1. Certificate of Limited Partnership: A written LP certificate must be filed centrally in the Secretary of State's Office, or the LP fails and a general partnership results. At filing, joint and several liability for all limited partners is cut off.

2. Name: The name must contain "limited partnership" or "L.P." and cannot contain the name of a limited partner. [§ 020]

3. Office for Records and Registered Agent: The LP's office address must be identified. The LP must keep a record of the contributions of every partner, financial statements, and tax returns for the last three years. A registered agent must be appointed for service of process and the LP's geographical address (not a post office box) must be specified. [§ 040]

4. General Partner: LPs require at least one general partner, which may be a corporation or other entity. The certificate must specify each partner and their geographical address. General partners have fiduciary duties of loyalty and care to the partnership entity and limited partners.

5. Foreign Limited Partnerships: Foreign LPs must register with the Secretary of State's Office before transacting business in the state. [§ 902]

6. Annual Reporting: All LPs must file an annual report.

7. Advantages: The chief advantage of an LP over a general partnership is that limited partners are liable only to the amount of their contributed capital. This is similar to corporate shareholders but with the advantages of partnership taxation and special allocations. [§ 190]

MEE Tip: Many LP, LLP, and LLC questions involve the liability for events and acts which occurred shortly before filing. This may split the liability status of the partners/members.

B. Prohibited Functions

1. Management and Name: A limited partner cannot actively participate in the control of the partnership or allow his name to be used in the partnership trade name. A limited partner who violates this rule is liable only to a third party who reasonably believed that the individual was a general partner.

2. Approved Functions: Without "participating in control of the business," a limited partner may act as a consultant, contractor, agent, employee, or surety for the entity. A limited partner may also bring a derivative action, and propose or approve incurring debt, a change in the nature of the business, or the admission or removal of a general or limited partner. [§ 190]

3. Service Contributions: A limited partner's contribution may now be in the form of cash, notes, or past or future personal services. [§ 270]

C. Liability to Third Parties

The broad list of approved functions of § 190 tends to restrict a limited partner's exposure to third parties. There are two exceptions which will create liability.

1. Named in Tradename: A limited partner who knowingly permits his name to be used in the tradename of the entity is liable to third parties who extend credit to the entity. The third party must lack knowledge that the limited partner is not a general partner.

2. Holding Out: If a limited partner represents to a third party that he is a general partner, he will at a later time be estopped to deny the liability of a general partner.

> **MEE Tip:** Many questions focus on a limited partner who becomes liable because of active participation in the management of the business or being held out as a partner.

D. Ownership Interests

1. General Partner Changes: Admission of a general partner(s) requires the written consent of all existing partners. Addition or deletion of a general partner requires an amendment to the filed certificate. [§ 220]

2. New Limited Partners: A limited partner can generally sell or assign his ownership interest without causing dissolution, unless otherwise provided in the partnership agreement. New limited partners may be subject to an agreement requiring general partners' consent.

3. Partner Bankruptcy: A general partner's bankruptcy creates a withdrawal or dissociation for that partner, and may subject the entity to claims by the partner's individual creditors to the extent of the general partner's ownership interest. A limited partner's bankruptcy has no effect on the partnership entity's existence.

4. Allocations: Absent a contrary agreement, profit and losses and distributions are allocated according to the capital contribution values as stated in the LP certificate. [§ 300]

> **MEE Tip:** Allocation of LP profits and distributions – capital account balances – are different from the general partnership default rule of equal sharing. Thus it makes for a good exam topic.

5. Fiduciary Duty: General partners have a fiduciary duty to limited partners. Secret profits from transactions between the general partner and the partnership will be disgorged.

6. Derivative Action: A limited partner may bring a partnership derivative action if the general partner having authority refuses to initiate such an action after demand.

7. Dissenter Rights: A limited partner may dissent from a merger of the entity and is entitled to receive the fair value of their partnership interest.

8. Other Partner's Rights: Most other limited partners' rights are the same as in a general partnership: the right to vote, receive annual financial statements, and inspect records.

E. Dissolution

Entity dissolution results when the last general partner dies or withdraws. [§ 440] In addition, any partner can apply for a court decree of dissolution. [§ 450]

X. LIMITED LIABILITY PARTNERSHIPS (LLP)

Not all states recognize Limited Liability Partnerships, in which partners are treated as corporate shareholders.   Partners are insulated from contract and tort liability (including malpractice), but not their own torts, or those of their directly supervised subordinates.

A. Formation and Trade Name

An "application" is filed instead of a certificate; errors in the application do not affect validity. The trade name must include the words "Limited Liability Partnership" or "LLP."

B. Contributions and Allocations

There are no restrictions on contributions, but like an LLC, allocation of profit and loss are determined by the agreed value of the partners' contribution.

C. Professional Practices

The LLP is usually available to all persons authorized to practice under the professional incorporation rules of the jurisdiction.

D. Partner's Liability

Typically malpractice insurance, a bond, bank letter of credit, or other deposit is required if the partners want to escape personal liability.

MEE Tip: Professionals using a PLLC or PLLP are individually liable for a threshold amount in many states if malpractice insurance is not carried to a defined amount. No practice entity will shield a professional from their own negligence or that committed by their subordinates.

PARTNERSHIP

Magic Memory Outlines®

I.   PARTNERSHIP INTRODUCTION
A. RUPA In General ....

B. Definition ....

    1. Types of Partnerships ....

    2. Co-Owner Requirement..

    3. No Presumption ....

    4. Share of Profits ....

    5. Capital and Profit ....

II. PARTNERSHIP ENTITY ORGANIZATION
A. Requirements..

    1. Statement of Partnership Authority...

    2. Statement of Denial ....

    3. Fictitious Name...

    4. Non-waivable Provisions..

B. Capacity..

C. Formation Methods...

    1. Express ....

        a. Statute of Frauds...

        b. Contributions ....

        c. Equal Capital Accounts ....

    2. Implied ....

        a. Sharing Profits ....

        b. Other Situations ....

    3. Estoppel...

III. PARTNERSHIP PROPERTY RIGHTS

A. Definition...

   1. Entity Ownership...

   2. Presumptions ....

B. Partners' Ownership Interest..

   1. Common Law...

   2. Modern Conveyance ....

C. Charging Orders ....

IV. PARTNERSHIP RIGHTS AND RELATIONSHIPS

A. Fiduciaries..

   1. General Standards ....

      a. Loyalty – **CAP** ....

         (1) **C**ompetition ....

         (2) **A**dverse Interests..

         (3) **P**artnership Benefits and Property......................................

      b. Care..

      c. Good Faith and Fair Dealing ....

      d. Partnership Transactions..

   2. Liability of Partner ....

B. Profit and Loss Sharing ....

C. Management Rule..

   1. Majority Rule ....

   2. Unanimous Approval ....

   3. Outside Ordinary Course ....

D. Right to Books and Records..

E. Information ....

F. Action by Partnership and Partners..

V. PARTNERSHIP LIABILITY TO THIRD PARTIES

A. General Liability...

B. Agency Rules...

   1. Contract Liability ....

      a. Ordinary Course..

      b. Not in Ordinary Course...

   2. Tort Liability ....

C. Joint and Several Liability...

D. Conveyance of Partnership Property ....

    1. Property Held in Partnership's Name ....

    2. Property Held in Individual Partner's Name ....

    3. Real Property Transfer ....

VI. PARTNERSHIP DISSOCIATION

A. Dissociation Events ....

    1. Express Will ....

    2. Expulsion ....

       a. By Partners ....

       b. Judicial ....

    3. Insolvency ....

    4. Death of Partner ....

B. Wrongful Dissociation ....

C. Dissociation Effect ....

D. Purchase of Dissociated Interest ....

    1. Price ....

    2. Non-Agreement ....

E. Dissociating Partner's Ongoing Liability ....

    1. Authority Terminates ....

    2. Two-Year Window ....

    3. Statement of Dissociation ....

    4. Prior Obligations ....

    5. Partner's Name Use ....

VII. PARTNERSHIP DISSOLUTION AND WINDUP

A. Events Causing Dissolution ....

    1. Partnership Agreement ....

    2. Illegality ....

    3. Judicial Determination ....

B. Partnership Continues After Dissolution ....

    1. Purpose ....

    2. Participation ....

    3. Liability ....

    4. Statement of Dissolution ....

C. Liquidation Distribution Priority – **CPU** ....

D. Settlement and Contribution Right ....

VIII. PARTNERSHIP CONVERSION AND MERGERS

IX. LIMITED PARTNERSHIPS

A. Requirements ....

   1. Certificate of Limited Partnership ....

   2. Name..

   3. Office for Records and Registered Agent..

   4. General Partner..

   5. Foreign Limited Partnerships..

   6. Annual Reporting ....

   7. Advantages ....

B. Prohibited Functions..

   1. Management and Name ....

   2. Approved Functions ....

   3. Service Contributions..

C. Liability to Third Parties ....

   1. Named in Tradename ....

   2. Holding Out ....

D. Ownership Interests ....

   1. General Partner Changes..

   2. New Limited Partners ....

   3. Partner Bankruptcy..

   4. Allocations..

   5. Fiduciary Duty..

   6. Derivative Action ....

   7. Dissenter Rights ....

   8. Other Partner's Rights..

E. LP Dissolution ....

X. LIMITED LIABILITY PARTNERSHIPS

A. Formation and Tradename ....

B. Contributions and Allocations...

C. Professional Practices..

D. Partner's Liability ....

CHAPTER 1

BUSINESS ASSOCIATIONS

Partnership Index

Action Against Partner .... T 1-61
Action Against Partnership .... T 1-61
Adverse Interests .... T 1-60
Agency .... T 1-62
Books and Records .... T 1-61
Capacity .... T 1-58
Capital Accounts .... T 1-58
Capital and Profit .... T 1-57
Charging Orders .... T 1-59
Co-Owner Requirement .... T 1-57
Common Property .... T 1-57
Competition with Partnership .... T 1-60
Contract Liability .... T 1-62
Contribution Right .... T 1-65
Conversions .... T 1-65
Conveyance of Partnership
    Interest .... T 1-59
Conveyance of Partnership
    Property .... T 1-62
Contributions .... T 1-58
Death of Partner .... T 1-63
Default Provisions .... T 1-57
Definitions .... T 1-57
Dissociation .... T 1-63
Dissolution .... T 1-64
Duty of Loyalty .... T 1-60
Entity Organization .... T 1-58
Express Partnership .... T 1-58
Expulsion .... T 1-63
Fair Dealing .... T 1-60
Fictitious Name .... T 1-58
Fiduciary Duties .... T 1-60
Formation Methods .... T 1-58
General Partner .... T 1-66
Good Faith .... T 1-60
Illegality .... T 1-64
Implied Partnership .... T 1-58
Information .... T 1-61
Insolvency .... T 1-63
Joint and Several Liability ...... T 1-58, 62
Joint Property .... T 1-57
Joint Tenancy .... T 1-57
Joint Venture .... T 1-57
Judicial Dissolution .... T 1-64
Judicial Expulsion .... T 1-63

Liability to Partnership .... T 1-61
Liability to Third Parties .... T 1-61
Limited Liability Partnership .... T 1-68
Limited Partner .... T 1-67
Limited Partnerships .... T 1-65
Loyalty .... T 1-60
Management .... T 1-61
Mergers .... T 1-65
Non-Waivable Provisions .... T 1-57, 58
Outside Ordinary Course .... T 1-61
Partner by Estoppel .... T 1-58
Partner's Creditors .... T 1-67
Partners' Ownership Interest .... T 1-59
Partnership at Will .... T 1-57
Partnership Creditors .... T 1-59
Partnership Dissolution .... T 1-64
Partnership for a Definite Term .... T 1-57
Partnership for a Particular
    Undertaking .... T 1-57
Prior Issue Distribution .... T 1-53
Professional Practice .... T 1-68
Profit and Loss .... T 1-57, 60
Property Rights .... T 1-59
Purchase of Dissociated Interest ... T 1-63
Real Property Transfer .... T 1-62
Records .... T 1-61
Relations of Partners to
    One Another .... T 1-60
Revised Uniform Partnership
    Act (RUPA) .... T 1-57
Right to Books and Records .... T 1-61
Rights of Partners .... T 1-72
Share of Profits .... T 1-57
Sharing Profits .... T 1-58
Statement of Denial .... T 1-58
Statement of Dissolution .... T 1-65
Statement of Partnership
    Authority .... T 1-57
Statute of Frauds .... T 1-58
Tenancy by the Entireties .... T 1-57
Tenancy in Common .... T 1-57
Tenancy in Partnership .... T 1-58
Tort Liability .... T 1-62
Transactions with Partnership ...... T 1-60
Types of Partnerships .... T 1-57

Withdrawal from Partnership........T 1-63
Windup...T 1-64
Wrongful Dissociation ....T 1-63

CHAPTER 1

PART C

CORPORATIONS

AND LLC

RIGOS BAR REVIEW SERIES

UNIFORM MULTISTATE ESSAY EXAM (MEE) REVIEW

CHAPTER 1

BUSINESS ASSOCIATIONS

CORPORATIONS AND LLCs

Table of Contents

A.	Sub-Topic Exam Issue Distribution	Text 1-79
B.	Opening Argument and Primary Issues	Text 1-83
C.	Text	Text 1-85
	I. Corporations Introduction	Text 1-85
	II. Corporations Formation Process	Text 1-85
	III. Domestic or Foreign Status	Text 1-87
	IV. Corporate Liability	Text 1-88
	V. Directors and Officers	Text 1-89
	VI. Stock Shares	Text 1-92
	VII. Shareholder Rights	Text 1-93
	VIII. Shareholder Liability	Text 1-95
	IX. Mergers, Share Exchange, & Affiliations	Text 1-97
	X. Dissolutions	Text 1-98
	XI. Professional Services Corporations	Text 1-99
	XII. Limited Liability Companies	Text 1-100
	XIII. Attributes of Business Entities	Text 1-104
D.	Magic Memory Outlines®	Magic Memory Outlines 1-105
E.	Corporations Essay Questions	Questions 1-111
F.	Corporations Essay Answers	Answers 1-115
G.	Corporations Index	Index 1-123
H.	Acronyms	Acronyms 15-624

RIGOS BAR REVIEW SERIES
MEE SUB-TOPIC FREQUENCY DISTRIBUTION

CORPORATIONS & LIMITED LIABILTY COMPANIES

	2/09	7/08	2/08	7/07	2/07	7/06	2/06	7/05	2/05	7/04	2/04	7/03	2/03	7/02	2/02	7/01	2/01
Opening Argument	/					/	/	/	/		/	/	/	/	/	/	/
Default Rules	/							/	/				/		/		
Formation Process (general)											/		/				
Promoter Liability								/			/		/		/		
Fiduciary Duty of Promoter								/			/		/				
Corporate Name Requirements								/					/		/		
Articles of Incorporation	//							/			/		/		/		
Filing Requirements								/			/				/		
Organizational Meeting								/									
Ratification																	
Undercapitalization													/				
Partnership Before Filing								/			/		/				
Corporate Liability												/		;			
Registered Agent														;			
Acts of Agents											/		/	;			
Ultra Vires Action																	
Tort Liability						/	/				/	/					/
Directors & Officers	/		/												/		
Election															/		

Course 5328. Copyright by Rigos Bar Review Series – MEE.

	2/09	7/08	2/08	7/07	2/07	7/06	2/06	7/05	2/05	7/04	2/04	7/03	2/03	7/02	2/02	7/01	2/01
Notice of Meetings							✓				✓					✓	
Removal of Officers/Directors											✓		✓	✓		✓	
Dividends											✓			✓			
Fiduciary Duties	✓		✓	✓				✓		✓	✓	✓	✓	✓	✓	✓	✓
Personal Liability	✓							✓			✓	✓	✓	✓		✓	
Interested Transaction	✓		✓					✓			✓	✓					
Conflict of Interest	✓		✓					✓	✓		✓			✓		✓	
Taking Corporate Opportunity								✓	✓		✓			✓			
Role of Officers	✓										✓						
Only One Officer							✓										
Agency Powers									✓			✓		✓			
Business Judgment Rule	✓								✓			✓			✓		
Indemnification	✓					✓								✓			
Stock Shares								✓	✓			✓	✓		✓		
Payment for Shares								✓			✓		✓		✓		
Price of Shares								✓			✓						
Preemptive Rights											✓			✓	✓		
Cumulative Voting														✓	✓		
Shareholder Rights						✓			✓			✓			✓	✓	✓
Notice of Meetings									✓			✓		✓	✓	✓	
Records and Financial Statements												✓					
Proxy Requirements							✓										✓
Legal Rights						✓									✓		
Derivative Action									✓					✓		✓	

	2/09	7/08	2/08	7/07	2/07	7/06	2/06	7/05	2/05	7/04	2/04	7/03	2/03	7/02	2/02	7/01	2/01
Dissenters' Rights																	
Ordinary Decisions						✓			✓			✓					
Fundamental Changes						✓	✓		✓			✓			✓	✓	✓
Changes Affecting SH Rights															✓		
Mergers						✓								✓			
Sale of Substantially All Assets									✓							✓	
Dissolution of Corporation												✓					
Dividends							✓										
Shareholder Liabilities						✓						✓				✓	✓
Statutory Duties												✓					
To Extent of Investment												✓	✓	✓		✓	
Equitable Liability								✓				✓	✓	✓	✓	✓	✓
Dissolution												✓				✓	
Resolution & SH												✓				✓	
Administrative Approval																	✓
Notice to Third Parties												✓					

OPENING ARGUMENT AND PRIMARY ISSUES

BUSINESS ASSOCIATIONS

There are a few thoughts that should usually be stated at the beginning of every answer. These will score you easy points and let the grader know you are in the right topic area.

Most essays should have an "opening argument": a brief, broad statement that shows you understand the broad significance of a legal topic. The opening argument also suggests to the grader that she is about to read a thoughtful and well-organized essay.

Many subjects also have "primary issues" that can be discussed up front or integrated into the essay answer. IMPORTANT: Do not merely regurgitate these statements on the exam without addressing the issues actually raised by the facts, or you will not pass.

<u>CORPORATIONS</u>

- **Corporations Opening Argument:** State law and the Revised Model Business Corporations Act control unless default provisions are modified by the Articles of Incorporation or bylaws.

- **Sample Primary Issue Statements:**

  - An incorporator/promoter is a fiduciary, owes the corporation a duty of good faith, loyalty, fair dealing, and can make no secret profit.

  - An incorporator/promoter is personally liable for any pre-incorporation contracts.

  - Articles of Incorporation must be filed, generally with the Secretary of State, and include the corporate name, registered agent, and stock information. Until the "de facto" corporation becomes "de jure," shareholders are treated as general partners with unlimited joint and several liability.

  - Corporate directors, officers, and senior executives have a fiduciary duty to stay informed about business affairs and avoid conflicts of interest, including usurping a corporate opportunity and trade secret appropriation.

  - Interested transactions (between directors or officers and the corporation) must be disclosed in the corporate minutes, be at market terms, and be approved by a majority of non-interested directors or shareholders.

  - The Business Judgment Rule protects directors and/or officers who make honest errors of judgment after reasonable investigation.

  - Corporate articles may restrict personal liability of directors, officers, and managers for simple negligence, but not for knowing violations of law, intentional misconduct, or personal benefit to which they are not properly entitled.

  - Shareholders have a right to vote for directors and resolutions at the annual meeting held after proper notice.

- Shareholders must receive annual financial statements within 120 days of the fiscal year end and have the right to inspect and copy corporate records upon demand.

- Shareholders dissenting from a fundamental corporate change shall receive the fair value of their shares in cash, as determined by agreement or the court.

- Shareholders are not liable for corporate acts unless they received dividends that caused insolvency, or the corporate veil is pierced to avoid unjust enrichment.

- A corporate veil may be pierced and shareholders held personally liable if the corporate shell was used for fraud.

- Shareholders' legal remedies are "direct action" if the act had a direct negative impact on personal finances, or "derivative action" if damage is to the corporation.

- A shareholder may seek a judicial dissolution if there were illegal or fraudulent activities, the majority is oppressing the minority shareholders, there is a waste of assets, or there is a corporate deadlock threatening irreparable corporate injury.

LIMITED LIABILITY COMPANIES

- **LLC Opening Argument:** A Limited Liability Company (LLC) has elements in common with both corporations and partnerships, but is neither. LLC members have limited liability like corporate shareholders, yet are taxed like partners in a partnership.

- **Sample Primary Issue Statements:**

  - Members of a properly formed LLC have personal liability only up to the value of their contribution.

  - Failure to properly file an LLC certificate with the Secretary of State will result in general partnership status with joint and several member liability.

  - All LLC members participate in management, unless the certificate of formation vests management power in a designated manager.

  - LLC managers owe the LLC a duty of care, but they are not liable for simple negligence. Grossly negligent and reckless conduct, intentional misconduct, and knowing violations of the law may lead to liability. Some states apply the business judgment rule, which protects LLC managers for good faith business decisions.

  - Members of an LLC may not maintain a direct action for mismanagement when the manager's alleged misconduct caused harm only to the LLC.

  - LLC members are not personally liable to third parties for torts unless the member participated in the tortious act.

  - Dissociation of an LLC member is caused by the member's death, expulsion, withdrawal, insolvency, or lack of capacity.

BUSINESS ASSOCIATIONS

CORPORATIONS AND LLCs

I.   CORPORATIONS INTRODUCTION

Three out of four MEEs have a corporations essay question. Most jurisdictions have adopted most of the provisions of the ALI's 2003 Revised Model Business Corporation Act (RMBCA) and subsequent amendments. Below are the general rules in effect in the majority of jurisdictions. A corporation is an entity separate and distinct from its shareholders, who generally have limited liability. A corporation has potentially perpetual life and is under the authority of the directors, who are elected by the shareholders.

II.   CORPORATIONS FORMATION PROCESS

> **MEE Tip:** If the facts indicate a lawyer was involved in corporate entity formation, consider discussing the 3 problem Cs of **c**ompetency, **c**onfidentiality, and **c**onflicts of interests.

A.   Incorporator / Promoter

The incorporator (in some jurisdictions, the "promoter") is the moving force in putting together the business plan. He acts as an agent in initiating and organizing the forming corporation. Usually, he also arranges for the initial capitalization of the corporation.

1. Fiduciary Status: An incorporator is a fiduciary and owes the corporation a duty of good faith, loyalty, and fair dealing. Full and effective disclosure is therefore required. An incorporator can make no secret profits or have any conflict of interest. Interested transactions may be ratified by the subscribers or the board of directors.

2. Personal Liability: An incorporator is always personally liable on pre-incorporation contracts. Because the corporation was not in existence, the corporation is not liable to a third party absent an adoption or novation. If the corporation expressly or impliedly adopts or ratifies the pre-incorporation contract, the third party can go against both the corporation and the incorporator. The incorporator may also seek indemnification from the corporation. [§ 2.04]

3. Undisclosed Principal: If the incorporator does not disclose the planned corporation to a third party, the agency rules of undisclosed principal apply, making the incorporator potentially personally liable.

4. Compensation: There is no absolute right to reimbursement for time or costs for pre-incorporation services and costs under the RMBCA. The Board of Directors may approve the payment of prior compensation, however.

B. Articles of Incorporation

Duplicate originals of the articles of incorporation signed by the incorporator(s) must be filed with the secretary of state. Filing begins the corporate legal existence.

1. Name Reservation: A corporate name may be reserved for 180 days. Tradenames must be distinguishable from any granted to and/or reserved by another corporation, LP, LLC, or LLP.

2. Contents:

a. Required Information – RINS: The articles must include at least minimal **RINS** information: **R**egistered Agent, **I**ncorporator(s), **N**ame, and certain **S**tock details.

(1) Registered Office and Agent: Street address of the office and the registered in-state agent are required. The agent must also affirmatively agree to serve.

(2) Incorporator(s): The names of each formal incorporator are required.

(3) Name: The name must contain one of the words "corporation," "incorporated," "company," or "limited," or an abbreviation, "corp.," "inc.," "co.," or "ltd."

(4) Stock Information: The number of authorized shares per class must be stated. If more than one class exists, a distinguishing description for each class is required. Preferences, limitations, voting powers, and relative rights must be the same for the whole class.

b. Optional Information: Other information is optional, but default provisions may apply if the articles are silent. The articles may not indemnify a director for **FICE** – **F**iduciary duty breach, **I**ntentional wrongdoing, **C**riminal act, or **E**xcess distributions to shareholders.

c. Compliance: Filing of the articles of incorporation by the secretary of state is conclusive evidence that the entity has complied with all legal conditions of incorporation.

3. Article Amendments: The board may amend the articles for most minor ministerial matters, but shareholders must approve any change that significantly affects the rights of shareholders. Shareholders must approve the proposal by a two-thirds vote, (or a majority, for public companies). Upon approval, the corporation must file restated articles of amendment.

> **MEE Tip:** Under the ALI model RMBCA almost all of the default provisions apply only if the articles do not specify to the contrary. Every answer should mention this treatment.

C. De Facto and De Jure Status

1. De Facto Corporations: A corporation is "de facto" when its articles have been rejected by the Secretary of State because they fail to comply with some provision of the state corporate laws, but the public treats the entity as if it were a "true" corporation. Purported shareholders of the de facto enterprise may be held jointly and severally liable as partners.

2. De Jure Corporations: A "de jure" corporation is one that substantially complies with the statute; shareholders then usually become insulated from personal liability.

D. Estoppel Status

When a third party deals to his detriment with what he believed to be a corporation, but which was in fact not perfected, a "corporation by estoppel" may result. After the corporation reaches "de jure" status, it is estopped from denying liability.

E. Organizational Meeting

An organizational meeting is required. This is where the corporation accepts stock subscriptions, shares are distributed, and the initial board of directors is elected, The initial board will go on to appoint the officers. At the organizational meeting, the newly elected board will commonly ratify and adopt the incorporator-promotor's pre-incorporation contracts. An actual in-person meeting is not necessary in most states if the meeting minutes are written.

F. Bylaws and Reports

1. Bylaws: The incorporators or board shall adopt corporate bylaws in the organizational meeting. The bylaws define and specify the day-to-day corporate governance rules and determine the number of directors.

2. Close Corporations: Many states have special requirements for private corporations owned by less than 10 to 50 members. Legal filings are required but significantly less than a public corporation. Instead of shares, close corporations have member's interest expressed as a percentage of the total ownership. Each member is entitled to participate in management and shareholder's agreements usually restrict or make outside ownership sales subject to right of first approval and non-competition agreements. Majority or controlling shareholders have heightened fiduciary duties to minority owners.

3. Initial Report: The corporation must usually file an initial written report with the secretary of state within 120 days of filing the articles, so the organizational meeting must be held within that time. The report must specify the officers, directors, registered agent with street address, and a description of the nature of the business.

G. Annual Report

Corporations must file a state annual report and pay the annual license fee. The requirement usually includes the names and addresses of the directors, principal officers, registered agent and a brief description of the nature of the business. Also required is the total authorized, issued, and outstanding shares by class and series.

H. Hierarchy of Authority

State corporate law is the ultimate authority, and no prohibition therein can be overruled by any corporate document. The corporate articles rank next, followed by the corporate bylaws which define and specify the day-to-day governance rules. Lowest in authority are corporate resolutions and the minutes of the ongoing corporate meetings.

III. DOMESTIC OR FOREIGN STATUS

Corporations are "domestic" in their state of incorporation; the laws of that state control internal corporate governance. A corporation is "foreign" in all other states, and lacks authority to transact business until it obtains a certificate of authority from the secretary of state's office.

A. Nexus to State

A corporation is deemed to be "transacting business" in a state if the in-state activities are permanent, substantial, and continuous. The in-state nexus must exceed isolated transactions, sales by mail, or through independent contractors. Appearing as a defendant in court, owning property, holding meetings, having a passive website, or borrowing money do not, by themselves, constitute minimum contacts sufficient for jurisdiction. A fixed permanent facility within the state or an active website taking orders generally qualifies as "transacting business." States continue to expand the definition of criteria necessary to tax foreign corporations selling to residents over the internet.

B. Consequences of Transacting Business

If "transacting business," the foreign corporation must incorporate or register as a foreign corporation by obtaining a certificate of authority and local licenses, appointing an in-state registered agent, and paying applicable state taxes. Failure to comply creates liability for a daily civil monetary penalty, and may also result in an injunction and personal liability to shareholders.

C. Effect on Legal Actions

Non-registration will deprive the corporation of the right to maintain suit in the state courts; this makes the corporation's contracts legally unenforceable. The right to defend against a lawsuit, however, cannot be denied under the Constitution.

D. Long-Arm Statutes

Foreign unregistered corporations may be subject to state legal process through the long-arm statute in effect in most states if the event creating the damages arose in the state. Examples include an automobile accident or physical injury caused by an authorized corporate agent.

IV. CORPORATE LIABILITY

A. Registered Agent

Proper service of process, notice, or demand upon a corporation may be made upon the corporate registered agent. Service on the secretary of state is adequate if the corporation has no registered agent or the registered agent cannot reasonably be served at the registered office.

B. General Liability

Corporate liability extends to the contracts of its officers and agents made with express, implied, or apparent agency authority. Ratification of a prior unauthorized contract may also create corporate liability. A corporation is vicariously liable for the torts of its employees if the agent was within the course and scope of employment under the doctrine of "respondeat superior." A corporation may attempt to defend against a third party's action by alleging the officer, employee, or agent exceeded his actual authority.

C. Purpose and Powers

1. Any Lawful Purpose: A corporation may engage in any lawful business unless the articles set forth a more limited purpose.

2. "Ultra Vires": The incapacity defense of "ultra vires" (outside the authority of corporate statute, articles, or bylaws) may be asserted only by a shareholder seeking to enjoin or set aside the corporate act.

a. Application: A frequently tested example is where a corporate act violates a statute, or a transaction is prohibited under the corporate articles.

b. Third Parties: A third party may not avoid a contract on the basis that the corporation was without authority to make the contract. Similarly, a corporation may not defend a suit on a contract on the basis that the contract is ultra vires, unless the third party had knowledge of the restriction in the articles of incorporation.

V.   DIRECTORS AND OFFICERS

A. Board of Directors

The board shall exercise all corporate powers, make tactical decisions, and manage the business to assure its profitability and long term success. An individual director does not have agency authority to act on behalf of the corporation unless specifically stated in the corporation articles. There is no minimum number of directors or state residency requirements.

1. Elections / Appointment: The corporate directors are elected by the shareholders. The articles may also grant the board authority to appoint directors under special circumstances.

a. Cumulative Voting Rule: "Cumulative voting" gives minority shareholders representation on the board of directors only if the articles so affirmatively provide. Each shareholder may cumulate his / her total votes (shares times open board seats) and cast them for one director-nominee. Prior notice of intent to cumulate is required.

> **MEE Tip:** Look out for this topic, as many states refused to adopt the no cumulative voting default provision of the Revised Model Act on the grounds that the change was anti-shareholder.

b. Removal: Directors may be removed by shareholders, with or without cause, upon a special meeting and prior notice. A director may also be removed by the court for gross abuse of duty, fraudulent conduct, or intentional wrongdoing. Officers cannot remove directors.

2. Dividends: The board has the sole power to declare dividends and distributions paid to shareholders. A dividend may not be paid if the corporation will be rendered insolvent by the distribution and thus unable to pay its liabilities as they become due. Directors who approve such a dividend will be personally liable.

3. Board Meetings: A quorum requires a simple majority of directors be present, but telephone attendance counts in most states. Articles or bylaws may reduce this to no less than one-third.

a. Regular Meetings: Regular board meetings may be held without notice unless the articles or bylaws provide otherwise. A director may also waive notice, and waiver is implied if they attend and participate in the meeting unless a specific objection is raised.

b. Special Meetings: Two days' notice must be given to hold a special meeting of the board. Oral notice may be allowed only if the articles of incorporation or bylaws approve.

c. Voting Proxy: Directors cannot give a voting right proxy to another director. They must usually attend board meetings in person or by phone / video conference. Directors present are deemed to have assented to a board action unless (1) they dissent or object at the beginning of the meeting, (2) their dissents or abstentions are entered into the minutes of the meeting, or (3) they deliver written notice of their dissent within a reasonable time thereafter.

d. Action Without Meeting: If every director signs written consent, an action may be proper without a formal meeting. A later ratification of the action may also qualify.

e. Electronic Transmissions: Notice by electronic transmission now qualifies in most states if the director or shareholder has consented to receiving notice in that form.

4. Fiduciary Duties: Members of the board of directors, officers, and senior executives are fiduciaries with a duty of loyalty to put the corporate best interest ahead of their own. A director is held to the standard of care that a prudent director would exercise under similar circumstances. The director must act in the best interests of the corporation and treat corporate assets as if they were their own. Private corporate affairs must be kept confidential.

a. Member Duties: Board members are under an affirmative, good faith duty to stay informed about the corporation's financial condition. The due care required is that of a reasonably prudent person in managing their own business affairs. Directors must direct the officers. They must also devote considerable attention to corporate affairs, exercise due diligence in decisions, remain loyal, and obey articles, bylaws, policies, and resolutions. [§ 8.30]

b. Conflicts of Interest – CUT: Directors and executives must avoid conflicts of interest, including "self-dealing" such as competing, or appropriating a business-related opportunity. Profits from such transactions must be disgorged. **CUT** conflicts are prohibited as follows:

(1) Competing With Corporation: Directors and executives must not compete during their employment term, especially if the activity is likely to harm the corporation.

(2) Usurp Corporate Opportunity: A director or executive may not take for themselves an existing or future corporate business-related opportunity. An exception may apply if the corporation affirmatively rejects the opportunity after full disclosure and the insider makes adequate disclosure that they intend to pursue the opportunity.

(3) Trade Secret Appropriation: Directors and executives may not appropriate a corporate trade secret. Some courts apply the "inevitable disclosure doctrine" to an executive who moves to a direct competitor, and may issue an injunction.

(4) Remedy: Such transactions may be set aside and/or their profits may be disgorged. Damages resulting from the breach of fiduciary duty may also be recovered.

c. Interested Transactions: Directors' inherent conflict requires that self-dealing transactions be disclosed and recorded in the corporate minutes. The price must be at market and fair with reasonable terms, and properly approved by a majority of non-interested directors and shareholders upon notice and full disclosure.

d. Close Corporation: Members in a close corporation are subject to all Directors' duties above. Restrictions on the members' ownership may include non-compete agreements and stock ownership transfer restrictions. The majority may not oppress the minority shareholders.

B. Officers

Corporate officers have authority to carry out the ordinary everyday business operations, as enumerated in the corporate bylaws. Agency authority to third parties is usual.

1. Corporate Positions: The officers usually consist of a president, vice-president, secretary, and treasurer, each of whom shall be appointed by the board. In most states, the same individual may simultaneously hold more than one or all of the offices.

2. Dismissal and Fiduciary Duties: Unless under contract, officers are at-will employees and may be dismissed by the board with or without cause. Officers are held to the same fiduciary duty as directors and are responsible to the corporation for negligent performance.

> **MEE Tip:** Look for a potential breach of fiduciary duty and/or conflict of interest transaction by a director and/or officer. Has the conflict of interest or interested transaction been disclosed and approved by the Board or Shareholders?

C. Business Judgment Rule – RIS

Directors and officers must exercise due care and diligence in managing the corporation. The "prudent business person" standard of care test is objective; liability is most likely if the behavior at issue was reckless or grossly negligent. Honest, good faith errors of judgment made after reasonable investigation do not usually lead to personal liability.

1. Reasonable Reliance: Directors and officers are entitled to rely upon information and assurances from officers, employees, and committees unless they know reliance is unwarranted. This includes experts' opinions, legal counsel, or public accountant's reports.

2. Criteria Applied: The test for the trier of fact is whether an ordinarily prudent business person under similar circumstances could have reasonably reached the same conclusion. There must have been a reasonable investigation made, an analysis of the investigation should be undertaken and deliberated. Any negligence cannot be gross. Courts are reluctant to second-guess the presumption of validity for most director and officer business judgments where fraud, illegal activity, or self-dealing were not present.

> **MEE Tip:** The Business Judgment Rule defense is on every exam. Remember **RIS**: the business decision appeared to be **r**easonable at the time, was made **i**n good faith, and **s**upported by a rational basis after an investigation appropriate to the importance of the matter.

D. Indemnification Agreements

Indemnification agreements require the corporation to pay for damages, legal costs, and attorney fees incurred by directors, officers, or employees personally named as a party to a suit. If permitted by the corporate articles, shareholders may vote to indemnify a defendant, unless she engaged in breach of fiduciary duty, a knowing violation of law, or received a personal benefit to which she was not entitled. A court may also order indemnification *sua sponte* if the defendant was fairly and reasonably entitled to such in view of all relevant circumstances.

> **MEE Tip:** The Business Judgment Rule and indemnification should always be mentioned when directors, officers or employees committed business error or were named as defendants.

VI.   STOCK SHARES

A.   Stock Subscriptions and Options

Stock subscriptions are a future shareholder's promise to purchase stock. These may be entered into before incorporation and are generally irrevocable for a period of six months. Subscriptions must be uniform as to all members of the stock class or series. A default in the stock subscription is treated as any other debt due the corporation. Contrast this to options, warrants, or rights which do not require purchase of the shares.

B.   Payment for Shares

Payment for shares may be in cash, promissory notes, other property or benefit, or past or future services performed for the corporation. Directors are required to sell shares only in a prudent manner. In the absence of fraud, a good faith determination by the board as to the value and adequacy of the consideration received from a stock sale shall be conclusive.

C.   Negotiable Securities

Stock shares are negotiable. Endorsement on the certificate by the named stockholder is necessary for the transfer of ownership. Any restraints on alienation or other transfer restrictions must be conspicuously noted on the stock certificate. Reasonable restrictions such as the corporation or other shareholders having a right of first refusal are permissible. A transfer is effected when the endorsed certificate is presented to the corporation. An owner whose certificate is lost, destroyed, or wrongfully taken must notify the issuer within a reasonable time.

D.   Preemptive Rights

Preemptive rights entitle shareholders to purchase pro rata shares of any new stock issue in order to maintain their proportional ownership interest. This is common in closely-held corporations. Parties may waive this right, and under the Revised Act, no preemptive rights exist unless specified in the articles of incorporation. Many states still require preemptive rights unless the articles provide to the contrary.

MEE Tip: Traditional preemptive rights differ from the RMBCA, and so may arise on the exam.

E.   Preferred Shares

Preferred shares may have superior rights to dividends and/or upon liquidation than common shares, but do not usually carry voting rights.

F.   Other Definitions

1.   Authorized Shares: The incorporation articles must specify the number and classes of shares that are permitted. Further issuance requires amendment by the shareholders.

2.   Outstanding Shares: Issued but unredeemed shares are "outstanding."

3.   Redeemed Shares: A corporation may repurchase or redeem its own shares. Redeemed shares may be cancelled or held in the treasury for potential reissue. Cancelled shares may not be reissued. Treasury shares do not have voting rights or receive dividends.

VII. SHAREHOLDER RIGHTS

MEE Tip: Shareholder rights are a common topic, and may be tricky to spot if the issue is fairly raised by a significant omission / failure to act, rather than an improper action.

A. Meetings and Voting

Shareholders have the right to vote for directors and resolutions at the annual meeting.

1. Shareholder Meetings: A corporation shall hold an annual regular meeting of shareholders. A special meeting may be called by the board or by at least 10% of the stockholders making written demand upon the corporation and specifying the meeting purpose(s).

2. Court-Ordered Meeting: Any shareholder may seek judicial remedy on the grounds that the annual meeting was not held, or a special meeting demand was disregarded.

3. Notice of Meetings:

a. Time Requirements: Shareholders must receive notice of the date, time, and place of any meeting no fewer than 10 days or more than 60 days beforehand. For special meetings, notice must describe the agenda. If the meeting includes action on fundamental changes which affects shareholders, plan of merger, sale of substantially all assets, or dissolution, notice must be given no fewer than 20 days before the meeting. Determination of shareholders entitled to meeting notice may not be set more than 70 days prior to the meeting.

b. Notice Waiver: Defects in notice are waived if the shareholder attends and does not object at the beginning of the meeting.

4. Resolutions and Obtaining Shareholder Lists: Shareholders owning 1% of outstanding certificates or shares valued at a minimum of $1,000 may usually submit business-related resolutions. Prior notice to the corporation may be required. The corporation must make available a list of eligible shareholders 10 days prior to the meeting.

5. Voting in Person or Proxy: A shareholder may vote their shares in person or by proxy. Proxy authority requires a signed appointment form and is effective for 11 months.

6. Quorum Requirements: A simple majority of the shares entitled to vote is sufficient to form a quorum unless the articles call for a higher percentage. Once the quorum is present, all actions conducted thereafter at the meeting are authorized. [§ 7.25]

MEE Tip: Corporate meetings and notice are heavily tested. Regular board meetings may be held without notice. All shareholder meetings require 10 days' notice. Special board meetings require two days' notice. Shareholder meetings re: fundamental changes require 20 days notice.

7. Electronic Transmissions: Notice, proxies, and consent may be given by electronic transmission, provided that the shareholder has consented to this communication mode.

8. Action Without Meeting: A meeting is not required if all the shareholders entitled to vote on the action so consent and sign a written waiver.

9. Voting Trusts and Agreements: A written voting trust confers on the trustee the power to vote on behalf of all the beneficial interests of members of the stock-block group. A voting trust must be in writing and is only valid for a maximum of 10 years.

10. Other Rights: Shareholders have the right to vote on any amendment to the articles or bylaws that affects their rights, and also to approve loans to officers and directors.

B. Records and Financial Statements

1. Corporate Records: A corporation shall maintain accounting records, a list of shareholders, the articles, bylaws, and minutes of meetings at its principal office.

2. Financial Statements: Shareholders must receive annual financial statements, including balance sheets and income statements, within 120 days of the close of the fiscal year.

3. Inspection Right: Any shareholder has the right to inspect and copy relevant books, records, and shareholder lists for a proper purpose. A written demand which includes the purpose of the inspection is required at least five business days beforehand. The corporation may impose a reasonable charge for copies.

4. Corporate Refusal: If the corporation refuses to permit examination, the court may compel access. The corporation may validly refuse a request if the shareholder intends to use the information for a wrongful purpose such as personal non-corporate business.

> **MEE Tip:** The right to receive financial statements and to inspect records is frequently tested.

C. Legal Remedies

Shareholders have a right to bring a suit against directors and/or officers for gross negligence, fraud, or breach of fiduciary duty. Suits can be undertaken individually or as a class action. There are two general types of shareholder lawsuits.

1. Direct Action: Shareholders allege a company action has had a direct negative impact on their personal finances. An example would be the directors paid dividends to only one class of shareholders.

2. Shareholder's Derivative Action: If the board's action damages the corporation itself, e.g., breach of fiduciary duty, shareholders "derive" the right to sue from the corporation. The corporation is the formal plaintiff. Shareholder(s) must first put written demand on the directors and/or officers to pursue the claim. If they are met with refusal or unreasonable delay, suit may be initiated after 90 days. If the derivative action results in substantial benefit to the corporation, it must pay legal expenses.

3. Business Judgment Rule Defense: Such lawsuits require a clear showing of abuse of discretion. This defense will shield the directors or officers in a close case. See a detailed discussion of the business judgment rule *supra*.

> **MEE Tip:** Look for a minority shareholder with grounds to sue under a direct or derivative action.

D. Shareholder Decision Control

    1. Ordinary Decisions: A simple majority of shareholders' votes usually determines ordinary corporate decisions.

    2. Fundamental Changes: Fundamental corporate changes must be approved by a mere majority of shareholders. 20 days' notice of the meeting is required. Fundamental changes are dissolution, mergers, share exchanges, bulk sales of over 75% of corporate assets not in the ordinary course, and any amendments which significantly impair the rights of shareholders.

> **MEE Tip:** A mere voting preponderance (greater than 50%) is all that is now required under RMBCA, but many states still require approval of at least two-thirds of the shareholders for a fundamental change and most states require a higher percentage for closely-held corporations.

E. Dissenter or Appraisal Rights

    Shareholders who dissent from a fundamental change (see above) have "appraisal rights" to receive the fair value of their shares in cash. This protects minority shareholders from being bulldozed by oppressive majority rule.

    1. Procedure: Prior to the vote, the dissenting shareholder must give the corporation written notice of their objections and intent to demand the appraisal rights if the proposed action is effectuated. Dissenter's stock certificates should be tendered to the corporation and they must not vote on the matter.

    2. Fair Value: The corporation has 30 days to pay the dissenter its estimate of the fair value of the shares plus any accrued dividends and interest. Payment must be accompanied by the corporate explanation of its calculation process and the last set of financial statements. The shareholder has 30 days to contest the corporation's determination. After 60 days, the corporation shall petition the superior court requesting a judicial determination of fair value.

    3. Minority Shareholder's Relief: The appraisal procedure is the only relief normally available to a minority shareholder. Such a shareholder may not challenge the corporate action creating the entitlement unless the act was unlawful or fraudulent.

> **MEE Tip:** Minority shareholders may dissent from a fundamental change and demand appraisal rights for the fair value of their ownership interest. This may be their only remedy.

F. Dividends

    Shareholders have no absolute right to dividend distributions no matter how profitable the corporation. Dividends are determined by the board's discretion. When the board declares a dividend, it becomes a corporate obligation, and the shareholders become unsecured creditors. Unless the articles differ, all shareholders in a stock class must have identical dividends per share.

VIII. SHAREHOLDER LIABILITY

A. General Rule

    A shareholder is not usually liable for the acts or liabilities of a corporation beyond the original investment in the shares. Because of corporate shell abuses, there are exceptions where there may be potential personal liability known generally as "piercing the corporate veil."

B. Statutory Liability

Most states recognize three situations that provide for potential liability to shareholders.

1. Subscription Agreement: A shareholder is responsible for the amount specified in her subscription agreement. Corporate bankruptcy trustees may enforce this right.

2. Equitable Insolvency: Dividends that create insolvency may expose shareholders (and the directors who authorized the distribution) to deficiency liability to creditors.

3. Balance Sheet Test: A dividend distribution is also illegal if after the distribution, the corporation's liabilities (including amounts due preferred shareholders) exceed its assets.

C. Veil Piercing Equitable Liability

Separate corporate existence is usually recognized by the courts. The corporate veil can be pierced through an equity action to avoid fundamental unfairness and unjust enrichment. If successful, the shareholder may be treated as a general partner for liability purposes. Two factors are required to pierce the corporate veil: (1) the corporate form was intentionally used to avoid or evade a duty and (2) disregarding the corporate form is necessary to prevent aiding the fraud or wrong upon an injured party. In some circumstances one corporation may be liable for the debts of another. This may apply in the following situations:

1. Concurrent Affiliates: Concurrent corporate affiliates (parent-subsidiary or brother-sister corporations) may be liable where there is a high degree of integration and deceptive cross-financing. This may apply if the entities were intended to operate as one or there was a commingling and confusion of records, assets, and personnel.

2. Successor Affiliates: If the new entity was a result of a de facto merger or consolidation, or is virtually the same as, and a mere continuation of, the bankrupt corporation, the successor corporation may be liable. If the new entity takes benefits derived from the old corporation, it should also take responsibility for its liabilities.

3. "Mere Sham": The shareholder treats the corporation as their "alter ego."

a. Fraud: Courts may order this form of equitable relief if the shareholder uses a corporate shell to perpetuate a fraud.

b. Failure to Separate: Failure to treat the corporation as a separate business entity and/or a total disregard for corporate formalities are frequent issues. This includes commingling personal and corporate funds and bank accounts, and failing to keep separate books and records. The gutting of a corporation by shareholders who later seek to avoid personal liability suffices to pierce the corporate veil. Material advances and loans to shareholders without proper documentation and authorization by the board may indicate a "mere sham."

4. Estoppel: If the shareholder intentionally and fraudulently misled a third party to believe the entity was a proprietorship or partnership, de facto partnership liability may follow.

MEE Tip: Piercing an insolvent corporate veil is a frequent topic. Look for owners' disregard for the corporate entity or where it would be unjust not to allow the third party a recovery.

IX. MERGERS, SHARE EXCHANGES, AND AFFILIATED GROUPS

Mergers are transactions that raise legal and organizational issues resulting from changes in ownership of the corporation. Mergers must not prejudice the rights of existing creditors. The RMBCA provides a structure and the procedures for mergers and share exchanges.

A. Mergers

A stock-for-stock statutory merger occurs when a surviving company absorbs all the merging entities.

1. Plan of Merger: Both corporations' boards must adopt a formal plan of merger, which discloses the terms and conditions and the manner of converting the shares. Both corporations' shareholders must receive due notice, but the formal plan need only be approved by shareholders of the target corporation. The RMBCA now requires only a mere majority of the shareholders to approve this fundamental change, but many states require two-thirds approval.

2. Articles of Merger: After a plan of merger is approved by the shareholders, articles of merger must be submitted to the secretary of state.

3. Fundamental Change: Mergers are a fundamental change requiring the appraisal buyout of any target corporation's dissenting stockholders.

B. Consolidations

A consolidation occurs when a new corporation is formed and the original corporations cease to exist. Consolidation proposals must also be submitted to a vote of the shareholders.

C. Holding Companies and Subsidiaries

A corporate holding company owns stock of other corporations. A subsidiary is a corporation in which the majority of the shares are owned by a parent corporation. Brother-sister corporations have common shareholders or a corporate parent. An exception to the usual required shareholder approval applies if a parent corporation owns at least 90% of its subsidiary target corporation.

D. Hostile Takeover Protection

Many states limit foreign corporations' ability to conduct hostile or unfriendly purchase attempts of an in-state based corporate target.

1. Equality Required: A tender offer must offer all the target corporation's shareholders the same price per share. This prohibits two-tier takeover attempts.

2. Procedure: The board must consider all bona fide written proposals, and respond in 30 days. The board may refuse the offer outright or decline to recommend it to shareholders.

3. Highest Price Duty: If the board indicates a willingness to sell to a "white knight" over a "raider," it has a duty to obtain the highest price for the shareholders.

E. Synergetic Factors

Business combinations can be categorized as either "horizontal" (involving actual competitors (e.g., Ford buying General Motors)); "vertical" (an upstream supply source and a downstream distribution channel (e.g., Ford buying General Tires)), or "conglomerate" (businesses in different industries or geographical markets (e.g., Ford buying General Foods)).

X.   DISSOLUTION

Dissolution is the legal termination of the corporate entity. Corporations have potentially unlimited life, so some affirmative action is necessary to begin the dissolution process.

A. Voluntary Dissolution

Voluntary dissolution occurs when the corporate charter is surrendered. If business has not commenced or shares been issued, the board may dissolve without shareholder approval.

B. Resolution and Shareholder Approval

To terminate business, the Board must pass a resolution recommending dissolution and notify all shareholders. Shareholders must meet and affirm the proposal with a majority vote. Corporate articles may alter this requirement, but less than a majority of shares will not suffice.

C. Articles of Dissolution

Articles of dissolution are then submitted to the secretary of state's office. A dissolved corporation may not carry on any business except winding up and liquidating its business.

D. Creditors' Claims

The dissolved corporation may dispose of any claims against it by actually notifying its known creditors that they have 120 days to put in a claim.

1. **Rejected Claims:** If the claim is rejected, the creditor has 90 days to file a lawsuit.

2. **Unknown Claims:** For unknown claims, notice must be published in a newspaper of general circulation in the county where the corporation's principal office was last located.

3. **Enforceable Against Shareholders:** Claims tendered within the time period may be enforced against the shareholders to the extent they have received corporate assets.

E. Administrative Dissolution

The secretary of state may move to dissolve a lapsed corporation because of non-filing of the annual report, nonpayment of license fees, or failure to maintain a registered agent or office in the state. The secretary of state will first send the corporation notice, and allow 60 days to cure the defect(s). A dissolved corporation has two years to apply for retroactive reinstatement.

F. Judicial Dissolution

A court may decree dissolution and direct the windup of the corporation's affairs.

1. Shareholder Suit: A shareholder may petition the court to dissolve the corporation if one or more of **FOWD** applies:

  a. Fraud: If directors / officers are involved in illegal or fraudulent activities.

  b. Oppression: Closely-held corporations shareholders often qualify for this relief if the majority shareholders oppress a minority shareholder. Oppression may be through a number of acts or omissions such as by withholding financial information, diluting the minority's proportional ownership interest, or effecting non pro rata stock redemptions.

  c. Waste of Assets: Clear waste or misapplication of corporate assets qualifies.

  d. Deadlock: The board and/or shareholders is deadlocked and corporate irreparable injury is threatened.

2. Creditor Proceeding: A creditor who has reduced a claim to judgment and execution has been returned unsatisfied may also move to dissolve the corporation.

3. Receivership or Custodianship: A court may appoint a receiver to wind up corporate affairs or custodian to carry on the business.

XI. PROFESSIONAL SERVICES CORPORATIONS

Most states now have a special corporate statute regarding professional services such as rendered by architects, attorneys, CPAs, engineers, and physicians.

A. Requirements

1. Only Licensed Professionals: Only professionals legally qualified in at least one state are allowed to be shareholders, directors, or officers of the corporation. All professional services must be rendered by qualified licensed individuals or their directly supervised staff.

2. Professionals Disqualified to Practice: The corporation must have provisions in its articles or bylaws to buy out members who become legally disqualified to practice in the state.

B. Prohibited Activities

1. Only Professional Services: Only professional services and related ancillary services may be performed by the corporation.

2. Idle Funds Exception: However, a professional service corporation may invest its idle funds in real estate, mortgages, stocks, bonds, insurance, or other passive investments.

C. Trade Name

1. Professional Ethics Control: State typically allow any tradename permitted by the relevant professional ethical standards.

2. Deceased Partner's Name: Professional names of deceased partners may be retained without liability to their estate.

3. Corporate Designation Requirement: Trade names must usually include the letters "P.S.," "P.C." or the words "professional service" or "professional corporation." A professional LLC or LLP may be abbreviated by PLLC or PLLP.

D. Death of Shareholder

1. Requirement to Purchase: If a shareholder dies or the shares are transferred by operation of law or court decree, the corporation or other members must purchase the shares.

2. Price Determination: The procedure for determining the fair value price (if no other agreement) parallels the corporate rules covering the rights of dissenting shareholders.

E. Shareholder Personal Liability Shield

An advantage to the corporate form is protection of shareholders from personal liability because the model statute does not prohibit a P.S. corporation from declaring bankruptcy.

1. Full Tort Liability: Corporate indemnification provisions apply to a P.S. corporation. Individual practitioners remain personally and fully liable for their own negligent acts, and those of subordinates under their direct supervision.

2. Dischargeable Contract Damages: Contract liability of the bankrupt entity will not usually be asserted against shareholders. An example is an outstanding corporate lease obligation.

XII. LIMITED LIABILITY COMPANIES (LLC)

A Limited Liability Company (LLC) has elements in common with both corporations and partnerships, but is neither. Members of an LLC usually have limited liability like the shareholders of a corporation and pass-through taxation like the partners in a partnership.

A. Filing Articles of Organization – NOMAD

One or more individuals or other entities may form an LLC by executing and delivering "articles of organization" or a "certificate of formation" to the Secretary of State for filing. Without filing, the entity is treated as a general partnership, with joint and several liability for all members. The articles must contain all **NOMAD** elements:

1. Name: The entity's trade name must include "Limited Liability Company" or "LLC." The entity may not use the words (or abbreviations) for "corporation," "incorporated," "cooperative," "partnership," "limited," "limited partnership," or limited liability partnership."

2. Organizer's Name and Address: Organizers need not be members of the LLC.

3. Manager Managed: Statement if the LLC is to be managed by a manager.

4. Address and Registered Agent: The name and address of a consenting registered agent must be included, and the street and mailing addresses of the principal place of business.

5. Date of Dissolution: The last possible date of dissolution, or a statement that the entity is perpetual. 30 years is the default period.

B. LLC Operating Agreement

The members may enter into a LLC operating agreement. The operating agreement, if any, may be written or oral and provide for the regulation and management of the affairs of the LLC in any manner not inconsistent with law or the articles of organization.

C. Management Authority

1. Managing Member: An LLC is member managed unless the articles vest power to manage the business to a designated managing member. The managing member's role is similar to that of the president in the corporate model. The managing member is elected or removed by a majority vote of the members. A manager may resign by giving written notice to the members and other managers. A resignation does not dissolve the LLC which becomes member managed unless new manager(s) are appointed within 90 days.

2. Third Party Notice: Filing is constructive notice to third parties that only the managing member has agency authority to contract with third parties.

3. All Members Manage: In a member-managed LLC, unless otherwise provided in the articles of organization or any operating agreement, each member has equal rights in the management and conduct of the LLC's business. Members may dissociate, but this does not dissolve the LLC. However a transferee of an ownership interest must be unanimously approved by the existing members for the new owner to be able to participate in management.

4. Duties of Managers: Managers owe a duty of care to the LLC, but they are not usually liable for simple negligence.

5. Manager Liability: Members of an LLC may not maintain a direct action for mismanagement when the manager's alleged misconduct caused harm only to the LLC. Courts may assign liability in derivative action lawsuits for gross negligence, reckless conduct, intentional misconduct, and knowing violations of the law. Some states instead assign liability based upon the business judgment rule, which protects LLC managers for business decisions acted upon on an informed basis, in good faith, and under the belief that the action was in the best interests of the LLC.

D. Ownership Issues

1. Number of Members: In a minority of states an LLC can be composed of just one member, and the LLC "agreement" can be the statement of the sole member.

2. Distribution Allocations: An LLC may make a distribution to a member only if, its manager(s) decides that the fair value of the LLC's assets remains greater than its liabilities plus funds to satisfy other members' superior preferential rights upon theoretical dissolution.

3. Members' Rights: LLC records are subject to inspection and copying at the reasonable request (and expense) of any member during ordinary business hours. Member-managed LLC members all have equal rights in the management and conduct of the business; and any matter relating to the LLC may be decided by a majority. Manager-managed LLC managers equally share managerial rights, and make decisions by majority-rule.

4. **Ownership Transfer:** An LLC ownership interest is transferable in whole or in part unless restricted in the LLC agreement. The assignee shares in profit, loss, and distributions, but can only participate in management as a member if all the other members approve.

E. Standard of Conduct

Members owe only two fiduciary duties to a member-managed LLC and its other members.

1. **Loyalty:** There is a duty of loyalty to account to the LLC and hold for it any property, profit, or benefit derived from business conduct, property, or winding up including the appropriation of an LLC opportunity and competing with the LLC.

2. **Due Care:** A member must exercise a duty of care in the conduct and winding up of the business including refraining from engaging in grossly negligent or reckless conduct, intentional misconduct, or a knowing violation of law.

F. Liability of Members

1. **LLC Authority:** Unlike a partner, an LLC member is not automatically an agent for the LLC. Whether the LLC is member-managed or manager-managed determines whether members have agency authority to bind the LLC. A third party must check the public record.

2. **Member to Entity and Other Members:** Members have standing to file derivative actions, just as shareholders would in a corporation. A member is not usually liable to the LLC itself or other members for ordinary negligence. Liability might exist for breach of contract, use of proprietary information, or breach of fiduciary duty (loyalty and due care). A member who knowingly receives a distribution that renders the LLC insolvent is liable to the LLC.

3. **Third Party Liability:**

a. **Contract Liability to Third Parties:** LLC members and managers are not personally liable for contractual obligations of the entity to third parties unless they were a co-maker, guarantor, or lacked authority to enter into the transaction. Apparent authority to bind the LLC itself in a third party contract is standard for member-managed LLCs.

b. **Tort Liability to Third Parties:** The LLC itself may be liable to third parties for employee's torts committed in the course and scope of business. Neither members nor managers are personally liable unless they participated in the tortious act or failed to supervise the harm creator. Members or managers may be personally liable to the LLC for torts involving their own gross negligence, intentional misconduct, breach of fiduciary duty, or knowing violations of law.

4. **Professional LLCs:** A professional is usually held liable for negligence committed by the professional herself or a subordinate under her direct supervision and control.

5. **Pierce LLC Entity Veil:** A court may "pierce the veil" of an LLC, exposing LLC members to personal liability, just as a corporate veil. Failure to observe LLC formalities (honoring the LLC agreement, annual filings, etc.) are factors in favor of piercing the veil.

G. Dissociation

1. Events of Dissociation: **WIDE** events cause the dissociation of an LLC member.

a. <u>W</u>ithdrawal: Withdrawal is effective upon receiving notice of express will to withdraw.

b. <u>I</u>nsolvency: If a member becomes a debtor in bankruptcy or a trustee, receiver, or liquidator is appointed, there may be a dissociation.

c. <u>D</u>eath or Incapacity: If an individual member person dies, there is dissociation, even though the economic rights continue in the decedent's personal representative. Incapacity is determined by a judicial order or the appointment of a conservator/ guardian.

d. <u>E</u>xpulsion: This may occur pursuant to a judicial order, breach of the operating agreement, or by unanimous consent of the other members.

2. Effect of Dissociation: If the dissociation of the member does not cause a dissolution of the LLC, the dissociating member is entitled to receive any distributions to which an assignee would be entitled.

H. Dissolution

1. In General: An LLC may be dissolved in a manner similar to a corporation. The written LLC agreement may specify a dissolution date, or an event that will automatically trigger dissolution. Written consent of all members (or dissociation of the last member) creates a dissolution unless the business is continued by an assignee within 90 days by voting to admit one or more members.

2. Distribution of LLC Assets: Unlike general partnerships, there is no contribution requirement for members in a dissolution. Assets are distributed, pro rata within each class:

- first, to creditors, including, to the extent permitted by law, creditor-members,
- second, to members and former members who are owed distributions, and
- third, unless contrary to the LLC agreement, return of members' contributions;
- and finally, the member's shares of profits.

MEE Tip: If the LLC certificate fails, or the contract / tort occurred before filing, members are treated as partners in a general partnership. Failure to properly organize an LLC may lead to partnership and joint and several liability issues.

XIII. ATTRIBUTES OF BUSINESS ENTITIES

Entity	Formalities Required	Owners	Management Authority	Agency Authority	Continuity of Life	Limited Liability	Free Transfer-ability of Interests
Sole Proprietor	None	Proprietor	Yes	Yes	Not beyond owner	No	Yes
General Partnership	None	Partners	All partners manage	All partners may commit	No	No	No
Limited Partnership	Filing	At least one general and one limited partner	General partner is sole manager	Only general partner can commit	No	Yes, for limited partners only	Limited partners' interests only
Limited Liability Partnership	Filing	Partners	All partners manage	All partners can commit	No	Yes	No
Corporation	Filing	Shareholders	Board of Directors	Officers and employees can commit	Yes	Yes	Yes
Limited Liability Company	Filing	One or more members	Unless mgmt by "managers" is elected, each member may participate	Only managers can commit LLC	No	Yes	No

RIGOS BAR REVIEW SERIES

UNIFORM MULTISTATE ESSAY EXAM (MEE) REVIEW

CHAPTER 1

BUSINESS ASSOCIATIONS

CORPORATIONS AND LLCs

Magic Memory Outlines®

I.   **CORPORATIONS INTRODUCTION**

II. **CORPORATIONS FORMATION PROCESS**
   A. Incorporator / Promoter ....
      1. Fiduciary Status ....
      2. Personal Liability ....
      3. Undisclosed Principal ....
      4. Compensation ....
   B. Articles of Incorporation ....
      1. Name Reservation ....
      2. Contents ....
         a. Required Information – **RINS** ....
            (1) **R**egistered Office and Agent ....
            (2) **I**ncorporator(s) ....
            (3) **N**ame ....
            (4) **S**tock Information ....
         b. Optional Information – **FICE** ....
         c. Compliance ....
      3. Article Amendments ....
   C. De Facto and De Jure Status ....
      1. De Facto Corporations ....
      2. De Jure Corporations ....
   D. Estoppel Status ....
   E. Organizational Meeting ....
   F. Bylaws and Special Agreements ....
      1. Bylaws ....
      2. Close Corporations ....
      3. Initial Report ....

    G. Annual Report ....

    H. Hierarchy of Authority..

III.   DOMESTIC OR FOREIGN STATUS

    A. Nexus to State ....

    B. Consequences of "Transacting Business" ....

    C. Effect on Legal Actions ....

    D. Long-Arm Statutes ....

IV.   CORPORATE LIABILITY

    A. Registered Agent ....

    B. General Liability ....

    C. Purpose and Powers ....

        1. Any Lawful Purpose ....

        2. "Ultra Vires" ....

            a. Application ....

            b. Third Parties..

V.   DIRECTORS AND OFFICERS

    A. Board of Directors...

        1. Elections – Appointment...

            a. Cumulative Voting Rule...

            b. Removal ....

        2. Dividends ....

        3. Board Meetings...

            a. Regular Meetings...

            b. Special Meetings ....

            c. Voting Proxy...

            d. Action Without Meeting...

            e. Electronic Transmissions ....

        4. Fiduciary Duties..

            a. Member Duties ....

            b. Conflicts of Interest – **CUT** ....

                (1) **C**ompeting With Corporation ....

                (2) **U**surp Corporate Opportunity ....

                (3) **T**rade Secret Appropriation ....

                (4) Remedy ....

            c. Interested Transactions..

            d. Close Corporations ....

    B. Officers...

        1. Corporate Positions...

        2. Dismissal and Fiduciary Duties...

   C. Business Judgment Rule – **RIS**..

      1. Reasonable Reliance ....

      2. Criteria Applied...

   D. Indemnification Agreements..

VI.   STOCK SHARES

   A. Stock Subscriptions and Options ....

   B. Payment for Shares...

   C. Negotiable Securities..

   D. Preemptive Rights ....

   E. Preferred Shares...

   F. Other Definitions ....

      1. Authorized Shares ....

      2. Outstanding Shares..

      3. Redeemed Shares ....

VII. SHAREHOLDER RIGHTS

   A. Meetings and Voting ....

      1. Shareholder Meetings..

      2. Court-Ordered Meeting..

      3. Notice of Meetings ....

         a. Time Requirements ....

         b. Notice Waiver ....

      4. Resolutions and Obtaining Shareholder Lists ....

      5. Voting in Person or Proxy..

      6. Quorum Requirements ....

      7. Electronic Transmissions ....

      8. Action Without Meeting ....

      9. Voting Trusts and Agreements ....

      10. Other Rights..

   B. Records and Financial Statements ....

      1. Corporate Records..

      2. Financial Statements ....

      3. Inspection Right ....

      4. Corporate Refusal..

   C. Legal Remedies ....

      1. Direct Action ....

      2. Shareholder's Derivative Action ....

      3. Business Judgment Rule Defense ....

   D. Shareholder Decision Control ....

      1. Ordinary Decisions..

      2. Fundamental Changes ....

E. Dissenter or Appraisal Rights..

    1. Procedure ....

    2. Fair Value...

    3. Minority Shareholder's Relief...

F. Dividends ....

VIII. SHAREHOLDER LIABILITY

A. General Rule...

B. Statutory Liability ....

    1. Subscription Agreement ....

    2. Equitable Insolvency ....

    3. Balance Sheet Test...

C. Veil Piercing Equitable Liability ....

    1. Concurrent Affiliates ....

    2. Successor Affiliates ....

    3. "Mere Sham" ....

        a. Fraud ....

        b. Failure to Separate ....

    4. Estoppel...

IX. MERGERS, SHARE EXCHANGE, & AFFILIATIONS

A. Mergers..

    1. Plan of Merger ....

    2. Articles of Merger..

    3. Fundamental Change ....

B. Consolidations..

C. Holding Companies and Subsidiaries...

D. Hostile Takeover Protection ....

    1. Equality Required ....

    2. Procedure ....

    3. Highest Price Duty...

E. Synergetic Factors..

X. DISSOLUTION

A. Voluntary Dissolution...

B. Resolution and Shareholder Approval ....

C. Articles of Dissolution ....

D. Creditors' Claims ....

    1. Rejected Claims ....

    2. Unknown Claims ....

    3. Enforceable Against Shareholders ....

E. Administrative Dissolution ....

F. Judicial Dissolution ....

    1. Shareholder Suit – **FOWD** ....

        a. **F**raud ....

        b. **O**ppression ....

        c. **W**aste of Assets..

        d. **D**eadlock...

    2. Creditor Proceeding...

    3. Receivership or Custodianship ....

XI. PROFESSIONAL SERVICE CORPORATIONS

  A. Requirements..

    1. Only Licensed Professionals...

    2. Professionals Disqualified to Practice ....

  B. Prohibited Activities...

    1. Only Professional Services ....

    2. Idle Funds Exception..

  C. Trade Name ....

    1. Professional Ethics Control...

    2. Deceased Partner's Name ....

    3. Corporate Designation Requirement ....

  D. Death of Shareholder..

    1. Requirement to Purchase ....

    2. Price Determination ....

  E. Shareholder Personal Liability Shield ....

    1. Full Tort Liability..

    2. Dischargeable Contract Damages...

XII. LIMITED LIABILITY COMPANIES

  A. Formation, Tradename, and Registered Agent – **NOMAD**..

    1. **N**ame..

    2. **O**rganizer's Name and Address..

    3. **M**anager Managed ....

    4. **A**ddress and Registered Agent..

    5. **D**ate of Dissolution..

  B. LLC Operating Agreement ....

  C. Management Authority ....

    1. Managing Member ....

    2. Third Party Notice ....

    3. All Members Manage..

    4. Duties of Managers ....

    5. Manager Liability...

    D. Ownership Issues ....

        1. Number of Members..

        2. Distribution Allocations ....

        3. Members' Rights ....

        4. Ownership Transfer ....

    E. Standard of Conduct ....

        1. Loyalty ....

        2. Due Care ....

    F. Liability of Members ....

        1. LLC Authority ....

        2. Member to Entity and Other Members ....

        3. Third Party Liability ....

            a. Contract Liability to Third Parties ....

            b. Tort Liability to Third Parties ....

        4. Professional LLCs ....

        5. Pierce LLC Entity Veil ....

    G. Dissociation..

        1. Events of Dissociation – **WIDE**..

            a. **W**ithdrawal ....

            b. **I**nsolvency..

            c. **D**eath or Incapacity..

            d. **E**xpulsion..

        2. Effect of Dissociating Member ....

    H. Dissolution ....

        1. In General..

        2. Distribution of LLC Assets ....

XIII. ATTRIBUTES OF BUSINESS ENTITIES

    A. Sole Proprietor ....

    B. General Partnership..

    C. Limited Partnership..

    D. Limited Liability Partnership..

    E. Corporation..

    F. Limited Liability Company ....

Essay Questions

Question Number 1

Fred's bicycle repair shop had occupied a small storefront on Main Street for as long as anyone could remember. Approaching his twilight years Fred was still spry and sharp, he felt running the shop by himself all these years had kept him young. Recently, however, Fred had convinced Son to come to work for him, with the incentive that someday they would share the business, and eventually Son would inherit it outright. Son agreed, providing they could modernize the shop's appearance, and Fred agreed to have new signage made for the storefront reflecting a more modern look, and offered to rename it "Fred and Son's bicycle repair shop" which pleased Son and he agreed to come to work for his dad.

Within months, word was out about the new products Son had convinced Fred to order, and the little shop was bursting at the seams with merchandise and new customers as well. The newly painted sign cost dearly, but really attracted a whole new crowd who never knew the shop was there before. One afternoon, Son announced he had just signed a three year lease on behalf of Fred and Son's for a large space in the new mall, at triple the cost of the current space which still has six years remaining on a ten year lease. Fred had renewed the current lease previously and had intended to again. While the original space was smaller than he might have liked, Fred felt there was real value in staying in the same location, and his rent was little more than what he had originally negotiated for, long ago when he first leased the space as a young man. Fred did not want to relocate his business.

Son convinced Fred the lesser of two evils was to move into the expensive space, so that the amount of their unpaid lease each month would be the smaller lease amount, until they found a way to mitigate their losses. Fred reluctantly agreed, and moved into the new space over a long holiday weekend, paying a moving crew to relocate his stock. Unable to sublease the original location over the next few months, Fred now seeks your help to determine his options.

1. Can Fred return to the original location free of liability on the new lease? Explain.

2. If not, under what authority would he be bound? Explain.

3. What are the duties and liabilities of Son and Fred to each other? Explain.

Question Number 2

Agent had worked as a carpet installer for Principal for ten years with little prospect of advancement. He decided to venture out and create his own drapery business to do on the side to supplement his income. Principal knew Agent began a drapery installation side business and was fine with it so long as it did not compete with the carpet company. Agent began asking carpet installation customers while he was in their homes if they would like to see his drapery sample books. If they chose to have him do the job within 30 days of carpet installation, he would knock 10 percent off the price. Carpet customer Carrie called Principal asking if he knew anything about the drapery offer, and Principal said he knew of the drapery work Agent was doing, and he was sure it would be of high quality.

Agent failed to properly measure and allow room for the brackets that hold the draperies he was installing at Carries, so he decided instead to cut away at the existing molding to make the needed bracket room. Notching out sections of what unbeknownst to him was a historical landmark window frame caused considerable damage. When Carrie discovered this after he left her house, she immediately called Principal and demanded he make it right. Principal told her he was not in the business of installing draperies, and she should call the company she dealt with. Carrie asserted this was his company, and she had even confirmed prior to service and received Principal's endorsement of Agent.

1. Who is liable to Carrie, Agent, Principal or both? Explain.

2. What theories can be argued for the Agent being solely liable? Explain.

3. What theories can be argued for the Principal having liability? Explain.

Question Number 3

Ralph and Fred were both seasoned land surveyors who decided to form their own surveying company. Their agreement stated that Ralph would handle the front end of the business and manage the customers and work crews, and Fred would handle behind the scenes administration such as the office staff, creditors, and keeping the books.

While out surveying a tract on a job site they had been working off and on for some time, Ralph learned that Fred personally received a company discount on a land purchase from the owner of this tract some time ago without telling him. When asked, Fred said, "We aren't in business together to buy and sell land, so it was none of your business," but Ralph began to wonder what else he didn't know about, so he asked to see the books, and an insulted Fred refused.

Fred abruptly decided that afternoon to quit the business, but Ralph told him he cannot, that he is the responsible party for the company books, and so he must wrap up the remaining administrative matters before being free to leave the business without incurring personal liability. Fred refused to stay partners with Ralph another minute, he gathered a few essentials from his office and left the building saying, "Ship the rest of my belongings to me, I'll pay the freight!"

This enrages Ralph, who grabs a golf club and walks outside, taking his anger out on a stranger's car, smashing out a passenger window with the prize putter. The car's owner sees the act, and then sees Ralph walk back into the surveying business. The car's owner calls the police to report the event. The car's owner wants to hold both Ralph and Fred liable, but Fred denies any affiliation with Ralph at the time of the incident.

1. What are the rights and duties of these business associates to one another? Explain.

2. Who will be responsible to the car's owner? Explain.

3. Can Fred quit the business if Ralph doesn't want to end the business? Explain.

Question Number 4

When Polly saw the welded steel yard art of the McKesh brothers, she knew it would sell in trendy galleries. The brothers had a local reputation for making fabulous gifts for friends and family. Polly had tried to convince them for some time that there was a ready-made business in it if they wanted. They continued to insist that they were artists, not businessmen, and couldn't negotiate purchases and sales with third parties and hope to make a profit. While attending a garden party that Spring, Polly overheard someone ask if the statuary, a McKesh original, was for sale, offering to pay $10,000.00 for it on the spot. In an effort to help the brothers out and make a profit herself, she struck up a conversation with the person, saying she might be able to work something out and said she would call them in three days time.

Approaching the brothers the next day, Polly made the following proposition. If the brothers would allow her a 30 percent brokerage fee, she would manage all the business particulars providing they would supply the workspace, tools, ingenuity and labor of producing the art. She agreed to only accept offers that kept her portion of the costs below 20 percent of the sale price, ensuring a full fifty percent of all revenues would be paid directly to the brothers. For her fee, she would incorporate their business as Ironworks, Inc., manage their business, and find them paying customers. This seemed acceptable to them, they agreed to begin work when she brought the first load of materials.

Polly went to Liberty Steel and began to pitch her vision for Ironworks, Inc. to the salesman. In her efforts to impress him about the quality of the art produced and thus the steel needed, Polly also managed to make a sale. The salesman agreed to give her the high-grade steel she requested with the smooth surface for an average grade price, if he could commission a nine-foot dragon for his patio. Polly struck the deal, and went over to deliver the steel to the brothers. Upon hearing the news that along with this truckload of steel comes an obligation to create a free sculpture, the brothers refuse. Polly says the deal is done, she can't unring a bell, and they have no choice but to produce the statuary. They refused so Polly found another artist to create the art.

The brothers learned of the substitution labor and complained to Polly. Polly asserts that she had their best interest in mind as she has not broken her promises. Liberty files suit against Polly and the brothers who cross-claim against Polly.

1. What is Polly's legal position in the above transaction? Explain.

2. Did Polly's actions create personal liability for her? Explain.

3. Can the Brothers be held liable, and if so, under what theories? Explain.

Question Number 5

Ann, Bill, and Cal decided to open an auto body shop known as Ann's Auto Body Repair, LLC (AABR). Ann, Bill, and Cal signed the Limited Liability Company Operating Agreement requiring Bill and Cal to contribute $2,000 each and Ann, experienced in the auto body business, to contribute her expertise and to manage AABR for no less than five years. The agreement carried a standard LLC member indemnification provision. The agreement gave Ann the exclusive right to manage and control the business. Ann and Bill signed the certificate of formation, which stated the management of AABR was vested in Ann. Using a power of attorney, Bill signed for Cal, a resident of an adjoining state.

Ann rented a building in the name of AABR from Dee for $2,000 per month and 10 days later she filed the LLC certificate of formation with the Secretary of State. Bill felt the business needed to attract more customers. Without the knowledge of Ann or Cal, Bill signed a written 12-month advertising contract with Eric's radio station at $1,000 per month in the name of AABR.

After learning of the advertising contract, Ann notified Eric, that AABR did not need advertising and would not make the payments. Ann then began to embezzle from the company. Six months later, Ann told Bill and Cal, "I am sick of this business. I quit." Ann handed them her written resignation. Each wrote, "Accepted" on the resignation and said, "We can run the business without you anyway." Dee received no payment on the lease and Bill and Cal later discovered the embezzlement.

Dee has sued Ann, Bill, Cal, and AABR for back due rent. Eric has sued them to enforce the advertising contract.

Discuss

1. What was the effectiveness of the LLC's formation?

2. What are the liabilities of all parties?

3. What is the effect of Ann quitting the LLC venture?

RIGOS BAR REVIEW SERIES

UNIFORM MULTISTATE ESSAY EXAM (MEE) REVIEW

CHAPTER 1

BUSINESS ASSOCIATIONS

AGENCY, PARTNERSHIPS, CORPORATIONS, AND LLCs

Essay Answers

Answer Number 1

Summary

As F's agent, S had express authority to make sales, but not to sign a legal document. F is liable if he ratified the lease, as he did by moving into the leased space. S had apparent authority if the lessor reasonably believed S had authority. S likely breached his fiduciary duty as an agent, and will remain personally liable if he did not disclose F as his principal.

Issues Raised

(1)   Agency / Principal Relationship
       (a) Agent acts on a principal's behalf in relationships with third parties
       (b) Agent must disclose principal to avoid personal liability
(2)   Apparent Authority
(3)   Ratification
(4)   Fiduciary Duties
       (a) Trust
       (b) Loyalty and Obedience
       (c) Honest dealing
       (d) Full disclosure to the principal
(5)   Liability of Principal
(6)   Liability of Agent

Sample Answer

(1)   Agency / Principal Relationship. An agency relationship exists where the agent acts on behalf of the principal in relationships with third parties. Here, Son is authorized to represent Fred within the shop as a salesman, but not to enter into lease agreements for his father's business. Whether Fred will be liable on the lease will depend on whether Son fully disclosed the principal before Fred ratified the lease by moving in.

(2)   Apparent Authority. This applies where no actual authority exists, but the principal's actions, conduct or manifestations lead an ordinary prudent person to reasonably believe the agent has authority. Here, after Fred was sole proprietor for many years, suddenly his signage changes and his Son is working in the shop daily. It may not be unreasonable to think the reason for this is that Son now has an ownership interest and therefore the authority to contract for a lease obligation. Even where no authority exists, the lease may be ratified by the principal creating liability.

(3)   Ratification. A principal is not normally bound by unauthorized contracts. Ratification by a disclosed principal usually cures the lack of authority. Here it is unclear whether Son disclosed Fred as the Principal, if not Son remains personally liable.

(4)   Fiduciary Duties. An agent has a duty of honest dealing, obedience, loyalty, and trust. An agent has the responsibility of full disclosure to the principal. Here, Son breached his fiduciary duty by exceeding the authority Fred granted him as his agent, by entering into a lease he was not authorized to, and this was disobedient.

(5)   Liability of Principal. Liability is imputed to the principal if the agent had implied/express or apparent authority, or if the principal expressly or impliedly ratified the agreement. Here, by moving into the space, Fred has impliedly ratified the lease by taking the benefits, providing Son had sufficiently disclosed him as the principal to the lessor.

(6)   Liability of Agent. Agents are not generally personally liable to a third party if they fully disclose that they are acting as an agent and they identify their principal. Personal liability is also possible if the agent misrepresented the scope of their employment, represented he was dealing for his own account, affirmatively stated that there is not an undisclosed principal or guaranteed performance of the contract. Here we are unclear as to the assertions of Son, so liability may, accordingly, be possible on one of those bases.

Answer Number 2

Summary

Here, Agent only created liability for P if he had agency authority to enter into contract on P's behalf. A had no express authority, but may have had apparent authority to contract for P. P may have assumed liability through ratification, but this does not appear to be the case, nor was A's action beneficial to P or within the course and scope of his employment. Independent contractors, as A is here, do not generally impute liability to their principal, unless their principal has granted express authority.

Issues Raised

(1)   Agency/Principal Relationship
    (a) Agent acts on a principal's behalf in relationships with third parties
    (b) Agent must disclose principal to avoid personal liability
(2)   Liability of Agent/Principal
    (a) Agent acts on a principal's behalf in relationships with third parties
    (b) Agent must disclose principal to avoid personal liability
(3)   Course and Scope of Employment
    (a) Intended to benefit the employer's business
    (b) Act is a normal duty
    (c) Act is conducted within the provided time and space parameters of the principal
    (d) Nexus between the act and the principal's business
(4)   Employee v. Independent Contractor
(5)   Ratification
(6)   Express Authority: Actual appointment of authority

Sample Answer

(1) Agency / Principal Relationship. The agency relationship is one in which the agent agrees to act on the Principal's behalf with third parties. This agency can create liability for the principal with third parties if the agent's actions are in the course of and for the benefit of the principal's business.

(2) Liability of Agent/Principal. Liability of contracts entered into by an agent is imputed to the principal if the agent had express, implied or apparent authority, or if the contract was ratified. Here, Carrie asserts that Principal "endorsed" the contract, but he was not the agent's principal regarding drapery installation, so that seems implausible. Principal may in fact have created an apparent authority on Agent's part in Carrie's mind by saying he was sure the work would be high quality. An agent may be personally liable if they misrepresent the scope of their authority, and the facts here are not clear what Agent told Carrie. While Agent was an employee for carpet installation, he was also a proprietor for the drapery business, and therefore was not acting as Principal's agent for the purposes of the drapery business.

(3) Course and Scope of Employment. Principal liability can be imputed if the agent's acts were for the benefit of the employer's business, or have a close nexus to his business. Merely being a similar installation contractor for home window treatments does not likely create the necessary nexus. The drape business benefits from the carpet business by getting access to potential customers, but the reverse is not true. Even if there is some overlap of service, Agent is not acting as an employee of Principal during his side job.

(4) Employee v. Independent Contractor. Generally, Principals are not responsible for torts of independent contractors. They are defined as agents not subject to the principal's control or supervision about the means and manner used to accomplish the task assigned. Here, even if Carrie somehow showed that through ratification Principal retained liability for the actions of Agent, clearly he would be seen as an independent contractor since Principal had no knowledge, must less control over the manner and method of his drapery work. It is unlikely Principal is involved at all, but if his mistaken endorsement granted any apparent authority, the independent nature of the work kept him from acquiring any liability.

(5) Ratification. A principal can create liability for themselves by ratifying actions of their agent's as discussed above. Here, by not expressly forbidding Agent to solicit the carpet customers for drapery sales, and by endorsing the work product to Carrie customer, it can be argued Principal ratified Agent's drapery work.

(6) Express Authority. When Principal tells Agent that engaging in the drapery business is fine, as long as it doesn't interfere with the carpeting business, he may have endorsed the work and given express authority to let the carpet company's good name stand behind the drapery business. This argument seems unlikely to prevail absent some benefit to the carpet company coming from the drape business.

Answer Number 3

Summary

Partners have various rights and duties. Rights include participation in management and to inspect the partnership's books. Obligations include non-competition and fiduciary duties of loyalty and care. Partners are always liable for their own intentional torts, but not the partnership. Here, dissolution was proper, and winding up should occur. Any activity outside the scope of winding up will incur personal liability for R.

Issues Raised

(1)   Property Rights
(2)   Fiduciary Duties
     (a) Duty of Disclosure
     (b) Competing with Partnership
(3)   Right to See the Books
(4)   Partners' Torts
(5)   Agents' Intentional Torts
(6)   Dissociating
(7)   Winding Up

Sample Answer

(1)   Property Rights. Partners have ownership interest in the entity itself and a right to participate in management. Fred cannot undertake significant business decisions unilaterally.

(2)   Fiduciary Duties. Partners have a duty of loyalty, care, good faith and fair dealing with each other and the partnership.

     (a) Duty of Disclosure. It is not clear if Fred had a fiduciary duty to disclose the property deal to Ralph since it was apparently an individual transaction that predated the partnership.

     (b) Competing with Partnership. The fiduciary duties also include not taking an opportunity of the partnership prior to its dissolution. Fred had no right to receive a company discount for a private purchase without Ralph's knowledge and approval during the partnership term. If so, this would be a breach of his duty to Ralph and the partnership.

(3)   Right to See the Books. Each partner has a right to see and copy the books under RUPA during business hours with proper notice. Fred acted improperly denying Ralph access.

(4)   Partners' Torts. All partners can create liability for the partnership during the normal course and scope of their business activities.

(5)   Agents' Intentional Torts. An agent is always responsible for their intentional torts, and the principal may be if within the scope of business activity or for benefit of business. This liability may exist even if the agent's act was unauthorized. Here, there does not appear there is a business nexus as Ralph is on a frolic of his own, so neither Fred nor the partnership is liable.

(6) Dissociating. Partners may leave the partnership voluntarily at any time, providing it does not violate the partnership agreement. They are also due the value of their ownership interest after dissociation or dissolution occurs. Here, Fred wanted to leave, but Ralph threatened him with additional liabilities if he left, warning he would incur an economically punitive result, denying his full ownership interest, which is improper.

(7) Winding Up. Is required if half or more of the partners dissociate, as is the case here. Activities during windup are confined to closing the business, anything beyond that scope creates personal liability for the partner. Ralph must limit his activities to only those concerning winding up the business, and must do so mindful of his duties of loyalty, care, good faith, and fair dealing discussed above. Any result that is less than fair will create personal liability for Ralph.

Answer Number 4

Summary

P was acting as incorporator / promoter, and purported to act on behalf of the corporation as its agent. As such, she is personally liable for all pre-formation contracts if the third party did not know incorporation had not been perfected. The brothers may assume liability for P's contract through express or implied ratification / adoption. If L recovers from P, P may seek indemnification from the corporation, as she received no personal benefit. P is liable for usurping the corporate opportunity.

Issues Raised

(1) Incorporator / Promoter
    (a) Fiduciary agency
    (b) Arranges for formation
(2) Promoter Liability
    (a) Always personally liable on pre-incorporation contracts
    (b) Once formed, corporation may ratify and adopt liability
(3) Adoption
    (a) Express adoption
    (b) Implied adoption
(4) Breach of Fiduciary Duty
(5) Indemnification

Sample Answer

(1) Incorporator. An incorporator or promoter acts as an agent arranging for the formation of the corporation. Here, Polly took on the tasks normally associated with a promoter and held herself out as one to both the first potential buyer and Liberty Steel. Polly is a fiduciary, owes the corporation a duty of good faith, loyalty, fair dealings, and can make no secret profit. While the corporation was never properly formed, and thus is not a formal entity, by the ratification of contracts prior to incorporation, the courts may hold the McKesh brothers liable.

(2) Promoter Liability. The incorporator who purports to be acting on behalf of the corporation is always personally liable on pre-incorporation contracts unless the third party knew there was no incorporation. Here, Polly promoter discusses Ironworks, Inc. with Liberty as though it is an existing entity, and Liberty has no opportunity to know that is not the case. She holds herself out as able to not only purchase materials for them, but also contract for their work, and as such, she has made herself personally liable.

(3)   Adoption.   The corporation can become liable for contracts entered into by the incorporator if they expressly or impliedly adopt or ratify such agreements. Here, an issue arises when the brothers admit they had been working with Polly who was going to get their business started, and they did not reject or return the steel she bargained for, so implied consent to adopt may exist.

(4)   Breach of Fiduciary Duty.   Corporate directors, officers, and senior executives, here Polly, have a duty to avoid conflicts of interest, including usurping a corporate opportunity and trade secret appropriation. Here Polly took the corporate contract with Liberty, but she would argue that the brothers affirmatively rejected the opportunity after full disclosure. If successful, the corporation may force Polly to disgorge the profit.

(5)   Indemnification.   If Liberty Steel were to manage to be wholly successful on the merits or otherwise, Polly may seek indemnification from the corporation. Here, she may be able to escape liability for the cost of the steel, as the brothers received the only benefit. She may also escape personal liability for specific performance, because she is not the artist. Damages are the difference in price between the two grades of steel that she bargained for.

Answer Number 5

Summary

The entity was likely a properly organized LLC with Ann as the managing member. The entity lease contract was executed pre-LLC filing and therefore all members have potential personal liability. A non-manager's act lacks authority to bind the LLC, but may have breached his warranty of authority to third parties. The LLC veil may be pierced and members held personally liable. Resignation of the manager does not terminate the LLC entity.

Issues Raised

(1)   Entity Formation
    (a) Separate legal entity
    (b) Filing requirements
    (c) Member-managed or manager-managed
(2)   Dee Lease Liability
    (a) Pre-filing obligation
    (b) General partnership status
    (c) Individual liability potential
(3)   Eric Advertising Liability
    (a) Non-manager had no authority to enter contract
    (b) Warranty of authority breached by agent
    (c) Apparent authority may be present
(4)   Piercing the LLC Veil
    (a) Akin to corporate piercing cases
    (b) Personal liability may apply

(5) Ann's Resignation
    (a) Entity not terminated
    (b) Potential breach of contract
    (c) Other members may continue business

Sample Answer

(1) Entity Formation. An LLC is a separate legal entity formed in compliance with the state Limited Liability Company Act. An LLC combines characteristics of a partnership and a corporation. The members of an LLC have limited personal liability (limited to the value of their contribution), but the entity receives the benefit of taxation as a partnership. In order to obtain LLC status, a proper certificate of formation must be filed with the Secretary of State. Contributions may take the form of tangible or intangible property, promissory notes, services, or agreements to perform services. Here, the contribution of cash and services is likely proper. An LLC may be member-managed, in which all members participate in management in proportion to their ownership interests, or manager-managed, where only the manager has authority to manage (akin to the corporate model). If a manager-managed form is chosen, that must be indicated in the certificate of formation. The manager need not be a member. Here, assuming all necessary information was included in the certificate, a manager-managed LLC was properly formed with the filing. If the power of attorney was valid, Bill could likely sign for Cal, as membership is not restricted to in-state residents.

(2) Dee Lease Liability. As this lease was entered into before the LLC certificate was filed, the LLC liability protection for members would be inapplicable. Instead, at the time the lease was entered into, Ann, Bill, and Cal (A, B, and C) would likely have been characterized as operating as a general partnership. A partnership is an association of two or more persons to carry on as co-owners a business for profit. Under partnership law, all partners have apparent authority to enter into transactions for carrying on the usual business of the partnership. Further, all partners are agents of the partnership and of each other. Given these principles, AABR is likely liable on the lease as within Ann's authority (either actual or apparent). In addition, by occupying the building after LLC filing, AABR may also have ratified the lease contract.   However, because the lease contract was executed prior to filing, all partners/members would be jointly and severally liable for the entity obligations. Dee may thus have grounds for recovering against AABR and if the entity fails to pay, secondarily against any or all of A, B, and C. A might also have liability akin to a corporate promoter.

(3) Eric Advertising Liability. If a manager-managed LLC was properly formed, the individual members are not considered agents of the LLC. Only the manager is an agent. Thus, Bill likely had no authority to enter the contract on behalf of AABR. Further, AABR did not ratify this contract, instead explicitly rejecting it. However, Bill himself might be liable to Eric on the theory of breach of warranty of agency authority. Eric could argue that by purporting to act on behalf of a principal (ABBR), Bill breached this warranty. In addition, Eric might try to argue apparent authority in order to bind AABR. Nonetheless, AABR could likely defend on the grounds of the constructive notice provided by the filed manager-managed LLC certificate.

(4) Piercing the LLC veil. In contrast to the general rule of no member liability, the LLC act provides for piercing the LLC veil under circumstances which would justify piercing in a corporate context. Failure to follow statutory formalities or gross undercapitalization, coupled with unfairness if piercing is not awarded, can be grounds for piercing the veil. Members would then be liable in proportion to their contributions.

(5) **Ann's Resignation.** Generally, a manager of an LLC may resign, and such resignation as a manager does not terminate their status as a member. Here, since both parties (B and C) accepted, the resignation may be proper. However, the resignation is also a breach of contract based on the agreement to contribute services for five years. The "Accepted" on the resignation was not an informed waiver and does not terminate the LLC's ability to sue Ann for breach of loyalty and fiduciary duty. The indemnification specified in the operating agreement is likely ineffective as embezzlement goes beyond simple negligence. AABR may thus have grounds for seeking damages from A. In addition, if B and C now intend to run AABR as a member-managed LLC, the certificate filed with the Secretary of State should be amended by a proper filing. Regardless, an LLC as a entity exists apart from its members, and is not dissolved by a resigning member. If Ann is also terminating her membership, a dissociation may occur, but remaining members may have the option of continuing the business.

CHAPTER 1

BUSINESS ASSOCIATIONS

Corporations and LLC Index

Action Without Meeting............... T 1-93
Administrative Dissolution .... T 1-98
Adoption of Pre-Incorporation
    Contracts................................... T 1-85
Alter Ego .... T 1-96
Annual Meeting........................... T 1-93
Annual Report .... T 1-87
Appointment of Directors............. T 1-89
Appraisal Rights .... T 1-95
Article Amendments .... T 1-86
Articles of Incorporation .... T 1-86
Attributes of Business Entities ... T 1-104
Authorized Shares .... T 1-92
Balance Sheet Test .... T 1-96
Board Meetings .... T 1-89
Board of Directors .... T 1-89
Business Judgment Rule......... T 1-91, 94
Bylaws... T 1-87
Canceled Shares .... T 1-92
Close Corporations..... T 1-87, 90, 92, 98
Competing with Corporation........ T 1-90
Concurrent Affiliates.................... T 1-96
Conflicts of Interest..................... T 1-90
Conglomerate Combinations........ T 1-97
Consolidations............................. T 1-97
Corporate Liability .... T 1-88
Corporate Records....................... T 1-94
Corporation by Estoppel............... T 1-87
Court Ordered Indemnification .... T 1-91
Creditor Proceeding..................... T 1-99
Cumulative Voting .... T 1-89
De Facto Corporations .... T 1-86
De Jure Corporations................... T 1-86
Deadlock...................................... T 1-99
Default Provisions .... T 1-86
Derivative Action .... T 1-94
Direct Action .... T 1-94
Directors...................................... T 1-89
Director Elections........................ T 1-89
Dismissal of Officers................... T 1-91
Dissenter Rights .... T 1-95
Dissolution .... T 1-98
Dividends .... T 1-89, 95
Domestic Corporations................. T 1-87
Election of Directors .... T 1-89

Electronic Transmissions.............. T 1-90
Equitable Insolvency .... T 1-95
Equitable Liability .... T 1-97
Estoppel Status .... T 1-87, 96
Failure to Separate .... T 1-96
Fiduciary Duties .... T 1-90, 91
Financial Statements.................... T 1-94
Foreign Corporations................... T 1-87
Formation .... T 1-85
Fraud................................ T 1-91, 96, 99
Frequency of Testing.................... T 1-85
Fundamental Changes .... T 1-97
Hierarchy of Authority .... T 1-87
Holding Companies...................... T 1-97
Horizontal Combinations.............. T 1-97
Hostile Takeover Protection .... T 1-97
Incorporator .... T 1-85, 86
Indemnification Agreements .... T 1-91
Initial Report............................... T 1-87
Inspection of Books and
    Records.................................... T 1-94
Interested Transactions........... T 1-85, 90
Judicial Dissolution .... T 1-98
Limited Liability Companies
    (LLC) .... T 1-100
    All Members Manage............. T 1-101
    Dissociation of Member......... T 1-103
    Dissolution .... T 1-103
    Fiduciary Duties.................... T 1-101
    Filing Articles .... T 1-100
    Management Authority .... T 1-101
    Managing Member................. T 1-101
    Manager Liability................... T 1-101
    Member Rights....................... T 1-101
    Name Restrictions.................. T 1-100
    Operating Agreement............. T 1-101
    Pierce LLC Veil .... T 1-102
    Third Party Liability............... T 1-102
Long-Arm Statutes .... T 1-88
Meetings .... T 1-93
Mere Sham.................................. T 1-96
Mergers....................................... T 1-97
Minority Shareholders Relief .... T 1-95
Name... T 1-86
Name Reservation .... T 1-86

Negotiable Securities ....T 1-92
Notice of Meetings.....................T 1-93
Officers................................T 1-89, 91
Oppression ....T 1-90, 99
Ordinary Decisions ....T 1-94
Organizational Meeting.................T 1-87
Outstanding Shares ....T 1-92
Payment for Shares ....T 1-92
Permissive Indemnification...........T 1-91
Piercing the Corporate Veil...........T 1-96
Powers.....................................T 1-88
Preferred Shares ....T 1-92
Preemptive Rights ....T 1-92
Prior Issue Distribution ....T 1-79
Professional Service
    Corporations ....T 1-99
    Death of Shareholder ....T 1-100
    Prohibited Activities.................T 1-99
    Requirements ....T 1-99
    Shareholder Personal
        Liability ....T 1-99, 100
    Trade Name Restrictions ....T 1-99
Promoter...T 1-85
Purpose...T 1-88
Quorum Requirements ....T 1-93
Ratification of
    Pre-Incorporation Contracts.......T 1-85
Receivership..................................T 1-99
Records and Financial
    Statements ....T 1-94
Redeemed Shares ....T 1-92
Registered Agent.....................T 1-86, 88
Registered Office ....T 1-86
Regular Board Meetings ....T 1-89
Removal of Directors ....T 1-89
Revised Model Business
    Corporation Act (RMBCA).........T 1-85
Shareholder Decision Control.......T 1-95
Shareholder Dissolution Action ....T 1-98
Shareholder Liability.....................T 1-95
Shareholder Meetings....................T 1-93
Shareholder Resolutions................T 1-93
Shareholder Rights........................T 1-93
Shareholder Voting ....T 1-93
Shareholder's Derivative
    Action...T 1-94
Special Meetings ....T 1-89
State Nexus ....T 1-88
Stock Fair Value.............................T 1-95
Stock Information...........................T 1-92
Stock Option ....T 1-92
Stock Right.....................................T 1-92

Stock Shares .... T 1-92
Stock Subscriptions .... T 1-92
Stock Warrant................................ T 1-92
Subsidiaries .... T 1-97
Successor Affiliates....................... T 1-96
Synergetic Factors .... T 1-98
Trade Secret Appropriation .... T 1-90
Transacting Business..................... T 1-88
Treasury Shares .... T 1-92
Ultra Vires .... T 1-89
Undisclosed Principal.................... T 1-85
Usurp Corporate Opportunity....... T 1-90
Veil Piercing.................................. T 1-96
Vertical Combinations................... T 1-97
Voluntary Dissolution .... T 1-98
Voting Proxy .... T 1-90, 93
Voting Trusts and Agreements..... T 1-94
Waste of Assets .... T 1-99

CHAPTER 2

CONFLICT OF LAWS

RIGOS BAR REVIEW SERIES

UNIFORM MULTISTATE ESSAY EXAM (MEE) REVIEW

CHAPTER 2

CONFLICTS OF LAW

Table of Contents

A.   Sub-Topic Exam Issue Distribution .... Text 2-129

B.   Opening Argument and Primary Issues .... Text 2-131

C.   Text .... Text 2-133

    I.   Introduction .... Text 2-133

    II.   Domicile .... Text 2-133

    III.   Jurisdiction of Courts .... Text 2-134

    IV.   Choice of Law Systems .... Text 2-135

    V.   Choice of Law in Specific Areas and Other Considerations . Text 2-138

    VI.   Judgments From Other States and Foreign Nations .... Text 2-140

D.   Magic Memory Outlines® .... Magic Memory Outlines 2-143

E.   Conflict of Laws Essay Questions .... Questions 2-147

F.   Conflict of Laws Essay Answers .... Answers 2-151

G.   Conflict of Laws Index .... Index 2-161

H.   Acronyms .... Acronyms 15-625

RIGOS BAR REVIEW SERIES
MEE SUB-TOPIC FREQUENCY DISTRIBUTION

CONFLICT OF LAWS

	2/09	7/08	2/08	7/07	2/07	7/06	2/06	7/05	2/05	7/04	2/04	7/03	2/03	7/02	2/02	7/01	2/01
Opening Argument						/			/				/				
Domicile	/	/			/								/		/		
Jurisdiction of Courts		/			/								/	/			
Divisible Divorce					/								/				
Forum Selection														/			
Service	/																
Foreign Parties	/																
Jurisdiction over Internet Business	/																
Most Significant Relationship	/																
Family Law		/			/	/											
Validity of Marriage						/											
Federal Supremacy									/				/				
Erie / Klaxon													/				
Full Faith & Credit									/	/			/			/	
Lack of Jurisdiction										/			/				
Premarital Contract		/															
Divorce Judgments		/			/								/				
Claim / Issue Preclusion										/							
Child Custody Judgments		/							/				/				
Child Support Judgments		/							/				/			/	

Course 5328. Copyright by Rigos Bar Review Series – MEE.

OPENING ARGUMENT AND PRIMARY ISSUES

CONFLICT OF LAWS

There are a few thoughts that should usually be stated at the beginning of every answer. These will score you easy points and let the grader know you are in the right topic area.

Most essays should have an "opening argument": a brief, broad statement that shows you understand the broad significance of a legal topic. The opening argument also suggests to the grader that she is about to read a thoughtful and well-organized essay.

Many subjects also have "primary issues" that can be discussed up front or integrated into the essay answer. IMPORTANT: Do not merely regurgitate these statements on the exam without addressing the issues actually raised by the facts, or you will not pass.

- **Conflicts of Laws Opening Argument:** Conflict of laws concerns matters having a nexus to more than one jurisdiction and problems that arise when jurisdictions' laws differ or conflict.

- **Sample Primary Issue Statements:**

  - "Domicile" is a fixed, principal, and permanent home. Establishing a domicile requires physical presence in a state with the intent to remain there indefinitely.

  - *Klaxon* requires that a federal district court hearing a diversity jurisdiction case apply the choice-of-law rules of the state in which it is located.

  - The Full Faith and Credit Clause of the U.S. Constitution creates a general right to have one state court's judgment recognized and enforced in another state.

  - Under the doctrine of "divisible divorce," when a court has personal jurisdiction over only one spouse, the court may dissolve the marriage, but cannot resolve issues of property division, alimony, child custody, or child support.

  - The Second Restatement resolves choice of law issues by applying the law of the state with the most significant relationship to the case.

  - A court may refuse to apply a foreign law that violates the public policy of the forum state.

  - State and federal child custody statutes work in tandem to prevent interstate custody disputes, deter custody-related child abductions, and keep custody-related litigation in the state with the closest connection to the parents and child.

I. INTRODUCTION

Conflict of laws ("conflicts") is the body of law that deals with matters having a nexus to more than one jurisdiction and the problems that arise when jurisdictions' laws differ.

A. Similarities with Civil Procedure

Conflicts are an advanced subset of civil procedure. Many civil procedure concepts, including personal jurisdiction, the *Erie* doctrine, and claim preclusion are detailed here.

B. MEE Focus

Conflicts questions are always cross-over questions, usually combined with federal civil procedure or family law. Typically, up to 2/3 of the points for the question come from conflicts issues. Conflicts law is technical and complicated, but MEE coverage is relatively superficial. The following material is oversimplified, but it should be all you will need for the exam.

C. Definitions of Key Terms

1. Forum: "Forum" refers to the jurisdiction where an action is pending. On the MEE, this is usually either the fictitious "State X" or "State Y."

2. Foreign: "Foreign" refers to both a state or a nation other than the forum.

II. DOMICILE

A. Definition

"Domicile" refers to one's fixed, principal, and permanent home – either a state or a similar political subdivision (e.g., the District of Columbia), or another nation. A person domiciled in State X is a "domiciliary" of that state.

B. Elements

1. Physical Presence: To establish a domicile, one must physically enter that state.

2. Intent to Remain: The other element needed to establish a domicile is the intent to remain indefinitely in that state and make it one's home. "Indefinitely" means lack of intent to leave the state permanently at a definite future time.

MEE Tip: One may establish a new domicile despite the intent to leave at some *unknown* time in the future. For example, a New Yorker who moves to California may become domiciled there even if she plans on returning to New York "someday."

C. Domicile Versus Residence

A person may have more than one residence simultaneously (e.g., a primary home in one state and a vacation home in another state), but only one domicile at any given time.

> **MEE Tip:** One may have a residence in a state even though that state does not consider her to be a "resident." "Resident" generally describes someone who is domiciled in that state.

D. No Minimum Time Requirement

1. General Rule: Once both physical presence and the requisite intent to remain exist, a new domicile is established immediately, and the former domicile is lost.

> **MEE Tip:** Look for key events that occur very shortly after the establishment of a new domicile, or a person who establishes a new domicile and then temporarily returns to the former domicile. The return visit will not destroy the new domicile.

2. Exceptions: A state may require a certain time lapse before it will treat a newcomer as being domiciled in that state for some purposes. An example is a public university requiring a person to have been domiciled in the state for at least 12 months to qualify for in-state tuition. Such restrictions may raise constitutional law issues concerning the right to interstate travel more than conflicts issues on the MEE.

III. JURISDICTION OF COURTS

Jurisdictional issues are traditionally associated with the general subject of conflicts. Jurisdiction is also explored in the Federal Civil Procedure chapter. Jurisdictional issues that implicate the Full Faith and Credit Clause are discussed in Section VI of this chapter.

A. Domicile and Personal Jurisdiction

1. General Rule: The courts of your domicile have personal jurisdiction. Such courts may hear any claim against you, even if the case has no other connection to the forum.

2. Scope of Divorce Decree: If a state court lacks personal jurisdiction over one spouse, under the doctrine of "divisible divorce," the court still has the power to dissolve the marriage. The court usually cannot resolve property division, alimony, or child custody or support issues without jurisdiction over all stakeholders.

> **MEE Tip:** The state where the spouses were domiciled immediately before separating has personal jurisdiction over both, even if one spouse later establishes domicile in a different state.

B. Limits on Exercise of Jurisdiction

In some circumstances, a court may decline to hear a case even though the exercise of jurisdiction would not violate constitutional limitations.

1. Choice of Forum by Agreement: Contracts often contain a forum selection clause providing that any related litigation occur in a specified forum. These clauses are generally enforceable, as long as the parties negotiated in good faith. In a minority of states, however, forum selection clauses are deemed to be void for public policy reasons.

2. Forum Non Conveniens: Under the doctrine of forum non conveniens, a court may refuse jurisdiction if it is shown that the forum is inconvenient for the parties or witnesses.

IV. CHOICE OF LAW SYSTEMS

"Choice of law" is rather self-explanatory: what jurisdiction's law should the forum use in deciding a case? There are three major choice of law systems used by state courts.

> **MEE Tip:** Unless the question states otherwise, or you have been instructed to use only the law of your state, discuss all three theories when analyzing a choice of law issue.

A. Traditional Restatement (First) "Vested Rights" Approach

The Restatement (First) of Conflict of Laws reflects the traditional "vested rights" approach to choice of law problems. A minority of states still follows the First Restatement.

1. Bright-Line Rules: The First Restatement has various bright-line rules for different areas of substantive law.

a. Torts: Under the First Restatement, the governing law is usually that of the state where the last event necessary to create liability occurred. Generally, this is the state where the injury occurred, even if a key event, e.g., the breach of duty, occurred elsewhere.

b. Contracts: Issues of contract formation are governed by the law of the state where the contract was made. Issues of contract performance (including excusable nonperformance) are governed by the law of the state where performance is to be rendered.

c. Property: Real property is governed by the law of the state where it is located. Personal property issues are governed by the law where the transaction occurred.

d. Corporations: Matters concerning the formation, dissolution, and internal affairs (e.g., rights and liabilities of shareholders, directors, and officers) are governed by the law of the state of incorporation. Corporate third-party dealings, such as contracts and tort liabilities, are governed by the rules that would apply if the corporation were a person.

2. Escape Devices – RADS: In order to avoid the inflexibility of the First Restatement's rules, courts sometimes employ "escape devices" to achieve a different result.

a. *Renvoi*: Although generally disfavored, a court may use the doctrine of "*renvoi*" ("send back," in French) to apply its own law even when choice-of-law rules point to the law of another jurisdiction. If a forum "accepts the *renvoi*," the court will interpret the indicated foreign law so as to point back to the interpreting court's forum, then apply its own law to break what would otherwise be an infinite loop.

b. Area of Substantive Law: The result of a choice of law analysis may vary depending upon what area of substantive law is used to label the issue. In one famous case, the defendant was a car rental agency located in Connecticut. The plaintiff, a passenger riding in a car rented from the defendant, was injured in Massachusetts by the driver's negligence and sought recovery in a Connecticut court. Under Connecticut's choice of law rules, classifying the action as a tort case would have mandated the application of Massachusetts law, which would not impose liability on the rental agency. However, the Connecticut court determined the matter to be a contract action, and thus applied Connecticut law, holding that the passenger could seek recovery from the rental company. *Daniels' U-Drive Auto Renting Co.*

        c. Dépeçage: The doctrine of *dépeçage* ("cutting up") is used by courts to apply the laws of different jurisdictions to different issues in the same matter. Cases are split into various issues and courts apply their forum's choice-of-law rules issue-by-issue.

        d. Substance Versus Procedure: The First Restatement generally provides that procedural issues will be governed by forum law, even if foreign law is applied to the substantive issues in the case. Under the First Restatement, statutes of limitation are usually considered to be procedural.

B. "Interest Analysis" Approach – CUT

        The rigidity of the First Restatement's rules led legal scholars to create alternative choice of law systems. The Interest Analysis approach rejects the Restatement's use of different rules for different areas of substantive law, and instead focuses on the policies underlying the laws. Interest Analysis asks whether each state involved has a legitimate interest, based upon its contacts with the case.

        1. Contact With the Case: To illustrate, in order to reduce tortfeasors' potential dependence upon State X's welfare programs, State X prohibits awards of punitive damages. State Y allows punitive damages to deter recklessness and negligence. Driver is domiciled in State Y, and Passenger is domiciled in State X. D drinks and drives in State Y, injuring P in the resulting crash. P sues D in State X for punitive damages. Because the forum should apply the law of the state with a bona fide interest in the application of its law, State X should apply the law of State Y and allow P to assert a claim for punitive damages.

MEE Tip: Under the Interest Analysis approach, the "contacts with the case" element usually assumes that a state has no interest in protecting or compensating people domiciled in a different state. The states' underlying policies are not stated explicitly; instead, briefly suggest possible policy justifications of your own. To hit all the analytical elements, remember our acronym **CUT**.

---

        2. "Unprovided-For" or "No-Interest" Case: In an "unprovided-for" or "no-interest" case, neither state has an interest in the application of its law. For example, State X imposes damages caps of $100,000 on medical malpractice actions in order to stop an exodus of physicians. State Y has no cap, because its primary policy concern is to fully compensate plaintiffs. Patient, a domiciliary of State X, undergoes surgery at a hospital in State Y. Doctor, a domiciliary of State Y who practices medicine in that state only, negligently performs the operation. P's resulting injury is valued at $500,000; P sues D in State Y.

        a. Interests: State X has no interest in the application of its damages cap because D is not a domiciliary of State X and does not practice there, so he cannot be part of the State X physician exodus. State Y has no interest in allowing P full recovery because P is not domiciled in State Y.

b. Rule and Result: In an unprovided-for or no-interest case, the rule is for the court to apply forum law. Therefore, even though State Y is deemed to have no interest, the forum should nonetheless apply its own law and allow P to seek total recovery.

3. <u>True Conflict</u>: In a true conflict situation, both states have an interest in the application of their respective laws. Assume that the Patient in the previous example is domiciled in State Y, the Doctor is domiciled in State X and practices medicine there, and Patient files suit in State X.

a. Interests: State X has an interest in not encouraging D to move his practice out of State X. State Y has an interest in its domiciliary, P being fully compensated.

b. Rule and Result: Most states would approach this conflict by applying of the forum law. So here, State X will apply its own law and cap P's damages at $100,000.

MEE Tip: Interest Analysis will usually bring you to the conclusion that the forum should apply its own law, except in false conflict cases where the forum has no interest in the application of forum law.

---

4. Substance Versus Procedure: Unlike the First and Second Restatements, the Interest Analysis approach does not distinguish between procedural and substantive laws.

C. <u>Modern Restatement (Second) Approach</u>

Currently a plurality of states follows this system. Probably the majority view for choice of law approaches is set forth in the Restatement (Second) of Conflict of Laws.

1. Issue-Specific: Choice of law determinations are made on an issue-by-issue basis. Under the Second Restatement, *dépeçage* is the preferred approach

2. Most Significant Relationship: The Second Restatement has fewer black-letter law rules than the First, and usually attempts to apply the law of the state with the "most significant relationship." General factors and "connecting factors" which vary among areas of substantive law are to be considered.

MEE Tip: The Second Restatement contains fewer black-letter law rules, and these are generally limited to very specific issues. You will not need to memorize them, and should instead apply the approaches set forth below.

---

a. General Factors – FINEBUD: The general choice of law factors under the Second Restatement are the **f**orum's policies, **i**nterested states' policies and interests, the **n**eeds of the interstate and international systems, protecting the parties' **e**xpectations, the **b**asic policies of the relevant field of law, **u**niformity/certainty/predictability, and the law's ease of being **d**etermined and applied.

b. Connecting Factors for Torts – CRIP: Section 145(2) specifies that four connecting factors control for tort issues. They are the **c**onduct that caused the injury, the **r**elationship among the parties, the **i**njury, and the locations of the **p**arties.

c. **Connecting Factors for Contracts – NSFPP:** For contract issues, the Second Restatement calls for consideration of the following connecting factors. They are the locations of the **n**egotiation, **s**ubject matter, **f**ormation, **p**erformance, and **p**arties.

3. Real Property: In theory, the Second Restatement also applies the most significant relationship analysis to real property issues. However, in practice, real property issues are governed by the law of the state where the land is located.

4. Corporations: Both the First and Second Restatement's approach to corporate issues of formation, dissolution and internal affairs is to apply the law of the state of incorporation. General choice of law principles apply to the corporation's external dealings.

5. Substance Versus Procedure: Like the First Restatement, the Second Restatement generally provides that procedural issues are governed by forum law.

a. **Statutes of Limitations:** This rule extends to statutes of limitations unless "exceptional circumstances" make a forum's shorter statute of limitations "unreasonable."

b. **Uniform Conflict of Laws Limitations Act:** A small number of states have adopted this statute, which rejects the Restatements' rule: if a claim "is substantively based" on the law of State X, then State X's statute of limitations is treated as substantive and applied.

6. Choice of Law Statutes: If a state has an on-point choice of law statute, it will trump any provision of the Second Restatement. This includes UCC choice of law provisions.

V. CHOICE OF LAW IN SPECIFIC AREAS AND OTHER CONSIDERATIONS

Some choice of law issues are clearer when separated from the three major systems.

A. Specific Areas of Substantive Law

1. Intestate Succession: Intestate succession of real property is governed by the law of the state in which the property is located. Intestate succession of personal property is controlled by the law of the decedent's final domicile.

2. Family Law: For family law questions, apply the following choice of law rules.

a. **Validity of Marriage:** If the validity of a marriage is challenged, a court will apply the law of the state where the marriage was officially celebrated, unless the marriage seriously violates the public policy of the forum, for example polygamous or incestuous marriages. States that do not allow common-law marriages to be formed will nonetheless recognize a common-law marriage that was legal at the time and place it was contracted.

> **MEE Tip:** Currently, some states recognize same-sex marriage or registered domestic partnerships, thereby raising issues concerning their legal effect in other jurisdictions. Because national policy is still developing, the MEE is unlikely to test conflicts issues involving same-sex marriage / partnership until courts provide more guidance.

b. **Grounds for Divorce, Separation, and Annulment:** Forum law always governs the question of whether sufficient grounds for divorce, separation, or annulment exist.

c. Jurisdiction over Divorce Proceedings: Jurisdiction over both spouses is not necessary to dissolve a marriage, so long as the plaintiff is domiciled in the forum state.

B. Other Choice of Law Considerations

1. Proof of Foreign Law: Federal courts and most state courts are bound to take judicial notice of law from foreign states and, to a lesser extent, foreign nations.

a. Parties Must Raise the Issue and Provide Proof: "Judicial notice" does not require courts to raise or research the applicability of foreign law on their own initiative ("*sua sponte*"). A party relying on foreign law must provide the court with the specific law(s) and enough information for the court to understand, which may require expert testimony.

b. Federal Courts and Law of Foreign Nations: Under Federal Rule of Civil Procedure 44.1, a party wishing to rely upon the law of a foreign country must notify the court. The court may use any source, even if not submitted by a party or inadmissible under the Federal Rules of Evidence, in making its "ruling on a question of law."

2. Choice of Law by Agreement: Many contracts contain a choice-of-law clause specifying that the law of a particular state will apply to, control, or govern any disputes concerning the contract.

a. Generally Enforced: These clauses are usually enforced as long as the parties contracted in good faith. The parties may even select the law of a jurisdiction that has no connection to the contract. For example, the parties to a business transaction may choose Delaware law because that state's corporate laws are considered quite favorable to businesses.

b. Avoiding *Renvoi*: To prevent a *renvoi* (see *supra*) back to the forum's law, a choice-of-law clause typically provides that disputes will be resolved by State X's "internal laws." This would exclude State X's choice-of-law rules. Similarly, the clause could explicitly declare that the chosen state's conflict of laws principles shall not apply.

MEE Tip: Don't confuse a choice-of-law clause with a forum selection clause. If a contract specifies a forum where suit must be brought, but does not indicate which state's law should apply, the forum will probably use its own choice-of-law rules, which could result in the parties' chosen forum applying the law of another state.

C. Defenses Against Application of Foreign Law

1. Local Public Policy: The forum may refuse to apply a foreign law on grounds that it seriously violates the public policy of the forum. One New York court held that to qualify, the foreign law must be "inherently vicious, wicked, or immoral, and shocking to the prevailing moral sense." *Intercontinental Hotels Corp.* This is a very high hurdle.

2. Penal Laws: The forum will not apply a foreign law that is "penal" in nature.

a. Criminal Laws: Criminal statutes are not enforced by foreign courts.

b. Civil Fines: Fines for a non-criminal offenses are penal.

c. Punitive Damages Exception: Punitive damages are not considered penal.

3. Revenue Laws: The forum will not enforce the tax laws of another jurisdiction. However, a tax judgment entered under the laws of State X by a State X court may subsequently be registered in State Y and enforced by the courts of State Y.

D. Constitutional Limitations

The United States Constitution limits state courts' choice of laws determinations, but the limitation is quite weak.

1. Due Process: To apply forum law without violating Due Process, a state court "must have a significant contact or significant aggregation of contacts, creating state interests. The showing must be that choice of its law is neither arbitrary nor fundamentally unfair." *Allstate Insurance*.

2. Full Faith and Credit: *Allstate* holds that the Due Process standard also determines whether a state's application of forum law violates the Full Faith and Credit Clause.

MEE Tip: The *Allstate* test has a superficial resemblance to the *International Shoe* standard for the exercise of personal jurisdiction. However, *Allstate* is a much lower hurdle than *International Shoe*. The forum state may choose its own law under the *Allstate* standard if it has a legitimate state interest to do so, and there is any meaningful connection between the forum state and the case.

E. Federal-State Conflicts

1. *Erie* Doctrine: The *Erie* doctrine has been extended to require that a federal district court hearing a diversity jurisdiction case apply the choice-of-law rules of the state in which it is located. *Klaxon*.

2. Federal Supremacy: The United States Constitution provides that federal law generally trumps state law.

VI. JUDGMENTS FROM OTHER STATES AND FOREIGN NATIONS

After a case has been fully adjudicated and judgment has been entered, what effect does that judgment have outside of the forum?

A. Constitutional Full Faith and Credit

1. General Rule: The Full Faith and Credit Clause creates a general right to have a State X court judgment recognized and enforced in State Y. By statute, federal courts must give Full Faith and Credit to state court judgments, and the U.S. Supreme Court has held that state courts must also give the same respect to federal judgments.

MEE Tip: Usually, State Y must give Full Faith and Credit even if the State X judgment is flawed due to an error of fact or law. A litigant wishing to correct the error should appeal in State X, not launch a collateral attack in State Y.

---

2. Exceptions: There are some exceptions to the Full Faith and Credit principle.

a. Jurisdiction: If State X lacked jurisdiction but nonetheless entered judgment, State Y usually need not give Full Faith and Credit. However, if the jurisdictional issue was previously raised in State X, and the State X court decided that it had jurisdiction, State Y must give Full Faith and Credit even if State X's jurisdictional ruling was wrong.

b. On the Merits: State Y may deny Full Faith and Credit to a State X judgment that was not on the merits; e.g., dismissal for lack of jurisdiction.

c. Finality: Until the State X judgment is final (i.e., all appeals have been exhausted or it is too late to appeal), State Y need not give Full Faith and Credit.

d. Penal Judgments: State Y need not give Full Faith and Credit to a State X judgment imposing a criminal or civil fine.

e. Inconsistent Judgments: A court faced with inconsistent judgments from other states should give Full Faith and Credit only to the most recent judgment.

3. Public Policy Exception: Just as a court may refuse to apply foreign law on public policy grounds (see *supra*), it may similarly deny Full Faith and Credit.

4. Divorce Judgments: Generally, divorce judgments – at least to the extent that they dissolve a marriage – are governed by Full Faith and Credit rules.

a. Jurisdiction: One key exception is that the issue of personal jurisdiction may be relitigated in State Y even if it was previously decided by the State X court.

b. Divisible Divorce: If a court that lacks jurisdiction over one spouse dissolves a marriage under the doctrine of "divisible divorce" (see *supra*), most states let the spouse seek spousal support in another state, even though the divorce itself is entitled to Full Faith and Credit. A minority of states disallow a subsequent action for alimony.

5. Claim and Issue Preclusion: A previous judgment from State X may create questions of claim preclusion (res judicata) or issue preclusion (collateral estoppel) in a subsequent State Y lawsuit. If so, the Full Faith and Credit Clause requires the State Y court to apply State X's law to decide whether the claim or issue is precluded by the State X judgment.

6. International Judgments: The Full Faith and Credit Clause does not expressly apply to judgments from other countries. However, modern courts equate international judgments to judgments from U.S. foreign state courts. A minority of states recognize foreign nation judgments only if that country gives reciprocal recognition to the state's own judgments.

B. Statutory Full Faith and Credit

Certain family law judgments are not constitutionally entitled to Full Faith and Credit because they are subject to modification and so "final." In response, federal and state governments have enacted laws to ensure that these judgments receive Full Faith and Credit.

1. Child Custody Judgments: The Uniform Child Custody Jurisdiction Act (UCCJA) the Uniform Child Custody Jurisdiction and Enforcement Act (UCCJEA), and the federal Parental Kidnapping Protection Act (PKPA) work in tandem. They prevent interstate custody disputes, deter custody-related abductions, and help ensure that custody litigation takes place "in the state with which the child and his family have the closest connection." If the court finds that a forum is "inconvenient" and that another forum would be more appropriate, it may decline jurisdiction. For custody disputes, a state court has jurisdiction if it satisfies one of the four following tests:

a. Home State Jurisdiction: A state court has "home state jurisdiction" if the child lived in that state when the custody action was commenced, or the child lived there within six months prior, and at least one parent / guardian continues to live there.

b. Emergency Jurisdiction: A state court may exercise "emergency jurisdiction" if the child is physically present in the state and needs protection from abuse or abandonment.

c. Significant Connection Jurisdiction: A state court may exercise "significant connection jurisdiction" if the child and at least one parent / guardian have a significant connection with the state. For purposes of interstate custody disputes, the PKPA recognizes significant connection jurisdiction only if no state can exercise home state jurisdiction.

d. Vacuum Jurisdiction: A state court may exercise "vacuum jurisdiction" if no state has home state jurisdiction and to do so is consistent with the child's best interests.

2. Abducted Child or Other Wrongful Conduct: A state may decline jurisdiction if the child was abducted from another state or if the parent seeking custody "has engaged in similar reprehensible conduct."

3. Child Support Judgments: The Uniform Interstate Family Support Act (UIFSA) has been adopted in all states pursuant to the federal Child Support Enforcement Act, as a condition of eligibility for federal child support programs. Under the UIFSA, a child support order issued in State X is entitled to Full Faith and Credit in State Y. Furthermore, as long as one of the parents or the child remains in State X, no other state may modify that order unless neither parent objects to the other state exercising jurisdiction.

MEE Tip: Divorce judgments and child custody issues are a very popular conflict of laws question area.

Magic Memory Outlines®

I.   **INTRODUCTION**
   A. Similarities with Civil Procedure..
   B. MEE Focus ....
   C. Definitions of Key Terms ....
      1. Forum...
      2. Foreign ....

II. **DOMICILE**
   A. Definition...
   B. Elements ....
      1. Physical Presence..
      2. Intent to Remain ....
   C. Domicile Versus Residence ....
   D. No Minimum Time Requirement ....
      1. General Rule ....
      2. Exceptions...

III. **JURISDICTION OF COURTS**
   A. Domicile and Personal Jurisdiction ....
      1. General Rule ....
      2. Scope of Divorce Decree ....
   B. Limits on Exercise of Jurisdiction ....
      1. Choice of Forum by Agreement ....
      2. Forum Non Conveniens ....

IV. **CHOICE OF LAW SYSTEMS**
   A. Traditional Restatement (First) "Vested Rights" Approach...................................
      1. Bright-Line Rules ....
         a. Torts...
         b. Contracts ....
         c. Property...

        d. Corporations ....

     2. Escape Devices – **RADS** ....

        a. *Renvoi* ....

        b. Area of Substantive Law ....

        c. *Dépeçage* ....

        d. Substance Versus Procedure ....

B. "Interest Analysis" Approach – **CUT** ....

     1. Contact With the Case ....

     2. "Unprovided-For" or "No Interest" Case ....

        a. Interests...

        b. Rule and Result...

     3. True Conflict ....

        a. Interests...

        b. Rule and Result...

     4. Substance Versus Procedure...

C. Modern Restatement (Second) Approach...

     1. Issue-Specific ....

     2. Most Significant Relationship ....

        a. General Factors – **FINEBUD**...

        b. Connecting Factors for Torts – **CRIP** ....

        c. Connecting Factors for Contracts – **NSFPP**................................

     3. Real Property ....

     4. Corporations ....

     5. Substance Versus Procedure...

        a. Statutes of Limitations..

        b. Uniform Conflict of Laws Limitations Act ....

     6. Choice of Law Statutes..

**V.   CHOICE OF LAW IN SPECIFIC AREAS AND
      OTHER CONSIDERATIONS**

A. Specific Areas of Substantive Law...

     1. Intestate Succession..

        a. General Rules ....

        b. Adopted Children ....

     2. Family Law..

        a. Validity of Marriage ....

        b. Grounds for Divorce, Separation, and Annulment.............................

        c. Jurisdiction Over Divorce Proceedings ....

B. Other Choice of Law Considerations ....

     1. Proof of Foreign Law ....

        a. Parties Must Raise Issue and Provide Proof.......................................

        b. Federal Courts and Law of Foreign Nations ....

2. Choice of Law by Agreement ....

    a. Generally Enforced ....

    b. Avoiding *Renvoi* ....

B. Choice of Law Systems ....

C. Defenses Against Application of Foreign Law ....

    1. Local Public Policy ....

    2. Penal Laws ....

       a. Criminal Laws ....

       b. Civil Fines ....

       c. Punitive Damages Exception ....

    3. Revenue Laws ....

D. Constitutional Limitations ....

    1. Due Process ....

    2. Full Faith and Credit ....

E. Federal-State Conflicts ....

    1. *Erie* Doctrine ....

    2. Federal Supremacy ....

VI. JUDGMENTS FROM OTHER STATES AND FOREIGN NATIONS

A. Constitutional Full Faith and Credit ....

    1. General Rule ....

    2. Exceptions ....

       a. Jurisdiction ....

       b. On the Merits ....

       c. Finality ....

       d. Penal Judgments ....

       e. Inconsistent Judgments ....

    3. Public Policy Exception ....

    4. Divorce Judgments ....

       a. Jurisdiction ....

       b. Divisible Divorce ....

    5. Claim and Issue Preclusion ....

    6. International Judgments ....

B. Statutory Full Faith and Credit ....

    1. Child Custody Judgments ....

       a. Home State Jurisdiction ....

       b. Emergency Jurisdiction ....

       c. Significant Connection Jurisdiction ....

       d. Vacuum Jurisdiction ....

    2. Abducted Child or Other Wrongful Conduct ....

    3. Child Support Judgments ....

RIGOS BAR REVIEW SERIES

UNIFORM MULTISTATE ESSAY EXAM (MEE) REVIEW

CHAPTER 2

CONFLICT OF LAWS

Note: On the MEE, conflict of laws is tested in crossover questions that usually involve issues of Family Law or Federal Civil Procedure.

Essay Questions

Question Number 1

In 2005, Donald, domiciled in State X, borrowed $10,000 from Peter, who is domiciled in State Y. According to their written loan agreement, in addition to repaying the principal, Donald would pay Peter a finance charge at an annual rate of 20%. Furthermore, because Peter did not trust the postal system, Donald was required to tender payments in person at Peter's home in State Y.

State X has a civil usury statute that imposes an annual finance charge ceiling of 15% and voids any loan agreement that purports to impose a higher rate. According to legislative history, the statute was enacted to prevent borrowers from becoming overextended on their debts and thereby becoming dependent upon welfare.

State Y had an identical statute at one time, but the legislature repealed it in 1985. According to the legislative history, the finance charge cap was repealed because it deterred the making of loans to State Y citizens, who often could not otherwise borrow money when they needed it.

Because Donald had incurred too much debt by borrowing the money from Peter, he could not make any payments on the loan. Peter sued Donald in a State X court to enforce the loan agreement. In his answer, Donald raised State X's finance charge as an affirmative defense and argued that the loan agreement was void.

Would the court agree with Donald? Explain. Assume that State X has not adopted the Restatement (Second) of Conflict of Laws.

Question Number 2

Harry married Wendy in 2010. At the time, both were domiciled in State A, and they remained domiciled there for the duration of their marriage. In 2012, Wendy gave birth to the spouses' only child, Christopher.

Unfortunately, the marriage was not a happy one, and in 2013, Harry left Wendy and Christopher, and established a new domicile in State B. Wendy and Christopher moved later that year and became domiciled in State C.

In 2016, Harry, who was still domiciled in State B, visited State C. During his trip, Harry tried to abduct Christopher. Fortunately, Wendy witnessed the attempt and rescued Christopher. However, Harry managed to get in his car and escape.

Wendy called the police, who caught up with Harry and pulled him over. But when Harry presented both his driver's license and a copy of Christopher's birth certificate, which listed Harry as the father, the police told Harry that he was free to go on his way. Harry promptly returned to State B. The police explained to an outraged Wendy that without a custody order, the abduction attempt was not a criminal matter and could be resolved in civil court only.

Shortly after the abduction attempt, Harry filed a divorce petition in State B. The petition asked the court to dissolve the marriage and award Harry full custody of Christopher. Service of process was made personally upon Wendy in State A. Wendy decided to ignore the petition because she believed that a court in State B could not dissolve the marriage or award custody of Christopher, as neither Wendy nor Christopher had even visited State B, let alone lived there.

The State B court entered an ex parte divorce decree that also gave full custody of Christopher to Harry. When Wendy learned of the judgment, she called a lawyer in State B, who informed her that the time for appealing the judgment had expired. Wendy now wants to start a collateral attack in a State C court for a declaratory judgment decreeing that the State B court lacked jurisdiction to dissolve the marriage or award custody.

Should the State C court enter the requested declaratory judgment? Explain.

Question Number 3

Irving had spent his entire adult life living in the same rented apartment in State X. A month ago, Irving's employer decided to move its State X office 50 miles away to a city in the adjacent State Y. While Irving was not terribly pleased about it, he nonetheless agreed to relocate because he enjoyed his job and had no desire to seek work elsewhere. In preparation for the relocation, Irving called an apartment complex that his employer recommended in State Y and made arrangements over the phone to sign the lease on a unit as soon as he arrived in State Y with his belongings.

On the day of his move, Irving followed the moving truck in his car from State X to State Y. After Irving and the moving truck arrived at the State Y apartment, the movers unloaded the boxes containing Irving's possessions. He made sure that everything was accounted for, signed the apartment lease, and then drove back to State X so he could clean the now-empty apartment there before returning the keys to the landlord.

Tragically, just one minute after crossing the border between the two states and reentering State X, Irving lost control of his car and hit a tree. The impact killed him instantly. Irving had not made a will before his death.

During the administration of his estate, the question arose as to which state's intestacy law would control. Under State X law, Irving's sole uncle would take all. But under State Y law, Irving's sole cousin would take all.

Who should receive Irving's estate? Explain.

Question Number 4

Plaintiff, an employer incorporated and headquartered in State A, hired Defendant, an individual domiciled in State B. The parties negotiated and executed a written employment contract at Plaintiff's headquarters, but the job itself was a position at Plaintiff's State B branch office.

Just a month after starting, Defendant resigned her employment with Plaintiff in order to accept a higher-paying job with Competitor. Plaintiff filed suit in State A court against Defendant on the grounds that by accepting her new job Defendant had violated a non-compete clause in their contract. Non-compete clauses are valid in State A, but void under the law of State B.

Defendant has moved for summary judgment on the grounds that State B law should govern the contract, and thus, the non-compete clause has no effect. Plaintiff has opposed the motion by arguing that State A law should control instead. The contract itself is silent on choice of law.

Should the court grant Defendant's motion? Explain. Assume that State A follows the Restatement (Second) of Conflict of Laws.

Question Number 5

Passenger, domiciled in State X, was riding on a train from State X to the adjacent State Y. She had purchased her ticket at Railroad's station in State X. Railroad is incorporated in State Y, headquartered in State Y, and has most of its tracks in State Y.

An employee of Railroad who works at its State X train yard had improperly coupled together two of the train's cars. As a result, the train derailed on a section of track in State Y, seriously injuring Passenger.

Passenger has filed a negligence lawsuit against Railroad in a State X court and requested trial by jury. The complaint seeks both compensatory and punitive damages. Under State X law, courts may award punitive damages. By contrast, State Y law prohibits punitive damages unless specifically authorized by statute.

In a pre-trial brief, Railroad has urged the court to apply State Y law and disallow Passenger's request for punitive damages. Passenger concedes that State Y law would not permit punitive damages for the particular harm she suffered. However, Passenger contends that State X law applies, and accordingly, she should be allowed to seek punitive damages.

Which state's law should the State X court apply? Explain. Assume that State X follows the Restatement (Second) of Conflict of Laws.

Answer Number 1

Summary

If State X uses the First Restatement ("Vested Rights") approach to resolving conflicts of laws, D's defense fails, since the law of the state where performance was to occur controls, and D was to pay in State Y. If the state uses Interest Analysis, his defense may succeed, because the court would consider the states' underlying policies for the laws and the legitimacy of the states' interest in applying their own laws. State X's policy relies on the welfare system to fulfill its legitimate interest in keeping citizens like D out of too much debt. State Y wants unlimited loans to be available to its citizens, but as domiciliary P is a lender, not a borrower, State Y's policy lacks contact with P. Only one state has an interest in the application of its law, so the case is a "false conflict," and therefore the court should apply the laws of State X, which has the legitimate interest. Using Interest Analysis, the court should impose the finance charge limit and void D's loan.

Issues Raised

(1)   First Restatement ("Vested Rights"): Contracts
      (a) Approach employed only by a minority of states
      (b) The law of the state where performance is to be rendered controls
(2)   Public Policy Exception
      (a) Refusal to apply law of another state if it violates the public policy of forum state
      (b) Policy violation must be very strong and morally shocking
(3)   Interest Analysis
      (a) Policy Considerations
      (b) False Conflict

Sample Answer

The outcome depends upon the choice of law system used by State X. Besides the Second Restatement approach, which is the most common system used by courts today, the two other major systems are the First Restatement approach and the "Interest Analysis" approach. If State X uses the former, the court should reject Donald's defense. If State X uses the latter, the court should accept the defense.

(1)   First Restatement ("Vested Rights"): Contracts. Under the First Restatement approach, which is still used in a minority of states, issues of contract performance are governed by the law of the state where performance is to be rendered. Here, because the contract required Donald to make his payments in person in State Y, the State X court should apply the law of State Y. Under the law of State Y, Donald's defense lacks merit because there is no finance charge limit that could be violated.

(2)   Public Policy Exception.   An attempt by Donald to invoke the "public policy" exception and persuade the State X court not to apply State Y law would likely fail. While a court may refuse to apply the law of another state on grounds that it violates the public policy of the forum state, the violation must be very strong and morally shocking. In practice, most policy violations will not meet this high standard. A state's desire to keep its citizens off welfare may be legitimate, but a person being dependent upon welfare does not seem morally shocking. Accordingly, the public policy exception seems inapplicable here. Under the First Restatement, the court should apply the law of State Y and reject Donald's defense, which requires the application of State X law.

(3)   Interest Analysis.   However, under the Interest Analysis approach, which only a few states use today, the court would consider the policies underlying the differences in the two states' laws. The court would focus on whether each state has a legitimate interest in its law being applied, based upon its contacts with the case.

   (a) Policy Considerations.   Here, State X's policy behind its finance charge cap is to prevent its citizens from getting too deeply in debt and thereby relying on the state's welfare system. Donald, a citizen of State X, has become too deeply in debt because of the loan at issue in this case. The policy behind the finance charge limit thus has a contact with State X, and accordingly, State X has an interest in enforcing its finance charge limit.

On the other hand, State Y has no finance charge limit because it wants loans to be available to citizens who need to borrow money. While Peter is domiciled in State Y, he is a lender, not a borrower in need of money. The policy underlying State Y's law lacks a contact with Peter, and thus State Y lacks an interest in having its law applied in this case. Furthermore, the availability of loans to Donald does not create a legitimate interest in the application of State Y law because Donald is not a citizen of State Y, and Interest Analysis usually assumes that a state has no legitimate interest in protecting or compensating non-citizens.

   (b) False Conflict.   When only one state has an interest in the application of its law, the case is classified as a "false conflict." In false conflict cases, a court should apply the law of the state that has the legitimate interest. Here, that state is State X. Under Interest Analysis, the court should agree with Donald, impose State X's finance charge limit, and void the loan.

Answer Number 2

Summary

Generally, state courts must recognize and enforce other states' judgments under the Full Faith and Credit Clause [FFCC]. Exceptions exist where the adjudicative state lacked jurisdiction (as State B, here). W had no apparent personal connection to State B – it was her ex's domiciliary, not hers, and she had never been physically present there. The doctrine of "divisible divorce" allows a court with jurisdiction over only one spouse (as State B has over H) to dissolve the marriage, but not to determine property division, child support, or alimony. H also submitted to State B's jurisdiction over dissolution by filing a claim there. State C must give Full Faith and Credit to the dissolution, but not the custody order. State courts have four types of jurisdiction over custody: "home state," "emergency," "significant connection," and "vacuum" (where no state has home state jurisdiction and jurisdiction is in the child's best interests).

State B had none of these, while State C had home state jurisdiction over C. Since State B lacked jurisdiction, State C need not give Full Faith and Credit to the custody award, and should give W custody.

Issues Raised

(1)   Constitutional Full Faith and Credit
    (a) Lack of Jurisdiction
       (i) Lack of minimum personal contacts
       (ii) Not physically present
    (b) Divisible Divorce
       (i) Court with jurisdiction over only one spouse may dissolve the marriage
       (ii) May not resolve property division, child support, and alimony issues
(2)   Child Custody Judgments
    (a) Jurisdictional Requirement
       (i) "Home state jurisdiction"
          a.   Child lives in forum state when custody action begins, or
          b.   Child had lived in the forum state within six months, and
          c.   At least one parent / guardian continues to live there
       (ii) "Emergency jurisdiction"
          a.   Child is physically present in forum state and
          b.   In need of protection from abandonment or abuse
       (iii)"Significant connection jurisdiction"
          a.   Child and one parent/guardian have significant connection to forum state
          b.   Significant connection considered only if no home state jurisdiction
       (iv) "Vacuum jurisdiction"
          a.   No state has home state jurisdiction
          b.   Jurisdiction in that forum is consistent with the child's best interests
(3)   Statutory Full Faith and Credit

Sample Answer

(1)   Constitutional Full Faith and Credit. The Full Faith and Credit Clause of the United States Constitution generally requires state courts to recognize and enforce judgments from other states. In most cases, this precludes a litigant from launching a collateral attack on a judgment from one state in the courts of another state, because the judgment from the first state binds the court in the second state. The preferred procedure for a litigant who is dissatisfied with a court's judgment is to appeal in that state, not start a collateral attack action elsewhere.

    (a) Lack of Jurisdiction. Various exceptions to the Full Faith and Credit Clause exist, and one of them commonly allows a court to deny Full Faith and Credit to a judgment from another state if the state that issued the judgment lacked jurisdiction. The State B court most likely lacked jurisdiction over Wendy as an individual, since she was not domiciled there, had never been physically present in the state, and the facts suggest no connection between Wendy and State B, other than her husband (or ex-husband) presently being domiciled there.

(b) Divisible Divorce. However, the lack of jurisdiction over Wendy is of no consequence. Under the doctrine of "divisible divorce," a court that has jurisdiction over only one spouse may nonetheless dissolve the marriage (although it may not resolve issues such as property division, child support, and alimony). State B courts have general jurisdiction over anyone domiciled in the state, including Harry. (Additionally, a party submits to the jurisdiction of a court by initiating an action in it, which is what Harry did.) Since the State B court had jurisdiction over Harry, the divisible divorce doctrine allowed it to dissolve the marriage. State C must give Full Faith and Credit to the State B decree of divorce and is thus precluded from entering a declaratory judgment to the contrary.

(2) Child Custody Judgments. The custody order portion of the State B judgment is another matter, and should not be enforced by the State C court.

(a) Jurisdictional Requirement. Every state has enacted either the Uniform Child Custody Jurisdiction Act (UCCJA) or the Uniform Child Custody Jurisdiction and Enforcement Act (UCCJEA). The UCCJA and UCCJEA gives state courts four types of jurisdiction over child custody disputes: "home state jurisdiction," "emergency jurisdiction," "significant connection jurisdiction," and "vacuum jurisdiction." Home state jurisdiction requires the child to be living in the forum state when the custody action begins, or that the child had lived in the forum state within six months before the start of the action and at least one parent/guardian continued to live there. Emergency jurisdiction requires that the child be physically present in the forum state and in need of protection from abandonment or abuse.

(b) Significant Connection. Significant connection jurisdiction requires that the child and at least one parent / guardian have a significant relationship to the forum state. The federal Parental Kidnapping Protection Act (PKPA) recognizes significant connection jurisdiction only if no state can exercise home state jurisdiction. Vacuum jurisdiction requires both that no state has home state jurisdiction and it is consistent with the child's best interests for the forum to exercise jurisdiction.

State B did not have any of these four types of jurisdiction. Christopher never lived in State B, so there was no home state jurisdiction. Christopher was never present in State B, so there could not have been emergency jurisdiction. Also, the facts here suggest no abandonment or abuse emergency. State C could have exercised home state jurisdiction in a custody dispute regarding Christopher, since he lived in State C at the time the State B action was commenced, so the PKPA would not recognize any claim of significant connection jurisdiction. Similarly, because State C could have exercised home state jurisdiction, State B could not have exercised vacuum jurisdiction.

(3) Statutory Full Faith and Credit. Under the PKPA, a state must give Full Faith and Credit to a child custody judgment from another state only if the state that issued the judgment had jurisdiction under the UCCJA or the UCCJEA. Since State B lacked jurisdiction to award Harry custody of Christopher, State C need not give Full Faith and Credit to the custody award, and the State C court should give Wendy the custody portion of her requested declaratory judgment.

Answer Number 3

Summary

Absent a contrary statute, the law of the decedent's domicile at death governs intestate succession of personal property. Irving died domiciled in State Y (he had physical presence and had the intent to stay). Irving arguably had two residences, but he can only have one domicile at a time. Neither his physical return to State X nor his death there revived Irving's domicile in State X, as he lacked the intent to stay indefinitely. Irving was still domiciled in State Y, so its law governs intestate succession of his personal property to the cousin.

Issues Raised

(1)   Intestate Succession: Personal Property
        (a) Law of State Where Domiciled Applies
        (b) True Under all Choice of Law Systems
(2)   Domicile
        (a) Creation Requirements
            (i) Physical presence in state
            (ii) Intent to remain
            (iii) New domicile immediately replaces old
        (a) Contrasted with Residence
        (b) Creation and Destruction
(3)   Domicile Revival

Sample Answer

(1)   Intestate Succession: Personal Property. The law of State Y will apply, and Irving's cousin should receive the entire estate. Absent a contrary statute, the law of the decedent's domicile at death governs intestate succession to personal property. This is true under all major choice of law systems (First Restatement, Second Restatement, and Interest Analysis). The facts do not indicate that Irving owns any real property, and given that he rents his residences, it is reasonable to assume that Irving probably does not own real estate.

(2)   Domicile. Irving died domiciled in State Y. The two elements needed to create a domicile are: 1) physical presence in the state; and 2) the intention to remain in the state indefinitely and make it one's home. Once these requirements are satisfied, the new domicile is established immediately and the old domicile ceases to exist. A person may have more than one residence simultaneously, but only one domicile.

    (a) Contrasted with Residence. In this case, Irving arguably had two residences: the old apartment in State X (which he still possessed at the time of his death) and the new apartment in State Y. While a person may have multiple residences, he can only have one domicile at a time.

    (b) Creation and Destruction. Irving's domicile in State Y was created when he followed the moving truck and crossed the border into State Y (physical presence). Since his move was triggered by his employer's relocation to State Y, and he had no desire to leave his job, Irving clearly entered the state with the requisite intent to stay there indefinitely and make it his home. At the moment he entered State Y, the new domicile was created, and his old domicile in State X was destroyed.

(3) Domicile Revival. Irving's return to State X did not revive his domicile there. Although he was physically present in State X, he lacked the intent to stay indefinitely. He was only in State X temporarily so he could clean his old apartment before surrendering possession of it. The fact that he died in State X does not change the domicile analysis. Thus, Irving was still domiciled in State Y when he died, and as explained above, the law of his domicile at death governs intestate succession of his personal property, all of which will go to the cousin under State Y law.

Answer Number 4

Summary

The Restatement 2d resolves choice of law problems by determining which state has the "most significant relationship" to the issue. Major factors in this determination are the forum's polices, the interested state's policies, the needs of the interstate and international systems, protecting parties' expectations, the basic policies of the area of law, ease of the law's application, uniformity, certainty, and predictability. Here, these general factors favor State A's law. For contract disputes, courts also consider connecting factors under the Restatement 2d: the location of the negotiation and formation (here, State A), the location of the subject matter and/ or performance (here, State B), and finally, the location of the parties. These connecting factors do not clearly favor either state, but the weight of the general factors dictates that the court should apply State A law. Thus, the non-compete clauses are valid, and D's motion for summary judgment should be denied.

Issues Raised

(1) Choice of Law: Modern Restatement (Second) Approach: Most Significant Relationship
(2) General Factors
    (a) Interested state's policies
    (b) Needs of the interstate and international systems
    (c) Protecting the parties' expectations
    (d) Basic policies of the area of law
    (e) Ease of the law's application
    (f) Uniformity, certainty, and predictability
(3) Connecting Factors for Contracts
    (a) Location of the negotiation and formation
    (b) Location of the subject matter and/ or performance
    (c) Location of the parties

Sample Answer

(1) Choice of Law: Modern Restatement (Second) Approach. Under the Restatement (Second) of Conflict of Laws, most choice of law problems are resolved by determining which state has the "most significant relationship" to the issue in question. In making this determination, the court considers general factors as well as other factors that are specific to certain areas of law.

(2)   General Factors. The Second Restatement specifies the following general factors:

(a) The forum's polices. The forum, State A, upholds non-compete clauses. This reflects the general contract law policies of protecting the parties' expectations and their freedom to contract.

(b) The interested states' policies. State A's policies are discussed above. State B's refusal to enforce non-compete clauses presumably stems from a policy of disfavoring restrictions on a person's ability to make a living for herself and contribute to the overall economy. These competing policies seem to cancel each other out.

(c) The needs of the interstate and international systems. Enforcing the non-compete clause would involve the State A court enforcing a contractual provision that is void in State B against a person in State B. On the other hand, declining to enforce the provision would involve a State A court applying State B law against an entity that incorporated in State A, is headquartered in State A, and likely relied upon State A law in making business decisions. Either way, a state's ability to set its own laws and be governed by them will be impaired somewhat, so this factor favors neither Plaintiff nor Defendant.

(d) Protecting the parties' expectations. The best reflection of the parties' expectations (and perhaps the only one that may be considered, due to the parol evidence rule) is the contract itself, which included a clause restricting Defendant's ability to work for a competitor of the Plaintiff. Enforcing the non-compete provision would protect this expectation.

(e) The basic policies of the relevant field of law. Again, contract law seeks to protect contractual freedom and expectations. Enforcing the non-compete clause upholds those policies.

(f) Uniformity, certainty, and predictability. Certainty and predictability would be served by applying State A law and enforcing the non-compete clause that the parties agreed to in writing. Uniformity favors neither party because the two states have diametrically opposing positions on the validity of non-compete agreements.

(g) The law's ease of being determined and applied. The law in both states is clear, so ease of determination favors neither party. Difficulty in application slightly favors the Defendant's position because upholding the non-compete clause would likely require the court to issue an injunction and may lead to future proceedings seeking to enforce the injunction.

As a whole, the general factors favor upholding and enforcing the non-compete clause against the Defendant pursuant to State A law.

(3) **Connecting Factors for Contracts.** Under the Second Restatement, the court also considers the following factors in contract disputes:

(a) Location of the negotiation. The parties negotiated the contract at Plaintiff's headquarters in State A.

(b) Location of the subject matter. The subject of the contract was rendering services in State B.

(c) Location of formation. The parties executed the contract in State A.

(d) Location of performance. Defendant was to perform her duties in State B.

(e) Location of the parties. Plaintiff is largely located in State A, but Defendant is entirely located in State B.

The connecting factors do not clearly favor either state. However, since the general factors weigh in favor of State A, the court should apply State A law. Because non-compete clauses are valid in State A, Defendant's motion for summary judgment should be denied.

Answer Number 5

Summary

The Restatement 2d resolves choice of law problems by determining which state has the "most significant relationship" to the issue. Major factors are the forum's polices (State X's punitive damages punish and deter tortfeasors), the interested state's policies (State Y discourages excessive damage awards), the needs of the interstate and international systems (State X's law denies protections against punitive damages), protecting parties' expectations (P's expectations of full legal compensation vs. the Railroad's expectation to avoid punitive damages), the basic policies of the area of law (tort law exists to compensate those harmed by another, not to punish or deter), ease of the law's application, uniformity, certainty, and predictability (none of these apply here to the directly conflicting laws). The court may also consider connecting factors for tort claims under the Restatement 2d: the location of the parties (divided), the location of the injury (State Y), and the location of the relationship between the parties (State X, where P bought her ticket), and the location of the conduct causing the injury (State X). Here, the general factors are inconclusive, but the connecting factors marginally favor State X law.

Issues Raised

(1)   Choice of Law: Modern Restatement (Second) Approach
(2)   General Factors
       (a) Interested state's policies
       (b) Needs of the interstate and international systems
       (c) Protecting the parties' expectations
       (d) Basic policies of the area of law
       (e) Ease of the law's application
       (f) Uniformity, certainty, and predictability

(3) Connecting Factors for Torts
   (a) Location of the parties
   (b) Location of the injury
   (c) Location of the relationship between the parties
   (d) Location of the conduct causing the injury (State

Sample Answer

(1) Choice of Law: Modern Restatement (Second) Approach. Courts that follow the Second Restatement in resolving choice-of-law issues attempt to apply the law of the state with the "most significant relationship" to the case. In making this determination, the court considers both general factors and "connecting factors" that are specific to a particular area of law.

(2) General Factors. Under the Second Restatement, general factors considered by the court are:

(a) The forum's polices. The forum, State X, generally allows punitive damage awards. This presumably reflects a policy of punishing egregious tortfeasors, deterring the tortfeasor from engaging in the same conduct in the future, and warning others who might act in a similar manner.

(b) The interested states' policies. State X's policy considerations are set forth above. State Y's general prohibition on punitive damages is presumably based upon a policy of discouraging excessive damage awards.

(c) The needs of the interstate and international systems. Applying State X law would deny a litigant domiciled in State Y of the protection against punitive damages provided by the law of that state. Similarly, applying State Y law would frustrate the State X court's ability to promote State X's policies underlying punitive damage awards. These competing problems seem to cancel each other out, and regardless of which law the court applies, a state's ability to govern entities domiciled in that state and promote the public policies of that state will be impeded.

(d) Protecting the parties' expectations. Although the facts do not state what the parties actually expected, it would be fair to assume that Passenger expected that she could recover damages to the full extent permitted in her state. Similarly, Railroad may have expected that it would be protected under State Y law from large punitive damage awards. Again, these competing expectations seem to cancel each other out.

(e) The basic policies of the relevant field of law. Perhaps the most fundamental policy of tort law is compensating those who suffer harm due to the fault of another. This policy is served by compensatory damages. By contrast, punitive damages go beyond compensating the injured party for the particular harm suffered and are arguably a windfall for a litigant who recovers them. This factor seems to weigh in favor of applying State Y's limit on punitive damages.

(f) Uniformity, certainty, and predictability. It seems that applying neither law would promote uniformity, certainty, and predictability. The two states have opposite positions on punitive damage awards, making uniformity impossible. Further, nothing in the facts suggest that the application of either state's law was predictable (e.g., the facts are silent on whether Railroad's contract of carriage contained a choice of law clause). This factor appears to be inapplicable to the case at hand.

(g) The law's ease of being determined and applied. Here, both states' laws concerning punitive damages have already been ascertained, and applying either law is simply a matter of instructing the jury accordingly. Thus, this factor favors neither state's law.

Considered as a whole, the general factors do not weigh significantly in favor of either state's law.

(3)   Connecting Factors for Torts. The Second Restatement specifies the following connecting factors to be considered in tort cases:

(a) Locations of the Parties. Passenger is domiciled in State X, and Railroad is domiciled in State Y, where it has most of its operations. Accordingly, this factor favors neither state.

(b) Location of the Injury. Passenger was injured when the train derailed in State Y.

(c) Location of the Relationship Between the Parties. The parties entered into their relationship in State X, where Passenger purchased her ticket.

(d) Location of the Conduct Causing the Injury. The wrongful conduct occurred in Railroad's State X train yard.

The connecting factors, when viewed as a whole, weigh slightly in favor of applying State X law since this is where the injury originated that caused the harm. Since the general factors do not favor either state, the connecting factors should control, and the State X court should apply its own law of awarding punitive damages.

CHAPTER 2

CONFLICTS OF LAW

Index

Abducted Child .... T 2-142
Annulment................................. T 2-138
Choice of Forum by
   Agreement .... T 2-134
Child Custody Judgments........... T 2-141
Child Support Judgments .... T 2-142
Choice of Law .... T 2-135, 138
Choice of Law by Agreement .... T 2-139
Civil Fines .... T 2-139
Claim Preclusion .... T 2-141
Collateral Estoppel .... T 2-141
Connecting Factors............. T 2-137, 138
Constitutional Limitations.......... T 2-140
Contracts............................ T 2-135, 138
Corporations .... T 2-135, 138
Criminal Laws .... T 2-139
Dépeçage Doctrine.................... T 2-136
Divisible Divorce .... T 2-134, 141
Divorce .... T 2-134, 138, 141
Domicile .... T 2-133
Due Process .... T 2-140
Erie Doctrine .... T 2-140
Escape Devices.......................... T 2-135
False Conflict .... T 2-137
Family Law .... T 2-138
Federal-State Conflicts.............. T 2-140
Federal Supremacy.................... T 2-140
First Restatement....................... T 2-135
"Foreign" .... T 2-133
Foreign Law .... T 2-139
Foreign Nations .... T 2-139
"Forum" .... T 2-133
Forum Non Conveniens .... T 2-135
Full Faith and Credit .... T 2-140
General Factors .... T 2-137
Inconsistent Judgments .... T 2-141
Intent to Remain .... T 2-133
Interest Analysis....................... T 2-136
International Judgments .... T 2-141
Intestate Succession................... T 2-138
Issue Preclusion........................ T 2-141
Jurisdiction of Courts .... T 2-134
Klaxon Doctrine .... T 2-140
Marriage .... T 2-138
Modern Approach .... T 2-137

Most Significant Relationship .... T 2-137
No-Interest Case .... T 2-134
Parental Kidnapping Protection
   Act (PKPA) .... T 2-141
Penal Laws................................ T 2-139
Penal Judgments .... T 2-141
Personal Jurisdiction................... T 2-134
Physical Presence .... T 2-133
Proof of Foreign Law .... T 2-139
Public Policy...................... T 2-139, 141
Punitive Damages....................... T 2-139
Real Property .... T 2-135, 138
Renvoi Doctrine .... T 2-135, 139
Res Judicata .... T 2-141
Residence.................................. T 2-134
Restatement (First) .... T 2-135
Restatement (Second)................. T 2-137
Revenue Laws .... T 2-140
Same-Sex Marriage .... T 2-138
Second Restatement.................... T 2-137
Separation .... T 2-138
Statutes of Limitations................ T 2-138
Statutory Full Faith and Credit ... T 2-141
Substance Versus
   Procedure................ T 2-136, 137, 138
Torts................................. T 2-135, 137
True Conflict .... T 2-137
Uniform Child Custody Jurisdiction
   Act (UCCJA) .... T 2-141
Uniform Child Custody Jurisdiction
   and Enforcement Act
   (UCCJEA) .... T 2-141
Uniform Conflict of Laws
   Limitations Act........................ T 2-138
Uniform Interstate Family Support
   Act (UIFSA) .... T 2-142
Unprovided-For Case .... T 2-136
Validity of Marriage................... T 2-138
"Vested Rights" Approach .... T 2-135

CHAPTER 3

FAMILY LAW

RIGOS BAR REVIEW SERIES

UNIFORM MULTISTATE ESSAY EXAM (MEE) REVIEW

CHAPTER 3

FAMILY LAW

Table of Contents

A.	Sub-Topic Exam Issue Distribution		Text 3-167
B.	Opening Argument and Primary Issues		Text 3-169
C.	Text		Text 3-171
	I.	Marriage	Text 3-171
	II.	Actions Prior to Final Dissolution	Text 3-172
	III.	Dissolution	Text 3-174
	IV.	Property Division and Maintenance	Text 3-175
	V.	Responsibility for Children	Text 3-176
D.	Magic Memory Outlines®		Magic Memory Outlines 3-181
E.	Family Law Essay Questions		Questions 3-185
F.	Family Law Essay Answers		Answers 3-189
G.	Family Law Index		Index 3-197
H.	Acronyms		Acronyms 15-625

RIGOS BAR REVIEW SERIES
MEE SUB-TOPIC FREQUENCY DISTRIBUTION

FAMILY LAW

	2/09	7/08	2/08	7/07	2/07	7/06	2/06	7/05	2/05	7/04	2/04	7/03	2/03	7/02	2/02	7/01	2/01
Marriage																	
Validity						/	/										
"Holding Out" as Husband & Wife							/										
Common Law		/					/										
Dissolution of Marriage	/	/	/		/	/	/	/	/	/	/	/	/			/	/
Jurisdiction	/				/				/				/			/	
Property Division		/			/	/					/	/	/				
Spousal Maintenance							/				/					/	
Need vs. Ability											/					/	
Parenting Plan	/		/					/	/	/			/	/		/	/
"Best Interests of the Child"	/		/					/	/				/			/	
Decision-Making Authority														/			
Modification of PP			/						/	/							
Residential Schedule	/								/	/							/
Visitation Right	/							/									

	2/09	7/08	2/08	7/07	2/07	7/06	2/06	7/05	2/05	7/04	2/04	7/03	2/03	7/02	2/02	7/01	2/01
Child Support	/	/	/					/	/			/					/
Deviation Allowed	/		/									/					
Modification of Child Support	/		/									/					
Uniform Parentage Act													/				
Determination of Paternity								/	/				/				
Acknowledge Paternity													/				
Presumption of Paternity								/	/				/				
Adoption			/			/											/
Rights of Natural Parent Terminated						/											/

OPENING ARGUMENT AND PRIMARY ISSUES

FAMILY LAW

There are a few thoughts that should usually be stated at the beginning of every answer. These will score you easy points and let the grader know you are in the right topic area.

Most essays should have an "opening argument": a brief, broad statement that shows you understand the broad significance of a legal topic. The opening argument also suggests to the grader that she is about to read a thoughtful and well-organized essay.

Many subjects also have "primary issues" that can be discussed up front or integrated into the essay answer. IMPORTANT: Do not merely regurgitate these statements on the exam without addressing the issues actually raised by the facts, or you will not pass.

- **Family Law Opening Argument:** Family law protects the rights of parties subject to a marital dissolution, including children.

- **Sample Primary Issue Statements:**

  - Most jurisdictions are no-fault divorce states; the petitioning party need only allege marriage is "irretrievably broken." If the dissolution is uncontested, it will be granted after 90 days.

  - Jurisdiction usually vests if one of the parties is a resident. Jurisdiction over both spouses is not necessary to dissolve a marriage, so long as the plaintiff is domiciled in the forum state.

  - Upon dissolution, all property (separate and jointly owned/community) will be distributed by the court in a "just and equitable" manner. The parties must be legally married for the Jointly Owned Property (JOP) rules to apply, but the court may apply the JOP rules by analogy if a meretricious relationship existed between the parties.

  - In any proceedings involving children, the court will look at the "best interest of the child" as a standard to determine the parents' responsibilities for the children.

  - Parenting plans allocate parental responsibilities of minor children, including residential schedules and decision-making authority.

FAMILY LAW

The American Law Institute (ALI) has model statutes that control domestic relations: marriage, dissolution, and the care of children. The below are general rules in most states.

I. MARRIAGE

A. Who May Contract

In most jurisdictions, marriage is a civil contract into which male and female persons 18 years or older and "who are otherwise capable" may enter. A marriage involving a person under 17 will be void unless waived by a superior court judge, generally with parental consent.

> **MEE Tip:** Currently, a few states recognize same-sex marriage. Other states recognize registered domestic partnerships. Because national policy is still developing, the MEE is unlikely to test on same-sex marriage / partnership issues until courts provide more guidance.

B. Validity Requirements – CALF SAW

1. Consanguinity: The parties cannot be closer kin than second cousins.

2. Not Already Married: Neither party to the present marriage may have another spouse living at the time of the marriage.

3. License: Parties must obtain a license from the county auditor. The license may not be used until three days after the application for the license and will expire 60 days after the application if the marriage is not solemnized. Obtaining a license is a regulatory requirement, so failure to obtain a license does not *per se* render a marriage invalid.

4. Filed Certificate: The marriage certificate must be signed by the witnesses and the person who solemnized the marriage, then filed with the county auditor and state registrar of vital statistics.

5. Solemnization: An authorized officer or person must solemnize the marriage contract. Judges of the superior court or above, superior court commissioners, or any regularly licensed or ordained clergy are authorized to perform marriage ceremonies.

6. Age of Majority: Both parties must be at least 18 years old to marry unless they both have their own parental consent. 17 year olds with parental consent may be married without a judge's order. Minors without parental consent, must obtain permission from a judge or court commissioner.

7. Witnesses: Two witnesses must be physically present to validate the marriage.

C. Common Law Marriages

Many states do not recognize common law marriages, but may recognize such marriages if valid in the state where established.

D. Registered Domestic Partnerships – SURE

Some states recognize Registered Domestic Partnerships between different-sex and same-sex couples. Generally, the requirements for domestic partnership can be remembered as **SURE**: **S**hare household, **U**nmarried to other person, **R**egistered, and **E**ighteen or Older.

II. ACTIONS PRIOR TO FINAL DISSOLUTION

A. Temporary Relief

Temporary relief pending entry of the decree of dissolution is available. Such relief includes temporary parenting plans, property allocations, child support orders, and restraining orders. Such temporary relief may be obtained by motion at a hearing on the Family Law Motions Calendar.

1. Temporary Parenting Plan: A temporary parenting plan provides for an established contact plan for children with each parent and any necessary safeguards for the children. The permanent plan is entered with the Decree when the divorce is finalized.

a. Best Interests Test: The court will use the "best interests of the child" test to determine the terms of the temporary parenting plan.

> **MEE Tip:** Whenever children are implicated in a divorce, e.g., parenting plans (primary residential placement) or visitation issues, specifically mention the "best interests of the child" test. It is the most important factor in all balancing tests used in family law.

b. Typical Provisions: Typical provisions in a parenting plan (whether temporary or final) include (1) designation of primary residential parent (*not* "custodial" parent); (2) residential schedule for both parents' contact with the child; (3) allocation of decision-making authority; (4) transportation arrangements of children between parents, and (5) any restrictions on contact.

2. Temporary Child Support Orders: States usually enter a Support Schedule, which is a table based on the parents' respective incomes that determines the amount of child support. Income may be imputed to a parent who is voluntarily unemployed or underemployed for purpose of avoiding support. Day care costs and other child-related expenses are paid proportionately to income.

3. Temporary Restraining Orders: TROs are issued to prevent (1) disposal or concealment of property, (2) interference with the peace of the opposing party or a child, (3) entry into either party's family home, and/or (4) removing a child from the court's jurisdiction.

4. Protection Orders / Domestic Violence: Emergency no-contact orders can be obtained to protect persons – usually abused spouses and/or children – who have been physically harmed or threatened. Protection orders require a high showing of potential domestic violence (physical harm, threats, stalking, fear of imminent harm). These types of civil court orders are separate from divorce proceedings.

B. Dissolution v. Legal Separation

The process for obtaining a Legal Separation is almost identical to a Dissolution in most states. The differences are:

1. Status of Marriage: Under a Decree of Legal Separation, the parties are still married. A Decree of Dissolution dissolves the marriage, and the parties are free to remarry.

2. Reconciliation: If the parties reconcile after obtaining a Legal Separation, they need only to dismiss their case. After a Dissolution is entered, they must remarry.

3. Waiting Period: There is often a waiting period (30 – 90 days) from the date of service and filing before orders may be entered in a Dissolution; there is no waiting period in a legal separation. Once a Decree of Legal Separation is entered, however, 180 days must pass before it can be converted into a Decree of Dissolution, upon simple motion by either party.

4. Conversion to Dissolution: If a Decree of Legal Separation is entered, parties do not "start over" when changing to Dissolution. Note that being actually physically separated is not the same as being "legally separated." "Date of separation" relates to the date of final, permanent physical separation, not the entry of a Legal Separation.

C. Declarations Regarding Validity

Either or both parties may petition the court for a determination of their marriage's validity. "Annulment" is a term used by various religious institutions to recognize that a marriage never took place; the legal term of art is "declared invalid." If the court finds that the marriage was invalid, it will enter a Decree of Dissolution. The process is the same as in a divorce if there are children, or if property has been accumulated.

1. Jurisdiction: At least one party must be a resident of the court's state.

2. Grounds for Declaration of Invalidity – DAFT LUV: If any of the following apply, then the petitioner has adequate support for a declaration of invalidity.

a. Duress: Inducement to marry by duress makes the marriage voidable by the forced party.

b. Already Married: A prior, undissolved marriage of either party at the time is grounds for invalidity of the second marriage.

c. Fraud: Inducement to marry fraud involving the essentials of the marriage makes the marriage voidable by the defrauded party.

d. Too Closely Related (Consanguinity): The parties must not be too closely related, usually closer than second cousins.

e. Lacked Capacity: Either of the parties lacked capacity.

f. Underage: A party was under the age of 18, without parental or court approval to marry.

g. Void Out of State Marriage: If the out of state marriage is void or voidable in that state's jurisdiction, there are grounds for invalidity.

3. Timeliness: Either party may petition for a declaration of invalidity at any time.

4. Effect on Children: Children are legitimate despite a declaration of marriage invalidity.

D. Personal Jurisdiction Required

A court must have personal jurisdiction to impose any financial burdens on a spouse such as child support or spousal maintenance.

III. DISSOLUTION

A. Jurisdiction

At the time of filing the petitioner must be domiciled in the state and either spouse must have a significant relationship to the state in order for the state to reasonably dissolve the marriage. Personal jurisdiction is required for a court to impose a financial obligation (i.e., spousal maintenance or child support) upon a party.

B. Venue

Venue exists in any county of the state, but may be filed in the county where either party or any child of the parties resides, or in any other county by agreement.

C. Grounds for Dissolution

The petition for dissolution must only contain an allegation that the marriage is "irretrievably broken." Most states are now "no-fault" states: a spouse is not required to prove allegations of misconduct for a dissolution to be granted. In fact, misconduct cannot be considered by the court in distributing property with a few narrow exceptions (such as dissipation of marital estate through gambling or abusive behavior requiring the other spouse to seek rehabilitation or therapy).

> **MEE Tip:** Use the language "no-fault dissolution" and "the marriage is irretrievably broken" (*not* "irreconcilable differences") in your essay answer.

D. Mediation and Settlement

Mediators are required to explain the mediation process, the law, and the parties' right to be represented by independent counsel. Parties must have enough information to ensure informed decision making and must understand the mediator is not their lawyer. A mediator must be impartial and disclose potential conflicts of interest. Where fraud, duress, coercive behavior, or a mediator's substantial misconduct results in an unfair agreement, the court may set aside a divorce settlement, particularly where the disadvantaged party was unrepresented by legal counsel. Some courts have held that when negotiating a divorce settlement, a represented spouse has a fiduciary obligation toward his or her unrepresented spouse.

E. 90-Day Waiting Period

The minimum waiting period for dissolving a marriage, where the parties agree on all terms, is 90 days from the date of filing and service. Many jurisdictions have a trial docket that may take up to one year for trial if settlement is not reached earlier.

F. Denial Required or Granted

If the respondent does not deny that the marriage is irretrievably broken, the court shall enter a decree of dissolution. If a denial is made, the court must make a determination that the marriage is irretrievably broken. The court may refer a couple to a counseling agency for a determination of either reconciliation or dissolution.

IV. PROPERTY DIVISION AND MAINTENANCE

A. Property Subject to Disposition

In any Dissolution, Legal Separation, or Declaration of Invalidity, all property (joint community and separate), is to be divided in a "just and equitable" distribution.

> **MEE Tip:** All property involved (joint, community, or separate), is subject to the court's disposition. Always state in your answer that "all property, joint, community, and separate is divided by the court in a just and equitable distribution."

B. Factors Affecting a "Just and Equitable" Distribution – DEP

Courts weigh the following factors to determine just and equitable property distributions:

1. Duration: Duration of the marriage in question. Five years or less is a clear "short-term" marriage, and the court will attempt to return the parties to their positions upon entering the marriage. Thirty or more years is a clear "long-term" marriage, which justifies an equalizing of assets and income. Anytime in between is subject to the court's discretion.

2. Economic Circumstances: The economic circumstances of the spouses at separation, including earning capacity, living expenses, and all resources available to each spouse from whatever source are to be considered.

3. Property Amount: The nature and extent of all property. The character of the property is not usually controlling (separate property can be awarded to the other spouse).

C. Joint and Separate Property Issues

The court must make a finding about the characterization of the property before it is awarded, even though its characterization as joint or separate does not control the distribution.

1. Compensation: All income and earnings, including compensation in the form benefits (401k, IRAs, pension, stock options, etc.), are subject to division. Federal law (ERISA) controls railroad, military, or government pensions.

2. Goodwill: Goodwill or the reputation of a spouse's professional services practice, if it can be valued, will also be considered as an asset to be divided. This would include a lawyer, CPA, or doctor's practice if well established. Expert testimony is used to establish this value. If the business is so intrinsically tied into the personal efforts of a spouse, the business may be a factor to be considered in arriving at a just and equitable division.

3. Joint v. Separate Property: Increases in separate property remain separate property if kept separate. Separate property never grows into community property. However, a joint property interest, or right of reimbursement, may be created for joint property contributions to separate property assets. This interest may be reduced by a benefit equal to or exceeding the contribution to the separate property.

4. "Hidden" Joint Property: If, after dissolution and asset distribution, an asset is discovered that was not brought before the court, both parties hold that asset as tenants in common and are entitled to 50% of its value, unless otherwise provided in the Decree.

D. Spousal Maintenance

While there is no absolute right to spousal maintenance, the court may grant temporary spousal maintenance to either spouse. The amount and duration of maintenance is determined on a case-by-case basis, in the court's discretion. The court weighs the following factors:

1. Need v. Ability: The financial resources of both spouses, the need of the maintenance seeker, and the ability of the other spouse to pay are all considered.

2. Standard of Living: The standard of living established during the marriage, and the age, physical, and emotional condition of the spouse seeking maintenance are considered.

3. Education: The education level of the spouse seeking maintenance and the time necessary to acquire sufficient education or training to find appropriate employment.

> **MEE Tip:** Some states provide for "rehabilitative maintenance," to temporarily assist where one spouse has achieved a high education or career position, and the other has not.

E. Non-Marital Dissolution

Where a relationship was not formalized by marriage (in some states, a "committed intimate relationship" or "meretricious relationship"), some states make a just and equitable distribution of jointly owned property (pseudo-community property). Separate property generally remains with its owner.

V. RESPONSIBILITY FOR CHILDREN

A. Policy Statement

Both parents have the responsibility to make decisions and to perform functions necessary for the care and growth of their minor children. If they are unable to agree on a Parenting Plan that is in the children's best interests, a Guardian ad Litem or Parenting Evaluator may be appointed for the child to investigate and make recommendations.

1. Child's Best Interest: The "best interests of the child" is the standard by which the court determines and allocates the parties' parental responsibilities. The relationship between the child and each parent is maintained and fostered unless inconsistent with the child's best interests.

2. Factors: The "best interests of the child" are served by a residential schedule that maintains a child's emotional growth, health and stability, and physical care. Emphasis is given to the strength of the relationship between the child and each parent.

3. Stability: The court seeks to maintain the existing pattern of interaction between a parent and child taking into account any changes that result naturally from a divorce situation. Protecting the child from physical, mental, or emotional harm takes precedence over maintaining any particular residential schedule.

B. Permanent Parenting Plans

Permanent parenting plans allocate parental responsibilities of minor children, including residential schedules and decision-making authority.

1. Primary Residential Placement: The court must name one parent the "primary residential parent" to satisfy federal laws requiring a "custodial parent." This does not affect the rights and responsibilities of the parents as spelled out in the Parenting Plan. The primary residential parent is the parent with whom the children spend the majority (51%) of their time.

2. Residential Schedule: The Parenting Plan sets forth where the children shall reside during the school year, holidays, vacation periods, and special occasions.

3. Factors: The court considers each parent's historical involvement in meeting the children's day-to-day needs, the strength of the relationship, the physical and emotional stability each parent can provide, and any harmful behaviors on the part of each parent.

4. Decision Making: Sole or joint decision-making authority is assigned regarding non-emergency health care, education, and religious upbringing. Conflict, domestic violence, and geographical separation may be bases for the court's assignation of sole decision making

5. Dispute Resolution: To reduce judicial intervention, a Parenting Plan must specify a dispute resolution process such as counseling, mediation, or arbitration. This requirement may be waived where there is a history of domestic violence.

6. Child's Input: A child's preference regarding residential placement is a factor that may be considered, but does not necessarily control. In many states, there is an "age of discretion" at which a child can choose to live with one parent or the other.

7. Restrictions on Contact with Children: A parent's residential time with a child will be limited if (a) the parent has willfully abandoned the child for an extended period of time; (b) the parent has refused to perform parental functions; (c) there has been physical, sexual, or emotional abuse of the child; or (d) there is a history of abuse or domestic violence.

8. Restrictions on Decision Making: A parent's decision-making involvement may be limited if he/she has (a) willfully abandoned the children for a period of time; (b) has refused to perform parental functions; (c) has abused a child emotionally, physically, or sexually; or (d) has a history of domestic violence.

9. Non-Parent Visitation: As a general rule, non-parents may not petition for visitation. Some states do recognize limited "grandparent rights." There is still a right to petition for Third Party Custody, but only if a parent is found to be unfit.

10. Modification of Parenting Plan: A petition to modify a parenting plan must show "adequate cause" because a substantial change has occurred in either a parent's or a child's situation. Examples include (a) there has been a substantial deviation from the original parenting plan with the consent of the other parent; (b) the current situation is detrimental to the child; (c) the other parent has been held in contempt at least twice within three years; or (d) the parents agree.

11. Relocation: Some states have notice requirements for a primary residential parent who seeks to relocate outside of the child's school district. The nonmoving party may object and seek court intervention. Courts use numerous factors to determine whether to allow the move, including the (a) relative strength of relationships between the child and family members; (b) relative harm of disrupting the relationship with the nonprimary parent; (c) reasons for relocation and good faith; (d) age, stage, and needs of child and overall impact of move on child's development; and (e) quality of life and benefits to child in new location.

12. Custodial Interference: Interference with a parenting plan or legal custody of a child is a crime in most states.

13. Failure to Comply: Failure by one parent to comply with a parenting plan does not excuse the other parent from his/her duties under the plan or any other court order. The parent's remedy is to seek enforcement from the court, to have the other parent found in contempt, or to petition for a modification. A parent cannot withhold child support in retaliation for the other parent's failure to follow the court-ordered parenting plan (or vice versa).

C. Child Support – SODA THIEF

Child support is based on a state schedule, taking into consideration the parents' income after allowable deductions. Income from new spouses is not included in the calculations. The Child Support Order provides for the following:

1. Standard Calculation: The basic support figure from the State Support Schedule, divided between the parents based on their portion of the total household net income.

2. Other Expenses: Day care costs, athletics, team sports, lessons, and camp fees are among other future expenses that may be shared by the parents *pro rata* as they arise.

3. Deviations: Deviations up or down from the standard State Support Schedule are possible. Reasons may be the support payments required for other children or for extraordinary time spent with the paying parent. Extreme financial hardship may also be a basis for downward deviation. An upward deviation may be granted where total household income exceeds a certain amount per month.

4. Adjustments and Modifications: Because income fluctuates, parents can review child support every two years by statute, or more frequently if they agree to do so. Support obligations cannot be changed retroactively. Tax returns and current pay stubs are the basis for recalculating support either by Motion (adjustment) or by Petition (modification).

5. Transportation: Costs related to long-distance travel to accomplish visitation are included in the Child Support Order, and are shared proportionate to the parents' incomes.

6. Health Care: Extraordinary health care costs in excess of some limit of the standard calculation in a given month are also allocated *pro rata*.

7. Life Insurance: The court may order a parent to obtain life insurance to ensure his/her prospective child support obligations in the event of his/her death.

8. Post-secondary Educational Support: There is no absolute obligation for a parent to support a child beyond the age of 18 or graduation from high school. The court may impose a post-secondary educational support responsibility on either or both parents based upon: (a) ability of the parents to contribute; (b) aptitude and ability of the child; (c) whether either or both parents obtained a post-secondary degree; (d) whether the parents intended to contribute toward post-secondary educational costs while they were married. If post-secondary educational support is reserved, it must be requested prior to the termination of support.

9. Federal Tax Exemptions: The income tax dependency exemption(s) may be allocated by the court to either parent, to be divided between parents, or to alternate between parents in any given year.

D. Uniform Parentage Act

Most states have a procedure to establish the legal relationship between a child and his natural parents. Parent-child relationships do not depend upon the marital status of the parents.

1. Presumption of Paternity: A man is presumed to be the natural father of a child if the child was born during the man's marriage to the child's natural mother, or within three hundred days after the marriage is terminated by death, annulment, declaration of invalidity, divorce or dissolution, or decree of separation. Or, he is the presumptive natural father if after the child's birth, he and the mother marry each other *and* he (a) acknowledges paternity in a writing filed with the registrar of vital statistics, or (b) agreed to be and is named on the child's birth certificate, or (c) promises in writing to support the child as his own.

2. Determination of Paternity:

a. Bringing Action: Any party with an interest may bring a paternity action, for the purpose of declaring the existence or nonexistence of a father and child relationship.

b. Child as Party: The child is not a necessary party, but if the court believes the child is not adequately represented, it will appoint a Guardian ad Litem.

c. Time Limit: A man presumed to be a child's father may seek a declaration of the nonpaternity, only if the action is commenced within two years of the child's birth. This time limitation does not apply if (a) the presumed father and the mother never cohabited or had sexual intercourse during the probable time of conception and (b) the presumed father never openly treated the child as his own.

d. Genetic Testing: If paternity is contested, the court (or a support enforcement agency) can require the child and any alleged father to submit to genetic tests to establish the statistical probability of the alleged paternity.

e. Denial of Genetic Testing: If genetic testing is denied, the presumed father will be adjudicated the father of the child. Genetic testing may be denied based upon (a) the time the presumed father waited between notice of possible nonpaternity and starting action; (b) length of time he has assumed the role of father to the child and the nature of that relationship; (c) facts surrounding the discovery of possible nonpaternity; (e) age of child; (f) harm to child if paternity is disproved; (g) chances of establishing paternity of other father; (h) other factors that might harm the child

3. Surrogate Parentage: Not all states have surrogate parentage rules, but the jurisdictions that do tend to cover the following topics.

a. Donors not Parents: A donor of either egg or sperm is not a parent of a child conceived by means of assisted reproduction.

b. Consenting Father is Parent: A husband who provides sperm for or consents to assisted reproduction for his wife is the father of any resulting child. Failure to sign a consent does not defeat paternity if the husband openly treated the child as his own.

c. Death or Dissolution Revokes Consent: If a marriage is dissolved or if a spouse dies before placement of eggs, sperm, or embryo, the former or deceased spouse is not a parent of a resulting child unless specifically stated in a record that parentage would occur for child born following death or divorce.

d. Revocation of Consent: Either parent may revoke consent in a record before placement of eggs, sperm, or embryo.

e. Alternate Agreements: The woman who gives birth to a child resulting from a donated egg is presumed to be the mother, unless a written agreement, signed by the donor, her doctor, the donee, and any other intended parents, states otherwise. Said agreement must be filed under seal with the registrar of vital statistics.

E. Adoption

State laws establish the procedures for the relinquishment of a child, termination of the parent-child relationship, certifying the fitness of prospective adoptive parent(s), and adoption.

1. Consent: The natural parent must consent in writing to the adoption or have his/her parental rights terminated. A consenting parent may not seek to set aside the adoption after a year has passed since the consent was approved by the court.

2. Notice: Any parent from whom consent is required must receive (a) 20 days' notice if served personally in-state; (b) 30 days notice if served personally out-of-state. If personal service cannot be given, then service must be made: (a) 30 days before the adoption proceeding via first class and certified mail and (b) once a week for three consecutive weeks by publication beginning 30 days before the hearing.

3. Legal Result of Adoption: The adoptee becomes the child, legal heir, and lawful issue of the adoptive parent, entitled to all rights and privileges (including rights of inheritance), and subject to all the obligations of a natural child.

F. Guardian ad Litem

Whenever the court finds it is necessary to represent the best interests of a minor child (or other person who lacks capacity), it may appoint a Guardian ad Litem.

Magic Memory Outlines®

I. MARRIAGE

A. Who May Contract ....

B. Validity Requirements – **CALF SAW** ....

   1. **C**onsanguinity ....

   2. Not **A**lready Married...

   3. **L**icense...

   4. **F**iled Certificate ....

   5. **S**olemnization ....

   6. **A**ge of Majority ....

   7. **W**itnesses ....

C. Common Law Marriages ....

D. Registered Domestic Partnerships – **SURE** ....

II. ACTIONS OTHER THAN DISSOLUTION

A. Temporary Relief...

   1. Temporary Parenting Plan ....

      a. Best Interests Test..

      b. Typical Provisions ....

   2. Temporary Child Support Orders ....

   3. Temporary Restraining Orders ....

   4. Protection Orders/Domestic Violence ....

B. Dissolution v. Legal Separation...

   1. Status of Marriage...

   2. Reconciliation ....

   3. Waiting Period ....

   4. Conversion to Dissolution ....

C. Declarations Regarding Validity ....

   1. Jurisdiction..

   2. Grounds for Declaration of Invalidity – **DAFT LUV** ....

        a. **D**uress ....

        b. **A**lready Married ....

        c. **F**raud...

        d. **T**oo Closely Related (Consanguinity) ....

        d. **L**acked Capacity ....

        e. **U**nderage...

        f. **V**oid Out of State Marriage ....

     3. Timeliness...

     4. Effect on Children ....

  D. Personal Jurisdiction Required ....

III. DISSOLUTION

  A. Jurisdiction ....

  B. Venue...

  C. Grounds for Dissolution ....

  D. Mediation and Settlement ....

  E. 90-Day Waiting Period...

  F. Denial Required or Granted..

IV. PROPERTY DIVISION AND MAINTENANCE

  A. Property Subject to Disposition..

  B. Factors Affecting a "Just and Equitable" Distribution – **DEP**.................................

     1. **D**uration...

     2. **E**conomic Circumstances ....

     3. **P**roperty Amount ....

  C. Community and Separate Property Issues ....

     1. Compensation ....

     2. Goodwill...

     3. Community v. Separate Property ....

     4. "Hidden" Community Property ....

  D. Spousal Maintenance...

     1. Need v. Ability ....

     2. Standard of Living ....

     3. Education..

  E. Non-Marital Dissolution..

V. RESPONSIBILITY FOR CHILDREN

A. Policy Statement ....
   1. Child's Best Interest ....
   2. Factors...
   3. Stability...

B. Permanent Parenting Plans ....
   1. Primary Residential Placement...
   2. Residential Schedule..
   3. Factors...
   4. Decision Making..
   5. Dispute Resolution...
   6. Child's Input...
   7. Restrictions on Contact with Children..
   8. Restrictions on Decision Making...
   9. Non-Parent Visitation...
   10. Modification of Parenting Plan...
   11. Relocation...
   12. Custodial Interference...
   13. Failure to Comply..

C. Child Support – **SODA THIEF** ....
   1. **S**tandard Calculation..
   2. **O**ther Expenses...
   3. **D**eviations...
   4. **A**djustments and Modifications...
   5. **T**ransportation...
   6. **H**eath Care..
   7. **I**nsurance..
   8. Post-secondary **E**ducational Support...
   9. **F**ederal Tax Exemptions...

D. Uniform Parentage Act..
   1. Presumption of Paternity..
   2. Determination of Paternity..
     a. Bringing Action...
     b. Child as Party...
     c. Time Limit..
     d. Genetic Testing..
     e. Denial of Genetic Testing..

      3. Surrogate Parentage ....

         a. Donors not Parents ....

         b. Consenting Father is Parent ....

         c. Death or Dissolution Revokes Consent ....

         d. Revocation of Consent ....

         e. Alternate Agreements ....

E. Adoption ....

      1. Consent ....

      2. Notice ....

      3. Legal Result of Adoption ....

F. Guardian ad Litem ....

Essay Questions

Question Number 1

Father and Mother both agreed the best thing that came out of their ten year marriage was Son, the eight year old wonder of their worlds, and the only child either parent had ever had. The marriage had been amicable for the most part, but in recent years, Father was on the road for business more than he was home, and touring with the band was no life for a family. Mother, a stay at home wife, had been the primary parent for Son for many years now; she had even coached his soccer team last year. When Father came home off the road, he made sure to make up for lost time with increasingly extravagant gifts and trips with Son, but failed to reaffirm his relationship with Mother.

As the marriage grew distant over time, Mother began to resent Father's willingness to "buy" their Son's love with gifts. She felt this only undermined her ability to remain the authoritative figure when left alone to parent. Once Son received a dirt bike from Father, he seemed to always be heading off somewhere unknown, much to Mother's dismay. Angry at not being consulted, Mother told Father that she made the decisions for Son and that Father was not allowed to just buy him gifts without asking her first.

The final straw came as Father proposed Son was old enough at 14 to go on tour with him, and that he should be allowed to miss a year of school to see the country as a roadie for the band. Mother filed for divorce requesting full custody and all the parental responsibilities because Father was never in town. Father said this was absurd, that he was only on the road so much because he was the breadwinner for his family, and they had ever increasing expenses. Father requested shared custody and shared child support. The divorce was granted and primary custody was given to Mother.

Three years later, Mother learned Father had been doing very well for some time now, earning ten times what she could at a normal job, and so she filed a request for the court to review his earnings for the last two years and require him to pay a greater percentage of Son's overdue tuition expenses. Father felt that as he had done increasingly better, he had shared that prosperity with his Son by buying him better gifts, and so he shouldn't be required to give Mother anything more toward the expenses that she asked to take on.

1. How will the court decide the original dissolution requests for parental rights of Son? Explain.

2. What responsibilities come with custody? Explain.

3. What can Mother do about Father's contribution to Son's expenses? Explain.

Question Number 2

When Child was born, Father and Mother had been living together for several years. Father even signed the birth certificate, and never disavowed the relationship with Child. When Mother suddenly announced she was marrying Stepdad, it took nearly everyone by surprise. The story finally came out that Mother had lived two lives in essence. While she had a home and family life with Father, Stepdad lived in a neighboring town, and residents there knew Mother and Stepdad as a couple and had seen her out on his property off and on for many years, and in recent years, with Child in tow. It was assumed by many that they were married and she traveled extensively, but in fact she had never been wed.

Child has been aware of both situations all her life, and does not want to live with Mother and Stepfather. Mother tells her she has no choice, and that Father isn't really her dad anyway. Shocked and needing answers, Child requests Mother, Father and Stepdad undergo paternity testing to learn the truth. Child and both men give samples and are not found to have a genetic relationship. Mother refuses Child's request to be tested, angry with the whole concept and unwilling to comply, asserting it is an invasive process she need not subject herself to.

Mother and Stepdad marry in an attempt to stabilize the family unit. Stepdad wants to adopt Child, but Child has spent many years thinking she would someday inherit Father's vacation cabin at the lake where her fondest childhood memories were formed, and does not want the adoption to occur unless she still inherits from Father as planned. Father has concerns with the adoption regard his ability to maintain his relationship with Child and he refuses to agree to the adoption unless he preserves his visitation rights. Advise the parties how the court will likely rule and why in the matters below:

1. How should the court proceed regarding the determination of paternity? Explain.

2. If adoption occurs, can Child still inherit from Father? Explain.

3. What visitation rights does Father have the ability to preserve? Explain.

Question Number 3

While the divorce was mutually agreed to, the division of marital assets certainly was not. Husband felt that despite his failure to get a pre-nuptial agreement, there was clear and convincing proof of his disproportional contributions to the marital assets. As the son of a physician, he arrived in the relationship with many nice possessions, he owned a condo in the city outright, and the sports car he bought after they were married was paid for largely by quarterly dividend checks he had been receiving as part of an inheritance.

Wife, conversely, had no worldly goods when they met, but invested all her efforts in helping Husband realize his dreams. She now resents that every dime that they earned during the course of the marriage was spent maintaining his lavish toys and keeping him up to date with the latest gadgetry. She finally convinced Husband to attend law school in hopes he could someday support his own lavish lifestyle choices. Wife supported them as a waitress while he finished school, and three weeks after graduation, he asked for a divorce so he could "actually" pursue the lifestyle he dreamed of. At this point, Wife was so estranged from who Husband had become, she agreed to the divorce, providing he supported her while she attended college. She felt this only fair, since she gave him nine years of her life.

Husband asserts he is just now arriving at the place where he will be earning any substantial money, and since they agree to not be together in the future, then Wife has agreed to not partake in his success. Wife asserts that she has lost opportunities to advance herself personally while she provided for his basic needs all through graduate school, and she is now 30 and an unskilled laborer, and Husband should help by offsetting those lost profits indefinitely, or assist in her education expenses and basic needs until she can achieve her own degree and become self- supporting.

1. How should the court distribute property? Explain.

   a. How are the assets held by the parties prior to dissolution? Explain.

   b. What should the court consider in making a determination? Explain.

2. Is spousal maintenance appropriate? Explain.

   a. What factors should be considered by the court in this instance? Explain.

Question Number 4

Father and Mother had one Son when their divorce was finalized two years ago. At that time, the court approved a permanent parenting plan, which determined primary residential placement should be with Mother. The approved plan provided a residential schedule allowing for Father to spend every other weekend with Son, and granted joint decision-making authority to both parents. Because both parents were in similar economic situations, the Court denied Mother's requests for spousal support. Additionally, the Court gave the family cabin to Father, despite it being a wedding gift given to the couple by Mother's parents.

After six months of lean living, Mother wants to return to court and request additional money from Father to pay for a proper upbringing for their Son. Mother will bring proof that Son is now subjected to living with 60% less income available to his care provider, and asserts Son has a right to be raised in an environment equal to the past arrangement, because the divorce was not a fault of his own. Mother tells Father if she is not successful in Court, she will no longer allow Father to see Son on the weekends as is provided for in the parenting plan. Mother seeks your counsel for the following issues:

1. Can the Court take her private property in the cabin, and if so, under what theory? Explain.

2. Does Son have a right to be raised in the manner he has come to expect? Explain.

3. Can Mother withhold visitation until she receives sufficient child support? Explain.

4. What is the proper course of action for Mother at this time? Explain.

Question Number 5

When Bobby Sue and Johnny Ray left the big city to become country music sensations overnight, they thought it might be best to get "hitched" before arriving in Nashville, to prevent anyone trying to break up their act. Late that night on the lonely highway, they pulled in to an all night "hitching post" attached to a combination restaurant/bar/casino and truck stop. The man behind the counter said the regular minister wasn't there that night and that half the town was down at Mirabelle's wedding across the tracks. Further he stated that he and his brother Cletis was standing in for him, as he had always wanted to be a preacher.

Cletis excused himself and returned in his proper marrying regalia with a bible in hand, and asked them to prove they were both of legal age to marry and confirmed they were. Cletis asked his Sister, the town Notary, to play the organ, another stand-in role, and so the wedding march sounded decidedly more like "chopsticks" but all in all the foursome thought it was a lovely service. Cletis and his Sister signed and notarized their statement witnessing the marriage and sent the newlyweds on their way. Years later, when Johnny Ray asked Bobby Sue if they were legally married even if the Preacher wasn't ordained, and she told him at the time Cletis was the court commissioner, so it was all perfectly legal.

1. What are the personal requirements to be eligible to enter a contract of marriage? Explain.

2. What are the proper procedural steps to becoming married that one must follow? Explain.

3. Is this marriage valid, and if invalid, on what grounds? Explain.

4. If invalid, is there a possibility for common law marriage to exist? Explain.

Essay Answers

Answer Number 1

Summary

Courts set parenting plans based upon the best interests of the child. Parenting plans allocate residential schedules, child support, and decision-making powers. Here, F should not be shut out of decision making, and should be allowed a reasonable custodial schedule, as comports with S's best interests. Support schedules may be modified, but here, M's attempt to do so is premature and cannot be effectuated retroactively.

Issues Raised

(1) Best Interests of the Child
(2) Parenting Plans
    (a) Decision Making
    (b) Residential Schedule
(3) Child Support Schedule
    (a) Basic calculation used to determine a non-custodial parent's amount of contribution
    (b) Award amount can deviate upward or downward
(4) Modification of Support Obligations
    (a) Every two years by statute
    (b) More frequently by agreement of the parties
    (c) No retroactive modification

Sample Answer

(1) Best Interests of the Child. Parents have a duty to their minor children, to provide care and support for them and promote their development. The determinations made by the court should be guided by the best interests of the child standard. A child's relationship with each of its parents should be fostered to the extent possible unless inconsistent with the child's best interests.

(2) Parenting Plans. A parenting plan allocates the various parenting responsibilities, and determines who will have residential custody of the child and have the decision-making authority for the child. When the court granted full custody to Mother, Father no longer was able to make these decisions for Son.

(a) Decision Making. Here, Mother received sole decision-making power over issues like school placement and religious affiliation. Since Father did not create a situation of conflict with Mother, there was no domestic violence in the fact pattern, and Father returns to the hometown regularly, sole decision-making authority should not be granted to Mother, as this violates Father's parental rights.

(b) Residential Schedule. The parenting plan sets out where the child will reside during the school year and during holidays. Here, Father requested his rights be preserved to live with Son for certain portions of the year, and unless this was inconsistent with Son's interests, such as continuity of routine and stability of his daily structure or school schedule, it should have been allowed. Son has an ongoing relationship with a loving parent who has not abused or neglected Son.

(3) Child Support Schedule. With every child support order a schedule is attached that shows the basic calculation used to determine a non-custodial parent's amount of contribution. That award amount can deviate upward or downward of the typical obligation based on family circumstances, but here, there is only one child, no great hardship or parent inability to meet the child's needs.

(4) Modification of Support Obligations. Support obligations can be modified every two years by statute, or more frequently by agreement of the parties. Here, Mother is requesting a modification perhaps prematurely as Father has just been doing better within this last two year period, and will presumably be ordered to pay more when the next review is authorized by statute. In either event, she cannot request a retroactive modification of his support obligation, as this is improper.

Answer Number 2

Summary

F may chose to bring an action to establish paternity, as may any party. M must submit to the court's order for a DNA test. F is not married to M, but if he were, paternity would be presumed. Adoption terminates all parental rights; the relinquishing parent must consent in writing or have their parental rights terminated. Here, C will not inherit from F via intestacy, but will need to be provided for by devise. Generally, third parties have no right to visitation. In order for F to petition for third party custody, he would have to prove M is unfit.

Issues Raised

(1) Determination of Paternity
   (a) Presumption of Paternity
   (b) Acknowledgement
   (c) DNA Testing
(2) Adoption
(3) Inheritance
   (a) Adoptee becomes legal heir of adoptive parents
   (b) All similar ties with former family as re: inheritance are severed
(4) Non-Parental Visitation

Sample Answer

(1)   Determination of Paternity.   Any party may bring an action for the purpose of declaring the existence or non-existence of a father and child relationship.   In this case, that may be something Father would like to establish, to preserve his rights.

(a) Presumption of Paternity.   A man is presumed to be the natural parent of a child if he is married to the Mother.   The marriage can even occur after the birth, if the man also appears on the birth certificate.   Here, the man is not married to the Mother so the presumption does not apply.

(b) Acknowledgement.   Occurs if the man marries the Mother after the birth, and also acknowledges paternity in a writing filed with the registrar of vital statistics, or agrees to be named on the birth certificate, or holds the child out as his own and promises to support it. Here, the failure to wed made any of these acknowledgements irrelevant.

(c) DNA Testing.   If paternity is contested, the court or support enforcement can order DNA testing of the Mother, Child and any potential Fathers.   Here, Mother must submit.

(2)   Adoption.   This is a termination of all parental rights, and so the relinquishing parent must consent in writing to the adoption or have their parental rights terminated for cause.   They then have up to a year to have the adoption set aside.   Here, Father has not been determined a non-parent by the court and has not relinquished his parental rights.

(3)   Inheritance.   An adoptee becomes the legal heir of their adoptive parents, and all similar ties are severed with their past family regarding right of inheritance.   Any provision for Child to inherit from Father will need to be provided for by devise, as she is no longer eligible to take if he dies intestate, as they are not related by consanguinity.

(4)   Non-Parental Visitation.   Similarly, visitation rights are generally restricted to parents only.   Some states have limited grandparent's rights, but generally, third parties have no right to petition for visitation with a child, so if the parties here cannot work it out amongst themselves, Father will not have a right to request visitation with Child.   In order to petition for third party custody, he would have to prove Mother unfit.

Answer Number 3

Summary

All property is subject to a "just and equitable" distribution by the court upon dissolution. In many states dividends from separate property become community property if commingled. Property acquired during marriage is jointly held and divisible. Property owned prior to the marriage, or acquired by gift, bequest or devise during the marriage is "separate," but is subject to just and equitable distribution. Professional reputation is an asset subject to consideration for a just and equitable division. W is invested in H's professional education, and there is a grave disparity in the spouses' relative prosperity. Thus, spousal maintenance may be assigned.

Issues Raised

(1) Dissolution of Marriage
    (a) Assets Prior to Divorce
    (b) Characterization of Property
    (c) Goodwill
    (d) Just and Equitable Distribution
(2) Spousal Maintenance
    (a) Need v. Ability
    (b) Education

Sample Answer

(1) Dissolution of Marriage. The dissolution of a marriage subjects all of the property of both spouses whether separately or jointly held to distribution by the court in an effort to affect a "just and equitable" distribution. Prior to distribution, the court determines the property's character.

(a) Assets Prior to Divorce. Here, Husband arrives with valuable possessions and a condo that seems to be his separate property. The dividends he receives during the marriage would be his separate property, but will not remain so unless he keeps them from being commingled. If used to make payments on a car bought during the marriage commingles the asset, then both the spouses have some interest in the car's value.

(b) Characterization of Property. Generally, all property onerously acquired during the marriage is jointly held and thus subject to division. That which was owned prior to the marriage, or is acquired by gift, bequest or devise during the marriage is generally characterized as being separately held, but of course is subject to a "just and equitable" distribution scheme and is thus not exempt from possible division.

(c) Goodwill. One's professional reputation is also an asset subject to consideration for a just and equitable division. Here, Husband becomes a lawyer while Wife forgoes all opportunity to provide for his basic needs for years, and so despite his ability to practice law just becoming viable, she has a multi-year investment in his professional education that should be recognized in the arrangements reached between the parties. Expert testimony would establish the figure.

(d) Just and Equitable Distribution. The court looks to the duration of the marriage, the economic circumstances of the parties and the property amounts in question to determine a "just and equitable" determination. This marriage is for a medium length of time, but has a grave disparity in the relative prosperity of one spouse over the other that was obtained at the second spouse's expense. This is the economic circumstances factor, and both earning capacity and resources available are vastly different for these two people.

(2) Spousal Maintenance. When the property amount disparity is considered relative to the earning capacity disparity, it would seem an unjust enrichment to allow him to escape some type of maintenance payments. Courts determine, based on the following factors:

(a) Need v. Ability. All of the resources of both parties are considered.

(b) Education. Court considers the education level and time to achieve degree.

Answer Number 4

Summary

All property, joint and separate, is divided by the court in a "just and equitable" fashion upon dissolution. M's parents gifted the cabin to both spouses, making it joint property, but a different just and equitable distribution as determined by the court is proper. Modifications of the parenting plan may be sought if substantial changes have occurred, or when circumstances become detrimental to the child's welfare, but not merely because M expected more support. Interference with the permanent parenting plan is a crime, and M's withholding of visitation is extortion. M must utilize the dispute resolution process for changes to the plan.

Issues Raised

(1) Disposition, Joint v. Separate Property
    (a) Character of all property both determined by the court
    (b) All property, joint and separate, divided in a just and equitable fashion
(2) Just and Equitable Distribution
    (a) Duration of the marriage
    (b) Economic circumstances of each spouse at separation
    (c) Amount of living expenses
    (d) All available resources for both spouses
(3) Modification
    (a) Every two years by statute
    (b) More frequently by agreement of the parties
    (c) No retroactive modification
(4) Custodial Interference/Failure to Comply
(5) Dispute Resolution

(1)   Disposition, Joint v. Separate Property. First, the character of all property involved, both separate and jointly held, is determined by the court. Then all property, both joint and separate, is to be divided in a just and equitable fashion, irrespective of ownership character.

(2)   Just and Equitable Distribution. In making this determination the court considers factors such as the duration of the marriage, what the economic circumstances of each spouse are at the time of separation, the amount of living expenses, and all available resources for both spouses. Here, Mother's parents gave the cabin to both spouses as a wedding gift, and thus in theory, both had some equity in the cabin during marriage. Still in a dissolution, the Court can award property in any manner to achieve a just and equitable distribution, and so this was proper.

(3)   Modification. If a substantial change has happened in the child's or either parent's situation, the Court can be petitioned for a modification of the parenting plan. This can occur when circumstances become detrimental to the child's welfare. Here, Mother expected a greater level of support than the Court awarded. That is not a change in circumstance. The Court approved the existing arrangements with the best interest of the child in mind and reversal of that decision seems unlikely.

(4)   Custodial Interference / Failure to Comply. Interference with the permanent parenting plan is a criminal act. Mother may not exercise self-help to obtain greater support payments and this amounts to extortion. Even if Father had not been making the payments required by the Court, Mother is not able to withhold visitation to compel child support payments, as the duties are not reciprocal. Here, a threat to withhold visitation may result in Mother being held in contempt of the Court, and if that occurs twice within three years, Father may have grounds to have the parenting plan modified in his favor.

(5)   Dispute Resolution. All parenting plans include an initial form of redress through an alternative dispute resolution option. This works to keep costs down, keep the courts from being overwhelmed, and provides quick and simple access to justice for the aggrieved. Here, Mother should have originally worked to get a proper plan that was just and equitable in the first place, but barring that, she must utilize the dispute resolution process for any questions she may now have regarding the plan's appropriateness for her Son.

Answer Number 5

Summary

To marry, neither party may be married already, the parties cannot be related more closely than second cousins, and both must be at least 18 years old or have the permission of their parents or the court. Parties must get a license from the county auditor at least three days prior, and use it within 60 days. The marriage must be solemnized, there must be two witnesses, and a marriage certificate must be filed. Here, there was no license, no signatures of the witnesses, and no filing. A lack of license does not invalidate a marriage, but there may have been improper solemnization and witnessing. If common law marriage was valid in the state where they joined, then the current state they reside in may choose to honor it.

Issues Raised

(1) Who May Contract
   (a) Neither party has another living spouse
   (b) Parties cannot be related more closely than second cousins
   (c) Parties must be 18 or have permission of their parents, a judge or court commissioner
(2) Procedural Steps Requirements
   (a) License from the county auditor
      (i)   License issued at least three days prior to marriage
      (ii) License used no later than 60 days after issuance
      (iii) Lack of a license does not necessarily render the marriage invalid
   (b) Marriage solemnized by an authorized person
      (i) Superior court judge or commissioner
      (ii) Ordained clergy member
   (c) Two witnesses who sign the marriage certificate
   (d) Marriage certificate must be filed with county auditor state registrar of vital statistics
(3) Validity Requirements
(4) Common Law Marriages

Sample Answer

(1)   Who May Contract. The personal requirements for eligibility to marry are that neither party to the current marriage have another spouse living at the time, that the parties cannot be related more closely than second cousins and both must be at least 18 years of age or have the permission of their parents. A judge, court commissioner, or ordained clergy must solemnize the marriage ceremony. Marriage occurs between one man and one woman who are otherwise capable to marry. Many states have Domestic Partnership statutes that require registration.

(2)   Procedural Steps. In order to properly be married, the parties must obtain a license from the county auditor at least three days prior to the marriage and the ceremony must be held not later than 60 days after issuance. A marriage license is a regulatory requirement and thus the lack of a license does not necessarily render the marriage invalid. The marriage must also be solemnized by an authorized person, either a superior court judge or commissioner, or an ordained clergy member. There must be two witnesses who sign the marriage certificate which must be then filed with the county auditor and state registrar of vital statistics.

(3)   Validity Requirements. Validity is questionable in this circumstance. While the parties are of suitable age, marital status, and consanguinity, questions remain as to whether proper procedure was followed. No license was obtained, thus no 3 day waiting period observed, and no signatures of the witnesses were placed on the non-existent license, which also has never been filed with state and county officials. Since that alone does not per se invalidate the marriage, we also look to the potential failure of the solemnization, which rests on whether Cletis is clergy or a commissioner, and even then he must be Superior Court or higher to qualify. Additionally, questions exist as to whether the two witnesses requirement is met by one witness and the clergy member, and so whether the formalities have been adhered to is a matter to be determined.

(4)   Common Law Marriages. Common law marriage is not recognized in many states, but if a common law marriage was valid in the state where the union was formed, then the current state they reside in may choose to honor it. Depending on where they end up actually residing, there is a possibility if they bring their notarized witness statement and explain their situation that their marriage may be recognized. While there are many problems with their procedural adherence, they seem otherwise capable to marry one another and so the easiest solution may ultimately be to "remarry" in the state where they now live.

Actions Prior to Dissolution .... T 3-172
Adoption .... T 3-180
Annulment .... T 3-173
Best Interests of the Child .. T 3-172, 176
Child Support .... T 3-178
Children .... T 3-172, 177
Committed Intimate
   Relationship .... T 3-176
Common Law Marriages .... T 3-172
Custodial Interference .... T 3-178
Decision Making .... T 3-177
Declarations Regarding
   Validity .... T 3-173
Determination of Paternity .... T 3-179
Dispute Resolution .... T 3-177
Dissolution .... T 3-173, 174
Domestic Violence .... T 3-172
Educational Support .... T 3-179
Federal Tax Exemptions .... T 3-179
Genetic Testing .... T 3-179
Goodwill .... T 3-175
Grounds for Invalidity .... T 3-173
Grounds for Dissolution .... T 3-174
Guardian Ad Litem .... T 3-180
"Hidden" Joint Property .... T 3-176
Invalidity .... T 3-173
Joint Property .... T 3-175
Jurisdiction .... T 3-173, 174
"Just and Equitable" Distribution
   of Property .... T 3-175
Legal Separation .... T 3-173
Life Insurance .... T 3-179
Maintenance .... T 3-176
Marriage .... T 3-171
Meretricious Relationship .... T 3-176
Modification of Parenting
   Plan .... T 3-178
Non-Marital Dissolution .... T 3-176
Non-Parent Visitation .... T 3-177
Parenting Plans .... T 3-172, 177
Paternity .... T 3-179
Permanent Parenting Plans .... T 3-177
Personal Jurisdiction .... T 3-174
Post-Secondary Educational
   Support .... T 3-179

Presumption of Paternity .... T 3-179
Primary Residential
   Placement .... T 3-177
Property Division .... T 3-175
Protection Orders .... T 3-172
Reconciliation .... T 3-173
Registered Domestic
   Partnerships .... T 3-172
Relocation of Child .... T 3-178
Residential Schedule .... T 3-177
Responsibility for Children .... T 3-176
Separate Property .... T 3-175
Separation .... T 3-173
Spousal Maintenance .... T 3-176
Surrogate Parentage .... T 3-180
Tax Exemptions .... T 3-179
Temporary Child Support
   Orders .... T 3-172
Temporary Parenting Plan .... T 3-172
Temporary Restraining Orders ... T 3-172
Uniform Parentage Act .... T 3-179
Validity Requirements .... T 3-171

CHAPTER 4

FEDERAL CIVIL

PROCEDURE

RIGOS BAR REVIEW SERIES

UNIFORM MULTISTATE ESSAY EXAM (MEE) REVIEW

CHAPTER 4

FEDERAL CIVIL PROCEDURE

Table of Contents

A.	Sub-Topic Exam Issue Distribution	Text 4-203
B.	Opening Argument and Primary Issues	Text 4-207
C.	Text	Text 4-209
	I. Commencement of Action	Text 4-209
	II. Jurisdiction and Service	Text 4-209
	III. Pleadings and Motions	Text 4-215
	IV. Parties	Text 4-220
	V. Discovery	Text 4-222
	VI. Pre-Trial Proceedings	Text 4-227
	VII. Trials	Text 4-230
	VIII. Judgment as a Matter of Law	Text 4-233
	IX. Verdicts and Judgments (other than JML)	Text 4-234
	X. Post-Trial Motions	Text 4-234
	XI. Appeals	Text 4-235
	XII. Preclusion	Text 4-237
D.	Magic Memory Outlines®	Magic Memory Outlines 4-239
E.	Federal Civil Procedure Essay Questions	Questions 4-249
F.	Federal Civil Procedure Essay Answers	Answers 4-253
G.	Federal Civil Procedure Index	Index 4-263
H.	Acronyms	Acronyms 15-626

RIGOS BAR REVIEW SERIES
MEE SUB-TOPIC FREQUENCY DISTRIBUTION

FEDERAL CIVIL PROCEDURE

	2/09	7/08	2/08	7/07	2/07	7/06	2/06	7/05	2/05	7/04	2/04	7/03	2/03	7/02	2/02	7/01	2/01
Rules of Civil Procedure	✓	✓	✓		✓	✓	✓	✓	✓	✓	✓	✓	✓	✓	✓		✓
Commencement of Action						✓											
Timeliness of Service						✓											
Personal Jurisdiction	✓						✓		✓	✓	✓			✓			
Person Out-of-State	✓						✓							✓			
Foreign Corp.	✓													✓			
Long-Arm Statute	✓						✓										
Internet Transactions	✓						✓										
Minimum Contacts		✓					✓										
Domicile		✓					✓										
Waiver														✓			
Consent														✓			
Subject Matter Jurisdiction		✓					✓✓		✓	✓✓	✓✓				✓✓		
Timing of Challenge										✓							
Federal Question							✓										
Affirmative Defense							✓										

	2/09	7/08	2/08	7/07	2/07	7/06	2/06	7/05	2/05	7/04	2/04	7/03	2/03	7/02	2/02	7/01	2/01
Counterclaim		✓															
Diversity Jurisdiction		✓					✓		✓	✓	✓				✓		
Domicile							✓		✓	✓					✓		
Corporation															✓		
Representative of Estate									✓								
Determined at Time of Filing									✓						✓		
Amount in Controversy		✓							✓	✓	✓				✓		
Aggregation of Claims									✓	✓							
Supplemental Jurisdiction									✓		✓				✓		
Third-Party Claims									✓	✓					✓	✓	
Venue									✓	✓				✓			
Change of Venue							✓							✓			
Motion or Objection Waiver		✓															
Amendment of Pleadings						✓											✓
Statute of Limitations						✓											
Relation Back		✓				✓											
Joinder of Parties		✓									✓				✓		
Impleader		✓															

	2/01	7/01	2/02	7/02	2/03	7/03	2/04	7/04	2/05	7/05	2/06	7/06	2/07	7/07	2/08	7/08	2/09
Class Action Requirements						/											
Prerequisites						/											
Common Questions						/											
Usual Claim						/											
Large Membership						/											
Protection of Class Members						/											
Discovery (general)	/			/									//				
Initial Disclosures	/												/				
Depositions				/													
Subpoena	/			/													
Duty to Cooperate	/																
Sanctions	/																
Injunctive Relief										/							
Temporary Restraining Order										/							
Preliminary Injunction										/							
Summary Judgment					/										/		
Issue of Material Fact					/										/		
Judgment as a Matter of Law															//		
Pre-Trial Conference	//																
Sanctions for Non-Compliance	/																
Modifying Final Pre-Trial Order	/																

	2/09	7/08	2/08	7/07	2/07	7/06	2/06	7/05	2/05	7/04	2/04	7/03	2/03	7/02	2/02	7/01
Juries, Voir Dire, and Misconduct		//														
Partial Judgment					/										/	
Appeal timing					/										/	
Appeal of Collateral Order					/											
Writ of Mandamus					/										/	
Res Judicata												/				
Final Judgment on Merits												/				
Scope of Prior Judgment												/				
Mutuality												/				
Close Relationship												/				/
Collateral Estoppel												/				/
Requirements																/
Final Judgment																/
Issue Actually Litigated												/				/
Same Issue																/
Mutuality												/				/
Effect of Settlement																

OPENING ARGUMENT AND PRIMARY ISSUES

FEDERAL CIVIL PROCEDURE

There are a few thoughts that should usually be stated at the beginning of every answer. These will score you easy points and let the grader know you are in the right topic area.

Most essays should have an "opening argument": a brief, broad statement that shows you understand the broad significance of a legal topic. The opening argument also suggests to the grader that she is about to read a thoughtful and well-organized essay.

Many subjects also have "primary issues" that can be discussed up front or integrated into the essay answer. IMPORTANT: Do not merely regurgitate these statements on the exam without addressing the issues actually raised by the facts, or you will not pass.

- **Civil Procedure Opening Argument:** Proper procedure promotes efficiency and courts generally require strict compliance.

- **Sample Primary Issue Statements:**

  - The Statute of Limitations (SOL) for this claim is [x] years from the time discovery/breach/tort occurred.

  - Actions commence when P files the Complaint. P then generally has 120 days to serve D.

  - A court must have personal jurisdiction through 1) notice (e.g., service of process by a person 18 or older who is not a party to the litigation) and 2) minimum contacts (physical presence, residency, long-arm jurisdiction).

  - Under the notice pleading system, P needs only to assert general allegations. Pleadings must include jurisdiction, factual events, a claim upon which relief can be granted, and relief desired.

  - D has 30 days to answer. Failure to object in the answer or by pre-trial motion to lack of jurisdiction, improper venue, or insufficient service waives D's right to object.

  - Removal of a case from a state court is appropriate if the federal court in that state would have original jurisdiction, and the defendant is not a citizen of that state.

  - If the pleadings show that there is no genuine issue as to any material fact remaining for trial, either party can move for a summary judgment

  - Discovery may not be unduly burdensome. The 5 forms of discovery are: 1) depositions; 2) interrogatories; 3) production of documents; 4) physical/mental exams; 5) requests for admission. Admissions of fact not objected to within 30 days are deemed admitted.

- Post trial motions include: 1) motion for a new trial – made within 10 days of entry of judgment, 2) motion for JML – made after either party rests or within 10 days of entry of judgment, or 3) motion to vacate judgment (if more than 10 have days elapsed).

- Issues for appeal must have been preserved below by making a timely objection.

- Before granting a preliminary injunction, a court considers whether harm to P outweighs the harm the injunction would cause D; P's likelihood of success on the merits; and the consequence, if any, on the public interest.

CHAPTER 4

FEDERAL CIVIL PROCEDURE

The controlling law is the Federal Rules of Civil Procedure (FRCP). Local district court rules may supplement the nationwide procedural rules, but must be consistent with them.

> **MEE Tip:** There is usually one civil procedure question on every MEE exam, which may also include conflict of laws issues. While we have listed the relevant FRCP number for reference, the numbers are not necessary in your answers.

I. COMMENCEMENT OF ACTION

A. Filing

A federal civil action is commenced by filing a complaint in a U.S. district (trial) court.

B. Pre-Filing Notice Requirements

In unusual situations, P may be required to give notice to D before formally commencing a lawsuit by filing.

1. Federal Tort Claims: Tort claims against the federal government must be submitted administratively before any lawsuit is commenced. If the federal government rejects the tort claim notice, or fails to make a final decision within six months, P may file suit.

2. Waiver: P's failure to comply with a pre-filing notice requirement is an affirmative defense, but D may waive the defense by not moving to dismiss within a reasonable time. If D pleads the defense, but then engages in discovery, pretrial motions, or other conduct inconsistent with an intent to seek a dismissal, the court may deny a later motion to dismiss.

C. Relationship to Service

After filing the complaint, the P must have a copy of the complaint and a summons served upon D. P generally has 120 days after filing to effect service, but the court has discretion to extend this deadline. However, if P fails to serve D before the deadline, the complaint will be treated as if it were never filed for statute of limitations purposes.

II. JURISDICTION AND SERVICE

> **MEE Tip:** Every Civil Procedure question raises jurisdiction issues. Be sure to separately address personal jurisdiction issues and subject matter jurisdiction issues.

A federal court may not assert personal jurisdiction unless the D named: (1) is given adequate notice and opportunity to be heard; and (2) has the minimum contacts with the state where the district court sits. An action commenced without jurisdiction will be dismissed, and any judgment entered in the absence of jurisdiction is void.

A. Service of Process

Notice to D is essential to personal jurisdiction. To satisfy due process requirements, notice must be "reasonably calculated, under all the circumstances," to reach the intended person. [*Mullane*] There are three acceptable methods of satisfying the service requirement: (1) D's waiver of service; (2) personal, hand-to-hand delivery, either to D or to someone authorized by law to accept service for D; and (3) any method allowed under the state law where the district court is located, or where D is served.

> **MEE Tip:** A P must comply with rules regarding service. Some states allow service of process by certified mail; others do not. Also, state law varies on whether service is effective if P substantially complies with procedural requirements, but commits some minor error.

1. Waiver of Service: P may mail D a written notice of suit, copy of the complaint, and request to waive service of process. The court may impose the costs of service and related attorney fees upon a D who receives such a notice but refuses to waive personal service. A D who grants a waiver of service does not waive any defenses, including lack of personal jurisdiction.

2. Personal Service on Individuals: Personal service upon individuals may be accomplished in the following ways:

a. Delivery to the Person: Personal, hand-to-hand service of both summons and complaint upon the D, regardless of where it is accomplished (e.g., at home, at work, on the street) is generally effective.

b. Abode: Leaving a copy of the summons and complaint with a resident of suitable age and discretion at the person's place of abode (home) is also an appropriate means of personal service. It is insufficient to leave the papers at a home in which D does not actually reside, or to leave the papers with a person who does not also reside in the home.

> **MEE Tip:** There is no bright-line rule on whether a person is of "suitable age and discretion." Service upon D's teenage child is probably effective, but describe the rule before dismissing it.

c. Who May Serve Papers: Summons and complaints may be served by anyone over 18 who is not a party to the action. P may not personally serve the papers.

d. Community Property Considerations: In community property states, service of process on either spouse is presumed sufficient to support an action on a community obligation. This presumption may be overcome by proof of the judgment debtor that the judgment is based solely on the separate obligation of one spouse. To be safe, most Ps serve both spouses personally or leave papers at place of their residence with a person of suitable age and discretion then resident therein.

3. Service by Publication: Service by publication is allowed under some circumstances. In general, though, publication is not sufficient if D's name and address are ascertainable. Publication may be proper where the D has concealed himself or left the state to avoid creditors, or has fled from service.

4. Service on the Federal Government: P may serve the federal government by: (1) personal or certified mail service upon the United States Attorney's Office for the district in which the action was filed; and (2) sending a copy of the summons and complaint by registered or certified mail to the U.S. Attorney General. If the complaint challenges an order by a non-party federal agency or officer, the summons and complaint must be sent to that agency or officer as well.

5. Service on Corporations and Other Business Associations: Every business entity (other than a general partnership) is required by law to designate a registered agent and address for service of process. The identity of the agent is a matter of public record.

6. Service in Specific Situations: Required methods of service may vary for specific entities in a variety of special situations. Examples include service on an *in rem* (property) D or a foreign government. These special requirements are unlikely to be tested, but may be significant in practice.

7. Service After Initial Service of Process: The rules relating to service of summons and complaints should not be confused with those governing service of papers (pleadings, motions, and the like) after the action has been commenced. Once the action has been commenced, papers may be served pursuant to less rigorous requirements including simple deliveries or mailings to opposing counsel of record.

B. Minimum Contacts

1. Generally: A federal court may not assert personal jurisdiction over a D unless the D has minimum contacts with the state where the district court is located. Over the years, the acceptable bases for asserting personal jurisdiction over an out-of state D have broadened, and state long-arm statutes normally govern.

2. Domicile: A person domiciled in a state, even if she has temporarily left, is subject to jurisdiction in that state.

3. No Contacts, But In-State Service: Service upon a nonresident who is physically present in the state is sufficient to confer personal jurisdiction. [*Burnham*]

4. Consent or Waiver: Jurisdiction exists if D consents to jurisdiction, or fails to challenge personal jurisdiction by a pre-answer motion or in the answer itself. FRCP 12.

5. Consent by Contract: Consent by contract is normally effective, e.g., "The parties agree that litigation arising out of this contract will be conducted in Alaska in accordance with Alaska law, and the parties consent to personal jurisdiction in Alaska."

C. Long-Arm Statutes

1. Generally: State long-arm statutes provide that a person submits to jurisdiction in that state by engaging in any of a long list of specified conduct. Common provisions allow the assertion of jurisdiction over a person who:

    a. Business: Transacts business within the state.

    b. Tort: Commits a tort within the state.

c. Property: Owns or uses any real property situated within the state.

d. Insurance: Contracts to insure any person or risk within the state.

2. Jurisdiction is Specific to In-state Activity: Jurisdiction under a long-arm statute is specific jurisdiction: jurisdiction to adjudicate a specific dispute arising out of D's activity in that state. Thus, if P seeks to base jurisdiction upon a business transaction, the dispute must arise from a transaction that occurred within the state. For jurisdiction based upon property in the state, P must show that the dispute arises out of the ownership of that property.

3. Transacting Business: Most of the provisions are self-explanatory.

a. Factors Considered: Factors considered under the "transacts business" clause vary, but courts commonly require the following three elements:

(1) The nonresident D or foreign corporation must purposefully act or consummate some transaction in the forum state.

(2) The cause of action must arise from, or be connected with, such act or transaction.

(3) The assumption of jurisdiction in the forum state must not offend traditional notions of fair play and substantial justice. Consideration is given to the quality, nature, and extent of the in-state activity, the relative convenience of the parties, the benefits and protection of state laws, and basic fairness.

b. Physical Presence not Required: The P's claim must arise from the D's actions occurring in the forum state, but D's physical presence in the state is not required. Extensive telephone or mail solicitations in-state may support jurisdiction.

c. Internet Transactions: In general, the test to determine whether D's website is sufficient to support personal jurisdiction is how "active" the website is. A passive website, which merely provides information, but does not allow for buying or selling online will not usually satisfy the requirements of minimum contacts. In comparison, an active website that both solicits business and takes orders may be sufficient to support jurisdiction.

d. Registered Agent Distinguished: An out-of-state corporation's appointment of a registered in-state agent (as required by law for service of process) does not provide minimum contacts.

4. Commission of Tort:

a. Generally: If D commits a tort in the state, jurisdiction usually attaches. A classic example is a nonresident motorist who causes an automobile accident.

b. Products Liability Cases: Product liability questions may involve products manufactured out-of-state that injure in-state residents. If D transacted business "in-state," the court may assert personal jurisdiction under the relevant long-arm statute. However, P must show that D placed the product in the general "stream of commerce," making it reasonably foreseeable that the product would be used in-state if it is not clear that D was transacting business in-state.

5. Ownership or Use of Property: Specific jurisdiction under a Long-Arm statute may be based upon D's ownership or use of property (real or personal) in the state. However, D's ownership of property in State X does not give a federal court sitting in State X jurisdiction over D for any lawsuit against D in State X. The court has jurisdiction only to resolve disputes arising out D's ownership or use of the in-state property. For example, if D's property is emitting noxious fumes, the court would have jurisdiction over D to resolve a dispute about the fumes, but not a dispute unrelated to the property.

6. Insuring Risk: Jurisdiction exists when an out-of-state D insures an in-state risk. The classic example is a suit by an insured State X resident to recover on a policy written by an out-of-state insurer.

7. Full Jurisdiction Obtained: Assuming the requirements of the long-arm statute have been satisfied, and assuming minimum contacts exist, the court obtains full jurisdiction – in rem and personal – and can proceed to determine all issues properly presented.

> **MEE Tip:** Civil procedure questions will involve federal courts, but your minimum contacts analysis must focus on the state where the court sits. Note that jurisdiction under Long-Arm Statutes is always "specific jurisdiction," and not "personal jurisdiction."

D. Challenges to Personal Jurisdiction, Consolidation, and Waiver

Unlike challenges to subject matter jurisdiction, challenges to personal jurisdiction (e.g., improper service of process, no minimum contacts) may be deemed waived under certain circumstances. Challenges to personal jurisdiction are subject to the consolidation and waiver provisions in FRCP 12.

1. Appearance: Appearance is not a waiver of the right to raise a timely objection to personal jurisdiction. However, if an objection is not timely asserted by motion or responsive pleading, the objection is waived under FRCP 12.

2. Method: Personal jurisdiction may be objected to by motion or in the answer to the complaint. If the challenger uses a motion, it must be in the first pleading, and filed before the answer to the complaint.

3. Exception: An exception is made for judgments entered by default, which may be vacated for lack of personal jurisdiction within the longer time allowed by FRCP 60.

4. Timeliness, Consolidation: A challenge to personal jurisdiction (whether based upon lack of notice, improper service, or lack of minimum contacts) must be asserted in a timely manner – by motion before filing an answer, or in the answer itself. An untimely challenge is deemed waived. Consolidation and waiver provisions in FRCP 12 apply.

5. Waiver: A challenge to personal jurisdiction may also be waived:

a. By Waiting Too Long to Move for Dismissal: D must make a timely objection to personal jurisdiction in the answer or by motion, and must also move to dismiss within a reasonable time. If D pleads the defense but then engages in discovery, pretrial motions, etc., a later motion to dismiss may come too late. Note that if a case is dismissed prior to trial, it is treated for purposes of the statute of limitations as if it had never been commenced.

Thus, courts are hesitant to grant a dismissal if D went through lengthy pretrial proceedings until the statute of limitations expired and prevents P from re-filing the case.

b. By Seeking Affirmative Relief: D may waive the defense by seeking affirmative relief from the court, on the theory that D has consented to jurisdiction.

MEE Tip: Personal jurisdiction is a popular bar topic. A challenge to personal jurisdiction must be made in the answer (or by motion before the answer) or else it is waived.

E. *In Rem* Jurisdiction

In very specific circumstances, a court lacking personal jurisdiction may take action in regard to D's real property in the state, pursuant to its *in rem* powers. The court may take such action (e.g., a partition or a quiet title remedy) without additional contacts because the property alone supplies sufficient contacts. Due process, however, still requires that D be given notice and opportunity to be heard. Modern long-arm statutes generally grant personal jurisdiction over D in the place of *in rem* jurisdiction.

F. Subject Matter Jurisdiction

Subject matter jurisdiction is the court's authority to hear and decide a particular case. Parties cannot create subject matter jurisdiction by consent. Subject matter jurisdiction (unlike personal jurisdiction) can be challenged at any time; even by post-trial motion or appeal. Federal district courts have subject matter jurisdiction over only certain defined categories of cases. The common grounds for federal subject matter jurisdiction are:

1. Federal Question: District courts may hear any case arising under a federal constitution, statute, or treaty. [28 U.S.C. § 1331] The mere existence of an affirmative defense under federal law is not sufficient, however, to create federal question jurisdiction.

2. Diversity Jurisdiction: District courts may hear cases between citizens of different states, provided that the amount in controversy is at least $75,000. Diversity must be "complete:" no P may be a citizen of the same state as any of the Ds. Note that an executor is a party to an action only insofar as he or she is a representative of an estate, for purposes of removal and diversity jurisdiction. Executors are thus treated as citizens of the same state as the decedents they represent.

3. Supplemental Jurisdiction: Usually, a federal court has subject matter jurisdiction over claims if they are related to other claims where federal subject matter jurisdiction exists. The test is whether the claims "form part of the same case or controversy under Article III of the United States Constitution." [28 U.S.C. § 1367]

4. Removal Jurisdiction: D may "remove" a state court case to federal court if subject matter jurisdiction exists and P could have originally filed the case there. However, if diversity is the only basis for federal jurisdiction, the case may not be removed if it was filed in a state where at least one D is a citizen.

MEE Tip: The P designates the state forum and may never remove the case to federal court, even if the D asserts a counterclaim against the P.

G. Venue and Change of Venue

Venue refers to the question of which federal district is the proper court to hear the case. Venue is frequently tested on the exam.

1. Basis: There are three general grounds for establishing proper venue.

a. Residence of D: Venue is proper in a district if any D resides in that district, provided that all Ds reside in the state where that district is located.

b. Location of Events or Property: Venue is also proper in a federal district where "a substantial part of the events or omissions giving rise to the claim occurred, or a substantial part of the property that is the subject of the action is situated." [28 U.S.C. § 1391]

c. Personal Jurisdiction: If there is otherwise no district where venue is proper, venue is proper in any district where any D is subject to personal jurisdiction.

2. Actions Against Corporations: A corporate D's "residence" is in the district where it has its principal place of business, any district where it transacts substantial business, and in any district in the state of its incorporation.

3. Improper Venue: If the case was filed in an improper venue, the court may either transfer the case to a district where venue is proper or dismiss the case.

4. *Forum Non Conveniens*: Even if venue is proper, the court may nonetheless transfer the case to another district where venue is proper if there is a compelling reason why the case should be heard there instead. D's burden is heavy when moving for transfer on *forum non conveniens* grounds. A court will not dismiss the case because of *forum non conveniens*.

> **MEE Tip:** Most federal civil procedure questions have multiple jurisdiction and venue issues.

III. PLEADINGS AND MOTIONS

A. Complaint and Answer

1. Complaint Contents – JARR: Despite the liberal rules about "notice pleading," a complaint must always give the D fair notice of all claims, the factual basis for each, and the legal basis for each. Undisclosed claims may not be asserted at trial. The complaint must include:

a. <u>J</u>urisdiction

b. <u>A</u>llegation of Facts Underlying the Claim

c. <u>R</u>ight to Relief: The legal theory must be specified (tort law, breach of contract, etc.). If the claim is based on a statute, the particular statute must be specified.

d. <u>R</u>elief Requested: P must specify the remedy that the lawsuit desires.

2. Joinder of Claims: P may assert multiple claims or theories of recovery in a single complaint, even if the claims do not all arise out of one transaction or occurrence. The court may later order separate trials in the interest of convenience, judicial economy, or to avoid prejudice.

3. Single Complaint: P must assert in a single complaint all claims arising out of one transaction or occurrence. "Claim splitting" is not allowed. For example, P may not file two separate lawsuits based upon one car crash, one for property damage and one for personal injury. The first judgment in the first lawsuit would preclude the second lawsuit.

4. Pre-Answer Motion to Dismiss: D may move to dismiss for lack of jurisdiction, insufficiency of service, failure to join a party, or failure to state a claim upon which relief can be granted (there is no interpretation of the facts under which the P could prevail). No "special appearance" by D is required. D does not waive the deficiency (typically lack of personal jurisdiction) by filing a motion to dismiss.

MEE Tip: A D who files a pre-answer motion to dismiss should allege all available defenses under FRCP 12, as certain omitted defenses cannot be made in a subsequent motion.

---

5. Answer: D must file an answer to the complaint within 30 days (60 days if D resides outside the U.S.). If D waived service, he has 60 days to respond (90 days if residing outside of the U.S.). Denials of allegations may be based on lack of knowledge. Affirmative defenses (e.g., the statute of limitations), must be expressly pleaded. If an answer contains counterclaims, then it may be amended once as a matter of right if the responsive pleading ("reply") has not yet been served. Otherwise, D has 20 days after service to amend the answer.

6. Post-Answer Motion to Dismiss: A summary judgment motion supported by affidavits or for judgment on the pleadings may be filed after or with the answer.

B. Notice Pleading – FRCP 8

The federal courts use the system of "notice pleading," which requires statements consisting merely of general allegations. General damages including pain and suffering, any disability, and loss on a contract, do not need to be specified in detail. Certain claims and defenses, however, must be specially pleaded.

C. Pleading Special Matters – FRCP 8 and 9

Fraud, mistake, and any denial of capacity need to be pleaded specifically and the relevant facts explained. Similarly, time, place, conditions precedent, and application of foreign laws shall be specified. Any special damages such as lost wages, medical expenses, and lost profits should also be specified in the complaint. [FRCP 9] Affirmative defenses (e.g., assumption of risk, contributory negligence, fault of nonparty, fraud, and statute of limitations) must be specifically pleaded. [FRCP 8(c)]

D. Signing of Pleadings, Sanctions – FRCP 11

Pleadings must be signed by the attorney of record, or the pleadings may be stricken. Rule 11 provides for sanctions if the attorney failed to make a reasonable inquiry into the factual basis or legal merits of a claim prior to filing a pleading. Pleadings must be well grounded in fact and warranted by existing law or a good faith argument for an extension or modification of existing law. If the pleading is frivolous, Rule 11 sanctions may apply.

E. **Challenges to the Pleadings** – FRCP 12

    1. In General: Pleadings may be challenged by a Rule 12 motion to dismiss. Rule 12 motions do not go to the facts, but rather address whether the law allows the specific claim or defense (e.g., improper jurisdiction, venue, service, or expired statute of limitations). A 12(b)(6) motion is for failure to state a claim upon which relief can be granted. A 12(c) motion is for judgment on the pleadings. A 12(f) motion is used to strike any invalid defense or any redundant, impertinent, or scandalous matter.

    2. Motion to Dismiss for Failure to State Claim: 12(b)(6) is the most common motion under FRCP 12 on the bar exam. The ground rules are as follows.

        a. Purpose: The rule offers a quick and convenient way for the D to avoid a claim when it is clear that the plaintiff will never prevail regardless of the facts proven at trial. Typical examples are claims barred by the statute of limitations, or causes of action that are not recognized under the law of the jurisdiction.

        b. Drastic Remedy: Judges consider dismissals for failure to state a claim a drastic remedy and grant them sparingly, only after careful scrutiny. The effect of granting the motion is to deny the P his or her day in court.

        c. Truth Inference: For purposes of deciding a 12(b)(6) motion, all the factual allegations in the complaint will be accepted as true. The motion will be granted only if the P could prove no set of facts that would entitle him or her to the relief requested.

        d. Amendment Allowed: Courts will generally allow a P to amend the complaint, in lieu of granting a dismissal. This relief may apply if by amendment the P may be able to state a new or additional cause of action.

        e. Too Vague: Despite notice pleading rules and P's ability to amend pleadings, courts will occasionally dismiss because the complaint was too vague to satisfy the D's due process right to notice (of both the fact of the claim and the nature of the claim).

F. **Consolidation and Waiver of Certain Defenses** – FRCP 12

    1. In General: Under FRCP 12, certain defenses must be raised timely and consolidated with certain other defenses, or they are deemed waived. These rules promote judicial economy by avoiding piecemeal challenges to the court's authority to proceed with the case. The ground rules for FRCP 12 are as follows.

    2. FRCP 12 Defenses: Defenses that may be subject to the consolidation and waiver provisions are (1) lack of subject matter jurisdiction, (2) lack of personal jurisdiction due to insufficient service or lack of minimum contacts, (3) improper venue, (5) failure to state a claim upon which relief can be granted, and (6) failure to join an indispensable party.

    3. Lack of Subject Matter Jurisdiction: Lack of subject matter jurisdiction can be raised at any time, even after judgment. Consolidation and waiver provisions do not apply.

    4. Lack of Personal Jurisdiction or Improper Venue: Lack of personal jurisdiction or improper venue may be challenged in two ways:

a. Challenge by Motion: D may challenge personal jurisdiction or venue by motion, prior to filing an answer. D must include all challenges to service of process, minimum contacts, and venue. Any challenges not included in the motion are waived.

b. Challenge in Answer: D must include in the answer all challenges to service of process, minimum contacts, and venue. Any challenges not included in the answer are waived. If the challenges are asserted in the answer, P may wait and file the actual motion to dismiss and/or for a change of venue later, to allow extra time to research and draft the motion.

G. Counterclaims

Counterclaims are causes of action made by the D against the P. There are two types of counterclaims: permissive and compulsory:

1. Compulsory: Compulsory counterclaims are any claims arising out of the same transaction or occurrence as the P's claim. They cannot be brought separately later by the D. Logically, P's complaint tolls the statute of limitations on any compulsory counterclaim by the D, or the P could prevent D's counterclaim by filing at the last minute.

2. Permissive: Permissive counterclaims arise from a separate set of facts.

H. Crossclaims – FRCP 13

Crossclaims are made by a D against other co-defendants. Cross claims must arise from the same transaction or occurrence as the P's claim again. Crossclaims are never compulsory.

I. Amended Pleadings – FRCP 15

1. Generally: A pleading may be amended as a matter of right (without leave of court) only: (1) once, before a responsive pleading is served, or (2) if no responsive pleading is permitted and the action is not yet on the trial calendar, within 20 days after it is served.

2. Leave of Court: Otherwise, pleadings may be amended only by leave of court, or with the written consent of the adverse counsel. FRCP 15 specifies that "leave shall be freely granted when justice so requires," giving considerable discretion to the trial court judge. Generally, judges will allow an amendment only if the other party will not be prejudiced.

3. Claims, Defenses, or Parties: Courts are more willing to allow amendments adding claims or defenses than to allow amendments adding new parties.

4. Relating Back: In time-sensitive situations (e.g., when the statute of limitations is close), a significant issue may be whether an amendment relates back to the date of the original pleading. The ground rules of FRCP 15 are as follows:

a. New Claim or Defense: An amendment adding a new claim or defense relates back if it arises out of the same transaction or occurrence, even if the amendment was necessitated by inexcusable neglect, or was the result of a conscious litigation strategy.

b. New Party: An amendment adding a new party relates back only if (a) it arises out of the same transaction or occurrence, (b) the added party receives due notice, and (c) the added party knew or should have known that, but for mistaken identity, the action would have been brought against him.

c. New Party – Restriction: An amendment adding a new party does not relate back if the amendment was necessitated by inexcusable neglect, or was the result of a conscious decision, strategy, or tactic.

d. New Party – Practical Effect: Courts almost never allow a claim against a new D to relate back if it would have otherwise been barred by the statute of limitations.

J. Appearance and Default – FRCP 55

A default judgment prevents the losing party from asserting defenses that might have otherwise been raised, and compulsory counterclaims arising from the original action. A default judgment is preclusive if the court had rightful jurisdiction over the D, and the D had proper notice and opportunity to appear.

1. General Overview: A summons instructs D to respond within 30 days (60 days if residing outside the U.S.). A D who waives service has 60 days to respond (90 days if residing outside the U.S.). If D fails to respond timely, P is entitled to a default judgment. P need not give D notice of the motion for default judgment.

2. Appearance: Even if D fails to file a timely answer, P must give D notice of the motion for default if D has "appeared" in the action. D may then prevent default judgment by serving and filing an answer before the hearing on P's motion. D counsel "appears" in an action by serving and filing a notice of appearance, but informal negotiations may constitute an appearance, if D was aware of P's claim and clearly intended to defend against it.

3. Entry and Judgment Amount: If the amount of a default judgment is uncertain, the court may order hearings or other procedures to determine the proper amount of damages. Normally the court may not award more than requested in the complaint.

4. Protection for Members of Military: Federal law protects members of the military against the entry of a default judgment.

5. Motions to Vacate – In General: A D typically learns of a default judgment after the judgment has been entered. The D's remedy, if any, is a motion to vacate the default judgment pursuant to FRCP 60.

6. Motions to Vacate – For Lack of Personal Jurisdiction: A motion to vacate a default judgment is often based upon an alleged lack of personal jurisdiction, for example if P resorted to substitute service (e.g., by publication) without using due diligence to locate D for personal service. A default judgment without personal jurisdiction may be vacated on motion of D, if filed within a "reasonable" time. Lack of personal jurisdiction is sufficient to vacate the judgment; D need not defend on the merits of the case.

7. Motions to Vacate – Other: Non-jurisdictional grounds to vacate default judgments are typically based upon D's admission of error, for example losing a summons or inadvertently failing to promptly retain counsel. When ruling on a motion to vacate, the court will examine the specific facts and take into account the following:

a. Meritorious Defense: Whether D has a plausible defense going to the merits of the case. If D has no defense, there is no point in vacating the default judgment.

b. Reason for D's Failure to Appear: Stubbornness or failure to appreciate the seriousness of a summons will not support D's motion to vacate. However, the courts may forgive misunderstanding or miscommunications among attorneys, clients, and insurers.

c. D's Diligence: If D did not move to vacate the judgment promptly upon learning of the default judgment, the court will be less inclined to vacate the judgment.

d. Effect Upon P: Similarly if P will be prejudiced by vacating the default judgment, the motion may be denied. This might apply if so much time has passed that crucial evidence is no longer available.

IV. PARTIES

> **MEE Tip:** The subject of parties has appeared only rarely on past exams, and questions have focused on joinder of parties and class actions. Only the most basic rules are covered below.

A. Generally – FRCP 17

1. Real Party in Interest: Every action must be prosecuted in the name of the real party in interest. This is roughly the equivalent of requiring that P must have "standing." Executors, administrators, guardians, trustees, and the like may qualify.

2. Capacity: Both P and D must have the "capacity" to sue or be sued. Minors and incompetent persons lack capacity and must sue or be sued via a guardian ad litem.

B. Compulsory Joinder of Indispensable Parties – FRCP 19

1. Generally: Although P's generally decide whom to name as a party, FRCP 19 requires that persons needed for just adjudication must be joined as parties if feasible. FRCP 19 is generally used to require joinder of other Ds, but it may require the joinder of Ps as well.

2. Complete Relief: Joinder is necessary if in the person's absence complete relief cannot be accorded among those who are already parties.

3. Rights Are Being Adjudicated: Joinder is necessary if the person claims an interest relating to the action and must be a party to adequately protect her interests, or to protect the interests of those who are already parties. This includes:

a. Indispensable Parties: In a contract dispute, all parties to the contract must be joined. In a property dispute, all affected property owners must be joined. In an insurance dispute, all named insureds must be joined.

b. Parties Who Are Not Indispensable: In a tort case, all the tortfeasors need not be joined. State law usually allows a P to sue multiple tortfeasors separately. (Do not confuse this rule with the rule prohibiting claim splitting. See "Joinder of Claims," supra.)

4. Procedure: If the parties do not voluntarily comply, the court will order joinder of a necessary party. If venue is improper, the joined party will be dismissed from the action.

5. Dismissal in Absence of Indispensable Party: If a person cannot be joined, thereby preventing the action from proceeding "in equity and good conscience," the court will dismiss the entire action. A person cannot be joined if the person is not subject to service of process or if venue would be improper.

C. Permissive Joinder of Parties – FRCP 20

1. Common Question of Law or Fact: FRCP 20 allows persons to join in an action if they have claims (or have claims asserted against them) arising from the same transaction or occurrence, involving some common question of law or fact. This rule encourages all interested persons to be joined in a single action to promote judicial economy.

2. Separate Trials: The court may, on motion, order a separate trial if the presence of a party would cause embarrassment, delay, undue expense, or prejudice.

D. Impleader (Third Party Practice) – FRCP 14

1. Generally: Impleader occurs when D#1 brings in D#2, on the theory that if D#1 is found liable to P, then D#2 will be liable to D#1. D#1 may then be termed the "third party P," and D#2 may be called the "third party D."

2. Procedure: D#1 may bring in D#2 by serving D#2 a summons and complaint within 10 days of answering P's complaint. After 10 days, D#1 needs the court's permission to bring in D#2. The court will deny permission if bringing in D#2 would be prejudicial.

3. Insurer as Party: In tort cases, D#1's insurer may not be brought in as a party. Under FRE 411, the jury may not be made aware of the presence or absence of insurance, due to the possibility of prejudice. An exception exists if the insurer would be directly liable to P.

E. Addition or Substitution of Parties – FRCP 25

1. Addition: A pleading may be amended to add a new P or D, subject to the limitations imposed by FRCP 15.

2. Procedure on Addition: A D who is added after the action is commenced must be served with a summons and complaint in the same manner as the original D.

3. Substitution: The addition of a new party should not be confused with the "substitution" of a new party. FRCP 25 gives the court broad authority to order the substitution of a new party for an original party when an original party dies, becomes incompetent, or transfers all interest in the subject matter of the action.

F. Class Actions – FRCP 23

1. Generally: In a class action lawsuit, one or more persons may sue or be sued as the representative of a class of Ps and Ds who have a common interest in the suit. Class actions allow for the efficient pursuit of claims that have a significant aggregate effect, but would be too small individually to justify legal action. Courts have considerable discretion to decide whether a case may proceed as a class action based upon guidelines in FRCP 23.

2. Requirements: A court will only certify a class action if **CULP** is satisfied:

a. Common Questions: There must be questions of law and/or fact common to the class.

b. Usual Claim: The claims or defenses of the representative parties are usual and typical of the claims or defenses of the other class members.

c. Large Membership: The class is so numerous that joinder of all members is impractical.

d. Protection: The representative parties will fairly and adequately protect the interests of all the class members.

3. Examples: CULP requirements were satisfied for a suit by customers of a paint that caused mold and mildew. CULP requirements were not satisfied in a discrimination suit brought by four university professors, as the court held that the facts and legal issues were likely to differ. The four Ps were allowed to proceed, but class action status was denied.

4. Additional Factors: Beyond the CULP requirements, a case may proceed as a class action only if the case fits within at least one of three categories:

a. Risks of Separate Actions: Separate actions would create the risk of: (1) inconsistent judgments, which would establish confusing standards of conduct for the party opposing the class; or (2) inadvertently affecting the rights or remedies of those who do not sue. For example, if all claims would be paid from a common fund on a first-come, first-served basis, the fund might be exhausted before all claimants have had an opportunity to litigate.

b. Conduct of Opposing Party: The class action's opponent has made final injunctive or declaratory relief appropriate. An example is company-wide discrimination against a large number of employees, who now seek a class-action remedy.

c. Common Questions: The questions of law or fact common to class members trump questions affecting individual members. A court determines whether a class action is the best way to adjudicate the controversy fairly and efficiently, by considering the possibility of individual claims, whether any litigation is already commenced, and possible difficulties in the management of a class action.

5. Notice Requirements:

a. In "Common Questions": For "Common Questions" class actions, the best notice practicable must be given to all class members who can be identified through reasonable effort. Each member must be notified that he or she may opt out of the class, and that the judgment will include all members who do not request exclusion.

b. Not In "Common Questions": For other types of class actions, notice requirements are decided by the court. Typically the class members are given notice of the proceedings, but they do not have the right to opt out and pursue individual claims.

V. DISCOVERY – FRCP 26-37

A. Methods and Scope of Discovery —PRIDE

1. Methods: In federal district court, five methods of **PRIDE** discovery are authorized following the initial disclosures (see infra): **P**roduction of documents, **R**equests for admission, **I**nterrogatories, **D**epositions, and **E**xaminations (physical and mental).

2. Timing and Sequence: Absent a local rule or court order, discovery may proceed at any speed and in any order, except that a party generally may not conduct discovery before the initial mandatory discovery conference is held between counsel. The parties are encouraged to agree by stipulation to a schedule for discovery. Stipulations are binding unless the court orders otherwise.

> **MEE Tip:** By local rule, many district courts establish rigid discovery schedules and deadlines that cannot be modified, even by stipulation. Always mention the possibility of local rules when responding to a question about discovery, particularly with respect to the timing and sequence of discovery and discovery deadlines. You need not recite the local rules.

3. Discovery vs. Ex Parte Contacts: In certain situations, counsel must use formal discovery rather than seeking information on an informal, ex parte basis. Ex parte contacts are improper when dealing with the opposing party (but not opposing counsel), and with the opposing party's experts, consultants, management-level employees, and treating physicians (except in workers' compensation cases). Ex parte contacts are proper with ordinary lay witnesses, and with lower-level former employees of a party.

4. Scope of Discovery Generally: The scope of discoverable information is broad, even beyond what would be admissible at trial. FRCP 26 requires only that information sought via discovery be relevant, and likely to "lead to" the discovery of admissible evidence.

5. Privileges Apply: Privileges (attorney-client, physician-patient, etc.) apply during discovery. Communications protected by a privilege are not discoverable unless the privilege has been waived.

6. Protective Orders: The court may enter a protective order to bar or limit proposed discovery that is oppressive, unduly burdensome, or unreasonably duplicative. A court may issue a protective order or seal a file to protect secret processes, formulas, customer lists, or other trade secrets.

7. Work-Product: An attorney's work-product is not discoverable. This includes all notes, investigative reports, legal research, impressions, and opinions prepared "in anticipation of litigation."

a. What is Protected: Documents and tangible items, including investigative reports, statements from witnesses, notes, research, photographs, videotapes, charts, diagrams, etc. If these were not prepared by the attorney, but at the request of the attorney, they are protected as well. For example, D's statement to an insurance investigator shortly after a car crash is protected. Note that the physical things themselves are protected, but not the facts therein, nor the sources of those facts. For example, an attorney's notes from interviewing a witness are work product, but opposing counsel may interview the same witness.

b. In Anticipation of Litigation: The prospect of litigation should suffice to trigger the "anticipation" rule, even if no litigation was actually in progress when made.

> **MEE Tip:** When you hire a consultant or investigator, the court will usually grant protection under the Work-Product Rule, as you are entitled to the advice you paid for without sharing it with your opponent.

c. Distinguish from Attorney-Client Privilege: The Work-Product Rule should not be confused with attorney-client privilege. The Work-Product Rule prevents the opposing party from discovering materials prepared in anticipation of litigation. The attorney-client privilege only protects confidential communications between attorney and client, but it applies at all stages of both civil and criminal proceedings

d. Court-Ordered Disclosure: Upon a showing of "substantial need," usually that the work-product is the only source of certain information, the court may order disclosure. The petitioning party must show the importance of the information to their case, and their difficulty obtaining equivalent information from other sources. In general, there is no justification for disclosure of a statement by a person who is available to be deposed.

e. Legal Malpractice: Where an attorney's work-product is directly at issue (e.g., in a malpractice action), the normal protections may evaporate.

f. Waiver by Disclosure to Witnesses: An attorney may waive the work-product privilege by allowing a witness to see work-product materials in preparation for testifying or giving a deposition. Opposing counsel has the right to examine and even introduce into evidence any materials used to refresh a witness' memory while testifying.

g. Attorney's Thought Processes: The courts tend to protect attorneys' impressions, legal theories, and strategies, even on the basis of "substantial need."

9. Insurance: Production of any insurance policy that may satisfy all or part of a judgment is a mandatory initial disclosure.

> **MEE Tip:** Remember that evidence regarding insurance is not admissible at trial on the issue of liability or negligence, but discovery may exceed the scope of what may be admitted at trial.

10. Using FOIA in Lieu of Discovery: When a P has a suit pending against a governmental entity, or a suit can be reasonably anticipated, the P may also use the Freedom of Information Act (FOIA) to obtain information. However, the scope of discovery under the FOIA is no broader than it would be under the civil discovery rules; privileges and the Work-Product Rule still apply.

B. Discovery With Regard to Experts

1. Testifying: Expert witnesses may be required to disclose their subject matter, substance of opinion, and grounds thereto. They may be formally deposed, but ex parte contact is improper. Failure to disclose an expert witness prior to trial may prevent her testimony, or may incur other sanctions.

2. Consulting: Discovery of experts not expected to be called at trial requires a showing of exceptional circumstances. The opinions of consulting experts are protected on the theory that they are part of the party's legal "team" and thus their opinions constitute work-product. A showing of undue hardship and inability to obtain information elsewhere may constitute "exceptional circumstances."

3. Fact or "Occurrence": A witness who would otherwise qualify as an expert witness, but who instead testifies on the basis of personal involvement in the case (e.g., a treating physician or project engineer), is termed a "fact expert" or an "occurrence expert." The test is whether opinions were obtained for the specific purpose of preparing for litigation. Fact experts are treated as ordinary lay witnesses without other "expert" protections. Labeling a fact expert a consultant cannot shield him from discovery. A fact expert may still be called as a witness by the opposing party and questioned regarding their professional expertise.

C. Initial Disclosures – FRCP 26(a)

In most federal civil actions, a party has a duty to automatically disclose certain basic information within 14 days of the initial discovery conference. This includes witnesses with discoverable information, documents, other tangible things the party may rely upon, computations of damages, and anticipated expert testimony (including the expert's qualifications, compensation, bases for expert opinions, the opinions themselves).

D. Depositions – FRCP 30

A deposition is an oral examination, and may be taken of anyone, even if not a party.

MEE Tip: While FRCP 31 allows for deposition questions to be submitted in writing, use of this procedure is not common and is unlikely to be tested on the exam.

---

1. Subpoena: A subpoena is required to compel the attendance of a non-party.

2. Recording Testimony: The questions and answers are recorded by a court stenographer, and videotaping is allowed.

3. Transcript: The witness' testimony is under oath and the deposition transcript is submitted to the witness for accuracy examination prior to publication.

4. Conduct During Depositions: Objections by counsel and instructions not to answer are only allowed to assert a privilege or to request a protective order. Witnesses must answer without evasion; private consultation between counsel and the deponent is not allowed.

5. Use of Deposition as Evidence at Trial: A deposition is an out-of-court statement and thus objectionable as hearsay. However, several exceptions to the hearsay rule apply. A deposition by a party is allowable as an admission by a party-opponent. If the deposition is by a nonparty, it will usually be admissible under FRE 801 to show prior inconsistent or consistent statements. If the deponent is unavailable for trial, the deposition will be admissible as former testimony.

E. Interrogatories – FRCP 33

1. Generally: Interrogatories are written questions. They can be addressed only to the parties to the lawsuit, and must be answered within 30 days of service. Interrogatories may be included with other written discovery requests. Supplementation is required if the answering party becomes aware of discoverable matter or additional experts expected to testify. Answers to interrogatories are not objectionable hearsay; they constitute admissions by party opponents.

2. Scope of Inquiry: Scope of discovery rules apply to interrogatories. Interrogatories may inquire about facts, or about the application of law to fact ("Do you contend that the facts alleged in the complaint give the plaintiff a cause of action under the Consumer Protection Act?"). Inquires about pure contentions of law, however, are not allowed ("Do you claim that Statute X prevails over Statute Y?").

F. Production of Documents – FRCP 34

Requests to produce, copy, and inspect documents must be answered within 30 days. The location of the requested information must be identified, and the other party must be allowed to examine and copy the records. Insurance contracts are discoverable.

G. Physical and Mental Examinations – FRCP 35

A party whose physical or mental condition is in controversy may be required to submit to a physical or mental examination (an independent medical exam, or "IME"). The examination cannot be conducted solely upon the demand of the party seeking discovery, but must be agreed to by stipulation or ordered by the court for good cause.

H. Requests For Admission – FRCP 36

Admissions of fact are deemed admitted if not affirmatively denied or objected to within 30 days, unless the court permits a withdrawal or amendment. As with interrogatories, the party seeking discovery cannot ask for an admission on a pure issue of law ("Do you admit that 42 U.S.C. § 1983 applies?"). One party may not request the other to admit to ultimate conclusions of law, e.g., negligence or proximate cause.

I. Supplementation of Responses – FRCP 26(e)

A party has no duty to supplement responses (including initial disclosures) unless:

1. Materially Incomplete or Incorrect: The party later learns that a response was in some material way incorrect or incomplete; and

2. Not Already Rectified: The information needed to correct or complete the response has not already been provided via other discovery or in writing.

J. Discovery Abuse – POSE

Before moving for a protective order of the court, counsel must certify that they have conferred with opposing council, or at least tried to, in an effort to resolve the discovery dispute. Once a discovery motion is filed, the court may bestow remedies for abuse of the discovery process ("discovery sanctions") under FRCP 37:

1. Protective Orders: If A believes B seeks excessive discovery or protected information, A's may file a motion for a protective order to limit the scope of discovery, based upon applicable law (e.g., work product rule, privilege).

2. Orders Compelling Discovery: If B resists A's request for discovery, A may seek a court order compelling B to cooperate.

3. Sanctions for Violation of Order or Rule: If a party refuses to comply with a protective order or an order compelling discovery, the court may impose sanctions.

a. Discretion: The court has broad discretion to determine the severity of the sanctions. The court may exclude evidence, find a party in contempt, or require the payment of costs and attorney fees.

b. Scale of Severity: Costs and attorney fees are considered routine sanctions. Harsher sanctions require explicit findings by the trial court.

c. Ultimate Sanctions: If a P engages in particularly egregious discovery abuse, the ultimate sanction is a dismissal with prejudice. For a D who engages in particularly egregious discovery abuse, the ultimate sanction is a default judgment in favor of the P.

4. Exclusion of Witness: If a party fails to identify a witness prior to trial, the court may refuse to allow the party to call the witness to testify at trial.

K. Spoliation

The duty to retain relevant evidence arises when it becomes apparent that the opposing party has a legal claim or defense expectancy that likely involves the evidence at issue.

1. In General: Intentional destruction of relevant evidence ("spoliation") is dealt with more harshly than other abuses of the discovery process. In addition to routine sanctions, the court may refuse to allow the offending party to introduce related evidence (e.g., if D destroyed the car, D's photo of the car will not be admitted).

2. Negative Inference: Evidence of the destruction is admissible to suggest that the destructive party had something to hide such as a "smoking gun" or dangerous product memorandums. Opposing counsel should be allowed a jury instruction which invites the jury to infer that the evidence must have been unfavorable to the party who destroyed it.

3. Electronically Stored Documents: The foregoing rules apply with equal force to electronically stored documents such as e-mails. Thus, a party to litigation has a duty to preserve even e-mails that may be relevant to the case.

4. Implications For Practice: Never destroy relevant evidence, or advise a client to do so. Clients must be advised to retain all documents, physical and electronic, that might be even arguably relevant to a case that has been filed, or is about to be filed. The duty to retain exists when awareness of the opposing parties' documentation expectation is clear to the spoliator.

5. Civil vs. Criminal Cases: Spoliation is usually used in the context of civil cases, but the same general rules apply to criminal cases. The State's duty to preserve exculpatory evidence in criminal cases stems from the defendant's constitutional right to due process. A violation of that duty may have consequences not associated with civil cases.

VI. PRE-TRIAL PROCEEDINGS

A. Preliminary Equitable Relief – FRCP 65(a)

A party may seek a preliminary injunction to restrain the other party from acting while the case is pending. If the restraining party eventually prevails on the merits, the court will usually make the preliminary injunction permanent.

1. Requirements – RAMP:
In considering a preliminary injunction motion, the court considers the following **RAMP** factors.

a. Risk of Irreparable Harm: The movant must have no adequate remedy at law; i.e., money damages are inadequate.

b. Appropriate Weight of Harm Distribution: The harm P will suffer without an injunction issuing outweighs the harm D will suffer if restrained.

c. Merit Success Likelihood: P must at least show that she is likely to succeed on the merits.

d. Public Interest: Whether the injunction will serve or harm the public interest.

2. Temporary Restraining Order:
If irreparable harm may occur before notice and opportunity to be heard can be afforded to the opposing party, the court may issue a temporary restraining order (TRO) *ex parte* (without the opposing party being heard).

a. Showing Required: The moving party must submit an affidavit setting forth the reason(s) why a TRO should be issued, the efforts made (if any) to notify the opposing party of the motion for a TRO, and the justification for issuing the TRO *ex parte*.

b. Limited Duration: A TRO must expire no later than 10 days after it is issued. During that time, the court will hold a hearing on the issue of whether the TRO should be dissolved or converted to a preliminary injunction.

B. Dismissals

> **MEE Tip:** Most exam questions involve motions to dismiss for lack of personal jurisdiction, rather than motions to dismiss under FRCP 41. Do not confuse the two.

1. Voluntary Dismissal – FRCP 41(a):
Actions may be dismissed voluntarily by the P, but the D may object if a counterclaim has been asserted. P may voluntarily dismiss as a matter of right, unless D has served an answer or motion for summary judgment. Otherwise, P must either have all parties stipulate to the dismissal or obtain leave of court. P's first voluntary dismissal is generally without prejudice, and P may refile the action. If P takes a second voluntary dismissal, however, the dismissal operates as an adjudication on the merits, and P cannot file the action a third time.

2. Involuntary Dismissal – FRCP 41(b):
The rule authorizes D to move for an involuntary dismissal of P's case. Grounds include failure to prosecute (undue delay), failure

to comply with a civil rule, and failure to comply with a court order. D may move for a dismissal at the close of P's case, on the basis that P has failed to demonstrate any right to relief. Such a dismissal is with prejudice (P may not refile), unless the court orders otherwise.

3. Coordination With Statute of Limitations: If a case is dismissed under FRCP 41, it is treated as if it had never been commenced for purposes of the statute of limitations. The statute is not tolled between the time of filing and the dismissal. Thus, even if a dismissal is without prejudice, the statute of limitations may bar P from refiling.

C. Summary Judgment – FRCP 56

Summary judgment is a procedural device designed to avoid the time and expense of an unnecessary trial. The formal requirements are set forth in a single rule of court, FRCP 56. The procedure is available to Ps and Ds alike.

1. Motion: A motion for summary judgment argues (1) that the case presents no genuine issues of fact (so the trier of fact has nothing to decide), and (2) that the moving party is entitled to a judgment as a matter of law. The first is a factual question resolved by the court on the basis of the evidence available. The second is a legal question, resolved by the court on the basis of briefs.

2. Issue of Material Fact: In most debatable cases, the issue is whether the case involves any genuine issues of material fact to be submitted to the trier of fact. The ground rules are as follows:

a. Affirmative Showing: The party opposing the motion may not simply rest on the pleadings, but must affirmatively show that the case involves one or more genuine issues of fact.

b. Materiality: Only material issues of fact will preclude summary judgment. Minor, inconsequential issues do not preclude summary judgment.

c. Admissible Evidence: In determining whether there are issues of fact, the court will consider only evidence that would be admissible at trial under the Rules of Evidence. Thus, for example, if a party submits an affidavit from an expert witness, the affidavit must set forth the witness's qualifications as an expert, just as would be necessary at trial.

d. Self-Contradiction: A party cannot create an issue of fact and prevent summary judgment simply by offering two different versions of the same story, e.g., by submitting an affidavit that contradicts his own statements in a prior deposition.

e. Credibility: The court does not consider credibility. Even if one affidavit lacks credibility, if the issue is material, a factual issue will be deemed to exist.

f. Typical Factual Issues: Certain issues, if disputed, are routinely considered material factual issues precluding summary judgment. Examples include an oral contract, negligence, proximate cause, reasonableness, and state of mind (e.g., intent, consent, knowledge, notice, mistake).

g. Any Doubt: Any doubt should be resolved in favor of allowing a trial.

3. Summary Judgment When Law Compels Result: Summary judgment may also be appropriate when discovery reveals that one party will prevail regardless of disputed issues of fact. For example, if D has an ironclad affirmative defense (e.g., the statute of limitations has run, or P signed a valid release) that P cannot overcome no matter how favorable the facts are for P. Summary judgment will likely be granted, because a trial would serve no useful purpose.

D. Pre-Trial Conference

The assigned judge will normally hold a pre-trial conference to discuss the details (scheduling, proposed witness list, document review, etc.) required in the proceedings. Motions in limine to exclude or limit trial evidence may be heard. Normally, a pre-trial order is issued after the conference. An order issued after a "final" pre-trial conference, shortly before the trial itself, will not be modified except as to prevent "manifest injustice." [FRCP 16]

MEE Tip: The standard for modifying a final pre-trial order has been tested on the MEE.

VII. TRIALS

A. Burden of Proof

1. More Likely Than Not: The preponderance of evidence – more likely than not – is the required proof standard. This applies to both P's claims and D's counterclaims.

2. Special Situations: Libel, slander, and fraud require a clear, cogent and convincing showing.

B. Procedure

1. Evidence Motion: Motions in limine are pretrial motions used to limit the presentation of inadmissible evidence.

2. Opening Statement: The party with the burden of proof opens the opening statement portion of the trial. The statement should be limited to the facts to be presented.

3. Timeliness of Trial Objections: In order to preserve the right to challenge a judgment by post-trial motion or by an appeal, counsel must voice objections to trial rulings at the earliest practicable opportunity. Objections to trial rulings cannot be voiced for the first time by post-trial motion or on appeal.

a. Rulings on Evidence: The preferred practice is to object before the witness answers the question "what did he tell you?" If the basis for the objection, here hearsay, does not become apparent until later, counsel must move to strike the inadmissible testimony at the earliest opportunity. "John told me . . . ."

b. Other Rulings: Counsel must seek other rulings during the course of trial – rulings on whether witnesses will be excluded from the courtroom, on whether testimony will be taken out of the usual order, etc., "on the record" by objecting at the earliest opportunity.

c. Constitutional Exception: An exception is made for constitutional issues, which may be raised for the first time on appeal.

4. Mistrials: Counsel may move for a mistrial on the basis of misconduct by the court, counsel, parties, or witnesses, or any other major irregularity in the trial. Examples include unwarranted statements by counsel, and jurors falling asleep.

a. Motion: A motion for a mistrial is similar to a motion for a new trial; the difference is largely one of timing. A motion for a mistrial is made during the trial itself and, if granted, renders the trial void. A motion for a new trial is made at the conclusion of the trial and, if granted, results in a new trial.

b. Timeliness: In order to be timely, a motion for a mistrial should be made as soon as practicable after the misconduct occurs. Counsel should not wait until the conclusion of the trial to voice an objection.

C. Jury Trials – FRCP 38

1. Of Right: Any party may demand that the judicial factual examination be by a jury of one's peers. This demand must be affirmatively made. Failure to comply with this demand requirement is deemed a waiver of a jury and the case is tried before a judge as a "bench trial." [FRCP 38] The jury shall have between six and twelve members. [FRCP 48]

2. Legal or Equitable Decisions: Juries are to decide questions of fact such as whether a breach of contract or tort occurred and the extent of the resulting damages. Judges decide questions of law, admissibility of evidence, and equitable actions such as specific performance or injunctive relief. The trial court has wide discretion to decide if the predominate nature of the case is legal or equitable.

3. Jury Selection: Voir dire is a process in which both parties' counsel select jurors. Questions are directed to the potential juror by the attorneys and judge.

a. Peremptory Challenge: A "peremptory challenge" is a challenge to a prospective juror for which no reason needs to be given. In a civil case, each party (not each side) is entitled to three peremptory challenges.

b. Restriction: The courts have created constitutional restrictions on the exercise of peremptory challenges. Most notably, a peremptory challenge cannot be based solely upon race or gender.

c. Challenge For Cause – LIB: A prospective juror may be challenged "for cause." There is no limit on the number of challenges for cause. Bases for challenge include:

(1) Lack of Qualifications: Under 18, not a US citizen, unable to communicate in English, or a convicted felon.

(2) Incapacity: Being of unsound mind or body, and thus rendered incapable of serving as an objective juror.

(3) Bias, Actual or Implied: This is the usual basis for challenge. For example a potential juror employed by, or related to, a party in the case.

4. Jury Instructions:

a. Generally: Jury instructions are the formal instructions given to the jury by the judge before the jury begins deliberations. The instructions are read orally by the judge and provided to the jurors in writing. Typically, instructions cover the role of the jury, the burden of proof, the required elements of P's cause of action, the required elements of defenses asserted by D, and any special instructions tailored to the individual case.

b. Content of Instructions: Instructions must accurately reflect applicable law and must be sufficient to permit each party to argue its theory of the case. They should be phrased in neutral language and not be argumentative.

c. Timing and Procedure: Under FRCP 51, proposed instructions are to be submitted at trial after all evidence has been presented, unless otherwise requested by the trial judge. As a practical matter, the timing and procedure for proposing instructions is usually governed in more detail by local rule, and even by the preferences of individual judges. At the time set by the judge, counsel generally meet with the judge to work out the language of the instructions to be used.

d. Objections to Proposed Instructions: Counsel must be given an opportunity to object to proposed instructions, or to the court's refusal to give a proposed instruction. In this context, the objection is often termed an "exception."

(1) Timeliness: The principle of timeliness applies. To preserve a point for appeal, an exception must be taken at the earliest opportunity. An exception made after the verdict is returned is usually too late.

(2) Preserve for Appeal: To preserve a point for appeal, exceptions must also be taken on the record. If the court has determined the content of the instructions in chambers with counsel, as is often the case, counsel must request an opportunity to go "on the record" with a court reporter to voice any exceptions.

5. Counsel's Closing Argument:
Each party addresses the jury at the end of the trial. The party with the burden opens and closes the comments on the evidence and the law as contained in the court's instructions. Counsel may only refer to evidence actually presented at trial and generally may not comment on insurance.

6. Jury Deliberations:
Jury deliberations are held in private. No other persons may be in the room. Court personnel may not discuss the case with jurors and may not pressure the jury to reach a verdict more quickly. The jurors are instructed that they are to consider only the evidence presented in the courtroom. The jurors may not conduct their own factual investigations or legal research. They are not to discuss the case with anybody outside the jury room until a verdict is reached.

7. Verdict:
When deliberations have concluded and the necessary votes have been cast, the presiding juror (the "jury foreman") reads the verdict. Unless the parties stipulate otherwise, the verdict must be unanimous. In the absence of a verdict, a mistrial is declared. Either party may usually poll the jury after the reading of the verdict.

8. Juror Misconduct, Setting Aside the Verdict:

a. Improper Actions: A party may move to set aside a verdict on the basis of juror misconduct or other improper actions by jurors. Whether the motion is granted will depend on the severity of the misconduct and the degree of prejudice to the losing party. Bases for this include discussing the case with friends or family before the verdict, independent investigation of the facts (e.g., by looking up information on the internet or visiting the scene of the accident), legal research, nonjurors present during deliberations, reaching a verdict "by chance or lot" (i.e., rolling dice or flipping a coin).

b. Improper Reasoning or Thought Process: The court will not set aside a verdict on the basis of improper or illogical reasoning, for example failing to follow instructions, failing to understand or consider specific evidence, attributing too much or too little importance to specific evidence, and calculation of damages. Similarly, the court will not entertain challenges to a juror's motives, intentions, or beliefs.

c. Life Experiences: As part of the deliberation process, the jurors may share their own life experiences with other jurors. For example, "I once had a injury similar to the plaintiff's injury, and I was not in any pain." The court will not set aside a verdict on this basis.

d. Bias or Prejudice: Traditionally, a juror's bias or prejudice against a party has not been considered a sufficient basis to set aside a verdict. It was believed that the *voir dire* process was sufficient to eliminate jurors with bias or prejudice. However, some courts have set aside verdicts on the basis of bias or prejudice that was deliberately concealed during *voir dire*, but which was expressed either during deliberations or outside the courtroom.

e. Error in Recording or Reporting Verdict: A clerical error in recording or reporting the verdict (e.g., clerk types $5,000 instead of $50,000, so the incorrect number is read aloud by the bailiff in court) may serve as grounds to set aside the verdict.

f. Procedure: Normally, a motion to set aside the verdict is brought as a motion for a new trial under FRCP 59, subject to time limits and other procedural requirements.

VIII. JUDGMENT AS A MATTER OF LAW (JML) – FRCP 50

A. Terminology

The procedures formerly known as motions (1) for judgment notwithstanding the verdict (JNOV), and (2) for a directed verdict (after P or D rests his case), are now obsolete, as they have been consolidated into a single procedure known as a motion for "judgment as a matter of law (JML)." Avoid using the obsolete terms on the exam.

B. Purpose and Timing

1. Purpose: The motion for JML is a procedural device to keep a case from being decided by the jury when there is nothing for the jury to decide; i.e., when one party has failed to produce even enough evidence to submit the case to the jury.

2. Timing: Either party may move for JML. A motion for JML may be made after P rests, after D rests, or even after the case has been submitted to the jury.

3. Comparison to Summary Judgment: A motion for JML is essentially a delayed motion for summary judgment. A motion for JML is made during the trial, instead of beforehand, and is based upon the failure of one party to produce enough evidence to create issues to submit to the jury.

C. Test For Sufficiency of the Evidence

1. Generally: The court's decision to grant a JML is based upon whether the evidence is sufficient to submit the case to the jury. The test for sufficiency is that it may be said, as a matter of law, that there is no evidence or reasonable inference therefrom to sustain a verdict on behalf of the party opposing the motion.

2. Burden on Motion: The burden is on the moving party. A motion for JML admits the truth of the evidence offered by the opposing party and all inferences therefrom. All evidence is interpreted against the moving party and favorably towards the opposing party. In close cases, doubts are usually resolved in favor of submitting the case to the jury.

3. Credibility Disregarded: Credibility is not taken into account when ruling on a motion for JML. The court will not grant the motion simply because it believes one party's witnesses and does not believe the other party's witnesses.

4. No Weighing of Evidence: When ruling on a motion for JML, the court does not "weigh" the parties' evidence. The question is simply whether the party opposing the motion for JML has produced enough evidence to submit the case to the jury.

IX. VERDICTS AND JUDGMENTS (OTHER THAN JML)

A. Jury Trials

The jurors may be asked to return a general verdict (in favor of one party) or a special verdict composed of answers to questions of fact. A special verdict question may be the determination of the proper judgment amount. It is also possible to have the jury answer interrogatories. The verdict is memorialized in a formal, final judgment.

B. Bench (Judge) Trials – FRCP 52

The trial judge makes findings of fact and conclusions of law, which are filed with the judgment.

C. Entry of Judgment – FRCP 58

The date a judgment is "entered" is of great significance because the date of entry starts the time running for most post-trial events, e.g., motions for new trial, motions to vacate, and appeals. A judgment is not entered when the jury returns a verdict or, when the judge announces his/her decision orally. "Entry" occurs later, when the judgment is reduced to writing, signed by the judge, and delivered to the clerk of court for filing in the judgment registry.

D. Costs and Attorney Fees

1. Litigation Costs: The prevailing party is usually entitled to recover costs from the losing party. Costs are specified by statute, and are relatively modest. Examples are fees for filing, witnesses, and service of process.

2. Attorney Fees: Under the so-called American rule, each side bears its own attorney fees, unless otherwise provided by statute or by contract between the parties. Specialized statutes (e.g., consumer protection, anti-discrimination, breach of fiduciary duty, family law, and probate) may allow an award of reasonable attorney fees.

X. POST-TRIAL MOTIONS

A. Motion for New Trial – FRCP 59

1. Grounds – JET: The grounds for a new trial include irregularity in the proceedings, misconduct by persons involved in the trial (including prevailing parties, witnesses, and jurors), excessive or inadequate damages (remittitur, additur), and newly discovered evidence that could not be discovered earlier with reasonable diligence.

a. Juror Misconduct: See Juror Misconduct, Setting Aside the Verdict above.

b. Errors of Law: Errors of law (the same sorts of errors that could be raised on appeal) may also serve as the basis for a motion for new trial. Thus, a motion for a new trial can often be a quick and inexpensive substitute for an appeal.

c. Timeliness: The principle of timely objection applies. Thus, in order to preserve the right to move for a new trial on the basis of an event or error occurring during trial, an objection should be made during trial, and as soon as practicable after the event occurs.

2. Timing and Procedure: A motion for new trial must be filed no later than 10 days after entry of judgment. The motion may be supported by the trial record, additional affidavits, or both. The court itself may also propose a new trial on its own initiative. The court must do so within 10 days after entry of judgment, and the parties are entitled to notice and a hearing. The time requirements are rigorously enforced.

B. Motion to Vacate Judgment – FRCP 60

1. Grounds: Relief from a judgment may be granted for clerical errors, excusable neglect or irregularity in obtaining the judgment, fraud, lack of jurisdiction, and newly discovered evidence that could not be discovered earlier with reasonable diligence. Unlike a motion for new trial, a motion to vacate is not a substitute for an appeal and cannot be based upon errors of law.

2. Timing and Procedure: In all cases, a motion to vacate must be brought within a "reasonable" time. Motions based upon mistake, excusable neglect, irregularity, fraud, or newly discovered evidence must be brought within one year after entry of judgment. The principle of timely objection applies, at least indirectly. A motion to vacate should be brought as soon as practicable after the basis for the motion becomes apparent.

XI. APPEALS

A. When an Appeal is Allowed – Final Judgment Rule

1. Appeal as of Right: An appeal is allowed as a matter of right from the final judgment, or from any other decision that terminates the action (e.g., a complete dismissal).

2. Discretionary Review: The appellate court has discretion to allow review of interlocutory (i.e., non-final) decisions of substantial importance, or to prevent the possibility of irreparable harm. The procedure is called "discretionary review."

3. Extraordinary Writs: In rare situations, a party may seek review of the district court's action before entry of judgment by seeking the "extraordinary writs" of mandamus and prohibition from the court of appeals. These writs are available only when no other form of review, such as an appeal, is available to remedy the error effectively, and justice requires that the writ be issued.

a. Writ of Mandamus: A writ of mandamus directs the district court to take some action that is required under the law.

b. Writ of Prohibition: By contrast, a writ of prohibition orders the district court to refrain from taking an action that is contrary to law, e.g., a court action beyond the scope of its subject matter jurisdiction.

B. Appeal Procedure

The Federal Rules of Appellate Procedure (FRAP), supplemented by any local circuit rules, control. Entry of judgment starts the clock running for the time parties may appeal.

1. Time for Notice of Appeal: An appeal is commenced by serving and filing a Notice of Appeal. The notice is filed in the trial court, not the appellate court. Generally, the notice must be filed within 30 days after entry of judgment (i.e., 30 days after the written judgment is delivered to the clerk for filing), unless the government is a party, in which case either side has 60 days. If a post-trial motion has been filed, the time to file an appeal begins to run when the order disposing the motion is entered. Cross-appeals must be filed 30 days after entry of judgment or 14 days after initial notice of appeal, whichever is later.

2. Extension: The district court may, in rare cases, extend the time limit in extraordinary circumstances. Generally, the principle of finality will prevail over a party's right to file an untimely appeal.

3. Standard of Review: The emphasis is on questions of law, not questions of fact.

a. Pure Questions of Law: Pure questions of law are reviewed *de novo* (i.e., without deference to the trial court's ruling). Examples are interpretation of statute or court rule, application of case law, substantive content of jury instruction, and interpretation of contract ambiguity.

b. Discretionary Rulings: Many rulings are within the discretion of the trial court, and are thus reviewed only for an abuse of discretion. Here, the appellate court will defer to the trial court's ruling, and reversals are less common. Examples are rulings with regard to discovery, granting or denial of a continuance, rulings as to the relevance of evidence, sanctions under FRCP 11, and rulings on motions to amend pleadings.

c. Factual Determinations: Factual determinations (jury's verdict, or judge's findings of fact) are given even more deference than discretionary rulings. Factual determinations will be affirmed if supported by "substantial evidence" (sufficient evidence to persuade a fair-minded, rational person of the truth of the premise). Reversals on factual issues are very rare, because the trier of fact is deemed to be in a better position than the appellate court to resolve factual issues.

d. Raised Below: Except for jurisdiction or constitutional questions, the alleged error must have been raised below in the trial court proceeding.

e. Sustain on Any Theory: Further, the trial court decision may be sustained on a theory different from the trial court's.

4. Circuit Court of Appeals: District Court decisions are reviewed by the United States Circuit Courts of Appeals. This first level of appeal is of right.

5. United States Supreme Court: Review of Court of Appeals decisions is usually discretionary.

a. Conflict: A petition for review may be granted if the Circuit Court of Appeals decision conflicts with another Circuit's decision (or a Supreme Court decision).

b. Question of Law: Review may be granted if a significant question of law is presented.

c. Substantial Public Interest: Review may also be granted if there is an issue of substantial interest that should be determined by the Supreme Court.

XII. PRECLUSION

To achieve judicial economy, litigants should get only one opportunity to try their case.

A. <u>Res Judicata</u>

Upon conclusion of litigation and a valid and final judgment, the judgment is binding and conclusive between the parties and any persons in privity with the parties. The same transaction or occurrence may not serve as the basis for a second lawsuit. Res judicata is often referred to as a rule of "claim preclusion." For example, if P obtains a judgment against D, she may not sue D again in an attempt to get more damages for the same injury.

B. Collateral Estoppel

Collateral estoppel is essentially a restriction on the relitigation of specific issues between the parties. An issue that was necessarily decided in reaching a final judgment is not subject to relitigation between the parties. Collateral estoppel is often referred to as a rule of "issue preclusion." For example, if P sues D for flood damages, and D unsuccessfully claims immunity, D may not claim immunity in a subsequent suit by P for damages from a second flood. D is barred from claiming immunity again, as the issue was resolved in the earlier suit.

I. COMMENCEMENT OF ACTION
  A. Filing ....
  B. Pre-Filing Notice Requirements ....
    1. Federal Tort Claims ....
    2. Waiver ....
  C. Relationship to Service ....

II. JURISDICTION AND SERVICE
  A. Service of Process ....
    1. Waiver of Service ....
    2. Personal Service on Individuals ....
      a. Delivery to the Person ....
      b. Abode ....
      c. Who May Serve Papers ....
      d. Community Property Considerations ....
    3. Service by Publication ....
    4. Service on the Federal Government ....
    5. Service on Corporations and Other Business Associations ....
    6. Service in Specific Situations ....
    7. Service After Initial Service of Process ....
  B. Minimum Contacts ....
    1. Generally ....
    2. Domicile ....
    3. No Contacts, But In-State Service Obtained ....
    4. Consent or Waiver ....
    5. Consent by Contract ....
  C. Long-Arm Statutes ....
    1. Generally ....

    a. Business ....

    b. Tort ....

    c. Property ....

    d. Insurance ....

  2. Jurisdiction is Specific to In-state Activity..

  3. Transacting Business ....

    a. Factors Considered ....

    b. Physical Presence not Required...

    c. Internet Transactions ....

    d. Registered Agent Distinguished ....

  4. Commission of Tort...

    a. Generally ....

    b. Products Liability Cases ....

  5. Ownership or Use of Property ....

  6. Insuring Risk ....

  7. Full Jurisdiction Obtained ....

D. Challenges to Personal Jurisdiction, Consolidation, and Waiver ....

  1. Appearance ....

  2. Method...

  3. Exception...

  4. Timeliness, Consolidation ....

  5. Waiver ....

    a. By Waiting Too Long to Move for Dismissal.......................

    b. By Seeking Affirmative Relief...

E. *In Rem* Jurisdiction ....

F. Subject Matter Jurisdiction...

  1. Federal Question..

  2. Diversity Jurisdiction...

  3. Supplemental Jurisdiction ....

  4. Removal Jurisdiction ....

G. Venue and Change of Venue ....

  1. Basis ....

    a. Residence of D ....

    b. Location of Events or Property...

    c. Personal Jurisdiction..

  2. Actions Against Corporations ....

3. Improper Venue ....

4. *Forum Non Conveniens* ....

III. **PLEADINGS AND MOTIONS**

    A. Complaint and Answer ....

        1. Complaint Contents – **JARR** ....

            a. **J**urisdiction ....

            b. **A**llegation of Facts ....

            c. **R**ight to Relief ....

            d. **R**elief Requested ....

        2. Joinder of Claims ....

        3. Single Complaint ....

        4. Pre-Answer Motion to Dismiss ....

        5. Answer ....

        6. Post-Answer Motion to Dismiss ....

    B. Notice Pleading ....

    C. Pleading Special Matters ....

    D. Signing of Pleadings, Sanctions ....

    E. Challenges to the Pleadings ....

        1. In General ....

        2. Motion to Dismiss for Failure to State Claim ....

            a. Purpose ....

            b. Drastic Remedy ....

            c. Truth Inference ....

            d. Amendment Allowed ....

            e. Too Vague ....

    F. Consolidation and Waiver of Certain Defenses ....

        1. In General ....

        2. FRCP 12 Defenses ....

        3. Lack of Subject Matter Jurisdiction ....

        4. Lack of Personal Jurisdiction or Improper Venue ....

            a. Challenge by Motion ....

            b. Challenge in Answer ....

    G. Counterclaims ....

        1. Compulsory ....

        2. Permissive ....

    H. Crossclaim ....

    I. Amended Pleadings ....

        1. Generally ....

        2. Leave of Court ....

        3. Claims, Defenses, or Parties ....

        4. Relating Back ....

           a. New Claim or Defense ....

           b. New Party ....

           c. New Party – Restriction ....

           d. New Party – Practical Effect ....

    J. Appearance and Default ....

        1. General Overview ....

        2. Appearance ....

        3. Proof of Service and Proper Venue ....

        4. Entry and Judgment Amount ....

        5. Protection for Members of Military ....

        6. Motion to Vacate – In General ....

        7. Motion to Vacate – for Lack of Personal Jurisdiction...........................

        8. Motion to Vacate – Other ....

           a. Meritorious Defense ....

           b. Reason for D's Failure to Appear ....

           c. D's Diligence ....

           d. Effect Upon P ....

IV. PARTIES

    A. Generally ....

        1. Real Party in Interest ....

        2. Capacity ....

    B. Compulsory Joinder of Indispensable Parties ....

        1. Generally ....

        2. Complete Relief..

        3. Rights Are Being Adjudicated..

           a. Indispensable Parties ....

           b. Parties Who Are Not Indispensable...

        4. Procedure..

        5. Dismissal in Absence of Indispensable Party.......................................

  C. Permissive Joinder of Parties ....

     1. Common Question of Law or Fact ....

     2. Separate Trials ....

  D. Impleader ....

     1. Generally ....

     2. Procedure ....

     3. Insurer as Party ....

  E. Addition or Substitution of Parties ....

     1. Addition ....

     2. Procedure on Addition ....

     3. Substitution ....

  F. Class Actions ....

     1. Generally ....

     2. Requirements – **CULP** ....

        a. **C**ommon Questions ....

        b. **U**sual Claim ....

        c. **L**arge Membership..

        d. **P**rotection...

     3. Examples..

     4. Additional Factors ....

        a. Risks of Separate Actions ....

        b. Conduct of Opposing Party ....

        c. Common Questions ....

     5. Notice Requirements ....

        a. In "Common Questions"...

        b. Not in "Common Questions"...

V. DISCOVERY

  A. Methods and Scope of Discovery ....

     1. Methods – **PRIDE**..

     2. Timing and Sequence ....

     3. Discovery vs. Ex Parte Contacts...

     4. Superior Court vs. District Court...

     5. Scope of Discovery Generally ....

     6. Privileges Apply ....

     7. Protective Orders ....

8. Work-Product ....

   a. What is Protected ....

   b. In Anticipation of Litigation ....

   c. Distinguish from Attorney-Client Privilege ....

   d. Court-Ordered Disclosure ....

   e. Legal Malpractice ....

   f. Waiver by Disclosure to Witnesses ....

   g. Attorney's Thought Processes ....

9. Using FOIA in Lieu of Discovery ....

B. Discovery With Regard to Experts ....

   1. Testifying ....

   2. Consulting ....

   3. Fact or "Occurrence" ....

C. Initial Disclosures ....

D. Depositions ....

   1. Subpoena ....

   2. Recording Testimony ....

   3. Transcript ....

   4. Conduct During Depositions ....

   5. Use of Deposition as Evidence at Trial ....

E. Interrogatories ....

   1. Generally ....

   2. Scope of Inquiry ....

F. Production of Documents ....

G. Physical and Mental Examinations ....

H. Requests for Admission ....

I. Supplementation of Responses ....

   1. Materially Incomplete or Incorrect ....

   2. Not Already Rectified ....

J. Discovery Abuse – **POSE** ....

   1. **P**rotective Orders ....

   2. **O**rders Compelling Discovery ....

   3. **S**anctions for Violation of Order ....

      a. Discretion ....

      b. Scale of Severity ....

      c. Ultimate Sanctions ....

  4. **E**xclusion of Witness ....

 K. Spoliation ....

  1. In General ....

  2. Negative Inference ....

  3. Electronically Stored Documents ....

  4. Implications for Practice ....

  5. Civil vs. Criminal Cases ....

VI. **PRE-TRIAL PROCEEDINGS**

 A. Preliminary Equitable Relief – FRCP 65(a) ....

  1. Requirements – **ROMP** ....

   a. **R**isk of Irreparable Harm ....

   b. P's Harm **O**utweighs the Harm to D ....

   c. Likelihood of Success on the **M**erits ....

   d. **P**ublic Interest ....

  2. Temporary Restraining Order ....

   a. Showing Required ....

   b. Limited Duration ....

 B. Dismissals ....

  1. Voluntary Dismissal ....

  2. Involuntary Dismissal ....

  3. Coordination With Statute of Limitations ....

 C. Summary Judgment ....

  1. Motion ....

  2. Issue of Material Fact ....

   a. Affirmative Showing ....

   b. Materiality ....

   c. Admissible Evidence ....

   d. Self-Contradiction ....

   e. Credibility ....

   f. Typical Factual Issues ....

   g. Any Doubt ....

  3. Summary Judgment When Law Compels Result ....

 D. Pre-Trial Conference ....

VII. TRIALS

A. Burden of Proof ....
   1. More Likely Than Not ....
   2. Special Situations ....
B. Procedure ....
   1. Evidence Motion ....
   2. Opening Statement ....
   3. Timeliness of Trial Objections ....
      a. Rulings on Evidence ....
      b. Other Rulings ....
      c. Constitutional Exception ....
   4. Mistrials ....
      a. Motion ....
      b. Timeliness ....
C. Jury Trials ....
   1. Of Right ....
   2. Legal or Equitable Decisions ....
   3. Jury Selection ....
      a. Peremptory Challenge ....
      b. Restriction ....
      c. Challenge For Cause – **LIB** ....
         (1) **L**ack of Qualifications ....
         (2) **I**ncapacity ....
         (3) **B**ias, Actual or Implied ....
   4. Jury Instructions ....
      a. Generally ....
      b. Content of Instructions ....
      c. Timing and Procedure ....
      d. Objections to Proposed Instructions ....
         (1) Timeliness ....
         (2) Preserve for Appeal ....
   5. Counsel's Closing Argument ....
   6. Jury Deliberations ....
   7. Verdict ....
   8. Jury Misconduct, Setting Aside the Verdict ....

        a. Improper Actions ....

        b. Improper Reasoning or Thought Process ....

        c. Life Experiences ....

        d. Bias or Prejudice..

        e. Error in Recording or Reporting Verdict...

        f. Procedure ....

VIII. JUDGMENT AS A MATTER OF LAW

    A. Terminology ....

    B. Purpose and Timing..

        1. Purpose ....

        2. Timing..

        3. Comparison to Summary Judgment...

    C. Test for Sufficiency of the Evidence ....

        1. Generally..

        2. Burden on Motion..

        3. Credibility Disregarded ....

        4. No Weighing of Evidence ....

IX.   VERDICTS AND JUDGMENTS (OTHER THAN JML)

    A. Jury Trials...

    B. Bench (Judge) Trials..

    C. Entry of Judgment..

    D. Costs and Attorney Fees ....

        1. Litigation Costs...

        2. Attorney Fees ....

X.   POST-TRIAL MOTIONS

    A. Motion for a New Trial..

        1. Grounds – **JET** ....

            a. **J**uror Misconduct...

            b. **E**rrors of Law...

            c. **T**imeliness..

        2. Timing and Procedure...

        3. Reopening Judgments...

B. Motion to Vacate Judgment...

    1. Grounds ....

    2. Timing and Procedure ....

XI. APPEALS

A. When an Appeal is Allowed – Final Judgment Rule.....................................

    1. Appeal as of Right...

    2. Discretionary Review ....

    3. Extraordinary Writs ....

        a. Writ of Mandamus...

        b. Writ of Prohibition ....

B. Appeal Procedure ....

    1. Time for Notice of Appeal..

    2. Extension ....

    3. Standard of Review ....

        a. Pure Questions of Law ....

        b. Discretionary Rulings ....

        c. Factual Determinations..

        d. Raised Below..

        e. Sustain on Any Theory ....

    4. Circuit Court of Appeals ....

    5. United States Supreme Court ....

        a. Conflict...

        b. Question of Law ....

        c. Substantial Public Interest ....

XII. PRECLUSION

A. Res Judicata ....

B. Collateral Estoppel ....

RIGOS BAR REVIEW SERIES

UNIFORM MULTISTATE ESSAY EXAM (MEE) REVIEW

CHAPTER 4

FEDERAL CIVIL PROCEDURE

Essay Questions

Question Number 1

On January 31, 2005, Biker punctured one of the tires on her motorcycle when she ran over a nail lying on the pavement of a State A highway. She pulled over to the shoulder and called a friend with her cell phone for assistance. While she was waiting for her friend to arrive, Motorist, who was driving on the same road, drifted out of his lane slightly. The side mirror on Motorist's car struck Biker, injuring her. At the time of the accident, both Biker and Motorist were residents of State A.

In 2006, Motorist moved to State B in order to accept a new job at the headquarters of Gadgets-n-Things, Inc., which was incorporated in State B.

On January 15, 2007, Biker filed a lawsuit against Motorist in the United States District Court for the District of State A. Her complaint asserted a state-law negligence claim against Motorist and sought damages of $100,000, the amount of Biker's medical bills stemming from the accident. The applicable statute of limitations was two years.

Motorist never filed an Answer. However, 20 days after he was properly served with the summons and complaint, Motorist responded with a motion to dismiss. In his motion, Motorist argued that venue was not proper in the District of State A.

After submitting their briefs, the parties began conducting discovery while awaiting a ruling on Motorist's motion. Biker noticed the deposition of Motorist, who testified that at the time of the accident, he was on his way to hand deliver a time-sensitive document on behalf of Widgets-4-U Corp., his employer at the time. Widgets-4-U was incorporated in State A, where its sole office was located. Motorist further testified that after the accident, he told his employer what happened and gave them a copy of the police report.

On April 1, 2007, with Motorist's motion to dismiss still awaiting a ruling, Biker filed a amended complaint that named Widgets-4-U as an additional defendant. A process server properly served Widgets-4-U with the amended complaint on the same date. Like Motorist, Widgets-4-U did not file an answer. Instead, the company filed its own motion to dismiss. Widgets-4-U's motion asserted that the amended complaint was untimely under the statute of limitations and, moreover, that the court lacked subject matter jurisdiction.

1. Should the court grant Motorist's motion to dismiss? Explain.

2. Is Biker's claim against Widgets-4-U barred by the statute of limitations? Explain.

3. How should the court rule upon Widgets-4-U's jurisdictional defense? Explain.

Question Number 2

Waldo, a citizen of State X, created and maintains a popular website that provides free car repair and maintenance advice. The server hosting the website is located in Waldo's basement.

Chris, a citizen of State Y, was the proud owner of a very rare, antique convertible and frequently consulted Waldo's website for advice. However, information on the website concerning fuel filter replacement was incorrect, and after Charlie followed the instructions to install a new filter, the car caught fire. Charlie survived the incident without injury, but the convertible — previously appraised at $500,000 — was damaged to the point where Charlie could do nothing but sell it for scrap metal.

Shortly thereafter, Chris learned that an estimated 1,000 car owners throughout the country had used Waldo's faulty fuel filter replacement instructions. While none of the other cars had caught fire, most of the owners had to pay approximately $500 each to replace parts damaged as a direct result of following Waldo's advice.

Chris hired an experienced class action attorney to sue Waldo on behalf of himself and the other affected car owners. Properly invoking diversity jurisdiction, the attorney filed the complaint in the United States District Court for the District of State Y. After filing the complaint, the attorney had her assistant send a copy of the summons and complaint to Waldo via First Class mail.

Waldo, who had never even set foot in State Y, received the summons and complaint in the mail. He responded by filing a pre-answer motion to dismiss for lack of personal jurisdiction. The long-arm statute in State Y provides that its courts may exercise personal jurisdiction "on any basis not inconsistent with the Constitution of this state or the United States."

1. Should the court grant Waldo's motion to dismiss? Explain.

2. If the court denies Waldo's motion, should it grant a motion for class certification by Chris? Explain.

Question Number 3

Orange Inc., a State A corporation, assembles and distributes a line of popular laptop computers. The parts used to build the laptops are manufactured by various companies, including MagnoMedia Co., a corporation in the Republic of Faroffistan that supplies the hard drives inside Orange computers.

MasterSpend Ltd., a credit card issuer incorporated in State B, ordered 1,000 laptops from Orange for use by MasterSpend employees. About one month after the computers were placed into service, over 500 of them suffered hard drive failures, which seriously disrupted MasterSpend's business operations.

MasterSpend's corporate counsel initially drafted a complaint that named both Orange and MagnoMedia as defendants. However, MagnoMedia was dropped from the lawsuit before it was even filed in order to avoid the difficulties posed by international litigation.

MasterSpend then sued Orange in federal court. Orange considered the possibility of impleading the hard drive manufacturer as a third-party defendant, but eventually made a strategic decision to file a separate action against MagnoMedia in the United States District Court for the District of State A.

As discovery progressed in *MasterSpend Ltd. v. Orange Inc.*, MasterSpend's attorneys received an anonymous tip claiming that Orange had intentionally destroyed key undisclosed documents that were directly responsive to previous requests for production served upon Orange. MasterSpend filed a motion for discovery sanctions, which the judge granted by entering a default judgment in favor of MasterSpend and against Orange. MasterSpend's pending motion for summary judgment, which asserted that the MagnoMedia hard drives were defective as a matter of law, was vacated as moot.

1. Did the court act properly in entering a default judgment against Orange? Explain.

2. If the court had denied the discovery sanctions motion and subsequently granted the summary judgment motion, could Orange have used the resulting judgment to establish that the MagnoMedia hard drives were defective in *Orange Inc. v. MagnoMedia Co.*? Explain.

Question Number 4

Severe animosity existed between former spouses Jack and Jill, both of whom live in Evergreen State. After a particularly heated argument over Jack's alleged failure to pay court-ordered child support, Jill printed up 100 flyers displaying the phrase, "DEADBEAT DAD COMMUNITY WARNING!" across the top. The flyers also included Jack's name, home and work addresses, home and work telephone numbers, and a picture of Jack that Jill had downloaded from Jack's personal website. Jill left the flyers in the mailboxes of Jack's neighbors.

When Jack learned of the flyers, he filed suit against Jill in federal court. The lawsuit alleged a violation of federal copyright laws and various claims under Evergreen State law, including defamation, invasion of privacy, and intentional infliction of emotional distress.

After some discovery, Jill filed a motion for summary judgment on the copyright infringement claim. Jill supported her motion with an affidavit from a photographer, who stated under oath that he had taken the picture of Jack and owned the copyright to the photo. Jack's opposition brief was not supported by any affidavits, but instead referred to statements in his complaint that contradicted the photographer's affidavit and asserted that Jack owned the copyright. The court granted Jill's motion, leaving Jack with the other claims in his complaint.

At trial, the jury found in favor of Jack and awarded him significant damages. Twenty (20) days ago, the clerk entered judgment against Jill, who has suddenly realized that all of claims resolved at the federal trial were Evergreen State law causes of action.

1. Did the court err in granting summary judgment on the federal copyright infringement claim? Explain.

2. What, if anything, can Jill do in light of her realization that no federal claims were heard or decided at the federal trial? Explain.

Question Number 5

In response to the growing problem of unsolicited commercial email ("spam"), the State of Jefferson enacted a law allowing the recipient of spam to sue the sender and recover statutory damages of $500 for each spam email. By contrast, federal spam laws then in effect allowed an email marketer to send spam unless the recipient specifically asked the sender to add the recipient to its "do-not-spam list."

Plaintiff, a resident of Jefferson, received an email promoting a get-rich-quick scheme from Defendant, a company that was incorporated in Jefferson and had its sole office there. In response, Plaintiff filed a lawsuit in Jefferson state court against Defendant for statutory damages of $500.

Defendant timely filed an answer that included an affirmative defense contending that the federal statute preempted the Jefferson statute and that Plaintiff had never asked to be added to Defendant's do-not-spam list. Along with its answer, Defendant also filed a notice of removal to federal court.

After the case was removed, Plaintiff filed a motion to remand the case back to state court. The federal court denied the motion.

Defendant then filed a motion for summary judgment on its claim that federal law preempted the Jefferson spam statute. The court denied Defendant's motion. Defendant filed a notice of appeal, but the Court of Appeals dismissed the appeal.

The case was then set for a jury trial. At least according to Plaintiff's testimony, all elements of the Jefferson spam statute were satisfied. The defense then presented its own case, including the testimony of its sole witness, Defendant's employee who handled all Internet marketing. The employee testified that Defendant's company policy strictly prohibited spamming and that he always abided by his employer's rules. During cross-examination, however, the employee admitted that he had been convicted two years ago for perjury due to false statements he made while giving a deposition in another spam lawsuit.

After the defense rested, Plaintiff moved for judgment as a matter of law. In his motion, Plaintiff noted that his own testimony "conclusively established liability under the Jefferson spam statute, and the defense's sole witness was a convicted perjurer whose testimony should be disregarded as lacking sufficient credibility." The court granted Plaintiff's motion.

1. Did the federal court err in not remanding the case back to state court? Explain.

2. Did the Court of Appeals err in dismissing Defendant's appeal? Explain.

3. Did the trial court err in granting judgment as a matter of law? Explain.

Essay Answers

Answer Number 1

Summary

D must file either an answer or a pre-answer motion to dismiss within 20 days. If the affirmative defense of improper venue is not raised in either in the answer or a pre-answer motion to dismiss (as M did here), it is waived. Venue is proper where any D resides at filing, or where a substantial part of the underlying facts occurred. M resided in State B, but all key facts occurred in State A, so venue is proper there. P may amend her complaint if no responsive pleading has been served. The complaint will "relate back" to the date of the original complaint only if: (a) the amendment arises out of the same facts; (b) the new D was put on actual or constructive notice of the lawsuit within 120 days after filing; and c) the added D knew or should have known that if not for a mistake concerning identity, he would have been originally named. Here, (a) and (b) are satisfied, but not (c), as the D's identity was not mistaken. It does not relate back, so the amended complaint was filed after the statute of limitations had run. Federal jurisdiction may be based upon a "federal question" and/ or "diversity." There is no federal question here, but M and P are citizens of different states, so diversity created federal subject matter jurisdiction. A corporation is a citizen where incorporated and also where its principal place of business is located. W and P are both citizens of State A, so the amendment adding W destroyed the court's diversity-based subject matter jurisdiction.

Issues Raised

(1) Responsive Pleading
    (a) Procedure for Challenging Venue
       (i) Affirmative defenses raised either in answer or a pre-answer to motion to dismiss
       (ii) Answer without challenging venue waives that defense
    (b) District Where Venue is Proper
(2) Amended Complaint
(3) Relation Back of Amendment
(4) Subject Matter Jurisdiction:
    (a) Federal Question Jurisdiction
    (b) Federal Diversity Jurisdiction
       (i)   At least $75,000 in controversy
       (ii) No P is a citizen of the same state as any D
       (iii) Diversity is determined at the time of filing
       (iv) Corporations are citizens where incorporated and primary place of business
       (v)   Amendment adding a non-diverse D destroys federal diversity jurisdiction

(1) Responsive Pleading. Unless the defendant (D) waives service, which did not occur here, a D must file either an answer or a pre-answer motion to dismiss within 20 days after service of the summons and complaint. Here, Motorist (M) filed his pre-answer motion to dismiss on the 20th day after service, so his motion was timely.

(a) Procedure for Challenging Venue. The affirmative defense of improper venue may be raised either in the answer or a pre-answer to motion to dismiss, but if D files an answer without challenging venue, that defense is waived. M properly asserted the defense by including it in his pre-answer motion.

(b) District Where Venue Is Proper. Venue is proper in a district where any D resides at the time of filing, if all D's reside in the same state, or in a district where a substantial part of the facts underlying the complaint occurred. Because M had moved to State B by the time the plaintiff (P) filed, residence is not a proper basis for venue in the District of State A. However, since all key facts in the original complaint occurred in State A, where the accident took place, venue is proper there, and the court should deny M's motion to dismiss for improper venue.

(2) Amended Complaint. The P may amend her complaint as a matter of right if no responsive pleading has been served. Here, neither M nor Widgets-4-U (W) had filed an answer by the time Biker (B) filed her amended complaint. (M's pre-answer motion is not a "pleading.")

(3) Relation Back of Amendment. An amended complaint adding a new party "relates back" to the date of the date of the original complaint (i.e., is deemed to have been filed then) only if: a) the amendment arises out of the same transaction or occurrence; b) the new D was put on actual or constructive notice of the lawsuit within 120 days after filing of the summons and complaint; and c) the added D knew or should have known that if not for a mistake concerning identity of the proper party, he would have been named in the original complaint. Here, a) is satisfied because W's potential liability arises out of the same accident, and b) is satisfied because W was put on actual notice of the lawsuit by being served with the amended complaint approximately 105 days after B filed her original complaint. However, c) is not satisfied because there was no "mistake" about the identity of the proper D's. Rather, B was ignorant of W's potential liability as a second D. The amended complaint will therefore not relate back; instead, it is deemed filed on April 1, 2007, after the statute of limitations deadline. B's claim against W is time-barred by the statute of limitations.

(4) Subject Matter Jurisdiction. Federal district courts are courts of limited jurisdiction. The two most common bases for federal jurisdiction are "federal question" and "diversity." Because B asserted only a state-law claim, there is no federal question jurisdiction here.

(a) Diversity Jurisdiction. Diversity jurisdiction requires: a) at least $75,000 in controversy; and b) that no P is a citizen of the same state as any D. Because diversity is determined at the time of filing, M is deemed to be a citizen of State B and is diverse as to P, a citizen of State A. Thus, subject matter jurisdiction existed under the original complaint.

(b) Citizenship. A corporation is deemed to be a citizen of both the state in which it was incorporated and where its principal place of business is located. W is a citizen of State A under either test, and since P is a citizen of the same state, the amended complaint adding W destroyed diversity jurisdiction. Thus, the court should dismiss the case for lack of subject matter jurisdiction.

Answer Number 2

Summary

Personal jurisdiction requires that the D get adequate notice and an opportunity to be heard, and has had at least minimum contacts with the forum state. Notice requires that the D be properly served, by either personal service or by leaving the summons and complaint with a person of suitable age and discretion who lives with the D. Without a waiver of service, First Class mail does not suffice, so the court lacks personal jurisdiction. D also lacks minimum contacts, such that requiring him to defend there will "offend traditional notions of fair play and substantial justice." The court may assert personal jurisdiction over an out-of-state D via a long-arm statute if D commits an act there or engages in conduct that has an effect in the forum state. A website may create sufficient minimum contacts, depending on how "active" the site is. A website that advertises and accepts orders generally has the requisite sufficient contacts. A "passive" website that merely provides information (as W's site, here) lacks sufficient contacts. To have a class action certified, the Ps must show (a) common questions of fact and law; (b) the representative's claim is typical for the potential class; (c) large class membership; and d) adequate protection by the representative. Here, P's damages of $500k are atypical, so the court should deny the motion for class certification.

Issues Raised

(1)   Personal Jurisdiction
      (a) Service of Process
      (b) Minimum Contacts
          (i) Websites to Provide Minimum Contacts
          (ii) Active vs. Passive Websites
(2)   Class Actions
      (a) Common Questions of Law and Fact
      (b) Representative's Claim is Typical of the Class
      (c) Large Class Membership
      (d) Adequate Protection by the Representative

Sample Answer

(1)   Personal Jurisdiction. A court may not assert jurisdiction over a person unless: a) the person is given adequate notice of the action and an opportunity to be heard; and b) the person has at least minimum contacts with the state where the court sits (regardless of whether the court is state or federal).

(a) Service of Process. Notice and opportunity to be heard is provided by serving the defendant (D) with a copy of the summons and complaint. Under the Federal Rules of Civil Procedure, service upon an individual is usually accomplished by either handing the papers to the D in person or by leaving them with a person of suitable age and discretion who lives with the D. Additionally, process may be served by any procedure allowed by the law of the state where the federal court sits. Absent a waiver of service, merely sending the summons and complaint via regular First Class mail does not comply with the federal rules and is almost always ineffective under state law. Thus, the court should grant Waldo's (W) motion to dismiss for lack of personal jurisdiction.

(b) Minimum Contacts. There also exists an independent alternative basis for the court to find that it lacks personal jurisdiction. The D must have sufficient "minimum contacts" with the forum state such that requiring him to defend himself in that state will not "offend traditional notions of fair play and substantial justice." While physical presence in the forum state is almost always sufficient, a court may assert personal jurisdiction over an out-of-state D via a "long-arm statute" providing for personal jurisdiction over a D who commits an act in the forum state or engages in conduct that has an effect in the forum state.

(c) Websites. Here, W's only contact with State Y is the operation of a website that may be accessed over the Internet from a computer in State Y. When assessing whether such a website creates sufficient minimum contacts with the state from which it is accessed, courts typically consider how "active" the site is. A website that advertises a product and accepts orders for that product will probably be deemed by State Y to have the requisite contacts. By contrast, a "passive" website that merely provides information, such as W's site, lacks sufficient contacts with another state from which it is accessed. Since the required minimum contacts do not exist here, the court should grant W's motion to dismiss for lack of personal jurisdiction.

(2) Class Actions. A class action allows a party to sue or be sued as the representative of a group of people with a common interest in the suit. The plaintiff (P) must satisfy four requirements to have his case certified as a class action: a) common questions of fact and law among class members; b) the representative having a claim that is usual and typical of the claims of the potential class; c) large class membership; and d) adequate protection by the representative.

(a) Application. In this case, joining the estimated 1,000 affected car owners as plaintiffs would be impractical, so the large membership requirement is satisfied. Since P's attorney has extensive class action experience, P would most likely protect the interests of the putative class members adequately. And since all potential class members have claims arising from the same specific faulty information on W's website, there are common questions of fact and law.

(b) Non-Typical Claim. The problem is that P's claim is not typical of that possessed by the potential class members. P suffered damages of $500,000, which is about 1,000 times the amount of damages incurred by the others. Due to this lack of typicality, the court should deny the motion for class certification.

Answer Number 3

Summary

A resisting party's failure to disclose requested documents is discovery abuse unless a protective order is granted by the court (not sought here by O). Intentional destruction of evidence, as here, is discovery abuse, also ("spoliation"). A court may impose sanctions upon a party and/or counsel for discovery abuse, including striking a document, excluding evidence, (including testimony), holding the offender in contempt of court, or awarding costs and attorney fees. For spoliation, the court may bar related evidence or invite the jury to infer that the evidence was unfavorable to the party who destroyed it. The ultimate sanction is a default judgment against the offending party, as was proper here for O's egregious discovery abuse. Issue preclusion (a/k/a collateral estoppel) restricts the relitigation of issues litigated and resolved in a prior lawsuit. Collateral estoppel has four required elements: (1) a valid and final judgment; (2) the issue is the same as the one litigated in the prior action; (3) the issue was actually litigated; (4) the party to be precluded had a full and fair opportunity to litigate the issue in the prior case. Here, summary judgment satisfies the first three elements, but not the fourth. MagnoMedia was not a party in the original suit, so it had no "full and fair opportunity" to defend itself—which also raises Due Process problems.

Issues Raised

(1)   Discovery Abuse
    (a) Spoliation
    (b) Sanctions
(2)   Issue Preclusion (Collateral Estoppel)
    (a) Valid and Final Judgment
    (b) Identical Issue
    (c) Issues Actually Litigated
    (d) Precluded Party Had Full and Fair Opportunity to Litigate

Sample Answer

(1)   Discovery Abuse. Failure to disclose documents that are responsive to a request for production is deemed a discovery abuse unless the party resisting production moves for and obtains a protective order. Here, Orange did not seek a protective order, let alone obtain one. Orange's failure to disclose the documents was thus an abuse of the discovery process.

(a) Spoliation. The intentional destruction of evidence, which occurred here, is called "spoliation" and considered an especially egregious form of discovery abuse. The spoliator must be aware the opposing party has a legal expectation and necessity to be provided the spoliated evidence. Upon gaining awareness the duty to retain vests.

(b) Sanctions. A court has a great deal of discretion in imposing sanctions upon a party and/or counsel that engages in discovery abuse. Possible sanctions include, but are not limited to: striking a document filed with the court, excluding evidence (including a witness' testimony), holding the offender in contempt of court, or awarding the other party its costs and attorney fees. Sanctions for spoliation may include barring related evidence (e.g., extrinsic evidence concerning the nature and content of the documents destroyed by Orange) or inviting the jury to infer that the evidence was unfavorable to the party who destroyed it. The ultimate sanction for discovery abuse, a default judgment against the offending party, is typically reserved for very serious cases of abuse, but spoliation is egregious enough to merit such a sanction. Thus, the court did not err by entering a default judgment in favor of MasterSpend and against Orange.

(2) Issue Preclusion (Collateral Estoppel). The doctrine of issue preclusion (a/k/a collateral estoppel) restricts the relitigation of specific issues that were litigated and resolved in a prior lawsuit. The modern approach to issue preclusion has four requirements. First, there must have been a valid and final judgment in the previous case. Second, the issue must have been the same as the one litigated in the prior action. Third, the issue must have been actually litigated, determined, and essential to the previous judgment. Fourth, the party to be precluded must have had a full and fair opportunity to litigate the issue in the original case. (The "full and fair opportunity" element replaces an older rule that generally required the parties in both actions to have been the same.)

The hypothetical summary judgment would have satisfied the first three elements. Summary judgment is a final judgment, and the issue (i.e., whether the hard drives were defective) would have been the same. Further, the issue would have been actually litigated (summary judgment is on the merits, unlike a dismissal without prejudice), and the defective nature of the hard drives was essential to the question of whether Orange was liable for the harm to MasterSpend that the computers allegedly caused.

However, the fourth element would not have been satisfied. Because MagnoMedia was not a party in the *MasterSpend v. Orange* case, it did not have a "full and fair opportunity" to litigate the issue of whether the drives were defective. Indeed, as a non-party, it had no opportunity whatsoever to defend itself, which raises Due Process considerations. Allowing Orange to collaterally estop MagnoMedia with the summary judgment from *MasterSpend v. Orange* would thus be improper.

Answer Number 4

Summary

The moving party is entitled to summary judgment as a matter of law where there is no genuine issue of material fact. Here, Jack asserted an issue of material fact by claiming to own the copyright, but merely resting on the pleadings, without an affirmative showing, is not sufficient. Parties may challenge federal subject matter jurisdiction [SMJ] (which cannot be created by consent) at any time, even by post-trial motion or appeal. Federal courts may hear any claim arising under federal law (e.g., Jack's copyright infringement claim), and may claim "supplemental" jurisdiction over claims related to other claims that are "part of the same case or controversy," where SMJ exists. Here, all claims arose out of Jill's flyer, so the federal court had SMJ over the state-law claims in Jack's complaint. That SMJ was destroyed, however, when the court resolved (via summary judgment) the lone federal cause of action. Lack of SMJ is grounds for a new trial only if a motion is filed within 10 days after entry of judgment, so since 20 days have passed here, Jill is too late to move for a new trial. Jill may still seek "relief from judgment" on SMJ grounds if she so moves within a "reasonable" time. Alternatively, since 30 days after entry of judgment has not yet passed, Jill still may seek relief in the Court of Appeals, as SMJ and constitutional claims may be raised for the first time on appeal.

Issues Raised

(1) Summary Judgment
(2) Subject Matter Jurisdiction
    (a) Parties cannot create SMJ by consent
    (b) Federal Question
    (c) Supplemental Jurisdiction
(3) Motion for New Trial
(4) Motion to Vacate Judgment
(5) Appeal
    (a) Filed within 30 days after entry of judgment
    (b) Issues are not to be first raised on appeal unless a SMJ or constitutional claim

Sample Answer

(1) Summary Judgment. The court did not err in granting summary judgment to Jill on the copyright claim. Summary judgment should be granted where there is no genuine issue of material fact, and the moving party is entitled to judgment as a matter of law. Here, if Jack did not own the copyright to the photo, then as a matter of law, Jill would be entitled to judgment in her favor on that claim.

(a) Defense. Jack tried to show that there was an issue of material fact by referring to the statement in his complaint that he owned the copyright. However, this was not sufficient. Once Jill submitted her motion and supporting affidavit, Jack needed to show affirmatively (e.g., through his own affidavit or with the fruits of discovery) that there was a genuine factual dispute as to copyright ownership. Merely resting on the pleadings, which Jack did, is not sufficient. Jill was entitled to summary judgment because Jack's opposition was insufficient.

(2) Subject Matter Jurisdiction. Federal courts are courts of limited jurisdiction. Parties cannot create subject matter jurisdiction (SMJ) by consent, and lack of SMJ may be challenged at any time, even via a post-trial motion or appeal.

(a) Federal Question. Federal courts may hear any claim arising under federal law, such as Jack's copyright infringement claim.

(b) Supplemental Jurisdiction. A federal court will have SMJ over claims that otherwise cannot be heard in federal court if they are related to other claim(s) where federal SMJ exists. The usual test is whether the supplemental claims are "part of the same case or controversy." Here, since all claims arose out of the flyer that Jill designed, printed, and distributed, the federal court originally had supplemental jurisdiction over the state-law claims in Jack's complaint. That SMJ was destroyed, however, when the court resolved via summary judgment the one federal cause of action, leaving only state-law claims.

(3) Motion for New Trial. An error of law, such as lack of SMJ, may be grounds for a new trial. However, a motion for a new trial must be made within 10 days after entry of judgment, and this deadline is strictly enforced. Since 20 days have passed here, it is too late for Jill to move for a new trial.

(4) Motion to Vacate Judgment. However, another post-trial motion possibility is seeking relief from judgment under FRCP 60. While a motion to vacate judgment usually cannot be based upon an error of law, a lack of SMJ renders the judgment completely void. While there is no strict deadline for a motion to vacate on SMJ grounds (most other grounds require filing within one year after entry of judgment), it must be brought within a "reasonable" time. If Jill wishes to use this procedure, she should file a motion to vacate the judgment as soon as possible.

(5) Appeal. Alternatively, since 30 days after entry of judgment has not yet passed, Jill still has the option of filing a notice of appeal and seeking relief in the Court of Appeals. While issues generally may not be raised for the first time on appeal, SMJ and constitutional claims are exceptions to this rule.

Answer Number 5

Summary

The court erred in not remanding the case back to state court. In order for a federal court to have SMJ there must either be a federal question or diversity of the parties, neither of which existed here. The court acted properly in dismissing Defendant's appeal. Appeals are allowed as a matter of right from the final judgment in the case or from any other decision that terminates the action, such as a complete dismissal. Here, there was not a complete dismissal and there was no final judgment therefore, the court dismissing the appeal was proper. The court should deny a motion for JML unless, as a matter of law, there is no evidence or reasonable inference therefrom to support a verdict on behalf of the opposing party. A motion for JML admits the truth of the evidence offered by the opposing party and all inferences therefrom. Accordingly, the court should not take credibility into account when ruling on a motion for JML. The court should deny a motion for JML unless, as a matter of law, there is no evidence or reasonable inference therefrom to support a verdict on behalf of the opposing party. A motion for JML admits the truth of the evidence offered by the opposing party and all inferences therefrom. Therefore, the court erred when it took credibility into account when ruling on a motion for JML.

Issues Raised

(1)   Subject Matter Jurisdiction
    (a) Removal Jurisdiction
    (b) Federal Question
(2)   Appeals
    (a) Final Judgment Rule
        (i) Appeal allowed as matter of right from final judgments that terminates the action
        (ii) No appeal without a final judgment
    (b) Discretionary Review of Interlocutory Decision
(3)   Judgment as a Matter of Law: Credibility Disregarded

Sample Answer

(1)   Subject Matter Jurisdiction. The federal court erred in not remanding the case back to state court, as the federal court had no subject matter jurisdiction (SMJ) over the case. Federal courts are courts of limited jurisdiction.

    (a) Removal Jurisdiction. Here, Defendant attempted to invoke federal SMJ by way of the removal jurisdiction statute. A defendant may "remove" a case filed by the plaintiff in state court if the case could have been initiated in federal court instead. The one major exception, which is not applicable here, is that if the only basis for federal jurisdiction is diversity of the parties, the case may not be removed if it was filed in a state where at least one defendant resides.

    (b) Federal Question. Here, the only apparent basis for Defendant's assertion of federal SMJ is federal question jurisdiction. Federal courts may hear any case arising under a federal constitution, statute, or treaty. However, merely pleading a federal affirmative defense is not sufficient to create federal question SMJ. Since the only federal law involved in this case was the one raised in Defendant's preemption defense, the federal court lacked SMJ and should have remanded the case back to state court.

(2)   Appeals. The Court of Appeals likely acted properly in dismissing Defendant's appeal.

(a) Final Judgment Rule. Appeals are allowed as a matter of right from the final judgment in the case or from any other decision that terminates the action, such as a complete dismissal. Conversely, an aggrieved party usually cannot appeal in the absence of a final judgment.

(b) Discretionary Review of Interlocutory Decision. The Court of Appeals has discretion to allow review of interlocutory (i.e., non-final) decisions that are of substantial importance or to prevent the possibility of irreparable harm. However, simple denial of summary judgment is almost certainly not "of substantial importance," at least under the facts here, and nothing suggests irreparable harm from requiring Defendant to wait until a final judgment before appealing. Indeed, even though the court denied summary judgment, the court could later grant the same requested judgment through judgment as a matter of law or a decision on the merits, either of which would moot Defendant's grounds for appeal. Accordingly, the appellate court did not err in dismissing the appeal.

(3)   Judgment as a Matter of Law: Credibility Disregarded. The court erred in granting judgment as a matter of law (JML). A motion for JML is akin to a summary judgment motion. The court should deny a motion for JML unless, as a matter of law, there is no evidence or reasonable inference therefrom to support a verdict on behalf of the opposing party. A motion for JML admits the truth of the evidence offered by the opposing party and all inferences therefrom. Accordingly, the court should not take credibility into account when ruling on a motion for JML.

Here, Defendant's employee testified that he always followed Defendant's policy against spamming. If this testimony was true, Defendant could not have violated the anti-spam statute. Plaintiff's argument that the employee lacked credibility may have had some merit, but it was not proper in the context of a motion for JML, and the court should not have granted the motion.

CHAPTER 4

FEDERAL CIVIL PROCEDURE

Index

Abode Service .... T 4-210

Actions Against
   Corporations .... T 4-211, 215

Addition of Parties .... T 4-221

Amended Pleadings.................... T 4-218

Answer .... T 4-215, 216

Appeals..................................... T 4-236

Attorney-Client Privilege .... T 4-224

Attorney Fees .... T 4-235

Attorney's Thought Processes.... T 4-224

Bench Trial .... T 4-231, 234

Burden of Proof........................ T 4-230

Capacity.................................... T 4-220

Challenge for Cause .... T 4-231

Challenges to Jurisdiction .... T 4-213

Challenges to the Pleadings........ T 4-217

Change of Venue....................... T 4-215

Claim Preclusion .... T 4-237

Claim Splitting .... T 4-216

Class Actions............................ T 4-221

Closing Argument .... T 4-232

Collateral Estoppel .... T 4-238

Commencement of Action .... T 4-209

Commission of Tort .... T 4-211

Community Property
   Considerations....................... T 4-210

Compelling Discovery................ T 4-227

Complaint.................................. T 4-215

Compulsory Counterclaims........ T 4-218

Compulsory Joinder .... T 4-220

Confer Requirement .... T 4-223

Consent to Jurisdiction .... T 4-211

Consolidation of Defenses . T 4-213, 217

Consulting Experts .... T 4-224

Costs... T 4-235

Counterclaims............................ T 4-218

Court of Appeals .... T 4-237

Crossclaim................................. T 4-218

Default....................................... T 4-219

Depositions............................... T 4-225

Discovery .... T 4-223

Discovery Abuse .... T 4-226

Discovery Sanctions .... T 4-226

Discretionary Review .... T 4-236

Dismissals.................................. T 4-228

Diversity Jurisdiction .... T 4-214

Domicile .... T 4-211

Electronically Stored
   Documents............................. T 4-227

Entry of Judgment .... T 4-234

Equitable Relief......................... T 4-227

Ex Parte Contacts .... T 4-223

"Exception" to Proposed Jury
   Instructions .... T 4-232

Exclusion of Witness................. T 4-227

Expert Witnesses .... T 4-224

Extraordinary Writs................... T 4-236

Fact Witness .... T 4-225

Failure to Appear .... T 4-220

Failure to Join Indispensable
   Party..................................... T 4-220

Failure to State a Claim .... T 4-217

Federal Question........................ T 4-214

Federal Tort Claims................... T 4-209

Filing.. T 4-209

Forum Non Conveniens .... T 4-215

Freedom of Information Act....... T 4-224

Impleader.................................. T 4-221

Improper Venue.................. T 4-215, 217

In Rem Jurisdiction.................... T 4-214

Indispensable Parties .... T 4-220

Initial Disclosures...................... T 4-225

Insurance Agreement
   Production.............................. T 4-224

Insurer as Party .... T 4-221

Insuring Risk .... T 4-212

Internet Transactions .... T 4-212

Interrogatories........................... T 4-225

Involuntary Dismissal................. T 4-228

Issue Preclusion .... T 4-238

Joinder of Claims....................... T 4-215

Joinder of Indispensable
   Parties .... T 4-220

Joinder of Parties .... T 4-221

Judgment as a Matter of Law ..... T 4-233

Juror Bias........................... T 4-231, 233

Juror Misconduct....................... T 4-233

Juror Qualifications .... T 4-231

Jury Deliberations...................... T 4-232

Jury Instructions .... T 4-232

Jury Selection .... T 4-231

Jury Size .... T 4-231

Jury Trials ....T 4-231, 234
Jury Verdict.................................T 4-232
Lack of Personal Jurisdiction......T 4-217
Lack of Subject Matter
   Jurisdiction.............................T 4-217
Legal Malpractice.......................T 4-224
Litigation Costs ....T 4-235
Long-Arm Statute ....T 4-211
Mcmbcrs of Military ....T 4-219
Mental Examinations ....T 4-226
Minimum Contacts......................T 4-211
Mistrials ....T 4-231
Motion for New Trial..................T 4-235
Motions in Limine.......................T 4-230
Motion to Dismiss.......................T 4-217
Motion to Strike Testimony ....T 4-230
Motion to Vacate Default
   Judgment ....T 4-219
Motion to Vacate Judgment ....T 4-235
Negative Inference ....T 4-227
Notice Pleading...........................T 4-216
Objections ....T 4-230, 232
Occurrence Witness ....T 4-224
Opening Statement......................T 4-230
Orders Compelling Discovery.....T 4-227
Ownership of Property ....T 4-212
Parties...T 4-220
Peremptory Challenge.................T 4-231
Permissive Counterclaims...........T 4-218
Permissive Joinder of Parties ......T 4-221
Personal Jurisdiction ....T 4-209
Personal Service on
   Individuals..............................T 4-210
Physical Examinations ....T 4-226
Pleading Special Matters.............T 4-216
Pleadings ....T 4-215
Polling the Jury ....T 4-232
Post-Trial Motions ....T 4-235
Pre-Answer Motion to Dismiss...T 4-216
Pre-Filing Notice
   Requirements ....T 4-209
Pre-Trial Conference...................T 4-230
Pre-Trial Order...........................T 4-230
Pre-Trial Proceedings.................T 4-228
Preclusion...................................T 4-237
Preliminary Equitable Relief.......T 4-228
Preliminary Injunction ....T 4-228
Privileges....................................T 4-223
Process Server ....T 4-210
Production of Documents............T 4-226
Products Liability........................T 4-212
Protective Orders.................T 4-223, 226

Real Party in Interest.................. T 4-220
Relating Back............................. T 4-218
Removal Jurisdiction.................. T 4-214
Requests for Admission .... T 4-226
Res Judicata............................... T 4-237
Rule 11 .... T 4-216
Rulings on Evidence................... T 4-230
Sanctions .... T 4-216, 227
Scope of Discovery .... T 4-223
Separate Trials........................... T 4-221
Service After Initial Service of
   Process.................................... T 4-211
Service by Publication................ T 4-210
Service of Process .... T 4-210
Service on Corporations and
   Business Associations .... T 4-211
Service on the Federal
   Government............................. T 4-211
Setting Aside the Verdict .... T 4-233
Signing of Pleadings.................. T 4-216
Spoliation .... T 4-227
Standard of Review .... T 4-236
Subject Matter Jurisdiction......... T 4-214
Subpoena .... T 4-225
Substitution of Parties .... T 4-221
Sufficiency of Evidence .... T 4-234
Summary Judgment..................... T 4-229
Supplemental Jurisdiction .... T 4-214
Supplementation of Discovery
   Responses .... T 4-226
Supreme Court............................ T 4-237
Temporary Restraining Order
   (TRO) .... T 4-228
Third Party Practice.................... T 4-221
Timeliness of Defenses .... T 4-213
Timeliness of Objection or
   Motion to Strike .... T 4-230
Trials.. T 4-230
Ultimate Sanctions .... T 4-227
Unanimous Verdict .... T 4-232
United States Supreme Court ..... T 4-237
Venue .... T 4-215
Verdict....................................... T 4-232
Voir Dire .... T 4-231
Voluntary Dismissal................... T 4-228
Waiver of Defenses .... T 4-217
Waiver of Jurisdiction .... T 4-211
Waiver of Privilege .... T 4-224
Waiver of Service....................... T 4-210
Work-Product............................. T 4-223
Writ of Mandamus .... T 4-236
Writ of Prohibition .... T 4-236

CHAPTER 5

TRUSTS, WILLS, AND

ESTATES

RIGOS BAR REVIEW SERIES

UNIFORM MULTISTATE ESSAY EXAM (MEE) REVIEW

CHAPTER 5

TRUSTS, WILLS, AND ESTATES

Table of Contents

A.	Sub-Topic Exam Issue Distribution		Text 5-269
B.	Opening Argument and Primary Issues		Text 5-273
C.	Text		Text 5-275
	I.	Introduction	Text 5-275
	II.	Types of Trusts	Text 5-275
	III.	Required Trust Elements – SIT – PA	Text 5-276
	IV.	Trust Organization Formation	Text 5-278
	V.	Trustee's Responsibilities and Liability – PIN CALL	Text 5-281
	VI.	Beneficiaries and Creditors' Rights	Text 5-283
	VII.	Charitable Trusts	Text 5-285
	VIII.	Third Party Liability	Text 5-285
	IX.	Termination of Trust	Text 5-286
	X.	Wills – SIT – MA	Text 5-287
	XI.	Will Challenges	Text 5-293
	XII.	Uniform Simultaneous Death Act	Text 5-294
	XIII.	Intestate Succession	Text 5-294
	XIV.	Related Documents	Text 5-296
	XV.	Probate Proceedings	Text 5-297
D.	Magic Memory Outlines®		Magic Memory Outlines 5-301
E.	Trusts, Wills and Estates Essay Questions		Questions 5-307
F.	Trusts, Wills and Estates Essay Answers		Answers 5-311
G.	Trusts, Wills and Estates Index		Index 5-319
H.	Acronyms		Acronyms 15-627

RIGOS BAR REVIEW SERIES
MEE SUB-TOPIC FREQUENCY DISTRIBUTION

TRUSTS, WILLS, AND ESTATES

	2/09	7/08	2/08	7/07	2/07	7/06	2/06	7/05	2/05	7/04	2/04	7/03	2/03	7/02	2/02	7/01	2/01
Opening Argument	/	/	//	/	//		/		/	/			/	/		/	/
Trusts																	
Trust Execution Validity	/	/	/	/	/		/		/				/	/		/	
Inter Vivos	/	/	/	/	/		/						/	/		/	
Testamentary Trust		/			/								/	/			
Revocable	/	/	/	/		/	/						/			/	
Property				/			/									/	
Intent	/	/	/	/	/		/			/						/	
Rule Against Perpetuities											/						
Taker Ineligible				/	/	/		/									
Trustee's Duties			/	/							/					/	
Fiduciary			/	/							/						
Loyalty			/								/						
Preserve Fund											/						
Trustee Personal Liability		/	/								/						
Reasonably Prudent Standard			/								/						
Spendthrift		/					/										
Distribution		/	/				/			/			/		/	/	
Exceptions			/										/				
Modification		/	/				/							/		/	

Course 5328. Copyright by Rigos Bar Review Series – MEE.

	2/01	7/01	2/02	7/02	2/03	7/03	2/04	7/04	2/05	7/05	2/06	7/06	2/07	7/07	2/08	7/08	2/09
Incorporation by Reference		/		/							/						
Future																	
Beneficiaries				/				/						/			
Termination		/			/												
Appointment										/				/			
Crossover Future Interest / Wills																	
Pourover Wills				/							/					/	
Reversion			/														
Wills																	
Validity of Will	/			/	/		/								/		
General Requirements				/	/		/		/						/		
Two Witnesses	/			/	/		/		/								
Acknowledgment					/		/										
Taker as Witness	/			/	/												
Advancement										/							/
Per Capita										/	/						
Per Stirpes										/	/						
Lapsed Devise	/							/		/	/						
Anti-Lapse Statute	/							/			/						/
Condition of Survival								/		/							
Omitted (Pretermitted) Child																	
Divestment of Ex-Spouse																	

	2/09	7/08	2/08	7/07	2/07	7/06	2/06	7/05	2/05	7/04	2/04	7/03	2/03	7/02	2/02	7/01	2/01
Advancement											/						/
Adopted Child Takes as Full											/						
Illegitimate Child							/				/						
Slayer Doesn't Take							/										
Exoneration							/										
Ademption	/				/				/				/		/	/	
Stock Splits & Dividends	/				/												
Codicils										/				/			
Witnessed							/			/							
Incorporation by Reference							/	/						/			
Revocation	/						/			/							/
Dependent Relative Revocation										/							/
Holographic Wills							/			/		/				/	
Joint Wills							/			/					/		
Will Challenge												/					

Course 5328. Copyright by Rigos Bar Review Series – MEE.

	2/09	7/08	2/08	7/07	2/07	7/06	2/06	7/05	2/05	7/04	2/04	7/03	2/03	7/02	2/02	7/01	2/01
Estates																	
Intestate Distribution					//		/		/		/					/	/
Probate			/								/						
Joint Tenancy With Right of Survivorship									/								
Life Insurance Contract								/	/								
Distribution to Beneficiaries	/				/	/	/	/		/	/					/	/
Residuary Estate Distribution	/				//			/			/			/	/	/	/

OPENING ARGUMENT AND PRIMARY ISSUES

TRUSTS, WILLS, AND ESTATES

There are a few thoughts that should usually be stated at the beginning of every answer. These will score you easy points and let the grader know you are in the right topic area.

Most essays should have an "opening argument": a brief, broad statement that shows you understand the broad significance of a legal topic. The opening argument also suggests to the grader that she is about to read a thoughtful and well-organized essay.

Many subjects also have "primary issues" that can be discussed up front or integrated into the essay answer. IMPORTANT: Do not merely regurgitate these statements on the exam without addressing the issues actually raised by the facts, or you will not pass.

- **Trusts and Wills Opening Argument:** The law of trusts controls the dispersal of personal property to others under the protection of a fiduciary. Will and probate law governs the disposition of assets upon death.

- **Trusts Sample Primary Issue Statements:**

  - A trust is a fiduciary relationship consisting of a settlor, intent, trustee, property, and ascertainable beneficiaries

  - The trustee must have legal capacity, can be court appointed if the named trustee fails, and must be someone other than or in addition to the beneficiary.

  - The trustee must administer the trust assets, inform beneficiaries, not delegate discretionary duties, not commingle trust assets with his own, litigate on behalf of the trust, and adhere to the fiduciary duty of loyalty.

  - Trustees have a duty to administer the trust in good faith, in accordance with its terms and the interests of the beneficiaries. In most states, trustees are duty-bound to invest trust assets prudently and diversify investments.

  - The trustee's fiduciary duty of loyalty excludes self-dealing unless the instrument expressly allows same. A trustee must not take an opportunity of the trust, borrow from the trust, or use trust assets as collateral for a personal loan.

  - A spendthrift trust prohibits assignment by the beneficiary or attachment of a future distribution by a beneficiary's creditor.

  - The trust's beneficiaries may bring suit against the trustees for diminution of the corpus and lost earnings. A court may order that a trustee be removed and appoint a successor. A declaratory action may order specific performance of the trustee's duties or enjoin the trustee in the future.

- **Wills Sample Primary Issue Statements:**

  - A valid will requires 1) a signature by the testator, 2) intent to devise, 3) testamentary capacity (18 and over), 4) mental capacity, and 5) attestation by two witnesses.

  - To contest a will on the basis of undue influence requires a showing of a large devise, the opportunity to unduly influence, active participation by the beneficiary, and a fiduciary relationship.

  - A will may incorporate by reference any separate writing if it is (1) in existence at the time the will is executed and (2) it is sufficiently described and identified.

  - A codicil modifying an original will or an interlineation changing or eliminating a beneficiary requires all the formalities of a will if it creates a new testamentary scheme or adds new beneficiaries, not merely adding to the residue.

  - Alternatives to probate include community property agreements, insurance policies, retirement plans, assets in trust, Pay on Death accounts, joint bank accounts, and property held as joint tenants.

  - Upon D's death, the original will and the death certificate must be submitted to court for probate within 30 days unless the will was destroyed or lost. A copy of the will can then be admitted if there is clear and convincing evidence that the will was not revoked and the court has proof of the proper execution and validity of the will.

  - If a person dies without a will, their heirs will take by intestate succession. In most states, the order of succession is: surviving spouse, issue, parents, siblings, sibling's issue, grandparents, grandparent's issue, and finally the state by escheatment.

I. INTRODUCTION

The subject of trusts may be combined with future interests, wills, and estates. Trust questions typically involve a settlor transferring the legal title of property to a trustee for beneficiaries who hold equitable title to the corpus or res. The MEE may ask for the specific amounts to be properly distributed to each party involved.

> **MEE Tip:** The area of trusts is ripe for various cross-over questions, including property, wills, intestacy, and probate. Look for trust property being willed to different beneficiaries.

II. TYPES OF TRUSTS

A. Express Trusts

Express creation is subject to the statute of frauds (SOF) if the trust is testamentary or the corpus is real estate. Also, if the trust expressly by its terms lasts more than one year, it must be written in most states. The trust instrument may also be called a "trust agreement" or a "deed of trust."

1. Instrument Controls: The specific provisions of the trust instrument usually control where there is a conflict with the statute, but trustees' duties of good faith and fair dealing cannot be waived. The intent of the settlor controls interpretation and is determined by looking at the "four corners" of the document as a whole.

2. Specific Directions: The trustee is usually provided specific, binding directions and powers in the trust instrument. Trust asset management and the trustee's degree of discretion are usually addressed in this document. Distinguish between directions of "hope, request, or wish" (precatory language) and a specific mandate.

3. Beneficiary Accounting Designation Conflict: The instrument may distinguish financially between income and principal also termed corpus or remainder. An example is "current earnings to my spouse for life with remainder to our children." Members of such classes have adverse interests concerning income and expense distributions. Conceptually earnings from corpus goes to the income beneficiary while improvements to corpus go to the remainder interest. Administration expenses are usually equitably allocated. If the trustee makes an improper allocation, there may be liability to the shorted beneficiary.

4. Distribution Decisions:

a. Distribution Discretion: The instrument may give the trustee absolute discretion over whether to make a distribution to the beneficiary. The trustee may also be allowed to "sprinkle" distributions among eligible members of a defined beneficiary class. In some states, the trustee may select a beneficiary from a defined class. Good faith and reasonableness are required.

b. Corpus Invasion: The trustee may also have discretion to invade the trust's corpus upon some occurrence. An example is "my trustee may invade principal if necessary to maintain my spouse's lifestyle and health."

B. Implied Trusts

1. Resulting Trust: Where there has been an unsuccessful but good faith effort to create a trust, a court may effect a resulting trust to satisfy the intent of the grantor.

2. Constructive Trust: A court may effect a constructive trust to repair inequity or to avoid unjust enrichment.

a. Wrongdoing Remedy: When a legal interest in property is obtained through theft, fraud, deception, duress, or breach of fiduciary duty, the wrongdoer becomes a constructive trustee for the properly entitled beneficiary of the property.

b. Secret Trusts: A trustee may have orally promised to hold property for a beneficiary, and failed to do so. For example, Sally's will leaves her property to Tom, who has promised to hold the property for the benefit of Sally's daughter, Sue. If Tom seeks sole legal ownership of the property, Sue may attempt to prove Sally's true intent by clear and convincing extrinsic evidence. The court may impose a constructive trust over the property.

> **MEE Tip:** Implied trusts are popular bar topics. Look for unjust enrichment by a fiduciary that may justify a judicial creation of a constructive trust.

C. Utility Of Entity

Trusts are useful vehicles for at least four purposes.

1. Reduce Estate Taxes: Trusts minimize estate taxes, because assets previously gifted to trust are valued for final estate tax purposes as of the gift date. The appreciation in value between the trust gift estate and the donor's death is not taxed.

2. Living Trust: A living trust effectively transfers assets when the donor dies. This may be preferable to a will if property is held in several states or the will might be contested. An example is parents who convey the title to their personal residence into trust naming both themselves and their children as beneficiaries.

3. Protect Assets: A donor may transfer assets into a trust to to put the property beyond the reach of creditors or the government. "Spendthrift" restrictions on the trust's distribution of assets may further protect the assets from a beneficiary's creditors.

4. Avoid Probate: Assets in trust usually avoid probate administration. When used as a will substitute, trusts maintain privacy and reduce delays in property distribution.

III. REQUIRED TRUST ELEMENTS – SIT – PA

Trusts involve a fiduciary relationship, in which the settler / donor / grantor / trustor intentionally places property into the hands of a trustee to keep or administer for the benefit of ascertainable beneficiaries.

The five required elements in most states are abbreviated by the acronym **SIT – PA** (as in "Sit down, Dad – so we can create a Trust").

MEE Tip: Begin with the statement, "a trust is a fiduciary relationship consisting of a settlor intentionally placing property for the benefit of ascertainable beneficiaries with a trustee."

A. Settlor / Donor / Grantor / Trustor

Settlor, donor, grantor, and trustor are four terms for the same person who establishes the trust – any of them may be used on the exam. Any person or entity who can validly transfer property (18 or older, of sound mind, etc.) can create a trust.

B. Intent to Properly Create

1. Objective Manifestation: This requires an objective manifestation of a present intent to create the trust for the benefit of another. Actual transfer is not necessary if the intent, *res*, and beneficiary are objectively sufficient. The "trustee" may also be the settlor ("I hold 200 Microsoft shares as trustee for my parents"), so no transfer of the shares is necessary.

2. Mere Desire: Contrast a settlor's clear intent with a mere wish to make a gift or create a trust sometime in the future. For example, "$5,000 to my son and I hope he will use it to pay my grandson's medical bills." The son would likely take the $5,000 outright.

3. Impermissible Purpose: The trust purpose cannot be illegal, or require the beneficiary to commit a crime or tort. A purpose that violates public policy is unenforceable, such as divesting a beneficiary's interest upon marriage to a person of a different religion or requiring the taker to divorce. But requiring that the trustee terminate a surviving spouse's interest upon remarriage does not usually violate public policy.

C. Trustee

The trustee is a fiduciary who holds legal title to and management authority over the *res*. Lack of appointment or directions for a method of appointment of a trustee may indicate lack of intent to create a valid trust.

1. Capacity: The trustee must have legal capacity. Corporate trustees, such as banks, are permissible.

2. Appointment: A trust will not usually fail for want of a trustee. A court will appoint a new trustee if the named trustee refuses to serve, resigns, or disclaims.

3. Merger: This occurs if the only trustee is or becomes the sole beneficiary. At least one person besides the trustee must own part of the legal or equitable title to the *res* or the trust fails and terminates.

D. Property / *Res*

The trust must be funded with the settlor's property ("*res*") that presently exists.

1. Specific Identity: Usually a written deed of trust or other document of title is transferred to the trustee. The property must be sufficiently identifiable.

2. Future Interest: To transfer property, the settlor must presently own the property, or must hold a vested future interest in it. Anticipated inheritances and potential future profits are not vested, but rather remain a mere expectancy. An exception is the right to receive life insurance proceeds, which can be the *res* of a trust despite being a future interest.

E. Ascertainable Beneficiaries

A beneficiary must be identifiable or a definite selection method must be indicated.

1. Acceptance Not Required: The beneficiary need not know of the interest.

2. Future Family Beneficiaries: Unborn beneficiaries (e.g., all my "children," "nephews," or "living descendants") are sufficiently susceptible of identification.

3. Class Beneficiaries:

a. Indefinite Class: If too indefinite ("my friends, employees, those of my drinking buddies my trustee shall select," etc.), the trust may fail.

b. Defined Selection: If the trust instrument directs the trustee to select the beneficiaries from a well specified class and the standard for selection is defined ("the best and brightest of our Law School's top scholars"), the trust is enforceable.

c. Remainder Class: A trust with a life estate and a remainder class at the end of a term is generally measured when the remainder class takes, so class members who die before the distribution (and their heirs) do not take.

d. "Surviving Heirs": A trust may be created with a term income beneficiary and heir remainder. "To my sister for five years after my death, then to my surviving children." If two of the four children die during the five years, the deceased children's share goes to their surviving issue, and not third parties that may be designated in their deceased children's wills.

4. Animal Beneficiaries: Some states recognize animals as valid trust beneficiaries, so long as the animals are alive at the time the trust was created. Commonly, the trust terminates upon the death of the last surviving designated animal. Any remaining corpus goes as directed in the instrument, the grantor's will, or according to the intestate scheme.

MEE Tip: If the trust fails **SIT – PA**, discuss a potential resulting or constructive trust. The court will examine all the facts and circumstances to determine whether the settlor showed sufficient creation intent.

IV. TRUST ORGANIZATION FORMATION

A. Promise to Create

A promise to create a future trust is unenforceable unless supported by consideration sufficient to form a contract, e.g., signing a prenuptial agreement, or waiving alimony rights.

B. "Inter Vivos" Trust

Trusts are "inter vivos" (between living people) if the grantor is alive. Inter vivos trusts take effect immediately upon funding. Such trusts become irrevocable upon the grantor's death and the provisions therein control over a will designation to the contrary.

C. "Testamentary" Trust

Trusts created by the grantor's will are "testamentary" trusts, which take effect only upon the death of the grantor. An example is a parent's will provision creating a trust for the benefit of minor children. All **SIT – MA** formalities of wills and **SIT – PA** formalities of trusts are required to create a valid testamentary trust. See Wills, *infra*.

D. Modification / Revocation of Trusts

1. Must Reserve Power: A gift to trust is irrevocable unless the donor specifically reserves the power to revoke, alter, or substitute assets. Explicit revocation power creates a "grantor trust," which is included in the donor's taxable estate.

2. By Agreement: A trust may be terminated if all the beneficiaries agree and it will not defeat a material purpose of the trust.

3. Petition for Judicial Proceeding:

a. Interested Party Required: An "interested party" (personal representative, trustee, living settlor, or beneficiary) may petition the court for a declaration of rights under an estate or trust. Generally, a state's Attorney General may petition on behalf of charitable trust beneficiaries.

b. Notification: All interested parties must be notified of the proceeding and all material facts.

c. Court Action: The court will hear all the evidence, ascertain the intent of the settlor, the effect on creditors or heirs, and direct the trustee to act or to refrain from acting.

4. Non-Judicial Resolution of Dispute: A nonjudicial settlement agreement is valid only to the extent the agreement does not violate a material purpose of a trust. Upon petition by an interested party, the court may approve informal resolutions of trust and estate disagreements. All persons who could have filed a petition to the court can by mediation enter into a written agreement to settle those matters in controversy.

E. Uniform Transfers to Minors Act

States may adopt this statute, which covers irrevocable custodian trusts for the benefit of minors. Property ownership is vested in the minor, but control, management, and investment decisions rest solely with the custodian / trustee, who may be the donor himself. The minor may petition to remove the trustee for cause. Unlike a spendthrift trust, a minor's creditors may usually reach custodial property. A custodian is not personally liable to third parties in contract, unless he fails to reveal the custodial relationship. Torts liability requires personal fault. Custodianship terminates when the minor comes of age and the corpus then goes to the minor.

F. Rule Against Perpetuities (RAP) Compliance – for Both Trusts and Wills

The RAP states that a nonvested property interest is invalid unless, when the interest is created, it is certain to vest or terminate within 21 years after the death of an individual then alive; or the interest must vest or terminate within 90 years after its creation. The RAP is designed to prevent burdensome contingent future interests.

> **MEE Tip:** The only future interests subject to the RAP are executory interests, open class remainders, and contingent remainders. The RAP does not apply to reversions, possibilities of reverter, rights of entry, vested remainders, and charitable trusts. In most states, non-charitable trusts may not be enforced for more than 90 years.

1. Period Begins: The RAP clock begins to run for an inter-vivos trust when corpus is delivered. For testamentary transfers, the clock is triggered by the testator's death.

2. RAP Applied:

    a. Example: "Blackacre into trust for A and her heirs, but if liquor is ever sold on the property, then to B and her heirs." A is the measuring life (person alive at the time the interest is created who can affect vesting). B's contingent remainder is void for violating the RAP because A and B could die and 21 years later liquor could be sold on the property.

    b. Distinguish: The measuring life is the key. "To A and her heirs, but if A ever sells liquor on the property, then to B and her heirs" would not violate the RAP because B's interest will necessarily vest or fail within A's lifetime.

3. Violating Portion: If a RAP violation exists, the court will merely strike that portion of the conveyance (and the related interest) that offends the rule.

4. Result: If the conveyance's conditional wording was "but if," the previous interest gets a fee simple absolute. If the wording was "so long as," the previous interest gets a fee simple determinable and the grantor retains a possibility of reverter.

> **MEE Tip:** Always ask, "Is there any way that the interest might fail or not vest within 21 years of the death of each measuring life?" Note that the RAP doesn't usually apply to charities.

5. Class Gifts: Class gifts that have "remainders subject to open," meaning the class might obtain a new member after the grantor's death, violate the RAP, unless the interest of each class member vests within 21 years of a life in being. An example is "To A and then to A's children who attain 20 years of age." Since A, the measuring life, could have a child more than one year after they take, the RAP would strike down the remainder.

> **MEE Tip:** Class gifts devised to grandchildren are usually valid because the measuring lives are established on the testator's death ("all my grandchildren" or "my daughter's children then alive"). If created in an inter-vivos ("grant" or "conveyance") or to the spouse's children, the chances of a RAP violation increase because after-born children are more likely.

6. Gifts to Charities: The RAP does not apply to trusts in which all vested interests are charitable. But if the interest goes first to a non-charitable interest and the charity's contingent interest is a remainder, the RAP applies. An example is "To Betty so long as used exclusively for farming, then to Land Conservatory." The contingent remainder to Land Conservancy would fail, unless "Betty" is a charity.

7. "Wait and See" Rule: States' RAPs often incorporate the "wait and see" principle, which means that the trust is not invalid upon creation. Rather the operation of the trust continues until the last possible time to see if vesting occurs.

8. "Fertile Septuagenarians" and "Test Tube" Babies: A minority of states acknowledge the possibility of heirs being born more than nine months after the testator's death. More commonly, when a state determines whether a nonvested interest is valid under its RAP, the possibility that a child will be born to an individual after the individual's death is disregarded.

> **MEE Tip:** The above future interest coverage should be sufficient for most trust and estate questions, but see Rigos MBE Volume 1 Property for extensive coverage.

V. TRUSTEE'S RESPONSIBILITIES AND LIABILITY – PIN CALL

The trustee is a fiduciary and subject to any directions and restrictions in the instrument. The acronym **PIN CALL** describes the trustee's basic duties.

A. Properly Administer

The trustee is charged with the responsibility of properly administering the trust assets according to the instruction in the instrument expressing the grantor's intentions.

1. Prudent Business Person Investment Standard: A trustee's standard of care is that which a prudent business person would exercise in managing and safeguarding her own affairs and investments. This is a higher criteria than the "reasonable person" standard.

a. Two Trustees: If there are two co-trustees, they must agree on administrative decisions, or a court must decide the question. On-going irreconcilable hostility between co-trustees substantially impairing the trust administration may be grounds for a court to appoint a new trustee.

b. Three or More Trustees: The majority control administrative decisions. All are potentially liable unless there is a written dissent by the minority trustee(s).

2. Preserve Principal and Diversification: Trustees have a duty to protect the corpus of the trust, which may override the productivity of assets. Assets should be insured. Diversification of the trust portfolio to reduce risk is required unless the settlor specifically directed to the contrary such as retaining all the stock of a closely-held family business. Significant non-routine transactions are subject to special scrutiny.

3. Productivity of Assets and Speculation: Trustees should attempt to maximize the return on principal assets, but should not heavily invest in highly speculative ventures. As return and risk are directly related, either extreme (too little return or too much risk) may violate the required prudent investment standard.

4. Total Asset Management Standard: The trustee shall consider the overall portfolio of assets, including probable income, safety of capital, investment marketability, economic conditions, trust duration, liquidity, taxes, and other assets of the beneficiary(s).

> **MEE Tip:** The prudent business person standard and the fact that this standard is higher than mere "reasonableness" should be mentioned if the facts indicate any trustee investment decision. Note that "prudence" is gauged at the time of the decision, not in hindsight. Look for investments in risky start-up companies, or lack of diversification to reduce overall risk.

B. Inform Beneficiaries

The trustee has a responsibility to keep sufficient detailed records required to inform the beneficiaries of the trust administration. Transactions involving more than 25% of trust assets require notice to the settlor and beneficiaries. The duty to inform beneficiaries may be negated if the settlor specifically directed the trustee to withhold information from the beneficiaries.

C. Not Delegate Decisions

The trustee cannot delegate decisions involving judgment or discretion, including investment decisions (to other than investment experts). Ministerial functions assigned to agents should be supervised and/or periodically reviewed by the trustee.

D. Commingling of Assets Not Allowed

The commingling of separate trusts, and also commingling trust assets with the trustee's personal assets are generally forbidden.

> **MEE Tip:** Commingling of fund assets frequently appears on the bar exam.

E. Account to Beneficiaries

The trustee must deliver to each adult trust beneficiary at least annually a written statement of all receipts and disbursements. Upon request the trustee must also furnish a statement of all the trust's assets. A breach of the trustee's allocation duty may be claimed by a class member of a beneficiary group that was under-allocated income or over-allocated expense.

F. Litigate on Behalf of Trust

The trustee may sue on behalf of the trust, and must defend the trust from legal attack. Jurisdiction and venue lie in the local county court of the "situs" of the trust, the trustee's regular business address or the trustee's residence.

G. Loyalty to Trust – SOB

The trustee's fiduciary duty is the most important responsibility. Breach lies for **SOB**.

1. Self-Dealings: The trustee may not buy, sell, or encumber trust assets, unless expressly allowed by the trust instrument, because the fiduciary duty owed the client and personal interests conflict. Many states extend the self-dealing prohibition to transactions with the trustee's close relations, by blood or marriage.

2. Opportunity of Trust: If the trustee takes an opportunity of the trust, such as acquiring property the trust could have purchased, it is usually a breach of fiduciary duty.

3. Borrowing from the Trust: If the trustee borrows from the trust, or uses the trust assets as collateral for a personal loan, he has breached his fiduciary duty.

> **MEE Tip:** Trustee **PIN CALL** questions are common, especially the fiduciary duty of loyalty. Lawyer trustees are also bound by the ethical rules of professional responsibility.

H. Liability of Trustee

1. Beneficiaries Enforce: Beneficiaries may bring suit to enforce the trust. The grantor may join if she is also a part of the beneficiary group. An order of specific performance, injunction, or assignment of damages are possible remedies.

2. Trustee Removal: A trustee appointed by the settlor may not usually be removed by court order, except for cause. Unfitness, unwillingness to serve, or a **PIN CALL** violation may result in removal for cause. The court may appoint a successor trustee.

3. Prior Trustee, Co-Trustee, and Agents: The trustee is liable for failure to pursue a prior trustee who failed to perform properly. Joint and several liability exists between co-trustees. A trustee may also be held liable for improper delegation of duties, or failure to properly select or supervise a negligent agent.

4. Trustee's Defenses:

a. Instrument Exculpatory Provisions: Courts dislike trust exculpatory clauses, but they may be enforced for mere negligence lacking bad faith. In comparison, if the trustee's breach of trust was intentional, grossly negligent, in bad faith, or in reckless disregard of a beneficiary's interest, related trust exculpatory or hold harmless provisions may be disregarded.

b. Consent: A beneficiary who knowingly consents to (or waives) a trustee's breach of duty may later be estopped from complaining. This is often implicitly applied to beneficiaries who benefited from the wrongful act. Consent by one beneficiary does not preclude a suit by other beneficiaries.

c. Statute of Limitations or Laches: If the beneficiaries failed to timely assert their claims, they may be time barred.

> **MEE Tip:** For any breach of **PIN CALL** duties, be sure to mention possible trustee defenses.

VI. BENEFICIARIES AND CREDITORS' RIGHTS

A. Beneficiaries Ownership Rights

Beneficiaries have absolute ownership interests unless the terms of the trust expressly or implicitly provide to the contrary. This includes the right of transfer if their interest has vested, even if it is a future remainder. Express restrictions may not violate public policy.

1. Transfer Rights: A beneficiary may usually transfer or devise their income and/or principal interest through an inter vivos or testamentary transfer. The transferee enjoys all the rights of the original beneficiary but is subject to any related restrictions.

2. Instrument Alienation Restrictions: In a close case, "no contest," restraints on alienation, or other restrictive conditions are more likely to be allowed in an inter vivos trust than in a will. The condition still may not violate public policy. In comparison, the settlor of the trust may dictate conditions on transfer such as ownership rights in a closely-held business may only be transferred to designated family members.

B. Creditors of Beneficiaries

The trust instrument may protect a beneficiary by specifying that a distribution is not subject to the claims of the beneficiary's creditors. Otherwise, a judgment creditor may place a "charging order" on the trustee, requiring income distributions to be paid to the creditor.

1. Spendthrift Trust: A spendthrift trust prohibits assignment by the beneficiary or attachment of a future distribution by a beneficiary's creditor. A creditor's charging order is ineffective. Exceptions usually honored include monetary claims deriving from necessaries provided to the beneficiary, taxes, or child support. A settlor cannot establish a spendthrift trust to protect property if he is also the beneficiary. A debtor may not transfer assets to a trust to fraudulently hinder, delay, or defraud a creditor.

2. Support Trust: The trustee is obligated to pay for the support of the beneficiary out of trust funds. A valid support trust must be limited to reasonable "necessities," e.g., food, clothing, shelter, and medical expenses.

3. Discretionary Trust: The trustee is given sole discretion to make or withhold distribution, so the beneficiary has no vested interest to be attached by creditors.

4. Exceptions: State statute and/or case law establishes exceptional public policy situations where vendor creditors have access to even a valid spendthrift or discretionary trust.

a. Necessities: Vendor creditors may execute upon a spendthrift trust for debts incurred for life necessities (food, shelter, medical expenses, etc.).

b. Family Support: Income to satisfy the beneficiary's responsibility to minor children can be attached. Most states extend this to alimony obligations due a former spouse.

c. Taxes: Income necessary to satisfy the beneficiary's tax responsibility can usually be attached.

d. Self-Serving Trusts: A settler cannot establish a spendthrift "self-settled asset protection trust" to protect property if the settler is also the beneficiary. This is against public policy. Case law extends this provision to trusts created by another if the consideration for the res was furnished by the beneficiary. A few states (Alaska and Delaware) allow self-settled spendthrift trusts if irrevocable and not created to defraud creditors.

e. Fraudulent Transfers: A debtor may transfer assets to a trust with an intent to hinder, delay, or defraud a creditor's claim. If the transfer occurred after the creditor's claim arose, the trust assets may be recovered by the creditor.

VII. CHARITABLE TRUSTS

A. Registration and Enforcement

Trusts created to benefit the public good must register with a state agency. The state attorney general may bring suit but not an expectant charitable beneficiary.

B. Exempt From RAP

Trusts created to benefit registered not-for-profit charities enjoy certain advantages, including exemption from the Rule against Perpetuities.

C. Cy Pres Doctrine

The court may substitute a similarly purposed charity to effectuate the grantor's intent if the stated purpose of the trust has become impossible, for example if the named charity taker no longer exists. When implementing the cy pres doctrine, the court examines the settlor's intent. If the settlor's charitable intentions were limited to a specifically named charity taker that no longer exists (and not a particular purpose), the gift usually becomes part of the residuary.

VIII. THIRD PARTY LIABILITY

A. Claim Against Trust

Third parties who enter into contracts with the trust or incur damages because of the trust's (or trustee's) torts usually have a claim against the trust. After judgment they may attach assets of the corpus.

B. Claim Against Trustee

1. Contracts: The trustee usually has no personal liability to third parties if the trustee is acting solely as a good faith agent for the trust principal. If this does not apply and the trustee is held liable, indemnification from the trust may be possible.

2. Torts: The trustee is personally liable to third parties for his own torts or the torts of his subordinates if there was a failure to supervise. Failure to obtain insurance for the trust property may be a breach of duty. Only if the tort damage arose from normal trust activities and the trustee was not at fault would indemnification from the trust be proper.

C. Claim Against Beneficiaries

Third parties have no rights against beneficiaries.

D. Third Party Liability to Trust

If a third party knowingly receives trust property for less than full and fair value, the transferee is liable to the trust and beneficiaries for damages. The trustee authorizing the transfer may also be liable if the transfer involved a SOB fiduciary duty breach. Similarly, if a third party dealing with a trust is aware a breach of duty exists, there may be liability to the transferee receiving trust assets.

IX. TRUST TERMINATION

A. Consolidation and Merger

Where there are multiple trusts, multiple trustees, and multiple settlors, but where the trusts have the same purpose and same beneficiaries, the trusts can be consolidated by a court.

B. Term Expiration

The trust instrument may specify a termination date and directions to then distribute or pour-over to another entity such as a probate administration.

C. Purpose Accomplished, Illegal, or Impossible

If the trust purpose has been accomplished, becomes illegal or impossible (such as the sole beneficiary dies without heirs), a court may order termination of the trust.

D. Merger

If all the beneficiaries and the trustee become the same, there is a merger and the trust terminates. This is because the legal and equitable title have merged and there remains no adverse interest.

E. Income Interest Terminates

Under the doctrine of acceleration, the corpus is to be distributed to the remainder beneficiaries if all the income beneficiaries die. In most states, this immediate remainder distribution will also follow an unequivocal disclaimer by the income beneficiary if it appears to the court no one will be harmed by the earlier corpus distribution.

F. Donor Termination

The donor may unilaterally terminate the trust if this right is retained in the instrument.

G. Court Petition

Income and remainder beneficiaries may successfully petition the court to terminate the trust where termination will not defeat any material purpose for which the trust was created. If the settlor and the beneficiaries all agree, a court may order termination even if a material purpose remains and/or the trustee objects.

1. Beneficiaries' Request: All of the income and remainder beneficiaries may petition a court to terminate the trust. If any beneficiary is a minor, a guardian ad litem should be appointed. Such termination will only be granted if the moving party can show it will not defeat any material purpose for which the trust was created. ("*Claflin* doctrine") This is rare because the settlor's purpose is almost always "material."

2. Spendthrift Provision: The traditional view is that a spendthrift provision is a material purpose because distribution would allow a beneficiary's creditor access to the property. The UTC does not contain a presumption in either direction and would require a finding that the trust grantor really intended the spendthrift provision to prohibit premature termination.

3. Settlor and Beneficiaries' Request: If the settlor and the beneficiaries all agree, a court may order termination even if a material purpose remains and/or the trustee objects.

X. WILLS

Most states have adopted the provisions of the Uniform Wills and Probate Code (UPC). Will questions may involve devises to multiple family generations and non-family entities, like ex-spouses, friends, or charities. It is important to keep the actors straight. Preparing a simple stick diagram may help clarify the factual setting of the question.

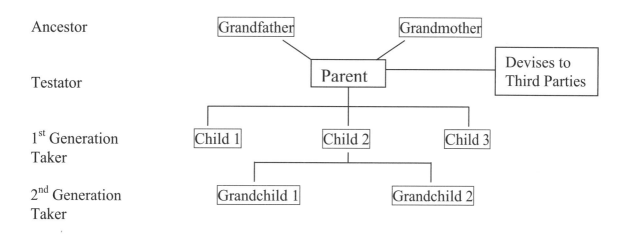

A. Traditional Formal Wills

A last will and testament indicates the decedent's desired allocation scheme for his separate assets and his share of community or tenancy in common property upon his death. To be valid, a will must comply with the law where the testator was domiciled at the time of its execution, or the state where the testator died. Generally, this requires five **SIT – MA** elements (as in "Sit, Ma; let's create a valid Will").

1. Requirements: Testate distribution applies where the decedent executed a will naming beneficiaries to all or part of her estate. A valid will must include:

a. Signed: The testator must, in front of two witnesses, either sign the will, direct another to sign for him, or acknowledge a previously made signature.

b. Intent: The testator must have testamentary intent at the will's execution.

c. Testamentary Age: The testator must be at least 18 years old.

d. Mental Capacity – POT: At execution, the testator must remember and understand her (1) **p**roperty nature and extent, (2) "natural **o**bjects of her bounty," such as the identity of family members, and (3) **t**estamentary effect of executing the devise. Rebuttal of the presumption of mental capacity requires substantial evidence that insane delusion caused an unnatural disposition.

MEE Tip: Many questions give details of testator's forgetfulness and incidents of erratic behavior, suggesting the absence of mental capacity. Watch also for a qualifying lucid moment even though lacking capacity before and after executing the will.

---

e. Attested to: In most states, a will must be properly attested to by two competent witnesses. Under the common law, a witness could not be an "interested party" (a beneficiary or "taker"). Today, a will attested by an interested witness is not necessarily thereby invalidated if there is no evidence of overreaching or undue influence. The witnesses must each see the testator sign the will or hear the testator acknowledge the signature and attest the will by signing their own names to it.

MEE Tip: Begin your essay answer with "a valid will requires a signature by the testator, intent to create, testamentary age, mental capacity, and proper attestation." Then analyze any **SIT – MA** issue that appears to be fairly raised in the facts of the question.

---

2. Court's Equitable Power: There is a presumption that the grantor's intent – however imperfect – should control over intestacy. The court's "dispensing power" may still allow probate admission, despite a small technical deficiency, when the grantor's intent is clear. Extrinsic evidence may be available to explain ambiguous terms and multiple interpretations of a taker's identity.

3. Components of a Will:

a. Integration: Identification of the whole will is best accomplished by having the testator initial each page and refer to the total number of pages at the end.

b. Incorporation by Reference: A will may incorporate a separate document (handwritten or signed by the testator) that describes items and recipients of personal property. The separate writing must be (1) in existence when the will is executed and (2) sufficiently described and identified. Beneficiaries named in the separate document who predecease the testator will not take absent specific language to the contrary. Provisions in the will control over inconsistencies in the separate writing.

4. Interpretation Issues: Where the decedent's language is ambiguous, the court will try to effectuate the grantor's intent by considering extrinsic evidence.

a. Identification of Beneficiaries: Class relative gifts such as "all my children," "the heirs of my body," or "issue of the decedent" are sufficient. Other takers must be specifically identified including "dependent heirs" or "family."

b. Independence Significant: A future taker may be determined under the UPC "by reference to acts and events that have significance apart from their effect upon the dispositions made by the will." Thus a $5,000 devise to the then appointed law school Dean in five years is likely enforceable since the administration and faculty are unlikely to decide their

Dean appointment based upon the $5,000 bequest. Thus the taker's designation has independent significance apart from the $5,000 bequest.

c. After-Acquired Property: All property acquired after execution of a will passes under the will unless the grantor's intent to the contrary is manifestly clear.

d. Doctrine of Worthier Title: Under the common law, the doctrine of worthier title applies where a grantor creates a life estate with remainder to the grantor's heirs. The future interest is treated as a vested reversion. The modern trend is to abolish this rule and give the future interest to the grantor's heirs, determined as of the death of the life estate.

e. Rule in Shelley's Case: The creation of a life estate with a remainder to the heirs of the life estate ("To A and then to his heirs") vests a remainder interest to the life interest's heirs, despite common law to the contrary.

f. Cy Press Doctrine: The court may modify the testator's bequest where the testator's charitable purpose has become impossible, impractical, or wasteful to carry out. Under the "cy pres doctrine,", a charitable bequest to an organization no longer in existence may be given to another charitable organization with a similar purpose.

5. Taker Problems: Until the testator's death, all takers have a mere expectancy.

a. Disinheritance: Evidence of a testator's intent to disinherit his existing spouse and/or children must be clear and convincing. This standard would be met if the non-takers were identified in the will and specifically disowned. Under the UPC and in most states, a clear intent to disinherit in a will operates to deny the heir any full or partial intestate distribution. If the disinherited heir is survived by children, they may still take by representation unless they were also specifically disinherited.

b. Adopted and Half-Blood Children: Adoption generally creates a full parent-child relationship for inheritance purposes. The child loses their intestate inheritance rights from their natural parents, unless the natural parent is the spouse of the adoptive parent. Half-blood siblings (share only one parent) are treated as whole blood.

c. Omitted (Pretermitted) Surviving Children: Surviving children born or adopted after the execution of the will ("post-testamentary" children) qualify for a forced share. This is equal to their share had the decedent died intestate. However, if a testator had living children when his will was executed but did not expressly provide for them, such children do not take a share of his testamentary estate.

d. Born out of Wedlock: For intestate succession only, a child born out of wedlock is entitled to a full share if paternity was established. The father may acknowledge paternity in a signed writing or be so adjudicated in a DNA paternity suit.

e. Divorce and Annulment: Upon divorce, unless a will specifies a different intent, all provisions in the will favoring an ex-spouse (including an executor appointment) are automatically revoked. An exception applies if the bequest specifically survives any divorce. Former spouses named in insurance policies and employee-benefit plans (e.g., federal ERISA) will still take unless the contractual beneficiary designation is changed.

f. Omitted Later Spouse: If the testator's will fails to name a later-married spouse (or a prenuptial contract) to the contrary, a surviving spouse will take half the community or joint property or an intestate share, whichever is higher.

> **MEE Tip:** Omitted children – intentional or inadvertent – divorced spouse, and omitted later-married spouse are frequent on the bar exam.

g. Lapsed Devise: If a devise is specifically conditioned upon the beneficiary surviving the testator and the beneficiary dies first, the devise "lapses" so the property is added to the residue of the estate. However, if the devise is not conditioned upon survival, the deceased beneficiary's descendants (if related to the testator by blood or adoption) may take by representation under an anti-lapse statute. Clear testamentary language that the non-survivors are not to take controls.

h. Disclaimer: A named beneficiary may refuse to accept ("disclaim") a devise. Unless there is an alternative taker specified the property is added to the residue, as if the disclaimant died before ("predeceased") the testator.

i. Class Beneficiaries: Membership in a class is determined as of the testator's death. The class must be sufficiently identifiable, e.g., "my grandchildren," or "my siblings." If too indefinite ("my friends"), the devise may fail. The will may direct the personal representative to select beneficiaries from a well-specified class, for example, "the best and brightest of our Law School's top scholars."

j. "Surviving Heirs": If a will creates a trust with a term income beneficiary remainder such as, "to my sister for five years after my death and then to any surviving children" the issue is whether the remainder class is determined on the date of the settlor's death or on the termination of the five years. The UPC construes the term to mean those surviving as of the date of distribution. The provision would allow the deceased children's share to be distributed to their surviving issue but not third parties such as a charity the deceased children may have designated in their will.

k. Devise to "Issue": "Issue" or "surviving issue" includes potentially all the descendant's blood descendants. This issue is tested when some of the descendant's children predeceased the descendant but they themselves are survived by issue. Do the grandchildren take their deceased parent's share? There are three different possible methods for determining shares of "issue." The method may be specified in the will, but if not, look to the state's intestate statute.

l. Power of Appointment Taxation: The testator may appoint a named person to decide who takes certain property of the decedent. A general power allows the holder to appoint anyone (including themselves) such as, "I leave my gold coins to whomever my daughter sees fit." This is taxed as part of the decedent's estate. A special power restricts the holder to distribute the property to a specified group or class such as, "I leave my gold coins to my twelve grandchildren with my daughter for her to choose who receives which coins." This is not taxed as part of the decedent's estate.

m. Slayers and Abusers: State statutes apply to property that would have passed by will, trust, or intestate succession to a person who was a slayer or an abuser of the decedent. The slayer or abuser is treated as if they had predeceased the decedent.

6. Property Problems:

a. Ademption: When a will specifies a devise of property that was subsequently transferred or destroyed prior to death, the taker takes nothing from the residuum. Under the "replacement property" doctrine, the beneficiary is entitled to receive any real property owned by the testator at death which was acquired as a replacement for the originally devised real property. Similarly the beneficiary may be entitled to the net proceeds from relevant insurance.

b. Accretions: If devised property increases in value between the will creation date and the testator's death, the property beneficiary usually takes the increase not the residuum. Stock splits and dividends go to the taker of the underlying shares and land added from a river movement accretes to the adjoining property.

c. Exoneration: If a specified asset going to a particular devisee becomes subject to a liability before the testator's death, the devisee takes the asset subject to the liability unless the will clearly specifies to the contrary.

d. Satisfaction: The issue is whether an inter vivos transfer should count against a testamentary devise. This is similar to advancement if the donor dies intestate. An example is father left son $50,000 in the will but gifted him $20,000 before death. Under the common law it was rebuttably assumed the $20,000 was a partial satisfaction of the $50,000. Under the UPC, such gifts are not to be treated as a satisfaction unless the donor so stated in writing.

7. Codicils: A codicil is a modification of an existing will, such as crossing out a line ("interlineation") to change or eliminate a devise or beneficiary.

a. New Scheme: If the codicil creates a new testamentary scheme, the instrument requires all the formalities of a will including two witnesses. Crossing out the name of one of three children will result in a larger bequest to each of the other children, so it is to be treated as a new testamentary scheme under many state's case law. But if the interlineation has the effect of merely decreasing the size of one gift by adding to the residue and does not augment specific gifts to specific takers, it will be allowed.

b. Republish by Reference: A codicil referring to an earlier will republishes it, and all directives in the original will (not overruled by the codicil) are reactivated.

> **MEE Tip:** The above codicil problems are often present in the fact pattern of the question. Frequently, the testator crosses out the name of one of the children or in a codicil specifically disowns a prior taker without witnesses. Is it a new testamentary scheme?

8. Revocation: A will may be revoked by being burned, torn, canceled, obliterated or destroyed, with the intention of revocation, by the testator, or by another person at the direction of, and in the presence of, the testator. Two witnesses must attest that destruction by a another person was at the direction of, and in the presence of, the testator. A will is also revoked by the execution of a subsequent will. Loss or accidental destruction is not sufficient and a copy may usually be admitted to probate.

a. Effect on Earlier Wills: Revocation by physical act revives a former instrument only if a revival was the testator's intent, as shown by extrinsic evidence.

b. Codicil Effect: Revocation of the will in its entirety revokes any codicil unless contrary to the grantor's clear intent.

c. Partial Revocation: A will may be partially revoked as long as it increases the residue of the estate. Specific gifts may be taken away (usually by drawing a line through the bequest), but none may be specifically added without **SIT – MA** formalities.

d. Dependent Relative Revocation (DRR): Most states have a DRR saving clause that operates to revive a previous will. The court must conclude the grantor would not have revoked the first will had he known the second will or codicil would fail.

> **MEE Tip:** Remember, changing a will (except revoking specific gifts, thereby increasing the residual) likely requires the testator to go through all the **SIT – MA** formalities.

B. Oral ("Nuncupative") and Handwritten ("Holographic") Wills

Oral ("nuncupative") wills are not valid in many states. In some states, legal enforceable status is allowed to oral personal property devises during the testator's last sickness or armed forces service. A will may be handwritten by the testator ("holographic") or another party, but proper witnessing and execution by the testator is still required.

C. Conditional Wills

If the testator intends that a condition precedent must occur before the will becomes operational, this must be clearly specified in the will document. An example is a will containing "if I do not return from my trip, you will receive..." Unless the conditional wording is such that the condition must occur before the will becomes effective, the failure of the condition to occur is not a defense against subsequent enforceability of the will.

D. Contract to Make a Device

A mere promise to make a future testamentary devise is not usually enforceable absent valuable consideration. An example is "I will leave you all my estate if you care for me for life without other compensation." If there is no other will and the beneficiary can prove the contract by clear and convincing evidence, a court may order recovery. A writing is required in most states.

E. Mutual or Joint Wills

This is a promise to devise in the same manner to certain third parties. This agreement may be done separately or in one joint will in which both parties agree not to revoke. Rescission is possible while both testators are alive but becomes irrevocable as to the survivor upon the death of the first testator.

F. Family Restrictions on Disposition

Family members may have rights superior to the decedent's testamentary scheme.

1. Spouse: The surviving spouse must ultimately end up with at least a minimum of one-half of all community and jointly-owned property. There is also a minimum "forced share" available on motion to the spouse in most states. This often includes a homestead interest in the family residence that is superior to all other interests except a recorded mortgage. A spouse's interest in a pension plan is protected under the federal ERISA laws and cannot be bequeathed to a third party.

> **MEE Tip:** Look for a residence that was the separate property of the deceased spouse or where the surviving spouse is the second wife.

2. Children: Protection for minor children is frequent and a court may create a care and support priority, especially if the surviving spouse parent has also passed. The state may appoint a guardian ad litem, conservator, or temporary fiduciary to protect the interests of minor dependent children during probate. Intestacy and pretermitted child provisions also usually provide protections for children.

3. Past Obligations: An ex-spouse who is bound by support obligations pursuant to a divorce decree cannot avoid the same by re-marrying and naming the new spouse beneficiary in lieu of the children. An example is Dad was required in the divorce to maintain insurance for kids so he could not name new wife as beneficiary to kids' detriment. Divorce decree provisions trump spouse's beneficiary status.

XI. WILL CHALLENGES

Contesting a will or testamentary trust usually requires that a petition be filed within four or six months immediately following the opening of probate. This petition must specify the external validity issue to be litigated. Only parties who would gain if the will was denied probate have standing to contest; grandchildren do not have standing if their parents are living.

A. Grounds To Contest

A successful challenge must be proven by clear and convincing evidence by the contestant and the burden of persuasion is on the contestant. Grounds include the below.

1. Failure to Adhere to SIT – MA Creation Formalities: The will was not in writing, was not signed, not witnessed, testator was not competent or 18 years old, etc.

2. Capacity Absent: Capacity exists if the decedent was able to understand the (1) nature and extent of her property and (2) natural objects of her bounty, including family members. Minor failure to understand every detail of a financial asset or remember remote family members is usually not enough to show lack of testamentary capacity. Similarly mild intoxication does not destroy testamentary capacity.

3. Fraud in the Execution: Misrepresentations were made to the testator as to the nature, content, or character of the physical will. An example is the testator thought he was signing to accept goods but the document was actually a will.

4. Fraud in the Inducement: Willful deceit or duress was imposed that induced the testator to make or change her will. For example, a son wrongly told his mother that his sister had died, causing his mother to delete her daughter from her will, benefiting the son.

5. Undue Influence – LOAF: Undue influence occurs if a vulnerable testator's normal will and decision making has been overcome, resulting in a donative transfer that the testator would not otherwise have made. If a will is the product of undue influence, the court will set it aside, or merely delete the relevant objectionable portion. The burden of establishing undue influence is on the contestant, who may rely upon circumstantial evidence. Contesting a will on the basis of undue influence requires a high showing, but a rebuttable presumption is created by all **LOAF** elements:

a. Large Devise: The beneficiary received an unusually and unnaturally large portion of the estate from what otherwise would have been bequeathed.

b. Opportunity: The benefactor had the opportunity to exert undue influence. The court may consider the circumstances in light of the age or health and mental vigor of the testator, and whether the testator had independent legal representation.

c. Active Participation: The beneficiary actively participated in the preparation or procurement of the suspicious will provision.

d. Fiduciary: The favored beneficiary stood in a fiduciary or confidential relationship with the testator involving special trust and confidence such that over-reaching was possible.

> **MEE Tip:** Will contests are quite frequent on the MEE. See *supra* for further details of required will execution requirements.

B. Dead Man's Statute

Dead Man's statutes prohibit an "interested party" (one who stands to gain or lose in a transaction) from testifying about the decedent's statements concerning the subject. Non-takers may testify, however, and documentary evidence may be introduced.

C. "In Terrorem" Clauses

No contest clauses provide that any beneficiaries contesting a will forfeit their share of the estate. Such clauses are generally enforceable (testator's intent controls) but will not usually operate where the contest is brought in good faith and with probable cause to believe that the will is a forgery or was revoked. The contest may be brought by a fiduciary acting on behalf of a protected person such as a guardian ad litem for a minor or incapacitated person.

D. Previous Will Revived

If the will is overturned, the most recent previous unrevoked will is revived. If there is no valid previous will, the decedent is said to have died intestate.

XII. UNIFORM SIMULTANEOUS DEATH ACT

Where persons die simultaneously who are intestate takers or whose wills name the other person, the heir is assumed to predecease the decedent (by the required 120 hours) unless there is clear evidence to the contrary. The property of each thus passes to their own alternative specified takers, not the heirs of the other. "Death" occurs when all brain function ceases, or when circulatory and respiratory functions irreversibly cease, per accepted medical standards.

XIII. INTESTATE SUCCESSION

Intestate succession is provided for by statute in every state. These rules apply where there is no will, a lapse, disclaimer, or the only will was successfully challenged. In addition, if the will does not cover all the decedent's property and there is no rest and residual provision, the non-specified property may be distributed per the intestate rules. Intestate succession is not favored under most state laws; the court will attempt to interpret extrinsic evidence to save any document which exists and adequately expresses the decedent's intent.

A. Advancement

Under the common law a beneficiary's inter vivos transfer to a beneficiary prior to the decedent's death was counted as an advancement towards their intestate share. The advancement is added to the remaining assets to determine the "hotchpot estate" subject to division among all of the beneficiaries. The new total is allocated according to the state's intestate share rule with the gift amount deducted as an advancement. In comparison, the UPC and many states today presume such a general gift is not to be an advancement against the intestate amount unless specifically stated in writing by the donor at the time of the gift.

B. Marital or Community Property

Under the common law the doctrines of dower and curtesy provided protection for the surviving spouse and children. Most states now have "elective share" statutes that require a minimum amount or percentage of the decedent's property at the time of death must pass within the family. The surviving spouse generally takes all the decedent's half-interest in community or jointly-owned property.

C. Separate Property

Separate property is generally distributed one-third to the surviving spouse and two-thirds to issue (children). Some states recognize a long-term co-habitation "common law marriage." The survivor of a same-sex couple is not a spouse under the intestate statute in most states. Stepchildren take nothing unless formally adopted by the decedent. If no surviving issue, the surviving spouse generally takes three-quarters and one quarter goes to surviving parents or the surviving issue of parents (siblings).

D. Determining Shares for "Issue"

"Issue" includes all blood descendants and is thus a broader group than children. There are three methods of determining the shares that grandchildren (or succeeding generations) take if their parent (decedent's child) predeceased the decedent.

1. Per Stirpes: The property is divided equally at the decedent's children level. For children who predeceased the decedent, their issue all share equally the amount their parents would have taken had they survived. This creates the potential that descendants of equal degree from the decedent will take uneven shares.

2. Per Capita: The division under a per capita scheme – by total head count – is only made at the level of first generation with live takers.

a. Per Capita with Representation: Where there is a deceased generation, the shares are pooled at the first level where there is a live taker (usually children) and the ultimate lower level takers share alike. This method also creates the potential that descendants of equal degree from the decedent will take unequal shares.

b. Per Capita at Each Generation: Again, the shares are pooled at the first level where there is a live taker. But the division at the final generation is equal among all takers, so all descendants of the same degree from the decedent take equal shares.

    3. Example: Assume T had three children, A, B, and C. A has no children, B has one child D, and C has two children, E and F. If C predeceases T, at T's death.

        a. If distribution is per stirpes, A takes one-third, B takes one-third, and E and F take one-sixth each because children split the distribution that went to their parents.

        b. If distribution is per capita, A, B, D, E, and F all take one-fifth each because descendents take equally regardless of their distance from the descendent.

MEE Tip: The states are split between the per stirpes and per capita with representation approaches. If the issue is raised in a question, the facts will likely state the state's statutory division rule.

E. Collateral Relatives

    If no surviving spouse, the issue (children, grandchildren, etc.) take all. If no surviving spouse or issue, look to collateral relatives. Any surviving parent(s) take all. Thereafter, the usual distribution scheme is to siblings (brothers and sisters – natural or adopted – and half-bloods are treated as whole bloods under the UPC), grandparents, aunts, uncles and first cousins. To determine the degree of relationship between the decedent and distant relatives, count the number of people up to a common ancestor and back down the family chain; the relative with the lowest number of people from the decedent takes.

F. Escheatment

    Collateral heirs beyond first or second cousins are not qualified intestate takers in most states. If no taker, the estate's property escheats to the state. A small exception applies if the decedent previously inherited property from a deceased spouse who has other children surviving; such property will pass to the deceased spouse's children (the stepchildren of the decedent) to avoid escheatment.

MEE Tip: The intestate succession rules are heavily tested on the bar exam. If the will is arguably ineffective and no previous will exists, always discuss the above statutory intestate scheme. If there are any children, collateral kin do not take.

XIV. RELATED DOCUMENTS

A. Power of Attorney

    1. Introduction: A durable power of attorney is an authorization of the principal to an agent to operate on their behalf if they later become disabled or incapacitated.

    2. Creation: The instrument creating the power must be in writing, using wording showing the grantor intends the authority to continue during disability or incapacity. Most states allow the wording "this power of attorney shall become effective upon the disability of the principal" or if continuing "this power of attorney shall not be affected by disability of the principal." Physician concurrence may be required. The principal's most recent nomination controls.

3. Scope: The instrument may itself dictate certain authority. If the designation authorizes "all the principal's powers of absolute ownership" or "all the powers the principal would have if alive and competent," the scope is all decisions about financial and legal matters. In most states such wording includes the right to convey the principal's assets. It is also usual to include health care decisions.

4. Excluded Powers: Certain economic powers must be specified in the document to be valid. This includes the power to make or amend life insurance contracts, the power to make wills, to make donative transfers, trust activities, or disclaim property.

B. Medical Powers

1. Health Care Directive: This durable power of attorney authorizes an agent to make medical decisions for an incapacitated principal. This may include the decision to withhold or withdraw life-sustaining treatment. There is no liability for wrongful death if the agent was acting in good faith under a valid durable health care power of attorney.

2. Living Will: A living will or directive to physician directs medical attendants to withhold life-extending procedures and life-sustaining maintenance if there is no reasonable hope of recovery in a terminal situation. Absent such a directive, physicians are ethically bound to continue life-support procedures even to a comatose patient with no hope of improvement.

C. Organ Donation Directives

The testator may will her organs and other body parts to a medical institution and/or for transplantation. This is usually accomplished by a special document referring to the institution and organs gifted.

XV. PROBATE PROCEEDINGS

Probate is a court-supervised process which establishes the rights of the beneficiaries, protects creditors, and ensures no beneficiary will have claims asserted against the assets they receive from an estate.

A. Jurisdiction and Venue

1. Original Jurisdiction: Probate of the will is in the jurisdiction where the decedent was domiciled at the time of death.

2. Ancillary Administration: State courts have jurisdiction over assets physically located in their state. There may be an original jurisdiction probate being conducted in another state. There may be some local dispute involving an asset in the estate such as the title to land which must be litigated locally. The two legal proceedings are separate.

3. Matters Covered: Probate courts have jurisdiction over the appointment or discharge of personal representatives (PRs), conservators, and guardians and will contests. Also included is the determination of heirship, title, rights in property, and the construction, administration and distribution of assets.

4. Court Determinations: Formal probate proceedings involve court hearings to determine whether: (1) to sell, lease, or mortgage assets; (2) to continue decedent's business; (3) to grant authority for partial/interim distributions; and (4) for approval of final reporting, accounting, and final decree of distribution,

B. Alternatives to Probate

Certain property is not subject to formal probate administration. This may reduce some of the costs of transferring the assets. The disadvantage is that creditor's claims against the non-probate assets may not be extinguished and may later be asserted against the possessor.

1. Community Property Agreements: In a number of states these written agreements apply if they contain three provisions: (1) that everything we own is community property; (2) everything we acquire will be community property; and (3) when I die, all community property goes to surviving spouse. Property passing to a surviving spouse pursuant to a community property agreement passes outside of probate. If there is no community property agreement, 100% of the community property becomes subject to probate administration. 100% of community property receives a stepped-up basis for tax purposes (fair market value) even though one-half may pass to other than the surviving spouse.

2. Insurance Policies and Pension Plans: A life insurance policy is a will substitute. Formal probate proceedings may be avoided for life insurance and employment pension proceeds, unless the contract names the estate itself as a beneficiary.

3. Joint Tenancies: A joint tenancy with right of survivorship avoids probate by vesting the subject property in the joint tenant, not the estate. Joint bank accounts may specify that surviving depositor(s) take the balance in equal shares, or that the funds belong to each proportionate to their deposits.

4. Pay-on-Death Accounts: The balance at death goes directly to the named beneficiary outside of probate. The advantage to this "Totten trust" arrangement is that, unlike a joint account, the prospective beneficiaries cannot withdraw funds prior to the testator's death.

5. Trust Res: A properly formed inter vivos trust removes the transferred property from the decedent's estate. This includes "living trusts" where both the beneficiary and the donor are beneficiaries; on the death of the donor, the remaining beneficiary takes outside probate.

a. Advantages: There is no need to file inventory with the court, giving greater privacy regarding assets and distribution.

b. Disadvantages: If assets change frequently, the trust must be modified often. There is also no four or six-month limitation on creditor claims.

6. "Pour-Over Wills": This type of will sends all assets at death into a trust created concurrently with or prior to the execution of the will.

C. Procedure

1. Personal Representative (PR): Probate estates are administered by a PR.

a. Designated or Appointed: The court appoints a PR, giving preference first to the executor named in the will, then the surviving spouse (or the spouse's nominee), then nearest kin (or that person's nominee). If a decedent has no named executor, spouse, or kin, the court may select a professional PR.

b. Fiduciary Role: The PR is a fiduciary, must be bonded, and must exercise reasonable care in fulfilling his duties. The PR is entitled to reasonable compensation from the assets in the probate estate.

2. Admission to Probate: Any interested person may petition the court for the appointment of a PR and for the probate of a will.

a. Petition Contents: A petition should specify whether the decedent had a will, the identity of would-be heirs or devisees, and that reasonable efforts have been made to locate them. An estimate of the estate's assets must be included.

b. Will Contest Disclosure: The petition should also state whether a will is being contested, and the values and nature of the estate's assets. The original will, or an authenticated copy if the original is unavailable, should be submitted to the court.

c. Lost or Destroyed Wills: Many states have a procedure that apples if the document cannot be located, but there is clear, cogent and convincing evidence of its existence and that it was not revoked. The court may take proof of the execution and validity of the will. Notice must be given to all persons interested in the will. The witnesses' testimony concerning the will's contents or the authenticity of a copy of the will must be reduced to writing. Examples on the exam have included the introduction of a photocopy and where the will was stolen as a part of the contents of a safe deposit box theft.

d. Non-Intervening Powers: Solvent estates may apply for non-intervention powers so the PR can conduct estate business without court intervention. A bond is required unless the will provides to the contrary.

3. Creditors:

a. Notice and Claim: The PR must publish a notice to interested persons for three consecutive weeks in a local newspaper. The notice must identify the decedent, the probate court, the PR's contact information, and must state that claims against the estate must be presented within four or six months of the first publication.

b. Claim Approval and Rejection: In most states claims under $1,000 are deemed allowed if not rejected within 6 months. Claims over $1,000 must be allowed or rejected. After 30 days, a claimant may notify the PR that he will petition the court to have the claim allowed. If the PR fails to respond within 20 days, the claimant may note the matter up for a hearing. If the claim is rejected, the claimant must bring suit within 30 days. If the claim is substantially allowed, the court may assess the estate reasonable attorney fees.

c. PR Personal Liability: A PR who fails to pay a known creditor becomes personally liable unless the non-payment was "without fault on his part." Also, a PR who pays an estate debt or makes a distribution without retaining sufficient assets to pay estate taxes becomes personally liable. Liability does not apply to costs of administering the probate, funeral, and last illness expenses, or any court-ordered family maintenance.

D. Traditional Administration Functions

The PR's administrative duties are to collect estate assets / debts, and make interim distributions to beneficiaries or run the estate's business. The PR is held to a "prudent person" standard in investment decisions, as if dealing with their own property. The PR has authority to sell property at public or private sales and execute deeds to real property.

MEE Tip: The PR is held to the fiduciary standard usually applicable to a trustee of a trust.

E. Insolvent Estate Priority

The priority of estate asset distribution in probate is as follows:

1. Costs of Administration: PR, accounting, and legal expenses all qualify.

2. Funeral and Last Illness Expenses: Such costs must be reasonable.

3. Family Maintenance: A probate court may grant a family allowance to a surviving spouse for living purposes and/or child support pending the final distribution and closing of the estate.

4. Taxes: In addition to federal estate taxes, the states take their share. States likely to assert taxation power potentially include the decedent's state of residence and any state where real property of the estate is located.

5. Judgment Debts: Judgments docketed against the deceased all qualify.

6. Unsecured Debts: This includes all other debts or obligations of the decedent.

7. Beneficiaries: If there is anything left in the estate, beneficiaries take in the following order: specific asset gifts, cash or demonstrative legacies, residuary gifts, intestate succession, and escheatment to the State.

F. Abatement

Priority of bequests becomes important when an estate has fewer assets than the decedent devised. The short-fall is controlled by the state Abatement of Assets statute. Such statutes will typically abate (reduce or eliminate) both real and personal property in the following order: (1) intestate property; (2) residuary gifts; (3) general gifts of money; and (4) specific gifts of non-monetary assets.

G. Taxation

A federal estate tax return must be filed within nine months of death, and the state also requires its own filing. State inheritance tax paid is allowed as a deduction on the federal return. If not specified in the will, estate taxes are apportioned by the value received by each person as to the value of the total estate. Charities are generally excluded from any tax apportionment, as the estate is allowed a deduction for charitable testamentary gifts.

RIGOS BAR REVIEW SERIES

UNIFORM MULTISTATE ESSAY EXAM (MEE) REVIEW

CHAPTER 5

TRUSTS, WILLS, AND ESTATES

Magic Memory Outlines®

I.   INTRODUCTION

II.   TYPES OF TRUSTS
   A. Express Trusts ....
      1. Instrument Controls ....
      2. Specific Directions ....
      3. Accounting Designation ....
      4. Distribution Decisions ....
         a. Distribution Discretion ....
         b. Corpus Invasion ....
   B. Implied Trusts ....
      1. Resulting Trust ....
      2. Constructive Trust ....
         a. Wrongdoing Remedy ....
         b. Secret Trusts ....
   C. Utility of Entity ....
      1. Reduce Estate Taxes ....
      2. Living Trust ....
      3. Protect Assets ....
      4. Avoid Probate ....

III. REQUIRED TRUST ELEMENTS – SIT – PA
   A. **S**ettlor / Donor / Grantor / Trustor ....
   B. **I**ntent to Properly Create ....
      1. Objective Manifestation ....
      2. Mere Desire ....
      3. Impermissible Purpose ....
   C. **T**rustee ....
      1. Capacity ....
      2. Appointment ....
      3. Merger ....
   D. **P**roperty / Res ....
      1. Specific Identity ....
      2. Future Interest ....
   E. **A**scertainable Beneficiaries ....
      1. Acceptance Not Required ....
      2. Future Family Beneficiaries ....
      3. Class Beneficiaries ....
         a. Indefinite Class ....
         b. Defined Selection ....

       c.   Remainder Class ....

       d.   "Surviving Heirs" ....

    4. Animal Beneficiaries ....

IV.   TRUST ORGANIZATION FORMATION

   A. Promise to Create ....

   B. "Inter Vivos" Trust ....

   C. "Testamentary" Trust ....

   D. Modification/Revocation of Trusts ....

    1. Must Reserve Power...

    2. By Agreement..

    3. Petition for Judicial Proceeding..

       a.   Interested Party Required ....

       b.   Notification Required ....

       c.   Court Action ....

    4. Non-Judicial Resolution of Disputes...

   E. Uniform Transfers to Minors Act ....

   F. Rule Against Perpetuities (RAP) Compliance...

    1. Period Begins...

    2. RAP Applied ....

       a.   Example ....

       b.   Distinguish...

    3. Violating Portion ....

    4. Result...

    5. Class Gifts ....

    6. Gifts to Charities..

    7. "Wait and See" Rule..

    8. "Fertile Septuagenarians" and "Test Tube" Babies ....

V.   TRUSTEE'S RESPONSIBILITIES AND LIABILITY – PIN CALL

   A. **P**roperly Administer ....

    1. Prudent Business Person Investment Standard...

       a.   Two Trustees ....

       b.   Three or More Trustees ....

    2. Preserve Principal and Diversification ....

    3. Productivity of Assets and Speculation ....

    4. Total Asset Management Standard..

   B. **I**nform Beneficiaries..

   C. **N**ot Delegate Decisions ....

   D. **C**ommingling of Assets Not Allowed ....

   E. **A**ccount to Beneficiaries ....

   F. **L**itigate on Behalf of Trust ....

   G. Loyalty to Trust – **SOB**..

    1. **S**elf-Dealings ....

    2. **O**pportunity of Trust..

    3. **B**orrowing from the Trust..

   H. Liability of Trustee ....

    1. Beneficiaries Enforce ....

    2. Trustee Removal...

    3. Prior Trustee, Co-Trustee, and Agents ....

       4. Trustee's Defenses ....
          a. Instrument Exculpatory Provisions ....
          b. Consent ....
          c. Statute of Limitation or Laches ....

VI.   BENEFICIARIES AND CREDITORS' RIGHTS

   A. Beneficiary Ownership Rights ....
       1. Transfer Rights ....
       2. Instrument Alienation Restrictions ....
   B. Creditors of Beneficiaries ....
       1. Spendthrift Trust ....
       2. Support Trust ....
       3. Discretionary Trust ....
       4. Exceptions ....
          a. Necessity ....
          b. Family Support ....
          c. Taxes ....
          d. Self-Serving Trusts ....
          e. Fraudulent Transfers ....

VII. CHARITABLE TRUSTS

   A. Registration and Enforcement ....
   B. Exempt from RAP ....
   C. Cy Pres Doctrine ....

VIII. THIRD PARTY LIABILITY

   A. Claim Against Trust ....
   B. Claims Against Trustee ....
       1. Contracts ....
       2. Torts ....
   C. Claim Against Beneficiary ....
   D. Third Party Liability to Trust ....

IX.   TRUST TERMINATION

   A. Consolidation and Merger ....
   B. Term Expiration ....
   C. Purpose Accomplished, Illegal, or Impossible ....
   D. Merger ....
   E. Income Interest Terminates ....
   F. Donor Termination ....
   G. Court Petition ....
       1. Beneficiaries' Request ....
       2. Spendthrift Provision ....
       3. Settlor and Beneficiaries' Request ....

X. WILLS

A. Traditional Formal Wills ....

    1. Requirements – **SIT – MA** ....

       a. **S**igned ....

       b. **I**ntent..

       c. **T**estamentary Age ....

       d. **M**ental Capacity – **POT** ....

       e. **A**ttested to ....

    2. Court's Equitable Power...

    3. Components of a Will ....

       a. Integration..

       b. Incorporation by Reference ....

    4. Interpretation Issues...

       a. Identification of Beneficiaries ....

       b. Independent Significance ....

       c. After-Acquired Property...

       d. Doctrine of Worthier Title ....

       e. Rule in Shelley's Case ....

       f. Cy Pres Doctrine ....

    5. Taker Problems...

       a. Disinheritance..

       b. Adopted and Half-Blood Children ....

       c. Omitted (Pretermitted) Surviving Children ....

       d. Born out of Wedlock ....

       e. Divorce and Annulment ....

       f. Omitted Later Spouse ....

       g. Lapsed Devise ....

       h. Disclaimer..

       i. Class Beneficiaries ....

       j. "Surviving Heirs" ....

       k. Devise to "Issue" ....

       l. Power of Appointment Taxation ....

       m. Slayers and Abusers ....

    6. Property Problems ....

       a. Ademption ....

       b. Accession...

       c. Exoneration..

       d. Satisfaction ....

    7. Codicils...

       a. New Scheme...

       b. Republish by Reference ....

    8. Revocation ....

       a. Effect on Earlier Wills..

       b. Codicil Effect...

       c. Partial Revocation ....

       d. Dependent Relative Revocation (DRR) ....

B. Oral ("Noncupative") and Handwritten ("Holographic") Wills...............................

C. Conditional Wills..

D. Contract to Make a Devise ....

E. Mutual or Joint Wills...

F. Family Restrictions on Disposition ....
    1. Spouse...
    2. Children ....
    3. Past Obligations ....

XI. **WILL CHALLENGES**
    A. Grounds To Contest..
        1. Failure to Adhere to **SIT – MA** Creation Formalities ....
        2. Capacity Absent..
        3. Fraud in the Execution..
        4. Fraud in the Inducement ....
        5. Undue Influence – **LOAF** ....
            a. **L**arge Devise...
            b. **O**pportunity...
            c. **A**ctive Participation ....
            d. **F**iduciary...
    B. Dead Man's Statute...
    C. "In Terrorem" Clauses ....
    D. Previous Will Revived ....

XII. **UNIFORM SIMULTANEOUS DEATH ACT**

XIII. **INTESTATE SUCCESSION**
    A. Advancement ....
    B. Marital or Community Property ....
    C. Separate Property..
    D. Determining Shares for "Issue" ....
        1. Per Stirpes..
        2. Per Capita..
            a. Per Capita with Representation ....
            b. Per Capita at Each Generation ....
    E. Collateral Relatives...
    F. Escheatment..

XIV. **RELATED DOCUMENTS**
    A. Power of Attorney...
        1. Introduction...
        2. Creation...
        3. Scope...
        4. Excluded Powers ....
    B. Medical Powers ....
        1. Health Care Directive ....
        2. Living Will...
    C. Organ Donation Directives ....

XV. PROBATE PROCEEDINGS

 A. Jurisdiction and Venue ....
  1. Original Jurisdiction ....
  2. Ancillary Administration ....
  3. Matters Covered ....
  4. Court Determinations ....
 B. Alternatives to Probate ....
  1. Insurance Policies and Pension Plans ....
  2. Joint Tenancies ....
  3. Pay-on-Death Accounts ....
  4. Trust Res ....
   a. Advantages ....
   b. Disadvantages ....
  5. Pour-Over Wills ....
 C. Procedure ....
  1. Personal Representative (PR) ....
   a. Designated or Appointed ....
   b. Fiduciary Role ....
  2. Admission to Probate ....
   a. Petition Contents ....
   b. Will Contest Disclosure ....
   c. Lost or Destroyed Wills ....
   d. Non-Intervention Powers ....
  3. Creditors ....
   a. Notice and Claim ....
   b. Claim Approval and Rejection ....
   c. PR Personal Liability ....
 D. Traditional Administration Functions ....
 E. Insolvent Estate Priority ....
  1. Costs of Administration ....
  2. Funeral and Last Illness Expenses ....
  3. Family Maintenance ....
  4. Taxes ....
  5. Judgment Debts ....
  6. Unsecured Debts ....
  7. Beneficiaries ....
 F. Abatement ....
 G. Taxation ....

RIGOS BAR REVIEW SERIES

UNIFORM MULTISTATE ESSAY EXAM (MEE) REVIEW

CHAPTER 5

TRUSTS, WILLS, and ESTATES

Essay Questions

Question Number 1

Sally Settlor was a widow with one daughter, Doris.

In 2000, Sally signed a document giving "my home to my brother Honest Henry to hold in trust for my use and at my death to my daughter if and when she marries. I also give Henry $100,000 cash to be invested for the benefit of the person who cares for me the most in the autumn of my years."

In 2005, Sally properly executed a will leaving her estate to brother Honest Henry to "hold one-half for the benefit of my daughter Doris and Henry may disburse principal and interest on her behalf as he sees fit. The other half of my estate shall be placed in a bank account for the care and support of my nephew David Drugey for life since he has failed at numerous drug treatment rehabilitation efforts. This portion of my estate shall not be subject to judgment or execution by David's creditors and he may not transfer any interest."

In 2006, Sally died. In 2007, David purchased a Harley Davidson motorcycle. He then fell into a bad biker crowd and began using drugs again. He negligently caused a serious automobile accident injuring a pedestrian. He also got behind in paying his rent and alimony to his ex-wife. All three claims against him were reduced to judgment and execution has begun.

1. Did Sally create a valid trust in 2000?

2. Did Sally create a valid will in 2005?

3. Do the accident tort victim, ex-wife, and/or the landlord have collection rights against the trust's bank account under the control of brother Honest Henry for the satisfaction of David's responsibilities?

Question Number 2

Alice had two adult daughters, Betty and Carol, who were distrustful of the influence each could exert over their mother. They pressured her into creating a revocable living trust document with her son David, a CPA-realtor, as trustee. The trust assets are to be distributed one-third to each child upon Alice's death. The trust gives David full management authority. The $9 million trust originally consisted of $2 million in commercial real estate, $3 million in stocks and bonds, and $4 million in negotiable instruments, with trust net income of $200,000 per year.

Twelve months after the trust was created, David transferred the proceeds of the negotiable instruments at maturity to First Bank, where David conducts his personal business, since that would be more convenient for him. Twenty-three months later, David sold the real estate for $3,000,000. Since no realtor was involved, David charged the trust a reduced real estate commission of three percent ($90,000), in addition to his regular agreed CPA trustee's fee of one percent per year of the value of the trust assets.

Part of the proceeds of the real estate sale were used to buy two houses of equal value, one in the name of each daughter. The remaining sales proceeds were used to buy stock in a three-year-old start-up "high tech" company, High Flyer, Inc., which does not pay dividends. Shortly thereafter, First Bank could not pay its obligations and went into receivership. The trust income is now $200,000 per year.

Carol pledged her interest in the trust as collateral for a $150,000 loan at Second Bank. Shortly thereafter, she defaulted on her loan payments and the bank made demand on Alice. Upon learning of this and her reduced income, Alice demanded David to return the assets to her, and David refused.

1. Were there any potential deficiencies in the trust creation?

2. Were the enumerated transactions proper? Discuss.

3. Was David's performance as trustee proper? Discuss.

4. Would Alice's demand for return of assets be enforced by a court?

Question Number 3

Frank was a single person who lived with his son, Sonny. In 2000, Frank signed a living trust agreement with himself as settlor, trustee, and income beneficiary, and conveyed Greenacre to the trust. Frank's signature on the trust was not witnessed. The trust provided that during his life he would receive all the income and that upon Frank's death, the trust was irrevocable and "distributable equally to Frank's children." The trust did not name a successor trustee.

In 2003, Frank married Wanda, moved out of Sonny's house, and they relocated from New York to Boston. Frank left the records of his living trust with Sonny in New York because Greenacre, the sole trust asset, was located there.

In 2004, George was born to Frank and Wanda. In 2006, Frank died intestate survived by Wanda, Sonny, and George. Frank's probate estate included all jointly owned property with

Wanda except Greenacre, which was Frank's separate property. Wanda was appointed personal representative of Frank's probate estate. Sonny petitioned the Superior Court for his appointment as successor trustee of Frank's living trust.

Wanda filed the following objections in response to Sonny's petition for this appointment as successor trustee: (1) Sonny has no statutory right to be a successor trustee; (2) Wanda should be appointed successor trustee because she is Frank's surviving spouse; (3) the trust agreement is void because it was not properly witnessed; (4) the trust agreement was also void because the trustor, trustee, and income beneficiary were one and the same person; (5) the assets of the trust should be distributed to Wanda as an omitted spouse; and (6) the venue for the trust should be changed to Boston.

1. Who should receive assets of the trust and Greenacre, and in what percentages?

2. How should the court rule upon Wanda's claims and objections?

Question Number 4

Adrian and Betty were a married couple with two children.

In 2000, Adrian passed away leaving a will giving Betty a small fortune with a direction "I hope you take care of the kids." Betty was then 68 and her two children lived in a distant city, so she shared her grief and loneliness with a local pastor at her local place of worship.

The pastor's wife passed away the next year and in 2001 the relationship between Betty and the pastor turned personal and serious. In 2002, Betty and the pastor were married and both of Betty's children told their mother they disapproved of the marriage.

In 2003, at the urging of the pastor, Betty decided to change her dispositive scheme. In the new will, Betty left all her assets 50% to the pastor and 50% to the pastor's church and "not my two children." The pastor told Betty this dispositive scheme would increase the chances she would enter the after life. The pastor and two other non-related church members signed the will as witnesses. Betty executed the will after declaring the document to be her final will and asking those present to witness her signature. The physical execution complied with state law. Betty did not tell her two children about the new will.

Betty developed Alzheimer's in 2004 and passed away in 2007. During the last two years of her life she completely lost her memory about her assets and could not identity her two children and four grandchildren.

Pastor submitted the 2003 will for probate. Betty's two children and four grandchildren timely filed a will contest action.

1. Do all six of Betty's children and grandchildren have standing to contest the will?

2. Does the Pastor witnessing the will invalidate the execution?

3. What theories will the will contest be based upon and what is the likely outcome?

Question Number 5

In 2001, Harry and Wanda were aging and their two children suggested they both agree on an estate distribution plan. Harry and Wanda agreed between themselves to execute parallel wills in a writing that stated "We both agree that the survivor takes all our separate and jointly owned assets. Upon the death of the survivor, the assets shall go one-half to our two children and one-half to a charity to be named in a document that we shall deliver to our attorney next year providing the charity raises an equivalent amount from other donors."

Three weeks later, they signed joint wills prepared by their attorney in accordance with their agreement. One year later, they identified the charity donee as the "Red Cross for use in preventing AIDS and treatment in Africa" in writing.

In 2003, Harry died and his estate valued at $300,000 was distributed in full to Wanda. In 2005, Wanda developed a romantic relationship with a veterinarian who headed up the local chapter of the Society for Prevention of Cruelty to Animals.

In 2006, Wanda exercised a new will leaving the new gold coin collection she had just purchased for $100,000 to her sister, $100,000 to "my heirs," and the balance of my estate to go to the Society for Prevention of Cruelty to Animals.

In 2007, the Executive Committee of the Red Cross decided their prior involvement in AIDS prevention outside the U.S. was ineffective under their management. They thus transferred all their Africa operations and related fund balances to the Gates Foundation.

In 2008, Wanda passed leaving an estate containing $500,000 in total value including the gold coins which were then worth $90,000. Both the Red Cross and Gates Foundation claim the charitable assets if they are not distributed to the Society for Prevention of Cruelty to Animals.

Discuss the issues determining to whom and in what amounts should Wanda's estate be distributed.

Essay Answers

Answer Number 1

Summary

To create a valid trust, a settlor must intentionally place property with a trustee for the benefit of ascertainable beneficiaries. Here the trust involves real property, so a written signed deed with a legal description may be required. The RAP may cause the trust to fail if S's daughter is not married when S dies, as marriage is a condition of the trust and there is no alternative provision if that never happens. The trigger of S's death does not violate the RAP since she is a life in being. There is a clear method of selection for the beneficiary. A valid will with a testamentary trust requires formal elements, which are met for Doris' trust. Trustees' discretionary decisions ("as he sees fit") must be exercised in good faith. The spendthrift trust will likely shield trust assets from the tort claims, but not family support obligations or rent.

Issues Raised

(1)   Trust Validity
  (a) Settlor intentionally placing property with a trustee
  (b) Trust is intended to benefit ascertainable beneficiaries.
(2)   Rule Against Perpetuities
  (a) Future interest must vest during the life of a person in being plus 21 years
  (b) Wait and See rule:
    (i) Trust is not invalidated until the last possible time
    (ii) Rule applied by most states
(3)   Trustee Discretion
(4)   2005 Will Testamentary Trust Validity Requirements
  (a) Signed by the decedent
  (b) Intent to create
  (c) Testamentary age (over 18)
  (c) Mental capacity
  (d) Attested to properly
(5)   Spendthrift Trust Invasion
  (a) Protects funds from beneficiary's creditors
  (b) Exceptions for family entity support obligations

(1)   2000 Trust Validity. To create a valid trust there must be a settlor intentionally placing property with a trustee for the benefit of ascertainable beneficiaries. Here all the above trust requirements seem to be met except the existing property rule may be violated. "My home" involves real property and statutes in most states require a written conveyancing document – usually a deed – signed by the settlor with a proper legal description of the property. While some states may allow "my home" to sufficiently identify the property, the legal description omission is fatal in most states.

(2)   Rule Against Perpetuities. The RAP requires that a future interest must vest, if at all, during the life of a person in being plus 21 years. Under the "wait and see" rule in most states the trust is not invalid upon creation but rather the operation of the trust continues until the last possible time under state law. If at Sally's death her daughter is not married, the trust will fail because marriage by that time is a condition of the trust and there is no alternative provision for where this trust property would go other than reverting to the settlor.

(3)   Trustee Discretion. The $100,000 cash portion of the trust appears valid. The property is existing and the testator's death does not violate the RAP since the settlor is a life in being. The "person who cares for me the most" is unnamed, but the beneficiary is ascertainable because there is a definite method of selection indicated and the designated class is limited. The trustee Henry will decide this person under his good faith duty to perform as a trustee. This is a permissible grant of discretion as there is a defined standard to guide the discretion.

(4)   2005 Will Testamentary Trust Validity. A valid will containing a testamentary trust requires testamentary age (over 18), intent to create, mental capacity, properly attested to, and signed by the decedent. All those requirements seem to be met for the one-half of Sally's estate placed into the testamentary trust for the benefit of her daughter Doris. The directive "as he sees fit" seems to lack an express limit, but such discretionary decisions are governed by the "good faith" standard imposed on trustees.

(5)   Spendthrift Trust Invasion. The one-half of the estate placed in the spendthrift trust for nephew David appears to be proper. The testator intended the trust to be spendthrift and not subject to judgment or execution by the beneficiary David's creditors. This will likely shield the trust assets from the claims of the pedestrian victim. However, most states have exceptions that apply to family entity support obligations such as alimony. The execution on the rent obligation is uncertain since if this entity is construed under state law as a support trust, a rent obligation is usually considered to be a support expenditure and thus subject to execution.

Answer Number 2

Summary

Undue influence is taking advantage of another's vulnerable position to influence a decision they would not otherwise have made. If undue influence is found, the court will terminate the trust. A is the sole beneficiary for her life; upon her death the remainder of the trust assets will go to residual beneficiaries with an expectancy interest (B, C, and D). A trustee's performance is judged under the "total asset management" approach, not asset-by-asset. Trustee D owes beneficiaries a fiduciary duty and must manage the assets under the "Prudent Person Standard." Real estate must be sold on the open market, or must be appraised, which D did not do. The beneficiaries have a cause of action against D for breach of trust. Since A has retained the power to revoke, the homes should be in the name of the trust, not B and C's names. C cannot pledge as security an expectancy interest that may never vest.

Issues Raised

(1)   Trust Creation Undue Influence
      (a) Taking advantage of vulnerable position to influence decision
      (b) Without the influence, person would not have made the decision
      (c) Beneficiaries
(2)   Total Asset Management Standard
(3)   Fiduciary Duty
      (a) Negotiable Instruments
      (b) Sale of Real Estate
      (c) Homes for Daughters
      (d) Pledge of Trust Interest
(4)   Revocable at Will

Sample Answer

(1)   Undue Influence. Depending on other circumstances including Alice's mental and physical health, undue influence can result when a person takes advantage of another's vulnerable position to influence her decision.

(a) Presumption. An important presumption of undue influence is that without the influence, the person would not have made the decision. If the court finds undue influence on the part of Betty and Carol, the trust will be terminated and the assets returned to Alice.

(b) Beneficiaries. The beneficiaries under the trust are those who are to benefit from the trust. Here, Alice is the sole beneficiary of the trust income for her life, with the remainder of the trust assets to go to the three children upon her death. Therefore, Betty, Carol, and David are residual beneficiaries under the trust with an expectancy interest.

(2)   Total Asset Management Standard. The Bank's failure happened after the High Flyer stock purchase and cannot be used to judge the prudence of the speculative investment. The trustee's performance will be judged under the "total asset management" approach – looking at the entire trust corpus to determine overall performance rather than on an asset-by-asset basis. In managing the trust assets, the trustee may consider a number of factors, including the size of the properties, the duration of the trust, the needs of the beneficiaries along with other assets and income each beneficiary has – as well as the effects of taxation.

(3) Fiduciary Duty. As trustee, David owes a fiduciary duty to the beneficiaries and must manage the assets under the "Prudent Person Standard." That standard is to deal with the trust properties as the trustee prudently would deal with his own assets in providing for permanent investments. Because the transfer is to the same bank David has his money in – he probably did not breach his duty as trustee despite the bank's eventual collapse – unless he had some prior notice of the insolvency.

(a) Proceeds of Negotiable Instruments. The fact that David transferred these instruments into the same bank where he has his own money suggests the conclusion that he is dealing with the proceeds in a prudent way. Within the prudent person standards, the trustee has wide discretion.

(b) Sale of Real Estate. The sale must be on the open market or the trustee must have the real property appraised to determine its fair market value. None of these safeguards were complied with here. No facts show the realty was sold on the open market even though the CPA-realtor was the trustee himself. In addition, David appears to have breached his fiduciary duty by charging a real estate commission in addition to his trustee fee of one percent a year – here $90,000. His trustee's fee is designed to cover these same activities – managing – including buying and selling assets. The beneficiaries have a cause of action against David for breach of trust and may recover what profits would have been made on the sale of the property had it been sold at fair market value. In addition, they can recover David's real estate commission.

(c) Homes for Daughters. The homes should be in the name of the trust, not the names of the individual beneficiaries – Betty and Carol only have an expectancy interest given Alice's power to revoke.

(d) Pledge of Trust Interest. Carol cannot pledge as security an expectancy interest that may never vest. The expectancy may be revoked prior to Alice's death. The trust is not liable in the event of her default and Bank must look to Carol personally.

(4) Revocable At Will. Since the facts state this to be a revocable trust, testator Alice can during her life revoke at any time with few formalities. The court will order trustee David to return the remaining assets to his mother.

Answer Number 3

Summary

Formation of an inter vivos trust requires a settlor intentionally placing property (Greenacre) with a trustee for the benefit of ascertainable beneficiaries. A trust must comply with the RAP, and is presumed to be irrevocable. A new trustee is needed merely to transfer title of the property, and the court may appoint S. Generally, a surviving spouse has an absolute right to act as executor / administrator of jointly-owned property, but not separate property. Here, F's separate property is passing outside of probate, so W has no right to administer. If a testator marries after validating his will, his spouse will have property rights as an omitted spouse, but F did not execute a will, so this statute does not apply. The venue for a trust containing real property is usually the property situs, so New York likely has jurisdiction.

Issues Raised

(1)   Formation of Inter Vivos Trust (SIT – PA)
(2)   Wanda's Claims
       (a) Trustee Appointment
       (b) Survivor Spouse as Successor Trustee
       (c) Trust Agreement Void Because Not Witnessed
       (d) Trust Agreement Void Because Trustor, Trustee, and Income Beneficiary Same Person
       (e) Assets Distributed to Omitted Spouse
       (f) Change in Venue
(3)   Distribution

Sample Answer

(1)   Formation of Inter Vivos Trust. Formation of an inter vivos trust requires a settlor intentionally placing property with a trustee for the benefit of ascertainable beneficiaries. Here, Frank appointed himself trustee, retaining a lifetime income interest and giving a future principal interest to his children as beneficiaries. Since there was a clear intention to form a trust, a signature is not necessary. The res was Greenacre. Greenacre was presumably properly conveyed (acknowledged writing). A trust is assumed to be irrevocable unless expressly stated otherwise. Here, Frank's trust was revocable during his lifetime. A trust must comply with the rule against perpetuities, which requires the trust vest within 21 years of the death of a life in being. The trust terminates at the end of his life, a life in being, and so is valid.

(2)   Wanda's Claims.

(a) Trustee Appointment. Where a sole trustee dies the court may appoint a successor trustee. A trustee must be competent – of age and capable of forming contracts. As there is no evidenced intent to have another manage the property, a resulting trust in favor of the children now exists. There is no need for a trustee except to transfer title of the property to Sonny and George. The court may appoint Sonny to carry out that task if he is competent.

(b) Survivor Spouse as Successor Trustee. A surviving spouse has an absolute right by statute in most states to act as executor / administrator of jointly-owned property. Here, Wanda has been properly appointed. However, a surviving spouse does not have an absolute right to administer separate property. As the *res* in the trust was Frank's separate property and is passing outside of probate, Wanda has no statutory right to serve as administrator.

(c) Trust Agreement Void Because Not Witnessed. The fact that the trust documents were not witnessed is irrelevant. An inter-vivos trust does not require a writing at all. So long as the title to Greenacre was properly conveyed, the trust will not fail because the writing was not witnessed.

(d) Trust Agreement Void Because Trustor, Trustee, and Income Beneficiary Same Person. An inter-vivos trust may be made by naming the settlor as trustee where the settlor gets income for life, with a future interest to other parties. In fact, this is a common form of inter-vivos trust used to avoid probate. Frank's trust will not fail because he retained an interest in the income.

(e) Assets Distributed to Omitted Spouse. Where an individual executes a valid will and is later married, the will is probated but the spouse will have rights in all property as an omitted spouse, usually in the amount she would have received by intestate distribution. Here, Frank did not execute a will and so the omitted spouse statute does not apply.

(f) Change in Venue. The proper trust venue containing real property is usually the situs of that property. The probate court may choose to consolidate the trust, but does not have to. Here, as all that exists is a resulting trust, New York, situs of Greenacre, likely has jurisdiction over the trust.

(3)   Distribution. A trust is a non-testamentary device – it passes property outside of estate probate. Here, Greenacre is transferred according to the trust terms, upon Frank's death, to his children. As he had two children, Sonny and George, each will get half interest in Greenacre as tenants in common from their common parent.

Answer Number 4

Summary

Only parties who stand to gain may contest a will, so here grandchildren do not have standing if their parents are alive. Deceased B's children have standing, but the grandchildren do not. If there is no valid will, intestacy applies. In most states, intestacy statutes give one-half of separate property to the surviving spouse and one-half to children. 2 out of 3 were not non-taking attestors, so though an interested witness may create a rebuttable presumption of undue influence, there are uninterested witnesses here, too. Likely grounds for a will contest here are mental capacity, undue influence, and fraud in the inducement. If any of these succeed in invalidating the will, the two children would take under the intestate statute.

Issues Raised

(1)   Standing to Contest
(2)   Interested Witness
(3)   Will Contest
    (a) Mental Capacity
    (b) Undue Influence
       (i) taking advantage of vulnerable position to influence decision
       (ii) without the influence, person would not have made the decision
    (c) Fraud in the Inducement

Sample Answer

(1)   Standing to Contest. Only parties who would gain financially if the will was denied probate have standing to contest a will. Grandchildren are not takers so do not have standing because their parents are living. If the will contest is successful and there is not a previous will that is revived, the decedent's estate is distributed intestate. The intestate rules in most states generally distribute one-half of separate property to the surviving spouse and one-half to children. Thus Betty's two children have standing to contest while her grandchildren do not.

(2)   Interested Witness. Under the common law, a will was invalid if one of the necessary attestation witnesses was also a taker under the will. Here there were three witnesses, so 2 out of 3 were still independent, non-taking attestors. In many states, however, an interested witness creates a rebuttable presumption of undue influence.

(3)   Will Contest. The will contest will likely proceed under at least three theories.

(a) Mental Capacity. At execution, the testator must remember and understand her property nature and extent, the natural object of her bounty including identifying her family, and the testamentary effect of making the devise. There is a presumption of mental capacity, so the burden is on the contestant. Here the facts state the decedent acknowledged her two children in the will and understood the testamentary effect of making the devise. The grandchildren were apparently not mentioned, but the facts do not say they were close and they would take through their parents. The incidents of the testator's memory loss occurred subsequent to executing the will.

(b) Undue Influence. The challenger may create a rebuttable presumption the devise beneficiary interfered with the testator's free will. The pastor did stand in a confidential relationship with the testator and he did actively participate in the will execution process. Since the pastor was a beneficiary and exercised undue influence, his witnessing of the will is invalid. Adrian's statement "I hope you take care of the kids" is extrinsic, but it is some evidence of intent to be considered.

(c) Fraud in the Inducement. The heirs could argue that their mother was deceived by the pastor's statement on entering the after life and that is why she left her entire estate to him and his church. However, the church's counter-argument would be there was no false statements made and the decedent was well aware of what she was doing at the time the new will was executed. The latter position seems likely to prevail as to fraud, but undue influence could apply, and if such a claim was successful, the two children could take under the intestate statute.

Answer Number 5

Summary

Parallel joint wills may devise in the same manner if the agreement specifically refers to the contract between the parties. This agreement became irrevocable by the survivor upon the death of the first spouse, so W's subsequent devise to the SPCA fails. The bequest to the unnamed charity raises the issue of the doctrines of incorporation by reference, Independent Significance, and Cy Pres. The gold coin collection is not a demonstrative legacy (a cash bequest to be satisfied from the sale of a particular asset), so the testator's sister takes the coins at present value. The residue is divided between the children (25% each) and the charity (50%).

Issues Raised

(1) Mutual / Joint Wills
    (a) Agree to execute parallel wills that devise in the same manner
    (b) Agreement must specifically refer to the contract between the parties
    (c) Clear intent to enter into contract not to unilaterally change distribution plans
    (d) Agreement became irrevocable as to the survivor upon the death of the first party

(2) Incorporation by Reference
    (a) Will may identity a new taker in a separate document
    (b) Document must be existence as of the will date

(3) Doctrine of Independent Significance

(4) Cy Pres Doctrine

(5) Demonstrative Legacy

Sample Answer

(1) Mutual / Joint Wills. Two people may agree between themselves to execute parallel wills that both devise in the same manner. The agreement must specifically refer to the contract between the parties. Here "we both agree" seems sufficient to indicate both spouses intended to enter into a mutual contract not to unilaterally change their plan of distribution after the first to die. This agreement became irrevocable in most jurisdictions as to the survivor upon the death of the first to pass. Thus Wanda's subsequent devise to the Society for Prevention of Cruelty to Animals is ineffective.

(2) Incorporation by Reference. The one-half bequest to the unnamed charity to be designated in an extrinsic document raises the issue whether the doctrine of incorporation by reference applies. A will may incorporate the identity of a taker in a separate document if it was in existence as of the will date. The document in question was to be delivered in the following year. Because this was not contemporaneous to the devise in question, incorporation by reference may not apply. But the facts do not specifically say the document was not in existence on the will execution date so it is unclear if the charity Red Cross will take.

(3) Doctrine of Independent Significance. Can the devise to the Red Cross be saved under the doctrine of Independent Significance? Usually a beneficiary must be specifically identified in the will. An exception is a devise to a taker determined by reference to acts that have significance apart from their effect upon the dispositions made by the will. Here the charity in question was dependent upon the volume of public contributions, which is an independent fact with an objective significance apart from the bequest. Thus the devise is likely enforceable.

(4) Cy Pres Doctrine. A court may modify the testator's bequest where the charitable purpose has become impossible to carry out. Here that is the specific purpose is the treatment of AIDS in Africa. Since the Red Cross is no longer fulfilling that purpose, the court may transfer the bequest of $205,000 to the Gates Foundation to effectuate the grantor's intent.

(5) Demonstrative Legacy (DL). The gold coin collection is not a demonstrative legacy which is a dollar bequest that is to be satisfied from the sale of a particular estate asset. Here the gift is merely that of a particular non-money asset. While the gold coins have apparently depreciated in value from $100,000 to $90,000, this is all the testator's sister takes.

    The residue of $410,000 should be distributed $205,000 to the two children ($102,500 each) and $205,000 to the charity, the Gates Foundation.

Trusts and Future Interests

Acceptance Not Required........... T 5-278
Account to Beneficiaries .... T 5-282
Accounting Designations .... T 5-275
Accretions................................. T 5-290
Administration of Trust............. T 5-281
Agent of Trustee....................... T 5-282
Animal Beneficiaries................. T 5-278
Appointment............................. T 5-277
Ascertainable Beneficiaries........ T 5-278
Attachment for Taxes................ T 5-284
Avoiding Probate...................... T 5-276
Beneficiaries' Rights .... T 5-283
Beneficiary Accounting
    Designation Conflict .... T 5-275
Borrowing from Trust .... T 5-283
Capacity................................... T 5-277
Charging Order......................... T 5-284
Charitable Trusts .... T 5-285
Claim Against Trust .... T 5-285
Claim Against Trustee............... T 5-285
Class Beneficiaries .... T 5-278
Class Gifts .... T 5-280
Commingling of Assets.............. T 5-282
Consolidation .... T 5-286
Constructive Trust .... T 5-276
Contingent Remainder............... T 5-280
Contrary Will Devise .... T 5-279
Corpus Invasion........................ T 5-276
Creditors' Rights .... T 5-283
Custodian for Minor .... T 5-279
"Cy Pres" Doctrine.................... T 5-285
Defense of Trustee .... T 5-283
Defined Selection of
    Beneficiaries.......................... T 5-278
Delegating Duties...................... T 5-282
Disabling Restraint on
    Alienation .... T 5-284
Discretionary Trust.................... T 5-284
Distribution Decisions............... T 5-275
Distribution Discretion.............. T 5-275
Diversification of Assets .... T 5-281
Donor....................................... T 5-277

Donor Termination .... T 5-286
Estate Taxes.............................. T 5-276
Executory Interest..................... T 5-280
Expiration of Term .... T 5-286
Express Trusts .... T 5-275
Family Support .... T 5-284
Fertile Septuagenarians .... T 5-281
Forfeiture Restraint on
    Alienation .... T 5-284
Fraudulent Transfers.................. T 5-284
Future Family Beneficiaries .... T 5-278
Future Interests .... T 5-278, 280
Gifts to Charities....................... T 5-280
Grantor..................................... T 5-277
Highly Speculative Investments . T 5-281
Illegality............................ T 5-277, 286
Impermissible Purpose .... T 5-277
Implied Trusts........................... T 5-276
Impossibility .... T 5-286
Income Interest Terminates .... T 5-286
Income Interests......................... T 5-275
Incorporation by Reference .... T 5-288
Indefinite Class......................... T 5-278
Inform Beneficiaries.................. T 5-282
Instrument Exculpatory
    Provisions .... T 5-283
Instrument Alienation
    Restrictions .... T 5-284
Intent to Properly Create .... T 5-277
Inter Vivos Trust....................... T 5-279
Joint and Several Liability of
    Co-Trustees............................ T 5-283
Judicial Review Petition............ T 5-279
Laches...................................... T 5-283
Liability of Trustee .... T 5-283
Life Insurance........................... T 5-278
Litigate on Behalf of Trust .... T 5-282
Living Trust.............................. T 5-276
Loyalty to Trust .... T 5-282
Mere Desire .... T 5-277
Merger .... T 5-277, 286
Modification of Trusts............... T 5-279
Multiple Trustees...................... T 5-281
Natural Objects of Bounty.......... T 5-288

Non-Judicial Resolution of
  Dispute ....T 5-279
Not Delegate Decisions...............T 5-282
Objective Manifestation of
  Intent ....T 5-277
Opportunity of Trust ....T 5-283
Petition to Terminate...................T 5-286
Pour-Over Provision ....T 5-279, 286
Power of Appointment................T 5-290
Power to Consume ....T 5-276
Principal Interests.......................T 5-275
Probate ....T 5-276
Productivity of Property..............T 5-281
Promise to Create ....T 5-278
Property Administer....................T 5-281
Protecting Assets........................T 5-276
Prudent Business Person
  Investment Standard.................T 5-281
Purpose Accomplished, Illegal,
  or Impossible...........................T 5-286
Reduce Estate Taxes ....T 5-276
Remainder Class.........................T 5-278
Required Trust Elements.............T 5-276
Remainders................................T 5-280
Res...T 5-277
Resolution of Dispute..................T 5-279
Restraints on Alienation..............T 5-284
Resulting Trust ....T 5-276
Reversion ....T 5-280
Revocation of Trusts ....T 5-279
Rule Against Perpetuities....T 5-280, 281
Rule in Shelley's Case ....T 5-289
Secret Trust ....T 5-276
Self-Dealings............................T 5-282
Self-Serving Trusts ....T 5-284
Settlor......................................T 5-277
Significant Non-Routine
  Transactions ....T 5-281
Spendthrift Trust ....T 5-284, 287
Split Interests............................T 5-275
Statute of Limitations.................T 5-283
Support Trust.............................T 5-284
"Surviving Heirs"................T 5-278, 290
Termination of Custodian for
  Minor.....................................T 5-279
Tax Attachments ....T 5-284
Term Expires.............................T 5-286
Termination...............................T 5-286
Testamentary Trust.....................T 5-279
Third Party Liability...........T 5-285, 286
Total Asset Management
  Standard ....T 5-281

Totten Trust ....T 5-298
Transfer Rights...........................T 5-284
Trust Elements...........................T 5-276
Trust Organization Formation....T 5-278
Trust Property............................T 5-277
Trustee.....................................T 5-277
Trustee Removal ....T 5-283
Trustee's Allocation Liability ....T 5-282
Trustee's Defenses ....T 5-283
Trustee's Responsibilities and
  Liability ....T 5-281
Types of Trusts..........................T 5-275
Uniform Transfers to Minors
  Act...T 5-279
Use Restriction ....T 5-284
Utility of Entity ....T 5-276
Vested Remainder ....T 5-278
Vested Remainder Subject to
  Open ....T 5-280
"Wait and See" Rule ....T 5-280
Wrongdoing Remedy ....T 5-276

Wills and Decedents' Estates

Abatement ....T 5-300
Accessions.................................T 5-290
Accretions.................................T 5-290
Acknowledged............................T 5-288
Ademption ....T 5-290
Adjudication of Testacy or
  Intestacy ....T 5-297
Administration Functions...........T 5-300
Admission to Probate ....T 5-299
Adopted Children ....T 5-289
Advancement..............................T 5-294
Affidavit Attestation...................T 5-288
After-Acquired Property ....T 5-289
After-born Children....................T 5-289
Alternatives to Probate ....T 5-297
Ancillary Administration............T 5-297
Anti-lapse Statute ....T 5-290
Attestation Requirement.............T 5-288
Beneficiary Accounting
  Designation Conflict ....T 5-275
Born Out of Wedlock ....T 5-289
Capacity Absent ....T 5-293
Cash Legacies............................T 5-300
Child Support ....T 5-292, 300
Claim Approval and Rejection... T 5-299
Claim Time Limit.......................T 5-299
Class Beneficiaries ....T 5-290

Codicils... T 5-291
Collateral Relatives .... T 5-296
Collect Estate Assets .... T 5-299
Community Property .... T 5-295
Community Property
   Agreement .... T 5-298
Competent Attestation................ T 5-288
Components of Will .... T 5-288
Conditional Wills .... T 5-292
Contract to Make a Will or
   Devise .... T 5-292
Corpus Management .... T 5-297
Costs of Administration .... T 5-300
Court's Equitable Power .... T 5-288
Creditors .... T 5-299
Cy Pres Doctrine .... T 5-289
Dead Man's Statute .... T 5-294
Defined Selection .... T 5-290
Demonstrative Legacy................ T 5-300
Dependent Relative
   Revocation............................... T 5-291
Destroyed Wills........................... T 5-299
Determining Shares for
   "Issue" .... T 5-290
Devise to "Issue"......................... T 5-290
Directive to Physician .... T 5-297
Disclaimer .... T 5-290
Disinheritance.............................. T 5-289
Distribute to Beneficiaries.......... T 5-300
Divorce .... T 5-289
Doctrine of Worthier Title.......... T 5-289
Equitable Power .... T 5-288
Escheatment .... T 5-300
Estate Taxes................................. T 5-300
Estates of Absentees................... T 5-297
Exoneration .... T 5-291
Extrinsic Evidence...................... T 5-288
Failure to Adhere to Statutory
   Formalities............................... T 5-293
Family Allowance .... T 5-300
Family Maintenance.................... T 5-300
Federal Estate Taxes................... T 5-300
Fiduciary........................... T 5-294, 298
Formal Wills................................ T 5-287
Former Spouse............................. T 5-289
Fraud in the Execution .... T 5-293
Fraud in the Inducement............. T 5-293
Funeral Expenses......................... T 5-300
General Legacies .... T 5-300
Grounds to Contest Will............. T 5-293
Half-Blood Children.................... T 5-289
Health Care Directive .... T 5-297

Holographic Wills or Codicils.... T 5-292
Homestead Interest .... T 5-292
Identification of Beneficiaries .... T 5-288
"In Terrorem" Clauses................ T 5-294
Incorporation by Reference .... T 5-288
Independent Significance .... T 5-288
Insolvent Estate Priority .... T 5-300
Insurance Proceeds .... T 5-298
Integration................................... T 5-288
Intent Requirement .... T 5-287
Interested Witnesses .... T 5-288
Interpretation Issues.................... T 5-288
Intestate Succession.................... T 5-294
Joint Bank Account .... T 5-298
Joint Tenancy.............................. T 5-298
Joint Wills................................... T 5-292
Judgment Debts .... T 5-300
Lapsed Devise .... T 5-290
Last Illness Expenses.................. T 5-300
Living Will .... T 5-297
Lost Wills .... T 5-299
Marital Property.......................... T 5-295
Medical Powers .... T 5-297
Mental Capacity.......................... T 5-288
Mutual Wills............................... T 5-292
Non-Intervention Powers........... T 5-299
Non-Monetary Gifts .... T 5-300
Non-Probate Asset Liability .... T 5-297
Non-Probate Assets .... T 5-297
Notice to Creditors .... T 5-299
Nuncupative (Oral) Wills .... T 5-292
Omitted Later Spouse................. T 5-289
Omitted Surviving Children .... T 5-289
Open Class................................... T 5-290
Oral Wills .... T 5-292
Order of Distribution When
   Assets Insufficient .... T 5-300
Organ Donation Directives......... T 5-297
Out of Wedlock Children .... T 5-289
Partial Revocation .... T 5-291
Past obligations........................... T 5-293
Pay-on-Death Accounts.............. T 5-298
Pension Plan .... T 5-298
Per Capita .... T 5-295
Per Capita at Each
   Generation .... T 5-295
Per Capita with
   Representation .... T 5-295
Per Stirpes................................... T 5-295
Personal Representative.............. T 5-298
Personal Liability of
   Personal Representative........... T 5-299

"Pour-Over Wills"........................T 5-298
Power of Appointment................T 5-290
Power of Attorney.......................T 5-296
Pretermitted Surviving
    Children...................................T 5-289
Previous Will Revived ....T 5-294
Probate Jurisdiction.....................T 5-297
Probate Proceedings....................T 5-297
Probate Venue ....T 5-297
Property Problems.......................T 5-290
Related Documents ....T 5-296
Requirements for Wills ....T 5-287
Republish by Reference ....T 5-291
Residuary Gifts ....T 5-300
Restrictions on Disposition ....T 5-292
Revocation ....T 5-291
Rule in Shelley's Case ....T 5-289
Satisfaction.................................T 5-291
Separate Property ....T 5-295
Shares for "Issue".......................T 5-295
Signature Requirement................T 5-287
Slayer and Abusers......................T 5-290
Specific Gifts..............................T 5-300
Spouse Forced Share...................T 5-292
State Taxes ....T 5-300
Subsequent Divorce ....T 5-289
"Surviving Heirs".......................T 5-290
Survivorship Property ....T 5-295
Taker Problems ....T 5-289
Taxation ....T 5-300
Tax Allocation............................T 5-300
Testamentary Age ....T 5-287
Testamentary Intent.....................T 5-287
Testimony Regarding
    Attestation ....T 5-288
Totten Trust................................T 5-298
Traditional Wills ....T 5-287
Trust Res ....T 5-298
Undue Influence..........................T 5-293
Uniform Simultaneous Death
    Act..T 5-294
Uniform Wills and
    Probate Code (UPC).................T 5-287
Unsecured Debts ....T 5-300
Will Challenges....................T 5-293, 299
Will Components ....T 5-288
Will Requirements ....T 5-287

CHAPTER 6

UCC ARTICLE 3

COMMERCIAL

PAPER

RIGOS BAR REVIEW SERIES

UNIFORM MULTISTATE ESSAY EXAM (MEE) REVIEW

CHAPTER 6

UCC ARTICLE 3 – COMMERCIAL PAPER

Table of Contents

A. **Sub-Topic Exam Issue Distribution**.. Text 6-327

B. **Opening Argument and Primary Issues**... Text 6-329

C. **Text** .... Text 6-331

    I. **Introduction** .... Text 6-331

    II. **Negotiable Instrument – NUTSS** .... Text 6-332

    III. **Holder in Due Course – FINNS** .... Text 6-335

    IV. **Real or Personal Defense** .... Text 6-337

    V. **Liability of Parties** .... Text 6-339

    VI. **Improper Negotiation** .... Text 6-343

    VII. **Article 4 – Bank Deposits and Collections** .... Text 6-344

    VIII. **Exam Approach to Negotiable Instruments Essay Answers** . Text 6-346

D. **Magic Memory Outlines®** .... Magic Memory Outlines 6-349

E. **UCC – Commercial Paper Essay Questions** .... Questions 6-353

F. **UCC – Commercial Paper Essay Answers** .... Answers 6-357

G. **UCC – Commercial Paper Index** .... Index 6-367

F. **Acronyms** .... Acronyms 15-630

RIGOS BAR REVIEW SERIES
MEE SUB-TOPIC FREQUENCY DISTRIBUTION

UCC ARTICLE 3 – COMMERCIAL PAPER

	2/09	7/08	2/08	7/07	2/07	7/06	2/06	7/05	2/05	7/04	2/04	7/03	2/03	7/02	2/02	7/01	2/01
Governing Law	/	/		/	/	/		/	/		/	/	/	/	/	/	/
UCC 3	/	/		/	/	/		/	/		/	/	/	/	/	/	/
UCC 4						/					/			/			/
Requirements (general)	/	/		/	/	/		/	/		/	/	/	/	/	/	
Negotiability Words															/		
Contradictory Terms												/					
Unconditional					/				/			/					/
Promise to Pay					/												/
Time Certain						/											/
Sum Certain						/											
Holder In Due Course	/			/	/			/	/			/	/		/		/
For Value				/	/			/									
Negotiation (general)				/	/			/									
Order Paper				/				/									
Exceptions to Negotiation Required					/			/									
Shelter Rule								/									

	2/01	7/01	2/02	7/02	2/03	7/03	2/04	7/04	2/05	7/05	2/06	7/06	2/07	7/07	2/08	7/08	2/09
Defenses		/			/		/			/		/	/	/		/	/
Personal (general)																	
Failure of Consideration					/											/	
Real (general)												/					
Forgery												/		/			/
Liability of Parties					/		/		/	/		/					
Primary Liability									/	/		/					
Joint and Several										/							
Right of Contribution										/							
Maker's Negligence												/					
Indorsers' Liability							/							/			/
Accommodation Parties									/				/				
Payment in Full											/		/			/	
Warranties			/	/	/		/									/	/
Transfer																/	/
Good Title					/												/
Presentment			/	/	/		/										/
Bank Deposits & Collections							//										/
Properly Payable							/										
Unauthorized Signature							/							/			/
Liability							/							/		/	/
Certification							/									/	/
Conversion		/		/		/	/									/	/

Copyright 5328. Copyright by Rigos Bar Review Series – MEE.

OPENING ARGUMENT AND PRIMARY ISSUES

UCC ARTICLE 3 – COMMERCIAL PAPER

There are a few thoughts that should usually be stated at the beginning of every answer. These will score you easy points and let the grader know you are in the right topic area.

Most essays should have an "opening argument": a brief, broad statement that shows you understand the broad significance of a legal topic. The opening argument also suggests to the grader that she is about to read a thoughtful and well-organized essay.

Many subjects also have "primary issues" that can be discussed up front or integrated into the essay answer. IMPORTANT: Do not merely regurgitate these statements on the exam without addressing the issues actually raised by the facts, or you will not pass.

- **Commercial Paper Opening Argument:** UCC Article 3 governs transactions involving negotiable instruments and Article 4 controls bank-customer relations.

- **Sample Primary Issue Statements:**

  - For an instrument to be negotiable (NI), it must have at issue (1) negotiable words such as "pay to the order of," (2) an unconditional promise to pay money with no other undertaking, (3) a time certain for payment, (4) a sum certain in money, and (5) signed by the maker or drawer.

  - Two-party commercial paper (notes, etc.) has (1) maker and (2) payee.

  - Three-party commercial paper (checks) has (1) a drawer, (2) a drawee bank, and (3) a payee.

  - An instrument is issued when the maker or drawer first delivers and transfers possession to a payee or bearer.

  - To be an HDC, a person must take the instrument (1) for value, (2) in good faith, (3) with no notice of imperfections, and (4) the instrument must be properly negotiated – indorsed and delivered for order paper or merely delivered for bearer paper.

  - An assignee who receives the NI as a gift may still qualify for HDC status under the Shelter Rule, if there is an HDC up the chain who passed HDC status by assignment.

  - Personal defenses are not valid against an HDC, but are good against the payee and include mutual mistake, unauthorized completion, unfulfilled condition precedent, fraud in the inducement, failure of consideration, and other claims.

- Real defenses are good against an HDC and they are fraud in the execution / factum, illegality, discharge in bankruptcy, duress, lack of capacity, statute of limitations, forgery, unauthorized signature, and material alteration.

- Forgery, unauthorized signature, and material alterations can be re-characterized from real to personal defense status if the maker / drawer's or indorser's negligence contributed to the defense.

- Primary liability is with the maker of a note or the drawer of a check. Secondary liability of indorsers depends upon the character and the extent and conditions associated with the indorsement.

- Transferors warrant that (1) they have good title and are entitled to enforce the instrument; (2) material alterations are not present; (3) they have no knowledge of maker's insolvency; (4) no defenses can be asserted against the warrantor; and (5) all signatures are genuine and authorized.

- Presenters to the drawee bank warrant (1) they have good title; (2) material alterations are not present; and (3) the drawer's signature is authorized.

- **Article 4 Banking Primary Issue Statements:**

  - A bank can be negligent by wrongfully honoring an instrument which was forged or irregular on its face or paying out over a valid stop payment order.

  - Under the "properly payable rule," a bank is liable to the customer for wrongful dishonor unless it would have created an overdraft.

  - As between the negligent drawer and the bank who wrongfully honored the instrument, monetary loss is to be allocated based upon comparative negligence.

UCC ARTICLE 3 – COMMERCIAL PAPER

I.   INTRODUCTION

Almost every MEE exam has a commercial paper question, usually involving a check drawn on a bank. Article 3 of the UCC covers most negotiable instruments. Articles 4 banking is also covered in this chapter where there has been or could be exam testing.

> **MEE Tip:** It is usually helpful to sketch out the facts identifying each party in the sequence from issue to the final holder who presents the instrument for payment. See page 345.

A. Advantages Over Ordinary Contracts

To be a readily accepted substitute for money, negotiable instruments (NI) are given certain advantages over the underlying ordinary contract. A holder in due course (HDC) of a NI is entitled to receive payment even though the maker or payor might not be required to pay the payee. Thus, an HDC may get greater or better rights than a mere assignee of the negotiable instrument. Personal defenses are not good against an HDC of a NI. The maker or payor may still assert real defenses against an HDC.

> **MEE Tip:** Always start your answer by writing, "Article 3 of the UCC controls." If the question includes a check and a bank, Article 4 may also apply. Next, write, "Personal defenses are not good against a holder in due course (HDC) of a negotiable instrument (NI)."

B. Two-Party Paper

Two-party paper includes primarily promissory notes. The maker promises to pay to the order of a named payee or bearer without specifying the source of funds. Notes may be made payable "on demand" (or "on sight") or on a stated future date.

Date

I promise to pay to the order of S. Donaldson or bearer $1,000 U.S. on or before May 1, 200x.

/s/ J. Rigos, maker

C. Three-Party Paper

Three-party paper includes checks and drafts. The drawer orders the drawee (usually a bank) to pay to the order of a named payee or bearer.

1. Check: A check is drawn on a commercial banking institution and the drawee must pay on demand. This category includes a cashier's check, teller's check, or money order.

2. Draft: A draft is the drawer's order to the drawee to pay the payee or the bearer. A sight draft is payable on presentment. A time draft is payable on or before a certain future date. The bank must present a draft to the drawer for acceptance; the drawer then deposits the necessary funds to cover the payment. The advantage of using drafts is that they delay the time a drawer must have funds on deposit at the bank to cover the charge. [UCC 3-104(c)]

Date
Pay to the order of payee J. Ainsworth or bearer $1,000 U.S. on or before May 1, 200x.
/s/ J. Rigos, drawer
First Bank: Drawee

D. Certificate of Deposit

A certificate of deposit is a bank's written acknowledgment of receipt of money and the bank's promise to repay the sum on demand or at a specified future date. [UCC 3-104(j)]

MEE Tip: For every instrument, identify the parties' capacity at issue (drawer/maker, drawee, payee, etc.).

II.   NEGOTIABLE INSTRUMENT – NUTSS

To be a readily accepted substitute for money, negotiable instruments (NI) are given certain advantages over ordinary contracts. The contract must rise to the dignity of a NI by meeting at issue all of the five elements discussed below, abbreviated by the acronym NUTSS.

A. Negotiable Words

Negotiable words are required (except for a check). [UCC 3-104]

1. Order Paper: If the payee is identified, there must be a statement "pay to the order of" on the face of the instrument. The magic word "order" is necessary unless there is an alternative to pay "bearer" such as "pay Jim Rigos or bearer." "Pay Jim Rigos," "I promise to pay Jim Rigos," or "IOU" is not sufficient; the necessary magic word is "ORDER." The negotiation (transfer) of order paper requires proper indorsement and delivery by the payee.

2. Bearer Paper: Negotiable bearer paper does not identify a payee and can state "pay to bearer" or "pay to cash." The negotiation (transfer) of bearer paper requires only transfer and delivery by the bearer. [UCC 3-109]

3. Contradictory Terms:

a. Handwritten, Typed, and Printed: A document may have handwritten, typed, and/or printed terms which are inconsistent. Handwritten terms control both typed and printed terms, and typed terms control printed.

b. Amount: If there is a contradiction between an amount written in numerals and also described by words, the words designation control (eighty thousand v. 8,000).

B. Unconditional Promise to Pay

The second requirement of a negotiable instrument is an unconditional promise to make payment at the place of business of the drawee or maker. This principle is heavily tested; the instrument must be payable in all events. Even if the contingency occurs before the due date, the instrument remains non-negotiable. [UCC 3-106]

1. Promise to Pay Only: The maker or drawer cannot undertake in the instrument to do any act (or give any instruction) other than pay money. An exception is that a maker or drawer may undertake to provide collateral securing the debt.

2. Future Contract: The promise to pay must not be subject to or governed by the future completion of a contingency. If it is contingent, it is in violation of the rule and the instrument would be non-negotiable. An example is, "I promise to pay to the order of S. Donaldson if he delivers his car to me." An instrument expressly limited by its terms to payment out of a particular future funded source (such as the proceeds of a future sale or payable out of revenue from a new computer product) is also non-negotiable.

3. Non-Violating Conditions: Implied or constructive conditions, statement of consideration or collateral given do not affect the negotiability of the instrument. Also, wording indicating the source of the agreement or reference to a past transaction from where the instrument arose does not defeat negotiability.

4. Surety Involvement: There may also be a guarantor or surety involved with the maker. They have joint and several liability.

5. Legal Right Retention Clause: A statutory or administrative law may specify that any assignee takes their rights subject to all claims or defenses that the issuer could assert against the original payee. Such a defense retention provision does not affect transferability.

C. Time Certain

Definite time certain for payment of the obligation principal (not interest accrual) is required. [UCC 3-108]

1. Face of Instrument: Time of payment is definite if on demand or can be determined from the face of the instrument. If no time for payment is specified, the instrument is payable on demand, such as a check. Payable at a fixed period after a stated date or event such as issue, acceptance, or presentment, is acceptable.

2. Dates and Substitution: There are at least four potential dates: issue by the maker/drawer, acceptance by the payee, presentation by the holder, and payment date. If the payment date is not specified, the presentment date controls. If the presentation and payment dates are not specified, the acceptance date controls. If the acceptance, presentment, and payment dates are not specified, the date of issue controls.

3. Extension or Acceleration Provisions: The holder may have an indefinite extension option, but the maker can only extend to a definite future time. Prepayment options by the maker or drawer do not defeat negotiability. A clause requiring acceleration of all the remaining principle balance in the event of a default also does not violate the rule.

4. Occurrence Time Uncertain: Watch out for an event which is uncertain as to time of occurrence. Examples include, "I will pay when I receive my inheritance" or "I will pay when I sell my automobile."

5. Undated Instrument: The instrument itself may be undated and still be negotiable as long as the date of payment is specified. An undated instrument payable "thirty days after date" is not payable at a definite time since the time of payment cannot be determined on the instrument's face.

D. Sum Certain in Money

Sum certain in money of the principal obligation must be stated. [UCC 3-104(a)]

1. Currency of Any Country: The money requirement is met by designating any country's currency or legal medium of exchange, including a Canadian Maple Leaf gold coin. [UCC 3-107]

2. Permissible Inclusions: The fixed amount requirement applies only to the principal of the obligation. Certainty is not destroyed by the inclusion of interest, discounts, penalties, collection costs, or attorney fees. The interest rate may be a fixed percentage or variable, increase after default, or be adjusted for foreign currency exchange rates. The term "prime rate" is deemed certain. [UCC 3-112]

3. Open Sum and Option: The sum can't be open, such as a certain price per unit where the units are not specified. Commodity notes (three tons of grain or an ounce of gold) or promises to pay future property taxes and insurance are not fixed in value and thus are not negotiable. Not even the payee may have the option to receive non-money in cancellation of the instrument. The instrument may not contain any other undertaking by the maker/drawer.

E. Signed by Maker/Drawer

Signature by the maker is required if a promissory note. If a check, draft, bill of exchange, or trade acceptance, the drawer must sign. [UCC 3-401]

1. Acceptable Signatures: This can be an actual signature, a machine signature, an engraving, a symbol such as X, a rubber stamp, or other present intent to authenticate. [UCC 3-401(b)]

2. Representative Liability: An agent or representative attempting to escape personal liability on the instrument must indicate both his principal's identity and his agency capacity. If both these requirements are met, only the principal will be liable. [UCC 3-402]

> **MEE Tip:** The second sentence in your answer should be "A negotiable instrument is a signed writing containing an unconditional promise to pay to order or bearer on demand or a date certain in the future a sum certain in money (no other undertaking)."

F. Issue and Incomplete Instruments

1. Issue Requirement: An instrument is issued when the maker or drawer first delivers (voluntarily transfers possession) to a payee or bearer. There must be an intent to give enforceable rights on the instrument to some other person. [UCC 3-105]

2. Incomplete Instruments: The bar questions often include facts indicating the instrument was incomplete when issued, but the signer intended it to be completed by the addition of words or numbers.

a. Enforceable When Properly Completed: If the maker or drawer intended for the payee to complete the instrument, the instrument is enforceable as completed.

b. Examples: If the date or amount are incomplete and both parties agree on the term, the payee may complete the instrument.

c. Payee Incomplete: If the payee's name is left blank, it is enforceable as a bearer instrument.

d. Improperly Completed: If the payee adds or fills in unauthorized words or numbers, there is an alteration of the instrument. The ultimate loss is usually placed on the party who left the instrument incomplete. [UCC 3-115]

> **MEE Tip:** The first threshold issue in your answer is whether the instrument meets all the NUTSS elements and thus is negotiable. If not negotiable, the holder takes subject to all contract defenses assertable against the payee. Many exam questions never get beyond this issue, but always briefly cover the remaining issues. Even if the document is not a negotiable instrument, there may still be contract issues worthy of discussion.

III. HOLDER IN DUE COURSE – FINNS

One of the advantages of a negotiable instrument is that it can be transferred (negotiated) to other parties by delivery with the necessary indorsements (see discussion below). A transferee of a negotiable instrument may achieve rights superior to other holders ("super P"). That prized status is called a "Holder in Due Course" (HDC) and is only realized if the transferee meets the following **FINNS** requirements. [UCC 3-302]

A. For Value

1. Gift Donee: The "for value" requirement prevents a gift donee from being an HDC.

2. Partial HDC: A holder qualifies as an HDC only to the extent that consideration has been given. Thus, a holder purchasing an instrument for less than full face value may stand as part HDC and part as mere assignee (split status). Value is also present when an HDC receives the instrument for collateral purposes (even if on account of an antecedent debt) or as a bank deposit.

3. Future Performance: A promise to perform in the future (deliver goods or render services at a later time) is inadequate value. [UCC 3-303]

B. In Good Faith

The "in good faith" ("honesty in fact") requirement calls into question whether the holder had actual knowledge of the claim or defense when she acquired the instrument. Examples include knowledge that the instrument is overdue (90 days for a check or a reasonable time for a demand instrument), had been dishonored, bears an unauthorized signature, is forged, altered, is otherwise contested or subject to a claim by any person.

C. No Notice

To achieve HDC status, the holder may not have constructive notice of a claim or defense against the enforceability of the instrument. Instruments which are irregular on their face or deeply discounted may call into question their authenticity or validity. Incomplete, overdue instruments, or knowledge of an uncured default often fall into this category. The objective test is whether a reasonable holder under the circumstances would have actual or constructive knowledge of the defect.

D. Negotiation

Proper negotiation is required if the transferee is to be allowed HDC status. [UCC 3-201]

1. Order Paper: For order paper (a specific payee named), negotiation requires delivery (transfer of possession plus proper indorsement by the payee). If two payees are named, separated by an "or," indorsement by either payee is adequate. If the payees' names are separated by an "and," both payees must indorse. Signatures are presumed to be authentic and authorized unless specifically denied. Lost or stolen instruments are not legally negotiated because proper delivery is absent.

2. Bearer Paper: Negotiation of bearer paper requires only a delivery or a transfer of possession, so an HDC can collect even if the bearer instrument was stolen. Blank and special indorsements may change the character of an instrument from order to bearer.

3. Prohibited Negotiation: The holder cannot acquire the rights of an HDC simply by purchasing the NI from an estate, in a bankruptcy, business bulk sale, or a creditor's sale.

E. Shelter Rule

Notwithstanding a failure to meet all of the FINNS elements above, a mere assignee may be allowed the rights of an HDC if his transferor was an HDC. This is a frequent exam topic. [UCC 3-203(b)]

1. Look Up the Ladder: Look up the sequence of assignees; if there is an HDC up the ladder, the subsequent holder receives the HDC's rights under the "shelter rule" through assignment. This assignment usually includes the status of an HDC. Even an assignee from a HDC who takes as a gift (such as a charity) will qualify under the shelter rule and can still collect on the instrument.

2. Example: Ace fraudulently induces Maker to make a NI payable to Ace. Ace negotiates the instrument to Brother who meets all of the FINNS requirements. Brother negotiates the instrument to Charlie as a gift; Charlie then presents it to Maker or the drawee and learns of the fraud in the inducement. Charlie succeeds to Brother's rights as an HDC through assignment, cutting off the defense which Maker could assert against Ace.

3. Cannot Improve Position: The shelter rule cannot improve an assignee's position. Thus a party to the fraud or illegality in the original transaction cannot wash the paper clean by passing it through an HDC and then repurchasing it. In the above example, Ace cannot receive HDC rights by purchasing the instrument from Brother or Charlie.

> **MEE Tip:** Do not forget the Shelter Rule! If there are multiple transferees include it in your FINNS analysis. Is there an HDC up the ladder? If so, the holder has all of the rights of an HDC through assignment.

F. Exceptions to Negotiation Requirement

Lack of proper negotiation, such as a forged indorsement (intent to impersonate another), means subsequent holders are mere assignees. Their assignor was a forger, and thus they receive only his rights on the instrument: none.

There are two exceptions where subsequent assignees are deemed to have HDC status. These exceptions are frequently tested on the bar exam. In both cases, the maker's or drawer's employee negligence contributed to the improper indorsement and they were in the best position to prevent this from occurring. Therefore public policy suggests that a HDC should prevail. [UCC 3-405]

1. Fictitious Payee: A fictitious payee is where the maker intended the named payee to have no real interest in the instrument. Examples include:

a. Dummy Vendor: The bookkeeper makes out a check to a fictitious company which does not exist. The bookkeeper then indorses the dummy vendor's name on the check and converts the funds to her own use.

b. Phantom Employee: A manufacturing supervisor creates a timecard for a worker who does not exist. The supervisor then indorses the phantom employee's name on the payroll check and converts the funds to his own use.

2. Impostor: An impostor is one who poses as another and thereby induces the maker to issue and execute the instrument payable to the person impersonated. [UCC 3-404]

> **MEE Tip:** The above exceptions to FINNS turn on whether the presenting party is an HDC or only a mere assignee. If the presenter fails under your FINNS requirements, discuss the contract default issues of an assignment of rights.

IV. REAL OR PERSONAL DEFENSE

The third step in the analysis is whether the defense asserted by the maker or drawer is effective. The issuer may assert a claim in recoupment against the payee to avoid payment on a note given for non-delivered goods. The effectiveness of defending against a third party HDC's claims depends upon whether the maker / drawer's defense is real or personal.

> **MEE Tip:** If the problem creating the defense is associated with the underlying contract such as a non-conforming tender of goods, the defense is likely personal. If the problem developed at issue of the NI or subsequently during transfer, the defense is likely real.

A. Personal Defenses – MUUFFO

If personal, the contract defense is not good against an HDC and the maker must pay. The major personal defenses tested on the bar exam are:

1. Mutual Mistake: A mutual mistake by both parties is a personal defense.

2. Unauthorized Completion: The payee completed the NI wrongfully. An example is if the payee fills in the wrong amount on a blank check.

3. Uncompletion of a Condition Precedent: If there was an extrinsic condition required before the contract payment was due, the defense is personal.

4. Fraud in the Inducement: The most frequently tested personal defense is fraud in the inducement (FIRD elements). An example is a salesman's misrepresentation intended to induce a buyer to enter into a transaction to purchase goods in exchange for a check.

5. Failure of Consideration: Failure of consideration includes negligence in performance of services, the goods purchased fail to conform to the contract specifications, or the goods were not delivered.

6. Other's Claims: This catch-all category applies if the defense does not fall into any other category. Therefore the UCC favors defenses being characterized as personal to allow a HDC to collect.

7. Federal Trade Commission: The Federal Trade Commission Act states that any assignee of a consumer credit contract, except a check, takes their rights subject to all defenses the consumer could assert against the seller. This right must be specifically stated in the contract. Thus, an HDC is treated as a mere assignee in a consumer credit sale with no greater rights than the original promisee. A consumer-buyer can assert personal defenses (such as fraud in the inducement) in such a situation against the HDC. [16 C.F.R. 433]

B. Real Defenses – FIDDLS FUM

Real defenses are effective (really good) in that the maker can assert them and does not have to pay the HDC. Real defenses are usually associated with events occurring at or after the issue of the NI, not deficiencies in the underlying contract.

1. General Real Defenses: Included in **FIDDLS FUM** are:

a. Fraud in Execution: Fraud in the factum or execution (D signed instrument believing it to be something other than a promise to pay).

b. Illegality: Illegality of the transaction or the creditor charging an usurious interest rate. In some jurisdictions, interest charged consumers in excess of 12% is usurious except for credit cards and retail sales agreements.

c. Discharge in Bankruptcy: Bankruptcy discharge of the debt is a real defense.

d. Duress: Extreme duress may be a real defense (gun held to head to get maker to sign).

e. Lack of Capacity: Lack of capacity such as infancy may be a real defense.

f. Statute of Limitations: Actions at law on the instrument must be commenced within six (6) years from the due date or demand. [UCC 3-118]

g. Forgery: Forgery (of maker's, drawer's or special indorsee's signature) is a real defense.

h. Unauthorized Signature: The signature on the instrument lacked actual or apparent authority. [UCC 3-403]

i. Material Alteration: An unauthorized material alteration of amount is also included as a real defense. [UCC 3-305] An HDC is allowed to collect the original tenor (amount) of an instrument that has been materially altered. A holder may have raised the amount from eight/$8 to eighty/$80; only $8 can be collected by an HDC. The $72 difference is subject to the real defense of material alteration. [UCC 3-407]

2. Forgery, Unauthorized Signature, Material Alteration Exceptions: The last three real **FUM** defenses (**f**orgery, **u**nauthorized signature and **m**aterial alteration) are subject to a special exception where the maker's, drawer's, or indorser's negligence substantially contributed to the defense. [UCC 3-406]

a. Examples: Frequent exam questions include the maker not controlling the signature stamp, mailing a bearer instrument to the wrong person, signing a blank check, or allowing another to fill in the amount later.

b. Recharacterizing From Real Defense to Personal: The negligence by the maker, drawer, or indorser recharacterizes the nature of these three defenses from real to personal; the consequence is that an HDC collects. The burden of proving negligence is on the party asserting the recharacterization.

c. Negligent Supervision: In addition, an employer is responsible for a fraudulent indorsement by an employee. [UCC 3-405]

d. Comparative Negligence: As between the negligent drawer and the bank who wrongfully honored the instrument, the loss is to be allocated based upon comparative negligence. The Code does not define what constitutes "failure to exercise ordinary care" or "substantially contributing to the alteration." [UCC 3-406]

> **MEE Tip:** Public policy allows the HDC to collect against these real defenses because the negligence of the maker or drawer caused the problem. More than 2/3 of the bar questions involve a personal defense. Remember personal defenses are not good against an HDC of a NI.

V. LIABILITY OF PARTIES

A holder may sue under (1) contract liability, (2) breach of (transfer or presenter) warranty, (3) conversion of the instrument, or (4) the underlying obligation.

A. Primary

Primary liability is with the person or institution who should pay in the ordinary course. This is normally the maker of a note, the drawer of a check, the drawee bank of a certified check (bank assumed place of maker when certified), or an acceptor of a draft. [UCC 3-414] An action must be commenced within six years of payment demand. [UCC 3-118]

1. Issue and Acceptance: A drawee only becomes potentially liable if they accept the instrument. Until delivery of the instrument to the payee, even the maker is not liable because there is no issue. Issue requires the maker-drawer to have the purpose of giving rights to another. [UCC 3-105]

2. Co-Makers: Joint and several liability applies to co-makers and a person entitled to enforce the instrument may recover from any maker. If a co-maker pays more than their proportional share, they may recover the excess from the other co-makers under the theory of contribution.

3. Liability for Dishonored Checks: In most states, a drawer of a dishonored check is penalized unless nonpayment resulted from a justifiable stop payment order. The payee or holder is usually entitled to a reasonable handling fee, 12% interest, costs of collection, and reasonable attorney's fees.

B. Secondary

1. In General: Secondary liability normally rests with the third-party indorsers; they are in effect sureties behind the maker and drawee bank (as agent for maker). [UCC 3-414] As to secondary parties, the character of the indorsement determines the extent and conditions of liability. (Note that the UCC uses "indorse." Most of the rest of the world uses "endorse." Pick one spelling and stick to it in your answer.)

a. Chronological Liability: Liability is chronological (up the ladder); you sue your transferors, and your transferees sue you. An HDC is an exception and can also go directly against the maker / drawer.

b. Conditions Precedent: Timely presentment (90 days after issue if a check or the due date specified in an instrument such as a note) and notice of dishonor are both conditions precedent to each indorser's liability. Indorser liability on a check is discharged 30 days after the indorsement was made.

c. Banks and HDC Limitations: The drawee bank is allowed until midnight of the next day to dishonor, and the HDC must notify his transferor within 30 days of receiving notice of dishonor. [UCC 3-503]

2. Types of Indorsements: The different types of indorsement include:

a. Unqualified / Blank: An unqualified or blank indorsement is a mere signature without specifying a particular indorsee. This converts order paper to bearer paper so that only delivery of the instrument is necessary for a subsequent negotiation. An assignee receiving an instrument without indorsement can generally demand an unqualified indorsement. [UCC 3-205(b)]

b. Special: A special indorsement identifies the next transferee who must indorse to further negotiate the instrument. Examples include "pay J. Ainsworth, J. Rigos," or "pay to the order of S. Donaldson, J. Rigos." A special indorsement converts bearer paper to order paper or continues order paper. [UCC 3-205(a)]

c. Restrictive: A restrictive indorsement is conditional or purports to prohibit further transfer. Examples include "pay T. Smith only," "to C. Rigos only," or "for collection only," or "to K. Tegland for deposit." These are ineffective to prohibit an assignment under the UCC. An exception is "for deposit only" which does prohibit transfer to any transferee except banks in the collection system. [UCC 3-206]

d. Qualified Without Recourse: A qualified indorsement of "without recourse" eliminates contractual liability on the instrument. However, even a "without recourse" indorser warrants that he has no knowledge of any defense good against him. (See warranty liability below.) [UCC 3-415]

e. Payment Guaranteed: A "payment guaranteed" indorsement means that if the instrument is not paid when due, the signer becomes primarily liable without resort by the holder to any other party.

f. Collection Guaranteed: A "collection guaranteed" indorsement means the signature party is only liable after the holder reduces the claim to a judgment against the maker or drawer. In addition, there must be a bona fide attempt to collect the judgment. [UCC 3-419(d)]

g. Accommodation Indorser: Accommodation (or "anomalous") indorser is a gratuitous surety who receives no compensation in return for the endorsing signature. An accommodation indorser becomes liable to all subsequent indorsers and has a right of indemnification or reimbursement from the party accommodated. Because the accommodation indorser is neither a holder nor involved in the chain of title, no implied warranties are imposed. [UCC 3-419]

h. Payment in Full: An instrument tendered with a conspicuous notation "payment in full" or "in full satisfaction" effects an accord and satisfaction if the claim was unliquidated or subject to a bona fide dispute. Crossing out the notation or adding "all rights reserved" is ineffectual to retain any rights on the underlying claim. An organization is given an exception and may designate a particular person, office, or place to which the accord must be tendered. In addition, the accord and satisfaction is defeated if the tendered check is returned within 90 days. [UCC 3-311]

C. Indorser's Skeleton

Exam questions usually involve multiple instruments with numerous parties who have indorsed in different manners. To keep the chronological order and type of indorsement straight, you may want to consider the following skeleton:

NAME   INDORSEMENT TYPE   LIABILITY   ORDER/BEARER PAPER

D. Warranty Liability

In addition to contract liability, warranty liability is possible. All transferors [UCC 3-416] or presenters [UCC 3-417] make certain implied warranties to their immediate transferees. If there is an indorsement, the warranty runs with the instrument. (Note that because presenters to the drawee bank are also transferors, the transfer warranties apply to a presenter as well as the presenter's warranties except in the case of an unaccepted instrument.) Any breach of warranty claim must be given to the warrantor within 30 days of learning of the breach. If notice is not timely given, the warrantor is not liable for any loss caused by the delay in giving notice of the claim.

1. Transfer Parties Warranties – GANDS:

a. Good Title: The warrantor has good title to the instrument and is entitled to enforce the instrument.

b. Alterations Not Present: All indorsers warrant that no material alterations have occurred to the instrument.

c. No Knowledge of Insolvency: All indorsers warrant that they have no knowledge of any commercial insolvency proceedings against the maker or drawer.

d. Defenses Not Present: All indorsers warrant that no defense can be asserted against the warrantor.

e. Signatures are Genuine and Authorized: All indorsers warrant that all signatures are authentic and authorized, so any prior unauthorized signature or forged indorsement creates liability.

2. Presentment Party Warranties – GAD:

a. Good Title: The warrantor has good title to the instrument and is entitled to enforce the instrument.

b. Alterations Not Present: Presenters warrant that no material alterations have occurred to the instrument.

c. Drawer's Signature is Authorized: The warrantor has no knowledge that the signature of the drawer is unauthorized.

3. Excluded Subjects:
The above warranties exclude any warranty that the instrument will be paid. But the indorser, in effect, guarantees payment to subsequent parties.

4. Exception to Warranty Liability: An exception is an accommodation indorser who makes no implied warranties because she is not involved in the chain of title.

5. Warranty Disclaimer: Transfer or presentment warranties may be disclaimed except in the case of checks. The Code requires specific reference to warranties such as "without warranties."

> **MEE Tip:** Warranties made upon transfer or presentment are common on the MEE. Often the transferring and/or presenting party lacks knowledge of problems in the instrument's history. If the transferor did not indorse a bearer instrument, there is no warranty liability to subsequent holders only to his immediate transferee.

E. Underlying Obligation

On issue of the instrument, rights on the underlying obligation are suspended. Upon dishonor, the suspension is lifted and the holder may sue on the original transaction obligation. [UCC 3-310]

> **MEE Tip:** Once a note is dishonored or check returned by the bank the payee seller may go directly against the maker / drawer customer on the underlying contract.

VI. IMPROPER NEGOTIATION

> **MEE Tip:** Instrument theft and forgery merit special emphasis in your essay answer. Contrast your analysis with the common law rule that theft constitutes conversion which prevents any assignee thereafter from receiving valid title. An HDC of bearer paper will prevail even if the instrument was previously lost or had been stolen. Order paper is more usual on the exam.

A. In General

Forgery is a signature by one other than the maker/drawer or an indorser made with an intent to impersonate another. The forger can steal an unsigned instrument and sign it; steal an order instrument and negotiate it to a third party through a payee forgery; or forge a required indorser's signature when the instrument is presented to the bank.

B. Maker's / Drawer's Signature Forged

If an unsigned instrument is stolen and the forger signs the proper maker or drawer's name, the bank's customer usually has no liability.

1. Bank Liability and Recovery: If the bank wrongfully honors such a check, it must return the money to the drawer; it may however be able to recover from the presenting party under a breach of title warranty theory. The law treats the forger as the maker of a new instrument so that there is no liability to even an HDC.

2. Exception for Owner's Negligence: The exception is where the owner's negligence contributed to the forgery such as placing checks in an unprotected place or leaving a signature stamp near the blank checks.

C. Payee Designation Incomplete

If an instrument is properly signed but fails to state the payee and the thief completes it in his favor (unauthorized completion), the maker/drawer is not liable to the thief. But, the drawer will be liable to a subsequent third party qualifying as an HDC. If the maker/drawer pays an HDC, the payee cannot recover.

D. Indorser's Signature Forged

If a properly issued negotiable instrument is stolen and the indorser's signature is forged, there is no liability to the indorser who was falsely represented (again, unless his negligence contributed to the theft). This breaks the chain of title and no subsequent transferee can become an HDC.

E. Enforcement of Lost, Destroyed, or Stolen Instrument

A payee from whom an instrument was stolen, lost, or destroyed can still enforce the contractual amount against the maker or drawer; instrument acceptance does not usually discharge the underlying obligation. A sworn declaration is required. The maker or drawer must be adequately protected against the claim of another trying to enforce the instrument. Adequate protection may be by any reasonable means. [UCC 3-309 and 312]

F. Forgery is a Crime / Tort

Forgery is also a crime in many jurisdictions and a tort action for conversion may also be possible. There must be intent to defraud. The statute applies both to the person making, completing, or altering an instrument and one who possesses, offers, or disposes of an instrument which he knows to be forged.

MEE Tip: Any time you see a forgery identify in your answer that in most states it is a criminal act for an easy half point. Remember it applies both to the forger and any subsequent holder with knowledge of the forgery.

VII. ARTICLE 4 – BANK DEPOSITS AND COLLECTIONS

MEE Tip: If one of the negotiable instruments on the exam is a check drawn on a bank, Article 4 has potential issues. Identify both Articles in the first sentence of your answer.

A. Drawee's Responsibilities

The provisions of this Article may usually be varied by agreement. [UCC 4-103] However, no contract term can disclaim a bank's responsibility for its own lack of good faith or failure to exercise ordinary care.

1. Wrongful Honor: The bank can be negligent by wrongfully honoring an instrument irregular on its face. The payment of a more than 90 day old stale check is potentially wrongful honor if the drawer complains.

2. No Duty to Presenter: The drawee bank has no duty to a presenter or other holder of an instrument unless the bank has certified the instrument. To avoid liability to the presenter, the drawee bank must return the check to the presenting party before midnight of the next business day. [UCC 3-503]

3. Overdue / Postdated / Overdraft: A check becomes stale 90 days from date. [UCC 3-304] The bank may pay a postdated check unless notified to the contrary by their customer. A bank may charge the customer's account with a transaction if it is properly payable, even if it creates an overdraft. [UCC 4-401]

4. Hold Periods: The federal Expedited Funds Availability Act allows the depository bank to hold its customer's funds for no more than 2 days for a deposit of a local check and 5 days for a deposit of a non-local check.

5. Multiple Payees: If an instrument is payable to "cash" or "A or B," either can indorse and the bank may pay to either A or B. But if payable to "A and B," both must indorse. If only one payee wrongfully indorses and cashes the check, they may also be sued for conversion by the other payee.

6. Wrongful Dishonor: Under the "properly payable rule," a bank is also liable to the customer for wrongful dishonor unless it would have created an overdraft. [UCC 4-402] Death or incompetence of the drawer terminates the bank's authority to pay any presenting party 10 days after the bank receives notice. [UCC 4-405] Regardless of any other arrangement, a bank has no obligation to honor checks presented more than six months after the date of issue unless the bank certified the check. [UCC 4-404]

B. Stop Payment Order and Transaction Sequence

A customer may order the bank to stop payment and not honor any or all items payable on their account. If the bank pays out over a valid stop payment order, it is a wrongful honor. [UCC 4-403]

1. Oral Order: An oral stop payment order is binding upon the bank for 14 days.

2. Written Order: A written stop payment order is effective for only six months unless renewed in writing.

3. Bank Decides Sequencing: Items may be accepted, paid or charged to the account in any order convenient to the bank. Once a check has been returned "stop payment," it cannot be presented again.

C. Unauthorized Signature or Alteration

1. Period to Report: The time period to report to the drawee bank that the drawer's signature was not authorized or that the instrument was altered depends on the drawer's category: [UCC 4-406]

a. Businesses: A business customer has a 60 day time period from receipt of the account statement to notify the bank of the unauthorized signature or material alteration.

b. Consumers: Personal, family, or household customers have one year from receipt of the canceled check to assert the claims of unauthorized signature or material alteration against the bank.

2. Forged Instrument Liability: Because the bank is expected to know the drawer's signature, it is usually liable for a forged instrument. If a forged instrument is paid, the bank may be able to recover against the presenting party or indorsers under a warranty theory.

3. Drawer's Negligence Exception: Exceptions where the bank is not liable include situations where the drawer was negligent. This includes leaving the signed check in a non-secured area, or situations involving a dummy vendor, phantom employee, or impostor.

D. Comparative Negligence

As between the negligent drawer and the bank who wrongfully honored the instrument, the loss is to be allocated based upon comparative negligence. The Code does not define what constitutes "failure to exercise ordinary care" or "substantially contributing to the alteration." [UCC 3-406]

E. Certification

If a holder procures a bank certification of the instrument, the drawer and former indorsers are discharged. After certification, a bank becomes solely liable to any holder in due course. Unless otherwise agreed, a bank has no obligation to certify a check. [UCC 3-411]

F. Subrogation Rights

A payor bank has full subrogation rights if it pays out over a stop payment order or other circumstances that are objected to by the drawer or maker. A bank may also go against other indorsers on their warranty liability.

VIII. EXAM APPROACH TO NEGOTIABLE INSTRUMENTS ESSAY ANSWERS

A. Introduction

The best sequential approach to use in addressing an essay answer is to follow the primary issues in order. If there is more than one instrument in the question analyze them sequentially. For each instrument, refer "supra" to your previous boiler plate language. Cover controlling law, negotiability, HDC, or mere assignee defenses – personal or real liability – as between parties.

B. Question Facts

On 4/15, Oscar received an insurance check for fire inventory damage to his store from InsureCo for $11,000, drawn on InsureCo's account at Big Banc. That day, his bookkeeper Betty fraudulently induced Oscar to endorse the check and transfer it to her to invest in a furniture cleaning company. On 4/16, Oscar changed his mind and called InsureCo to ask them to stop payment on the check. InsureCo directed Big Banc to stop payment, but Betty had already taken the check to Credit Union, which gave her $11,000 cash even though Betty's account was habitually and currently overdrawn. Credit Union presented the check to Big Banc, which refused to pay. Betty is missing, Oscar has no money, and Credit Union wants reimbursement from someone.

Oscar's second check from InsureCo for building damage was for $28,000, mad out to "Oscar and Ned" (his childhood friend who held a mortgage on the store property). InsureCo sent the check to Ned, who signed his name and deposited it at Rock Bank. Ned then withdrew the money and skipped town.

C. Questions Requirements

1. Are the $11,000 and $28,000 checks negotiable instruments? Explain.

2. Is any party a holder in due course? Explain

3. Are there defenses and which party is liable? Explain

D. Fact Sequential Diagram (not to be submitted as part of your written answer)

$11,000 check

Drawer, InsureCo ⇒ Payee, Oscar ⇒ fraudulent endorsement to Betty ⇒ Credit Union, presentor to

Big Bank
Drawee, dishonored

$28,000 check

Drawer, InsureCo ⇒ Payee, Oscar and Ned ⇒ Only Ned endorsed ⇒ RockBank, presentor to

Big Bank
Drawee, dishonored

E. Model Answer

Controlling Law. Commercial paper is governed by UCC Article 3. Banks and their customer relations are governed by UCC Article 4.

Negotiability. For an instrument to be negotiable, it must have at issue (1) negotiable words such as "pay to the order of," (2) an unconditional promise to pay with no other undertaking, (3) a time certain for payment, (4) a sum certain in money, and (5) signed by the maker or drawer. Here, Insure Co.'s check for $11,000 appears to meet all these requirements.

Holder in Due Course (HDC). To facilitate commerce, an HDC has greater rights than a mere assignee. Personal defenses are not valid against an HDC. To be an HDC, a person must take the instrument (1) for value, (2) in good faith, (3) with no notice of imperfections, and (4) the instrument must be properly negotiated – endorsed and delivered for order paper and merely delivered for bearer paper. If someone does not qualify as an HDC (because he receives the item as a gift, for example) he can still be an HDC under the Shelter Rule, if there is an HDC up the chain who passed HDC status by assignment. Here Betty did not take the instrument in good faith. She fraudulently induced Oscar to endorse the check to her. Therefore, Betty does not qualify as an HDC.

Credit Union is an HDC. They took from Betty who is not an HDC, but they could be an HDC in their own right. They gave value, in good faith, with no notice, and presumably with proper endorsement. By the time Credit Union presented the check to Big Banc, Big Banc's customer had placed a stop payment on the check. The drawee bank is an agent for their customer, therefore the check was not properly payable and Big Banc cannot pay Credit Union or they would be liable to their customer InsureCo. for wrongful honor.

Liability. Credit Union, as an HDC, can go against the maker, InsureCo, which stopped payment (which is notice they are not going to pay) or Credit Union's transferor, Betty. The facts state Oscar has no money, but Oscar is not liable to Credit Union as he is not the maker or their transferor. Credit Union's only recourse is from their transferor, Betty. At transfer Betty warranted she had good title and had the right to enforce the instrument, no material alterations were present, she had no knowledge of maker's insolvency, no defenses can be asserted against the her, and all signatures are genuine and authorized. Credit Union should not have paid out on uncollected funds, especially as they had notice Betty had financial problems and was currently overdrawn. They are allowed to hold funds on a deposited instrument from a local bank for 2 days and non-local banks for 5 days.

Check for $28,000. This instrument also appears to meet all the negotiability requirements listed supra.

Negotiation. A check can be payable to two or more people. If the payees are A "or" B, either can endorse it. However, if the payees are A "and" B, then both must endorse the check. Here, Oscar did not endorse this check and therefore it was not validly negotiated to Rock Bank, and Rock Bank should not have accepted it for deposit. The check will not be paid by Big Banc and will be sent back to Rock Bank which can recover only from its customer, Ned.

Liability. If Ned had forged Oscar's endorsement, Rock Bank would still not get paid by Big Banc. However, they would not have known they should refuse the deposit because they have no way of verifying Oscar's endorsement. Oscar can sue Ned for conversion of his share of the $28,000 check. The fact that Ned "skipped town" does not relieve him of liability.

RIGOS BAR REVIEW SERIES

UNIFORM MULTISTATE ESSAY EXAM (MEE) REVIEW

CHAPTER 6

UCC ARTICLE 3 – COMMERCIAL PAPER

Magic Memory Outlines®

I. **INTRODUCTION**
   A. Advantages Over Ordinary Contracts...
   B. Two-Party Paper ....
   C. Three-Party Paper ....
      1. Check ....
      2. Draft ....
   D. Certificate of Deposit..

II. **NEGOTIABLE INSTRUMENT – NUTSS**
   A. **N**egotiable Words ....
      1. Order Paper...
      2. Bearer Paper...
      3. Contradictory Terms ....
         a. Handwritten, Typed, and Printed...
         b. Amount ....
   B. **U**nconditional Promise to Pay ....
      1. Promise to Pay Only ....
      2. Future Contract ....
      3. Non-Violating Conditions...
      4. Surety Involvement...
      5. Legal Right Retention Clause ....
   C. **T**ime Certain ....
      1. Face of Instrument ....
      2. Dates and Substitution ....
      3. Extension or Acceleration Provisions...
      4. Occurrence Time Uncertain..
      5. Undated Instrument...
   D. **S**um Certain in Money..
      1. Currency of Any Country ....
      2. Permissible Inclusions ....
      3. Open Sum and Option...
   E. **S**igned by Maker/Drawer..
      1. Acceptable Signatures...
      2. Representative Liability ....
   F. Issue and Incomplete Instruments..
      1. Issue Requirement...

2. Incomplete Instrument ....
    a. Enforceable When Properly Completed ....
    b. Examples ....
    c. Payee Incomplete ....
    d. Improperly Completed ....

III. HOLDER IN DUE COURSE – FINNS
  A. **F**or Value ....
    1. Gift Donee ....
    2. Partial HDC ....
    3. Future Performance ....
  B. **I**n Good Faith ....
  C. **N**o Notice ....
  D. **N**egotiation ....
    1. Order Paper ....
    2. Bearer Paper ....
    3. Prohibited Negotiation ....
  E. **S**helter Rule ....
    1. Look Up the Ladder ....
    2. Example ....
    3. Cannot Improve Position ....
  F. Exceptions to Negotiation Requirement ....
    1. Fictitious Payee ....
      a. Dummy Vendor ....
      b. Phantom Employee ....
    2. Impostor ....

IV. REAL OR PERSONAL DEFENSE
  A. Personal Defenses – **MUUFFO** ....
    1. **M**utual Mistake ....
    2. **U**nauthorized Completion ....
    3. **U**ncompletion of a Condition Precedent ....
    4. **F**raud in the Inducement ....
    5. **F**ailure of Consideration ....
    6. **O**ther's Claims ....
    7. Federal Trade Commission ....
  B. Real Defenses – **FIDDLS FUM** ....
    1. General Real Defenses ....
      a. **F**raud in Execution ....
      b. **I**llegality ....
      c. **D**ischarge in Bankruptcy ....
      d. **D**uress ....
      e. **L**ack of Capacity ....

  f. **S**tatute of Limitations ....

  g. **F**orgery ....

  h. **U**nauthorized Signature ....

  i. **M**aterial Alteration ....

 2. Forgery, Unauthorized Signature, Material Alteration Exceptions ....

  a. Examples...

  b. Recharacterizing From Real Defense to Personal ....

  c. Negligent Supervision ....

  d. Comparative Negligence ....

V. LIABILITY OF PARTIES

 A. Primary ....

  1. Issue and Acceptance...

  2. Co-Makers ....

  3. Liability for Dishonored Checks ....

 B. Secondary ....

  1. In General ....

   a. Chronological Liability...

   b. Conditions Precedent ....

   c. Banks and HDC Limitations...

  2. Types of Indorsements...

   a. Unqualified / Blank...

   b. Special..

   c. Restrictive ....

   d. Qualified Without Recourse ....

   e. Payment Guaranteed ....

   f. Collection Guaranteed ....

   g. Accommodation Indorser ....

   h. Payment in Full..

 C. Indorser's Skeleton ....

 D. Warranty Liability ....

  1. Transfer Parties Warranties – **GANDS** ....

   a. **G**ood Title...

   b. **A**lterations Not Present..

   c. **N**o Knowledge of Insolvency ....

   d. **D**efenses Not Present...

   e. **S**ignatures are Genuine and Authorized ....

  2. Presentment Party Warranties – **GAD**...

   a. **G**ood Title...

   b. **A**lterations Not Present..

   c. **D**rawer's Signature is Authorized ....

  3. Excluded Subjects...

  4. Exception to Warranty Liability ....

  5. Warranty Disclaimer...

 E. Underlying Obligation...

VI. IMPROPER NEGOTIATION
    A. In General ....
    B. Maker's/Drawer's Signature Forged ....
        1. Bank Liability and Recovery ....
        2. Exception for Owner's Negligence ....
    C. Payee Designation Incomplete ....
    D. Indorser's Signature Forged ....
    E. Enforcement of Lost, Destroyed, or Stolen Instruments ....
    F. Forgery is a Crime / Tort ....

VII. ARTICLE 4 – BANK DEPOSITS AND COLLECTIONS
    A. Drawee's Responsibilities ....
        1. Wrongful Honor ....
        2. No Duty to Presenter ....
        3. Overdue / Postdated / Overdraft ....
        4. Hold Periods ....
        5. Multiple Payees ....
        6. Wrongful Dishonor ....
    B. Stop Payment Order and Transaction Sequence ....
        1. Oral Orders – 14 Days ....
        2. Written Orders – 6 Months ....
        3. Bank Decides Sequencing ....
    C. Unauthorized Signature or Alteration ....
        1. Period to Report ....
            a. Businesses – 60 days ....
            b. Consumers – 1 year ....
        2. Forged Instrument Liability ....
        3. Drawer's Negligence Exception ....
    D. Comparative Negligence ....
    E. Certification ....
    F. Subrogation Rights ....

VIII. EXAM APPROACH TO ESSAY ANSWERS
    A. Introduction ....
    B. Question Facts ....
    C. Question Requirements ....
    D. Fact Sequential Diagram ....
    E. Model Answer ....

Essay Questions

Question Number 1

Andy Parks found it a conversation starter that his name was similar to a giant star in the music industry, with only the addition of the "s" in their last name being different. This similarity may even have originally attracted Andy to become a roadie with a band, but despite developing the "Rock Star" appearance and swagger, all it had ever been good for was as a pickup line in bars. This changed backstage at a concert one night, when Andy convinced Promoter that he was the real rock star he merely shared a name with. Later in the evening, Andy negotiated a $15,000 deal to be the opening act at the next Rockapalooza festival.

Soon after, the Promoter received from Andy an extensive list of demands for the appearance, including a lavish catered food and beverage spread and a RV equipped with a hot tub for the band's private dressing room. Andy also demanded half the payment beforehand to cover some traveling expenses and costume and equipment purchases. Promoter sent a check for half the agreed amount, $7,500, made out to Andy Park, but no band showed up on performance day. Promoter checked with his Bank to find the check had been cashed by a Mr. Andy Parks three days earlier.

Promoter disputes the Bank's honoring of the check when he determines the famous Mr. Park had never heard of Promoter and had not agreed to perform at Rockapalooza. Promoter claims he was fraudulently induced, and is therefore not responsible. Bank asserts they had no way of knowing there was a problem and are therefore not responsible.

1. Was the instrument properly issued? Explain.

2. Was negotiation properly affected? Explain.

3. Is Promoter liable for payment? Explain.

Question Number 2

Adapt-a-car began its biodiesel rent-by-the-day vehicle leasing business with a fleet of older family sedans they had acquired over time to keep pace with their business's growing demand. When it became obvious that gasoline was getting more expensive, Manager made the decision to purchase a fleet of new vehicles gradually to replace the aging low-mileage fleet vehicles as they were retired. He approached Wholesale Auto Sales with his requirements, who showed him three European vehicles from different makers, all of which they boasted would get over

60 MPG on biodiesel fuel. Manager was then offered a large one-time discount if Adapt-a-car purchased at least three vehicles initially to begin the fleet upgrade. Adapt-a-car agreed to the purchase and issued a check for $60,000.00 to Wholesale Auto Sales.

The owner of Wholesale properly endorsed the check and transferred it to his Distributor for additional vehicles and accessories. Distributor had been waiting for a large influx of cash to help his Son pay his college tuition, so Distributor properly endorsed the $60,000 check and gave it to Son as a gift towards his law school tuition. Son took the check to Adapt-a-car's Bank, who advised they had received a stop payment order.

Son contacted Adapt-a-car, who stated they would not be making payment on the three vehicles, but were returning them. This was due to their misrepresented fuel efficiency and already failing fuel systems which they had just learned are not covered under manufacturer's warranty due to the unauthorized biodiesel fuel used in them. Furthermore, they learned the price they paid per vehicle was identical to the price Wholesale offered retailers in the Sunday paper.

Son explained to Adapt-a-car that he acquired the check legitimately, and he demands payment regardless of whatever vehicle arrangements the previous parties engaged in. Please advise Son of his rights and obligations regarding the following:

1. Was the instrument properly negotiated amongst the parties? Explain.

2. What will determine liability for payment? Explain.

3. Who, if anyone, owes payment to Son? Explain.

Question Number 3

After attending a worldwide church conference, Polly Purity receives desperate email requests for her help from another friendly Attendee. She learns that the friend lives in Nigeria, and his Brother is arriving in her home city soon and needs watching over as an impulsive youth. Polly agrees to help. In a subsequent email attendee describes how there is an inheritance now owed to both he and his Brother, but he cannot find a way to get his Brother's $40,000 share to him without losing most of it in wire transfer fees and currency exchange costs.

Attendee asks Polly to accept a check from him for $50,000, and for her efforts to help him he would like to give her $10,000 of that check. She would be helping him by depositing it into her Bank and making sure Brother is given cashier's checks made out in his landlord's name and the names of his various debtors so he would not squander his inheritance.

Hearing nothing back from Polly, Attendee signs the back of the $50,000 check drawn on an account at the Nigerian Bank "pay Polly Purity, /s/Attendee Abroad." He sends the endorsed check to Brother, who now approaches Polly saying he will lose his entire inheritance if she is not able to help, and seeing the endorsement, reluctantly, she agrees. Polly deposits the Nigerian check into her Bank, draws out eight cashier's checks totaling $40,000 in the names directed by Attendee and gives them to Brother. Several days later the Nigerian Bank $50,000 check bounces and Brother is nowhere to be found.

Further investigation reveals there was no such account at the Nigerian Bank, and the origin of the email requests Polly received was some internet cafe right in her home state. The cashier's checks had all been cashed immediately. Polly's account is now overdrawn, and she has no idea who Attendee and Brother actually are, so she seeks your advice in determining liability.

1. What is the liability of the Nigerian Bank? Explain.

2. Did Polly legitimately acquire the instrument and was it properly transferred? Explain.

3. Can any party assert wrongful honor against Polly's Bank, and if so, what would be their defenses? Explain.

Question 4

When Abner Curmudgeon left work early to attend his sister's funeral saying he would not return for several days, his staff was stunned. Abner owned the company and had not missed a day's work in thirty two years, and never trusted anyone else to lock up. In his absence, the staff acted like school children, having free reign with no supervision, they blasted the radio, took long breaks and were generally unproductive.

By Friday when Abner had not yet returned, Buster was determined to get his paycheck, to avoid an eviction notice from his landlord. Even though Buster was just the maintenance man, he knew the checks and signature stamp were kept in the top drawer of Abner's unlocked file cabinet, and asserting he had earned it and deserved it, Buster wrote out the check for his regular salary amount and stamped it with Abner's signature.

On his way home that evening, Buster stops in the Loopy Lady tavern, and asks old Hank to cash his paycheck so he can spend some money in the tavern. Hank looks the check over, and it appears like every other payroll check he has cashed for Buster, so with Buster's endorsement, he cashes it. Five days later Hank then deposits the check into the tavern's bank account, and three days later receives notice that the check was denied because Abner, upon his return, reported the check stolen once he realized one was not accounted for.

Now Hank wants Abner to make good on the check that was bounced, and Abner confronts Buster and fires him. Buster asserts the money is owed to him by Abner anyway, so Abner has no justification to deny payment.

1. Is this a negotiable instrument? Explain.

2. Is presenter an HDC? Explain.

3. What defenses might Abner assert? Explain.

Question Number 5

When Branford saw the lovely landscaping the neighbor had done to his yard and garden, he wanted to know which company had done the great work so he could hire them to transform his home, too. The neighbor kindly shared the name of the Landscaper and said the work was done in two days time, and that he was pleased with the value he got for his money.

Branford called Landscaper and had him come and bid the job to create a new outdoor living space. After the two discuss about what work will be done, Landscaper issues an estimate on the spot and lets Branford know there is one customer in front of him, but he is available to start after that. Wanting to have an end-of-summer party in a fabulous new outdoor living space, Branford writes two checks on the spot totaling the entire amount hoping this will avoid any further delays, one with "first half of the job" and one with "second half of the job" written in the memo sections.

Excited at the yard and garden changes they discussed, Branford begins planning his first outdoor event in the new space. He calls 45 of his closest friends and the best caterer in town, arranging a luau in his new tropical paradise this weekend. When Thursday arrived and still no Landscaper, Branford grew very nervous, and checked his bank account to find the first check to Landscaper had been cashed. Later that afternoon, Landscaper arrived with a truckload of tropical plants and began digging up the back yard. Furious that things looked worse not better on his return home that evening, Branford accused Landscaper of taking payment for the first half of a job he hadn't done yet.

Landscaper informed him that the previous job he had to do was very large, taking up more of his time and operating capital than expected, and he had not received payment from them yet, so he had to cash Branford's check to buy supplies. Branford explained his party plans, but Landscaper said the yard simply could not be ready in time. Branford stopped payment on the second check and cancelled the party.

1. Was Landscaper's cashing the first check improper? Explain.

2. Does Branford have a defense against honoring the second check? Explain.

3. Is the bank liable for improperly honoring the first check? Explain.

Course 5328. Copyright by Rigos Bar Review Series – MEE.

Essay Answers

Answer Number 1

Summary

Negotiable instruments (NI) require (1) negotiable words, (2) an unconditional promise to pay, (3) at a time certain, (4) a sum certain in money, and (5) the signature of the drawer or maker. Here, issuance meets these five requirements. To be a holder in due course (HDC), one must acquire the NI for value, in good faith, with no notice of a claim against its enforceability, and through proper negotiation. Here, A lacks all of the elements. An HDC takes free of personal defenses, but since A is not an HDC, he is liable for fraud in the inducement. The presenter to the drawee bank warrants he has good title, that material alterations have not occurred, and that the drawer's signature is authorized. Real defenses are good against a HDC and personal defenses are good against the payee. Here, A defrauded P and forged the indorsement that the Bank wrongfully honored. Thus, P is not liable. Liability goes upstream chronologically by transferor. Here, bank would have a claim against A, who cannot pursue the maker (P), as A is not an HDC.

Issues Raised

(1) Issue and Negotiability Requirements
 (a) Negotiable words
 (b) Unconditional promise to pay
 (c) Time certain
 (d) Sum certain in money
 (e) Signature of the drawer or maker
(2) Holder in Due Course
 (a) For value
 (b) In good faith
 (c) No notice of a claim against its enforceability
 (d) Negotiation proper
(3) Presentment Warranties
 (a) Good title
 (b) No material alterations
 (c) Drawer's signature is authorized
(4) Defenses
 (a) Fraud in the inducement
 (b) Unauthorized signature
 (c) Material alteration

(5) Bank – Parks Liability
    (a) Creates obligation to refund any payment on the NI
    (b) Precedes chronologically up the ladder
    (c) "You sue your transferors, your transferees sue you"
(6) Bank – Promoter Liability
    (a) Improper honor
    (b) No stop payment order
    (c) Promoter assumes bank rights

Sample Answer

Authority: UCC Article 3 governs transactions involving negotiable instruments (NI) and Article 4 controls bank-customer relations.

(1) Issue and Negotiability Requirements. A NI must meet the five requirements of negotiable words, an unconditional promise to pay, at a time certain, a sum certain in money, and signed by the drawer or maker. Here, the instrument payable to Park possesses all the requisite elements by the maker to create valid payment, and thus was properly issued.

(2) Holder in Due Course (HDC). To be an HDC, one must acquire the instrument for value, in good faith, with no notice of a claim against the enforceability of the instrument and through proper negotiation. Here, Andy Parks by impersonating another lacks good faith and is not planning to give value. An HDC takes free of personal defenses, but Andy is not an HDC because of his lack of good faith, etc.

(3) Presentment Warranties. The presenter to the drawee bank asserts they have good title, that material alterations have not occurred to the instrument, and the drawer's signature is authorized. Here, Andy knows the check has been fraudulently procured thus he does not have good title to the check and the intended payee's signature is forged. Therefore when Parks cashed it, he violated the required presentment warranty elements.

(4) Defenses. Personal defenses arising from the underlying contract are not good against an HDC, but may be asserted against the payee. These include mutual mistake, unauthorized completion, uncompletion of a condition precedent, fraud in the inducement, and failure of consideration. Real defenses at or after issuance of the NI are good against an HDC and they are fraud in the execution, illegality, discharge in bankruptcy, duress, lack of capacity, statute of limitations, forgery, unauthorized signature, and material alteration. The last three can be re-characterized as personal defenses if the maker/drawer's or endorser's negligence contributed to the defense. Here, Andy Parks fraudulently induced Promoter into issuing payment, altered the instrument to his own name or improperly endorsed it with his own name. As between the maker and payee, Promoter is not liable.

(5) Bank – Parks Liability. Liability precedes chronologically up the ladder, one sues their transferors after their transferees sue them. Here, Promoter's Bank that Andy Parks presented the check to for payment would have a claim against him for breach of presentment warranties, and since he is not an HDC, he would not be able to pursue the Promoter as maker. The payment the drawee bank gave Andy for the instrument will be his obligation to refund.

(6) Bank – Promoter Liability. The Bank may have improperly honored the instrument which was presented to them by the Payee Park. The signature of the drawer Promoter was authorized. The facts do not state whether the Bank asked the presenter for identification; if they did they should have realized that Parks was an imposter and if they did not they were negligent. Promoter may have been contributorily negligent himself, but likely the Bank will have to credit the amount back to Promoter's account and then sue Parks for breach of presentment warranties.

Answer Number 2

Summary

Negotiable instruments (NI) require (1) negotiable words, (2) an unconditional promise to pay, (3) at a time certain, (4) a sum certain, and (5) the signature of the drawer or maker. Here, the $60,000 check appears to be a valid NI. To be a holder in due course (HDC), one must acquire the NI for value, in good faith, with no notice of a claim against its enforceability, and through proper negotiation. Personal defenses are good against the payee, Wholesale Auto Sales, here, fraud in the inducement and failure of consideration. All NI transferors warrant good title, alterations not present, no knowledge of insolvency, defenses not present, and the signatures are genuine and authorized. Here, Wholesale transferred the check to Distributor with knowledge of defenses and is liable to Distributor. Though they are not acquired for value, gifted NIs from a previous HDC offer that same protection to their recipients under the "shelter rule." Here S gets the shelter rule equivalent of HDC status. Implied warranties upon presentment are good title, that material alterations have not occurred, and that the drawer's signature is authorized. S and D would sue the dealership, Wholesale, who is liable.

Issues Raised

(1) General Requirements
    (a) Negotiable words
    (b) Unconditional promise to pay
    (c) Time certain
    (d) Sum certain in money
    (e) Signature of the drawer or maker
(2) Holder in Due Course
    (a) For value
    (b) In good faith
    (c) No notice of a claim against its enforceability
    (d) Negotiation proper
(3) Personal Defenses
    (a) Fraud in the inducement
    (b) Failure of consideration
(4) Transfer Warranties
    (a) Good title
    (b) Alterations not present
    (c) No knowledge of insolvency
    (d) Defenses not present
    (e) Signatures are genuine and authorized
(5) Shelter Rule
(6) Presentment Warranties
    (a) Good title
    (b) No material alterations
    (c) Drawer's signature is authorized

(7) Liability
    (a) Creates obligation to refund any payment on the NI
    (b) Precedes chronologically up the ladder
    (c) "You sue your transferors, your transferees sue you"

Sample Answer

(1) General Requirements. UCC Article 3 governs transactions in negotiable instruments (NI) and Article 4 controls bank-customer relations. For a NI to be valid, it must contain negotiable words, make an unconditional promise to pay, at a time certain, a sum certain in money, and it must be signed by the maker or drawer. Here, the check instrument appears to have been validly issued by drawer Adapt.

(2) Holder in Due Course. To attain the status of a HDC, the holder must acquire the instrument for value, in good faith, having no notices of defenses to the enforceability of the instrument, and through proper negotiation. Here, the question turns on Wholesale's good faith, both in their representations about the suitability of their product for the customer's topics, and about the price discount. These are somewhat subjective areas, and without specific knowledge of unsuitability or industry standards, proving bad faith of a car dealer may be difficult. Conversely he was in the best position to know what the manufacturer's warranty covered.

(3) Personal Defenses. Wholesale is the payee and personal defenses are good against the payee. Personal defenses which might be relevant here include fraud in the inducement and failure of consideration. The fraudulent inducement would be the salesman's claims about the vehicles and mileage. The failure of consideration was the actual product being unable to satisfy those claims.

(4) Transfer Warranties. All transferors of an instrument offer an implied warranty of good title, alterations not present, no knowledge of insolvency, defenses not present, and the signatures are genuine and authorized. Here, Wholesale Auto Sales transferred the check to Distributor with knowledge of defects and is therefore liable to Distributor. Distributor qualifies as an HDC as he gave value in good faith with no knowledge of the defenses to payment.

(5) Shelter Rule. Despite not acquiring for value, gifted instruments that have a previous HDC offer full protection to their recipients. Here, Son assumes the shelter rule equivalent of HDC status from Distributor who appears to be a proper HDC.

(6) Presentment Warranties. These are the warranties the presenter to the drawee bank makes when presenting an instrument for payment. They include good title, no material alterations, and that the drawer's signature is authorized. Here, Son presents the check for payment with no knowledge of any of these defenses.

(7) Liability. A holder pursues their claims up the ladder, one sues their tranferors after their transferees have sued them. Here, since Son is an HDC through the shelter rule and Distributor is an HDC, Son could go directly against Wholesale Auto Sales for payment. In comparison, Son could not go against his transferor since the gift lacked consideration.

Answer Number 3

Summary

Negotiable instruments (NI) require (1) negotiable words, (2) an unconditional promise to pay, (3) at a time certain, (4) a sum certain in money, and (5) the signature of the drawer or maker. Here, A had no valid account at the Nigerian Bank, so no valid NI was created. To be a holder in due course (HDC), one must acquire the NI for value, in good faith, with no notice of a claim against its enforceability, and through proper negotiation. Here, the NI was not transferred in good faith, there was notice of a defense, and it was not properly negotiated, so none of the mandatory requirements were present to achieve HDC status. All NI transferors warrant good title, alterations not present, no knowledge of insolvency, defenses not present, and the signatures are genuine and authorized. Here, A knew the issuing account did not exist, while P unknowingly presented the bad check but still breached her warranty in doing so. Implied warranties upon presentment are good title, that material alterations have not occurred, and that the drawer's signature is authorized. Here, P's bank was unable to present the NI for payment, and thus properly denied payment to P. Forgery is a relevant real defense good even against an HDC. P must identify her transferor before she can sue for her loss.

Issues Raised

(1)   General Requirements
    (a) Negotiable words
    (b) Unconditional promise to pay
    (c) Time certain
    (d) Sum certain in money
    (e) Signature of the drawer or maker
(2)   Holder in Due Course
    (a) For value
    (b) In good faith
    (c) No notice of a claim against its enforceability
    (d) Negotiation proper
(3)   Drawee Bank
(4)   Transfer Warranties
    (a) Good title
    (b) Alterations not present
    (c) No knowledge of insolvency
    (d) Defenses not present
    (e) Signatures are genuine and authorized
(5)   Presentment Warranties
    (a) Good title
    (b) No material alterations
    (c) Drawer's signature is authorized
(6)   Real Defenses
    (a) Fraud in the execution
    (b) Forgery
    (c) Unauthorized signature
    (d) Material alteration

Sample Answer

(1)   General Requirements. UCC Article 3 governs transactions in negotiable instruments (NI) and Article 4 controls bank-customer relations. A NI must contain negotiable words, make an unconditional promise to pay, at a time certain, a sum certain in money, with the authorized signature of the drawer or maker. Here, Attendee had no valid account at the Nigerian Bank, and thus no valid instrument was created. Nigerian Bank is in fact a victim of this crime as well, their good name has been discredited.

(2)   Holder in Due Course. One must acquire the instrument for value, in good faith, with no notice of a defense to the enforceability of the claim and through proper negotiation. The shelter rule allows gift recipients to receive HDC status if one existed earlier in the instrument's journey. The instrument was not transferred in good faith, there was notice of a defense to enforceability, and it was not properly negotiated, so none of the mandatory requirements were met to achieve HDC status.

(3)   Drawee Bank. A drawee bank has no duty to the presenting party unless they certified the instrument. It also appears that the drawee bank returned the false check timely to the presenter. Nigerian Bank thus has no liability unless it could be shown they knew Attendee was negotiating false checks containing their name as drawee.

(4)   Transfer Warranties. The transferor of an instrument warrantees they have good title, that material alterations are not present, no knowledge of insolvency, no defenses are present and the signature is authorized. Here, Attendee issued a $50,000 check on an account which did not exist. He therefore knew that he failed all of the transfer warranty provisions, and was in fact committing check fraud. Polly, however, unknowingly transferred a bad check to her bank but nonetheless breached her warranty in doing so.

(5)   Presentment Warranties. The presenter warrants that they have good title to the instrument, and are entitled to enforce the instrument, that no material alterations are present and they have no knowledge that the drawer's signature is unauthorized. Here, Polly's bank was unable to present the instrument for payment, and accordingly properly denied payment to Polly.

(6)   Real Defenses. Real defenses include fraud on the part of the maker or drawer in issuance such as the forgery present here. Polly did not negotiate the $50,000 check so there is no HDC. The liability moves chronologically backwards through the transactions. Here, Polly's bank was unable to present the instrument for payment and therefore properly returned the checks to the presenting party. This was not a properly issued negotiable instrument that was stolen and then transferred with a forged maker's signature. Here, no such account existed, so this check amounts to counterfeit money that Polly received and tried to negotiate unsuccessfully. Sadly, her Bank has properly exercised recourse for their conditional acceptance of the check, but Polly must first identify and locate her transferor before she can consider suing for her loss.

Answer Number 4

Summary

Negotiable instruments (NI) require (1) negotiable words, (2) an unconditional promise to pay, (3) at a time certain, (4) for a sum certain, and (5) the signature of the drawer or maker. Here, B is the intended payee, not the real drawer or maker, and so cannot issue this check from A's account. To be a holder in due course (HDC), one must acquire the NI for value, in good faith, with no notice of a claim against its enforceability, and through proper negotiation. H meets these requirements and is thus an HDC. The presentment warranties to the drawee bank are good title, that material alterations have not occurred, and that the drawer's signature is authorized. H breaches unknowingly because the drawer's signature was not authorized. Real defenses include fraud in the execution, illegality, discharge in bankruptcy, duress, lack of capacity, statute of limitations forgery, unauthorized signature, and material alterations. Here, forgery, unauthorized signature and material alteration apply. Even if the instrument had been properly negotiated by H, these real defenses are good against a HDC, and the maker need not pay. An exception to the real defenses of forgery, unauthorized signature, and material alteration exists where the maker's negligence contributed to the defense. A's failure to lock up the payroll checks and signature stamp may make him liable to the HDC, H.

Issues Raised

(1) General Requirements
    (a) Negotiable words
    (b) Unconditional promise to pay
    (c) Time certain
    (d) Sum certain in money
    (e) Signature of the drawer or maker
(2) Holder in Due Course
    (a) For value
    (b) In good faith
    (c) No notice of a claim against its enforceability
    (d) Negotiation proper
(3) Presentment Warranties
    (a) Good title
    (b) No material alterations
    (c) Drawer's signature is authorized
(4) Real Defenses
    (a) Fraud in the execution
    (b) Forgery
    (c) Unauthorized signature
    (d) Material alteration
(5) Liability
    (a) Creates obligation to refund any payment on the NI
    (b) Precedes chronologically up the ladder
    (c) "You sue your transferors, your transferees sue you"

Sample Answer

(1)   General Requirements. UCC Article 3 governs transactions in negotiable instruments (NI) and Article 4 controls bank-customer relations. A NI must include the five requirements of negotiable words, an unconditional promise to pay, at a time certain, a sum certain in money, and signed by the drawer or maker. Here, Buster is not the legal drawer or maker, but rather the intended payee, and cannot properly issue this check from Abner's account.

(2)   Holder in Due Course. To be a holder in due course (HDC), one must acquire the instrument for value, in good faith, with no notice of a claim against the enforceability of the instrument and through proper negotiation. Hank apparently meets the requirements of an HDC here taking from B as there were no suspicious circumstances.

(3)   Presentment Warranties. The warrantor asserts they have good title, that material alterations have not occurred to the instrument and the drawer's signature is authorized. Here again, with Hank as presenter, he meets the criteria except the drawer's signature was not authorized. Thus Hank breached his presentation warranty as knowledge that the signature is unauthorized is not required.

(4)   Real Defenses. Include fraud in the execution, illegality, discharge in bankruptcy, duress, lack of capacity, statute of limitations forgery, unauthorized signature, material alterations. Forgery and unauthorized signature apply here. Even if the instrument had been properly negotiated by Hank, these real defenses are good against a HDC and the maker need not pay providing he does not fall into the exception to this rule where the drawer's negligence substantially contributed to the loss.

(5)   Liability. Generally, liability proceeds chronologically up the ladder, you sue your transferors, your transferees sue you. An HDC takes free of personal defenses, but real defenses can be asserted against an HDC and payment is not required. An exception to the real defenses of forgery, unauthorized signature and material alteration exists where the maker's negligence contributed to the defense. Abner's failure to lock up the payroll checks and signature stamp was negligence and substantially contributed to the wrongful issue. This recharacterizes the real defenses to personal defenses thereby allowing the HDC Hank to collect.

(6)   Claims against Buster. A may here have a cause of action against his employee. While the amount may have been due, such theft and forgery are crimes so A could file a criminal complaint and sue B for at least all costs associated with the incident.

Answer Number 5

Summary

Negotiable instruments (NI) require (1) negotiable words, (2) an unconditional promise to pay, (3) at a time certain, (4) a sum certain in money, and (5) the signature of the drawer or maker. A properly drafted check would have said pay to L on X date Y amount. To be a holder in due course (HDC), one must acquire the NI for value, in good faith, with no notice of a claim against its enforceability, and through proper negotiation. The value here was a promise to perform labor; L's failure to perform is a breach of contract, not a reason to deny payment. The warrantor asserts good title, that material alterations have not occurred to the instrument and the drawer's signature is authorized. Here, L meets all these requirements. An HDC takes clear of personal defenses. Generally, liability proceeds chronologically up the ladder. B must honor the check, as it was properly payable. Barring any real defenses which generally cover the legitimacy of the actual instrument issuance, as opposed to a personal defense, which usually addresses issues with the underlying contract, the Bank is not liable.

Issues Raised

(1)　General Requirements
　　　(a) Negotiable words
　　　(b) Unconditional promise to pay
　　　(c) Time certain
　　　(d) Sum certain in money
　　　(e) Signature of the drawer or maker
(2)　Holder in Due Course
　　　(a) For value
　　　(b) In good faith
　　　(c) No notice of a claim against its enforceability
　　　(d) Negotiation proper
(3)　Presentment Warranties
　　　(a) Good title
　　　(b) No material alterations
　　　(c) Drawer's signature is authorized
(4)　Personal Defenses
　　　(a) Fraud in the inducement
　　　(b) Failure of consideration
(5)　Liability
　　　(a) Creates obligation to refund any payment on the NI
　　　(b) Precedes chronologically up the ladder

Sample Answer

(1)　General Requirements. UCC Article 3 governs transactions in negotiable instruments (NI) and Article 4 controls bank-customer relations. A NI must include the five requirements of negotiable words, an unconditional promise to pay, at a time certain, a sum certain in money, and signed by the drawer or maker. Here, a properly drafted check would have said pay to Landscaper on this date this amount. Here, the notation "first half of job" did not create a condition precedent to issue or bank payment rather only a reference to the portion of the job. The unconditional promise to pay means once issued, the check was negotiable.

(2)   Holder in Due Course. To be a holder in due course (HDC), one must acquire the instrument for value, in good faith, with no notice of a claim against the enforceability of the instrument and through proper negotiation. The value here was a promise to perform future labor, Landscaper had not done so by the time he cashed the check, but this is a breach of the underlying contract, not a reason to deny the holder's presentment rights to the drawee bank.

(3)   Presentment Warranties. The warrantor asserts they have good title, that material alterations have not occurred to the instrument, and the drawer's signature is authorized. Here, Landscaper meets all the necessary elements to present the checks for payment. There was no timeline for completion of the job, so Landscaper had no knowledge that Branford intended to create a condition precedent which might have affected the check's negotiability.

(4)   Personal Defenses. Branford will assert that by adding "first half of job" in the memo line he restricted the endorsement, and made a condition precedent that Landscaper failed to complete. Restrictive endorsements limit who can endorse the check, not impose a condition when they can be presented for payment. There was no contract agreement for a specific timeframe such that a breach had occurred, and an HDC takes clear of personal defenses even if one were found.

(5)   Liability. Generally, liability proceeds chronologically up the ladder, you sue your transferors, your transferees sue you. Bank rightfully honored and had no reason not to honor the check, it was properly payable. Not having received a stop payment order, the Bank had no way to know there was an underlying contract dispute between the parties, and barring any real defenses which generally cover the legitimacy of the actual issuance, as opposed to a personal defense, which usually addresses deficiencies with the underlying contract terms, the Bank is not liable to return the funds to the drawer's account.

CHAPTER 6

UCC ARTICLE 3 – COMMERCIAL PAPER

Index

Acceleration Clause.................... T 6-333
Acceptable Signatures .... T 6-334
Accommodation Indorser.......... T 6-341
Advantages Over Ordinary
   Contracts................................. T 6-331
Agent Liability .... T 6-334
Alterations Not Present .... T 6-342
Amount Contradiction............... T 6-332
Article 3 .... T 6-331
Article 4 .... T 6-331, 344
Bank Certification .... T 6-346
Bank Deposits and Collections .. T 6-344
Bank Liability and Recovery for
   Forged Signature .... T 6-343
Bank Sequencing....................... T 6-345
Bankruptcy .... T 6-338
Bearer Paper .... T 6-332, 336
Blank Indorsement .... T 6-340
Capacity.................................... T 6-339
Certificate of Deposit .... T 6-332
Certification.............................. T 6-345
Check.. T 6-331
Check Hold................................ T 6-345
Chronological Liability .... T 6-340
Collection Guaranteed
   Indorsement .... T 6-341
Comparative Negligence .... T 6-339
Contradictory Terms .... T 6-332
Conversion .... T 6-344
Currency of Any Country.......... T 6-334
Dates... T 6-333
Defenses .... T 6-337
Defenses Not Present .... T 6-342
Destroyed Instrument .... T 6-344
Discharge in Bankruptcy .... T 6-338
Dishonored Checks .... T 6-340
Draft .... T 6-332
Drawee's Responsibilities.......... T 6-344
Drawer's Negligence.................. T 6-346
Drawer's Signature Authorized.. T 6-342
Dummy Vendor.......................... T 6-337
Duress....................................... T 6-338
Exceptions to Negotiation
   Requirement .... T 6-337

Expedited Funds Availability
   Act .... T 6-345
Extension Provision................... T 6-333
Failure of Consideration .... T 6-338
Federal Trade Commission........ T 6-338
Fictitious Payee .... T 6-337
For Value................................... T 6-335
Forged Instrument Liability........ T 6-346
Forgery .... T 6-339, 344
Fraud in Execution .... T 6-338
Fraud in the Inducement............ T 6-338
Future Contract.......................... T 6-333
Future Performance .... T 6-335
General Real Defenses .... T 6-338
Good Faith................................. T 6-335
Good Title.................................. T 6-342
Gift Donee .... T 6-335
Handwritten Terms..................... T 6-332
Holder in Due Course (HDC)..... T 6-335
Illegality.................................... T 6-338
Impostor.................................... T 6-337
Improper Negotiation .... T 6-343
Improperly Completed................ T 6-335
Incomplete Instruments .... T 6-335
Indorsement............................... T 6-340
Indorsement Without Recourse .. T 6-341
Indorser Liability .... T 6-340
Indorser's Signature Forged .... T 6-344
Issue Requirement .... T 6-334
Knowledge of Insolvency........... T 6-342
Lack of Capacity........................ T 6-339
Legal Right Retention Clause..... T 6-333
Liability of Parties .... T 6-339
Lost Instrument.......................... T 6-344
Material Alteration .... T 6-339
Midnight Deadline...................... T 6-340
Multiple Payees .... T 6-345
Mutual Mistake.......................... T 6-338
Negligence .... T 6-339, 343, 346
Negligent Supervision .... T 6-339
Negotiable Instrument................ T 6-332
Negotiable Words....................... T 6-332
Negotiation .... T 6-336
No Knowledge of Insolvency..... T 6-342

Non-Violating Conditions............T 6-333
Notice of Claim or Defense ....T 6-336
Notice of Dishonor......................T 6-340
Occurrence Time Uncertain ....T 6-334
Open Sum...................................T 6-334
Order Paper ....T 6-332, 336
Other's Claims ....T 6-338
Overdraft Check ....T 6-345
Overdue Check............................T 6-345
Owner's Negligence....................T 6-343
Partial HDC ....T 6-335
Payable on Demand ....T 6-331
Payable on Sight.........................T 6-331
Payee Designation Incomplete....T 6-344
Payee Incomplete ....T 6-335
Payment Guaranteed
    Indorsement............................T 6-341
Payment in Full Indorsement ......T 6-341
Personal Defenses ....T 6-338
Phantom Employee ....T 6-337
Postdated Check ....T 6-345
Prepayment Options....................T 6-333
Presentment Party Warranties .....T 6-342
Primary Liability ....T 6-340
Printed Terms ....T 6-332
Prohibited Negotiation ....T 6-336
Promise to Pay Only ....T 6-333
Qualified Indorsement.................T 6-341
Real Defenses.............................T 6-338
Representative Liability ....T 6-334
Restrictive Indorsement ....T 6-341
Secondary Liability ....T 6-340
Shelter Rule................................T 6-336
Signature Forged ....T 6-342
Signature Form...........................T 6-334
Signatures Genuine and
    Authorized...............................T 6-342
Signed by Maker/Drawer ....T 6-334
Special Indorsement....................T 6-341
Stale Check ....T 6-344
Statute of Limitations.................T 6-339
Stolen Instrument ....T 6-344
Stop Payment Order ....T 6-345
Subrogation Rights......................T 6-346
Sum Certain in Money ....T 6-334
Three-Party Paper.......................T 6-331
Time Certain ....T 6-333
Time Uncertain...........................T 6-334
Transfer Parties Warranties........T 6-342
Two-Party Paper ....T 6-331
Typed Terms ....T 6-332
Unauthorized Alteration..............T 6-345

Unauthorized Completion ....T 6-338
Unauthorized Signature...... T 6-339, 345
Uncompletion of Condition
    Precedent ....T 6-338
Unconditional Promise to Pay....T 6-333
Underlying Obligation.................T 6-343
Unqualified Indorsement............T 6-340
Warranty Disclaimer ....T 6-343
Warranty Liability ....T 6-342
Warranty Liability Exception.....T 6-343
Wrongful Dishonor ....T 6-345
Wrongful Honor ....T 6-344

CHAPTER 7

UCC ARTICLE 9

SECURED

TRANSACTIONS

RIGOS BAR REVIEW SERIES

UNIFORM MULTISTATE ESSAY EXAM (MEE) REVIEW

CHAPTER 7

UCC ARTICLE 9 – SECURED TRANSACTIONS

Table of Contents

A.   Sub-Topic Exam Issue Distribution .... Text 7-373

B.   Opening Argument and Primary Issues .... Text 7-377

C.   Text .... Text 7-379

    I.   Introduction .... Text 7-379

    II.   Collateral Category .... Text 7-379

    III.   Creditors and Purchase Money Security Interest (PMSI) .... Text 7-381

    IV.   Security Agreement (SA) .... Text 7-382

    V.   Attachment – ARV .... Text 7-385

    VI.   Perfection – PCFMT .... Text 7-385

    VII.   Repossession Right .... Text 7-390

    VIII. Priority Rules .... Text 7-391

    IX.   Exam Approach to Essay Answers .... Text 7-394

D.   Magic Memory Outlines® .... Magic Memory Outlines 7-397

E.   UCC – Secured Transactions Essay Questions .... Questions 7-401

F.   UCC – Secured Transactions Essay Answers .... Answers 7-405

G.   UCC – Secured Transactions Index .... Index 7-413

H.   Acronyms .... Acronyms 15-630

RIGOS BAR REVIEW SERIES
MEE SUB-TOPIC FREQUENCY DISTRIBUTION

UCC ARTICLE 9 – SECURE TRANSACTIONS

	2/09	7/08	2/08	7/07	2/07	7/06	2/06	7/05	2/05	7/04	2/04	7/03	2/03	7/02	2/02	7/01	2/01
Opening Argument		//	/		/	/	/	/	/	/	/	/		/	/	/	
Collateral Classification			/				/		/								
Tangible							/		/	/	//	/			/	/	
Inventory							/				/	/			/	/	
Equipment									/		/	/					
Consumer Goods							/										
Intangible and Documents										/	/						
Chattel Paper										/							
Accounts										/	/						
Purchase Money Security Interest		//							/						/	/	
Security Agreements (general)			/							/	/				/	/	
Proceeds							/										
After-Acquired Property											/				/		
Description of Collateral			/								/						

Course 5328. Copyright by Rigos Bar Review Series – MEE.

	2/01	7/01	2/02	7/02	2/03	7/03	2/04	7/04	2/05	7/05	2/06	7/06	2/07	7/07	2/08	7/08	2/09
Attachment		/	/							/	/				/		
Debtor Rights in Collateral		/	/								/				/	/	
Creditor Gave Value		/	/														
Perfection		/	/	/					/	/	/	/	//		/	//	
By Possession			/	/					//	/	/				/	/	
By Filing				/					/	/	/	//			/	/	
Financing Statement Requirements							//		//							/	
Filing							/		/	/						/	
Authorized by Debtor							//										
Wrong Location									/								
20-day Grace Period (PMSI)			/						/								
Consignment											/						
Notice to Prior Creditors											/						
Remedies				/			/		/	/	/	/					
Right to Peaceful Repossession				/		/				/	/	/					
Disposition Sale										/	/	/					
Commercially Reasonable											/	/					

	2/09	7/08	2/08	7/07	2/07	7/06	2/06	7/05	2/05	7/04	2/04	7/03	2/03	7/02	2/02	7/01
Actual Damages					/					/						
Statutory Damages					/											
Right of Redemption					/											
Notice to Debtor/Other Creditors					/		/									
Other Creditors' Security Interests		/		/		/										
Senior Interests		/		/		/										
Deficiency Judgment						/		/				/				
Account Debtors		/		/	//		/		/							
Priorities		/		/	/		/		//					/	/	/
Perfected PMSI		/	/	/	/		/							/	/	/
Competing Perfected Interests		/	/		/		/									
Attached Interests		/		/			/	/								
Judgment Creditor		/						/								
Fixtures								/								

OPENING ARGUMENT AND PRIMARY ISSUES

UCC ARTICLE 9 – SECURED TRANSACTIONS

There are a few thoughts that should usually be stated at the beginning of every answer. These will score you easy points and let the grader know you are in the right topic area.

Most essays should have an "opening argument": a brief, broad statement that shows you understand the broad significance of a legal topic. The opening argument also suggests to the grader that she is about to read a thoughtful and well-organized essay.

Many subjects also have "primary issues" that can be discussed up front or integrated into the essay answer. IMPORTANT: Do not merely regurgitate these statements on the exam without addressing the issues actually raised by the facts, or you will not pass.

- **Secured Transactions Opening Argument:** UCC Article 9 controls a creditor's secured interest in a debtor's collateral.

- **Sample Primary Issue Statements:**

  - A security interest (SI) is obtained by possession / control of the collateral or is contained in a security agreement (SA).

  - There are 4 types of UCC Article 9 tangible goods qualifying as collateral: 1) inventory, 2) equipment, 3) consumer goods, and 4) farm products. If collateral is used for mixed purposes, the primary use in the debtor's hands will control.

  - A SA is a written contract between a creditor and a debtor authenticated by the latter, identifying the collateral in reasonable detail, its primary use, and its county location.

  - Attachment establishes the creditor's rights against the debtor and is necessary for the secured party to repossess the collateral or related proceeds from the debtor. Attachment requires: 1) a SA, 2) debtor has rights in the collateral, and 3) creditor gives value. Attachment alone may not be sufficient if the debtor has given more than one security interest, the collateral has been transferred, or against a bankruptcy Trustee.

  - Perfection is necessary to protect the creditor against third parties. Perfection can be accomplished by attachment plus 1) possession, 2) control, 3) filing, 4) mere attachment if PMSI in consumer goods, or 5) title certificate. Filing of a financing statement (FS) is at the location of the debtor – at the appropriate state or local agency.

  - Filing gives constructive notice to all other creditors and is effective at the time of filing.

- Creditors who have a purchase money security interest (PMSI) are afforded special rights to perfect by mere attachment for consumer goods. PSMIs are given a 20 day-grace period to file for non-inventory collateral and perfection is deemed to relate back to the date of attachment.

- A filed PSMI interest in their own collateral other than inventory is superior to a preceding PSMI's "hereafter acquired" clause.

- A PSMI providing new inventory collateral must inform all prior creditors with "hereafter acquired" clauses.

- Upon a debtor's default, the creditor may repossess the collateral (replevin right) and retain it or dispose of it at a commercially reasonable sale and offset the proceeds against the creditor's debt. Notice of the sale must be given to all other known creditors.

- The priority rules are as follows: Perfected creditors have priority over unperfected. Between perfected creditors, the first to perfect is first in right. A perfected PMSI has priority over other secured creditors in the PMSI collateral.

- An attached creditor with a SA prevails over unsecured creditors lacking a SI.

I.   INTRODUCTION

Three or four out of five MEEs contain a secured transactions question. Article 9 of the UCC covers any transaction intended to create a security interest (SI) in collateral including personal property, fixtures, agricultural liens, and certain intangibles. Most jurisdictions have now adopted the 1998 Revised American Law Institute model UCC statute.

> **MEE Tip:** Always begin, "Revised Article 9 of the UCC governs security interests (SI) in collateral including personal property, fixtures, agricultural liens, and certain intangibles."

A. Purpose of Article 9

Creditors can reduce their monetary risk if a debtor defaults because there is specific collateral available as a source of repayment. Such a creditor only stands as a general creditor for the unsecured balance of the debt.

B. Question Facts

The typical exam question facts involve one debtor (usually a business person), two or three creditors who provide collateral and/or make cash loans to the debtor, and one transferee who receives some items of collateral from the debtor.

II. COLLATERAL CATEGORY

Collateral is the property subject to a SI. There are two general categories of collateral; tangible goods and intangibles. The collateral categories are important because the rules concerning perfection, filing requirements, and priorities vary between classes.

A. Tangible Goods

1. Classification: All goods are moveable and classified as inventory, equipment, consumer goods, or farm products. [UCC 9-102 *et seq.*]

a.   Inventory: Inventory is goods held for sale or lease in the ordinary course of business. This includes raw material, work in process, and materials used or consumed in a business. Farm product inventories are excluded.

b.   Equipment: Equipment is goods, other than farm products or consumer goods, used or bought for use in the productive capacity of a business. Machinery, manufacturing equipment, furniture, computers, and office equipment are examples.

c.   Consumer Goods: Consumer goods are used or bought for non-business, personal, family, or household purposes. Household furniture, a home television, or a personal laptop computer are examples. There is no dollar limit for this category.

d. Farming Products: This includes crops (growing or harvested), livestock (unborn or born), and supplies used or produced in farming operations. Wheat, potatoes, cows, and fertilizer are examples. Machinery used on a farm is equipment.

e. Manufactured Homes: This is a structure of over 320 square feet designed to be used as a dwelling and includes contained plumbing, heating, air conditioning equipment, and electrical systems.

2. Primary Use Controls: The emphasis is upon the use of the collateral in the debtor's hand. If used for more than one purpose, the primary use controls. The collateral's category is established as of the date of attachment. This characterization is unaffected by other later uses of the collateral by this debtor.

3. Example: A horse offered for sale by a horse dealer is inventory. In a riding stable's hands, it would be equipment used in a business. In the hands of a person buying the horse for personal recreational riding purposes, it would be consumer goods. Last, in a farmer's hands, the horse could be farm products (livestock) if held for breeding.

MEE Tip: The good's collateral category stays constant in the debtor's hands and is determined upon attachment. The debtor's use may change (business to consumer, usually) and the collateral may be transferred to third parties who change the use. Identify each change.

B. Intangible and Documentary Collateral

1. Instrument: A negotiable instrument or other writing, such as a promissory note, evidences a right to receive payment. Transfer requires delivery with proper endorsement. The security interest in collateral is perfected by possession.

2. Document of Title: A document of title is that which, in the regular course of business or financing is treated as evidencing that the person in possession of it is entitled to receive the goods it covers. Examples include UCC Article 7 bills of lading and warehouse receipts. They represent intangible ownership to goods held by others.

3. Chattel Paper: Chattel paper is a record which evidences both a monetary obligation and a security interest in specific goods or software. This record may be in tangible or electronic or digital medium. A secured party may sell the security agreement (SA) itself along with his interest in the collateral. An example is a consumer's installment or purchase agreement which is assigned to a finance company.

4. Account: An account is an unsecured right to payment of a monetary obligation whether or not earned by performance. This includes business accounts receivables and credit card balances.

5. Deposit Account: This is a bank demand, time savings, or passbook account other than a consumer's checking account.

6. Investment Property: This includes certificated and uncertificated securities, commodity accounts, and commodity contracts to buy or sell in the future.

7. Commercial Tort Claims: This is the right to pursue a judgment arising from a cause of action in the claimant's business or profession other than personal injury or death.

8. Letter of Credit Rights: This is the right to receive payment or performance under a UCC Article 5 letter of credit.

9. Policy of Insurance: Insurance is bifurcated as potential collateral. Original insurance – say a life insurance policy covering the debtor / obligor, is not collateral to the extent that the creditor's interest varies from the beneficiary designation in the insurance contract. But insurance claims based upon the destruction or involuntary conversion of secured collateral may be treated as "proceeds" (see infra).

10. General Intangibles: This is the residual category and includes copyrights, trademarks, patents, franchise rights, software, and royalties.

> **MEE Tip:** Most of these categories were added by the 2001 Revised Act. The exam testing has continued to focus primarily on tangible goods.

C. Proceeds

This is whatever the debtor acquires or collects from the sale, trade, or other disposition of the primary collateral. Proceeds are categorized as cash or non-cash.

> **MEE Tip:** Early in your answer state, "UCC tangible collateral categories are inventory, equipment, consumer goods, and farm products, and proceeds therefrom." If applicable in the facts, also state, "There are also intangible categories, including instruments, documents of title, chattel paper, accounts, deposit accounts, investment property, commercial tort claims, letter of credit rights, policy of insurance, and general intangibles."

D. Description Importance

Collateral must be reasonably identified. The more particular and detailed the identification and description the better, as the creditor has the burden to show that the good at issue is their collateral. Generic descriptions as "all collateral," "all assets," or "all personal property" are too vague in the security agreement (SA). Likewise "collateral to be purchased in the future" might not qualify. In comparison, "all inventory" does qualify. An address and description of the property is usually required for timber, crops, or minerals. [UCC 9-108]

> **MEE Tip:** Vague descriptions of collateral are very frequent. Distinguish between SA and FS treatment – the latter is more liberal in allowing general collateral description.

III. CREDITORS AND PURCHASE MONEY SECURITY INTEREST (PMSI)

A creditor is anyone owed money by the debtor. A creditor who has a purchase money security interest (PMSI) in goods is allowed special or extra rights in perfecting their security interest. A PMSI has a "close nexus" between the collateral and the secured obligation. This applies where the collateral purchased by the debtor secures repayment of the purchase price owed to the creditor. A creditor may be part PMSI and part non-PMSI if more than one item of collateral is specified (such as equipment and after-acquired property); this is called "dual status." There are two acceptable methods of creating a PMSI [UCC 9-103]:

A. Collateral Sale

This method applies where a creditor sells goods to a debtor and takes back a paper receivable secured by the same goods. For example, when a consumer purchases an appliance on credit from a department store, the seller may retain a PMSI in the appliance collateral transferred to the buyer.

B. Loan for Specific Collateral

This method applies when a creditor, such as a commercial bank, loans a debtor money to buy a specific asset from a third party. If the purchase money is used to acquire the same assets from the designated third party, the creditor has a PMSI in that collateral.

C. Working Capital Loan

A bank loan for working capital purposes, such as a general business line of credit, does not qualify as a PMSI because it is not associated with specific collateral. While such a party still enjoys the usual rights of a creditor, they are not allowed the special privileges of a PMSI.

D. Burden of Proof

The secured party claiming PMSI status has the burden of proof to establish her status.

MEE Tip: PMSI is a key concept in every Article 9 question. Discuss the two types of PMSIs, and the advantages of potential "super priority" PMSI status. Look for "dual status" and the working capital loan exception to status attainment. Analyze the status of PMSI for every creditor given in the question.

E. Advantages to PMSI Status

1. Household Goods: A PMSI in household goods is effective to create a valid security interest for the seller. Any other non-PMSI security interest in household goods is not allowed under FTC rules.

2. Mere Attachment Perfection: PMSI interests are allowed the right to perfect by mere attachment if the PMSI is for consumer goods.

3. 20-day Grace Period: A PMSI interest in non-inventory goods (equipment or fixtures) is allowed a 20-day grace period to perfect its security interests through filing.

4. Super Priority on Inventory: A PMSI in inventory gets a super priority as long as they provide advance notice to other creditors who have a SI in inventory. This notice requirement is to prevent a previous creditor claiming collateral under an after-acquired clause that they did not actually provide the debtor. The PMSI providing the collateral is given a priority.

IV. SECURITY AGREEMENTS (SA)

MEE Tip: Most secured transactions questions include a security agreement (SA). Discuss the collateral description and other relevant provisions contained therein.

A. In General

A security agreement (SA) creates the security interest (SI) in the collateral. This contract between a creditor and a debtor must either be written or be an "authenticated record." If on paper the debtor must physically sign; if some other record, the debtor may encrypt or identify the authentication agreeing to the record. The creditor's signature is not required. The debtor agrees that the creditor may claim the described collateral for debt repayment.

B. Collateral Description

The SA must describe and identify the collateral in reasonable detail; collateral categories are sufficiently descriptive unless a consumer transaction or a commercial tort claim. Super-generic descriptions such as "all debtor's assets," "all collateral," or "all personal property" are insufficient in the SA. These descriptions are usually sufficient in the financing statement (FS) used to perfect by filing. At a minimum, the SA must specify the collateral's primary use in the debtor's hands. The SA may also include the following provisions:

C. Proceeds

"Proceeds" include whatever is received by the debtor upon the sale, exchange, or other disposition of the primary collateral. This may include cash or non-cash property received from a sale of the collateral, such as deposit accounts, accounts receivable, insurance proceeds, or other substituted property. It also includes license revenue and infringement claims arising from collateral.

1. Collateral Interest Continues: The SI in the collateral itself continues against third party transferees if the interest in the original collateral was attached or perfected. The creditor may repossess the collateral from the transferee unless so specified to the contrary in the SA or the sale or disposition was with the secured party's consent

2. SI Automatic: An attached or perfected SI in proceeds may continue for 20 days automatically. After 20 days, the security interest survives only in identifiable cash proceeds which the creditor can trace, and the interest in non-cash proceeds ceases to be perfected unless a new FS has been filed. The new filing requires particular identification of the new non-cash proceeds. [UCC 9-315]

D. After-Acquired Property

An "after-acquired property" clause in the SA includes in the covered category all future collateral the debtor may acquire or manufacture later. This may create a conflict with the rights of a subsequent creditor providing and/or financing the new collateral. Notice filing requires only that the provision be stated in the SA. [UCC 9-502] Clauses covering consumer goods are limited to collateral received within 10 days after the secured party gives value such as making a loan. An after-acquired property interest is junior to a subsequent PMSI in the collateral provided by the new creditor. Commercial tort claims not yet matured are also excluded from after-acquired property. [UCC 9-204(a)]

E. Future Advances

A "future advances" clause will allow further cash advances to be secured by collateral covered by an earlier SA. As with proceeds, this SI is automatic. Thus, if the bank makes a new loan, the existing collateral may apply as security for the new loan. [UCC 9-204(c)]

F. Floating Lien

A "floating lien" is a variety of a SA where the collateral turns over, such as automobiles on a car lot. In such a situation it is not practical to execute a new agreement as the individual items of collateral change. Floating liens that cover aggregations of particular items (such as retail inventory) may also be subject to an after-acquired property clause.

G. Other Provisions

1. Set-off or Recoupment Rights: A SA may specify that any other right of the creditor (such as another loan to the same debtor) may be set-off against property of the debtor subject to the agreement. A depository bank priority to offset funds prevails over any other creditor's claim including cash proceeds of collateral deposited into the account. [UCC 9-340]

2. Debtor Duties: Unless specified to the contrary, the debtor has a duty to pay insurance and taxes and to repair the collateral.

3. Default: Circumstances constituting a default in performance under the SA are usually broadly defined. Included are such acts as a failure to pay an invoice in the ordinary course of business, failure to pay a tax, bankruptcy, and entry of a judgment against the debtor.

4. Remedies: In the event of default, the creditor is usually granted the replevin right to enter onto the debtor's property, take possession of the collateral, and liquidate same. The entering must be reasonable as to time and extent, and must not involve a breach of the peace.

5. Costs and Attorney Fees: Most seller-oriented agreements provide that the secured party is entitled to costs and reasonable attorney fees.

6. Good Faith Required: A SA may not waive the creditor's obligations of good faith, diligence, reasonableness, and due care. A creditor has 14 days following request to provide a debtor a requested accounting of unpaid obligations and/or assets collateralizing the debt. [UCC 9-210]

H. Prohibition on Assignment of Security Interest

Contract terms which prohibit transfer of the debtor's right in collateral are usually ineffective. Similarly unenforceable is a provision specifying that a transfer is deemed to be a default. [UCC 9-401(b)]

I. Agreement Not to Assert Defenses

Normally, a buyer can assert defenses such as fraud in the inducement or failure of consideration against a seller's lawsuit seeking enforcement of a SA. A buyer may waive the right to assert a defense against an assignee of the SI even though the defense might be good against a seller. [UCC 9-403]

1. Commercial Contract: Such a waiver can be enforced by an assignee who takes the SI **F**or value, **I**n good faith, and with **N**o notice (**FIN**) of the defense. The buyer may still assert real defenses that would be good against a HDC under Article 3.

2. Consumer Credit Contract: The Federal Trade Commission provides that any assignee takes their rights subject to all defenses the consumer could assert against the seller. [16 C.F.R. 433]

> **MEE Tip:** Look for a cross-over question combining Sales and Secured Transactions in which the sales contract and SA contain a waiver of defense provision. Did the sale involve a consumer? If so, the federal rule may override the Model UCC statute.

V. ATTACHMENT – ARV

Attachment establishes the creditor's rights against the debtor and some third parties who have knowledge of the SI. Attachment prevails over most unsecured or normal trade creditors. Attachment is necessary for the secured party to have the legal replevin right to repossess the collateral or related proceeds from the debtor. Attachment requires three **ARV** elements **A** **R**ecreational **V**ehicle and is effective when the last of the three events occur. [UCC 9-203]

A. A Security Agreement – SA

1. Writing Required: Unless the secured party has possession or control of the collateral, the parties must have entered into a written SA authenticated by the debtor.

2. Reasonable Identity: The SA must reasonably identify the location and use of the collateral in the debtor's hands. The identity on the SA cannot be super-generic such as "all collateral," "all debtor's assets," or "all personal property." The comments to the UCC state that category listings such as "all inventory" or "all equipment" do qualify.

3. Consumer Goods: The generalized collateral types alone are insufficient for the collateral categories of consumer goods, a commercial tort claim, a commodity account, a security account, or entitlement. [UCC 9-108]

B. Rights in Collateral

The debtor must have rights in the collateral. If the debtor has not received the goods, there must at least be a legally enforceable ownership right, such as a warehouse receipt.

C. Value Given

Value must have been given; the creditor must make the loan or deliver the collateral to the debtor. A binding commitment to extend credit is sufficient if legally enforceable under state law.

> **MEE Tip:** Every answer requires discussion of the ARV elements required for attachment. Cover the three elements in detail in your discussion of the first creditor. For subsequent creditors say "see supra discussion."

VI. PERFECTION – PCFMT

Perfection is the highest form of a creditor's protection for collateral rights against third parties who may also have claims against the debtor's property. A debtor may have given more than one creditor a SI, the debtor may have conveyed the collateral to a third party, or a bankruptcy trustee may be asserting ownership of the collateral. Attachment is insufficient to protect against these third parties; perfection is necessary. Perfection requires attachment plus one of the following 5 PCFMT (**P**erfection **C**alls **F**or **M**any **T**hings) methods of perfection.

> **MEE Tip:** List the 5 PCFMT methods of perfection in your discussion of the first creditor who perfected. For subsequent creditors, write "see supra discussion of perfection methods."

A. Possession

Possession of the collateral by the secured party is a way to accomplish valid perfection. [UCC 9-313]

1. Application: Possession is required for money. It is also the highest form of perfection for collateral in which a transferee may have greater rights than the transferor. For negotiable collateral, possession places a higher priority with the transferee / possessor (such as a HDC) than with the transferor/creditor. [UCC 9-304]

2. Examples of Possession Collateral: Examples include checks, promissory notes, certificates of deposit, bearer bonds, negotiable instruments, warehouse receipts, bills of lading, and investment securities. The possessor must exercise reasonable care to protect and preserve the collateral.

3. Effective Date: Perfection is effective as of the date of possession. Filing is still possible and will prevail over the bankruptcy trustee, but it is ineffective against an HDC with possession. [UCC 9-308]

B. Control

The Revised Act shifts the focus of notice filing to "control" by creating a new perfection category of "constructive possession." [UCC 9-314]

1. General Application: Perfection by control applies to deposit accounts, electronic chattel paper, investment property, and letter of credit rights. If the depository is the secured party, control is automatic. Control may also be achieved by the debtor and secured party entering into an agreement with the depository.

2. Specific Application: Four types of collateral are subject to control.

a. Deposit Account: A bank, the debtor, and the creditor all agree in an authenticated record that the bank will comply with the secured party's instructions directing disposition of the funds in the "blocked" deposit account. Control is the only way to perfect an interest in a deposit account. [UCC 9-104]

b. Electronic Chattel Paper: Either control or filing will perfect a SI in electronic chattel paper. [UCC 9-105]

c. Investment Property: This category includes commodity contracts, stock certificates, and other related items of collateral as covered under UCC Article 8. Either filing or control is allowed. [UCC 9-106]

d. Letter of Credit Rights: Control is the only method of perfection for a letter of credit under which the payee has consented to assignment of the proceeds. [UCC 9-107]

3. Continuation: Perfection by control continues only as long as the secured party retains control of the collateral.

C. Filing

Perfection by filing a standardized financing statement (FS) form is the preferred method and is the only permissible way to perfect a SI in most intangibles. This applies to accounts receivable, commercial tort claims, copyrights or patents, fixtures, and farming crops. This is also the method for most tangible collateral such as inventory and equipment except for vehicles. Constructive notice to the world of the creditor's SI in the collateral is accomplished. Filing also avoids the potential problem of the consumer transferee discussed *infra* under mere attachment. [UCC 9-310]

1. **Financing Statement (FS):**

   a. **Contents:** The multi-page FS form must sufficiently indicate the collateral covered. The description on the FS may be more super-generic than the SA; "all assets," "all property," or "all personal property" all qualify. The filing must be authorized by the debtor (although a signature is not required), and must include the names and addresses of both the debtor and the creditor. "After acquired property" need only be mentioned in the SA. [UCC 9-502, 503, and 504]

   b. **Seriously Misleading Change:** If the debtor's name is erroneous or changes so the financing statement becomes "seriously misleading" to subsequent creditors (more than minor errors), the original creditor must file a new FS within 4 months. Examples are a proprietor incorporating using a different corporate name or a debtor using a new married name. This is required because a third party uses the specific wording in the debtor's name in a filing search. [UCC 9-508]

2. **Filing Place:** The state of the debtor's principal residence or place of business controls where to file (or that of the chief executive officer if the debtor has more than one place of business). [UCC 9-301 and 307]

   a. **Proper:** Generally, filings are to be made with the State Department of Licensing. Central filing does not apply to fixtures, minerals, oil, gas, timber, and farm crops; these interests in land must be filed at the county where the real property is located. There must be an adequate description of the related real property's location.

   b. **Improper:** If the filing statement is filed in an improper place, it is ineffective to create perfection except against those with actual knowledge of its contents; attachment is still effective.

MEE Tip: Many FS questions contain one or more of three issues; fuzzy collateral descriptions – is it too super-generic? – the FS allows more vagueness that the SA; a change in debtor's name – is it too "seriously misleading"?; and filing in the wrong place – only fixtures, minerals, oil, gas, timber, and farm crops are to be filed locally.

---

3. **Effective Date:**

   a. **General Rule:** Perfection is generally effective as of the date and time of filing the FS. If the filing occurs before the debtor acquires rights in the collateral, perfection is effective upon attachment.

   b. **Filing 20-Day Grace Period:** A PMSI for non-inventory (equipment, consumer goods (generally perfected by mere attachment), or farming products) is allowed a 20-day grace period in which to file. The effective date of filing relates back to the date of attachment (usually when the debtor received the collateral). The 20-day grace period is also applicable to and overrides an "after acquired property" clause of a previous creditor. [UCC 9-324(a)]

c. Inventory Rule: Besides not being eligible for the 20-day grace period, there is one additional requirement when the collateral is inventory and another secured party previously filed. Typically an inventory financier makes cash advances against incoming inventory. Therefore, to gain a priority, the new PMSI must send an authenticated notification in writing to the holder of a prior after-acquired inventory interest. To get priority the new PMSI must provide this notice before delivering the new inventory to the debtor. This notification is to be addressed to the location specified on the FS, even if that address is or becomes incorrect. [UCC 9-324(b)]

d. Proceeds 20-Day Grace Period: The debtor may transfer the collateral to a third party without the creditor's permission. The SI continues in any identifiable proceeds under the "lowest intermediate balance rule." If the debtor sells the collateral and uses the proceeds to purchase new non-cash assets of a different collateral category, the SI becomes unperfected on the 21st day thereafter unless there is a new filing. A creditor avoids the refilling requirement if the original FS specified "all debtor's property. [UCC 9-315]

> **MEE Tip:** Filing rules may be the most common secured transactions issue on the MEE. To qualify for the 20-day grace rule, the creditor must be a PMSI and the goods collateral must be other than inventory, usually equipment. If the collateral is inventory or proceeds, the above special rules apply.

e. Effective Period: Filing is usually effective for five years, but may be extended by filing a continuation statement within six months of the end of the original period. [UCC 9-515]

f. Termination: The secured party is penalized $500 for failure to file a termination statement within 20 days after receipt of a proper request by a debtor. [UCC 9-625(c)]

4. Consignment: A consignee merchant sells inventory goods owned by others. A consignor's objective is to make sure the delivered goods are not subject to levy by the consignee's other creditors. A consignor must comply with the filing requirements and send an authenticated notification to any previously perfected inventory creditors. This notice must state that the consignor expects to deliver certain described goods on consignment to the consignee. Such a procedure will be effective to create PMSI status and override an "after-acquired property" clause of the previous creditor and will include any identifiable cash proceeds. [UCC 9-324(b)]

5. Multi-State Transactions: The debtor's location determines the applicable state law and filing rules.

a. Collateral Location Not Controlling: Interested parties must check the filings in the debtor's state even if the collateral is located in a different state. [UCC 9-307(i)]

b. Debtor Movement and 4 Month Refiling: If the debtor's location moves to another state, the SI becomes unperfected after 4 months. This puts a duty on a perfected creditor to know the location of the debtor and refile in the new state within 4 month. [UCC 9-316(a)(2)]

c. New State and New Debtor: Creditors with a SI in collateral which is transferred to a new debtor in a new state must re-file in the new state within one year. [UCC 9-316(a)(3)]

D. Mere Attachment

1. Requirements: The UCC authorizes perfection by mere attachment. This perfection method applies where the creditor has a PMSI, and the collateral is consumer goods of any value or farm machinery equipment under $2,500. Automobiles do not qualify. This is intended to save from ex post facto invalidation those assignments which not reasonably would be thought of as subject to filing. Perfection under mere attachment is effective as of the date of attachment. [UCC 9-309]

2. Consumer Transferee Problem: A creditor's perfection by mere attachment is not effective against a bona fide transferee of the debtor who also uses the collateral for personal or household purposes. The transferee must give value and be without knowledge of the creditor's SI in the transferred goods. The creditor can't repossess the collateral from such a transferee. Look for a consumer to consumer transferee.

3. Equipment or Inventory Purposes: A transferee of the debtor using the collateral as equipment or inventory takes an interest junior to the prior perfected interest. Notice that only consumer use is allowed this privilege to take free and clear of perfection by mere attachment. [UCC 9-320(b)]

4. Example: A debtor sells his home workshop power saw (consumer goods), upon which a PMSI creditor had previously perfected a SI by mere attachment. If sold to a dealer who intended to resell it (inventory) or to a cabinet-making shop who intended to use it as equipment in a business, both transferees take subject to the prior perfected interest. A transferee using the saw in a home workshop (consumer goods) takes a priority over the perfected interest. Finally, if the creditor files, it defeats even the consumer transferee.

> **MEE Tip:** Perfection by mere attachment is a common bar topic. To qualify, there must be a PMSI and the collateral must be consumer goods. Look for collateral transfer to another consumer who may take free and clear if they gave value without knowledge of the PMSI.

E. Title Certificate

1. State or Federal Statute: A federal or state statute may create a fifth perfection category. Most states have a title certificate system that applies to motor vehicles, mobile homes, boats, and trailers. The Federal Government registers airplanes. [UCC 311(a)(2)]

2. Notation Required: A SI in such collateral can only be perfected by notation on the title certificate issued by the relevant governmental agency. For an automobile, the SI is usually referred to as a "lien." Filing of a FS form is ineffective for such collateral.

3. Exception: "Vehicle" dealers who are in the business of selling automobiles, trailers, etc., (where the automobiles are inventory) are the exception. A SI held by an auto wholesaler must perfect by filing under the usual code rules.

> **MEE Tip:** Every answer requires a discussion of the **PCFMT** methods of perfection. Filing and by mere attachment are historically the heavy areas. An oral SI is not a valid SI at all.

VII. REPOSSESSION RIGHT

> **MEE Tip:** Know the repossession and disposition sale process for any SI. Usually the call of the question is from the creditor's standpoint. This is the essence of any Article 9 question.

A. Retention of Collateral

1. Repossession Details: An attached creditor has the replevin right to repossess the collateral from the debtor with or without judicial process; self-help is authorized. If the creditor's SI is perfected, the repossession right is also good against third-party transferees. The creditor is allowed a limited privilege against the tort of trespass to enter onto the debtor's property. The entering must be reasonable under the circumstances as to time and extent, and not involve a breach of the peace. [UCC 9-609]

2. Retention Requirements: Following repossession, the creditor may propose to simply retain the collateral ("strict foreclosure") and waive any deficiency against the debtor. Written notice of this proposal must be sent to the debtor and any other known secured parties of record. Partial strict foreclosure with the affirmative consent of the debtor is also allowed. If the debtor or a junior lienholder objects to retention within 20 days, the secured party must hold a disposition sale. The creditor himself may also elect to conduct a disposition sale of the collateral. Such a disposition sale liquidates the repossessed assets. [UCC 9-620, 621, and 622]

3. Bankruptcy Exception: The Federal Bankruptcy Court issues an automatic "stay" when a bankruptcy petition is filed. This stops all creditor actions against the collateral owned by the debtor. The secured party must file a motion seeking relief before she can repossess or dispose of the collateral.

B. Disposition Sale

The creditor is allowed to conduct a non-judicial disposition sale of the collateral and obtain a deficiency judgment against the debtor. The Code specifies the required procedures which must be followed.

1. Sale Details: The liquidating creditor must conduct a lien search and notify the debtor and other perfected parties by sending authenticated notice of the time and place of the disposition sale at least 10 days prior to the sale. [UCC 9-611] The disposition sale may be public or private. The creditor may purchase the collateral in a public sale, [UCC 9-610(c)] but significantly low price sales to a related party or affiliate organization are subject to special judicial scrutiny. [UCC 9-615(f)] A debtor may redeem the collateral by tendering the full balance plus repossession expenses prior to the disposition sale.

2. Reasonable Aspects: Every aspect of the disposition sale including the method, manner, time, place, and terms must be commercially reasonable by industry standards. [UCC 9-610(c)] This right may not be waived. If the secured party's compliance is placed at issue, the creditor has the burden to show "reasonableness." A secured party who fails to adhere to this standard or fails to give the required notification is liable for actual damages. If consumer goods, this may be up to 10% of the debt. [UCC 9-625(c)(2)]

3. Creditor Warranty: The creditor warrants title, possession, and quiet enjoyment to the disposition sale purchaser unless expressly disclaimed at the sale. [UCC 9-610(d) and (e)]

4. Proceeds Application: Disposition proceeds are applied first to the costs of repossession and disposition sale expenses and second to the indebtedness owed to the creditor conducting the sale.

5. Other Creditors' Security Interests: There may be other creditors who have existing SIs in the collateral sold at the disposition sale. It is important that you distinguish between junior and senior creditors as they pertain to a disposition sale on the exam.

a. Senior Interests: Senior-superior interests created prior to the interest of the liquidating creditor are not discharged. They survive the disposition sale as a priority lien against the collateral.

b. Junior Interests: Junior-subordinate interests receive any proceeds above the amount due the liquidating creditor. The purchaser of the collateral at a disposition sale takes free and clear of everything except senior interests. All subordinate interests are discharged. [UCC 9-617(a)(3) and 622(b)]

6. Surplus and Deficiency: Any surplus must be returned to the debtor. A deficiency judgment against the debtor is also possible if the collateral brings less than the debt. [UCC 9-608(a)(4)]

C. 60% Payment by Debtor

The creditor must hold a disposition sale within 90 days of repossession if the debtor has paid at least 60% of the price for consumer goods. This right may be waived by the debtor after default. [UCC 9-620] The secured party must submit to the debtor a record of the surplus or deficiency calculation. [UCC 9-616]

D. Unauthorized Sale, Removal, or Conversion

In most jurisdictions a debtor is guilty of at least a misdemeanor if they sold, removed, concealed, or converted collateral upon which they know that a valid SA exists. This must be done without permission of the secured party and with intent to hinder, delay, or defraud the collateral rights of the secured party.

> **MEE Tip:** Always discuss any defects in the creditor's notification or repossession process.

VIII. PRIORITY RULES

After determining the classification of the SI, the next step is to decide which interests have priority in each piece of collateral. The laws of the jurisdiction where the collateral is located control the rights of competing claimants. [UCC 9-301] Within each below category, apply the "first in time, first in right" approach.

> **MEE Tip:** Commonly, a seller of goods or a bank advances funds to purchase specific collateral. If a PMSI, look at the collateral category. Equipment is subject to the 20-day grace period for perfection by filing and consumer goods are eligible for perfection by mere attachment.

A. First to Attach

If no creditor has perfected (or perfection failed), the priority would be determined by which interest attached first. Attachment occurs as soon as all three of the requirements are met: **A** Security Agreement, **R**ights in Collateral, and **V**alue Given. [UCC 9-322(a)(3)]

B. Perfection Prevails over Attachment

Any method of perfection will prevail over creditors whose SI has only attached. This includes proceeds if the SI in the original collateral was perfected or if a proceeds perfection in non-cash collateral occurs within 20 days of the collateral disposition date. [UCC 9-315(d)] For deposit accounts and letters of credit, control will triumph over any other method of perfection. [UCC 9-322(d)]

C. Competing Perfected Interests

The priority between competing perfected creditors is usually a question of "first in time, first in right." The earlier of the first to file or to perfect has a priority claim to the collateral. [UCC 9-322(a)(1)]

1. PMSI Two Advantages: Remember the 20-day grace rule (PMSI and non-inventory) and perfection by mere attachment (PMSI and consumer goods).

2. Inventory PMSI v. Non-PMSI: A perfected PMSI inventory creditor will prevail if they notify the prior perfected non-PMSI creditor (asserting a claim under an after-acquired clause). [UCC 9-324(a) and (b)]

D. Judgment Creditor

A judgment creditor perfects on the date the judgment is registered at the county seat. The judgment becomes a lien on all the debtor's real property and related fixtures in the county. The judgment creditor must actually levy to perfect an interest in personal property.

E. Bankruptcy Trustee

A bankruptcy trustee becomes perfected as of the date the petition is filed in federal bankruptcy court. This priority attaches to any collateral in which a valid perfection was not previously accomplished.

F. Unsecured Creditor

Unsecured creditors are the lowest priority in liquidation; they are termed "general" creditors if the debtor is in bankruptcy. "Oral SI" are ineffective and such creditors fall into this category. Any balance due a secured creditor after collateral liquidation is treated as unsecured and all creditors in this class share pro rata.

G. Exceptions to Priorities – RAP

There are three big exceptions or "super priorities" to the above rules:

1. Retail Inventory: Except for farm products purchased from a farmer, a retail buyer of inventory in the ordinary course of business (BIOCOB) takes the title and ownership free and clear of any senior interest created by her seller. Therefore any sale by a retailer conveys title to the buyer free from any claims of the retailer's creditors. An example is the purchase of a watch from a jewelry store. [UCC 9-320(a)]

a. Buyer in the Ordinary Course: The retail buyer must be purchasing inventory in the ordinary course of business from a person who regularly sells that kind of goods. This excludes a purchaser at a bulk sale. The new law also specifies that purchases from a pawnbroker do not usually qualify for the exclusion; such purchasers take subject to a prior interest. [UCC 9-320(c)]

b. Collateral Category Irrelevant: Notice this result applies regardless of the use of the collateral in the hands of the buyer.

c. Actual Knowledge Irrelevant: If consumer goods, this rule of receiving unencumbered title usually applies even if the buyer has actual knowledge of the existence of the prior SI.

d. Prior Filing Irrelevant: Finally, even if there was a prior filing by a secured creditor, the retail buyer of inventory takes the collateral free and clear.

e. Entrusting to a Merchant: It follows that any entrusting to a merchant or bailee who regularly deals in goods of that type (as inventory) empowers him to transfer all ownership rights to a buyer in the ordinary course of business. Such purchasers take free and clear of any prior SI.

f. Farm Products: To take free and clear, the purchase must be from other than the farmer, such as a roadside stand or grocery store.

MEE Tip: Be aware of the retail purchaser exception. The facts may state that the retail buyer knew of the prior secured interest. Even unclean hands will not defeat this super-priority.

---

2. Adding Value to Collateral – Laborer's and Materials Liens: This exception applies to both the personal labor performed by workmen and materials furnished by suppliers which have added value to the collateral. The collateral is worth more because of their labor and/or material so it is equitable that the prior SI should stand junior to the charges which have created the increase in value. [UCC 9-333]

a. Chattel and Real Property Liens: In most jurisdictions a person or firm that has performed labor or furnished material in the construction or repair of any chattel or real property has a lien. Labor is usually given a priority over material. In most states the chattel possessory lien right loses its effectiveness if the collateral is returned to the debtor.

MEE Tip: The UCC model statute extinguishes the super-priority if the collateral is returned to the debtor. Many jurisdictions are to the contrary and allow the lien to continue.

---

(1) Filing of Lien: The lien claimant must usually file a formal lien notice with the jurisdiction's designated office or Department of Licensing within 90 days of the last day of work. Absent timely filing, the lien is extinguished.

(2) Lien Priority: The lien is superior to any interest which attached previously that was not perfected. The lien is also superior to any interest created subsequent to the labor or material being provided. To override a prior perfected interest, the statute must so authorize. Examples are labor liens on timber harvested and the costs of a processor of agricultural products (crops or hay) which are superior to a prior perfected interest.

> **MEE Tip:** In many states a typical labor or material lien is senior to any perfected SI.

(3) Filing and HDC Exception: If the lienholder does not file in 90 days, a new chattel owner who acquires title for value, in good faith, and without actual notice takes free and clear of the lien interest.

b. Warehouse and Carrier Lien: A warehouseperson or public carrier has a lien for storage and transportation charges. This lien is lost if the lienholder voluntarily redelivers the collateral to the owner. [UCC 7-209 and 7-307] A federal maritime lien also has super-priority.

c. Lien Foreclosure: The secured lienholder's priority interest must be formally executed upon. This may require holding a disposition sale of the debtor's assets. The lienholder must give prior notice of the legal action to the debtor and any secured parties. Any bidder must be informed of the existence of any prior lien or SI given in payment for antecedent debts on the eve of the foreclosure disposition sale.

3. Preferential Bankruptcy Interests Avoided: The Federal Bankruptcy law may have an impact on a secured interest. When a bankruptcy petition is filed, the bankruptcy court appoints a trustee to represent the unsecured or general creditors. The bankruptcy court has the power to set aside a debtor's bargain sales of assets and any SI given in payment for antecedent debts on the eve of bankruptcy.

a. Asset Bargain Sale: This is a transfer of assets for less than full and fair consideration. This will also usually constitute the unauthorized sale or conversion.

b. Preferential SI Given: The debtor granting the SI must have owed an antecedent debt to the creditor receiving the SI. This potential to set aside does not apply to a current transaction such as a purchase of new collateral and giving back a SI (PMSI).

c. 90 Days from Petition: This window usually applies to a sale or SI given in the 90 day period immediately preceding the bankruptcy petition date.

d. One Year Extension: The 90 day time period is expanded to one year if the transferee is an "insider," a related party, or if the transfer was fraudulent.

e. Interest Voided: If the above requirements are met, the trustee files a motion with the bankruptcy judge. The judge may void the sale or SI so the asset is available to the unsecured creditors.

> **MEE Tip:** Look for an insolvent debtor who sold assets at a bargain price or gave an SI to provide collateral for a previous (antecedent) obligation on the eve of filing for bankruptcy.

IX. EXAM APPROACH TO ESSAY ANSWERS

A. Overall Coverage

The typical exam question facts involve one debtor (usually a businessman), two or three creditors who provide collateral and/or cash loans to the debtor, and one or two transferees who receive items of collateral from the debtor.

B. Basic Approach

The most effective approach is to begin by discussing the four subjects of collateral categories, purchase money SI, attachment, and perfection. Much of this will begin by use of the Rigos Primary Issues boilerplate. Then analyze each creditor's security interest (SI) in their collateral (did they attach or perfect?). Conclude who has priority in each item of collateral. For the creditors with priority include a brief discussion of their right of replevin and execution ("strict foreclosure," or disposition sale details). Finally, analyze any transferee's position.

C. Skeleton for Analysis

Creditor Entity	PMSI	Collateral	Attached / Perfected	By	Filing Date	Effective Date

Examine every creditor's position in a separate short paragraph. Use the left margin alongside the facts to write the creditor's name and whether they are a PMSI. In the right margin write the collateral category and the date the creditor attached and/or perfected.

D. Question Facts

On 7/5. Friendly Finance lent Abe $100,000 and took a written security interest in "all collateral" signed by Abe. Friendly filed at the local Department of Licensing.

On 7/8, Abe received approval for a bank business loan to purchase a computer and for general working capital purposes. On 7/10, Abe received the cash and signed the bank's loan contract, SA, and financing statement which included "a Compact computer model ASST, all existing equipment, and after-acquired collateral." The bank's financing statement form was filed on 7/12 in the state Department of Licensing. On 7/13, Abe incorporated his business under the tradename "Honest Abe Inc." and assigned all the assets to the new entity.

On 7/15, Acme Equipment filed a financing statement under the name Honest Abe Inc. covering a 7/8 delivery of equipment on credit. On 7/25, Ida Inventory delivered inventory to Abe without filing or notifying the bank. Abe orally agreed this inventory would be subject to a security interest in favor of Ida Inventory.

On 8/1, Abe sold the computer to a computer shop; the next day the shop, in turn, sold the same computer to a retail buyer. On 8/2, Abe filed bankruptcy and the trustee is alleging that the previous two conveyances were fraudulent and that one of the transferees was a related party. Which creditor has priority to the collateral in liquidation?

ANALYSIS SKELETON

Creditor Entity	PMSI	Collateral	Attached / Perfected	By	Filing Date	Effective Date
FrFin (FF).	N	All	Perfected	ARV	7/5	7/5
Bank (B)	Y	Computer	Perfected	Filing	7/12	7/10
Bank (B)	N	After-acquired	Perfected	Filing	7/12	7/12
Acme Eq. (AE)	Y	Equipment	Perfected	Filing	7/15	7/8
I. Inventory (II)	Y	Inventory	Neither			
Bank/Trustee (B)	N	All Assets	Perfected	Auto	8/2	?

E. Model Answer

Controlling Law: Article 9 of the UCC governs security interests (SI) in collateral including personal property, fixtures, agricultural liens, and certain intangibles.

Collateral: The UCC tangible collateral categories are inventory, equipment, consumer goods, and farm products, and the proceeds therefrom. There are also intangible collateral categories such as instruments, documents of title, and chattel paper.

PMSI: A Purchase Money Security Interest (PMSI) has a "close nexus" with the collateral such as a goods seller who takes back paper receivables or a bank loaning money to buy a particular piece of collateral. A general working capital loan does not qualify. A PMSI is allowed to perfect by mere attachment for consumer goods and has a 20-day grace period to perfect non-inventory collateral by filing.

Attachment: Attachment gives the creditor rights against the debtor, the collateral, and third parties who know of the SI. This requires a SA authenticated by the debtor which identifies the collateral, the debtor to have rights in the collateral, and value given by the creditor.

Perfection: Perfection protects the creditor's SI against other SIs, most transferees for value, and the bankruptcy trustee. Perfection may be achieved by attachment plus one of the following: possession, control, filing the financing statement (FS) (in the debtor's principal state), mere attachment (consumer goods and PMSI), or title certificate. Certain collateral must be perfected using certain methods.

Friendly Finance (FF) was not a PMSI, so not eligible for the 20-day grace rule. FF attached on 7/5 since this is the date the creditor gave value. "All collateral" is too generic a description in a SA but qualifies in the FS. The creditor filed locally rather than centrally as required for goods; this was not an interest attached to land. This is ineffective to perfect a SI except as against other creditors with knowledge of the improper filing.

Bank (B) has a "dual status" as a PMSI for the computer equipment collateral, but a non-PMSI for all existing equipment and after-acquired collateral. Perfection by filing the FS for the computer related back and was effective on the date of attachment under the 20-day grace rule allowed a PMSI for non-inventory collateral. For the other collateral, perfection was effective 7/12 since B was not a PMSI for such collateral.

Name Change from Abe to Honest Abe Inc. was seriously misleading because a new creditor could not index it under "Honest Abe Inc." However, since 4 months have not elapsed, filing a new FS is not yet required.

Acme Equipment (AE) was a PMSI since they sold the collateral and took back a receivable. Because the collateral was non-inventory equipment, the 20-day grace period allows perfection to relate back to the date of attachment of 7/8 and thus they prevail over B for their after acquired property.

Ida Inventory (II) was a PMSI, but failed to even acquire a SA which is required for attachment. An oral SI is no SI at all; any attached creditor beats II.

8/1 disposition by the debtor was unauthorized. Since the original creditor was perfected, any traceable cash would be deemed "proceeds" and subject to B's perfected interest. Because the non-pawnshop transferee sold the collateral to a retail purchaser in the ordinary course of business, the retail buyer takes free and clear of all prior SIs.

Bankruptcy trustee has the power to set aside a bargain sale of assets if full value was not received by A or a security interest was given on account of an antecedent debt. The 90-day window is extended to one year if the transferee was a related party. Here, both financing statements were filed after May 2 so they are within the 90 day window period and thus could possibly be set aside.

Prevailing Creditors: Unless set aside, Bank has a perfected SI in the Compact computer for which they provided the financing and all "after-acquired" collateral. AE is perfected in the equipment they sold to Abe.

Magic Memory Outlines®

I. INTRODUCTION
    A. Purpose of Article 9 ....
    B. Question Facts ....

II. COLLATERAL CATEGORY
    A. Tangible Goods..
        1. Classification ....
            a. Inventory...
            b. Equipment...
            c. Consumer Goods ....
            d. Farming Products...
            e. Manufactured Homes..
        2. Primary Use Controls ....
        3. Example ....
    B. Intangible and Documentary Collateral..
        1. Instrument ....
        2. Document of Title...
        3. Chattel Paper...
        4. Account ....
        5. Deposit Account ....
        6. Investment Property..
        7. Commercial Tort Claims ....
        8. Letter of Credit Rights ....
        9. Insurance Policies ....
        10. General Intangibles...
    C. Proceeds..
    D. Description Importance ....

III. CREDITORS AND PURCHASE MONEY SECURITY INTEREST (PMSI)
    A. Collateral Sale..
    B. Loan for Specific Collateral...
    C. Working Capital Loan ....
    D. Burden of Proof ....
    E. Advantages to PMSI Status ....

      1. Household Goods ....

      2. Mere Attachment Perfection...

      3. 20-Day Grace Period ....

      4. Super Priority on Inventory ....

IV. **SECURITY AGREEMENTS (SA)**

    A. In General ....

    B. Collateral Description..

    C. Proceeds...

      1. Collateral Interest Continues ....

      2. SI Automatic ....

    D. After-Acquired Property...

    E. Future Advances ....

    F. Floating Lien ....

    G. Other Provisions ....

      1. Set-off or Recoupment Rights ....

      2. Debtor Duties...

      3. Default ....

      4. Remedies ....

      5. Costs and Attorney Fees ....

      6. Good Faith Required ....

    H. Prohibition on Assignment of Security Interest ....

    I. Agreement Not to Assert Defenses ....

      1. Commercial Contract...

      2. Consumer Credit Contract...

V. **ATTACHMENT – ARV**

    A. **A** Security Agreement ....

      1. Writing Required...

      2. Reasonable Identity ....

      3. Consumer Goods ....

    B. **R**ights in Collateral...

    C. **V**alue Given ....

VI. **PERFECTION – PCFMT**

    A. **P**ossession..

      1. Application ....

      2. Examples of Possession Collateral ....

      3. Effective Date..

    B. **C**ontrol...

      1. General Application...

      2. Specific Application ....

        a. Deposit Account ....

        b. Electronic Chattel Paper ....

        c. Investment Property...

        d.   Letter of Credit Rights ....

    3. Continuation ....

  C. **F**iling...

    1. Financing Statement (FS) ....

        a.   Contents ....

        b. Seriously Misleading Change ....

    2. Filing Place ....

        a.   Proper...

        b. Improper...

    3. Effective Date ....

        a.   General Rule ....

        b. Filing 20-Day Grace Period...

        c.   Inventory Rule ....

        d. Proceeds 20-Day Grace Period..

        e.   Effective Period ....

        f.   Termination..

    4. Consignment ....

    5. Multi-State Transactions..

        a.   Collateral Location Not Controlling...

        b. Debtor Movement and 4 Month Refiling ....

        c.   New State and New Debtor ....

  D. **M**ere Attachment ....

    1. Requirements ....

    2. Consumer Transferee Problem ....

    3. Equipment or Inventory Purposes ....

    4. Example ....

  E. **T**itle Certificate...

    1. State or Federal Statute ....

    2. Notation Required...

    3. Exception ....

VII. REPOSSESSION RIGHT

  A. Retention of Collateral..

    1. Repossession Details ....

    2. Retention Requirements...

    3. Bankruptcy Exception ....

  B. Disposition Sale ....

    1. Sale Details ....

    2. Reasonable Aspects ....

    3. Creditor Warranty ....

    4. Proceeds Application ....

    5. Other Creditors' Security Interests ....

        a.   Senior Interests ....

        b. Junior Interests..

    6. Surplus and Deficiency...

C. 60% Payment by Debtor ....

D. Unauthorized Sale, Removal, or Conversion ....

VIII. PRIORITY RULES

A. First to Attach ....

B. Perfection Prevails over Attachment ....

C. Competing Perfected Interests ....

   1. PMSI Two Advantages ....

   2. Inventory PMSI v. Non-PMSI ....

D. Judgment Creditor ....

E. Bankruptcy Trustee ....

F. Unsecured Creditor ....

G. Exceptions to Priorities – **RAP** ....

   1. **R**etail Inventory ....

      a. Buyer in the Ordinary Course ....

      b. Collateral Category Irrelevant ....

      c. Actual Knowledge Irrelevant ....

      d. Prior Filing Irrelevant ....

      e. Entrusting to a Merchant ....

      f. Farm Products ....

   2. **A**dding Value to Collateral – Laborer's and Materials Lien ....

      a. Chattel and Real Property Liens ....

         (1) Filing of Lien ....

         (2) Lien Priority ....

         (3) Filing and HDC Exception ....

      b. Warehouse and Carrier Lien ....

      c. Lien Foreclosure ....

   3. **P**referential Bankruptcy Interests Avoided ....

      a. Asset Bargain Sale ....

      b. Preferential SI Given ....

      c. 90 Days from Petition ....

      d. One Year Extension ....

      e. Interest Voided ....

IX. EXAM APPROACH TO ESSAY ANSWERS

A. Overall Coverage ....

B. Basic Approach ....

C. Skeleton For Analysis ....

D. Question Facts ....

E. Model Answer ....

RIGOS BAR REVIEW SERIES

UNIFORM MULTISTATE ESSAY EXAM (MEE) REVIEW

CHAPTER 7

UCC ARTICLE 9 – SECURED TRANSACTIONS

Essay Questions

Question Number 1

On March 5th, Debtor as sole proprietor opened Counterculture, a custom countertop company. He ordered his initial supply of 45 sheets of marble on credit from Marble Distributor on March 11th. Debtor signed a loan agreement, security agreement, and financing statement on that date which granted Marble Distributor a security interest in collateral described as "now owned or hereafter acquired inventory and equipment." The financing statement was filed centrally with the Department of Licensing on March 25th. The goods were delivered March 30th.

On March 20th, Debtor met with Granite Distributor who offered 20 sheets of granite on credit. Debtor signed a loan agreement, financing statement, and security agreement that granted Granite Distributor a security interest in collateral described as "all now owned or hereafter acquired inventory" and was filed with the Department of Licensing the same day. The goods were delivered April 6th. Debtor completed 32 countertops and installed them before realizing a monkey could run a router all day and he no longer wanted to make countertops.

In pursuit of happiness, Debtor approached a sculptor who convinced him to take up artistic use of the medium, and also convinced him to relinquish a good share of the fine marble he still possessed in exchange for a chance at an apprenticeship. Debtor followed this advice and while he became enlightened in the coming weeks, he also lacked the cash to make payments on his supply obligations and ultimately announced to his creditors he was closing shop. Both Granite and Marble Distributors assert priority for repayment.

1. Was valid creation of the security interests achieved here? Explain.

2. Who has priority interest in what remaining collateral exists? Explain.

3. What are the possible remedies? Explain.

Question Number 2

On August 6th, Borrower purchased $40,000.00 worth of ski resurfacing gear from Smoothski for his wildly successful Chalet Latte at the bottom of the slopes that provides "hot-java-and-ski-resurfacing-while-you-wait." Borrower signed a security agreement containing the terms of repayment for the resurfacing machines. A financing statement was filed with the state Department of Licensing on August 24th and listed "Latte Chalet" as debtor.

As that winter season approached, Borrower firmly attached the gear to the built-in counters so the machinery would be more stable. He resurfaced half the townspeople's skis, but the snow never came, and sales soon grew dismal. With no skiers around to even buy lattes, Borrower could not make his rent, much less his agreed upon payments to Smoothski. In an act of desperation, Borrower attempted to use the equipment to prepare water Skimboards in hopes of attracting that sports' business and perhaps relocating on the coast. Unfortunately, the result was to damage the resurfacing equipment irreparably, causing Borrower to close shop for good.

Now Smoothski demands priority repayment regardless of any previous creditors Chalet Latte may have, asserting they have a security interest for the equipment at the very heart of this business, and are owed more than the ski shop is even worth. Borrower asserts they can take their broken machines or wait their turn for repayment, since they failed to timely file a proper financing statement to secure their interest. Smoothski has no use for the broken machines.

1. Was a security interest properly acquired by Smoothski for the machines? Explain.

2. Was the security interest perfected? Explain.

3. What right has Smoothski in realizing their collateral? Explain.

Question Number 3

On June 3rd, Borrower walked into MegaVision, a retail electronics distributor, and signed a purchase agreement for a complete home theatre system on credit, agreeing to pay $300 each month for 22 months that granted MegaVision a security interest in the equipment. Borrower loved the system at first, but after a year had passed and there was still nearly a year left to pay, Borrower no longer thought it was such a great deal because newer electronic equipment available was superior to the MegaVison system.

When offered a chance to take over payments of a better home theatre system that Friend had, Borrower thought this might be a solution, if he could just sell the old system for enough to pay it off. Three months after making payments on both systems while using only one, Borrower was desperate, and decided to sell the old system components separately. He found Buyer, who was willing to pay $500 for the theater screen, but was not interested in the projector or sound system. Borrower took the money proceeds for the screen and paid his rent.

Borrower was unable to sell any of the remainder of the system, and ended up giving Brother the all the remaining sound system components, and soon after stopped making payments altogether. MegaVision now wants either full payment, or return of the equipment. Borrower asserts that as far as he is concerned they can recapture their equipment, and gives them the names and addresses where the various parts can be found, saying it is no longer his responsibility.

1. Is Borrower liable when no security agreement was filed? Explain.

2. Does Store have the right to peaceful recapture? Explain.

3. What are the other potential remedies for creditor MegaVision? Explain.

Question Number 4

Bob's plans for his communal pottery studio and kiln in an unused wing of his house were grandiose. He spent several years dreaming up the ideal workspace, where he could teach students to throw clay on the wheel, and then charge for kiln use and materials. He also saw a benefit in that this would offset the cost of his own pottery artistic endeavors. By opening the studio up to outsiders, he could increase the size of his workspace and the type of equipment available for his own use.

Bob contacted Distributor, and ordered four pottery clay throwing wheels so he could begin teaching. Distributor delivered the wheels that week, and Bob signed a security agreement for them. Distributor didn't rush in submitting the filing statement, because he had been told he had a grace period. Unfortunately, Bob panicked two weeks after opening his doors, when still no one had rented a pottery wheel for even an hour, and decided to cut his losses.

At an out of town weekend workshop for glazing techniques, Bob networked and made two pottery wheel sales, one to the owner of Chug's Mugs, a pottery studio that creates and sells ceramic mugs, and the other wheel sold to Randall, an absolute beginner hobbyist. A few days later, returning from submitting the filing statement properly, Distributor stops in at Bob's to collect a payment, and when he sees two wheels missing, he demands full payment or return of all the equipment. Bob refuses, and asserts there was no security interest when the wheels were sold, and Distributor will have to take what he is given whenever Bob can afford to give him more, as others are in line wanting money, too.

1. What is the collateral classification? Explain.

2. How does classification affect the Filing statement? Explain.

3. What is the Distributor's rights against Chug's and Randall? Explain.

Question Number 5

Bailey was a proficient guitar maker, but not as clever at running his business. When friends asked to buy his guitars on credit, it always made him cringe, for fear he'd somehow lose the guitar, payment, and a friend in the deal. He began requiring buyers to sign very detailed purchase agreements containing full descriptions of the particular guitar sold and details where both creditor and debtor lived. Bailey hoped this would reduce the number of folks who skipped out after half the payments were made.

When Bailey made a sale, he went down that very day and filed a statement of what he sold, and to whom. This seemed to work for a time, until Fred came along and wanted five guitars at once. This made Bailey very anxious because he thought Fred might resell some, and so first he made Fred accompany him to the filing department before releasing the guitars. Fred packed his vehicle with the new guitars and then laughed at Bailey before driving away. He yelled out that Bailey had it all backwards and it would be a while before he'd be making a payment. He added that there was nothing Bailey could do, since he failed to perfect his security interest.

Bailey had no idea what he meant, but when he showed copies of his security agreement and filing statement to a business associate, he learned he may have reason to doubt their effectiveness. Bailey asks you if his interest is protected and what he can do.

1. Did Bailey perfect a PMSI? Explain.

2. Can Bailey repossess the guitars? Explain.

3. If Fred sells a guitar to make payment, can Bailey repossess that guitar from Fred's customer? Explain.

Essay Answers

Answer Number 1

Summary

Marble and granite stone are tangible goods, and if the raw material requires preparation before sale, it is classified as inventory. Attachment gives the creditor rights against the debtor, the collateral, and all third parties who know of the security interest (SI). This requires a security agreement (SA). Perfection protects a creditor's SI against other SIs, most transferees for value, and the bankruptcy trustee. Perfection may be achieved by attachment plus possession, control, filing, mere attachment, or title certificate. A purchase money security interest (PMSI) goods seller sells the collateral and takes back paper receivables. A PMSI is allowed to perfect by mere attachment for consumer goods and has a 20 day grace period to perfect non-inventory by filing. For inventory, as here, mere attachment will not perfect and the 20-day grace period does not apply. First in time to perfect is first in right to collect. Here GD filed first. Attached creditors have the right of repossession; replevin self-help is authorized. The creditor then may retain the collateral ("strict foreclosure"), thereby waiving any deficiency. If the creditor elects to hold a disposition sale, the debtor must receive notice, and may object within 20 days. Proceeds from the sale are applied first for repossession and sale expenses, and then disbursed to creditors with senior interests. The debtor receives any remainder and is liable for a deficiency judgment. Here, G will take first; M will take remainder.

Issues Raised

(1) Collateral classification
(2) Attachment – description sufficient?
(3) Perfection
(4) PMSI
    (a) close nexus with collateral
    (b) 20 day grace period for filing on non-inventory collateral
(5) Marble status
(6) Granite status
(7) Remedies
    (a) transferee
    (b) repossession
    (c) disposition sale

(1) Collateral Classification. The collateral here concerns tangible goods which UCC Article 9 includes inventory, equipment, consumer goods, or farm products. Slabs of marble and granite stone that are raw materials needing further tooling before being a retail sale are considered inventory.

(2) Attachment. Attachment gives the creditor rights against the debtor, the collateral and third parties who know of the security interest (SI). This requires a security agreement (SA), the debtor to have rights in the collateral, and value given by the creditor. "All inventory" is generic but meets the minimum standard required in the security agreement (SA).

(3) Perfection. Protects the creditor's SI against other SI, most transferees for value, and the bankruptcy trustee. Perfection may be achieved by attachment plus one of the following: Possession, control, filing a financing statement, mere attachment or title certificate.

(4) PMSI. A purchase money security interest (PMSI) has a close nexus with collateral, including the goods seller who takes back paper receivables. A PMSI may perfect by mere attachment for consumer goods and has a 20 day grace period to perfect non-inventory by filing.

(5) Marble Status. Here, the slabs of stone are not consumer goods, but rather inventory. Therefore, mere attachment is insufficient to perfect so the creditor must take additional steps. Since it is inventory, the 20-day perfection grace period does not apply. Without this exception, the basic rule is first in time to perfect is first in right to collect. Here, both distributors achieved attachment, but Marble Distributor perfected by properly filing first and thus has first claim to the marble over Sculptor.

(6) Granite Status. If a creditor's security agreement contains a "hereafter acquired" clause they are entitled to collateral the debtor subsequently acquires. An exception applies if the subsequent creditor was a PSMI furnishing new collateral. However, if the collateral in question is inventory, the subsequent creditor must search the record and send written notice to the previous creditor. Here it is not stated if Granite complied with that requirement.

(7) Remedies. An attached creditor has the right of repossession, even without judicial process; self-help replevin is authorized for a PMSI. If the interest is perfected, the right is also good against third-party transferees. The creditor is given a limited replevin privilege against the tort of trespass to enter onto the debtor's property, but it must be reasonable as to time and extent, and not involve a breach of the peace. "Strict foreclosure" allows the creditor to retain the collateral, but usually the creditor waives any deficiency claim against the debtor.

Written notice must be given the debtor if the creditor repossesses, and if objected to within 20 days, a disposition sale of the collateral must be held. The creditor must conduct a lien search and give other creditors of record notice. The proceeds from the sale must be used first for repossession and disposition sale expenses, and then disbursed to creditors with priority interests senior to the creditor conducting the sale. Any junior interests take after the creditor conducting the sale. Any remainder or deficiency judgment is given to or is the responsibility of the debtor. Here, Granite will take first, Marble will take the remainder and receive a deficiency judgment for the remainder owed. The interest in the marble transferred to a third party transferee might also be recovered unless Sculptor is deemed to be a purchaser in the ordinary course of business.

Answer Number 2

Summary

The resurfacing machines are classified here as equipment or fixtures. Attachment gives the creditor rights against the debtor, the collateral, and all third parties who know of the security interest (SI). This requires a Security agreement (SA). Here, an SI was properly created. Perfection protects a creditor's SI against other subsequent SI, most transferees for value, and the bankruptcy trustee. For equipment, either possession or filing perfects. A purchase money security interest (PMSI) has a close nexus with collateral, including the good seller who takes back paper receivables. A PMSI is allowed to perfect by filing and has a 20 day grace period to perfect non-inventory by filing. Here the grace period to file applies 18 days later, but the filing error of inverting the name was not corrected. So the improperly filed SI may cost S priority over senior creditors. The first to file or perfect has priority, and S will take only once they are satisfied. S cannot demand a super priority over other creditors who perfected first. If S is the only creditor, it can affect a strict foreclosure and repossess the equipment, or hold a disposition sale. If the proceeds are not sufficient, S may obtain a deficiency judgment against D.

Issues Raised

(1) Collateral Classification
(2) Attachment
(3) Perfection
   (a) filing
   (b) name error fatal
 (4) PMSI
   (a) close nexus with collateral
   (b) 20 day grace period for filing
(5) Priority
(6) Remedies
   (a) repossession right
   (b) disposition sale

Sample Answer

(1) Collateral Classification. Under UCC Article 9 tangible goods may be inventory equipment, consumer goods or farming products. Here, the resurfacing machines are used in a productive capacity for the business, and therefore are classified as equipment.

(2) Attachment. Gives the creditor rights against the debtor, the collateral and third parties who know of the security interest (SI). This requires a security agreement (SA), the debtor to have rights in the collateral, and value given by the creditor. Here, "resurfacing equipment" in the SA is sufficiently descriptive for the collateral and a security interest was thus properly created.

(3) Perfection. Protects the creditors SI against other subsequent SIs, most transferees for value, and the bankruptcy trustee. Perfection may be achieved by attachment plus possession, control, filing a financing statement (FS), mere attachment, or title certificate. Here, the facts indicate that Smoothski perfected their security interest in the collateral by filing.

(4) PMSI. A purchase money security interest (PMSI) has a close nexus with collateral, including a goods seller who takes back paper receivables or a bank loaning money to buy a particular piece of equipment. A PMSI is allowed to perfect by mere attachment for consumer goods and has a 20 day grace period to perfect non-inventory by filing the FS. Here the grace period to file applies so filing 18 days later is timely, but the filing error of inverting the name was not corrected. This may have made the filing statement seriously misleading since a third party would reference the debtor's name in performing a filing search. Here there is a SI granted to Smoothski, but failure to file properly may cost them priority if there are other creditors.

(5) Priority. The first to file or perfect has priority. Here, we only know of the one secured debt, although there presumably was a rental agreement on the Chalet itself which might define the "gear" as an attachment (fixture) the removal of which could damage the landlord's reversion. Any other debts the Chalet had incurred while doing business prior to the resurfacing equipment purchase would have priority if their filings included a "hereafter acquired" clause since Smoothski did not check the record. The basic rule is first in time to perfect is first in right to collect. Smoothski is subordinate to the senior creditors and takes only once they are satisfied. They cannot demand the inventory super priority over other creditors who perfected first.

(6) Remedies. Smoothski's improper filing name negates perfection but not attachment against the debtor. Since there are no other attached creditors, attachment prevails as to that collateral. They can affect a strict foreclosure and repossess the equipment, or with written approval from the Debtor can receive a partial strict foreclosure if less than a whole recovery is available. This waives any potential deficiency judgment against the debtor. A collateral disposition sale is also an available remedy, and if the proceeds are not sufficient to pay the sale costs and underlying debt, Smoothski can obtain a deficiency judgment against Chalet Latte. This would be satisfied pro rata with the debtor's other general creditors.

Answer Number 3

Summary

The home theatre equipment is a tangible good for personal use, and so is classified as a consumer good. Attachment gives the creditor rights against the debtor, the collateral and third parties who know of the security interest (SI). This requires a Security agreement (SA), the debtor to have rights in the collateral, and value given by the creditor. Here, a SI was properly created. Perfection protects the creditors SI against other SI, most transferees for value, and the bankruptcy trustee. A purchase money security interest (PMSI) has a close nexus with collateral, and is allowed to perfect by mere attachment for consumer goods (as M did here). Following replevin and a commercially reasonable disposition sale, a deficiency judgment against the debtor is available to the creditor for the balance due, but it is unsecured.

Issues Raised

(1) Collateral Classification
(2) Attachment
(3) Perfection
    (a) control
    (b) filing
    (c) mere attachment

   (d) title certificate
(4) PMSI
   (a) close nexus with collateral
   (b) 20 day grace period for filing
(5) Consumer-to-Consumer Transfer
(6) Brother not a bona fide transferee
(7) Repossession
   (a) self help acceptable with exceptions
   (b) possible against third-party transferees if SI is perfected
   (c) strict foreclosure waives deficiencies

Sample Answer

(1) Collateral Classification. UCC Article 9 tangible goods includes inventory, equipment, consumer goods and farm products. Here, the home theatre equipment is a tangible item, for personal use, and therefore is classified as a consumer good.

(2) Attachment. Gives the creditor rights against the debtor, the collateral and third parties who know of the security interest (SI). This requires a security agreement (SA), the debtor to have rights in the collateral, and value given by the creditor. Here, a security interest was properly created because all of the requirements were apparently met.

(3) Perfection. Protects the creditors SI against other SI, most transferees for value, and the bankruptcy trustee. Perfection may be achieved by attachment plus one of the following: Possession, control, filing, mere attachment or title certificate. For consumer goods, mere attachment perfects, and here Borrower signed a purchase agreement and accepted the consumer equipment, so the security interest was deemed perfected.

(4) PMSI. A purchase money security interest (PMSI) has a close nexus with collateral, including the goods seller who takes back paper receivables or a bank loaning money to buy a particular piece of equipment. A PMSI is allowed to perfect by mere attachment for consumer goods. MegaVision has properly perfected their PMSI here by mere attachment. MegaVison could thus secure a judgment against Borrower.

(5) Consumer-to-Consumer Transfer. A creditor who perfects by mere attachment loses the perfection priority if the consumer debtor transfers the collateral to s bona fide consumer who uses the collateral for personal purposes. It is likely that the transferees, Buyer qualifies as a bona fide consumer transferee since it was a "home system." Therefore, MegaVision may have no rights to the theater screen in Buyer's possession.

(6) Brother not a Bona Fide Transferee. The consumer-to-consumer exception requires the transferee to be bona fide. Here, the transferee paid no value and is a relative which suggests knowledge of the underlying creditor's SI. This would seem contrary to the legal policy exception. Further since the transfer was as a gift there are no proceeds to pursue. Borrower can likely thus still be sued, a judgment for the balance obtained, and the creditor could begin execution.

(6) Repossession. Assuming the transferees Buyer and/or Brother use for other than personal use, an attached creditor has the right to repossess the collateral for non-payment with or without judicial process; self-help is authorized. If the creditor's interest is perfected, the repossession right is also good against third-party transferees such as Brother. The creditor is granted a limited replevin privilege against the tort of trespass to enter onto the debtor's property, providing it is reasonable as to time and extent, and does not involve a breach of the peace.

Answer Number 4

Summary

If the merchandise here is used in a productive capacity of a business, it should be classified as equipment, but if it was intended for resale then it is inventory. The parties here will likely assert a different category. Generally, to perfect a security interest (SI), a filing statement must be properly filed. For consumer goods, perfection occurs by mere attachment. If the item is intended as equipment, there is a 20 day filing grace period, which allows the SI to relate back to the date of the agreement. A SI was properly formed with B either way. Attachment gives the creditor rights against the debtor, the collateral, and third parties who know of the interest. This requires a SA, the debtor to have rights in the collateral, and value given by the creditor. Perfection protects the creditor's interests against other interests, most transferees for value, and the bankruptcy trustee. Perfection may be achieved by attachment plus possession, control, filing, mere attachment, or title certificate. D perfected here by filing. If filing was timely, D may affect a strict foreclosure and repossess the equipment. With written approval from the debtor, D can also affect a partial strict foreclosure since less than a whole recovery is available. If the sold merchandise is inventory, a retail buyer in the ordinary course of business takes the title free and clear of creditors' claims against the retailer.

Issues Raised

(1)   Collateral Classification
(2)   PMSI
      (a) close nexus with collateral
      (b) 20 day grace period for filing uncertain
(3)   Attachment
(4)   Perfection
      (a) filing not timely if equipment
      (b) mere attachment if consumer good
 (5)   Remedies
      (a) repossession
      (b) disposition sale
(6)   Priorities

Sample Answer

(1)   Collateral Classification. Here the collateral classification is vital. If the merchandise is used in a productive capacity for Bob's business, it would be classified as equipment. If intended for resale then it would be considered inventory in the hands of the debtor. Since Bob also used the pottery wheels for his own use it may be characterized as consumer goods. The primary use controls. Usually the use is designated in the security agreement. The fact pattern here does not tell us what the original agreement designated the use as, if at all. The parties likely will assert a different category.

(2)   PMSI. Has a close nexus with collateral, including a goods seller who takes back paper receivables as Distributor did here. In order to perfect the security interest, a filing statement must usually be properly filed. If the merchandise is determined to be consumer goods perfection by a PSMI occurs by mere attachment. If the item is intended as other than inventory, including equipment, there is a 20 day filing grace period, which allows the security interest to relate back to the date of the agreement.

(3) Attachment. Gives the creditor rights against the debtor, the collateral, and third parties who know of the interest. This requires a written Security Agreement, the debtor to have rights in the collateral, and value given by the creditor. A security interest appears to have been properly formed with Bob regardless of the collateral category.

(4) Perfection. Protects the creditors interests against other interests, most transferees for value, and the bankruptcy trustee. Perfection may be achieved by attachment plus possession, control, filing, mere attachment, or title certificate. Here, Distributor's interest is perfected by mere attachment if consumer goods. If consumer goods in the original debtor Bob's hands, a bona fide consumer transferee takes free and clear under the "consumer-to-consumer" transferee exception to perfection by mere attachment. If the pottery throwing machines are deemed to be equipment and the filing occurred, as here, within 20 days of the debtor receiving the collateral, their interest has a priority. If the collateral is deemed inventory held for resale, there is no 20-day grace period so Distributor's filing was too late.

(5) Remedies. Distributor can affect a strict foreclosure and repossess the equipment remaining in Bob's possession. This waives any deficiency judgment. With 10 days notice to the debtor and other creditors of record the creditor may hold a disposition sale. Every aspect of the disposition sale must be commercially reasonable by industry standards.

(6) Priorities. If the merchandise sold to Randall is deemed inventory in the debtor's hands a retail buyer in the ordinary course of business takes the title free and clear of the retailer's creditors. The seller is required to be a person who sells that kind of goods, and since two wheels were sold, it is arguable this is a part of Bob's business.

Answer Number 5

Summary

Guitars are classified as consumer goods, unless intended for resale in which case they are inventory. Attachment gives creditor rights against a debtor, the collateral and third parties who know of the security interest (SI). This requires a security agreement (SA), for the debtor to have rights in the collateral, and value given by the creditor. Here these criteria seem to be all met. Perfection is achieved by attachment plus either possession, control, filing, mere attachment or filing the financing statement (FS) at the state department of licensing. A FS must adequately identify each item. A PMSI is allowed to perfect by mere attachment for consumer goods, so failure of filing may be irrelevant. For remedies, a creditor may repossess and retain the collateral and waive any deficiency against the debtor. The creditor may also conduct a disposition sale. Unauthorized sale, removal, or conversion of the property by the Debtor is at least a misdemeanor. An attached creditor may repossess with or without judicial process; self-help is authorized. For perfected SIs, repossession rights are also good against third party transferees.

Issues Raised

(1)   Collateral Classification
(2)   Attachment
(3)   Perfection
      (a) control
      (b) filing
      (c) mere attachment
      (d) title certificate
(4)   PMSI
      (a) close nexus with collateral
      (b) 20 day grace period for filing
(5)   Remedies
      (a) repossession
      (b) disposition sale

Sample Answer

(1)   Collateral Classification. Guitars are usually considered a consumer good, unless the contract was with a distributor for resale, and then it is classified as inventory or used in a band where it would be classified as equipment. If mixed use, the primary use in the hands of the debtor controls. Here, there is no detail as to whether these goods purchased by Fred were primarily for personal use, for resale as inventory, or as equipment such as being used in a band.

(2)   Attachment. Gives creditor rights against a debtor, the collateral, and third parties who know of the security interest. This requires a security agreement, the debtor to have rights in the collateral, and value given by the creditor. Here these criteria were apparently met.

(3)   Perfection. Is achieved by attachment plus one of the following: possession, control, filing, mere attachment, or title certificate. A financing statement must adequately identify each item of collateral and list the addresses of both creditor and debtor. It is not clear here if proper filing occurred at the required state office. Since filing occurred before transfer, Bailey did not need the 20 day grace period allowed for equipment.

(4)   PMSI. A PMSI is allowed a creditor providing goods to a debtor. Perfection by mere attachment applies to PMSIs in consumer goods. Therefore any failure to properly file is irrelevant if consumer goods was the primary use of the guitars in Bailey's hands.

(5)   Repossession Remedies. A creditor may repossess and retain the collateral by waiving any deficiency against the debtor. Partial strict foreclosure is also allowed with permission of the debtor. The creditor may also conduct a formal disposition sale, but the unauthorized sale, removal, or conversion of the collateral by the Debtor is a violation and at least a misdemeanor in most jurisdictions.

(6)   Rights Against Transferees. If the interest is perfected, the creditor's repossession right is also good against third party transferees. This right is not applicable to a bona fide consumer transferee purchasing from a consumer where perfection was by mere attachment Also a purchase of collateral sold as inventory to a buyer in the ordinary course of business who regularly deal in those goods takes free and clear. Here the facts do not disclose if Fred regularly deals in guitars. If so, Fred can sell a guitar at retail and Bailey cannot repossess the guitar from those purchasers.

CHAPTER 7

UCC ARTICLE 9 – SECURED TRANSACTIONS

Index

20-Day Grace Period.......... T 7-382, 387
Account .... T 7-380
Adding Value to Collateral .... T 7-393
Agreement Not to Assert
    Defenses .... T 7-384
After-Acquired Property .... T 7-384
Asset Bargain Sale .... T 7-394
Attachment .... T 7-385
Attorney Fees .... T 7-384
Automobile Dealers.................... T 7-389
Bankruptcy Preferences.............. T 7-394
Bankruptcy Stay .... T 7-390
Bankruptcy Trustee .... T 7-392
Bona Fide Consumer
    Transferee.............................. T 7-389
Buyer in the Ordinary Course of
    Business.................................. T 7-392
Carrier Lien .... T 7-395
Chattel Liens .... T 7-393
Chattel Paper .... T 7-380
Collateral Categories .... T 7-379
Collateral
    Description ...... T 7-381, 383, 385, 387
Collateral Sale .... T 7-381
Commercial Tort Claims............ T 7-380
Competing Perfected Interests ... T 7-392
Consignment.............................. T 7-388
Consumer Credit Contract.......... T 7-384
Consumer Goods .... T 7-379
Consumer Transferee .... T 7-389
Continuation of Perfection .... T 7-386
Control....................................... T 7-386
Costs and Attorney Fees............. T 7-384
Creditors .... T 7-381
Creditors' Remedies................... T 7-384
Debtor Duties .... T 7-384
Debtor Movement .... T 7-388
Debtor's Name Change or
    Error .... T 7-387
Default....................................... T 7-384
Deficiency Judgment.................. T 7-391
Deposit Account................. T 7-380, 386
Description of
    Collateral .... T 7-381, 383, 385, 387

Disposition Proceeds
    Application .... T 7-390
Disposition Sale......................... T 7-390
Document of Title...................... T 7-380
Documentary Collateral.............. T 7-380
Equipment................................. T 7-379
Equipment Transferee .... T 7-389
Electronic Chattel Paper............. T 7-386
Entrusting to Merchant .... T 7-393
Exceptions to Priorities.............. T 7-392
Farming Products................ T 7-380, 393
Filing of Financing Statement .... T 7-386
Filing of Lien............................. T 7-393
Filing Place .... T 7-387
Financing Statement................... T 7-387
Floating Lien .... T 7-383
Future Advances........................ T 7-383
General Intangibles..................... T 7-381
Good Faith Required .... T 7-384
Household Goods .... T 7-382
Instrument.................................. T 7-380
Insurance Policy .... T 7-381
Intangible Collateral .... T 7-380
Inventory................................... T 7-379
Inventory PMSI .... T 7-392
Inventory Transferee .... T 7-389
Investment Property............ T 7-380, 386
Judgment Creditor .... T 7-392
Junior Interests.......................... T 7-391
Laborer's Lien .... T 7-393
Lien Filing .... T 7-393
Lien Priority.............................. T 7-393
Letter of Credit Rights........ T 7-381, 386
Loan for Specific Collateral .... T 7-382
Materials Lien............................ T 7-393
Mere Attachment
    Perfection...................... T 7-382, 389
Multi-State Transactions .... T 7-388
Perfection.................................. T 7-385
Policy of Insurance.................... T 7-381
Possession................................. T 7-386
Primary Use Controls .... T 7-380
Priority Exceptions .... T 7-392
Priority Rules............................. T 7-391

Preferential Bankruptcy
    Interests Avoided ....T 7-394
Proceeds ....T 7-381, 383, 388
Prohibition on Assignment of
    Security Interest ....T 7-384
Purchase Money Security
    Interest (PMSI)........................T 7-381
Real Property Liens.....................T 7-393
Recoupment Rights ....T 7-384
Remedies.....................................T 7-384
Repossession Right ....T 7-389
Retail Inventory..........................T 7-382
Retention of Collateral ....T 7-390
Rights in Collateral ....T 7-385
Security Agreements ....T 7-382, 385
Senior Interests...........................T 7-391
Set-Off Rights ....T 7-384
Super Priority on Inventory........T 7-382
Tangible Goods ....T 7-379
Termination Statement................T 7-388
Title Certificate ....T 7-389
Title Transferee ....T 7-389
Unauthorized Sale, Removal,
    or Conversion by Debtor..........T 7-391
Value Given ....T 7-385
Vehicle Dealers ....T 7-389
Warehouse Lien ....T 7-394
Working Capital Loan.................T 7-382
Writing Required........................T 7-385

CHAPTER 8

ABA PROFESSIONAL

RESPONSIBILITY RULES

RIGOS BAR REVIEW SERIES

UNIFORM MULTISTATE ESSAY EXAM (MEE) REVIEW

CHAPTER 8

ABA PROFESSIONAL RESPONSIBILITY RULES

Table of Contents

A.   Opening Argument and Primary Issues.................................... Text 8-419

B.   Text .... Text 8-421

    I.   Competence, Scope of Representation, and Fees .... Text 8-421

    II.   Confidentiality and Conflicts of Interest................................ Text 8-427

    III.   Disqualification, Client Funds, and Withdrawal.................... Text 8-436

    IV.   Counselor, Advocate, and Third Party Dealings.................... Text 8-443

    V.   Law Firms, Marketing, and Professional Integrity .... Text 8-451

C.   Magic Memory Outlines® .... Magic Memory Outlines 8-461

D.   Professional Responsibility Essay Questions .... Questions 8-465

E.   Professional Responsibility Essay Answers .... Answers 8-469

F.   Professional Responsibility Index .... Index 8-475

G.   Acronyms .... Acronyms 15-630

OPENING ARGUMENT AND PRIMARY ISSUES

ABA PROFESSIONAL RESPONSIBILITY RULES

The following material is a brief overview of most, but not all, of the key issues in Professional Responsibility. NCBE and a growing number of states are now testing professional responsibility issues in traditional essay question subjects. The following essay questions and answers assume the state follows the ABA's model rules, 2007 edition (MRPC). Candidates should check with the local authority to determine if the individual jurisdiction's ethics rules are tested and if they vary from the model rules.

Candidates in jurisdictions that test professional responsibility in the MPRE should consult the *Rigos Bar Review Series – MPRE* for complete textual coverage, Magic Memory Outlines® software, and over 350 multiple-choice questions with Make Your Own Exam™ drills. This book and other Rigos Bar Review Series publications are sold at law school bookstores throughout the nation and online at http://lawschool.aspenpublishers.com.

There are a few thoughts that should usually be stated at the beginning of every answer. These will score you easy points and let the grader know you are in the right topic area.

Most essays should have an "opening argument": a brief, broad statement that shows you understand the broad significance of a legal topic. The opening argument also suggests to the grader that she is about to read a thoughtful and well-organized essay.

Many subjects also have "primary issues" that can be discussed up front or integrated into the essay answer. IMPORTANT: Do not merely regurgitate these statements on the exam without addressing the issues actually raised by the facts, or you will not pass.

- **Professional responsibility Opening Argument:** The Rules of Professional Conduct (RPCs) set the minimum standard that no lawyer may fall below without being subject to professional discipline.

- **Sample Primary Issue Statements:**

  - A lawyer must provide a client reasonably competent representation which is the legal knowledge, skill, thoroughness, and preparation necessary for the representation.

  - A lawyer must communicate sufficiently to allow the client to make informed decisions about objectives and settlement offers and report all malpractice to the client.

  - A lawyer's fees shall be reasonable considering the skills required, amount involved, novelty and difficulty, time involved, opportunities foregone, average customary fee in the locale, relationship, expertise, reputation, experience, and result.

  - A lawyer may reveal client confidential information to the extent necessary to prevent reasonably certain death or substantial bodily injury.

- A lawyer may reveal confidential information to prevent the client from committing a crime or fraud resulting in substantial injury in furtherance of which the client has used or is using the lawyer's services.

- A lawyer shall not represent a client if that representation will be directly adverse to another client.

- A lawyer shall not represent a client if that representation is materially limited by other clients or the lawyer's personal considerations.

- A lawyer who has formerly represented a client in a matter shall not represent another person with adverse interests in the same or a substantially related matter.

- While lawyers are associated in a firm, none of them shall knowingly represent a client when any one of them practicing alone would be prohibited from doing so.

- A lawyer shall withdraw if the representation would result in a violation of the RPCs, if the lawyer has an impaired ability, or the lawyer is discharged by a client.

- A lawyer may withdraw if the client is pursuing criminal action, the lawyer is being used to commit a crime, the objective is repugnant, the burden on the lawyer is unreasonable, or other good cause for withdrawal exists.

- A lawyer shall not knowingly make a false statement of fact or law to a tribunal and must promptly notify the court of past falsity.

- A lawyer shall not falsify evidence or counsel, assist, or induce a witness to testify falsely or flee the jurisdiction.

- A lawyer is responsible for the improper conduct of subordinates if they directly order the conduct or with knowledge of the specific conduct fail to avoid, correct, or mitigate the consequences.

- A lawyer with actual personal knowledge of a committed violation of the MRPCs that raise a substantial question as to another lawyer's honesty, trustworthiness, or fitness shall inform the appropriate professional authority.

- A lawyer is in violation of MRPCs if they engage in conduct involving dishonesty, fraud, deceit, or misrepresentation even if not related to the practice of law.

ABA PROFESSIONAL RESPONSIBILITY RULES

This material is a summary of the ABA's Model Rules and includes the Ethics 2000 recommendations. Many states and the NCBE Uniform MEE test the professional responsibility (PR) subjects as a part of other substantive essay questions. Look for the word "lawyer" or "attorney" in the facts. Examples include a corporate governance question in which a lawyer is advising both the entity and another adverse constituent or conflicting shareholders. Discuss the PR issues either before or after the substantive portion; do not mix the two.

I. COMPETENCE, SCOPE OF REPRESENTATION, AND FEES

The following ethical rules are often combined on the MEE.

> **MEE Tip:** A lawyer-client relationship may be express or implied and may be created by a failure to affirmatively reject a prospective client's reasonable belief of representation.

A. Competence – MRPC 1.1

Lawyers must be legally competent. Competent representation requires the legal knowledge, skill, thoroughness, and preparation reasonably necessary for the case.

1. Proficiency Required: Competent representation is usually based on personal experience and lawyers should not accept employment beyond their competency. Lack of experience in a given area is not conclusive evidence of incompetence because all persons who pass the bar exam are presumed competent to research and practice any general area of law. However, a lawyer cannot charge the client for excessive research time spent learning details of the substantive law that an experienced lawyer would know. A lawyer may associate with another attorney who has the necessary competency, but the client must consent to the association arrangement.

2. Required Standard: The standard is usually that of a general practitioner, but may be elevated if the lawyer held himself out as an expert such as an LL.M. in taxation.

3. Emergency Situation: In an emergency, a lawyer may make a best effort until it is possible to refer the client to a more competent practitioner.

4. Maintaining Competence: A lawyer must keep abreast of changes in the area of practice. Usually this means participating in relevant continuing legal education (CLE).

> **MEE Tip:** Incompetence is often combined on the exam questions with delay (MRPC 1.3) and a failure to communicate with the client (MRPC 1.4).

5. Legal Malpractice Relationship: Legal malpractice theories include breach of contract (reasonable care implied), tort (misrepresentation or negligence), or breach of fiduciary duty (confidentiality, loyalty, and honest dealings).

a. Standards Differ: The MRPCs do not create a civil claim or necessarily set the standards of practice for purposes of civil liability, and evidence of a disciplinary violation or alleged violation may not be introduced in a malpractice lawsuit. However, an expert may incorporate the concepts underlying the MRPCs into an opinion on the reasonable legal standard of care to which the lawyer should have adhered.

b. Proof Required: The client generally must prove that but for the lawyer's malpractice, the client would have prevailed in the underlying matter ("case within a case").

B. Scope of Representation and Authority Allocation – MRPC 1.2

This Rule includes a variety of representation matters including who – the client or lawyer – makes which decisions and addresses related ethical restrictions on the client's directions over the lawyer. The scope of the lawyer's undertaking is also examined.

1. Representation Objectives: The client has the ultimate authority in determining the representation objectives. This includes all of the major outcome-determinant decisions.

2. Lawyer's Decisions: Unless specified to the contrary, the lawyer has implied authorization to decide the means and tactics to achieve the objectives. This includes making most strategic and procedural decisions such as which causes of action to plead, the extent of discovery, professional courtesy to be extended to opposing counsel, and trial witness presentation choices. The lawyer should consult with the client on such details.

3. Client's Decisions – AJET: The client has the ultimate authority to make major litigation decisions. These include the questions of whether to (1) **a**ccept or reject a settlement offer; or in a criminal case, (2) **j**ury trial waiver, (3) **e**ntering a plea, or (4) **t**estifying at trial.

4. No Endorsement: A lawyer's representation of a client does not constitute approval or an endorsement of the client's political, social, or moral views and activities.

5. Counsel a Crime or Fraud: A lawyer shall not counsel or assist a client in perpetrating conduct that the lawyer knows is criminal or fraudulent. Prohibitions include planning and concealing ongoing unlawful activities, which is aiding and abetting; the lawyer must withdraw. However, the lawyer may attempt to determine the validity, scope, meaning, or application of the law to a past offense and discuss the legal consequences. A lawyer may in good faith counsel a client on how to gain legal standing necessary to challenge the law.

6. Client Urging MRPC Violation: If the client expects assistance from the lawyer not permitted by the MRPCs, the lawyer must consult with the client concerning the ethical limitations on the lawyer's conduct. The lawyer must tell the client that he cannot violate the disciplinary rules. If the client insists, the lawyer must attempt to withdraw.

7. Client Authority: In some states, a lawyer shall not willfully purport to act as a lawyer for any person without the prior authority of that person.

8. Limit of Representation: Clients usually employ a lawyer contractually to handle all aspects of a matter, such as pursuing or defending all legal representation in a pre-defined cause of action. In many states, the scope of representation by a lawyer may be "limited" to a particular discrete aspect of a matter, such as only the trial court representation, but not an appeal. Scope restrictions must be reasonable under the circumstances. The client must give informed consent after consultation.

MEE Tip: A lawyer unilaterally making the client's **AJET** decisions is frequently tested.

C. Diligence – MRPC 1.3

A lawyer shall act with reasonable diligence and promptness in representing a client.

1. Dilatory Practices: The lawyer must act promptly and forcefully in pursuing the client's interests. Dilatory practices include an unreasonable delay in filing a lawsuit, procrastination in pursuing the matter, or neglecting to return the client's calls or requests for information concerning the status of the case. If a lawyer is leaving the practice of law, substituted counsel must be appointed to handle the ongoing client representation. The client must be informed of the situation and the succeeding attorney. The client may decide to go elsewhere.

2. Legal Rules: Court deadlines control. A plaintiff's lawyer's worst nightmare is a statute of limitations (SOL) violation – usually failure to file a claim timely is automatic malpractice. Effective calendaring and docket control systems are critical.

3. Representation Completion: Diligence includes carrying through the representation until the case is complete and/or the lawyer properly withdraws. The client must be informed of completion and any appeal possibility – preferably in writing – so she understands the lawyer's responsibility has ended and she needs to look elsewhere for advice and monitoring.

MEE Tip: To violate MRPC 1.3, the lawyer's delay must be patently unreasonable.

D. Communication – MRPC 1.4

A lawyer shall keep the client reasonably informed about progress and developments in the status of the matter, any issues requiring informed consent, and any limitations on the lawyer. Any MRPC limitations should be explained if the client's expectations could involve a violation. All bona fide offers of settlement must be communicated to the client.

1. Informative Explanations: An explanation may be necessary so that clients can participate in making informed decisions and have a full understanding upon which informed consent is based. Any request for information by the client should be answered timely. Client telephone calls, emails, and letters should be returned promptly. If for some reason the time schedule or agreed timeline slips, the lawyer should inform the client before the due dates.

2. Written v. Oral: Oral communications are worth the paper they are written on. While the expectations of both parties start with the representation agreement, it is also a good idea to send a letter at various intervals summarizing the status of the matter and what is ahead.

3. Special Situations: There are two exceptions to the communication duty.

a. Court Order or Rules: A court order may prohibit or limit the lawyer from sharing sensitive information with the client. For instance, a judge may issue a protection order forbidding the lawyer from communicating to the client trade secrets of a competitor that the lawyer learned in the discovery process.

b. Client Imprudent Reaction: If the disclosure of adverse information would cause the client to harm herself, the lawyer may delay the communication.

4. Communicate Mistakes: Ethical rulings direct that any mistake a lawyer makes must be communicated to the client. This could create a conflict of interest requiring client consent to allow the lawyer to go forward in the representation.

5. Communicate Termination: The client must be informed when the attorney-client relationship has ended. This requirement intends to make it clear to the client that the lawyer's responsibility has terminated, and she is no longer monitoring the client's situation or changes in the law that may have adverse consequences.

> **MEE Tip:** A failure to communicate (MRPC 1.4) and failure to act in a diligent manner (MRPC 1.3) both suggest an incompetent lawyer (MRPC 1.1).

E. Fees – MRPC 1.5(a)

A lawyer may not charge an unreasonable fee (or recover unreasonable expenses), regardless of how characterized or calculated. Therefore, all the client charges shall not be unreasonable.

1. Reasonable Factors: In determining the reasonableness of a fee, there is no single bright-line test. Rather there is a multi-factor analysis in most states. Consider the following **SANTA** (case-related) and **REBER** (attorney-related) factors.

a. Skill Required: A complex antitrust class action will require more skill than an uncontested divorce and thus may be billed at a higher rate.

b. Amount Involved: Value added is currently a favored justification for higher fees. An attorney pursuing a personal injury case seeking millions of dollars in damages could bill more per hour than for a small dollar collection action.

c. Novelty and Difficulty: The novelty and difficulty of prevailing in the case is a factor in determining appropriate fee levels.

d. Time Involved / Opportunities Foregone: The time and labor required are probably the most widely accepted factors in setting fees. A case that the client knows will absorb all a lawyer's time and preclude other employment may be billed at a higher rate.

e. Average Customary Fee: This is the amount normally charged in the locality for similar legal services.

f. Relationship: The nature and length of the attorney's professional relationship with the client is a factor in determining the fee level. Frequently a lawyer demands a fee and cost advance from a new client.

g. Expertise: An attorney who is the world's expert on corporate tax-free reorganizations would command a higher billing rate than a novice.

h. Basis of Fee: Whether the fee is fixed, hourly, or contingent is an important factor in determining the reasonableness question.

i. Experience / Reputation: The more experience in the area and better the reputation of the attorney, the higher the attorney's fee is to be expected.

j. Result: The result achieved in the controversy matters; winning attorneys usually are paid more than losing attorneys.

MEE Tip: No one factor is conclusive in the **SANTA REBER** analysis. If the fee is questioned, the burden is on the lawyer to show that the fee is not unreasonable.

---

2. Double Billing: The ABA in Formal Opinion 93-379 stated that double billing the same time or work product to two clients is improper. This may involve billing two clients for the same research or the same transportation time.

3. Fee Agreement Required – MRPC 1.5(b): Fee agreements (alone or as a part of a more inclusive representation agreement) are often determinant or quite important to the reasonableness of the amount to be charged.

a. Includes: There must always be a fee agreement that allows the client to receive a reasonable and fair disclosure of all material elements of the engagement and billing practices. Some states require a writing if the fee exceeds a threshold amount, such as $1,000 or involves a nonrefundable arrangement. The MRPCs suggest a simple memorandum avoids misunderstandings and clarifies expectations. Still, the Rule does not preclude an oral agreement as long as the lawyer is able to prove that the oral agreement gave the required reasonable and fair disclosure.

b. New Client: When the lawyer does not have an established business relationship with the client, an agreement is required. This communication will preferably be communicated before or within a reasonable time after commencing the representation.

c. Substantially Different: If the services to be performed or the fee details are substantially different from a previously-existing arrangement between the lawyer and client, the new factors involved in determining the charges must be communicated to the client.

d. Change in Circumstances: If developments occur that make an earlier fee estimate impossible, a revised estimate should be timely submitted to the client.

e. External Fee Split: There must be client informed consent if a fee split involves a lawyer external to the firm, and it is not proportional to services performed. All associated lawyers must take joint responsibility for the matter. See *infra* under G2 at 427. Fee splits with non-lawyers are not allowed. See MRPC 5.4(a) *infra* at 452.

f. Writing Request: Upon the request of the client in any matter, the lawyer shall communicate in writing the details requested, the rate, or basis of the fee.

g. Withdrawal Writing: Depending on the particular situation at hand, the lawyer may conclude that the safest course of action is to withdraw rather than complete the representation. The client's non-payment of fees, failure to provide required information, or expressed intent to defraud the court may create such a situation. If the matter is in litigation, a formal motion to withdraw may be necessary. See also MRPC 1.16 *infra* at 439 for additional detail concerning withdrawals.

4. Client Fee Objection: The question of fee reasonableness usually develops when a client objects to a billing. If there was a client fee prepayment, the disputed amount should remain in trust pending a resolution. A lawsuit by a lawyer to collect a fee from a client usually draws both a counterclaim for malpractice and a complaint to the disciplinary authority alleging the fee is unreasonable.

MEE Tip: Any disputed portion of client advances and prepayment funds should be left in trust pending a resolution.

F. Contingency Fee Agreement – MRPC 1.5(c)

A fee may be contingent in whole or in part on the outcome of the matter except in the two situations where a contingent fee is prohibited; see subsection 3 *infra*.

1. Writing Requirement: A contingent fee is determined by the outcome of the representation. Such an agreement must always be in writing and signed by the client. A contingent fee cannot be unreasonable in amount considering the effort and outcome. The writing should clearly state the method by which the lawyer's fee is to be determined. Details of the percentages that would accrue to the lawyer in the event of settlement, trial, or appeal should be explained. Examples, including case outcome dollar hypotheticals, may also be helpful.

2. Treatment of Costs: The agreement must set forth litigation and other expenses to be deducted from the recovery. In addition, whether such expenses are to be deducted before or after the contingent fee is calculated must be disclosed.

3. Prohibited Matters – MRPC 1.5(d): A lawyer cannot enter into a contingency fee arrangement for the following matters:

a. Domestic Relations: This includes an attempt to secure a dissolution or custody of a child, or the amount of property awarded, alimony, or child support. In contrast, a contingent fee is proper for collection of alimony or support in arrears.

b. Criminal Matter: Representation in a criminal case may not be undertaken on a contingency basis.

4. Client Termination: The client may terminate an "at-will" lawyer at any time. Substantial completion is usually achieved if the lawyer obtains a firm settlement offer in an amount that the client had approved. If substantial completion has been delivered, a recovery is allowed under a theory of quantum meruit for the reasonable value of the services rendered.

5. End of Case: Upon conclusion of a contingency matter, the lawyer must provide the client with a written statement of account. This should itemize the dollar recovery outcome, all chargeable costs, and the calculation of amounts going to both the lawyer and the client.

G. Division of Fees – MRPC 1.5(e)

The rules on an allowable division of fees between lawyers depends on whether they practice in the same law firm.

1. In Same Firm: There are no restrictions on intra-firm split of fees paid by a client for representation. Many firms have formula revenue and expense allocation systems. For example, a rainmaking partner may receive some portion of the billing for supervising the law firm's representation of certain of her clients. Similarly, the firm may pay a former partner a percentage of fees earned after her retirement or sale of her interest.

2. Not in Same Firm: This involves a single fee billing to a client when the lawyers are not in the same firm. This facilitates association of external expertise on a client's matter. There are two allowed methods of permissive fee splits.

a. Proportional: Fees proportional to services each lawyer performs are allowed.

b. Non-Proportional: An external fee division not proportional to services performed by each lawyer may be proper if both lawyers assume joint responsibility for the whole representation, and

c. Client Consent: Under either of the above arrangements, the client must consent to the arrangement, including the non-proportional share each lawyer is to receive, and the agreement must be confirmed in writing. For instance, the client could agree that her friend, the overseeing lawyer, would receive a substantially higher fee per hour than the lawyer doing most of the work.

3. Referral Services: External referral fees may be paid only to a bar association or local bar-approved referral service. Any other forwarding, referrals, or commissions on fees may not be paid to any person, even if that person is another lawyer.

4. Overall Reasonable Restraint: Finally, the total fee all the lawyers receive in the matter and the fee allocation scheme must be reasonable.

II. CONFIDENTIALITY AND CONFLICTS OF INTEREST

A. Confidentiality of Information – MRPC 1.6

1. In General: This topic includes both the evidence rules of the attorney-client privilege and work-product doctrine, as well as the ethical rule of confidentiality.

a. Core Values: The core legal professional value here is to promote candid and complete communications from the client to the attorney so all the details and complexities of the problem become known. Only with this full information can lawyers provide the best possible comprehensive advice to their clients. If a client believes the lawyer will reveal her representation information to third parties outside the law firm, it necessarily puts a chilling effect upon the desirable candid communications. Confidential information usually may be shared within the firm for consultation or to prepare for trial.

b. Attorney-Client Privilege: The attorney-client privilege is an evidence rule of exclusion for non-public communications that an actual or potential client communicates to his lawyer. Preexisting documents do not become subject to the privilege merely by transmitting them to an attorney, but all work product created by a lawyer or her subordinates generally is privileged. The confidential privilege survives the death of the client. The general rule is there is no litigation privilege between jointly-represented clients – see MRPC 1.7 *infra*.

2. Representation Information: In some jurisdictions, the rule distinguishes between confidences and secrets. "Confidences" include the substance of client communications to the lawyer and a lawyer's work product protected by the evidentiary attorney-client privilege. "Secrets" refers to other information gained in the professional relationship concerning the client, the disclosure of which would be embarrassing or would likely be detrimental to the client. Profits made by the lawyer from the use of confidential client information may be disgorged.

3. Exceptions: There are important exceptions to the general rule of non-disclosure outside the law firm absent informed client consent. The lawyer should usually first seek to persuade the client to take the action necessary to obviate the need for disclosure and, if unsuccessful, warn the client that the lawyer will reveal the confidential information. If disclosure is still necessary, the scope should be minimized.

a. Future Death or Substantial Bodily Injury: A lawyer may reveal confidential information to the extent necessary to prevent the client from committing a future crime causing reasonably certain death or substantial bodily harm of a human. This includes a client's plan to take his own life. The overriding value of life controls. Even if the lawyer concludes that disclosure should be made, it is permissible only to the extent necessary to prevent the offense. This might not even require disclosure of the identity of the client.

> **MEE Tip:** A growing number of states elevate the future death and substantial bodily harm confidentiality exception "may" to "must" reveal.

b. Lawyer Being Sued or Related: A lawyer may also reveal relevant client confidential information only to the extent necessary concerning a:

(1) Claim or Defense Against Client: Disclosure is allowed to establish a "claim or defense" on behalf of the lawyer in a controversy between the lawyer and the client. If the client brings a malpractice claim against a lawyer, she waives the confidentiality right, at least as it relates to the relevant details of the representation. A lawyer entitled to a fee may reveal client confidences to the extent reasonably necessary to effectuate collection.

(2) Lawyer's Involvement: A lawyer may disclose client crimes, fraud, or substantial financial injury in which the client used the lawyer's services. Such involvement could create legal complicity and lead to a criminal charge or civil claim against the lawyer because of client activities. A lawyer may also make disclosures in the process of securing legal advice about his own degree of compliance with the MRPCs.

(3) Bar Complaint: Disclosure may be made to respond to allegations in any proceeding concerning the lawyer's representation of the client (such as a bar association grievance filed by a client). Some jurisdictions, however, require client approval as a prerequisite to disclosure of confidential information in a disciplinary action against the lawyer.

(4) Court Order: Disclosure may be made pursuant to a court order issued by a judge.

c. Sarbanes-Oxley Act (SOX): The ABA Model Rule now allows federal securities lawyers to disclose externally corporate client frauds.

(1) Breadth: Disclosure may be made to prevent the client from committing a crime, financial fraud, or breach of fiduciary duty that involved the lawyer's services, if reasonably certain to result in substantial injury to the financial interests or property of another.

(2) Corporate Reporting Up: SOX § 307 states that a lawyer learning of evidence of (1) material, clear violations of federal security laws or (2) breach of fiduciary duty must disclose such evidence internally within the company. If the corporate chief legal officer (CLO) or CEO does not "appropriately respond" – basically stop the wrongdoing – the lawyer is required to then report the matter to the company's board of directors or audit committee. If that internal reporting fails to result in a corporate "appropriate response," external disclosure to the SEC is authorized to the extent necessary to prevent certain injury to the corporation or its investor-owners. See also MRPC 1.13 *infra* for organizational reporting and whistleblowing issues.

d. Representation Withdrawal: The lawyer may give reasonable notice to a third party of the fact that she has withdrawn. Also, any relevant opinion document or other "questionable information" prepared by the lawyer based on client provided fraudulent information may be withdrawn or disaffirmed.

e. IRS Form 8300: Another "no reveal" exception involves IRS Form 8300, which must usually be filed if the client pays the lawyer $10,000 or more in cash. The ABA suggests that unless the client approves, the lawyer can file the form but must leave the secret of the client's name and Social Security number off the form. The IRS can issue a summons, and if the U.S. District Court judge so orders, the lawyer could then make full disclosure.

f. Client Waiver: If the client communication is not private or the client releases a substantial portion of the information to third parties, confidentiality may be waived.

g. Breach of Court-Appointed Fiduciary Responsibility: Many states also allow a lawyer to reveal to the tribunal information that discloses significant breach of fiduciary responsibility by a client who is a guardian, personal representative, receiver, or other court-appointed fiduciary.

MEE Tip: Confidentiality issues are heavily tested. The extent and manner of disclosure under the above exceptions must be the minimum necessary under the circumstances.

B. Conflict of Interest: Current Clients – MRPC 1.7

MRPC 1.7, 1.8, and 1.9 have a variety of restraints to ensure there are no impairments to a lawyer giving undivided loyalty to a client. A lawyer must decline new representation for a person whose interest concurrently conflicts with that of an existing client. If the conflict becomes apparent later, after the representation is underway, the lawyer must withdraw from both. Under MRPC 1.10, this conflict disqualification is imputed to all lawyers in a firm.

1. Client-to-Client: There are two degrees of present and potential concurrent client conflicts. The lawyer's benefit to one client is also a detriment to the other client.

a. Representation of Two Directly Adverse Clients – MRPC 1.7(a)(1): "Direct Adversity" is the highest level of present conflict of interest and applies to a matter that is in litigation. A lawyer shall not represent a client if the representation is directly in opposition to the interests of another of the lawyer's clients.

> **MEE Tip:** Representation while simultaneously opposing the same client puts a client in the difficult position of considering the same lawyer as both trusted friend and frightening foe.

b. Lawyer's Responsibilities Materially Limited – MRPC 1.7(a)(2): This potential conflict applies if there is significant risk that a lawyer's action on behalf of one client will materially limit her future effectiveness in representing other client(s). Another client may be substantially affected by the resolution of the matter.

(1) Lower Level: "Materially limited" is a lower level of conflict than present "direct adversity," and formal litigation may not be involved. The conflict may arise because of the lawyer's responsibilities to another client, a third party, or her own interests.

(2) Examples: Examples include the conflicts that could result from joint representation of the driver and passenger against a common defendant in an automobile accident. Representing one client against a second client in an unrelated matter, representing both a buyer and seller in the same transaction, or mediating a dispute between clients are favorite exam facts (see MRPC 2.2 *infra* at 443).

c. Exception – MRPC 1.7(b): Dual representation may be allowed if:

(1) No Harm to Attorney-Client Relationship: The lawyer must reasonably believe that the representation of one client would not adversely affect the competent and diligent representation relationship with the other client. This is an objective foreseeability standard of a prudent, disinterested lawyer.

> **MEE Tip:** The lawyer's belief that there will not be an adverse effect on the representation of either client must be objectively reasonable. Would a disinterested lawyer so conclude?

(2) Informed Consent Confirmed in Writing: Each client must give prior informed consent after receiving full disclosure of all material risks and dangers that the lawyer's conflict could create. This informed consent must then be confirmed in writing.

(a) Adverse Clients Identification: The lawyer's disclosure to the clients must usually include the identification of the other conflicting client(s) and lack of the attorney-client privilege between clients in jointly represented matters.

(b) Confidential Information Authorization: Full disclosure to one client may require the other client's authorization if it contains his confidential information.

(c) Revoking Consent: Conflict consent may be withdrawn by either client. The employment of the lawyer also may be terminated by either client. The lawyer ordinarily will be forced to withdraw from representing any and all the clients if the joint representation fails.

> **MEE Tip:** Look for a situation in which an incident occurred that strongly suggests future representation of a client may be materially limited by the duty of loyalty to another client. The lawyer must withdraw from representing both clients without disclosing any confidences.

(3) Same Litigation Prohibition: The ABA Model Rule does not allow the above consent to abate a present directly adverse conflict if the matter is in litigation.

> **MEE Tip:** In both direct adversity and materially limited situations, representation is only possible if (1) the clients give informed consent confirmed in writing and (2) there is not an adverse effect on the representation. Both requirements must be met.

(4) Fundamentally Antagonistic: The comments to the Model Rules state that if the clients are fundamentally antagonistic, they are not capable of giving reasonable consent. A husband and wife dissolution may be a good example due to the high level of animosity that frequently develops between the parties in a divorce proceeding.

d. Related Attorneys: A possible conflict of interest relates to personal relationships between opposing counsel. A lawyer is prohibited from representing a party if an attorney who is related to the first lawyer represents a directly adverse party. Related attorneys include husband-wife, domestic partner, parent-child, or two siblings. The informed consent of both clients may abate this restriction, and a writing is not required. The prohibition is not imputed so another lawyer in the firm could handle one of the representation positions.

e. Organizational Clients: This conflict rule addresses organizational groups. Examples include a lawyer for one corporation in a corporate-affiliated group or one governmental agency that is a part of an upstream government control organization.

(1) General Rule: A lawyer representing one corporate or governmental unit does not necessarily represent any other constituent or affiliated organization. Thus, such a lawyer may accept representation of a case adverse to the affiliate.

(2) Exceptions: The no-conflict outcome does not apply if (1) the related affiliate is considered to be a client of the lawyer, (2) there is a prior understanding that the lawyer will avoid representation adverse to the affiliate, or (3) the representation would in fact place a material limitation on the loyalty afforded to either client.

f. Lawyer Board Member: A lawyer for an entity who is also an official member of the board of directors may be conflicted in advising board actions when the lawyer's prior work is at issue. This could create a conflict for the lawyer. The lawyer may be required to withdraw from the board to eliminate the conflict. Further, other board members should be advised that the attorney-client privilege does not apply if the lawyer is in a director's capacity. (See MRPC 1.13 *infra* for additional details.)

MEE Tip: MRPC 1.8, discussed in detail below, contains a variety of restrictions and/or prohibitions where the conflict of interest is between the lawyer and the client. The client trust inherent in the fiduciary relationship creates a disparity in bargaining power. Any prohibition on a lawyer is generally imputed to all the lawyers associated in the law firm.

    2. Current Client / Prohibited Transactions: Business transactions between a lawyer and a client could create divided loyalties, and thus are subject to special scrutiny.

    a. No Business Relationship Unless TIC – MRPC 1.8(a): The lawyer shall not enter into a business relationship with a client (including an estate) she represents in the same transaction because there is a clear possibility of overreaching. Examples are loaning to or borrowing money from a client or entering into a partnership with a client. An exception allows the client transaction if all three **TIC** transaction elements are met:

    (1) Terms of Transaction Are Fair: The financial transaction and all material terms must be fair at a reasonable market price and fully disclosed to the client in writing. The disclosure must be stated in language that the client can clearly understand.

    (2) Independent Counsel: The client must be advised in writing to seek the advice of independent counsel in the transaction. Notice it is only a requirement that the client has reasonable opportunity to seek advice from another attorney, not that he actually receives it. Certainly, the safest posture is if the client secures independent advice and financial valuation.

    (3) Consent in Writing: The client must consent in a signed writing. The informed consent must go to both the transaction's essential terms and the lawyer's conflict of interest disclosure, not only the terms of the underlying transaction.

MEE Tip: The disparity in bargaining power is significant since the client inherently trusts the lawyer to protect her financial and legal interests. This creates a presumption of overreaching and undue influence justifying setting aside a client-to-lawyer transaction, such as a bargain purchase or loan from a client.

    b. Information Disadvantaging the Client – MRPC 1.8(b): The lawyer must not use information to a client's disadvantage unless the client gives informed consent. For instance, a lawyer may not purchase assets in competition with a client she is representing. In a later transaction or business dispute, the lawyer cannot use information derived from a prior representation to the client's disadvantage unless informed consent was given.

    c. No Gifts from Clients – MRPC 1.8(c): A lawyer may accept a gift from a client only if the transaction meets general standards of fairness and does not involve overreaching. However, a lawyer cannot solicit a gift or prepare an instrument bestowing upon herself or her family members a substantial gift from a client. This includes a testamentary device, such as a will, unless the lawyer is related to the donor. Lawyers can prepare their parents' wills and name themselves and their children as takers. Gifts given to a lawyer without a prepared instrument – say a cash bonus at the end of a case – are not per se improper as they are for a judge.

    d. No Agreement for Literary or Media Rights – MRPC 1.8(d): A lawyer may not negotiate an agreement to receive the client's publication rights to information based in substantial part on the lawsuit prior to the conclusion of the representation. A client waiver and consent is ineffective. A lawyer has to wait until the case is over before the client can agree to give the lawyer the book and movie rights of the trial. This rule guards against a lawyer trying to publicize an upcoming book during a trial, which could jeopardize the client's position.

e. No Financial Assistance – MRPC 1.8(e): A lawyer shall not advance or guarantee financial assistance to a client for living expenses, advances for family support, or medical treatment because this would be acquiring an interest in litigation. There are three exceptions:

(1) Litigation Expenses: A lawyer may lend a client funds to pay or guarantee a third party's payment of litigation costs – such as expert witness fees, court costs, medical examinations, and discovery costs – but the client must remain responsible for those costs. Still, repayment of these costs may be contingent on the outcome of the matter.

(2) Contingency Cost Allocation: There are three possible ways to charge costs in a contingency recovery. First, the costs come off the top before the percentage split between the attorney and client. That's probably all right because the client bears most of the costs. Second, the client bears 100% of the costs from his portion – that's permissible even though the client may not like it. Third, the lawyer bears all the costs from her share – in theory, that is a violation even though the client would usually prefer it.

(3) Indigent Client: Court costs and expenses may be paid on behalf of an indigent client regardless of whether these funds will be repaid. Some jurisdictions also have a class-action exception, which is justified because of the public service aspect, since it otherwise might be too difficult to get plaintiffs to join the class.

MEE Tip: A lawyer may refer a client seeking funds to a financing institution or bank as long as the lawyer does not guarantee the loan.

---

f. No Fee Payment by Third Parties – MRPC 1.8(f): Payment of attorney fees by a third party is not allowed. Examples include parents who pay for their child's DUI defense or the corporate payment of attorney fees incurred by a co-defendant officer. Another example is the defendant's insurance company that may be responsible for the ultimate damage claim and is also paying for the defendant's legal defense. Exceptions apply if:

(1) Informed Consent and No Interference: The primary client may consent to the lawyer representing joint clients after consultation – a writing is not required – if there is no interference by the third-party payor with the lawyer's independence, professional judgment, or loyalty to the client. A future conflict waiver demanded by an insurance company third party payor is problematic. It may be ineffective because the client may lack sufficient information about possible future third-party interference acts to give an informed consent until a fact-specific conflict actually develops.

(2) Confidentiality: The client's confidential information must not be compromised. This may be tricky because information the lawyer conveys to the fee paying third party in a billing statement is protected by the confidentiality rules. The lawyer cannot disclose sensitive client information that could damage the client, such as a "reservation of rights" notice being issued by the insurance company based on the billing information. Insurers may not impose "litigation management guidelines" on a lawyer if it will harm the representation of the insured. If any of these conditions occur, a lawyer may have to withdraw.

> **Rigos Tip:** Look for payment by a third party, such as an insurance company, a parent or other relative offering to pay for the legal services and wanting input on how to proceed in the matter. The fee payment arrangement can be allowed if the client gives informed consent, there is no conflict of interest, and the attorney retains independent judgment.

g. No Aggregate Settlement if Multiple Clients – MRPC 1.8(g):

(1) Criminal Case: When a lawyer represents more than one client in a criminal matter, the lawyer must not participate in making an aggregate agreement as to guilty or *nolo contendere* pleas. The potential for conflict in representing multiple criminal defendants is so grave – they may need to take inconsistent positions – that ordinarily a lawyer should decline to represent more than one co-defendant. An exception applies if each client gives informed, written consent. The lawyer must make disclosure of the existence and nature of all the claims or pleas involved and the participation of each person in the settlement agreement.

(2) Civil Case: This lawyer representation restraint applies to multiple clients who would share as plaintiffs in an aggregate dollar settlement or co-defendants in a civil case with joint and several liability. There may be cross-claims or disputes relating to award recovery or cost allocations between the clients. Again, there is an exception if each client gives informed consent in a signed writing after disclosure that includes all information about the claims being settled and the amount each client will receive or be required to pay.

h. Limiting Liability – MCPR 1.8(h): A lawyer who is representing a client shall not limit the client's right to file a bar complaint or pursue a claim for future or past malpractice.

(1) Prospective Limitation: The lawyer's representation agreement cannot state that the "client agrees not to sue for malpractice if the lawyer fails to exercise reasonable care" unless the client is separately represented by counsel in the negotiation. A mere warning that "you should talk to a lawyer" is insufficient; actual independent representation is required.

(2) Malpractice Settlement: A client may assert a malpractice claim against her lawyer, for example, because the lawyer complied with the requirement that he communicate his lack of competent performance and the client is unhappy about it. The attorney and client may reach agreement as to an equitable settlement. The client must be advised in writing to seek independent counsel, but need not do so. However, there must be reasonable opportunity to seek such advice; settlement cannot be made "on the spot."

> **MEE Tip:** Notice the client must actually have independent representation for prospective malpractice limitations. In contrast, after-the-fact limitations only require the client to receive such advice and a reasonable opportunity to seek representation.

i. No Proprietary Interest in Cause of Action – MRPC 1.8(i): A lawyer shall not acquire an actual ownership interest in the client's cause of action or legal claim. There is no exception, even if the client agrees. Still allowed are:

(1) Fee Security: A lawyer may take a promissory note or acquire a lien allowed by law to secure the lawyer's fee or expenses. This is a business or financial transaction with a client requiring the three **TIC** transaction elements.

(2) Contingent Fee: A lawyer may contract with a client for a reasonable contingent fee in a civil case.

j. No Sexual Relations – MRPC 1.8(j): Lawyers in most jurisdictions are prohibited from having sexual relations with current clients or representatives of their clients, such as the parent of a child in a personal injury action. This restriction is not imputed to other firm members who are not working on the representation. Also, an exception exists if there was a prior consensual relationship between the lawyer and client before the lawyer undertook the case. This sexual relationship prohibition terminates at the end of the representation.

(1) Definition: The definition of "sexual relationship" is not in the Model Rule – and many people differ in their views of how much it takes to have a "sexual relationship." Some states attempt a definition such as California's "sexual intercourse or the touching of an intimate part of another…." Disciplinary cases focus on lawyers going to bed with their clients; in most states this meets the threshold definition.

(2) Consent Ineffective: A client's consent or waiver, even in writing, does not abate the violation. In such a situation, there could easily be overreaching by the lawyer where a client is emotionally vulnerable and therefore might feel forced to accept an imposed quid pro quo personal relationship. A sexual relationship could impact the attorney's fiduciary duty, in which the lawyer occupies the highest position of trust and confidence. From a lawyer's standpoint, your independence and objectivity may be put at risk – can you tell a lover client that her case objectively lacks merit or that she would make a bad witness?

(3) Client Affections: If the client wants an affair, the attorney needs to say no. Explain to the client that you could get disciplined. Say no to gifts, and no dinners or drinks after work. If the client's aggressive affections do not stop, it would be prudent to transfer the client to another attorney in the firm.

MEE Tip: The 1.8 restrictions (except 1.8(j)) usually are imputed to all lawyers in the firm.

C. Conflict of Interest: Duties to Former Clients – MRPC 1.9

Lawyer loyalty and confidence rules survive the representation, and these ongoing duties to a former client may conflict with a current client's interests. Under MRPC 1.10, the conflict disqualification is imputed to every lawyer in a law firm.

1. Subject Matter Relationship: The current matter must be substantially related to the factual context of the prior client's matter. This provision relates to MRPC 1.7 in that if a lawyer withdraws from representing one client, the client then becomes a prior client.

2. Informed Consent Possible: A lawyer usually cannot, in the same or a substantially related legal dispute, represent another person who has an adverse interest to her prior client. Representation in different unrelated matters is permissible. This conflict may be waived if both the former and new client give informed consent after full disclosure, confirmed in writing.

3. Substantially Related Example: Suppose a lawyer represented both spouses in a property transaction, and three years later, the wife wants the same lawyer (or the lawyer's partner) to represent her in a divorce. If the same property is subject to the dissolution proceeding, the matter may be sufficiently factually related to disqualify the lawyer. The lawyer needs both spouses' informed consent, or the attorney is conflicted out in the divorce representation.

4. Confidential Information Restriction: Even if the former client consents to the representation, and it is confirmed in writing, there is a separate restriction on using the former client's confidential information to his disadvantage. The duty of information confidentiality continues after the client-lawyer relationship has terminated unless the information is then public knowledge.

5. Example: Suppose a corporate client asked a lawyer's opinion about hiring an employee whom the lawyer had defended in an embezzlement case five years ago. The lawyer probably cannot disclose to the corporation what she knows about her former client's fraud potential even though one could argue the matter is not exactly the same. The test is "substantial subject matter relationship." Still, the common nexus concerns the former embezzlement, so the similar subject matter test is arguably satisfied in this fact pattern.

> **MEE Tip:** For purposes of former client disqualification under Rule 1.9, the matter at issue must be substantially related to the prior client's matter. Note this subject-matter nexus is not necessary to create a disqualifying conflict under Rule 1.7 for present "direct adversity" and future "materially limited" conflicts where mere adverse client identity may be sufficient.

III. DISQUALIFICATION, CLIENT FUNDS, AND WITHDRAWAL

A. Imputed Disqualification – MRPC 1.10

1. Conflicts of Interest: While lawyers are associated in a law firm, none of them shall knowingly represent a client when any one of them practicing alone would be prohibited from doing so by the conflict of interest rules. If any one lawyer is disqualified, this disqualification is imputed to all other lawyers in the firm.

2. Joining a Firm: When a lawyer who, as opposing counsel, represented an adverse party at their old firm becomes associated with a new firm, both the new firm and all members in it are disqualified. Neither the firm nor the "personally disqualified lawyer" may knowingly represent a person with adverse interests to the prior represented client in any same or related matter unless:

a. Screening: The personally disqualified lawyer must be effectively screened from participating in or discussing the matter with the litigation team. No material confidential information can be revealed by the personally disqualified lawyer and she may not be apportioned any part of the fee obtained from that representation,

b. Notice to Former Client: The former client of the personally disqualified lawyer must receive notice of the conflict and the details of the screening mechanism used to prohibit dissemination of secret or confidential information, and

c. Affidavit: The personally disqualified lawyer must serve on her former law firm and the client an affidavit stating she will not participate in or discuss the case with members of her new law firm. Judicial review and supervision of the screening procedures is possible to ensure compliance.

3. Leaving a Firm: A law firm may represent a person with interests directly adverse to a client represented by a lawyer who has left the firm. Representation is only precluded if (1) the matter is the same or substantially related and (2) any lawyer remaining in the firm has relevant confidential information protected by RPC 1.6.

B. Successive Government and Private Employment – MRPC 1.11

This applies to a government attorney who goes into private practice, such as a prosecutor, public defender, or representative attorney for a government agency.

1. Personal and Substantial Participation: Such a previous government lawyer may not represent a private client in a matter in which she previously personally and substantially participated, unless the agency consents with confirmation in writing. The "matter" must involve the same party or parties. This disqualification is imputed to any other lawyer in the firm, but (1) a screening arrangement is possible with (2) written notice to the agency of the screening procedures employed, if (3) the screened lawyer does not share in the fee. The prohibition extends to use of any agency confidential information.

2. Employment Negotiation: A government lawyer may not negotiate for private employment with parties and attorneys appearing before the agency if the lawyer participated personally and substantially. If the lawyer did not participate in a matter for or against the party – she only worked for the same agency – it is not improper to pursue such employment.

3. Confidential Government Information: In subsequently representing a client in private practice, a lawyer may not use "confidential government information" that was prohibited by law from disclosure to the public. The prohibition extends to confidential government information about a person who is an adversary of the client. Information available under the Freedom of Information Act is not deemed confidential.

C. Former Judge, Arbitrator, Mediator, or Neutral – MRPC 1.12

This provision parallels MRPC 1.11.

1. Restrictions: A former or retired judge, adjudicative officer, or third-party neutral (including their law clerks) may not act as a lawyer in a matter in which she formerly served as a judge. Prior participation in the matter must have been personal and substantial to disqualify the former judge – for example, she personally adjudicated a case where the client was a party. Mere remote involvement or incidental administrative responsibility is insufficient to create a conflict. A partisan member of an arbitration panel is not prohibited from subsequently representing that party.

2. Employment Negotiation: A judge or law clerk shall not negotiate for private employment with parties appearing in her court. This restriction does not block all work for a former litigant in front of the judge – only those matters in which the former judge or law clerk was involved. A law clerk nearing the end of a clerkship may negotiate for employment with a law firm appearing in the court; however, the clerk must first tell the judge of the employment search and specifically identify the law firms with which she is interviewing.

3. Consent or Screening Exception: Subsequent representation is permitted if all parties to that proceeding consent after disclosure. Even if no consent is given, a law firm is not disqualified if its tainted lawyer is timely screened and written notice is promptly given to the parties and appropriate tribunal.

D. Organization as Client – MRPC 1.13

A corporate attorney owes the primary duty to the organizational entity, not the directors, officers, employees, shareholders, or other human constituents. A lawyer for a business entity may usually also represent a majority owner.

1. Dual Representation: Dual representation of both the corporation and a human constituent may be a RPC 1.7 conflict, but informed consent by both clients may avoid the disqualification. A lawyer may not concurrently represent a constituent whose interest the lawyer determines is adverse to the organization, such as an employee accused of committing a criminal act involving the corporation. Such parties must be told the lawyer does not represent them or give them advice and that no attorney-client privilege exists as to anything they disclose.

2. Private Organization Internal Reporting: A lawyer should report violations of law to the involved wrongdoer(s). If not corrected, and the matter is clearly a violation of law that will result in substantial injury to the organization, the lawyer "may" (not "must") reveal "up the ladder" to the chief executive officer or full Board of Directors. The lawyer must minimize any risk of the information being revealed externally. A lawyer discharged by a corporate manager for revealing such wrongdoing shall inform the Board of the discharge or withdrawal details.

3. Public Organization External Reporting: If the corporation is publicly-traded, the lawyer "must" report to the SEC under the Sarbanes-Oxley Act. While noisy withdrawals are not encouraged, a lawyer may externally withdraw his own prior writings relied upon by third parties, even if this is not normally permitted by Rule 1.6.

4. Governmental Organizational Client: When a lawyer who is not a public officer or employee represents a discrete governmental agency that is part of a broader governmental entity, the lawyer's client is the particular governmental agency or unit represented, not the broader governmental entity. An exception may apply if so indicated by both agencies in writing.

E. Client with Diminished Capacity – MRPC 1.14

Usually we assume a client has the ability and capacity to maintain a normal client-lawyer relationship, including making adequately considered decisions and assisting in preparation of her case.

1. Disability: If the client cannot adequately act in her own interest because she is under a significant disability – e.g., incapacity, minority, unconsciousness, mental impairment, elderly with diminished capacity – the lawyer may seek court appointment of a guardian ad litem.

2. Preserve Confidences: The application for appointment should not disclose any unnecessary client confidences protected under MRPC 1.6.

F. Safeguarding Property – MRPC 1.15

1. Separation Required: All property of clients and third persons must be safeguarded. Client and third person funds should be held separately from the lawyer's own property and may not be used, commingled, converted, borrowed from, or pledged by the lawyer. A small exception is that a lawyer's funds may be used to pay bank service charges. Commingling is a serious fiduciary offense even if the client approves of the "loan" and all funds are repaid.

2. Retainers and Trust Advances: The ABA Model Rules do not distinguish between retainers and advances. In many jurisdictions, retainers are client payments that are fully earned when received as compensation for taking on the case and being available concerning the matter. Such retainers are non-refundable and should not be deposited in a trust account. All other funds that clients advance for future fees and costs must be deposited in trust accounts in the state where the lawyer's office is situated, and must be kept separate from the law firm's regular operating account. In most states, split deposits (part retainer and part earned fees in one check) must be deposited into a trust account.

3. Transfers from Trust: As lawyers bill, they should withdraw that portion from the trust account unless the client objects. The usual prudent approach is to wait 10 to 20 days after sending out a fee statement before transferring the funds between accounts; this gives the client a reasonable time to contest the billing. A lawyer's failure to withdraw uncontested billed fees from the trust account results in impermissible commingling.

MEE Tip: Any client disputed amount must be left in trust until the dispute is resolved.

---

4. All Client Property Kept Identifiable and Accountable: Client property must be identifiable, segregated, and held in a secure place such as a locked safe deposit box. Complete records of all client property shall be preserved for five years.

a. Notice of Receipt of Property and Funds: A lawyer shall promptly notify a client of the receipt of funds, securities, or other property, including a settlement check.

b. Identify and Label Securities and Properties: A lawyer shall identify and label securities and properties of a client promptly upon receipt. Such assets shall be placed in a locked safe deposit box or other place of safekeeping as soon as practicable.

c. Third Parties' Claims: If a third party has a lawful claim – usually an unsatisfied judgment – against client funds or other property in the lawyer's possession, the lawyer may file an action to have a court resolve the dispute. The funds at issue in the controversy should be interpleaded into the registry of the court for a judicial determination of the third party's claims.

d. Promptly Return Property: At the client's request or at the end of the representation, a lawyer must promptly deliver to the client all the client's property. This includes all client-related assets in the lawyer's possession and any interest earned during custody of the client's funds. If the client disputes the fee and / or other split amount items as calculated by the lawyer, the undisputed portion due the client should be paid. If the dispute cannot be liquidated, the balance may be interpleaded into the registry of a court.

5. Escrow Funds: Escrow and other funds held by a lawyer involving multiple party transactions are treated as client funds subject to these rules. Examples include funds for the closing of a real estate property transfer, or the sale and purchase of a business. This applies regardless of whether the lawyer, the law firm, or the parties view the funds as belonging to clients or non-clients. Many jurisdictions require bar authorities to perform random audits to promote proper client funds management.

G. Declining or Terminating Representation – MRPC 1.16

The rule on declining or terminating representation provision has two sections – one where the lawyer must withdraw and another where withdrawal is optional.

1. Must Terminate / Withdraw – VID: Withdrawal is mandatory if any of the following three **VID** reasons apply.

a. Violate MRPCs: A lawyer shall withdraw from the representation of a client if the representation would result in a violation of the MRPCs, a court order, or other laws. Examples include a client's refusal to comply with discovery orders or the lawyer's conclusion that the client's case cannot be supported by a good faith argument for the extension, modification, or reversal of existing law. [MRPC 3.1]

b. Impaired Ability to Represent: A lawyer must decline or withdraw from the representation of a client if the lawyer's physical or mental condition materially impairs his ability to represent the client.

c. Discharged: A lawyer must withdraw if discharged by the client.

MEE Tip: The "must" withdraw rules, especially MRPC violations, are frequently tested.

---

2. May Terminate / Withdraw – CURBSO: The second prong of the Rule gives a lawyer discretion to withdraw from representing a client. The withdrawal usually must be accomplished without a material adverse effect on the client's interests, but certain specifically approved **CURBSO** grounds allow withdrawal notwithstanding adverse effects. These include:

a. Client Pursuing Criminal Action: A lawyer may withdraw if the client persists in a course of action involving the lawyer's services that the lawyer reasonably believes is criminal or fraudulent (future actions).

b. Used Lawyer to Commit Crime: A lawyer may withdraw if the client has used the lawyer's services to perpetrate a crime or fraud (past actions).

c. Repugnant Objective: A lawyer may withdraw if the client insists on pursuing an objective the lawyer considers repugnant or very imprudent.

d. Burden on Lawyer Unreasonable: A lawyer may withdraw if the representation will result in an unreasonable financial burden on the lawyer or the client has been unreasonably difficult.

e. Serious Client Failure: This includes a client's unsatisfied commitment to pay fees, refusal to obey a court order, or failure to comply with required discovery. The lawyer should warn the client that withdrawal will occur unless the obligation is satisfied timely. Still, a failure to pay fees when due may be insufficient to justify withdrawal.

f. Other Good Cause for Withdrawal Exists: This is a catchall category where the burden is on the attorney asserting the good cause argument. Client difficulties short of actual discharge, such as non-cooperation in preparing for trial, may fall into this category.

> **MEE Tip:** Distinguish between the **VID** reasons for which a lawyer must withdraw (especially RPC violations) and those **CURBSO** reasons in which she may withdraw but it is not required even in situations that arouse suspicion.

3. Court Order: Formal withdrawal may be required if the matter is in litigation. Where ordered by a tribunal, a lawyer must continue representation notwithstanding a good cause for terminating the representation.

4. Notice, Surrender, and Refund: A lawyer must take reasonable steps to protect a client's interests. This includes giving reasonable notice of intent to withdraw, allowing time to hire other counsel, surrendering appropriate papers and property to the client, and refunding any unearned advance payment of fees.

a. No Client Prejudice: The withdrawal should not prejudice the client's rights or create a material adverse effect on her interests. A withdrawing lawyer must allow sufficient time before trial so the client can get a new attorney.

b. Surrender Papers and Property: The lawyer must surrender papers and property to which the client is entitled. The files belong to the client unless the retainer agreement specifically states to the contrary. It makes no difference if the document is the lawyer's work product or not. Any unearned balance in the trust account shall be refunded.

c. File Lien: In many jurisdictions an attorney's possessory lien provision may apply to the client's judgment award. This lien provision may not be used to hold the client's legal files hostage unless the retention would not prejudice the client. Such a circumstance is rare if the litigation is still going forward with new counsel. If withholding the file materially interferes with the ability of a new lawyer to represent the client, the court or professional authority may order the file transferred to the succeeding attorney.

d. Other Lien Restraints: A lawyer seeking or enforcing a lien to tie up the client's judgment or property must be sure the underlying proceeding is not frivolous [MRPC 3.1] or interposed strictly to embarrass or burden a person [MRPC 4.4].

5. Formal Notice: Many jurisdictions require filing of a formal Notice of Withdrawal with the tribunal a minimum of 10 days before withdrawal may be effective. The notice must specify the trial date and identify any succeeding lawyer. If the client does not have a new lawyer substituting in, the address of the client must be stated. If anyone objects to the withdrawal, the court will hold a hearing. If it is too close to trial or other prejudice will result, the court may deny the motion, and the lawyer must stay on the case.

6. Malpractice Concern: Prudence suggests that a lawyer with any concern about a possible present or future malpractice claim should copy the file at her own expense.

7. "Noisy" or "Flag-Waving" Withdrawals: To alert third parties, the federal Sarbanes-Oxley Act (SOX) allows a noisy withdrawal for a corporate attorney learning of an ongoing client fraud. This aspect of SOX is controversial because most jurisdictions require that a lawyer's withdrawal not create a material adverse effect on a client. A lawyer can withdraw any of her own prior opinions given to third parties that now appear to be fraudulent. It is proper to author a letter to a third party stating that "facts have come to my attention such that you should not rely on my prior opinions," without saying anything negative about the client.

> **MEE Tip**: A good summary of a lawyer's 4R withdrawal requirements are that a lawyer must allow a **r**easonable time for the client to **r**etain succeeding counsel, **r**eturn client papers, and **r**efund all unearned fees.

H. Sale of Law Practice – MRPC 1.17

This rule focuses on the sale of a law practice by a retiring lawyer or by the estate of a deceased attorney. There are confidentiality restrictions imposed on potential buyers making a purchase investigation. Notice must be given to clients of the transfer and client consent for file transfer is required. This may be inferred if the client does not affirmatively object within 90 days after receiving notice of the transfer of account. A single buyer must purchase the entire practice or an entire substantive practice area; cherry-picking and piecemeal sale of client accounts is not allowed. The sales price may be set at a percentage of future fees collected from the book of business the buyer purchased. The purchaser cannot increase client fees to finance the purchase.

I. Duties To Prospective Client – MRPC 1.18

A growing number of jurisdictions recognize some duty to a prospective client. A typical example is where a potential client telephones a lawyer to discuss whether the lawyer will take on the representation of their case.

1. Conflict Question: The prospective client must always reveal enough information to allow the lawyer to perform a conflict check and determine if the lawyer is competent and willing to undertake representation of the matter. As long as the discussion stops before "significantly harmful" information is shared, the lawyer will not be personally disqualified from later representing the other side in the same or a substantially related controversy.

2. Screening Possible: Even if "significantly harmful" information has passed and the client does not consent, the Rule allows a "screening" procedure. This permits others in the firm to undertake representation of someone on the other side of the controversy, with written notice to the prospective client.

3. Fair Warning: A lawyer receiving a prospective representation inquiry usually may avoid disqualification by affirmatively stating that "our law firm has many clients who may be adverse to your interest in this dispute. Therefore, nothing you disclose in this prospective conversation should be considered confidential unless we enter into a formal written representation agreement." Website inquiry submission forms should contain a specific disclaimer disavowing an attorney-client relationship until a writing is signed.

4. Duty Not to Mislead: If the client expects that a lawyer will represent her in a matter, the lawyer must affirmatively reject the association expectation.

5. Confidential Information Protected: Even if the lawyer disavows the representation, MRPC 1.6 protects preliminary discussions with the prospective client of any harmful non-public information.

IV. COUNSELOR, ADVOCATE, AND THIRD PARTY DEALINGS

A. Counselor – TITLE 2

Title 2 focuses on a lawyer functioning not as a partisan, but rather as an advisor, intermediary, preparer of an evaluation for use by a third party, or neutral.

1. Advisor – MRPC 2.1:

a. Independence: A lawyer in an advisory role shall exercise independent professional judgment. A lawyer cannot, for example, write an opinion letter she knows is misleading because the client told her to do so. The lawyer must give the client honest and candid advice, which may refer to relevant moral, economic, social, political, and ethical considerations. If the necessary objective advice is unpleasant, try to put it in as acceptable a form as honesty permits. Sometimes lawyers have to tell their clients what they don't want to hear.

b. Offering Advice: There is normally no duty to give advice until asked by the client. But if the client's action is likely to result in substantial adverse legal consequences, there may be a communication duty under Rule 1.4. A lawyer should attempt to tell the client that such activity is likely to result in serious legal or ethical problems.

2. Intermediary: The ABA has deleted MRPC 2.2 (intermediary between clients) and now treats the intermediary role as a Rule 1.7(b) conflict where there is a "material limitation" on the lawyer concurrently serving two clients. See *supra*. Many jurisdictions have retained this role and related restraints in a separate rule.

a. General Rule: A lawyer may act as intermediary between existing clients. The general conflict of interest rules still apply here since parties may have or develop adverse interests; the theoretical difference is that the lawyer is functioning as a counselor, not as an advocate. Examples include putting a transaction together for both a seller and a buyer, or representing two individuals in forming a corporation or partnership without any apparent adverse interest in sight. The lawyer seeks common ground between clients where both benefit rather than seeking to obtain an advantage for one party over the other.

(1) Consultation and Consent: The lawyer consults with each client concerning the implications of the common representation, including the advantages and risks involved and the effect on the attorney-client privilege. Each client must give written consent to the common representation.

(2) Client's Best Interests: The client's best interests controls. The lawyer must reasonably believe the matter can be resolved on terms compatible with each client's best interests. This is an objective standard. The lawyer must also believe that each client will be able to make adequately informed decisions in the matter and there is little risk of material prejudice to any of the clients if the contemplated resolution is unsuccessful.

(3) Impartiality: The lawyer must also reasonably believe that the common representation can be undertaken impartially and without improper effect on other responsibilities the lawyer has to any of the clients.

(4) Attorney-Client Privilege: The prevailing view is that the evidentiary privilege and duty of confidentiality does not attach to communication with commonly represented clients as to one another. Both affected clients should be so advised in advance.

b. Withdrawal: A lawyer shall withdraw as intermediary if one of the clients so requests or any of the above conditions is no longer satisfied. Upon withdrawal, both clients receive Rule 1.9 prior client protections, and the lawyer cannot continue to represent any of the clients in any matter that was a subject of the intermediation.

3. Evaluation for Use by Third Party – MRPC 2.3:

a. Role: This is preparing an evaluation or opinion letter for the primary use of a third party. An example is a lawyer giving an opinion on a client's property title for a buyer or lender. Another is a corporate client planning to sponsor a public stock offering who wants its lawyer to author an opinion letter that states the corporation is current on all its state filings. Factual matters limited, excluded, or scope restrictions should be disclosed in the evaluation.

b. Two Requirements: The lawyer must reasonably believe that making the evaluation is compatible with other aspects of the attorney-client relationship. If the evaluation may create adverse effects, the client must give informed consent. The consent to disclose confidential information and secrets in an evaluation may be oral.

c. Uncertainties: The attorney function is much like a CPA in an audit role. There is potential negligent misrepresentation liability to third parties who rely on the lawyer's evaluation and thereby suffer losses. Some jurisdictions authorize withdrawing a false evaluation relied upon by a third party. See also MRPC 1.6, 4.1, and 8.4(c).

4. Lawyer Serving as Third-Party Neutral – MRPC 2.4: Lawyers serving non-clients as neutrals in mediation, arbitration, conciliation, or in a similar capacity must inform unrepresented parties that the lawyer is not representing them and it might be prudent to seek independent legal advice. A former neutral may not later become an advocate in the same dispute unless all the parties give informed consent, confirmed in writing. However, a partisan member of an arbitration panel is not prohibited from subsequently representing that party. [MRPC 1.12]

MEE Tip: The treatment of subsequent representation of a party involved in a prior intermediary and neutral role is related to MRPC 1.9 prior client protections.

B. Advocate – TITLE 3

1. Meritorious Claims and Contentions – MRPC 3.1:

a. Civil Case: The required ethical basis in bringing or defending a civil lawsuit is that lawyers must present a non-frivolous good faith argument in support of their clients' positions. This is similar to Civil Rule 11, under which the court may impose sanctions when an attorney signs a pleading lacking minimal merit. Civil Rule 11 requires a "reasonable basis," while MRPC 3.1 requires a basis that is "not frivolous." The required ethical standard thus appears lower than the legal threshold.

(1) Not Frivolous: It is not frivolous to advance an action merely because the facts have not been fully substantiated, discovery is necessary to develop vital evidence, or it involves a new legal theory. The fact that the lawyer believes that the client's position ultimately will not prevail also does not necessarily mean a claim or defense is frivolous.

(2) Is Frivolous: The action is frivolous if the lawyer is unable to make a good faith argument for the extension, modification, or reversal of existing law. Also, if the claim was asserted merely to delay a trial or harass or maliciously injure the opposing party, it is frivolous. If the client insists on a frivolous position, the lawyer must withdraw. [MRPC 1.16]

b. Criminal Case: This standard is somewhat relaxed in a criminal case. A frivolous defense may be asserted at least to the extent it forces the state to prove every element required to prosecute the crime.

MEE Tip: If the client insists on a frivolous position or extreme delay, the attorney must withdraw.

---

2. Expediting Litigation – MRPC 3.2: A plaintiff is entitled to obtain her day in court. Dilatory practices done with no intent besides delaying proceedings or harassing the opposing side are not allowed. Multiple postponements are to be avoided. Defendant counsel's dilatory actions must thus have some substantial purpose and rationale other than naked intent to delay.

MEE Tip: This lawyer litigation violation is often combined with inadequate competency (1.1) and diligence (1.4). Try **DEC** – diligence, expediting litigation, and competency.

---

3. Candor Toward the Tribunal – MRPC 3.3: These restraints focus on the duties the lawyer owes as an officer of the court.

a. False Statements of Law / Fact: A lawyer shall not knowingly make a false statement of law or material fact to a tribunal or fail to correct a previous false statement. Although the lawyer may not have personal knowledge of all factual matters, he should verify legal authority. For example, a lawyer cannot cite or quote a case for controlling authority when the case held to the contrary or was overruled. The lawyer may also refuse the client's request/demand to offer evidence that the lawyer reasonably believes to be false.

b. Facts Believed False: A lawyer may not offer evidence that the lawyer reasonably believes or actually knows to be false. It is also improper for a lawyer to facilitate a client or witness giving false testimony. This includes narrative answers the lawyer knows will be false such as asking, "What happened next?" The lawyer's duty is less clear if the client or a witness commits perjury when called by the opposing party since the lawyer is not "offering" anything.

c. Later Falsity Discovery: If the client or lawyer offered material evidence that later is discovered to have been false, the lawyer must take reasonable remedial measures.

(1) Persuade Client: The lawyer should first make reasonable efforts to persuade the client to consent to curative disclosure.

(2) Withdrawal: If the client refuses, the lawyer should seek to withdraw.

(3) Required Tribunal Disclosure: Disclosure of the falsity to the tribunal is required if the motion to withdraw is denied or the lawyer's withdrawal will not undo the effect of the false evidence.

d. Continuing to End of Proceeding: The duty to make disclosure to the court continues to the end of the proceeding, including the trial court appeal period. Thus, withdrawal does not necessarily terminate the duty to disclose to the court. If the lawyer first learns of the fraud after final judgment, the Rule 1.6 confidential duty precludes disclosure.

e. Ex Parte Proceeding: In some states, a lawyer may appear ex parte before a judge without the opposing party or his attorney present. The appearing lawyer shall inform the ex parte tribunal of all material facts reasonably necessary to make an informed decision, even if such facts are adverse to the lawyer's client. This enhanced duty of candor is necessary because the usual checks and balances of the adversarial process are missing.

MEE Tip: Every exam has numerous questions focusing on the above restraints. In the end, the lawyer's duty as an officer of the court prevails over blind obedience to the client's cause.

---

4. Fairness to Opposing Party and Counsel – MRPC 3.4: These restraints focus on litigation discovery abuses and a lawyer's improper statements at trial.

a. Cannot Interfere with Evidence: A lawyer shall not unlawfully suppress or obstruct another party's pre-trial access to relevant evidence or participate in the altering, destroying (spoliation), or concealing a document or physical instrument having potential evidentiary value. The duty to preserve evidence arises when the commencement of a relevant proceeding becomes reasonably foreseeable. A lawyer also may not counsel or assist another in doing such an act. There is no duty to disclose voluntarily the existence of evidence, only to preserve it.

b. Falsify Evidence or Witness Inducement: A lawyer shall not falsify evidence or counsel, assist, or induce a witness not to give relevant information, to testify falsely, or to flee the jurisdiction to avoid testifying. Subornation of perjury is the corrupt procurement of false testimony; this is a crime in most jurisdictions. Agents, employees, and relatives of clients may properly be instructed not to voluntarily give information to an opposing party or attorney unless subpoenaed. Only payments of usual expenses, including loss of time, are proper for fact witnesses. In contrast, expert witnesses may be paid at a usual professional hourly rate. Neither type of witness may be paid on a contingent testimony or outcome basis.

MEE Tip: The ethical dilemma between a lawyer's duty not to reveal client secrets (1.6) and the duty not to offer false testimony (3.4) is usually resolved in favor of candor to the court.

---

c. Discovery Standards: In pretrial procedure, a lawyer shall not make a frivolous or unduly burdensome discovery request for facts or documents. A lawyer must also reasonably comply with a legally proper discovery request propounded by an opposing party. Litigation sanctions may be imposed for repeated discovery non-compliance.

d. At Trial:

(1) Improper Arguments: A lawyer shall not allude to any matter that is not relevant or that has not been or will not be supported by admissible evidence. Examples include mentioning the defendant's previous settlement offers to imply culpability or referring to the defendant's enormous wealth in an attempt to inflame the jury.

(2) Closing Arguments: In summing up, a lawyer must not refer to evidence not introduced during the trial, including a criminal defendant's refusal to testify.

e. Personal Opinion During Trial: At trial, a lawyer may usually argue on the analysis of the evidence for or against any position or conclusion, but should not assert personal knowledge or related opinions on the facts, unless the lawyer is also a trial witness.

(1) Prohibited Statements: During trial, a lawyer shall not state a personal opinion as to the justness of a cause, credibility of a witness, culpability of a civil litigant, or the guilt or innocence of the accused. The lawyer should not use or imply the word "I," "me," or "we" during trial argument. An example is "Everyone in this courtroom believes the defendant is a liar and not credible." "Everyone" includes the lawyer, so this is improper.

(2) Witness Questions: A lawyer may not ask a witness questions that will draw answers that imply another witness was or was not credible. An example is, "Do you think witness B was testifying truthfully?" But in closing arguments, it would not be improper for a lawyer to sum up to the jury with "You saw in cross-examination that C was not truthful."

MEE Tip: Watch for a lawyer using "I," "we," or "everyone here" in the closing argument, such as, "We all know that the defendant is guilty . . ." This goes beyond the scope of permissible evidentiary argumentation.

---

5. Impartiality and Decorum of the Tribunal – MRPC 3.5:

a. Improper Influence: A lawyer shall not seek to illegally influence a judge, juror, or potential juror. Gifts or loans to judges are only allowed if permitted by state judicial conduct rules. Disruptive, harassing, or abusive conduct in court is also prohibited.

b. Ex Parte Communications: Ex parte communications with the court or jurors are ordinarily prohibited because the opposing lawyer's position cannot be considered. An exception applies if the lawyer's ex parte communication was purely procedural, such as inquiring about a scheduling matter. Even a lawyer not connected with a case must not discuss the case with an impaneled juror. Post-trial communication with jurors in an attempt to prove juror impropriety must not involve coercion, duress, or harassment.

MEE Tip: A lawyer's ex parte communications with the court or attempts to create judicial partiality in a question usually involves several violations of candor to the tribunal and fairness to opposing party and counsel.

---

6. Trial Publicity – MRPC 3.6: Extrajudicial trial publicity by lawyers and prosecutors is restricted if it would be disseminated and materially prejudice the proceeding.

a. Prohibited Criminal Case Statements – TOPIC: Prohibited extrajudicial statements and comments by a lawyer that may create a heightened public condemnation of the accused include the **TOPIC** subjects of:

(1) <u>T</u>est Results: The performance or results of any investigative test, such as a polygraph examination (lie detector test) or a lab test or failure to submit to such a test.

(2) Opinion or Future Witness Testimony: Any opinion as to the guilt or innocence of any suspect or defendant, or the credibility or anticipated testimony of a prospective witness.

(3) Plea or Confession: The possibility of a guilty plea or the existence or contents of a confession, admission, or statement given by a suspect or defendant or that person's refusal or failure to make such a statement.

(4) Inadmissible Evidence: Information the lawyer knows or reasonably should know is likely to be inadmissible as evidence in a trial.

(5) Character: Statements about the character, credibility, reputation, or past criminal record of a witness, suspect, or defendant are generally prohibited (except for impeachment purposes in some circumstances).

MEE Tip: The **TOPIC** prohibited extrajudicial statements made by a lawyer or their subordinate are heavily tested on the exam.

---

b. Permitted Disclosures: A lawyer's out-of-court statements should be limited to the general nature of the claim or defense, the procedural or scheduling status of the case, and public record information, including identities of designated witnesses. A lawyer also has a right to publicly rebut the prejudicial effect of negative publicity generated by another.

c. Safety Information: The public has a right to know about threats to its safety and measures aimed at assuring public security. A public prosecutor or other lawyer involved in a criminal case may state that an investigation is in progress, identify involved parties (if allowed by law), request assistance in obtaining evidence and information, and warn of danger concerning the behavior of a person involved. There must be reason to believe there is a likelihood of substantial harm to an individual or to the public interest.

d. Civil Case Statements: Statements that have a substantial likelihood of materially prejudicing an adjudicative proceeding are prohibited in civil matters. This usually involves a lawyer's discussion of inadmissible evidence or evidence of negative statements about an opposing party's character or credibility.

MEE Tip: Any extrajudicial publicity by an attorney or their subordinates that could materially prejudice the proceeding – especially on a **TOPIC** subject in a criminal case – deserves a full paragraph in your answer.

---

7. Lawyer as Witness – MRPC 3.7: The role of a trial partisan-advocate may conflict with that of an independent witness. Serving as a fact witness subject to cross-examination may also reduce the effectiveness of the lawyer's advocacy role.

a. Improper to Act as Advocate and Witness: A lawyer shall not act as advocate at a trial where the lawyer is likely to be a necessary witness concerning a material contested question of fact. Some states limit this prohibition to jury trials.

b. Exceptions: An attorney may be a witness if any **HULA** reason applies:

(1) Hardship on Client: A lawyer may testify when the evidence is otherwise unobtainable or the lawyer has been called by the opposing party, and/or that disqualification of the lawyer would work a substantial hardship on the client. Some states also require that the likelihood of the lawyer being a necessary witness was not reasonably foreseeable before trial.

(2) Uncontested or Formality: A lawyer may testify if the testimony relates to a minor factual issue that is either uncontested or a mere formality. An example is testifying as a witness to the execution of a will or a corporate document.

(3) Legal Services Rendered Value: A lawyer may testify if the testimony relates to the nature and value of legal services rendered in the case.

(4) Another Firm Lawyer Witness: Unlike the firm-wide disqualification provisions of MRPC 1.10, a lawyer is not disqualified as an advocate merely because another lawyer in the same firm is a witness unless the firm itself has a Rule 1.7 or 1.9 conflict.

8. Special Responsibilities of a Prosecutor – MRPC 3.8: A prosecutor in a criminal case has several elevated duties as the role turns from being an advocate of a private client to being an advocate of the public in the pursuit of justice.

a. Probable Cause Necessary: A prosecutor cannot bring a charge or prosecute a criminal case that the prosecutor knows is not supported by probable cause. This includes being able to present believable evidence on every element of the offense.

b. Accused's Right to Counsel: The prosecutor has a duty to advise the accused of the right to counsel and provide the opportunity to obtain a lawyer. The absence of *Miranda* warnings is usually grounds for reversal of a subsequent conviction based upon admissions made during unrepresented interrogation.

c. Honor Pretrial Rights of Accused: The prosecutor has a duty to refrain from seeking a waiver of important pretrial rights from an unrepresented accused (rights against self-incrimination, waiver of preliminary hearing, or demand for jury trial).

d. Timely Disclosure of Exculpatory Evidence: The prosecutor may not suppress and must make timely disclosure to the defense of all material exculpatory evidence or information known to the prosecutor that tends to negate the guilt of the accused or tends to mitigate the severity of the offense. During sentencing, the prosecutor has a duty to disclose to the defense and the tribunal all unprivileged mitigating information known to the prosecutor.

e. Lawyer Discovery: Prosecutors shall not subpoena a lawyer to secure client evidence in a criminal proceeding. An exception allows such discovery on a lawyer if the evidence is not privileged, it is essential or extremely important, and there is no feasible alternative source.

f. Prohibited Extrajudicial Statements: The prosecutor shall not make prohibited extrajudicial statements and must supervise paralegals and other subordinates. Investigators, law enforcement personnel, employees, paralegals, or other persons assisting or associated with the lawyer in a criminal case likewise are prohibited from making extrajudicial statements that the prosecutor would be prohibited from making. (See also MRPC 3.6)

g. Post-Conviction Duty: In February 2008, the ABA House of Delegates voted to require prosecutors to take reasonable affirmative steps to rectify a potentially wrongful prior conviction. This applies if new credible legal or factual evidence later comes to light that clearly and convincingly creates substantial doubt about the fundamental fairness of the defendant's guilt. A prosecutor must promptly disclose such information to an appropriate court or other authority. Some argue this new requirement may put prosecutor immunity at risk.

MEE Tip: Look for fact patterns where the prosecutor over-reaches the scope of probable cause to bring charges, fails to preserve the defendant's right to counsel, fails to disclose to the defendant's attorney exculpatory or mitigating information, or fails to prevent subordinates from making inappropriate remarks.

---

9. Advocate in Nonadjudicative Proceeding – MRPC 3.9: A legislative or administrative tribunal or agency will likely give special weight to a lawyer's opinions on a question of law or rulemaking. If the lawyer is giving opinion testimony and simultaneously representing a client with an interest in the subject, disclosure of the attorney-client relationship is required. This permits the agency to make an assessment of any relevant biases of the lawyer. If the jurisdiction allows practicing lawyers to hold public office concurrently, they may not use their public positions to obtain special advantage that is clearly contrary to the public interest.

C. Transactions with Persons Other than Clients – TITLE 4

1. Truthfulness in Statements to Others – MRPC 4.1

a. False Statement: A lawyer shall not knowingly make a false statement of material fact or law to a third person in the course of representing a client. Third parties include opposing counsel. Misrepresentations can also occur by partially true but misleading statements. While a lawyer need not disclose all facts, omissions that are the equivalent of affirmative false statements are improper. A lawyer's puffery to opposing counsel in representing estimates of price, value, or dollar settlement maximums are not usually considered statements of fact.

b. Duty to Disclose: There is also a duty to make disclosure of a material fact to a third party when disclosure is necessary to avoid assisting a client's criminal or fraudulent act. Most jurisdictions do not allow disclosures violating MRPC 1.6, but withdrawal may be required. Beyond withdrawal, a lawyer may have to disaffirm affirmatively documents she created that now appear to be fraudulent to avoid being deemed to have personally assisted.

c. Liabilities to Third Parties: Some jurisdictions, including California, have adopted a multi-factor test and held there is potential legal liability to unrepresented third parties if it is clear they will rely to their detriment on the lawyer's statements.

2. Communication with Persons Represented by Counsel – MRPC 4.2: A lawyer shall not communicate with a person represented by another lawyer in the same matter unless that person's lawyer consents or direct communication is authorized by law or court order. If the lawyer is contacted by the opposing party, she should say, "I cannot talk to you directly; you need to talk to your own lawyer." Simultaneous communication, such as mailing a letter directed to both the opposing party and his lawyer, is still a violation.

a. Includes: Direct communications by a lawyer about the subject of the representation are prohibited. This might include a lawyer using an investigator to record conversations surreptitiously to obtain damaging admissions from a represented opposing party. If an organization such as a corporation is a party, the Rule protects all directors and employees with managerial responsibility and those personally involved in the wrongdoing.

b. Limited Representation: An opposing party with only limited representation is considered unrepresented unless the opposing lawyer knows of or has received a written notice of appearance. This means the lawyer may usually communicate directly with such a party. This Rule promotes filing a limited Notice of Appearance.

MEE Tip: Opposing counsel must consent to communication with the opposing party. This absolute "no contact" rule applies even if the opposing party initiates the communication with the lawyer. Opposing parties themselves may directly communicate with each other.

---

3. Dealing with Unrepresented Person – MRPC 4.3: A lawyer shall not state or imply that the lawyer is disinterested to a person who is not represented by counsel.

a. Correct Any Misunderstanding: The lawyer shall make reasonable efforts to correct any misunderstanding the unrepresented person has of the lawyer's role in the matter. This rule suggests the lawyer must affirmatively state that (1) she is a lawyer, (2) who represents an identified opposing party, and (3) you should secure your own counsel.

b. Giving Legal Advice: A lawyer should avoid giving legal advice to an unrepresented party if that party is or may be adverse to a current client.

4. Respect for Rights of Third Person – MRPC 4.4: A lawyer shall not use means that have no substantial purpose other than to embarrass, delay, or burden a third person who is not a party, such as a witness.

a. Depositions: Third parties may be compelled to give deposition testimony, but a lawyer should avoid subjects involving unwarranted intrusions. The lawyer may also not use methods to obtain evidence that are oppressive or violate the legal rights of third parties.

b. Receipt of Inadvertently Sent Documents: A lawyer may receive documents or e-mails that the lawyer knows were mistakenly sent to him by opposing parties or their lawyer. The lawyer must promptly notify the sender in order to permit him to consider initiating protective measures. The ABA comments suggest it is best to return such documents unread. The rule specifically excludes evidence provided by the client that the lawyer knows was wrongfully obtained. Using stolen information could become a criminal offense by the lawyer.

V. LAW FIRMS, MARKETING, AND PROFESSIONAL INTEGRITY

A. Law Firms and Associations – TITLE 5

1. Responsibilities of Partners, Managers, and Supervisory Lawyer – MRPC 5.1: Law firms are not usually subject to professional discipline – only the involved lawyer(s).

a. Partner Responsibility: A partner or one with comparable managerial authority must ensure the organization has in place quality control policies and procedures that give reasonable assurance that all lawyers in the firm conform to the MRPCs.

b. Supervisory Lawyer Responsibility: A lawyer with direct supervisory authority over an associate lawyer must make reasonable efforts to ensure the associate conforms to the MRPCs. Whether a lawyer may be civilly vicariously liable for negligence damages in non-supervision of another lawyer's conduct is not addressed in this ethical rule.

c. Responsibility for Associates' Acts: A supervisory lawyer is responsible if the lawyer directly orders improper conduct or, with knowledge of the specific improper conduct, ratifies the unethical conduct involved. If she knows of the conduct at a time when the consequences can be avoided or mitigated, she must take reasonable remedial action.

2. Responsibilities of a Subordinate Lawyer – MRPC 5.2:

a. General Rule: Even though a subordinate (associate) lawyer acts under the direction of another person, that associate lawyer is personally bound by the MRPCs.

b. Exception: A subordinate lawyer does not violate the MRPCs if she acts in accordance with a supervisory lawyer's ethical decision, and the question involved a reasonably arguable ethical issue. An example is whether the conflict provisions of MRPC 1.7(b) are put at risk by two different clients' interests that might foreseeably become adverse. Another example is where an associate files a frivolous pleading at the direction of a partner, and reasonably relied on the supervisor's analysis of the relevant factual questions.

> **MEE Tip:** An associate's reliance on a supervising lawyer's decision is frequently tested.

3. Responsibilities Regarding Non-lawyer Assistants – MRPC 5.3: Any lawyer with supervisory authority over non-lawyer employees (office managers, law school interns, paralegals, investigators, and clerical staff) must review their work, and the lawyer must always maintain a direct client relationship. If the non-lawyer was engaged in conduct that would be a violation of the MRPCs, the supervisory lawyer might be vicariously responsible. Liability applies if the lawyer orders or, with knowledge of the specific conduct, ratifies the conduct involved. The lawyer will be liable if he knows of the conduct at a time when its consequences can be avoided or mitigated, but fails to take reasonable remedial action.

> **MEE Tip:** ABA Opinion 1203 requires external reporting of clear ethical violations by lawyers in the firm. Simply "reporting up" within the law firm is insufficient.

4. Professional Independence of a Lawyer – MRPC 5.4:

a. Improper to Share Fees with Non-Lawyer – MRPC 5.4(a): A lawyer or law firm shall not share legal fees with a non-lawyer. This is the principal deterrent to multi-disciplinary practice. Even splitting fees with a charity is disallowed. There are four **PEND** exceptions where fee sharing with non-lawyers is permitted.

(1) Purchase of Practice: Under a law firm purchase agreement, the acquisition price may be paid to the seller. Similarly, payment to the estate of the deceased, disabled, or disappeared lawyer is proper.

(2) Employee Payment Plans: A firm may include non-lawyer employees in a compensation or retirement plan. This exception is allowed even though the firm's compensation and retirement plan funding sources are derived from the legal fees.

(3) Nonprofit Organization: Court-awarded legal fees may be shared with a nonprofit organization that employed, retained, or recommended the lawyer in the matter.

(4) Death or Disability of Lawyer: A firm or partner may pay the pro-rata law firm capital account benefits to a lawyer's estate or beneficiaries. Such death benefit payments may not extend beyond a reasonable period of time after the lawyer's death.

b. Non-Law Partnerships – MRPC 5.4(b): A lawyer shall not form a partnership with a non-lawyer if any of the activities of the partnership consist of the "practice of law." The "practice of law" is defined by the jurisdiction in question. The broadest definition is "the application of legal principles and judgments to resolve a problem or how to proceed under the law." This broad definition produces uncertainty as to whether the state could move against others, such as CPAs, financial planners, etc., for the unauthorized practice of law.

> **MEE Tip:** This is a common fact pattern on the Bar and easy to spot. To violate the rule, the business venture with the non-lawyer must be related to a legal matter.

c. Improper to Direct Lawyer's Professional Judgment – MRPC 5.4(c): A third party who employed, retained, or recommended a lawyer in a matter or pays the lawyer may not direct, regulate, or exercise influence over the lawyer's professional judgment. This exam issue arises if a third party "calls the shots." There should not be any interference with the lawyer's independent professional judgment. The student should also review MRPC 1.8(f), No Fee Payment by Third Parties *supra*.

> **MEE Tip:** This issue is likely to arise where a third party is paying the client's bills (such as a parent or insurance company) and the payer tries to interfere with the attorney's judgment.

d. Professional Corporation or Association – MRPC 5.4(d): A lawyer shall not practice law with a non-lawyer (or suspended lawyer). This applies if a non-lawyer owns any interest in the law firm or is a law firm director or officer. An ownership exception allows a fiduciary representative of the estate of a deceased partner to own a nominal interest for a reasonable time during administration of the estate.

5. Unauthorized and Multi-jurisdictional Practice of Law – MRPC 5.5:

a. Unauthorized Practice: A lawyer may not assist a non-lawyer in the performance of any activity that constitutes the unauthorized practice of law, as defined by state law. Counseling with pro se representation is usually allowed. Delegation of legal work to non-lawyer assistants is allowed if the lawyer adequately supervises the details of the work and maintains a direct relationship with the client. Unauthorized practice usually includes engaging in the practice of law while on inactive or suspended status. It also typically includes participating in the practice of law with a unadmitted, disbarred, or suspended lawyer.

b. Multi-jurisdiction Practice: A lawyer shall not practice law in a jurisdiction in which she is not admitted. This prohibition includes non-isolated transactions such as entering a formal court appearance, opening an office, holding out, or other systematic and continuous presence in the jurisdiction. Local admission may not be required for services provided on a temporary basis in a matter reasonably related to a controversy arising in the lawyer's home jurisdiction, or for mediation and arbitration proceedings in some states like California and New York. Most jurisdictions have *pro hac vice* (for a specific matter) admission in association with local counsel and permission of the tribunal. If the local rule is not met, the lawyer's home state licensing authority may also impose discipline for the unauthorized practice in another state.

6. Restrictions on Right to Practice – MRPC 5.6:

a. Non-compete Agreements: Entering into an employment agreement that restricts the rights of a lawyer to represent firm clients after leaving a law firm is improper. The client has the right to decide their own legal representation, and may switch lawyers or follow a lawyer to a new firm. A small exception is that a lawyer's non-compete agreement may be given in return for retirement benefits or the sale of a law practice.

b. No Further Representation Clause: A lawyer cannot make or sign an agreement not to represent her client or other persons or claims against the opposing party in the future. For example, a settlement agreement prohibiting the lawyer from bringing future suits against the same corporate defendant is contrary to the public interest. These anti-competitive restrictions apply even if the client urges the lawyer to agree to such a condition.

> **MEE Tip:** Two lawyers participating in an agreement prohibiting a lawyer from representing a client or bringing a different lawsuit against the opposing party are both acting improperly.

7. Responsibilities Regarding Law-related Services – MRPC 5.7: A lawyer may engage in law-related ancillary services (such as title insurance, trust services, or financial planning), but all the MRPCs apply whether services are provided through the law firm or a separate entity. If the provider is a separate entity, the customer must understand the services are not legal representation. Disclosure must affirmatively be made that regular law firm protections, such as the attorney-client privilege and restrictions on conflicts of interest, do not apply. If the customer is also a law firm client, the conflict rules of MRPC 1.7 and transaction **TIC** rules of MRPC 1.8 may apply.

B. Public Service – TITLE 6

1. Pro Bono Publico Service – MRPC 6.1: A lawyer should aspire to render pro bono public interest legal service and contribute to the community by serving people of limited means and charitable organizations at no charge or for a reduced fee. This is not usually mandatory; 50 hours per year is the ABA aspirational goal. Public service representation may not violate the civil sanction provisions of Civil Rule 11 or any MRPCs, such as conflicts with the interests of other clients.

> **MEE Tip:** Pro bono representation and public service is aspirational, but it does not excuse a violation of the civil sanction of Civil Rule 11 or any MRPC, such as conflicts with the interests of other clients.

2. Accepting Appointments – MRPC 6.2: A judge may appoint a lawyer to represent indigents and unpopular parties. The appointment should not be declined except for good cause. Good cause includes representation that would lead to likely violation of the MRPCs (including violation of MRPC 1.1 – competency requirements) or create an unreasonable financial burden on the lawyer. If the client or cause is so repugnant to the lawyer as to impair the client-lawyer relationship or the lawyer's ability to represent the client as an effective advocate, the appointment may also be declined. But mere unpopularity of the matter or disapproval by other clients is not considered good cause.

> **MEE Tip:** Financial burden must be extreme; just because a lawyer would not make as much money by taking the case, he/she is not excused from appointment. Likewise, repugnancy of the case must actually interfere with the attorney's ability to advocate for the client. Even the worst of offenders deserve some counsel.

3. Membership in Legal Services Organization – MRPC 6.3: Legal services organizations serve the public. A lawyer may serve as a director, officer, or member even if the organization serves persons whose interests are adverse to a client of the lawyer's firm. The lawyer must not knowingly participate in a decision or action of the organization if the decision or action would be incompatible with the conflict of interest rules.

4. Law Reform Activities Affecting Client Interests – MRPC 6.4: Participation in a law reform organization is acceptable even where reform measures may affect the interests of a client. If the lawyer learns that the interests of a client may be materially benefited by an organizational decision in which the lawyer participates, the lawyer must disclose that fact to the organization but need not identify the client. Note that there is no duty to disclose circumstances where a client may be hurt by the actions of the organization.

5. Nonprofit and Court-annexed Limited Representation – MRPC 6.5: This provision focuses on a lawyer sponsored by a nonprofit organization or appointed by a court to provide short-term legal services to a client without expectation of continuing representation. Examples are the completion of legal forms in a walk-in clinic or advice given on a hotline. The client must agree to the limited scope of representation and be informed if further assistance of counsel is desirable. The imputed firm-wide disqualification conflict of interest rules [MRPC 1.10] do not apply unless the lawyer has personal knowledge of a conflict.

C. Information About Legal Services – TITLE 7

1. Communications Concerning a Lawyer's Services – MRPC 7.1:

a. Includes: The Rule prohibits false and misleading communications or failure to disclose information that is necessary to make the statement not materially misleading.

b. Unjustified Expectations: Many states have not adopted the ABA 2003 Rule 7.1 changes and still require that communications may not create unjustified expectations about results the lawyer can achieve. False statistics, claims to experience, or statements of "influence with the tribunal" may create unjustified expectations and be a basis for discipline. Statements of prior law firm case dollar recoveries should include a disclaimer as to future recoveries.

c. Comparisons: Any comparisons of the lawyer's services with other lawyers' must be factually substantiated or otherwise verifiable. An example is, "We are the best tax lawyers in New York City"; such a marketing statement would be very difficult to verify factually. The burden is on the lawyer to show sufficient support for the statement.

> **MEE Tip:** False, misleading, or unverifiable marketing is improper. While advertising may not create unjustified expectations for potential clients, good taste is not directly required.

2. Advertising – MRPC 7.2: This rule is heavily related to MRPC 7.1. Commercial speech is protected by the 1st and 14th Amendments. (*Bates*) Still, narrowly drawn regulations such as a 30-day ban on mass-disaster blanket mailings are permitted.

a. Use of Public Media: A lawyer may advertise services through public media such as radio, television, telephone directories, electronic search engines, yellow pages, legal directories, newspaper and other periodicals, and other electronic and written communications. Impersonation of a lawyer, client, celebrity spokesperson and/or depiction of accident scenes, injuries, or related are not allowed in many states.

b. Records of Advertisement Kept: Many jurisdictions (but not the MRPC since 2003) require retention of a copy or recording of an advertisement for two years after its last dissemination. This includes video, online, or television advertisements. The lawyer has the burden to show the basis of any factual claims advertised.

c. No Compensation for Recommendations: A lawyer may not directly or indirectly compensate an individual or organization for recommending or referring a client, except a bar-approved, nonprofit referral service. A lawyer may pay to purchase a law practice or for reasonable costs of advertising. The payment of compensation to for-profit referral services, including paid online legal matching services, is not allowed in some states.

> **MEE Tip:** Although direct, person-to-person solicitation is not allowed, blanket 'wide-net' mailings are permitted. Look for a lawyer – or their third-party agent – approaching a person who has just been injured at the accident scene, soliciting patients at hospital emergency rooms, or strangers at a social event.

d. Name in Advertisement: In many jurisdictions, advertisements must include the name and address of the law firm. Some states require publishing the name of at least one lawyer responsible for its content.

3. Direct Contact with Prospective Clients – MRPC 7.3: The concern is that the lawyer using direct communications to solicit employment will overwhelm a potential client.

a. Solicitation Breadth and ROFF Exceptions – MRPC 7.3(a): Direct solicitations by a lawyer to prospective clients are restricted whether oral, in person, live telephone, or real-time electronic communication. Oral solicitation seeking future employment from other than **ROFF** – **r**elatives, **o**ther lawyers, **f**ormer clients, or **f**riends – is prohibited.

(1) Examples: A lawyer may not solicit a stranger at a social event or use an agent, such as a "runner" or "capper," to pass out business cards at an accident scene or hospital emergency room. In comparison, setting up a booth at a street fair with signs stating "Legal questions answered" is not usually a violation since the lawyer waits for the potential client to approach and does not directly solicit.

(2) Referrals: A lawyer may agree to refer clients to another lawyer or non-lawyer professional in return for the undertaking of that person to refer back to the lawyer, as long as no fee or other remuneration is involved. Reciprocal referral agreements that are not exclusive (do not apply to any and all clients) and do not interfere with the lawyer's professional independent judgment are also permissible. The client must be informed of the reciprocal agreement.

MEE Tip: A lawyer giving value as a quid pro quo for legal referrals is frequently tested.

b. Written Solicitation – MRPC 7.3(b) and (c): A lawyer's written offers to represent, such as sending letters to individuals who had a foreclosure action filed against them, are now permissible (*Shapero*), but must state "advertising material." An exception applies if the non-client has indicated that no communication from the lawyer is desired.

4. Communication of Fields of Practice and Specialization – MRPC 7.4: A lawyer may communicate that she practices certain types of law and not others.

a. No "Specialists": A lawyer shall not state or imply that he is a specialist such as a "Tax Specialist Attorney." Historical exceptions include "patent attorney" if the attorney is admitted to practice before the United States Patent and Trademark Office. A "Proctor in Admiralty" designation is also usually allowed.

b. Certification: A lawyer may make statements about certifications, awards, or recognition she has been issued, as long as they are not misleading and identify the certifying organization. Included are a viable designation or earned award by a bona fide group that is authorized to issue such certifications (e.g., CFP issued by the Certified Financial Planning Institute). The ABA may also accredit the organization. An attorney-CPA may designate her dual credentials. (*Ibanez*)

c. Additional Required Disclosure: Some jurisdictions require that the reference to acceptable credentials must state that the supreme court of the state does not recognize specialties in the practice of law. Some even go further and require a statement that the certificate, award, or recognition is not a requirement to practice law in the state.

MEE Tip: The exam often combines advertising, solicitation, and specialization designation.

5. Firm Names and Letterheads – MRPC 7.5:

a. Trade Names: Trade names and web sites may be used in most jurisdictions by a law firm in private practice unless they are misleading or imply a connection with a government related agency (e.g., "New York City Legal Clinic" or "IRS Tax Law Firm") or charitable legal service organization (e.g., "Community Legal Center").

(1) Misleading Prohibition: The trade name and any web sites used by the law firm may not be misleading or communicate an unauthorized specialty designation. It is usually considered inherently misleading for a sole practitioner to use the term "and associates" in a firm's trade name if there are no associates in the firm.

(2) Former Partners: A law firm may use the names of deceased or retired partners in the firm name where there has been a continuing succession in the firm's identity.

b. Multiple Offices: A law firm with offices in multiple locations may use the same firm name on the individual offices' letterhead. If individual attorneys are listed on the letterhead, the jurisdictions in which they are admitted must be specified.

c. Holding Public Office: A lawyer holding a public office shall not use her name in the law firm trade name or in communications on its behalf during any substantial period when the lawyer is not actively and regularly practicing with the firm.

d. Professional Organization v. Solo Practice: Lawyers practicing out of the same office who are not partners or shareholders of a professional corporation may not join their names together. Lawyers may state or imply that they practice in a partnership or other organization only when that is the fact. Solo separate letterheads, cards, pleading papers, etc. are required unless the lawyer is a partner, employee or "of counsel" to the firm.

MEE Tip: The question of trade names or attorneys who share office space without having a formal partnership has appeared on the bar. The rule for sole practitioners is no joint holding out such as letterheads or business cards.

---

6. Improper Political Contributions – MRPC 7.6: Political contributions or solicitation of another's contributions by a lawyer is usually not improper. But if such contribution or solicitation is made for the purpose of obtaining assigned work or judicial appointment, it is not allowed. This rule prohibits only political contributions or solicitations that would not be made "but for" the consideration of an appointment or legal work.

D. Maintaining the Integrity of the Profession – TITLE 8

1. Bar Admission and Disciplinary Matters – MRPC 8.1: This communication rule addresses an applicant for admission to the bar or a lawyer in a disciplinary matter.

a. Admission Application: A lawyer's recommendation of an applicant for admission must be accurate and based on personal knowledge following a reasonable investigation as to the applicant's character, fitness, and qualifications. Any misstatements in an applicant's admission application must be corrected by a recommender because a lawyer must not assist an unfit or unqualified candidate in gaining admission.

b. Disciplinary Proceeding: All statements made by participants in any bar proceeding must be true and accurate, with full disclosure. Both an applicant and a lawyer must respond to all lawful state bar admission authority demands for information.

2. Judicial and Legal Officials – MRPC 8.2: The objective is to maintain public confidence in the legal system and the integrity of the involved jurists.

a. False or Reckless Statements: Lawyers must not make false or reckless statements about the qualifications, integrity, or record of a sitting judge, public legal officer, or candidate for election or appointment to a judicial or legal office.

b. Objectivity Required: A lawyer's candid opinions concerning a judge that are objective, factually accurate, and honest are allowed. A candidate for judicial office must comply with the Code of Judicial Conduct (CJC). A lawyer should defend judges and courts from unjust or uninformed criticism.

MEE Tip: An attorney's outrageous statements about the integrity of a judge are clear grounds for discipline.

---

3. Reporting Professional Misconduct – MRPC 8.3: Under the ABA Model Rules, a lawyer is required to ("shall" or "must") report substantial misconduct of another lawyer. Many jurisdictions differ as to the required degree of reporting compliance (such as non-mandatory "should" or "may").

a. Knowledge of MRPC Violation: A lawyer with actual personal knowledge of a committed violation of the MRPCs by another attorney shall promptly inform the appropriate authority. The perceived violation must raise a substantial and clear question as to that individual's honesty, trustworthiness, or fitness as a lawyer. A failure to report a serious violation by another lawyer has led to discipline being imposed on the non-reporter. In addition, it is improper to threaten reporting as a bargaining chip in negotiating a settlement.

b. Knowledge of MCJC Violation: A lawyer with actual, personal knowledge of a judge's violation of the MCJC shall promptly inform the appropriate authority. Again, this is mandatory under the ABA Model Rules, not merely suggestive. The perceived violation must raise a substantial and clear question as to the judge's fitness for office.

> **MEE Tip:** To raise the reporting issue there must be at least two lawyers in the facts.

c. Appropriate Authority: If the matter is in litigation, the appropriate authority for a lawyer would usually be the trial judge. Otherwise it ordinarily would be the state lawyer disciplinary authority. For reporting a judge, it would be the Judicial Conduct Commission in the jurisdiction.

> **MEE Tip:** Some states also require self-reporting to the state bar under some circumstances.

d. CAD Exceptions: There are three **CAD** situations where reporting misconduct is not required: if the information to be reported is protected under the MRPC 1.6 duty of **c**onfidentiality to clients; if the information was received through an approved lawyers' or judges' **a**ssistance program, or if a lawyer is retained to **d**efend the attorney in question.

> **MEE Tip:** The Rules comments specify that judgment is required in applying the reporting obligation. The "substantial" requirement refers to the seriousness of the offense. Actual knowledge of a clear violation by a lawyer goes beyond "mere suspicion."

4. Misconduct – MRPC 8.4: This catch-all category includes lawyers who:

a. Violate MRPCs: Violate or attempt to violate the MRPCs, knowingly assist or induce another to do the same, or do so through the acts of another, such as a legal assistant.

> **MEE Tip:** A lawyer may not use an agent to do indirectly that which a lawyer must not do.

b. Commit a Criminal Act: Commit a criminal act or act of public moral turpitude that reflects adversely on the lawyer's honesty, trustworthiness, or fitness as a lawyer in a professional capacity.

(1) Included: Qualifying acts include willful failure to file an income tax return, violence (such as an unjustified assault), "indifference to legal obligation," threatening witnesses, jurors, other lawyers, and judges, or other offenses relevant to the practice of law.

(2) Excluded: In comparison, matters of personal morality are usually insufficient. Examples include a single personal use of marijuana, act of marital infidelity, or comparable offenses lacking a specific connection to fitness for the practice of law. Repeated occurrences of minor personal morality offenses may cumulate, thus elevating the level of misconduct and increasing the chances of professional discipline.

c. Engage in Dishonesty or Fraud: This includes engaging in conduct that clearly demonstrates intentional dishonesty, fraud, deceit, misrepresentation, breach of trust or fiduciary duty. This is not limited to the practice of law, and a criminal conviction is not necessary.

d. Conduct Prejudicial to Administration of Justice: This includes a significant expression of disrespect to or about a tribunal. Rule Comment 3 makes it clear that conduct or statements in employment or while representing a client that manifest prejudice or bias on the basis of sex, race, age, creed, religion, color, national origin, disability, sexual orientation, or marital status are a violation if they are prejudicial to the administration of justice. Discriminatory peremptory juror challenges do not usually violate the rule.

e. Improperly Influence Government: A lawyer should not state or imply to a client or prospective client an ability to influence improperly a government agency, official, or tribunal. A statement promising to achieve results also is prohibited by the MRPCs.

f. Knowingly Assist Judge in Violation: Knowingly assist a judge or judicial officer in conduct that is a violation of applicable rules of judicial conduct or other law is prohibited.

g. Abuse of Public Position: Lawyers holding public office assume responsibilities beyond ordinary citizens. They may not use the public position to obtain special advantage for themselves or a client if such action is not in the public interest.

5. Disciplinary Authority – Choice of Law – MRPC 8.5: This rule addresses disciplinary power over lawyers in multi-jurisdiction practice.

a. Foreign Lawyer in State: This rule subjects a foreign lawyer admitted to appear under the *pro hac vice* rule to discipline by the local bar authority. *Pro hac vice* status usually requires the sponsorship of an attorney admitted in the jurisdiction. This temporary practice privilege usually is not available to persons who have failed the local bar exam.

b. Lawyer Outside State: Similarly, a state lawyer disciplinary authority may discipline a lawyer who is admitted even if the wrongful action occurred outside the licensing jurisdiction. If there are different rules between the licensing jurisdiction and the jurisdiction in which the violating effect of the conduct occurred, the latter jurisdiction's rules control.

c. Unlicensed Practice Practicality: Beyond the theoretical requirements, there is a practical problem for Ls practicing in a jurisdiction where they are not admitted. *Birbrower v. Superior Ct. of Santa Clara County*, 17 Cal.4th 119, 70 Cal. Rptr.2d 304, 949 P.2d 1 (1998), held that a L not admitted to the California state bar may be denied recovery of the legal fees charged a California C. This case involved a New York L who made multiple visits to California to advise a California client on California law. In comparison, *Winterrowd v. American*, 321 F.3d 933, 2009 (9th Cir. 2009) allowed an Oregon L to collect a fee from a California client when the Oregon L was engaged by a California L in a federal ERISA matter. At least on matters of federal law this opinion approves a multi-jurisdictional partnership.

Magic Memory Outline®

I. COMPETENCE, SCOPE OF REPRESENTATION, AND FEES
- A. Competence ....
  - 1. Proficiency Required ....
  - 2. Required Standard..
  - 3. Emergency Situation..
  - 4. Maintaining Competence ....
  - 5. Legal Malpractice Relationship ....
    - a. Standards Differ ....
    - b. Proof Required ....
- B. Scope of Representation and Authority Allocation ....
  - 1. Representation Objectives ....
  - 2. Lawyer's Decisions ....
  - 3. Client's Decisions – **AJET** ....
  - 4. No Endorsement ....
  - 5. Counsel a Crime or Fraud..
  - 6. Client Urging MRPC Violation ....
  - 7. Client Authority ....
  - 8. Limit of Representation ....
- C. Diligence..
  - 1. Dilatory Practices..
  - 2. Legal Rules ....
  - 3. Representation Completion ....
- D. Communication..
  - 1. Informative Explanations..
  - 2. Written v. Oral ....
  - 3. Special Situations..
    - a. Court Order or Rules ....
    - b. Client Imprudent Reaction..
  - 4. Communicate Mistakes..
  - 5. Communicate Termination ....
- E. Fees..
  - 1. Reasonable Factors – **SANTA REBER**...
    - a. **S**kill Required ....
    - b. **A**mount Involved ....
    - c. **N**ovelty and Difficulty ....
    - d. **T**ime Involved / Opportunities Foregone ....
    - e. **A**verage Customary Fee ....
    - f. **R**elationship..

        g. **E**xpertise ....

        h. **B**asis of Fee ....

        i. **E**xperience / Reputation ....

        j. **R**esult..

    2. Double Billing ....

    3. Fee Agreement Required ....

        a. Includes..

        b. New Client...

        c. Substantially Different...

        d. Change in Circumstances ....

        e. External Fee Split ....

        f. Writing Request...

        g. Withdrawal Writing ....

    4. Client Fee Objection ....

  F. Contingency Fee Agreement ....

    1. Writing Requirement ....

    2. Treatment of Costs ....

    3. Prohibited Matters ....

        a. Domestic Relations..

        b. Criminal Matter ....

    4. Client Termination...

    5. End of Case...

  G. Division of Fees ....

    1. In Same Firm ....

    2. Not in Same Firm ....

        a. Proportional ....

        b. Non-Proportional...

            (1) Joint Responsibility ....

            (2) Client Consent ....

    3. Referral Service ....

    4. Overall Reasonable Restraint ....

II.   CONFIDENTIALITY AND CONFLICT OF INTEREST

  A. Confidentiality of Information ....

    1. In General ....

        a. Core Values ....

        b. Attorney-Client Privilege ....

    2. Representation Information ....

    3. Exceptions ....

        a. Future Death or Substantial Bodily Injury ....

        b. Lawyer Being Sued or Related..

            (1) Claim or Defense Against Client..

            (2) Lawyer's Involvement...

            (3) Bar Complaint ....

            (4) Court Order...

        c. Sarbanes-Oxley Act ....

            (1) Breadth ....

            (2) Corporate Reporting Up ....

        d. Representation Withdrawal ....

        e. IRS Form 8300 ....

  f. Client Waiver...

  g. Breach of Fiduciary Responsibility ....

 B. Conflict of Interest: Current Clients ....

  1. Client-to-Client ....

   a. Representation of Two Directly Adverse Clients ....

   b. Lawyer's Responsibilities Materially Limited ....

    (1) Lower Level...

    (2) Examples..

   c. Exception ....

    (1) No Harm to Attorney-Client Relationship..

    (2) Informed Consent Confirmed in Writing ....

     (a) Adverse Clients Identification ....

     (b) Confidential Information Authorization ....

     (c) Revoking Consent...

    (3) Same Litigation Prohibition..

    (4) Fundamentally Antagonistic ....

   d. Related Attorneys ....

   e. Organizational Clients ....

    (1) General Rule ....

    (2) Exceptions..

   f. Lawyer Board Member..

  2. Current Client/Prohibited Transactions and Related ....

   a. No Business Relationship Unless **TIC**...

    (1) **T**erms of Transaction Are Fair ....

    (2) **I**ndependent Counsel ....

    (3) **C**onsent in Writing ....

   b. Information Disadvantaging the Client ....

   c. No Gifts from Clients ....

   d. No Agreement for Literary or Media Rights ....

   e. No Financial Assistance ....

    (1) Litigation Expenses ....

    (2) Contingency Cost Allocation...

    (3) Indigent Client ....

   f. No Fee Payment by Third Parties..

    (1) Informed Consent and No Interference ....

    (2) Confidentiality ....

   g. No Aggregate Settlement if Multiple Clients ....

    (1) Criminal Case ....

    (2) Civil Case...

   h. Limiting Liability...

    (1) Prospective Limitation...

    (2) Malpractice Settlement ....

   i. No Proprietary Interest in Cause of Action ....

    (1) Fee Security ....

    (2) Contingent Fee ....

   j. No Sexual Relations ....

    (1) Definition...

    (2) Consent Ineffective ....

    (3) Client Affections...

C. Conflict of Interest: Duties to Former Clients ....
  1. Subject Matter Relationship ....
  2. Informed Consent Possible ....
  3. Substantially Related Example ....
  4. Confidential Information Restriction ....
  5. Example ....

III. **DISQUALIFICATION, CLIENT FUNDS, AND WITHDRAWAL**
  A. Imputed Disqualification ....
    1. Conflicts of Interest ....
    2. Joining a Firm ....
      a. Screening ....
      b. Notice to Former Client ....
      c. Affidavit ....
    3. Leaving a Firm ....
  B. Successive Government and Private Employment ....
    1. Personal and Substantial Participation ....
    2. Employment Negotiation ....
    3. Confidential Government Information ....
  C. Former Judge, Arbitrator, Mediator, or Neutral ....
    1. Restrictions ....
    2. Employment Negotiation ....
    3. Consent or Screening ....
  D. Organization as Client ....
    1. Dual Representation ....
    2. Private Organization Internal Reporting ....
    3. Public Organization External Reporting ....
    4. Government Organization Client ....
  E. Client with Diminished Capacity ....
    1. Disability ....
    2. Preserve Confidences ....
  F. Safeguarding Property ....
    1. Separation Required ....
    2. Retainer and Trust Advances ....
    3. Transfers from Trust ....
    4. All Client Property Kept Identifiable and Accountable ....
      a. Notice of Receipt of Property and Funds ....
      b. Identify and Label Securities and Properties ....
      c. Third Parties' Claims ....
      d. Promptly Return Property ....
    5. Escrow Funds ....
  G. Declining or Terminating Representation ....
    1. Must Terminate / Withdraw – **VID** ....
      a. **V**iolate MRPCs ....
      b. **I**mpaired Ability to Represent ....
      c. **D**ischarged ....
    2. May Terminate / Withdraw – **CURBSO** ....
      a. **C**lient Pursuing Criminal Action ....
      b. **U**sed Lawyer to Commit Crime ....
      c. **R**epugnant Objective ....

        d. **B**urden on Lawyer Unreasonable ....

        e. **S**erious Client Failure ....

        f. **O**ther Good Cause for Withdrawal Exists ....

    3. Court Order ....

    4. Notice, Surrender, and Refund ....

        a. No Client Prejudice ....

        b. Surrender Papers and Property ....

        c. File Lien ....

        d. Other Lien Restraints ....

    5. Formal Notice ....

    6. Malpractice Concern ....

    7. "Noisy" or "Flag-Waving" Withdrawals ....

  H. Sale of Law Practice ....

  I. Duties to Prospective Client ....

    1. Conflict Question ....

    2. Screening Possible ....

    3. Fair Warning ....

    4. Duty Not to Mislead ....

    5. Confidential Information Protected ....

IV.   **COUNSELOR, ADVOCATE, AND THIRD PARTY DEALINGS**

  A. Counselor ....

    1. Advisor ....

        a. Independence ....

        b. Offering Advice ....

    2. Intermediary ....

        a. General Rule ....

            (1) Consultation and Consent ....

            (2) Client's Best Interests ....

            (3) Impartiality ....

            (4) Attorney-Client Privilege ....

        b. Withdrawal ....

    3. Evaluation for Use by Third Party ....

        a. Role ....

        b. Two Requirements ....

        c. Uncertainties ....

    4. Lawyer Serving as Third-Party Neutral ....

  B. Advocate ....

    1. Meritorious Claims and Contentions ....

        a. Civil Case ....

            (1) Not Frivolous ....

            (2) Is Frivolous ....

        b. Criminal Case ....

    2. Expediting Litigation ....

    3. Candor Toward the Tribunal ....

        a. False Statements of Law / Fact ....

        b. Facts Believed False ....

        c. Later Falsity Discovery ....

            (1) Persuade Client ....

          (2) Withdrawal ....

          (3) Required Tribunal Disclosure...

     d. Continuing to End of Proceeding ....

     e. Ex Parte Proceeding ....

  4. Fairness to Opposing Party and Counsel...

     a. Cannot Interfere with Evidence..

     b. Falsify Evidence or Witness Inducement ....

     c. Discovery Standards..

     d. At Trial ....

          (1) Improper Argument..

          (2) Closing Argument ....

     e. Personal Opinion During Trial ....

          (1) Prohibited Statements ....

          (2) Witness Questions ....

  5. Impartiality and Decorum of the Tribunal...

     a. Improper Influence ....

     b. Ex Parte Communications ....

  6. Trial Publicity...

     a. Prohibited Criminal Case Statements – **TOPIC** ....

          (1) <u>T</u>est Results ....

          (2) <u>O</u>pinion or Future Witness Testimony ....

          (3) <u>P</u>lea or Confession...

          (4) <u>I</u>nadmissible Evidence...

          (5) <u>C</u>haracter ....

     b. Permitted Disclosures..

     c. Safety Information..

     d. Civil Case Statements..

  7. Lawyer as Witness...

     a. Improper to Act as Advocate and Witness ....

     b. Exceptions – **HULA** ....

          (1) <u>H</u>ardship on Client ....

          (2) <u>U</u>ncontested or Formality ....

          (3) <u>L</u>egal Services Rendered Valuation ....

          (4) <u>A</u>nother Firm Lawyer Witness ....

  8. Special Responsibilities of a Prosecutor...

     a. Probable Cause Necessary...

     b. Accused's Right to Counsel ....

     c. Honor Pretrial Rights of Accused..

     d. Timely Disclosure of Exculpatory Evidence...

     e. Lawyer Discovery ....

     f. Prohibited Extrajudicial Statements ....

     g. Post Conviction Duty ....

  9. Advocate in Nonadjudicative Proceeding ....

C. Transactions with Persons Other than Clients..

  1. Truthfulness in Statements to Others ....

     a. False Statement...

     b. Duty to Disclose ....

     c. Liabilities to Third Parties..

2. Communication with Persons Represented by Counsel ....
   a. Includes ....
   b. Limited Representation ....
3. Dealing with Unrepresented Person ....
   a. Correct Any Misunderstandings ....
   b. Giving Legal Advice ....
4. Respect for Rights of Third Person ....
   a. Depositions ....
   b. Receipt of Inadvertently Sent Documents ....

V. LAW FIRMS, MARKETING, AND PROFESSIONAL INTEGRITY
  A. Law Firms and Associations ....
     1. Responsibilities of Partners, Managers, and Supervisory Lawyer ....
       a. Partner Responsibility ....
       b. Supervisory Lawyer Responsibility ....
       c. Responsibility for Associates' Acts ....
     2. Responsibilities of a Subordinate Lawyer ....
       a. General Rule ....
       b. Exception ....
     3. Responsibilities Regarding Non-lawyer Assistants ....
     4. Professional Independence of a Lawyer ....
       a. Improper to Share Fees with Non-lawyer – **PEND** Exceptions ....
         (1) **P**urchase of Practice ....
         (2) **E**mployee Payment Plan ....
         (3) **N**onprofit Organization ....
         (4) **D**eath or Disability of Lawyer ....
       b. Non-Law Partnerships ....
       c. Improper to Direct Lawyer's Professional Judgment ....
       d. Professional Corporation or Association ....
     5. Unauthorized and Multi-jurisdictional Practice of Law ....
       a. Unauthorized Practice ....
       b. Multi-jurisdictional Practice ....
     6. Restrictions on Right to Practice ....
       a. Non-compete Agreements ....
       b. No Further Representation Clause ....
     7. Responsibilities Regarding Law-related Services ....
  B. Public Service ....
     1. Pro Bono Publico Service ....
     2. Accepting Appointments ....
     3. Membership in Legal Services Organization ....
     4. Law Reform Activities Affecting Client Interests ....
     5. Nonprofit and Court-annexed Limited Representation ....
  C. Information About Legal Services ....
     1. Communications Concerning a Lawyer's Services ....
       a. Includes ....
       b. Unjustified Expectations ....
       c. Comparisons ....

2. Advertising ....
    a. Use of Public Media ....
    b. Records of Advertisement Kept ....
    c. No Compensation for Recommendations....................................
    d. Name in Advertisement...
3. Direct Contact with Prospective Clients..
    a. Solicitation Breadth and **ROFF** Exceptions.............................
      (1) Examples ....
      (2) Referrals ....
    b. Written Solicitation ....
4. Communication of Fields of Practice and Specialization....................
    a. No "Specialists"..
    b. Certification..
    c. Additional Required Disclosure ....
5. Firm Names and Letterheads ....
    a. Trade Names..
      (1) Misleading Prohibition ....
      (2) Former Partners ....
    b. Multiple Offices...
    c. Holding Public Office...
    d. Professional Organization v. Solo Practice ....
6. Improper Political Contributions ....
D. Maintaining the Integrity of the Profession...
  1. Bar Admission and Disciplinary Matters ....
    a. Admission Application..
    b. Disciplinary Proceeding ....
  2. Judicial and Legal Officials...
    a. False or Reckless Statement ....
    b. Objectivity Required ....
  3. Reporting Professional Misconduct ....
    a. Knowledge of MRPC Violation ....
    b. Knowledge of MCJC Violation...
    c. Appropriate Authority ....
    d. **CAD** Exceptions...
  4. Misconduct ....
    a. Violate MRPCs..
    b. Commit a Criminal Act ....
      (1) Included ....
      (2) Excluded ....
    c. Engage in Dishonesty or Fraud ....
    d. Conduct Prejudicial to Administration of Justice........................
    e. Improperly Influence Government ....
    f. Knowingly Assist Judge in Violation...
    g. Abuse of Public Position ....
  5. Disciplinary Authority – Choice of Law ....
    a. Foreign Lawyer in State ....
    b. Lawyer Outside of State ....
    c. Unlicensed Practice Practicality ....

RIGOS BAR REVIEW SERIES

UNIFORM MULTISTATE ESSAY EXAM (MEE) REVIEW

CHAPTER 8

ABA PROFESSIONAL RESPONSIBILITY RULES

Essay Questions

Question Number 1

In January 2009, Lessee and Lessor visited Attorney at her office. They asked if she would prepare a lease between them. Attorney agreed. In February, after drafting the agreement to their specifications, she met jointly with both clients. Attorney explained the lease, including a clause be created for a $250 late fee assessment for each month Lessee failed to make his payment. Lessor asked, "If Lessee doesn't pay, will you represent me to collect my money?" Attorney did not reply. When Lessor did not persist, the meeting ended with the lease's execution.

In November, Lessor contacted Attorney complaining, "Lessee has missed three lease payments. He owes $1500 in rent payments and $750 in late fees. I want you to sue Lessee and get my rent payments and late fees from him." Attorney agreed.

Inexplicably, Attorney did nothing until July 2010 when she sent Lessee a demand letter for just the late lease payments. Attorney had failed to review the agreement's late-fee clause and disregarded Lessor's instructions. Attorney's letter resulted in Lessee tendering just his overdue lease payments, which Lessor rejected.

Attorney billed Lessor $1800 for her collection services.

Discuss the issues raised under the ABA Model Rules of Professional Conduct.

Question Number 2

Ann and Larry, two sole proprietor lawyers, shared an office suite. Ann had worked as an insurance defense lawyer. Larry had criminal defense experience. They advertised as "Ann and Larry, personal injury and criminal defense experts" but were not actual partners.

Pam, the passenger, was injured while riding with Dave, the driver, when Dave's car hit a tree while rounding a curve. Dave said his brakes failed, but he was charged with reckless driving by the police. Larry saw the accident occur and approached Dave telling him that he would represent him in the criminal matter. Further, he stated that his partner Ann could represent Dave and Pam for civil damages against GimmeaBrake, Inc., the shop that had recently replaced Dave's brakes.

Dave and Pam met with Larry and Ann. Larry said the prosecutor was a friend, so he thought that he could get Dave's charge reduced to negligent driving. Dave pleaded guilty to negligent driving.

Ann had previously defended GimmeaBrake on similar claims. After Ann offered to pay the costs of litigation, Dave and Pam signed her contingent fee agreement. GimmeaBrake offered Pam reasonable compensation for her injury if Dave would drop his property damage claim. After consultation with Ann, both accepted the offer.

Discuss the issues raised under the ABA Model Rules of Professional Conduct.

Question Number 3

Deputy Prosecuting Attorney Joe filed assault charges against Bill. After working on the case for months, Joe left the prosecutor's office and established a private practice with attorney Steve. Bill then asked Joe and Steve to represent him in the assault case. Joe declined, as did Steve.

Bill retained Mack, a former Judge, to defend him in the assault case. Bill liked Mack because Mack was the judge who acquitted him in a prior criminal matter.

Mack tried to explain trial strategies to Bill even though Bill was mentally disabled and could not understand. Bill then gave Mack a check to cover witness fees. Mack put the check in his pocket and forgot about it. In fact, Mack was forgetting many things, and it became apparent to him that he had suffered a stroke. Mack continued representation of Bill nonetheless because he needed the work. Mack eventually found the check and deposited it into his personal savings account.

Bill also had a dispute with his landlord and, pleading poverty, asked the court for a pro bono attorney. The court appointed lawyer Harry to the case. Bill told Harry about Mack's shortcomings. After consideration, Harry refused to represent Bill as he had been Bill's victim in a former burglary case.

Discuss the issues raised under the ABA Model Rules of Professional Conduct.

Question Number 4

Attorney Jennifer hired Attorney Kevin to work at her law firm. As part of his employment contract, Kevin agreed not to practice law locally for six months if Jennifer terminated his employment. Kevin's first client advised he would be on vacation on their scheduled court date. Kevin advised, "No problems; I'll continue the matter."

Kevin appeared in court and moved for a continuance because the client "was in surgery." The continuance was granted, conditioned upon Kevin submitting a doctor's note. Kevin flew into a rage, yelling, "No one ever trusts defendants!" The court reprimanded Kevin and ordered he submit a doctor's note.

Kevin advised Jennifer and she suggested Kevin author the note himself. Kevin complied, signing it "Doctor Smith," and filing it with the court.

Subsequently, Kevin met Lisa, a disbarred attorney working as a bail-bond agent, who said they could make tons of money if she referred clients and they split attorney fees. Kevin eagerly agreed, and Lisa started referring clients. Jealous of Kevin's success, Jennifer fired him, demanding he not practice law locally for six months. Kevin moved his law practice into Lisa's office, continuing their arrangement.

Discuss the issues raised under the ABA Model Rules of Professional Conduct.

Question Number 5

Attorney Andy represented infamous XYZ Development Corporation and its controversial CEO, Sam. Sam and his date Darlene were having dinner with Andy at Sam's penthouse. Darlene and Sam argued, and Sam slapped Darlene. While calling 911 to report the incident, Darlene accidentally dropped the phone, a fact mentioned in the police report. The police arrived and arrested Sam.

Deputy prosecutor and avid environmentalist Patty charged Sam with fourth-degree assault and interfering with a 911 call. Andy represented Sam and outside of the courtroom before Sam's arraignment told reporters, "At trial, I will prove that Patty's politics caused both false charges against Sam." Patty responded, "Sam treats women like he treats the land."

Andy's nephew and legal intern, Frank, was completing his bar admissions application. Andy told Frank, "Don't mention your juvenile shoplifting conviction. Your record was expunged.

Andy and Frank were preparing Sam for testimony before the state Environmental Committee examining one of Sam's development proposals. Andy told Sam, "Don't worry. The chair owes me a favor." At the administrative board hearing, Andy testified that he was one of many concerned citizens in favor of the project.

Discuss issues raised under the ABA Model Rules of Professional Conduct.

Essay Answers

Answer Number 1

Issues Raised

(1)   Intermediary
(2)   Keeping Client Informed
(3)   Taking Representation
(4)   Diligence
(5)   Scope Of Representation
(6)   Competence
(7)   Fees

Sample Answer

(1)   Intermediary. A L acting as an intermediary between two clients whose interests are not currently adverse but could become so must consider the likelihood of the conflict occurring and the potential for materially limiting the lawyer's independence of professional judgment. The L must inform clients of the nature of the potential conflict, advise them of the wisdom of seeking independent counsel, inform them he will withdraw from representing both if the conflict arises and confirm the informed consent from both of them in writing. L should also discuss the implications on the attorney-client privilege of joint representation. L has violated the MRPCs by not complying with these requirements, since the interests of lessees and lessors are likely to come into future conflict.

(2)   Keeping Client Informed. A L must keep the client reasonably informed and respond to requests for information. When Lessor asked about future representation, A should have responded. Mere silence, as here, is insufficient. L should have informed Lessor that if such a conflict developed later she would withdraw from representing both clients.

(3)   Taking Representation. When a L acts as intermediary and the potential conflict becomes an actual conflict, the attorney must withdraw from representing both parties. Here A agreed to represent one party against another and therefore violated the MRPCs.

(4)   Diligence. A L must be reasonably competent and diligent in pursuing resolution of a client's matter. Matters must not be neglected. Here, failure to act for 8 months without reason is neglect and an MRPC violation.

(5)   Scope of Representation. The client sets the goals and objectives of a matter and the L can decide the process (tactics) after consultation with the client. The L must comply with the client's requests when reasonable and not in violation of the MRPCs. A failed to comply with Lessor's instructions by sending an insufficient demand letter.

(6)   Competence. A L must provide competent services necessary in the representation. Failing to complete a full demand letter or to review the lease contract violates competency. In addition, A may have been incompetent in drafting the lease agreement since it has led to a legal dispute.

(7)   Fees. Ls may not charge unreasonable fees. The rate and basis for calculating fees should be communicated to the client before or soon after the start of the representation, preferably in writing. The amount of fees must be reasonable. This can be based on the difficulty of the matter, the experience and reputation of the attorney, the average customary fee in the locale, etc. Here, $1800 seems to be a high fee for the services rendered and probably unreasonable, especially given A's incompetent representation of the client.

Answer Number 2

Issues Raised

(1)   Advertisement
(2)   Solicitation
(3)   Conflict of Interest
(4)   Fee-splitting
(5)   Influence
(6)   Former Client
(7)   Financing Litigation
(8)   Contingency fee
(9)   Aggregate Settlement

Sample Answer

(1)   Advertisement. An advertisement must not contain false or misleading information. A false or misleading statement includes misrepresentation of facts, creating unjustified expectations, or comparing one's services to another's without capability of substantiation. Here, Ann and Larry are each sole proprietors yet imply that they are partners or associates. The MRPC also prohibits claiming "expertise" as likely to create unjustified expectations. Further, no specialty can be claimed except for patent and trademark law, and certifications must be true. Thus, here, stating they are "experts" is improper under the MRPC. Instead, the advertisement could say "limited to" or "with emphasis in."

(2)   Solicitation. A L may not personally solicit, in person or by phone, a potential client unless they are relatives, other Ls, former clients, or friends. Larry violated the MRPC by his solicitation of Dave.

(3)   Conflict of Interest. Potential conflicts of interest occur when an actual conflict exists between two Cs or is foreseeable in the future. The courts will consider likelihood of actual conflict and whether representation could be materially limited. Here, driver-passenger cross-claims are possible. Ann should have explained to Dave and Pam the existing and potential conflict that may arise, what she will do if it does (withdraw), suggest independent counsel, and obtain informed consent which is at least confirmed in writing.

(4)   Fee-splitting. Ls may not split fees with Ls from other firms unless the fee is proportional to services rendered or both attorneys remain liable on the case, the fee is reasonable, and the client does not object. Here, Pam and Dave were unaware that Larry and Ann were separate firms and thus a potential violation.

(5)   Influence. A L should not state or imply that he has influence over a government official or an adjudicator. Larry's statements regarding the prosecutor were improper.

(6)   Former Client. A L cannot represent a client against a former client in the same or substantially related matter, unless informed consent is given and confirmed in writing. The facts stipulate the claims here were similar. Thus, Ann should not represent Pam against GimmeaBrake without consent. Even so, at no point may Ann use confidential information obtained during the representation against the former client.

(7)   Financing Litigation. A L may not make a client loan or financial assistance except to finance the litigation. Ann acted permissibly by her offer because these were merely allowable costs of litigation.

(8)   Contingency fee. A L's fees must be reasonable in light of the work done, the complexities of the issues, the reputation of the attorney, etc. Contingency fees must be in writing and clearly explain how fees will be calculated and the treatment of costs. The fee agreement here appears proper.

(9)   Aggregate Settlement. Aggregate settlement of multiple clients' claims are a potential violation. Each client is owed a duty of loyalty and full disclosure of all aspects of the monetary settlement for all participants. Ann potentially breached this loyalty by settling Pam's claim and dismissing Dave's claim.

Answer Number 3

Issues Raised

(1)   Former Government Employee
(2)   Former Judge
(3)   Disabled Client
(4)   Retainer
(5)   Competency
(6)   L Appointment
(7)   Imputed Disqualification
(8)   Duty to Report

Sample Answer

(1)   Former Government Employee. A L cannot represent a C in a matter in which he had substantially worked on as a government employee unless the Agency consents after consultation. Here, J declined the representation, but if he accepted, the Agency's consent would be necessary. Any privileged information gained in government work must not be revealed / used in private practice.

(2)   Former Judge. Mack (M) cannot represent client in a matter that he had substantial prior participation in. Here it was a prior criminal case but this is a different matter and case and civil in nature so may be OK if there was consent.

(3)   Disabled Client. A L must try to maintain a normal client-L relationship and request the court to appoint a guardian or obtain a protective order if L feels necessary. Here M may have authority to request a guardian for Bill (B) since he could not understand.

(4)   Retainer. Any fees given to L for representation must be placed in a separate trust account, and C must be promptly notified of any funds received. After the conclusion of the case a written itemized accounting must be provided to client and excess funds returned. Here M held in pocket, forgot about it, placed in personal bank account (L's funds must not be commingled with C funds) and did not promptly notify B of receipt.

(5)   Competency. A L must provide legal skills, thoroughness, preparation, and research to reasonably represent Client in the matter. If L cannot, must withdraw from representation especially if the physical or mental condition materially impairs duties. Here M was very forgetful due to his stroke but continued to represent B.

(6)   L Appointment. Pro bono is encouraged and appointment should be declined only for good cause. Here the past victimization has likely made it extremely repugnant to L. This is likely to impair his ability to represent the client zealously. H could also argue he may be called on as a witness and therefore should not be required to represent B.

(7)   Imputed Disqualification. If Steve or Joe had a conflict of interest with prosecution C / former C may also be disqualified personally unless screened, notice given to other party, no leaks of secrets / confidences prior to screening.

(8)   Duty to Report. A L who has credible reason to know that another L has committed a violation of the MRPCs that raises a substantial question as to that L's fitness shall inform the appropriate professional authority. Here L H seems to have credible knowledge of M's shortcomings and should so report.

Answer Number 4

Issues Raised

(1)   Covenant not to Compete
(2)   No Unreasonable Assurances
(3)   Duty of Candor Toward Tribunal
(4)   Duty of Professional Conduct
(5)   Judge's Authority to Sanction
(6)   Supervising Lawyer Duties
(7)   No Unauthorized Practice of Law
(8)   Client Referral Fees
(9)   Non-Lawyer Issues

Sample Answer

(1)   Covenant Not to Compete. A L shall not participate in an agreement restricting the L's right to practice after employment termination. A client is free to select professional legal representation of their choosing. Jennifer violated the MRPCs by forcing Kevin to sign the covenant, then by trying to enforce it later.

(2)   No Unreasonable Assurances. In communicating with a C, a L must not give a C unreasonable or false assurances of outcomes. The "no problem" to continuance representation may have violated this rule by promising to get a continuance.

(3)   Duty of Candor Toward Tribunal. A L owes the tribunal a duty of candor and they may not lie, or support a C in lying. Kevin violated the MRPCs by lying to the court about the reason for the continuance, then by forging the doctor's note.

(4)   Duty of Professional Conduct. Ls must behave professionally and may not display behavior that reflects poorly on attorneys as a profession. Kevin's display of rage and statements are improper because they reflect poorly on Ls and discredit the profession.

(5)   Judge's Authority to Sanction. A judge possesses the ability to control their courtroom and may reprimand or sanction a L officer in her court as deemed appropriate; the judge could properly reprimand Kevin for his outburst and report the matter to the bar disciplinary authorities.

(6)   Supervising Lawyer Duties. Any supervising L must ensure their subordinates know and follow the MRPCs and may not counsel any violation of the MRPCs. Jennifer violated this duty by suggesting Kevin forge the doctor's note. A supervised subordinate L also has an independent duty to follow the MRPCs and must not follow a supervising L's orders if such orders are an ethical violation; Kevin has violated the MRPC by following Jennifer's order.

(7)   No Unauthorized Practice of Law. No one without a license may practice law, including a disbarred L. A L may not assist a non-attorney or disbarred attorney in practicing law; Kevin may be in violation of the MRPCs if he has been helping Lisa practice law.

(8)   Client Referral Fees. A L may not pay or receive referral fees to any entity except one authorized by the state or county bar association; Kevin has violated the MRPCs by agreeing to give Lisa a referral fee.

(9)   Non-Lawyer Issues. A L may not share legal fees with a non-L; Kevin violated the MRPCs by so doing. A L may not share an office with a non-L to assist them in practicing law without a license. Kevin might be in violation of the MRPCs if he is assisting Lisa practice law (see above).

Answer Number 5

Issues Raised

(1) Prosecutor Duties
(2) Lawyer As Witness
(3) Prejudicial Public Statement
(4) Misleading Statements
(5) Statement to third Parties
(6) Bar Application misstatements
(7) Non-Adjudicative Proceedings
(8) Lawyer Dishonesty

Sample Answer

(1) Prosecutor Duties. Prosecutor must only pursue charges if probable cause exists. Patty (P)'s politics may explain her charges as Sam (S) clearly did not interfere with the 911 call. Political independence is not a prosecutor's requirement. Probable cause likely exists for 4th degree assault.

(2) Lawyer As Witness. Cannot represent C if reasonably believe L will be witness. Here, Andy (A) is only possible witness to the assault/911 interference charges. The exception for mere formalities or court permission probably do not apply as the testimony is criticized– A should realize problem and decline representation.

(3) Prejudicial Public Statement. Communications reasonably expected to be disseminated widely to public cannot impugn the opposing L's character or prejudice the proceeding. A suggests P abdicating procedural responsibilities, politically motivated, and falsely charging is a likely violation. Also cannot comment on character of the defendant. P insults S's treatment of women/land.

(4) Misleading Statements. L must not mislead client or create unjustified expectation about results. A's public statement that charges are false may reasonably cause S to expect acquittal. A suggests to S that A can exert influent on a government agent.

(5) Statement to 3rd Parties. L may not state to 3rd parties materially false statements unless protecting client confidences. Telling reporters the charges are "false" is inaccurate given that A saw the assault. Perhaps A defends that Rule 1.6 protects "confidences" and the guilt of S is implicitly "inviolate" or "embarrassing."

(6) Bar Application. This appears to be a materially false statement or at least materially misleading failures to disclose information. Frank (F)'s incomplete disclosure on shoplifting could lead to Bar declining to admit / license F. A counseling F to conceal on his application is a violation of MRPC's so A breached the duty not to counsel MRPC violations.

(7) Non-Adjudicative Proceedings. A lawyer must disclose representative capacity. A here is posing as a mere concerned citizen and not a paid advocate.

(8) Dishonesty. It is generally impermissible to engage in conduct that is dishonest, prejudicial to the administration of justice, and reflect poorly on our proud and honorable profession. Here all the above lies and misstatements independently violate the MRPCs.

CHAPTER 8

ABA PROFESSIONAL RESPONSIBILITY RULES

Index

Accepting Appointments............... T 8-454

Admission Truthfulness .... T 8-458

Adverse Authority Disclosure .... T 8-445

Advertising................................. T 8-456

Advisor Role .... T 8-443

Advocate Role .... T 8-444, 450

Aggregate Settlements................... T 8-434

Assist Judge in Violation.............. T 8-460

Attorney-Client Privilege .... T 8-428

Bar Admission Matters................. T 8-458

Business Organization Internal
   Reporting................................. T 8-438

Business Transaction with Client.. T 8-432

Candid and Honest Advice............ T 8-440

Candor Towards Tribunal .... T 8-445

   Ex Parte Proceeding .... T 8-446

   False Statement .... T 8-445

   Later Falsity Discover .... T 8-445

Certification Designation .... T 8-457

Choice of Disciplinary Authority.. T 8-460

Client Urging MRPC Violation..... T 8-440

Client Communications................. T 8-423

Communication with
   Represented Persons.................. T 8-451

Compensation for
   Recommendations .... T 8-456

Competence................................. T 8-421

Confidentiality Restraints............. T 8-427

   Exceptions .... T 8-428

Conflict of Interest .... T 8-430

   Direct Adversely .... T 8-430

   Fundamentally Antagonistic ...... T 8-431

   Informed Consent...................... T 8-430

   Materially Limited..................... T 8-430

   No Harm to Relationship............ T 8-430

   Organizational Clients............... T 8-431

   Prior Client .... T 8-429

Contingency Fee Agreement......... T 8-426

   Prohibited Matters .... T 8-426

   Writing Requirement.................. T 8-426

Corporate Client .... T 8-438

Counsel a Crime or Fraud .... T 8-422

Court Appointment....................... T 8-429

Criminal Act by Lawyer............... T 8-459

Diligence .... T 8-423

Decisions – Client and Lawyer...... T 8-422

Decorum of Tribunal .... T 8-447

Depositions of Third Parties.......... T 8-451

Diminished Capacity .... T 8-438

Direct Solicitation........................ T 8-456

Directing Lawyer's Judgment .... T 8-433

Disciplinary Matters .... T 8-458

Disclosing Confidences .... T 8-428

Discovery of Lawyer .... T 8-449

Dishonesty or Fraud .... T 8-460

Disqualification .... T 8-436

Double Billing .... T 8-425

Emergency Situation .... T 8-421

Escrow Funds .... T 8-439

Evaluation for Third Party............ T 8-444

Ex Parte Proceedings.................... T 8-446

Expediting Litigation.................... T 8-445

External Fee Splits........................ T 8-427

Exculpatory Evidence Disclosure.. T 8-449

False Statement by Lawyer .... T 8-450

False Statements About Judges ..... T 8-458

Fair Warning to Prospective
   Clients..................................... T 8-442

Fairness to Opposing Party............ T 8-446

   Discovery Standards.................. T 8-446

   Interference with Evidence......... T 8-446

   Falsify Evidence .... T 8-446

   Trial Abuses...................... T 8-446, 447

   Witness Inducement .... T 8-446

Fees... T 8-424

   Agreement Required................... T 8-423

   Contingencies .... T 8-426

   Cost Treatment .... T 8-426

   Divisions of Fees .... T 8-427

   Locality Average .... T 8-424

   Reasonable Factors..................... T 8-424

   Referral Services .... T 8-456

   Share with Non-Lawyer .... T 8-452

Fields of Practice Communication T 8-457

Financial Assistance to Clients...... T 8-433

Firm Names and Letterheads......... T 8-457

Former Client Conflicts................ T 8-435

Former Judge or Neutral............... T 8-437

Frivolous Position........................ T 8-444

Future Death Disclosure .... T 8-428

Gifts from Clients........................T 8-432
Good Faith Argument ....T 8-444
Government to Private Practice .....T 8-437
Governmental Organization Client T 8-438
Holding Public Office ....T 8-457
Human Future Death......................T 8-428
Improper Government Influence....T 8-460
Improper Judicial Influence ....T 8-447
Improper Political Contributions....T 8-458
Imputed Disqualifications ....T 8-436
Inadvertently Sent Documents ....T 8-451
Independence of Lawyer........T 8-443, 452
Information About Legal Services .T 8-455
    Advertising...................................T 8-455
    Comparisons................................T 8-455
    Unjustified Expectations ....T 8-455
Informed Consent........................T 8-430
Insurance Company Fee Payments T 8-433
Intermediary Role ....T 8-443
IRS Form 8300.............................T 8-429
Law Firm and Associations...........T 8-451
    Associate Responsibility ....T 8-452
    Non-Lawyer Assistants ....T 8-452
    Partner Responsibilities..............T 8-451
    Supervisor's Responsibilities......T 8-452
Law Reform Activities...................T 8-455
Law-Related Services ....T 8-454
Lawyer Board Member ....T 8-431
Lawyer Defendant..........................T 8-428
Lawyer Outside State ....T 8-460
Legal Malpractice...........................T 8-422
Legal Services Organization ....T 8-455
Limiting Liability – Prospective ....T 8-434
Literary and Media Rights ....T 8-432
Malpractice Settlement....................T 8-434
Mediation ....T 8-444
Meritorious Claims ....T 8-444
Misconduct.....................................T 8-459
Multi-Jurisdiction Practice ....T 8-453
Multiple Law Offices ....T 8-457
Neutral Role ....T 8-444
No Further Representation Clause .T 8-454
Noisy Withdrawal ....T 8-441
Non-Adjudicative Proceedings ......T 8-450
Non-Compete Agreements..............T 8-454
Non-Profit Limited Representation T 8-455
Office Sharing ....T 8-434, 455
Opinion Letters ....T 8-444
Opinion Withdrawal.......................T 8-444
Organizational Clients............T 8-431, 438
Partnership with Non-Lawyer........T 8-452
Personal Opinion During Trial.......T 8-447

Political Contributions...................T 8-458
Post-Conviction Duty.....................T 8-450
Practice with Non-Lawyer ....T 8-453
Pro Bono Service............................T 8-454
Prohibited Client Transactions......T 8-432
Prohibited Trial Publicity ....T 8-447
Professional Misconduct ....T 8-458
Proficiency Required......................T 8-421
Property of Client ....T 8-439
Proprietary Interest in Claim.........T 8-434
Prosecutor's Responsibilities ....T 8-449
Prospective Clients................ T 8-439, 442
Public Office .... T 8-457, 460
Public Organization Client ....T 8-455
Public Service.................................T 8-454
Recommendation for
    Compensation.............................T 8-456
Related Attorneys..........................T 8-431
Reporting Misconduct........... T 8-458, 459
Reporting up in Organization T 8-431, 438
Representation Withdrawal............T 8-429
Represented Person ....T 8-450
Reservation of Rights Clause ....T 8-433
Retainers and Advances ....T 8-439
Safeguarding Property....................T 8-438
Safety Information..........................T 8-448
Sarbanes-Oxley Act............... T 8-429, 441
Sale of Law Practice......................T 8-442
Screening.............................. T 8-436, 437
Scope of Representation................T 8-422
Sexual Relations with Clients ....T 8-435
Solicitations of Prospective Clients T 8-456
Subsequent Discovery of Falsity...T 8-445
Termination of Representation......T 8-440
Third Party Claims to Funds ....T 8-439
Third Party Fee Payors..................T 8-433
Third Party Neutral........................T 8-444
Third Party Rights ....T 8-451
Trade Names for Law Firms ....T 8-457
Trial Publicity Prohibited..............T 8-447
Trust Accounts ....T 8-439
Truthfulness in Statements ....T 8-450
Unauthorized Practice of Law.......T 8-453
Unlicensed Practice Practicality....T 8-460
Unauthorized Practice ....T 8-453
Unrepresented Person....................T 8-451
Using Information Disadvantaging
    the Client ....T 8-432
Whistleblowing .... T 8-427, 438
Withdrawals ....T 8-440
Witness-Lawyer Conflict ....T 8-448
Written Solicitation ....T 8-457

CHAPTER 9

COMMON LAW

CONTRACTS AND

UCC SALES

CHAPTER 9

COMMON LAW CONTRACTS AND UCC SALES

Table of Contents

A.   Sub-Topic Exam Issue Distribution .... Text 9-485

B.   MEE Subject Coverage 9-489

    I.   Opening Argument 9-489

    2.   Primary Issue Statements 9-489

    3.   Text .... MBE Volume 1

    4   Magic Memory Outlines® .... MBE Volume 1

C.   Common Law Contracts and UCC Sales Essay Questions 9-493

D.   Common Law Contracts and UCC Sales Essay Answers 9-497

E.   Acronyms 15-632

CONTRACTS & UCC SALES

Beginning in 2010 we have distributed all NCBE Contracts and UCC Sales essay questions released since they began testing the subject.

	2/09	7/08	2/08	7/07
OPENING ARGUMENT				
Common Law Applies – Contracts for Services, Intangibles, or Real Estate		/		/
UCC Article II – Contracts for Sales		/		/
FORMATION				
Requirements for Contracts: **OACLLS**				/
Offer and Acceptance (general)				/
Material Terms Objectively Definite & Certain				/
Intent to be Bound				/
Unilateral Contracts				
Rejection & Counter Offer				//
Mirror Image Rule				/
Form of Acceptance				/
Acceptance Timing (Mailbox rule)				/
CONSIDERATION				
Mutual Promise Ok for Bilateral Ks				
Pre-existing Duty				
Legal Claim Surrender				
Required for Modification				
LEGAL CAPACITY				
Intoxication				
Infants				
LEGAL SUBJECT MATTER				
Public Policy Violation				
Non-Compete Agreements				

	2/09	7/08	2/08	7/07
STATUTE of FRAUDS				
Can be Performed Within One Year				/
Part Performance Resulting in Windfall				/
Integration/Merger				
PERFORMANCE				
Objective Standard for Satisfactory Performance		/		
Mistakes		/		
Mutual Mistakes		/		
Unilateral Mistakes		/		
Fraud in the Inducement & Fraud in Factum		/		
Non-Fraudulent Misrepresentation; Misrepresentation by Omission		/		
Interpretation & Ambiguity		/		
Parol Evidence Rule		/		
Conditions Precedent & Subsequent				
Time of the Essence				
Substantial Performance				
Excusable Non-Performance				
Frustration of Purpose		/		
Subsequent Illegality or Incapacity				
Impossibility and Impracticability		/		
Allocation of Risk				
Accord and Satisfaction				
Novation, Cancellation or Waiver				
Void Versus Voidable				

	2/09	7/08	2/08	7/07
BREACH of CONTRACT				
Anticipatory Repudiation				/
Divisibility of Contract				/
REMEDIES				
Money Damages		/		/
Compensatory/ Expectation Profits/ Benefit of Bargain		/		
Position Materially Changed in Reliance		/		
Foreseeable & Not Speculative (Reasonably Certain)		/		
Mitigation Duty		/		
Incidental Damages		/		
Consequential Damages		/		
No Punitive Damages				
Restitution & Rescission				
Specific Performance				/
Promissory Estoppel				
Quantum Meruit/ Quasi Contract		/		
Unjust Enrichment				
Statute of Limitations				
Third Party Beneficiaries				
Creditor Beneficiary				
Donee (gift) Beneficiary				
Incidental Beneficiary- No Recovery				
Assignment or Delegation of Contractual Duty		/		
Delgator remains Liable				
Marital Community Liability				
Apparent Authority				
Joinder not Required				

OPENING ARGUMENT AND PRIMARY ISSUES

COMMON LAW CONTRACTS AND UCC SALES

The following material is a brief overview of some, but not all, of the key issues in Common Law Contracts and UCC Sales. Candidates in jurisdictions that administer MEE essays on the six MBE subjects should consult the two-volume *Rigos Bar Review Series – MBE* Volume 1 at page 1-23 for complete textual coverage and Magic Memory Outlines® software. These books and other Rigos Bar Review Series publications are sold at law school bookstores throughout the nation and online at http://lawschool.aspenpublishers.com.

There are a few thoughts that should usually be stated at the beginning of every answer. These will score you easy points and let the grader know you are in the right topic area.

Most essays should have an "opening argument": a brief, broad statement that shows you understand the broad significance of a legal topic. The opening argument also suggests to the grader that she is about to read a thoughtful and well-organized essay.

Many subjects also have "primary issues" that can be discussed up front or integrated into the essay answer. IMPORTANT: Do not merely regurgitate these statements on the exam without addressing the issues actually raised by the facts, or you will not pass.

- **Contracts Opening Argument:** The common law of contracts governs contracts for services, intangibles, and real estate, but the court may apply a UCC Article 2 "goods" provision by analogy. UCC Article 2 eases strict common law contract requirements to provide more certainty in goods transactions.

- **Sample Primary Issue Statements:**

  - A bargained for exchange contract requires an offer expressing definite terms, present willingness and intention to be bound, acceptance by the intended offeree before revocation, consideration in the form of a benefit reserved by the promisor or detriment incurred by the promisee, legal capacity of the parties, legal subject matter, and compliance with the statute of frauds.

  - Acceptance may be express or implied. A bargained for exchange contract requires the trilogy of offer, acceptance, and consideration or implied by performance of the parties, so the last communication of terms between the parties would control under "the master of the bargain" or "last shot" theory.

  - Additional consistent terms in an acceptance do not violate the "mirror image rule" and therefore are not a rejection. Usually they are if treated as a mere inquiry or request. Demand for inclusion may be a rejection.

  - Consideration is a benefit received by the promisor or a detriment incurred by the promise. The statute of frauds applies to contracts performed over one year, over $500 if for UCC goods (except part performance, admission by D, written M to M confirmation, or specially manufactured goods), land sale or lease over one year, and suretyship promises.

- The parol evidence rule (PER) excludes extrinsic evidence to show intent that contradicts the terms of a final written "integrated" contract. Exceptions which may be introduced include defects in formation, UCC performance, dealings, and trade terms, condition precedent unfulfilled, ambiguity clarification, and subsequent modifications.

- Valid excuses for nonperformance include: cooperation withheld, illegality, source of supply destroyed, subject matter destroyed, and failure of a presupposed condition.

- Remedies available to the non-breaching party include money damages, rescission, specific performance, declaratory judgment, accounting, injunctions, and in quasi-contract recovery. The claim must be filed before the statute of limitations has run.

- Damages must have been reasonably foreseeable by D and established with reasonable certainty by P. The non-breaching party has a duty to mitigate.

- **UCC Opening Argument:** UCC Article 2 eases strict common law contract requirements to provide more certainty in goods transactions which are movable.

- **Sample Primary Issue Statements:**

  - The UCC applies to the sale of goods, but a court may apply a UCC provision to the common law.

  - Special provisions apply to "merchants" who are defined as parties who deal with goods of the kind or hold themselves out to have special knowledge or expertise in the goods.

  - All contracting parties must perform in good faith under the UCC. Merchants are held to a higher standard – honesty in fact and reasonable commercial standards of fair dealing.

  - A valid contract requires offer, acceptance (mutual assent), consideration, legal capacity, and legal subject matter. The contract must comply with the Statute of Frauds if the contract is for the sale of goods for $500 and over unless an exception exists such as a merchant confirming memo, specially manufactured goods, admissions, or part performance.

  - Under the UCC, a missing term does not invalidate a contract as long there is reasonable basis to provide a remedy and the contract contains the quantity. The court provides terms with the UCC default rule or in preferential order, course of performance, past course of dealings, and usage of trade.

  - Additional consistent terms between two merchants become part of the contract unless they materially change the essence of the bargain, the offeror objects to their inclusion within a reasonable time, or any changes were precluded in the offer.

- Upon a buyer's breach, a seller may cancel and sue for the difference between the contract and market price derived from a commercially reasonable resale of the goods and incidental damages.

- A "perfect tender" is required and a buyer may accept none, all, or any commercially reasonable portion of a non-conforming shipment.

- A buyer's remedies after rightful rejection is to "cover" their requirements by purchasing equivalent substitute goods elsewhere and recover the difference between the "cover" and contract price together with incidental and consequential damages.

RIGOS BAR REVIEW SERIES

UNIFORM MULTISTATE ESSAY EXAM (MEE) REVIEW

CHAPTER 9

COMMON LAW CONTRACTS AND UCC SALES

Essay Questions

Question Number 1

Able purchased a house with a majestic formal living room. The previous owners had left the living room carpet rather dirty, so Able decided to have it cleaned. He did some research and determined that the industry average price for carpet cleaning in his town was $.15 per square foot.

On October 1st, he sent an email with the following text to various local carpet cleaning companies: "I'm soliciting bids for a carpet cleaning job in my living room. The dimensions of the carpet are 50 feet by 20 feet. I'd like to have this done during the week of November 19th. I'm at 1776 Independence Drive. If you're interested, please respond to me with your best price."

The next day, Baker replied to Able's email: "We can do that for you. Our rate is $.30 per square foot, so it'd be $300 for your living room. Do we have a deal?" Able immediately responded with, "I'm afraid that's more than I was planning on spending. I really don't want to pay more than $100." Insulted and feeling that Able was trying to "lowball" him, Baker decided not to continue the negotiations.

During the next few weeks, Baker began experiencing cash flow problems and regretted that he had broken off negotiations with Able. Figuring that $100 was better than nothing, Baker printed out Able's original email, wrote "$100" on it, and stuck it in his appointment book.

On the morning of November 19th, Baker went to Able's house. Able was surprised to see Baker, but figured that since they'd never reached an agreement, he could get a free carpet cleaning if he kept quiet. Baker gave the carpet a thorough cleaning and told Able, "I'll send you the bill in the mail." When the bill for $100 arrived, Able replied with a letter that said, "Sorry, but we had no deal. Maybe this will teach you a lesson about trying to overcharge customers."

Baker has filed a lawsuit against Able. What, if anything, can Baker recover? Explain.

Question Number 2

On July 1st, the purchasing manager at SuperOffice, a retailer that sells office supplies and equipment, made a telephone call to VividView, a manufacturer and wholesaler of computer monitors. The manager placed an oral order for 100 monitors at VividView's standard wholesale price of $100 each, to be delivered no later than August 31st. VividView immediately faxed an order confirmation back to SuperOffice that accurately reflected the agreed-upon quantity and price. The confirmation also stated, "VividView reserves the right to deliver the merchandise to SuperOffice in multiple lots."

On July 15th, SuperOffice received a shipment from VividView. Upon discovering that VividView had sent only 50 monitors, SuperOffice's purchasing manager called VividView to complain. The VividView sales representative responded, "We've still got a month and a half to get the rest of the monitors to you. Look at your order confirmation, and you'll see our standard clause about multiple shipments. In fact, the freight company just picked up the other 50 monitors yesterday, and you should have them in a week or so."

The purchasing manager angrily replied, "I don't care what the confirmation says! That wasn't part of our deal. I have a very low tolerance for suppliers who pull bait-and-switch scams on us. Cancel the rest of the order, because we're taking our business elsewhere!" After hanging up the phone, the purchasing manager sent VividView a check for $5,000 to pay only for the monitors already delivered.

    1.   What rights and remedies does SuperOffice have against VividView, if any? Explain.

    2.   What rights and remedies does VividView have against SuperOffice, if any? Explain.

Question Number 3

Charlie is a concert promoter and booking agent in Anystate. Every Labor Day weekend, he stages a large outdoor music festival called Rockapaloopa. Charlie hired the world-famous band Purple Freud to headline the 2008 event for $100,000. The written contract between Charlie and Purple Freud, executed six months before the festival, provided that the band would perform their best-selling album *Long Flight of the Loon* in its entirety. The contract ended with a clause stating, "This contract is the final, total agreement between the parties."

Purple Freud concerts typically feature an extravagant laser light show. The contract specified that Purple Freud was responsible for any "lights, lasers, or other visual effects, if any," that would accompany the music. Accordingly, Purple Freud entered into a contract with a company called Professional FX that agreed to provide and operate lasers during the concert in exchange for $10,000.

A month before the concert, the Anystate legislature passed a "light pollution" statute that banned, among other things, outdoor laser displays. Purple Freud suggested that a stunning high-tech video display would be a sufficient substitute, but Professional FX declined, even though it was capable of providing such a display, and told the band that it would not be rendering any services.

Shortly thereafter, Purple Freud contacted Charlie and explained that they'd never performed *Long Flight of the Loon* without a visual show and felt that such a performance would not provide "the complete *Long Flight* experience." In exchange for a reduction of the performance fee to $50,000, Charlie orally agreed that the band could instead perform one of its lesser-selling albums, *Glad That You're Gone*.

When the media reported that Purple Freud would not be performing *Long Flight of the Loon* at Rockapaloopa, many people who were planning on purchasing tickets decided not to attend the festival. A week before the event, almost half of the available Rockapaloopa tickets remained unsold. Charlie called Purple Freud's manager and demanded that they play *Long Flight of the Loon* per the original contract. When the band's manager protested that Charlie had already allowed the band to play *Glad That You're Gone* instead, Charlie replied, "You should have gotten that in writing. Our written agreement says your band will play *Long Flight of the Loon*, and that's what you're going to play, with or without lasers."

1. If Charlie sues Purple Freud for a court order of specific performance requiring the band to perform *Long Flight of the Loon*, who will prevail? Explain.

2. If Purple Freud sues Professional FX for damages, who will prevail? Explain.

Question Number 4

Henry owns and operates a farm with a large chicken coop for the purpose of selling eggs and poultry at wholesale. Sam, who runs a nearby grocery store, called Henry and asked to purchase 50 cartons of Grade AA eggs. Henry quoted a price of 50 cents per carton and said that he could get the eggs to Sam in two days. Sam agreed and asked Henry to send the bill via mail.

Two days later, Henry delivered the eggs to Sam's grocery store, left them on the loading dock, and drove away. When Sam went to the loading dock an hour later to start carrying the eggs inside, he noticed that Henry had delivered Grade B eggs, which are almost never sold directly to retail consumers due to quality issues. Grade B eggs are typically purchased by bakeries, foodservice providers, and manufacturers of food products that contain eggs.

An angry Sam immediately called Henry to demand that Henry take away and replace the substandard eggs. Henry's voice mail picked up the call and answered with the following greeting: "Hi, you've reached Henry. I've gone on vacation to the Caribbean for the next month. There's no phone service where I'm staying, but please leave me a message, and I'll get back to you after I return on September 1st." Sam left the following voice mail: "Henry, this is Sam. I ordered Grade AA eggs, and you sent me Grade B eggs. That wasn't our deal. I'm returning the eggs to your farm."

Sam hung up the phone and went outside for a walk to calm down. He encountered his friend Roger, who operates a local restaurant. Roger asked, "Why the long face?" Sam replied, "You know Henry, the chicken farmer? He sold me Grade B eggs when I specifically ordered Grade AA. If they were Grade A, I probably could sell them, but Grade B is unacceptable."

"You're in luck," said Roger. "I've been hired to prepare and serve a large brunch this Sunday. The main course will be omelets, and I usually use Grade B for those. I could take up to 50 cartons off your hands at 25 cents each." "Thanks for the offer," replied Sam. "But I don't want to send the wrong message to Henry. When I order Grade AA, I expect to receive Grade AA, and he needs to understand that. When he gets back from vacation, he's going to find a lot of rotten eggs sitting on his front porch."

Sam then returned to his store and called Jerry, another farmer who sold eggs at wholesale. Jerry said he could sell Sam 50 cartons of Grade AA eggs, but the price had increased to 75 cents per carton on the previous day due to an unexpected shortage of eggs caused by the avian influenza (bird flu) virus. Sam reluctantly agreed to buy Jerry's eggs as replacements for Henry's Grade B eggs.

What recourse does Sam have against Henry? Explain.

Question Number 5

In January, anticipating his retirement, 63-year-old Al entered into signed written agreement with Peggy to keep house and care for him at his home in San Francisco, California, for five years, commencing in January 2006, for $12,000 per year.

In February, Al's friend Brad warned Al that Peggy had imminent plans to leave the state. Doubtful about Peggy's dependability, Al wrote her a letter requesting assurance that she "would live up to her end of our bargain." Peggy ignored the letter. Late in February Al told Peggy her services were not needed.

In March, Al entered into a written agreement with Michelle identical to the agreement with Peggy.

In April, embarrassed Brad admitted to Al that he had mistaken Peggy, who was, in fact, a long-time, stable resident, for someone else. Al immediately apologized to Peggy, who demanded compensation. They agreed in writing to settle for $30,000 payable by year-end if Peggy, after reasonable efforts, was unable to find comparable work. In May, after announcing her engagement to a wealthy suitor, Peggy told Al, "Never mind about the $30,000; you need it more than I do."

Michelle started work in June. In July, Al became ill, diagnosed with a condition requiring frequent medication and other specialized ministrations that Al insisted Michelle perform. On August 31, Michelle stopped work, telling Al, "You've always paid me promptly, sir, but I wasn't hired to be a nursemaid."

Al then entered into a written agreement with his niece Suzanne, who promised to provide two years of care at her home in exchange for periodic payment of her $30,000-per-year beauty school tuition during his stay. Al paid $30,000 and moved in. In September Suzanne remodeled a room to accommodate Al's medical requirements. In October Al's medical condition went into remission and he moved in with his sister.

On December 25 Peggy and Suzanne respectively demanded $60,000 and $30,000 from Al. He demanded $60,000 from Michelle. All demands were refused.

Discuss the rights and liabilities of these parties under each agreement.

Essay Answers

Answer Number 1

Issues Raised

(1)   Governing Law
     (a) Common Law
     (b) UCC Article II
(2)   Offer
     (a) Termination of Offer: Rejection
     (b) Counteroffer
     (c) Termination of Offer: Passage of Time
(2)   Quasi-Contract / Quantum Meruit
     (a) Reasonable Expectation
     (b) Recovery Amount
        (i) value of benefit
        (ii) industry standard

Summary

The common law governs contracts for services, but the court may apply UCC Article 2 by analogy. All material terms in an offer must be must be unambiguous, clear, and definite. A valid offer must indicate the offeror's clear intent and willingness to be bound upon acceptance. A mere solicitation for bids (A's first email) is not an offer, but B's reply was. A rejected and thereby terminated Baker's offer. A's statement that he didn't "want to pay more than $100" was not definite enough to constitute a counteroffer, but even if it had, B did not accept timely. Absent an express promise not to revoke, an unaccepted offer terminates within a reasonable time. Even without a contract, B may seek recovery in quasi-contract ("quantum meruit"), if A knowingly received unjust enrichment, and B reasonably expected compensation in good faith. Here, the value of the benefit conferred would be set by the industry standard.

Sample Answer

(1)   Governing Law. Because the parties were negotiating for a service, the common law of contracts governs, although the court may apply the provisions of UCC Article 2 (sale of goods) by analogy.

    (a) Offer. An offer must be unambiguous, clear, and definite on all material terms. It must also indicate the offeror's clear intent and willingness to be bound if the offeree accepts. Mere solicitations seeking bids, such as Able's first email, do not normally constitute an offer. By contrast, Baker's initial reply was an offer, as it contained a specific price based upon the details of the work to be performed and implied that a binding contract would be formed if Able accepted ("Do we have a deal?").

(b) Termination of Offer: Rejection. If instead of accepting, the offeree responds with a refusal or rejection, no contract is formed, and the offer terminates. When Able said that $300 was "more than [he] was planning on spending," he rejected and thereby effectively terminated Baker's offer.

(c) Counteroffer. A rejection that proposes different or additional terms may be a counteroffer if it meets the requirements of an offer. Here, Able said that he didn't "want to pay more than $100." Although this communication proposed different terms, it was likely not definite enough to constitute an offer. Able did not say he was willing to pay a specific price; rather, he indicated what range of prices was acceptable to him. Thus, Able's response was not a counteroffer.

(d) Termination of Offer: Passage of Time. Even if Able's reply had been a counteroffer, Baker failed to accept it, which would have caused any such counteroffer to terminate. Absent an express promise not to revoke, such as an option contract or UCC "firm offer," an offer terminates if it is not accepted within a reasonable amount of time. Here, Baker did nothing for over a month after Able's reply. This passage of time would likely have terminated any counteroffer.

(2) Quasi-Contract / Quantum Meruit. Although no contract was formed, Baker may seek recovery in quasi-contract (a/k/a quantum meruit). The purpose of this equitable remedy is to promote fairness and prevent unjust enrichment. Able knowingly received a benefit from Baker (i.e., the carpet cleaning), and Baker had an expectation of being compensated.

(a) Reasonable Expectation. To recover in quasi-contract, the plaintiff's expectation of compensation must be reasonable. Arguably, Baker's expectation of payment was not reasonable because he initially chose to ignore Able's suggestion of a lower price and ended the negotiations. Nonetheless, the facts suggest that Baker acted with little bad faith, if any. When Baker arrived at Able's house, Able could have simply turned him away. Instead, Able invited Baker in with the culpable intent of getting a free carpet cleaning. Under the circumstances, Baker's expectation of payment for the work was most likely reasonable.

(b) Recovery Amount. A plaintiff who prevails under a quasi-contract theory is entitled to the value of the benefit provided to the defendant, regardless of what the contract price (if any) might have been. Since the local industry average for carpet cleaning was $.15 per square foot, and Able's carpet was 1,000 square feet, the court would likely award Baker $150 for cleaning Able's carpet as the value of the work done.

Answer Number 2

Issues Raised

(1) Governing Law
    (a) Common Law
    (b) UCC Article II, Sales
(2) Merchant v. Casual Party
(3) Statute of Frauds: Written Merchant to Merchant Confirmations
(4) Delivery Terms

(a) Acceptance with Demand for Different Terms
(b) Merchant to Merchant
(5)   Breach: Anticipatory Repudiation
(6)   Seller's Remedies: Lost Profit Remedy

Summary

UCC Article 2 governs the sale of goods, supplemented by the common law. If either party is a merchant (one who deals in the specified type of goods, or holds himself out as an expert as to the goods), as VV and SO here, special rules apply. The SOF states that sales contracts for more than $500 must be in writing, but a written merchant-to-merchant confirmation sent within 10 days of an oral contract satisfies this unless there is an objection. VV faxed a confirmation the day of the order, thus satisfying the SOF. All goods must be tendered in a single delivery unless the parties agree otherwise. The UCC does not require acceptance to be a "mirror image" of the offer. Merchant-merchant contracts, as here, may add minor terms in the acceptance unless the other party objects within a reasonable time. SO likely breached contract, as SO accepted only half the agreed goods. Anticipatory repudiation applies, and VO may immediately suspend performance and sue for damages (lost profit).

Sample Answer

(1)   Governing Law. UCC Article 2 governs the sale of goods. The common law of contracts supplements the UCC provisions where Article 2 is silent.

(2)   Merchant v. Casual Party. Article 2 has special provisions that may apply if one or both parties to a contract is a "merchant." A merchant is one who deals in the type of goods specified in the contract or holds himself out as an expert having special skill and knowledge with respect to those goods. Wholesalers, such as VividView, and retailers, such as SuperOffice, are usually merchants.

(3)   Statute of Frauds: Written Merchant to Merchant Confirmations. Under the Statute of Frauds (SOF), UCC sales contracts for $500 or more generally must be written. Here, SuperOffice placed an oral $10,000 order, so it is within the SOF. However, the UCC provides that a written merchant-to-merchant confirmation, sent within 10 days of an oral contract, satisfies the writing requirement and binds both parties unless there is an objection. Since VividView faxed a written confirmation to SuperOffice on the same day that SuperOffice placed the order, the parties satisfied the SOF.

(4)   Delivery Terms. Under the UCC, all goods must be tendered in a single delivery unless the parties agree otherwise.

   (a) Acceptance with Demand for Different Terms. The UCC does not follow the common law's rule that an acceptance must always be a "mirror image" of the offer. Here, the acceptance by VividView contained a provision (delivery in multiple lots) not in SuperOffice's order. Absent that change, the UCC default of single delivery would apply.

   (b) Merchant to Merchant. If the contract is between merchants, such as VividView and SuperOffice, a minor additional term in the acceptance becomes part of the contract unless the other party objects within a reasonable amount of time. An additional term is "minor" if it does not materially alter the bargain. The additional term here, which allowed VividView to deliver the monitors in multiple shipments, probably does not materially alter the parties' bargain. SuperOffice asked for delivery before August 31st, and as long as VividView delivered all 100 monitors by that date, it would be hard to identify any meaningful harm suffered by SuperOffice. Because SuperOffice did not object until after two weeks had passed, the clause permitting delivery in multiple shipments became part of the contract and trumped the UCC default rule of single delivery. Accordingly, SuperOffice has no recourse against VividView.

(5) Breach: Anticipatory Repudiation. By contrast, VividView has a claim against SuperOffice for breach of contract. SuperOffice agreed to buy 100 monitors, but accepted only 50 and told VividView it would not buy or pay for any more. When a party unambiguously expresses its intent not to render any performance due, the other party may immediately suspend its performance and sue for damages.

(6) Seller's Remedies: Lost Profit Remedy. Under the UCC, when a buyer breaches a contract by refusing to accept goods, and the seller routinely sells the same goods at the same price to all buyers, the seller's remedy is the lost profit. Here, since VividView sells monitors at wholesale and charges a "standard price," the lost profit remedy is appropriate for the 50 monitors that VividView refused to accept.

Answer Number 3

Summary

The common law governs contracts for services, but the court may apply UCC Article 2 by analogy. The PER excludes evidence of prior or contemporaneous extrinsic discussions or agreements that contradict the terms of a written "integrated" contract, but not subsequent modifications (if supported by consideration), as here. The SOF requires only certain types of contracts/ modifications to be written; none apply here, so the modification need not have been in writing. Specific performance is not generally awarded as a remedy for personal service contracts. Even though Professional FX refused to provide contracted services nonperformance was excusable because subsequent legislation barred legal performance.

Issues Raised

(1) Governing Law
    (a) Common Law
    (b) UCC Article II, Sales
(2) Parol Evidence Rule
    (a) Integration
    (b) Subsequent Modifications
    (c) Statute of Frauds
(3) Remedies: Specific Performance
(4) Excusable Nonperformance: Illegality After Formation

Sample Answer

(1) Governing Law. Contracts for services, such as performing at a concert, are governed by the common law of contracts. The court may also apply the provisions of UCC Article 2 by analogy.

(2) Parol Evidence Rule. The parol evidence rule (PER) excludes evidence of prior or contemporaneous extrinsic discussions or agreements that contradict the terms of a written "integrated" contract.

(a) Integration. A contract is integrated if the parties intend it to be the final expression of their entire agreement concerning the included terms. A "merger clause," such as the one at the end of the contract between Charlie and Purple Freud, will generally be sufficient to raise the PER.

(b) Subsequent Modifications. The PER does not bar evidence of subsequent modifications to an integrated contract, even if the modification conflicts with the original contract. Common-law contracts, such as the one between the promoter and the band, require modifications to be supported by consideration (a benefit to the promisor or a detriment to the promisee) on both sides. Here, both Charlie and Purple Freud gave consideration sufficient to support the oral modification. Charlie benefited by a 50% reduction in the performance fee, which was detrimental to the band. Purple Freud benefited by being allowed to change the music it would play to something it felt was more appropriate, which was a detriment to the promoter because the substituted music was less popular and generated fewer ticket sales. Thus, the oral modification to the performance contract is effective, and Charlie has no grounds for a lawsuit based upon the band's intent to play *Glad That You're Gone* instead of *Long Flight of the Loon*. Purple Freud will prevail.

(c) Statute of Frauds. Charlie's argument that the modification should have been written has no merit. The Statute of Frauds requires only the following types of contracts (or contract modifications) to be written: contracts with marriage as consideration, contracts that expressly require performance for over one year, UCC sales of goods for $500 or more, land sales/leases, and suretyship promises. Because a contract to perform a concert is not within any of those categories, the modification concerning the music to be performed did not need to be written.

(3) Remedies: Specific Performance. Charlie's lawsuit will also lose because it seeks an order of specific performance. Such a remedy is generally not available to enforce a personal service contract, such as a band's agreement to perform a concert, due to practical and constitutional problems with involuntary servitude.

(4) Excusable Nonperformance: Illegality After Formation. Professional FX would prevail if sued by Purple Freud. Even though Professional FX refused to provide any services to the band, despite having earlier contracted to do so, the nonperformance was excusable. If legislation enacted after contract formation (such as the "light pollution" statute here) prevents a party from performing its duties legally (here, operating an outdoor laser show), the contract is discharged.

Answer Number 4

Summary

UCC Article 2 governs the sale of goods, supplemented by the common law. If either party is a merchant (one who deals in the specified type of goods, or holds himself out as an expert as to the goods), as H, J, and S here, special rules apply. UCC Art. 2 requires sellers to make a "perfect tender," not merely substantial performance. If the seller delivers non-conforming goods, the buyer may accept them all, reject them all, or accept some and reject the rest. The eggs were non-conforming goods, so S's rejection was proper. S had a right to inspect goods; doing so within an hour of delivery was fine. Rejection must specify reasons and must be communicated within a reasonable time. S properly rejected here, even though H did not get the message. Breach is generally remedied by money damages: the difference between the market price for substitute goods purchased ("cover"), here $12.50. S's recovery may be reduced because he failed to mitigate damages. Even upon rejection, a buyer has a duty to make a reasonable effort to sell perishable non-conforming goods on behalf of the seller.

Issues Raised

(1) Governing Law
    (a) Common Law
    (b) UCC Article II, Sales
(2) Merchant v. Casual Party
(3) Perfect Tender Rule
    (a) Inspection Right
    (b) Communication of Rejection
(4) Remedies
    (a) Cover Damages
    (b) Damage Mitigation: Merchant

Sample Answer

(1) Governing Law. Contracts for the sale of goods, such as the contract between Henry and Sam, are governed by Article 2 of the UCC. If the UCC is silent on a particular issue, the court will apply the common law of contracts.

(2) Merchant v. Casual Party. UCC Article 2 contains special provisions that apply when one or both parties is a "merchant." A merchant is one who deals in goods of that type or holds himself out as an expert with special knowledge and skill related to the goods at issue. Wholesalers, such as Henry and Jerry, and retailers, such as Sam, are usually deemed to be merchants.

(3) Perfect Tender Rule. UCC Article 2 rejects the common-law rule of substantial performance and requires that a seller make a "perfect tender" of the goods in full conformity with the contract specification. If the seller delivers goods that do not conform to the contract, the buyer may accept them all, reject them all, or accept some and reject the rest. Here, the goods did not conform to the contract between Henry and Sam because the contract called for Class AA eggs, and Henry sent Class B eggs, which are generally unacceptable for retail sale. Sam's rejection of Henry's eggs was proper.

    (a) Inspection Right. A buyer has a reasonable right to inspect goods before payment or acceptance. Sam acted within his rights when he inspected the eggs just an hour after delivery.

    (b) Communication of Rejection. A buyer who rejects non-conforming goods must do so within a reasonable amount of time, communicate the rejection to the seller, and specify why the goods do not conform. Here, Sam properly communicated his rejection by immediately calling Henry after the inspection and complaining that the eggs were a lower grade than what he ordered. Even though Henry would not actually receive the voice mail rejection until after a month had passed, Sam's rejection was sufficient because Henry had left on vacation and was (by his own admission) unreachable. Further, Sam followed Henry's specific instruction for callers to leave a voice mail message.

(4)   Remedies. The usual remedy for breach of a UCC sale of goods contract is money damages.

(a) Cover Damages. When the seller breaches the contract, the buyer may "cover" by purchasing equivalent goods from another supplier at a commercially reasonable price. The buyer's damage amount is the difference between the market price for the substitute goods (at the time the buyer learned of the breach) and the contract price. Here, the market price for 50 cartons of eggs was $37.50 when Sam discovered that Henry's eggs were deficient, but Sam had contracted to buy them for $25.00. Therefore, Sam's cover damage amount is $12.50.

(b) Damage Mitigation: Merchant. However, Sam's recovery may be reduced because he failed to mitigate his damages. When a merchant buys perishable goods, such as eggs, that are non-conforming, and the seller provides no instructions to the buyer (e.g., returning them immediately), the buyer must make a reasonable effort to sell them on behalf of the seller. Sam made no effort at all to sell. In fact, Sam had a willing buyer for the Class B eggs, but he declined to sell to Roger because he wanted to "send a message" to Henry.

Answer Number 5

Summary

The common law governs personal service contracts but the court may apply UCC Article 2 by analogy. Here a request for assurances would be allowed after repudiation. The accord had consideration but the implied condition precedent was not met. Breach allows a claim for compensatory damages including incidental and consequential damages.

Issues Raised

(1)   Governing Law
(2)   Formation Proper
(3)   Non-Performance Assurances
(4)   Modification v. Accord and Satisfaction
(5)   Michelle Contract
    (a) Repudiation and Breach
    (b) Materiality of Breach
    (c) Damages
(6)   Suzanne's Damage

Sample Answer

(1)   Governing Law. The common law governs contracts for services although a court may apply a UCC provision to a common law contract dispute through analogy.

(2)   Al (A) v. Peggy (P) – Formation Proper. A valid contract requires mutual assent including the trilogy of offer and acceptance and consideration. A contract that cannot be performed within 1 year must be in writing and signed by the defendant to satisfy the statute of frauds. The agreement between A and P appears to satisfy these requirements.

(3) Non-Performance Assurances. When one party has grounds to reasonably believe the other will not contractually perform, the insecure party may request assurances. If reasonable assurances of performance are not received within a reasonable time, the party may treat the contract as cancelled. This is not a common law rule, but the court may apply the assurance requirement by analogy. Al was thus entitled to cancel the contract.

(4) Modification v. Accord and Satisfaction. A modification is an agreed revision of contractual terms that discharges the original agreement. An accord is a new agreement (the accord) and satisfaction is discharge by payment of the reduced sum. The original obligations are not discharged until the accord and satisfaction is completed. A novation is substitution of new contractual parties for old ones. Both modification and novation require new consideration, which can be an agreement not to further pursue a dispute about the original terms. Because the agreement (the original one) was already cancelled, the agreement between Al and Peggy for $30,000 was most likely an accord and satisfaction.

Peggy Recovery. Because the condition precedent (her making reasonable efforts to find work) does not seem to have occurred, she cannot demand that Al perform under the $30,000 agreement. Performance is only due when there are no conditions to be satisfied or excused. Al rightly treated her failure to respond to his request for assurances as a material breach, entitling him to suspend his own performance, Peggy cannot recover under the original agreement. In any event, since Peggy is the one who has ensured that the condition precedent under the accord and satisfaction has not occurred, the original obligations have not sprung back. She cannot recover from Al.

(5) Michelle Contract. See contract formation discussion supra rule above. Here there is a valid contract.

(a) Michelle Repudiate. Breach is non-performance when performance is due. Repudiation is a clear expression that one party does not intend to perform. The breach here is material and allows the other party to suspend its own performance since it goes to the heart of the bargain. Michelle repudiated when she quit work. Her performance was not discharged by impossibility, impracticability, or frustration because she should have foreseen that an elderly man might get sicker. It does not seem impossible or unduly burdensome to keep doing what she was originally hired to do while refusing to do the extra / new tasks.

(b) Al's Damages. Any breach no matter how slight entitles the other party to compensatory damages measured by the expectation interest, or where he would have been had the contract been performed. Al can recover the costs he paid Suzanne minus the amount paid to Michelle under the contract. He is also entitled to both incidental and consequential damages that were certain, foreseeable, and unavoidable through mitigation.

(6) Contract with Suzanne. See contract formation rules supra. Consideration is a bargained-for exchange of legal value. If the "periodic" payments were not set and either within Al's discretion or to be determined later, there was no valid contract. Even if there is no contract, Suzanne could recover reliance damages. Promissory estoppel occurs when a party makes a promise that reasonably induces justifiable reliance to the promisee's detriment. Suzanne could recover remodel costs. Or she could recover in quasi-contract the reasonable value of any services provided above the $30,000 paid.

CHAPTER 10

TORTS

RIGOS BAR REVIEW SERIES

UNIFORM MULTISTATE ESSAY EXAM (MEE) REVIEW

CHAPTER 10

TORTS

Table of Contents

A.	Sub-Topic Exam Issue Distribution		10-509
B.	MEE Subject Coverage		10-513
	I.	Opening Argument	10-513
	2.	Primary Issue Statements	10-513
	3.	Text	MBE Volume 1
	4.	Magic Memory Outlines®	MBE Volume 1
C.	Torts Essay Questions		10-515
D.	Torts Essay Answers		10-519
E.	Acronyms		15-636

RIGOS BAR REVIEW SERIES
MEE SUB-TOPIC FREQUENCY DISTRIBUTION

TORTS

Beginning in 2010 we have distributed all NCBE tort essay questions released since they began testing the subject.

	2/09	7/08	2/08	7/07
OPENING ARGUMENT:	/	/		
Intentional Torts				
Transferred Intent: *Intent to commit a tort against P1, resulting in tort against P2*				
Battery: *Intentionally causing harmful or offensive contact with plaintiff's body or connected item*				
Assault: *reasonable apprehension of an immediate harmful or offensive contact*				
False Imprisonment: *intentional confinement/ restraint by physical barriers, threat, or force*				
Trespass to Land: *intentional entry onto land without express/ implied consent;*				
Trespass to Chattels: *intentionally cause harm or use, without taking possession*				
Conversion: *distinguish from trespass to chattels– requires serious interference*				
Intentional Infliction of Emotional Distress				
Defenses to Intentional Torts:				
Self-Defense				
Defense of Others				
Defense of Property				
Mistake of Fact				
Lack of Capacity				
"Reasonable Child" Standard				
Damages for Intentional Torts:				
Punitive Damages				
Community Liability for Intentional Torts				
Negligence (general)	/		/	
A Legal Duty: *reasonable care standard; reasonable person in similar situation*	/		/	
Breach: *reasonable person standard; unreasonable action with foreseeable result*	/		/	
Res Ipsa Loquitur	/		/	

	2/09	7/08	2/08	7/07
Causation & Foreseeability	/		/	
Actual : *"but for"*	/		/	
Proximate Causation: *requires foreseeable plaintiff and foreseeable injury*	/		/	
Superseding Cause/ Negligence of Intervening Third Party				
Harm	/		/	
Damages for Negligence & Mitigation	/		/	
Professional Malpractice: *reasonable specialist standard, e.g., reasonable doctor*				
Rescuers				
Duty to Act With Reasonable Care				
Liability: *breach of duty must lead to greater harm*				
Good Samaritan Defense				
Injury to Good Samaritan / Rescuer				
Professional Standard of Care				
Tortfeasor's Duty to Rescue Victim				
Tortious Interference With a Rescue Effort				
Medical Malpractice				
Medical Battery/ Nonconsensual Medical Procedure: *offensive & harmful contact*				
Respondeat Superior / Vicarious Liability: *employer liability for employees' torts*				
Within Scope of Employment				
Intentional torts not generally 'within scope' unless employer authorized force, friction inherent to job, or employee furthering business interests				
Negligent Supervision: *duty, breach, harm, causation (actual or proximate)*				
Negligent Hiring: *duty, breach, harm, causation (actual or proximate)*				
Independent Contractors				
Land/ Property Owners' Duties to:	//			
Business Invitees	/			
Licensees	/			
Trespassers				
Attractive Nuisance (child)				
Automobile Use & Negligent Entrustment				
Commercial Venders of Alcohol				

	2/09	7/08	2/08	7/07
Comparative Fault & Contributory Negligence	/			
Joint & Several Liability				
Contribution				
Defenses to Negligence: Consent & Assumption of Risk	/		/	
Misrepresentation/Fraud				
Fraud in the Inducement				
Strict Liability			/	
Animals and Strict Liability				
Abnormally Dangerous Activity				
Products Liability (general)			/	
Manufacturer's Liability				
New Product				
Design Defect – RAD				
Risk-Utility Balancing Test				
Strict Products Liability: *if physical harm, manufacturer's due care irrelevant*			/	
Construction/ Manufacturing Defect			/	
Ultra-hazardous Activity				
Warranties			/	
Sellers' Liability			/	
Seller's Negligence: Failure to Warn; Proximate Cause				
Defenses to Product/Seller's Liability			/	
Statute of Limitations				
Assumption of Risk & Indemnification				
Useful Life				
Use of Product in Foreseeable Manner				
Foreseeability of Third Parties Victims			/	
Nuisance				
Defamation: Libel (written) and Slander (spoken)				
Publication of False Statement				
Standards of Intent for Public vs. Private Figure				
Defamation Defenses: *truth; provocation ("hot blood")* and Damages				

	2/09	7/08	2/08	7/07
Invasion of Privacy: *intrusion on private domain; objectionable to reasonable person*				
Consumer Protection Act				
Interference with a Business Expectancy & Trade Libel				
Alienation of Affection				
Interfamilial Immunity; Parental Liability for Children's Torts				

The following material is a brief overview of some, but not all, of the key issues in Torts. Candidates in jurisdictions that administer MEE essays on the six MBE subjects should consult the two-volume *Rigos Bar Review Series – MBE* Volume 1 at page 2-269 for complete textual coverage and Magic Memory Outlines® software. These books and other Rigos Bar Review Series publications are sold at law school bookstores throughout the nation and online at http://lawschool.aspenpublishers.com.

There are a few thoughts that should usually be stated at the beginning of every answer. These will score you easy points and let the grader know you are in the right topic area.

Most essays should have an "opening argument": a brief, broad statement that shows you understand the broad significance of a legal topic. The opening argument also suggests to the grader that she is about to read a thoughtful and well-organized essay.

Many subjects also have "primary issues" that can be discussed up front or integrated into the essay answer. IMPORTANT: Do not merely regurgitate these statements on the exam without addressing the issues actually raised by the facts, or you will not pass.

- **Opening Argument:** The common law of torts protects the interests of those who have suffered harm.

- **Sample Primary Issue Statements:**

  - Intentional torts start with an intentional act (or failure to act) that creates harm. Intent or motive to cause harm is not required, only the intent to commit the act, even if the resulting harm was not intended.

  - Five torts – battery, assault, false imprisonment, trespass to land, and trespass to chattels – expand D's liability through the "transferred intent" doctrine. If D intends one of these five torts and instead (or also) commits a different tort, D will be liable for the other tort as if he actually intended it. Intent may be transferred between victims if the intended consequence is the same.

  - In order for the P to make out a prima facie case of negligence there must exist **a** legal duty to exercise reasonable care to that particular P, a **b**reach of that duty, **c**ausation ("but for" and proximate), and resulting **d**amages.

  - The jury may be instructed to use a balancing test to weigh the risks against any social value created by D's activity. Judge Learned Hand employed an equation weighing D's burden of precaution against the probability of harm (P) times the magnitude of harm that would occur.

  - Creating danger invites rescue and it is foreseeable that a rescuer may herself be injured, or may cause additional injury to P in her rescue attempt. The original tortfeasor is liable for these additional harms.

- In an emergency situation, the standard of care is one of a reasonable person in a similar emergency situation.

- Agency vicarious liability to the employer – "respondeat superior" – applies if the tortious act was within the course and scope of the agency, was in furtherance of the business, or was inherently dangerous. The principal may also be liable if there was negligent hiring or supervision.

- The defense of contributory negligence requires D to take reasonable care to protect himself, similar to assumption of the risk, and is a total bar to recovery under the common law. Comparative fault is now the rule in most states and operates to diminish proportionally the amount P is awarded for damages.

- Fraud is a false statement of a material fact, intention by D that P be misled, reliance by P both "in fact" and objectively reasonable that results in damages.

- Strict liability of D applies to undomesticated dangerous animals, abnormally dangerous activities, and product liability arising from a defective new product sold by a merchant.

- Defamation is an unprivileged false statement of fact concerning P, publicized to a third person, with the requisite intent, thereby exposing the P to hatred, contempt, ridicule, or disgrace and thus damaging P's reputation.

Essay Questions

Question Number 1

Gus applied for a job as a chef at Tamara's Diner. At the interview, Gus told Tamara, the owner, that he had six years of experience as a chef, although he had none, and loved to slave over a hot stove. Tamara was impressed by his work experience and hired him on the spot.

Three days into the job, Gus complained that he hated "slaving over a hot stove", and numerous customers complained about their food. Tamara approached Gus while at work, and in front of her other employees, she yelled, "I don't want any lazy morons working for me! You're fired!"

Gus pleaded his case, but this made Tamara irate. Stepping in front of Gus and waving her finger, Tamara shouted "If I ever see you again, I'll punch your lights out!" Then she grabbed the steak knife out of Gus' hand.

The next day, Gus went to the local kitchen supply store to purchase some equipment to open his own catering business. At the register, Clerk said, "Hey, I heard about you from Tamara – you are a lazy moron and probably a thief too!" Clerk locked the exits to the store and said "You are staying here until the police come." Gus waited patiently for 45 minutes until the police arrived and found he did nothing wrong.

Gus went elsewhere to purchase his equipment, including a state of the art blender manufactured by Studer & Sons. That afternoon while he was making a milkshake, the blade of the blender became dislodged, causing a severe wound to his arm. Gus could not work for two months until his arm healed.

1. Discuss the claims Gus can bring against the following, and the defenses they can assert:

   a. Tamara's Diner

   b. Clerk

   c. Studer & Sons

2. Does Tamara have any recourse against Gus? Explain.

Question Number 2

When Rocco and Stella moved into a new neighborhood, they went to introduce themselves to their neighbors, the Clarkson family. Ignoring the "No Trespassing" sign at the foot of the driveway, they proceeded to the front door and knocked. While waiting for an answer, Stella noticed a shovel leaning against the house, and realizing it would be useful in digging their new garden, she picked it up intending to return it the next day.

Disappointed that no one was home, Rocco and Stella turned to leave, but were instead greeted by Butch, the Clarksons' pet wolf, who growled and bit Rocco on the ankle. They fled the Clarksons' land, shovel in hand.

To make matters worse, Butch's loud and constant howling bothered them so much, they were unable to sleep at night. After two weeks of sleepless nights, Rocco and Stella left a note for the Clarksons that said "Shut that beast up!"

The Clarksons' 12-year-old son Eric, prone to violent tantrums and angered that his pet wolf was called a "beast," began throwing pebbles at Rocco and Stella's window. Instead of hitting the window, one pebble struck Stella who was outside watering the grass. Stella, a hemophiliac, had to be rushed to the hospital for extensive medical treatment.

    1. The Clarksons are upset over their missing shovel. What claims can they bring against Rocco and Stella? Discuss.

    2. What legal claims do Rocco and Stella have against the Clarksons for Butch's behavior? Explain.

    3. Who can Stella sue for her injuries, under what claim, and for what damages?

Question Number 3

Rosie asked Brooke if she could borrow her pickup truck in order to transport her used furniture to a local charity. Brooke was hesitant because of Rosie's propensity for speeding and her numerous prior traffic violations, but decided to give her the keys because it was for a good cause.

That night, Rosie drove carefully and dropped off her furniture. Glad to have the job done, Rosie sped up to 10 miles over the legal speed limit on her drive home. She rounded a curve while taking a freeway exit and lost control of the truck. The truck tumbled off the road and down a hill.

Sherman, witnessing the whole thing, ran down the hill to help, and stumbled in a hole severely spraining his ankle. Rosie emerged dazed, but without a scratch. The truck was wrecked. An ambulance took Sherman to the hospital.

The emergency room physician, Dr. Vera, taped up Sherman's ankle and gave him crutches, but the injury prevented him from opening his new landscaping business for another two months.

1. Can Sherman recover his medical costs? From whom? Explain.

2. Can Sherman recover the income lost from the two-month delay of the opening of his business? From whom? Explain.

3. Discuss any issues of joint & several liability as applied to Sherman's claims.

Question Number 4

Larry Land owned and operated the "Hideaway Bed and Breakfast" which was located on half of his property. The other half was a wooded forest that he left in its natural state and carefully marked with "Keep Out!" signs.

The Hideaway had a swimming pool in the back yard for their paying guests to use. The tiles surrounding the pool were uneven and loose. Larry meant to fix them but was waiting on the delivery of the new tiles.

During a warm summer day, Jeannine Jolly, a paying weekend guest, went with her 8-year-old daughter Karin for a refreshing splash in the pool. When Karin protested, Jeannine told her to go find somewhere to play.

Karin wandered off in to the wooded area of Larry's land. She noticed an old and rotting tree house and began to climb up. Once she set foot inside the tree house, the floorboards gave in and Karin fell to the ground, resulting a large gash on her head that required ten stitches. Hearing her daughter's screams, Jeannine jumped out of the pool, ran across the pool deck, and tripped over a loose tile, cutting her heel and breaking a toe.

When Peter Paramedic arrived to tend to Jeannine, he walked around the Hideaway to reach the swimming pool. As he pushed his way through some bushes, he fell into a sinkhole that Larry did not know existed, spraining his wrist as he pulled himself out. When Peter reached Jeannine, he applied a tourniquet to help ease the bleeding, but left it on for too long, which resulted in permanent nerve damage to her left foot.

Larry thought to himself, "Thank goodness I have all my guests sign a waiver saying they cannot sue me!"

1. Explain Larry's liability to:

   a. Jeannine

   b. Karin

   c. Peter

2. Will Larry's mandatory guest waiver relieve him of liability? Explain.

Question Number 5

Gabriela, an advertising salesperson for KRZY radio, ended her long-time romance with Mario, an advertising salesperson at the local television station. She began dating Theodore, the popular host of a highly-rated KRZY talk show which emphasized family values.

Mario still saw Gabriela at the weekly meetings of the Success for Salespersons support group. At the next meeting, Mario overheard Gabriela saying she was wrapping up an advertising deal with Wild Waters Theme Park worth $50,000 on KRZY radio.

That afternoon, Mario observed Theodore entering an HIV (human immunodeficiency virus) testing clinic. Unbeknownst to Mario, Theodore was researching a story for an upcoming radio program.

Mario tuned in to Theodore's radio program that evening and heard him announce, "Next month I am getting married to my sweetheart Gabriela!" In a jealous rage, Mario phoned into Theodore's show and said on-air, "Have you told Gabriela you got a HIV test this afternoon? And did you know Gabriela wears bunny slippers to bed?" Theodore was stunned and speechless.

Gabriela was listening to the show and became so distressed that she sought psychiatric help. Meanwhile, the ratings for Theodore's show plummeted, and the show was cancelled the next week.

Not satisfied with the damage he already caused, Mario hounded Wild Waters Theme Park to advertise on his television station instead of the radio. Sensing the bitter dispute, Wild Waters decided not to advertise on either KRZY or the television station. Gabriela lost her commission.

1. Does Gabriela have any recourse against Mario for:

   a. her lost deal with Wild Waters? Explain.

   b. her distress? Explain.

2. Discuss the claims, defenses, and potential damages resulting from Mario's on-air remarks in the following law suits:

   a. Theodore v. Mario.

   b. Gabriela v. Mario.

Answer Number 1

Summary

Under the theory of respondeat superior, G can sue the diner for the actions of its agent, T. Causes of action are (1) Defamation/Slander (a false statement of fact, publicized to a third person, with the requisite intent, thereby causing damage). T can argue that the statement was merely her subjective opinion. (2) Assault (an unprivileged, intentional act resulting in a reasonable apprehension of imminent harm or offensive contact). T can argue that a mere finger and a threat was one of a potential future contact did not cause reasonable apprehension. (3) Battery (intentional harmful or offensive contact with a person / object closely associated with same). (4) False imprisonment (intentional, unprivileged confinement of against one's will, leaving no reasonable means of escape). C may try the "shopkeepers privilege" defense (shopkeepers may detain suspected shoplifters for a reasonable amount of time). (5) Strict Products Liability (product was defective by design or manufacturing, was being used in an ordinary manner, and posed an unreasonable risk). (6) Fraud (false statement of material fact intended to mislead, and causing reliance and foreseeable damages).

Issues Raised

(1)   Defamation/Slander
      (a) False statement of fact
      (b) Publicized to a third person
      (c) With the requisite intent
      (d) Thereby causing damage
      (e) Defense: Mere subjective opinion
(2)   Assault
      (a) Intentional, unprivileged act
      (b) Resulting in a reasonable apprehension of imminent harm or offensive contact
(3)   Battery
      (a) Intentional harmful or offensive contact with a person or an object closely associated
      (b) Defenses: defense of property or recapture of chattels
(4)   False Imprisonment
      (a) Intentional, unprivileged confinement of against one's will
      (b) No reasonable means of escape
      (c) Defense: Shopkeeper's Privilege
(5)   Strict Products Liability
      (a) Product was defective by design or manufacturing
      (b) Product was being used in an ordinary manner
      (c) Product posed an unreasonable risk

(6) Fraud
     (a) False statement of material fact
     (b) Intended to mislead

Sample Answer

Because Tamara (T) was acting as an agent of Tamara's Diner, presumably in the course and scope of her duties as owner, Gus can sue the principal, Tamara's Diner for:

(1) Defamation/Slander. T made a false statement of fact ("lazy moron") that was publicized to a third person (T's employees) with a wrongful intention (mere negligence required for private parties here) to expose G to ridicule or contempt that created damage to G's good reputation (known as a thief in town, was refused service at the shop). T will likely be successful in arguing that is not defamation because calling someone lazy or a moron is not a statement of fact, but rather her mere subjective opinion. G may also have trouble showing specific monetary damages.

(2) Assault. Assault is an unprivileged, intentional act resulting in a plaintiff's reasonable apprehension of imminent harm or offensive contact. By angrily stepping close to G, waving a finger at him, and saying she will punch him, T may have assaulted G. However, because T waived a finger as opposed to a fist, and her threat was one of a potential future contact, it is unlikely G had an imminent fear of harm.

(3) Battery. Battery is intentional harmful or offensive contact with the dignity of the person of the plaintiff. This extends to the touching of an object closely associated with the plaintiff. Here, when T grabbed the knife G was holding, she harmfully contacted G without his consent or privilege, thus battering him. T can claim the defense of self although it will fail. While it may have been reasonable force for her to grab the knife away from G, there is no indication G was threatening imminent assault or battery of her. T could argue defense of property or recapture of chattels, since the knife belonged to her business, but this will also fail because there is no indication G was taking the knife.

(4) False Imprisonment. Gus can sue Clerk for false imprisonment, which is the intentional, unprivileged confinement of a plaintiff against his will. Here, Clerk intended to restrict G within the shop by locking all exits, thereby leaving no reasonable means for G to leave. Although G was patient, he did not give consent. Clerk will use the "shopkeepers privilege" defense, which allows merchant shopkeepers to detain a suspected shoplifter for a reasonable amount of time and in reasonable physical confinement to conduct an investigation. Here, Clerk had no reasonable basis to suspect G was shoplifting, nor was 45 minutes a reasonable amount of time to keep him confined.

(5) Strict Products Liability. Gus can sue Studer & Sons, the manufacturer of the blender, for strict products liability. (Note, he could also sue the retailer, provided they are a merchant engaged in the commercial business of selling such products.) The blender was a household product that had a defective condition (either by design or manufacturing) that posed an unreasonable risk, was being used in an ordinary manner without substantial change from its original condition. G can collect damages for his injury, but not lost wages, as only personal injury and a consumer's personal property damages are recoverable under a strict liability theory.

(6)   Fraud. Tamara has claims against Gus for fraud. Fraud is a false statement of material fact intended to mislead the plaintiff, which causes actual reliance and foreseeable damages. Here, G misled T by saying he had years of experience and enjoyed working over the stove and he likely did this to induce T to give him the job. T relied on his statements and caused damage to her business in lost business and unhappy customers.

Answer Number 2

Summary

Cs can sue R and S for (1) trespass to land (physical invasion upon real property without privilege, with no harm required) for walking on Cs' land, (2) trespass to chattels (minor use or intermeddling with another's personal property without consent or privilege) for using Cs' shovel, and (3) conversion (wrongful dominion and control of property, entitling Cs to the full market value). R and S may sue the Cs for (1) negligence under a strict liability theory for the wild animal bite, and (2) nuisance (substantial and unreasonable interference with use or enjoyment of private real property), although R and S may have assumed the risk by "coming to the nuisance." E is liable for his own torts, but his parents may be vicariously liable as they knew of his violence and failed to properly supervise him in the face of foreseeable harm. S may sue for battery (intentional harm or offensive contact) under a transferred intent theory (from the tort of trespass to land – the property was invaded by the thrown pebbles). Damages are presumed for battery and the tortfeasor takes his victim as he finds her so liable for full damages.

Issues Raised

(1)   Trespass to Land
    (a) Unprivileged physical invasion upon real property
    (b) No harm required, just intent to enter land
(2)   Trespass to Chattels
    (a) Minor use or intermeddling with another's personal property
    (b) Without consent or privilege
(3)   Conversion
    (a) Wrongful dominion and control of property
(4)   Negligence: Animal Owners
(5)   Nuisance
(6)   Family Relationships: Parent-Child
(7)   Battery
    (a) Trespass to Land
    (b) Transferred Intent
    (c) Damages

Sample Answer

The Clarksons (Cs) can sue Rocco and Stella (R&S) for trespass to land, trespass to chattels, and conversion.

(1)   Trespass to Land. The tort of trespass to land, an intentional physical invasion on the Clarksons' real property without privilege, occurred when R&S walked on to the Clarkson property despite the "no trespassing" sign. There need not have been an intention to harm or any actual harm caused, just the intent to enter their land.

(2)   Trespass to Chattels. The tort of trespass to chattels occurs when there is minor use or intermeddling with another's personal property without consent or privilege. Here, S did just so by borrowing and using the Clarksons' shovel. However, actual damages must be shown in order to prevail on a trespass to chattels claim, which the Clarksons cannot show. The Clarksons could sue R&S for conversion, which requires a showing that S exercised wrongful dominion and control over the shovel, such that the Clarksons are entitled to the full market value of the shovel. S's taking does not rise to the level of her making a claim of ownership over the tool, so this claim will fail.

(3)   Negligence: Animal Owners. Because R was bitten by a wolf which is a wild animal, although now their "pet," the Clarksons are strictly liable to R for his injuries. There is no "one free bite" rule for wild animals, even if the Clarksons exercised the utmost care, which they did not by leaving him outside unleashed. The Clarksons cannot raise a defense (such as R&S should not have been on their property), as liability is strict.

(4)   Nuisance. R&S can also sue C for the tort of nuisance, which is a substantial and unreasonable interference with one's significant use or enjoyment of their private real property. Here, two weeks of being unable to sleep probably makes the interference substantial, rising above a mere annoyance. However, to recover, R&S must prove that the howling is causing actual harm to the property, including diminution in value. The Clarksons can defend by saying R&S "came to the nuisance," if they can prove R&S knew of the constant howling prior to purchasing their house (assumption of risk).

(5)   Family Relationships: Parent – Child. In general there is no per se vicarious liability for parents whose child commits an intentional tort. Eric is individually liable. However, liability for Eric's parents may exist under the exception that his parents knew of his dangerous proclivity (violent tantrums) and failed to supervise him in a situation where foreseeable harm would occur.

(6)   Battery. Through the doctrine of transferred intent, S can recover for <u>battery</u>, which is intentional harmful or offensive contact.

(a) Trespass to Land. The intended tort was trespass to land, which occurred because Eric intentionally physically invaded R&S's land with the throwing of the pebbles.

(b) Transferred Intent. Although the intent to make contact with the pebbles is missing, the intent from the intended tort (trespass to land) is transferred to the resulting tort (battery) which created the injury.

(c) Damages. When the tort of battery occurs, damages are presumed. The tortfeasor takes his victim as he finds her so E is liable for full damages.

Answer Number 3

Summary

Negligence requires a duty of reasonable care to protect foreseeable plaintiffs in the zone of danger; and a breach which causes (in fact and proximately) resulting damages. S may sue B for negligent entrustment, for knowingly allowing a reckless driver to use her car. S was injured while coming to the rescue of R. The injury was foreseeable (as "danger invites rescue"), so B is liable. The chain of causation allows S to sue R for negligence, established by R's speeding law violation. S can sue R or B (who are jointly and severally liable) for medical bills, and pain, and suffering. S must prove actual damages, but the amount of lost business is only speculative.

Issues Raised

(1)   Negligence
    (a) Negligent Entrustment
    (b) Rescuer: Tortfeasor Liability
    (c) Negligence
    (d) Damages: Medical expenses / pain and suffering
    (e) Damages: Lost Wages
(2)   Joint and Several Liability

Sample Answer

(1)   Negligence. A prima facie case of negligence requires a duty of reasonable care to protect foreseeable plaintiffs in the zone of danger; breach of that duty; causation (cause in fact and proximate cause); and resulting damages.

(a) Negligent Entrustment. Sherman has a claim against Brooke for negligent entrustment. The owner of an automobile has a duty not to allow a known negligent or reckless driver to use the vehicle. Here, despite knowing that Rosie was a habitual speeder with many traffic violations, Brooke breached this duty by lending the truck to Rosie. Brooke is liable under negligent entrustment for any foreseeable damages caused by Rosie's driving.

(b) Rescuer: Tortfeasor Liability. Here, Sherman voluntarily came to the aid of Rosie, injuring himself in the process, which is foreseeable under the "danger invites rescue" doctrine: a tortfeasor is liable for injuries that a rescuer suffers in attempting a rescue. Thus the chain of causation is not broken here.

(c) Negligence. Sherman can sue Rosie for negligence. Rosie had a duty to drive safely which she breached by speeding. Violation of speeding statute will be evidence of negligence in most states. Her speeding was the cause in fact and proximate cause of Sherman's injuries under the "danger invites rescue" doctrine (above).

(d) Damages. Sherman must prove actual damages and economic losses for a claim of negligence. Medical expenses are quantifiable and therefore recoverable. Sherman would be able to recover from Rosie or Brooke for his medical expenses and pain and suffering. Lost wages are recoverable if it was foreseeable they would occur as a result of the negligent conduct. Here, it is foreseeable that Sherman would not be able to work because of his injury. However, the amount of business he lost is purely speculative. Since it is a new business with no history of profits, Sherman cannot prove with reasonable certainty the amount of profits expected or lost.

(2)   Joint and Several Liability. Where two or more tortfeasors act in concert or cause indivisible injury to a plaintiff, all defendants are jointly and severally liable for the full amount of damages. Here, Sherman's injury and resulting damages are the result of both Rosie and Brooke, and not capable of apportionment between them. Thus, because Sherman is not at fault, he can go after both of them or either one of them for the full amount. The trier of fact must then apportion percentages of fault for negligence between the co-defendants.

Answer Number 4

Summary

Negligence requires a duty of reasonable care to protect foreseeable plaintiffs in the zone of danger, and a breach which causes (in fact and proximately) resulting damages. L's duty of care depends on the status of the injured party. J is an invitee, so land-owner L is liable for known and unknown hazards; he breached his duty to inspect and warn invitees of potential hazards and to prevent foreseeable injury. P's error was foreseeable as subsequent medical malpractice, resulting from L's original tort, so the chain of causation is unbroken and L is liable. In states with the relevant law, L may assert J was also comparatively at fault for running barefoot. Landowners owe no duty to trespassers (K), but where a child is injured by an artificial attractive nuisance, the landowner is strictly liable if K cannot appreciate the risk, the condition was dangerous in itself, and the risk greatly outweighs the cost of correcting or removing the hazard. Emergency workers (P) are licensees, so L is liable to P only for known hazards, not the sinkhole. The "danger invites rescue" doctrine does not apply to paid medical professionals. L's assumption of risk defense will fail, as the waiver was vague, and courts disfavor blanket exculpatory clauses.

Issues Raised

(1)   Negligence
       (a) Duty of reasonable care
       (b) Protect foreseeable plaintiffs in the zone of danger
       (c) Breach which causes resulting damages
            (i) causation in fact
            (ii) proximate cause
(2)   Land Owner / Possessor's Duty
(3)   Causation: Superseding Causes
(4)   Comparative Fault
(5)   Land Owner / Possessor's Duty: Trespassers
(6)   Land Owner / Possessor's Duty: Attractive Nuisance
(7)   Land Owner/Possessor's Duty: Licensees
(8)   Assumption of Risk: Express

(1) Negligence. The parties will sue Larry for negligence, which requires a duty of reasonable care to protect foreseeable plaintiffs in the zone of danger; breach of that duty; causation (cause in fact and proximate cause); and resulting damages. Larry's standard of care (duty) depends on the status of the injured party.

(2) Land Owner / Possessor's Duty. Invitee. As a paying customer, Jeannine is an invitee because she is benefiting the owner. Larry is therefore liable for known and unknown hazards, which imposes a duty of Larry to inspect and warn the invitees of potential hazards. Here, Larry knew the loose tiles were a hazard; in fact he meant to fix them. However, there were no signs or warnings of the danger, and failing to take these reasonable steps to prevent injury, Larry breached his duty of care. The loose tiles directly caused the foreseeable injury of Jeannine's broken toe and cut heel.

(3) Causation: Superseding Causes. Larry will argue that he is not liable for damages resulting from her permanent nerve damage because Peter's error was an unforeseeable, intervening force that breaks the chain of causation. However, subsequent malpractice by a medical professional tending to injuries caused by the original tortfeasor is considered foreseeable. Thus Larry can be liable for the permanent nerve damage as well.

(4) Comparative Fault. Larry will defend Jeannine's claim by arguing that she is also comparatively at fault. In a comparative fault state, any fault by the plaintiff prior to the injury will proportionally diminish the amount she is awarded. Here, a jury would be entitled to consider how running barefoot on loose and probably wet tiles contributed to her injuries.

(5) Land Owner / Possessor's Duty: Trespassers. In general, landowners owe no duty to trespassers. Here, Karin wrongfully entered the marked wooded area and thus trespassed.

(6) Land Owner / Possessor's Duty: Attractive Nuisance. However there is strict liability for the owner where a child is injured by an artificial attractive nuisance, as long as the child is too young to appreciate the risk and the condition was dangerous in itself. The man-made tree house qualifies as an artificial attractive nuisance, and at the age of 8, she is likely not able to understand the dangers a rotting tree house poses. Larry's warning signs do not serve to avoid his liability since the risk to a child greatly outweighs the cost of correcting or removing the hazard.

(7) Land Owner / Possessor's Duty: Licensee. Peter, as an emergency worker, qualifies as a licensee, therefore Larry is liable to Peter only for known hazards on his land. As Larry had no knowledge of the sinkhole, nor did he have a duty to inspect and seek it out, he did not breach his duty of care to Peter under this theory. Larry is not liable for Peter's injuries under the "danger invites rescue" doctrine because it applies only to volunteer bystanders. Here, Peter is a paid medical professional who is injured on the job and the general rule applies: the original tortfeasor is not liable to a professional rescuer who injures himself.

(8) Assumption of Risk: Express. Larry can defend by stating that Jeannine (and Karin) expressly assumed the risk of injury through their exculpatory agreement. Such waivers must be negotiated for and particular as to the type of liability being disclaimed. Here, the waiver was broad and vague, simply saying that a guest cannot sue Larry, presumably for anything at all. Because it is not specific and courts disfavor such blanket exculpatory clauses, Larry will not be able to escape liability.

Answer Number 5

Summary

G has a cause of action against M for intentional interference with a business expectancy, as the contract was nearly final, M knew of the deal and intentionally (and with the requisite malice) caused it to fail, causing actual damages of $50k. G may have a claim for intentional infliction of emotional distress ("outrage") against M, but she was exceptionally sensitive, and M did not know she was listening. T has a claim against M for defamation (a false statement of fact about him, publicized to a third party with wrongful intention, causing damage). M's statement about the HIV test was slander (spoken defamation). If T is a public figure, he must show M acted recklessly (not merely negligently), unless HIV is considered a public matter, in which case T must show M's intent was malicious. Since the slander was of a loathsome disease, T may claim damages without pecuniary loss. Possible defenses (truth, mere opinion, consent, privilege, and retraction) don't apply here, unless consent was implied by the invitation to call. T also has a claim for publication in false light, resulting in actual damages. If she can prove damages, G also has a claim for publication of a private matter (not of public concern), that a reasonable person would expect to remain private.

Issues Raised

(1) Interference with business expectancy
    (a) Elements
    (b) Defenses
(2) Outrage
    (a) Elements
    (b) Defenses
(3) Defamation
    (a) Intention
    (b) Damages
    (c) Defenses
(4) Publication in False light
(5) Public disclosure of private matter

Sample Answer

(1) Interference with business expectancy.

(a) Cause of action. Mario induced Wild Waters to disrupt its nearly complete contract with Gabriela, and she has a cause of action for interference with a business expectancy. The expectancy was reasonably certain as the contract was nearly final; Mario had knowledge of the deal; intended to interfere with it; and he played an active role is causing it to fail since he was "hounding" Wild Waters. Mario need not have gained an economic advantage himself (e.g., by getting the deal instead), but merely have caused Gabriela to lose out. She now must prove actual pecuniary damages, which we know is $50,000.

(b) Defenses. Mario will defend himself by saying it was legitimate business competition to offer advertising on television, even if it was perhaps aggressive. However, he loses this privilege since his motive was primarily malice as opposed to economic advantage. Even Wild Waters sensed a "bitter dispute." Mario may also argue that since there was no actual contract, there was only a potential, prospective deal. However, it appears the deal was all but finalized, thus reasonably certain.

(2) Outrage.

(a) Cause of action. Intentional infliction of emotional distress, known as outrage, is extreme and outrageous conduct causing the plaintiff to suffer severe emotional or mental distress that is manifested by objective symptoms. Here, Gabriela suffered distress because of Mario that caused her to seek psychiatric help (actual damages proven). Mario's conduct of embarrassing her on the radio to a wide audience most likely qualifies as "exceeding the bounds of common decency."

(b) Defenses. Mario can defend by saying that his statements were not directed at Gabriela. In fact, he had no way of knowing that she was listening. He could also argue that to a reasonable person, his words would not have caused such severe distress or caused one to seek psychiatric help. In other words, Gabriela is exceptionally sensitive.

(3) Defamation. Theodore has a claim against Mario for defamation, which is a false statement of fact about the plaintiff, publicized to a third party, with a wrongful intention to subject them to contempt, hatred or ridicule, which damages the plaintiff's good name or reputation. When Mario said that Theodore needed an HIV test, this was slander (spoken defamation). Mario in fact did not have an HIV test; it was publicized to a third party (to a wide audience in fact); and brought damage to his reputation as a "family values" advocate in that his show was cancelled.

(a) Intention. The degree of fault required (intention) hinges on whether the plaintiff is a public figure or private, and whether the matter is a private or public one. Here, because of the immense popularity of his show, Theodore likely qualifies as a public figure. HIV is private, personal matter. Thus, Theodore must show that Mario acted recklessly (not merely negligently), in that he had actual or constructive doubt as to the truth of the statement yet said it anyway. Mario did not know why Theodore went to the HIV clinic and failed to do any investigation, which qualifies as reckless. If HIV is considered a public matter, the intent that must be shown is malice, which is also clearly present here.

(b) Damages. Theodore must prove special damages to his reputation that resulted from the reaction to the defamatory act, which he can do here by calculating his lost wages from losing his "family-values" audience and consequently losing his job. In addition, since the accusation is one of a loathsome disease, Theodore is entitled to substantial damages, even without proof of special pecuniary loss.

(c) Defenses. Of the defamation defenses available – truth of the statement, consent, mere opinion, privilege, and retraction – only implied consent may prevail. Theodore gives permission for his audience to call in and speak their mind, unedited, on the air. He cannot now object that he did not like the content of a caller's message. Also, Theodore did not object or deny the accusation although he had the opportunity.

(4)   Publication in a false light. Theodore can also sue Mario for publication in false light – publication of a false attribution that casts a false light on the plaintiff in the public's view, resulting in actual damages. Here, the false attribution that is now in the public's view is that Theodore has HIV or perhaps implying that he is promiscuous. He can prove actual damages.

(5)   Public disclosure of private matter. In addition to suing Mario for outrage (above), Gabriela has a claim against him for publication of a private matter, which is disclosure of private information to the public that a reasonable person would expect to remain private. Here, a reasonable person would expect what they wear to bed to be kept private, thus finding it objectionable and not a matter of public concern. She must prove actual damages.

CHAPTER 11

REAL PROPERTY

AND

FUTURE INTERESTS

RIGOS BAR REVIEW SERIES

UNIFORM MULTISTATE ESSAY EXAM (MEE) REVIEW

CHAPTER 11

REAL PROPERTY AND FUTURE INTERESTS

Table of Contents

A.   **Sub-Topic Exam Issue Distribution**..11-533

B.   **MEE Subject Coverage**..11-535

    1.   **Opening Argument**..11-535

    2.   **Primary Issue Statements**..11-535

    3.   **Text**..MBE Volume 1

    4.   **Magic Memory Outlines®**..MBE Volume 1

C.   **Real Property and Future Interests Essay Questions**................................11-537

D.   **Real Property and Future Interests Essay Answers**................................11-541

E.   **Acronyms**..15-637

RIGOS BAR REVIEW SERIES
MEE SUB-TOPIC FREQUENCY DISTRIBUTION

PROPERTY

Beginning in 2010 we have distributed all NCBE Property essay questions released since they began testing the subject.

	2/09	7/08	2/08	7/07
OPENING ARGUMENT:	/	/		/
Concurrent Estates	//			
Joint Tenancy	/			
Community Property	/			
Tenancy in Common	//			
Easements: *grant of an interest in land entitling use of land possessed by another*				
Appurtenant,				
In Gross				
Prescription				
Tacking of time				
Implied Easement: *needs no written document —exception to the statute of frauds*				
By Necessity				
By Express Grant				
By Estoppel & Irrevocable License: *licensee made substantial repairs in reliance*				
Overuse				
Termination: *by prescription (e.g., given permission) or intentional abandonment*				
License: *a privilege granted to use property, revocable by nature*				
Profit				
Nuisance: *unprivileged, unreasonable interference with others' use/ enjoyment of his land*				
Public vs. Private Nuisance				
"Coming to the Nuisance"				
Trespass: *intentional invasion of possessor's interest in exclusive possession of land*				
Covenants/Equitable Servitude				
Intent for successors in interest to be bound				
Notice: Presumed if covenant is in a recorded deed				

	2/09	7/08	2/08	7/07
Horizontal and Vertical Privity				
Touch and concern: *e.g.*, a negative covenant restricting use of the land				
Enforcement: *by injunction unless acquiescence or "unclean hands"*				
Reciprocal Negative Servitude ("common plan")				
Recording and Race-Notice Recording	//			
Government Restraints and Environmental Impact				
Zoning				
Due Process: Notice; Opportunity to be Heard; Appearance of Fairness				
Variance and Spot Zoning				
Constructive Taking Under the Fifth Amendment				
Earnest Money Agreement Requirements				
Conveyance by Deed—Formalities: Identify Land; SoF Writing & Signature; Delivery	//			//
Joinder for Married Persons				
Warranties				
Quitclaim Deed				
Adverse Possession: Requirements; Statutory period				//
Landlord & Tenant Law: Rights, Duties, and Warranties		//		
Lease Formalities and Compliance with Statute of Frauds		/		
"At-Will" and Periodic Month-to Month Tenancies		//		
Constructive Eviction		/		
Damages		/		
Termination, Abandonment, and Eviction		/		
Personal Property				
Estates & Interests in Land				/
Fee Simple & Defeasible Fee Simple				/
Determinable				
Condition Subsequent				
Life Estate & Life Estate *Pur Autre Vie* (measured by someone else's life)				
Waste				
Remainders & Executory Interests				
Reversion / Right of Reentry				
Rule Against Perpetuities				

OPENING ARGUMENT AND PRIMARY ISSUES

REAL PROPERTY AND FUTURE INTERESTS

The following material is a brief overview of some, but not all, of the key issues in Real Property and Future Interests. Candidates in jurisdictions that administer MEE essays on the six MBE subjects should consult the two-volume *Rigos Bar Review Series – MBE* Volume 1 at page 3-465 for complete textual coverage and Magic Memory Outlines® software. These books and other Rigos Bar Review Series publications are sold at law school bookstores throughout the nation and online at http://lawschool.aspenpublishers.com.

There are a few thoughts that should usually be stated at the beginning of every answer. These will score you easy points and let the grader know you are in the right topic area.

Most essays should have an "opening argument": a brief, broad statement that shows you understand the broad significance of a legal topic. The opening argument also suggests to the grader that she is about to read a thoughtful and well-organized essay.

Many subjects also have "primary issues" that can be discussed up front or integrated into the essay answer. IMPORTANT: Do not merely regurgitate these statements on the exam without addressing the issues actually raised by the facts, or you will not pass.

- **Real Property Opening Argument:** The common law of property applies.

- **Sample Primary Issue Statements:**

  - An easement is an assignable, nonpossessory right to cross over or use anothers' land. An easement is created by prescription, implication, necessity, or express grant. A prescriptive easement must be continuous for the statutory period, hostile to the true owner's interest, and the use must be open and notorious so the owner has actual or constructive notice.

  - A covenant is a promise in a deed burdening the "servient" tenement for the benefit of the "dominant" tenement. Enforcing a covenant requires a writing, the intent that the promise run with the land, and an effect that touches and concerns the land. An equitable servitude imposes similar restrictions based upon actual or constructive notice of the burden.

  - Zoning regulates property use and controls development. Zoning is a quasi-judicial function; it requires that notice be given to affected parties, who have the right to be heard. There must be an appearance of fairness in the decision-making process. Judicial review requires standing, exhaustion of administrative remedies, ripeness, and that the agency has issued a final determination.

- A nonconforming property use that was legal when established but violates the current zoning code may remain (is "grandfathered"), so long as the nonconforming use is continuous from the time it was legal. The use cannot be substantially expanded or changed to a different nonconforming use. An intensification of the same use is usually allowed (if it does not impact the neighbors) as opposed to a different use (gravel mining to coal mining). If the nonconforming use is abandoned, the grandfather protection lapses forever.

- Adverse possession (or an easement by prescription) can ripen into a title of record through a quiet title action if the possession is exclusive, continuous for [x] years, and is hostile to the true owner. The use must also be "open and notorious," to assure the property owner has actual or constructive knowledge of the adverse possession.

- A lease gives the tenant/lessee (T) a nonfreehold possessory estate, while the landlord/lessor (LL) retains a reversionary interest. It establishes a tenant's right to use property for a period of time in exchange for rent.

- The classification of an interest in land is determined by the granting language used to convey the property. With the exception of a fee simple absolute, all present interests in land are accompanied by future interests in the same land. The SOF requires transfers (deeds) and encumbrances (mortgages) of real property to be in writing.

RIGOS BAR REVIEW SERIES

UNIFORM MULTISTATE ESSAY EXAM (MEE) REVIEW

CHAPTER 11

REAL PROPERTY AND FUTURE INTERESTS

Essay Questions

Question Number 1

Lisa is a widow who rented out the basement apartment of the townhouse she owned. A recent housing inspection of the townhouse revealed that there was a substantial crack in a main water pipe running underneath the apartment. Not wanting to make the costly repairs, Lisa advertised the house for rent "as is."

Teddy responded to Lisa's ad and visited the house. The only question he asked Lisa was "How much is rent?" Lisa volunteered no information about the fragile cracked pipe. Teddy and Lisa orally agreed that Teddy would pay $425 a month for 10 months.

Teddy moved in and paid rent monthly. That winter, when temperatures dropped below freezing, the cracked pipe ruptured, creating a hole in the floorboards and flooding the entire basement. Teddy's antique sofa was ruined. In addition, there was no running water.

Teddy asked Lisa to repair the pipe and the hole in the floor, restore running water, and remove the two inches of standing water on the floor. Lisa refused, saying, "I was afraid this would happen. That's why I rented the apartment to you 'as is.'" Teddy repaired the floorboards himself and tried to tough it out by remaining there for five more days. But the standing water remained and there was still no running water.

Teddy told Lisa, "I can't live here. I'm moving out and terminating the lease!" Teddy had to live in a nearby motel for 14 days until he found another place to live. There were three months remaining on the lease.

1. Is the lease valid? What type of tenancy was created between Lisa and Teddy?

2. Did Lisa breach her duties to Teddy? Explain.

3. Does Teddy owe rent for the remaining term of the lease? Explain.

4. Can Teddy collect from Lisa for the ruined couch? For repairing the floor? For his motel stay? Discuss.

Question Number 2

Debra is a land owner in the town of Springfield. Springfield zoning ordinances allow only residential structures to be built. As Debra's children all grew up and moved out of her house, she no longer wanted all 30 acres of her land. Debra kept five acres to herself and divided the rest into four unequal parcels, which she sold with the "prohibition against commercial and agricultural activities by the owner and all successors in interest," as written in the deed.

The outermost parcel of land was slow to sell because it was only accessible by a rough dirt lane that crossed over the adjoining parcel now owned by an aging and cranky Nathan. The plot was finally sold to Amanda, who negotiated a deal with Nathan. They signed an agreement that Amanda can use the dirt lane "for access to Amanda's new house."

Amanda built a new house as well as a large chicken coop. Amanda began selling the chicken eggs, which became renowned as the best tasting, largest, and healthiest organic eggs in the area. People from all over the state began flocking to Amanda's house to purchase the exquisite eggs. The increased amount of traffic prompted Amanda to put a sign on the entrance to the dirt lane that said "Welcome to Amanda's Eggs!"

Nathan was upset by the noise and congestion caused by the traffic to Amanda's Eggs. In addition, he complained to her about the pungent stench from the chicken coop that offended him and his guests. When Amanda refused to do anything about it, Nathan built a barricade over the entrance to the lane that went over his property. "I said *she* could cross over my land, but not all these customers! Besides, she can't do business here anyway!" Additionally, Debra was not pleased that Amanda was making a fortune.

1. What type of easement was created between Amanda and Nathan? Can he rightfully barricade the lane? Explain.

2. Discuss any nuisance claims Nathan could bring against Amanda.

3. What are the consequences of Amanda building "a non-residential structure" contrary to the zoning laws?

4. How can Debra seek damages from Amanda for her commercial and agricultural activities? Explain.

Question Number 3

In 1985, the parents of Luke and William deeded to them some family acreage in the mountains that included part of an old-growth forest. The deed, which was proper in form and recorded, stated "To Luke and William, but if any old growth trees are cut down, then to their sister Jean."

William was never interested in caring for the land, so he decided to sell his interest to Harold. They executed and recorded a valid Real Estate Contract that provided that Harold would acquire William's interest in the property for $100,000 payable in ten equal annual installments. Harold paid the first two years' installments but then ceased making payments, leaving an open balance of $80,000. Meanwhile the land remained untouched and overgrown.

In 1995, Harold gave his daughter Barbara a quitclaim deed to the land for her birthday, which was signed but not recorded. Barbara knew of the contract between her father and William, but assumed it had been fulfilled. Barbara took care of the land, paid the property taxes, and cut down several of the old growth trees in order to make room for a cabin that she built.

In 2007, Barbara finally recorded the deed in the proper county and asked William for a fulfillment deed on the contract. William refused, saying that he had sold his interest to Amber in 2005 because he was never paid on the contract with Harold. When Amber heard that Barbara was making this claim to the land, she promptly recorded the deed.

1. What type of estate in land was created in the original deed? What type of concurrent estate? Explain.

2. What is Jean's interest in the original deed? Does she have a claim to the land now? Explain.

3. Discuss Barbara's possible claims to the land.

4. Did William rightfully refuse to hand over the deed? Assuming this is a race-notice jurisdiction, who has priority between Barbara and Amber? Discuss.

Question Number 4

The Claiborne Fields subdivision, located in Chester County, was established with the filing of an approved plat. It was in an area zoned "Residential." Each lot was subject to real covenants declared "for the exclusive, mutual benefit of the lot owners herein." The covenant provided that each lot was for single-family residence and "not for any business purpose."

Colleen, a boat builder, bought a home in Claiborne Fields. Colleen usually drove a large flat-bed truck to and from her office that carried thick pieces of wood to build the ships. She also kept a large trailer in her driveway that she used for both business and recreation.

The following year, Megan purchased the land bordering Colleen's in Claiborne Fields with a pond view and built a house. She found, however, that her view of the pond was often blocked by Colleen's truck with its stacks of lumber. Megan complained to Chester County about her blocked view. The County investigated and concluded that Colleen was operating a business on her land and cited her for violating the zoning laws.

Colleen responded by filing with the county planning commission an application for a rezone of the subdivision to "Light Industrial," where both residences and ship-building yards were permitted. The rezone was approved by the County Commissioners the following day.

Two weeks later, Megan saw Colleen diligently building a hull for a new ship in her driveway. "I thought the County made you stop!" protested Megan.

"Oh, didn't you hear? They allow ship building yards now," gloated Colleen.

Megan rushed to Superior Court where she appealed the County's granting of the rezone. She also sued Colleen for violating the real covenants and for blocking her view.

1. Discuss the claims Megan can bring against Colleen for conducting business on her land, whether she is entitled to enforce it, and what remedies she can seek.

2. Upset she cannot see the pond, Megan claims "breach of view easement" and nuisance against Colleen. Will she succeed? Explain.

3. Was the rezone properly granted? How should the Court rule? Assume Megan exhausted all her administrative remedies and has standing. Explain.

Question Number 5

Oscar held fee simple absolute title to a ten acre farm in Easton County, which has an adverse possession and prescription statute that requires continuous possession for 12 years. In 1990, Oscar sold the lot, which had a farmhouse and small country store, to Melvin. In return for the purchase price, Oscar gave Melvin an unacknowledged deed. Melvin moved into the farmhouse, built an attached garage, and began paying property taxes.

In 1992, a windstorm destroyed the boundary fence between Melvin's farm and the neighboring land, owned by Bridget. After the storm, Melvin and Bridget together rebuilt an improved fence to mark the boundary, but inadvertently placed the fence nine feet inside Melvin's property.

Along the fence in those "extra" nine feet, Bridget built a walkway for the neighborhood children to walk along on their way to school to prevent them from trampling over her nicely landscaped yard like they usually did.

Meanwhile, Melvin rented the building that Oscar had used as a country store to Ernest. Their valid written lease stated Ernest would pay $1000 a month for the next three years. Ernest took possession, added new shelving, and began selling homemade jams and jellies. However, business was not good enough for Ernest to make a profit, and after only six months of paying rent, Ernest abandoned the store and stopped paying rent, taking with him the shelving which severely damaged the floor.

In 2006, Melvin realized the new fence was put in the wrong place and politely informed Bridget he would be moving the fence to "where it belonged" and planting rows of corn where the path had been. Bridget said "You can't do that to the school children! Besides, I own that land now!"

Later that year Oscar passed away. His valid will stated that he bequeathed "all real property owned at the time of my death to my only son Junior."

1. Between Melvin and Junior, who owns the farm? Discuss.

2. What recourse under common law does Melvin have against Ernest? Explain.

3. Discuss Bridget's claims to the "extra" nine feet and to the walkway.

Essay Answers

Answer Number 1

Summary

A term tenancy (granting the tenant (T) a possessory interest, measured by a definite period of time, with a reversionary interest to the Landlord (LL)) was created here. LL failed her common-law duty to disclose any known serious, hidden, or dangerous defects. Renting the apartment "as is" does not disclaim LL's duties, as T was under no duty to detect the defect himself. LL also breached her duty under the theory of implied warranty of habitability by failing to provide running water and by leaving the standing water. Generally, LL can sue for each rent payment as it becomes due, but when LL is in breach, T may vacate the premises and terminate the lease. T has no duty to pay rent if he was "constructively evicted," (LL has breached the implied covenant of quiet enjoyment by failing to keep the premises in a condition suitable for T's use and enjoyment). T properly gave notice to LL and vacated, but even if he had not, LL had a duty to mitigate her damages by making reasonable attempts to re-rent the premises promptly. T may be entitled to damages to his couch under a negligence theory, and for his motel expenses under a breach of contract theory. T is responsible for day-to-day repairs, but LL is responsible for major, structural repairs. In most jurisdictions, T had the option of repairing the floor and deducting his costs from his rent.

Issues Raised

(1) Term Tenancy
  (a) Tenant has a nonfreehold, possessory estate
  (b) Landlord retains a reversionary interest
  (c) Over one year:
      (i) In writing to satisfy the statute of frauds
      (ii) Otherwise, an oral lease is valid.
(2) Fitness of Premises
  (a) Common Law
  (b) Implied Warranty of Residential Habitability
(3) Tenant's Remedies for Landlord's Breach
  (a) Vacate and Terminate the Lease
  (b) Constructive Eviction
(4) Landlord Duties: Mitigation Duty
(5) Tenant's Remedies for Landlord's Breach: Action for Damages
(6) Landlord's and Tenant's Duties: Repairs
  (a) Landlord Duties: Action for Damages
  (b) Landlord Duties: Deduct Costs of Restoring Habitability from Rent

(1)   Term Tenancy. A lease gives the tenant a nonfreehold, possessory estate with the landlord retaining a reversionary interest at the end of the lease. A lease for over one year must be in writing to satisfy the statute of frauds; otherwise an oral lease is valid. Here the term was 10 months, so it is valid. A term tenancy was created because it is measured by a definite period of time.

(2)   Fitness of Premises. A landlord-tenant relationship imposes certain duties upon the landlord.

(a) Common Law. Under the common law, a landlord has a duty to disclose any serious, hidden, dangerous defects of which she has actual knowledge. Here, Lisa knew of the substantial crack in the water pipe. By failing to disclose this, she violated her duty to Teddy. Lisa's defense that she rented the apartment "as is" does not disclaim her duties. She can argue that such a provision put Teddy on notice of problems. However, Teddy is under no duty to detect the defect himself. In addition, leasing a place "as is" usually implies the landlord will not make such changes as painting or other cosmetic additions, as opposed to implying there is a major structural defect.

(b) Implied Warranty of Residential Habitability. Under the theory of implied warranty of habitability, a landlord must provide habitable premises throughout the duration of a residential lease. Here, Lisa breached this warranty by failing to provide running water or remove the standing water following the pipe's rupture. Lisa cannot use the "as is" provision as a defense because these conditions arose after Terry took possession.

(3)   Tenant's Remedies for Landlord's Breach. The general rule is that a landlord can hold the tenant to his contractual obligation and sue for each rent payment as it becomes due.

(a) Vacate and Terminate the Lease. However, when a landlord is in breach, one remedy for the tenant is to vacate the premises and terminate the lease, as Teddy did here. This rescinds the contract, and Teddy is not liable for the remaining three months of rent.

(b) Constructive Eviction. In addition, a tenant has no duty to pay rent if he has been constructively evicted. Constructive eviction occurs if the landlord breached the implied covenant of quiet enjoyment: failure to keep the premises in a condition required for the tenant's use and enjoyment of the property, making it uninhabitable. Since there were two inches of standing water and still no running water, Teddy was constructively evicted. He properly gave notice of the conditions to Lisa and vacated the apartment. Lisa will try to argue waiver, in that Teddy did not exercise his right to leave within a reasonable time. However, five days is probably not long enough to constitute a waiver or acceptance of the unlivable conditions.

(4)   Landlord Duties: Mitigation Duty. Finally, even if Teddy wrongly vacated, Lisa has a duty to mitigate her damages under contract law. Lisa would not be able to collect all three month's rent from Teddy as she would be required to make reasonable attempts to re-rent the premises promptly.

(5)   Tenant's Remedies for Landlord's Breach: Action for Damages. A tenant is entitled to seek relief from a landlord's breach, including an action for damages. Here, Teddy may sue

Lisa for the damage to his antique couch under a negligence theory. He may sue Lisa for the cost of his motel stay under a breach of contract theory.

(6) Landlord's and Tenant's Duties: Repairs. While a tenant is responsible for ordinary, day-to-day repairs, the landlord is responsible for major, structural repairs. When Lisa did not repair the hole in the floor, as was her duty, Teddy took it upon himself.

(a) Landlord Duties: Action for Damages. Teddy may collect the costs of his repair in a suit for negligence or breach of contract against Lisa.

(b) Landlord Duties: Deduct Costs of Restoring Habitability from Rent. In most jurisdictions, Teddy would have had the other option of doing the required repairs to the floor, in his attempt to restore the apartment to habitability, and then deduct the costs from his rent due.

Answer Number 2

Summary

An easement is an assignable, non-possessory right to cross over or use the land of another. Here, N granted Amanda an express easement, which must be in a signed and notarized writing, with a full and accurate description of the property, scope, and duration. If the prior common owner divided the land and sold a portion that has been subject to prior continuous, apparent, and reasonably necessary use, there may also have been an implied easement. An easement by necessity can occur where there was once a common ownership of the land and there is strict necessity (e.g., no other access to a public road). Here, the easement is necessary because the land (formally owned by D) was "only" accessible via that lane. Reasonable modification or expansion of an easement is allowed, but A may not overburden the servient (N's) estate, as she did here by expanding the access. Overuse does not terminate A's easement. N may not self-help by physical blockage. A private nuisance is an unreasonable interference with a right to enjoy one's own property (as the coop's smell and busy road are, here) unless the utility of the activity outweighs the severity of the damages. Defenses include "coming to the nuisance" (here, N was there first), or that the use is reasonable by an "ordinary person" standard (unlikely here). If A is in violation of zoning laws, the city can seek an injunction and levy a fine. The only exception is for prior nonconforming uses of new zoning restrictions, which is not the case here. A is breaching the real covenant in her deed (a written promise restricting the use of her property for the benefit of another's property) by conducting business, so D may get damages. A real covenant must be in writing (per the SOF), have intent to bind successors in interest, touch and concern the land, and there must be privity of estate. Here, these conditions are met.

Issues Raised

(1) Easement
   (a) Express
      (i) signed and notarized writing
      (ii) full and accurate description of the property, scope, and duration
   (b) Implied
      (i) prior common owner divided the land and sold a portion

(ii) portion was subject to continuous, apparent, and reasonably necessary use
(iii) no practical alternative route
(c) Necessity
(i) once a common ownership of the land
(ii) strict necessity such that there is no other access to a public road
(d) Termination
(i) no self help
(ii) injunction, unless utility of the activity outweighs severity of harm
(2) Nuisance
(a) Private
(b) Public
(c) Defenses
(i) coming to the nuisance
(ii) reasonable use by an "ordinary person" standard
(3) Violation of Zoning law
(i) prior, continuous use
(ii) injunction and a fine
(4) Breach of Real Covenant
(a) In writing to satisfy Statute of Frauds
(b) Implied intent to bind
(c) Restriction on land use touches and concerns the land
(d) Horizontal privity

Sample Answer

(1)   Easement. An easement is an assignable, non-possessory right to cross over or use the land of another.

(a) Express. Nathan granted Amanda an express easement, which must be in a signed and notarized writing, with a full and accurate description of the property, scope, and duration. Here the easement was specifically for Amanda to access her own home. The easement is appurtenant—the holder of the easement (Amanda) is directly benefited by the physical use of Nathan's land.

(b) Implied. This may also be an implied easement, which requires that the prior common owner divided the land and sold a portion that has been subject to a prior easement-like use. The prior use must have been continuous, apparent, reasonably necessary and with no practical alternative route. Here, the extent to which the prior use was continuous or apparent is unclear; all other elements are met.

(c) Necessity. An easement by necessity can occur where there was once a common ownership of the land and there is strict necessity such that there is no other access to a public road. Here, the easement may be necessary because it was "only" accessible via that lane, and the land was formerly owned commonly by Debra.

(d) Termination. Amanda and her customers improperly used the easement as a driveway for her business, thus she violated the express easement. However, despite her violation, physical blockage is not effective to terminate an express easement, so Nathan may not use self-help. While reasonable modification or expansion of an easement is allowed, Amanda may not overburden the servient (Nathan's) estate, as she did here by expanding the access from personal driveway to commercial access. Overuse does not terminate the easement, but Nathan can seek an injunction. (Amanda's overuse can create a nuisance as well.) If the driveway is determined to be an easement of necessity, the barricade will not terminate the easement. Only lack of necessity (if another access is built to Amanda's house) will rightfully terminate it.

(2) Nuisance.

(a) Private. A private nuisance is an unreasonable interference with an individual's right to enjoy his own property. The pungent smell from the chicken coop and the noise and disruption from overuse of the easement both qualify, and Nathan may bring an action to enjoin it and seek damages. The court will balance the utility of the activity against the severity of the damages. Here it is likely the balance tips in Nathan's favor because of the substantial interference with his peace and comfort in his own house. While this is now Amanda's means of making a living, she is doing so in violation of the zoning laws and restrictive covenant.

(b) Public. A public nuisance is an unreasonable interference with the public's right to enjoy public facilities. Although possible, there are no facts to indicate the odors or traffic affected public facilities.

(c) Defense. Defenses to a claim for nuisance include "coming to the nuisance" or that the use is not unreasonable. Clearly, Nathan did not come to the nuisance since he was there first. The reasonableness of the use is tested by an 'ordinary person' standard. Here, the odors and traffic are likely to be offensive to a reasonable person, and there is no indication that Nathan is particularly sensitive.

(3) Violation of Zoning Law. Where a property owner is in violation of zoning laws, the city can seek to enjoin the violation in addition to assessing a fine. The only exception is for prior nonconforming uses, which become nonconforming after a rezoning, which is not the case here. The chicken coop is a commercial building, thus she is violating the zoning laws, and Springfield can seek an injunction to close down or remove the chicken coop.

(4) Breach of Real Covenant. Amanda is also subject to the real covenant in her deed, which she is violating by conducting business. The legal remedy for a breach of covenant claim is damages. A real covenant is a written promise restricting the owner's use of her property for the benefit of another's property, including this restriction on commercial buildings and activities. To be effective, the covenant must be in writing (satisfy the Statute of Frauds), have intent to bind successors in interest, touch and concern the land, and there must be privity of estate. Here, the writing was the deed, intent to bind is implied in a deed, the restriction on land use touches and concerns the land, and there is horizontal privity between Debra and Amanda. Therefore, Debra can sue to enforce the covenant and seek monetary damages.

Answer Number 3

Summary

A fee simple subject to an executory interest creates an interest so long as conditions specified by the deed are satisfied. If the condition is unsatisfied, a third party's executory interest automatically becomes possessory. L and W own as tenants in common: they have separate, undivided interests that are alienable, and each has an unrestricted right to possess the entire property. J's interest in the future estate is a shifting executory interest, so cutting down the trees vested her future interest and possession shifted to her. However, executory interests are subject to the RAP (a contingent future interest must vest within 21 of a life in being), and the trees could be cut down after L and W die. Thus, J's conveyance will be stricken, leaving a fee simple absolute for L and W. H's quitclaim deed conveys all the grantor's interest to the grantee, without covenants or warranties: B takes subject to any encumbrances, liens, or judgments. A valid deed transfers title of W's interest (fee simple absolute as a tenant in common) to B. B may also claim title by adverse possession (exclusive physical possession, with continuous use for the statutory period of time, that is hostile to the true owner's interest, and is both open and notorious). Under a Real Estate Contract, when a buyer pays the entire balance directly to the seller (in installments), the title is finally transferred. H stopped payments, forfeiting title transfer to B, who took subject to the debt. The buyer must record the deed at the county recorder's office where the property is located. In a "race-notice" jurisdiction, a subsequent grantee (who must be a bona fide purchaser for value without notice of a prior interest and be the first one to record) may claim priority. Here, B recorded first, but she knew of the prior contract, and no value was given (since it was a gift). Thus, A has priority.

Issues Raised

(1) Estates in Land: Fee Simple Subject to Executory Interest
(2) Concurrent estates: Tenancy in common
    (a) Separate, undivided interests
    (b) Interests are alienable
    (c) Each tenant in common has an unrestricted right to possess the entire property
(3) Future Interests
    (a) Shifting Executory Interest
    (b) Rule Against Perpetuities
        (i) contingent future interest
        (ii) must vest within 21 of a life in being
(4) Quitclaim Deed
    (a) Conveys grantor's entire ownership interest to the grantee
        (i) without covenants or warranties
        (ii) seller warrants only that they are transferring all of their ownership interest
    (b) Grantee takes subject to any encumbrances, liens, or judgments
(5) Adverse Possession
    (a) exclusive physical possession of the land
    (b) use is continuous for the statutory period of time
    (c) use is hostile to the true owner's title and interest
    (d) use is open and notorious.
(6) Real Estate Contract
(7) Recording Statute: Race-Notice
    (a) subsequent grantee may claim if files deed first
    (b) subsequent grantee must be a "bona fide" purchaser
        (i) takes for value
        (ii) without notice of a prior interest
        (iii) first to record in order to have priority

Sample Answer

(1)   Estates in Land: Fee Simple Subject to Executory Interest. A fee simple subject to an executory interest is an estate that creates an interest in the first grantee so long as the person acts as specified in the deed. When that condition is no longer satisfied, an executory interest held by a third party automatically becomes possessory (no requirement of entry within a reasonable time). The language to create such a deed is satisfied here, for "but if" creates in Luke and William a fee simple subject to an executory interest.

(2)   Concurrent Estates: Tenancy in Common. Absent language to the contrary, Luke and William own as tenants in common. They have separate, undivided interests that are alienable, and each has an unrestricted right to possess the entire property.

(3)   Future Interests.

    (a) Shifting Executory Interest. Jean's interest in the future estate is a shifting executory interest, whereby the triggering of the event (cutting down trees) causes possession to shift to her. Jean can claim that once Barbara cut down the trees, Jean future interest had vested.

    (b) Rule Against Perpetuities. However, executory interests are subject to the Rule Against Perpetuity (RAP), which requires that a contingent future interest must vest within 21 of a life in being. In this case, the measuring lives are Luke and William. The deed violates RAP because they may pass away and 21 years later trees may be cut down. Therefore that portion of the conveyance to Jean will be stricken, resulting in a fee simple absolute for Luke and William. Thus, Jean has no claim to the land.

(4)   Quitclaim Deed. A quitclaim deed conveys all the grantor's ownership interest to the grantee, without covenants or warranties. The seller warrants only that they are transferring all of their ownership interest. Here, Harold transferred his interest (although what the interest was is in question). Barbara takes subject to any encumbrances, liens, or judgments. The deed appears to meet the requirements in order to be valid (complies with Statute of Frauds, notarized, legal description, and delivery) and therefore effectively transfers title of William's interest (fee simple absolute as a tenant in common) to Barbara, and she takes subject to the outstanding Real Estate Contract.

(5)   Adverse Possession. Barbara can also claim title to the entire land by adverse possession if she brings a quiet title action. Adverse possession requires physical possession of the land to be exclusive, continuous for the statutory period of time, hostile to the true owner's title and interest, and open and notorious. Here, she had exclusive and continuous possession for at least 12 years that was not secret or hidden. It was hostile to Luke's possession because there is no evidence he gave her permission or knew of her possession and did not object; and it was hostile to William's possession because she was operating under "color of title" from the quitclaim deed. In addition, payment of property taxes is strong evidence of the "hostility" requirement.

(6)   Real Estate Contracts. A Real Estate Contract is an agreement to sell property whereby the buyer pays directly to the seller in installments until the balance is paid. Title is not transferred until the full balance of the debt is paid. If the buyer stops paying, the seller can declare the contract forfeited. Here, Harold stopped payments after only 2 installments, leaving a large outstanding balance. William may thus declare the contract forfeited and properly refuse delivery of the title to Barbara, who took subject to her father's debt. (Barbara can bring a quite title action to get title via adverse possession.)

(7) Recording Statutes: Race-Notice. To protect against a third party buyer later acquiring a superior interest from a seller, the buyer must record the deed at the county recorder's office where the real property is located. In a "race-notice" jurisdiction, a subsequent grantee must be a bona fide purchaser for value without notice of a prior interest and be the first to record in order to have priority. Here, Amber was the first one to both record and be a bona fide purchaser for value. Although Barbara recorded first, she knew of the prior contract with her father and failed to investigate (on notice) and it was gifted to her (no value given). Amber has priority.

Answer Number 4

Summary

A real covenant is a written promise restricting an owner's use of her property for the benefit of another's property. The covenant must be in writing (per the SOF), intended to bind successors in interest, "touch and concern" the land, and have horizontal privity (as here, from the original developer). Here, privity does not exist between M and C, so M may not enforce the covenant against C. M may, however, pursue her claim in equity: an equitable servitude may restrict the owners' uses of their lots to maintain a "common scheme" if there is a writing, intent to bind, and touch and concern the land. Privity is not required, but the successor in interest must have notice of the servitude when she acquired the interest. Here, all parties had actual notice, so C was bound under the "common scheme," and may be enjoined. M's claim for breach of view easement will fail, as C's property ownership includes the airspace above the ground, up to a reasonable height, unless a zoning rule or covenant otherwise limits it. Nuisance is an unreasonable interference with the use or enjoyment of one's property. Here, M's view is only blocked at times, and the court will balance the utility of C's action against M's damages. Also, because C (and her truck) were there first, Megan came to the nuisance. Rezoning is proper only if neighborhood conditions have substantially changed, unlike here. Further, rezoning violated constitutional requirements of substantive due process by not having the appearance of fairness, and by failing to give owners notice and an opportunity to be heard.

Issues Raised

(1) Real Covenants
   (a) Writing to satisfy the statute of frauds
   (b) Intended to bind successors in interest
   (c) Touches and concerns the land (affects its usage)
   (d) Horizontal privity
   (b) Remedy
(2) Equitable Servitude
   (a) Notice
   (b) Remedy
(3) "View Easement"
(4) Nuisance
   (a) Private
   (b) Public

        (c) Defenses
            (i) coming to the nuisance
            (ii) reasonable use by an "ordinary person" standard
(5) Zoning laws
    (a) Rezone
    (b) Due Process Violation
        (i) appearance of fairness
        (ii) notice and opportunity to be heard

Sample Answer

(1) Real Covenants. Megan may choose to enforce the covenant at law or in equity as an equitable servitude. A real covenant is a written promise, usually in a deed, restricting an owner's use of her property for the benefit of another's property. All owners here in Claiborne Fields are subject to the covenant (the burden runs to them from the developer as a successor in interest) because it is in writing (satisfies the statute of frauds), it is presumably intended to bind successors in interest, it touches and concerns the land (affects its usage), and there is horizontal privity (from the original developer). The covenant here expressly forbids "any business purposes" on the lots, and Colleen is violating it by doing construction and using the trailer as an office.

   (a) Privity. However, privity does not exist between Megan and Colleen, which is required in order to enforce a real covenant. Thus Megan is not entitled to enforce the covenant at law against Colleen.

   (b) Remedy. If Megan did try to enforce the covenant at law, she can seek the legal remedy of damages.

(2) Equitable Servitude. Because privity is missing, Megan should pursue her claim in equity against Colleen. An equitable servitude is used here to restrict the owners' uses of their lots to maintain a "common scheme." As with a real covenant, there is a writing, intent to bind, and touch and concern the land. A "common scheme" is apparent because the language in the covenant states the developer intended all lots to be similarly restricted for the benefit of all other lots.

   (a) Notice. While privity is not required, the successor in interest must have notice of the servitude at the time of acquiring the interest. Here, all parties had actual notice in writing. Thus, Megan, as owner of land bound under the same "common scheme", may enforce the servitude against Colleen.

   (b) Remedy. If Megan elects to enforce the covenant in equity as an equitable servitude, the equitable remedy would be an injunction to prevent Colleen from conducting business on her land.

(3) "View Easement." Megan's claim for breach of view easement is not persuasive. Generally, property ownership includes the airspace above the ground, up to a reasonable height. Colleen may use her airspace as she wishes absent an express easement, zoning rule or covenant that otherwise limits it. Nothing in the facts suggests that any of these exist, so her claim will fail, as she has not established her right to a view of the pond.

(4)   Nuisance. Nuisance is an unreasonable (to an ordinary person) interference with the use or enjoyment of one's property. The conduct must substantially interfere with safety, peace, or comfort in the use of the property or violate an ordinance. Here, Megan is claiming a private nuisance, in that Colleen is unreasonably interfering with her right to enjoy her view of the pond. Here, Megan's view is blocked not by a permanent structure, but by a mobile vehicle only when parked in the driveway. This probably does not rise to the level of significant or substantial interference since it is only blocked part of the time. In addition, the court will balance the utility of Colleen's action (parking her own vehicle in her own driveway) against the severity of the damages suffered by Megan (probably minimal). In addition, Colleen will argue that because she and her truck were there first, Megan came to the nuisance. Megan will not prevail.

(5)   Zoning Laws. Government zoning laws are used to regulate property use and control development. Zoning is presumed to be valid if it reasonably relates to police power objectives.

(a) Rezone. A rezone, or change in zoning laws, can be applied for if conditions in the neighborhood have substantially changed. That was not the case here, so the rezone should probably not have been granted.

(b) Due Process Violation. Megan will succeed on overturning the rezone because of the substantive due process violation by failing to meet the appearance of fairness. Neighboring property owners must receive actual notice so they may have an opportunity to be heard on the proposed changes. Given Megan's ignorance of the rezone and the quick approval by the Commission, it appears the specific proposed change was not publicized or disclosed. Thus the court should strike down the rezone as unconstitutional.

Answer Number 5

Summary

O had a fee simple absolute, so his land was freely inheritable and transferable during life. M received a deed conveying title to real property (which requires a signed writing, acknowledgment (notarized), an accurate legal description, and delivery. M may own the land despite the defective (unacknowledged) deed if he makes a successful claim in equity under the part performance exception: he had possession, made significant improvements (the garage), and paid the purchase price. M may also claim ownership via adverse possession: his possession was exclusive, continuous for more than the 12-year statutory period, hostile, and open and notorious. M was also acting under "color of title", so the statutory period is even shorter. M and E entered into a valid commercial lease agreement, giving E (tenant) a nonfreehold possessory estate, while M (landlord) retained a reversionary interest. E has violated his duty to pay rent. M may take possession and terminate the lease, or he may hold E responsible for the rent owed under the lease as each payment becomes due, so long as he properly attempts to mitigate by re-letting the store. If M re-rents, he may hold E liable for any deficiency. E also caused waste (damage beyond ordinary wear and tear) while removing the shelving, and is liable for repair costs. If the shelving was a fixture (attached to the structure), E is liable for the damage caused in the removal. B may not claim the nine feet through adverse possession, as her use was not exclusive. However, B may claim that the footpath is a valid easement (a nonpossessory right to cross over the land of another). Easements may be created by prescription (as here), implication, necessity, or express grant/reservation. If the easement was never recorded, M can terminate and regain possession by blocking it for a 12 year period.

Issues Raised

(1)   Fee Simple Absolute
(2)   Deed
      (a) Formalities
          (i) written and signed to comply with the Statute of Frauds
          (ii) acknowledgment (notarized)
          (iii) accurate legal description
          (iv) delivery
      (b) Part Performance Exception
          (i) possession
          (ii) significant improvements consistent with ownership
          (iii) paid the purchase price.
(3)   Adverse Possession
      (a) Requirements
          (i) exclusive physical possession of the land
          (ii) use is continuous for the statutory period of time
          (iii) use is hostile to the true owner's title and interest
          (iv) use is open and notorious.
      (b) Continuous: Color of Title
(4)   Lease
      (a) Breach of Lease: Landlord's Remedies
      (b) Waste
(5)   Adverse Possession
(6)   Easement
      (a) Creation: Prescription
      (b) Termination

Sample Answer

(1)   Fee Simple Absolute. As Oscar held his land in fee simple absolute, it was freely inheritable and transferable during life. Had Oscar still owned it, it would go to Junior according to his will.

(2)   Deed. However, it appears Melvin owns the land despite the defective deed.

    (a) Formalities. A deed conveying title to real property requires compliance with the Statute of Frauds (written and signed), acknowledgment (notarized), accurate legal description and delivery. It appears three of the four requirements are met, but it was unacknowledged.

    (b) Part Performance Exception. Although the conveyance failed to meet all the formalities, Melvin has a claim in equity under the part performance exception. Melvin meets these three requirements: he had possession, made significant improvements (built a garage), and had paid the purchase price; all are consistent with ownership.

(3)   Adverse Possession.

    (a) Requirements. Melvin also has a claim of ownership via adverse possession, which requires that possession be exclusive, continuous for the statutory period), hostile, and open and notorious. Here, Melvin's possession was exclusive (not shared), hostile (as evidenced by his payment of taxes), and open (visible and known).

(b) Continuous: Color of Title. It was also continuous for at least 16 years and counting, which is longer than the 12 year statutory period. The period is even shorter for those acting under "color of title", such as here when the deed is defective. Thus, all elements of adverse possession are satisfied, and Melvin will win in a quiet title action.

(4) Lease. Melvin and Ernest entered in to a valid commercial lease agreement that gave Ernest, the tenant, a nonfreehold possessory estate with Melvin, the landlord, retaining a reversionary interest at the end of the term.

(a) Breach of Lease: Landlord's Remedies. Ernest has violated his obligation under the lease by failing to pay rent, giving Melvin several options under common law. He may take possession of the store and relieve Ernest of further obligation by terminating the lease. He may choose to hold Ernest responsible for the rent owed under the lease as the payments become due. However, Melvin will be required to mitigate his losses by re-letting the store, so he probably will not be able to get rent for all two and a half years. If Melvin chooses to re-rent the premises, he could hold Ernest liable for any deficiency in rent, such as if he is only able to rent it for $800 a month.

(b) Waste. Ernest also violated the common law obligation not to cause waste – damage beyond ordinary wear and tear – by damaging the floor while removing the shelving. Ernest will be liable for the cost of repairing the floor to its original condition. In the alternative, if the shelving was considered a fixture attached to the structure, Ernest should not have removed them and is liable for the damage caused in the removal.

(5) Adverse Possession. Bridget's claim of ownership of or title to the "extra" nine feet through adverse possession will fail. Same elements as above apply. It was continuous for 14 years and counting, which is long enough under the statute. Melvin will try to argue it is not hostile because he gave permission, in essence, by letting her use it. However, the fact that he was unaware it was his property does not defeat the hostility (or open and notorious) requirement because it is against his interest in the land which he legally owns. Reciprocally, Bridget's use was hostile as well, even though inadvertently so. Its use was open and notorious. However, Bridget's possession is not exclusive – she shared it with the school children and it was open to the public in general. Thus she has not come to own the "extra" nine feet.

(6) Easement. Bridget can claim that the footpath is a valid easement, which is a nonpossessory right to cross over the land of another.

(a) Creation: Prescription. Easements can be created by prescription, implication, necessity, or express grant/reservation. Here, only prescription is possible. The requirements are the same as adverse possession, except it need not be exclusive. Thus, it does not matter that she shared it with the students and public in general. It was continuous, open, as well as hostile to Melvin's interest. Therefore, Bridget has an easement by prescription.

(b) Termination. If the easement was never made of record, Melvin can terminate and regain possession by blocking it for a 12 year period.

CHAPTER 12

EVIDENCE

RIGOS BAR REVIEW SERIES

UNIFORM MULTISTATE ESSAY EXAM (MEE) REVIEW

CHAPTER 12

EVIDENCE

Table of Contents

A.   **Sub-Topic Exam Issue Distribution** 12-557

B.   **MEE Subject Coverage** 12-559

     I.   **Opening Argument** 12-559

     2.   **Primary Issue Statements** 12-559

     3.   **Text** .... MBE Volume 2

     4.   **Magic Memory Outlines®** .... MBE Volume 2

C.   **Evidence Essay Questions** 12-561

D.   **Evidence Essay Answers** 12-565

E.   **Acronyms** 15-640

RIGOS BAR REVIEW SERIES
MEE SUB-TOPIC FREQUENCY DISTRIBUTION

EVIDENCE

Beginning in 2010 we have distributed all NCBE Evidence essay questions released since they began testing the subject.

	2/09	7/08	2/08	7/07
Governing Law	/		/	
Federal Rules of Evidence	/		/	
Preliminary Determinations				
Judicial Notice				
Relevance	/			
Probative Value	/			
Unfair Prejudice	/			
Confusion				
Character Evidence	/		/	
Criminal Proceeding	/			
Other Crimes, Wrongs, or Acts	/			
Admissible for Other Purposes			/	
Subsequent Remedial Measures				
Offers of Compromise				
Liability Insurance				
Competency of Witness				
Personal Knowledge				
Judge as Witness				
Witness Credibility/Impeachment	/			
Prior Inconsistent Statement	/			
Character of Witness	/			
Witness Presentation and Interrogation	/			
Leading Questions				
Calls for Narrative				
	2/09	7/08	2/08	7/07

Topic		
Compound Question		
Argumentative		
Writing Used to Refresh Memory	✓	
Opinion Testimony by Lay Witness		
Expert Testimony		
Hearsay		
Rule of Exclusion		✓
Non-Hearsay		✓
Prove Statement Was Said		
State of Mind		
Prior Statement by Witness		
Party-Opponent Admission		
Agent		
Assertive Conduct		
Availability Immaterial		
Present Sense Impression		
Excited Utterance		
State of Mind		
Recorded Recollection		✓
Business Records		✓
Government Records		
Medical Diagnosis and Treatment		✓
Declarant Unavailable		✓
Definition		✓
Privilege		✓
Statement Against Interest		
Hearsay Within Hearsay ("Double Hearsay")		✓
Authentication and Identification		✓
Voice Identification		
Self-Authentication		
Trade Inscriptions		
Best Evidence Rule		

OPENING ARGUMENT AND PRIMARY ISSUES

EVIDENCE

The following material is a brief overview of some, but not all, of the key issues in Evidence. Candidates in jurisdictions that administer MEE essays on the six MBE subjects should consult the two-volume *Rigos Bar Review Series – MBE* Volume 2 at page 4-23 for complete textual coverage and Magic Memory Outlines® software. These books and other Rigos Bar Review Series publications are sold at law school bookstores throughout the nation and online at http://lawschool.aspenpublishers.com.

There are a few thoughts that should usually be stated at the beginning of every answer. These will score you easy points and let the grader know you are in the right topic area.

Most essays should have an "opening argument": a brief, broad statement that shows you understand the broad significance of a legal topic. The opening argument also suggests to the grader that she is about to read a thoughtful and well-organized essay.

Many subjects also have "primary issues" that can be discussed up front or integrated into the essay answer. IMPORTANT: Do not merely regurgitate these statements on the exam without addressing the issues actually raised by the facts, or you will not pass.

- **Evidence Opening Argument:** The Federal Rules of Evidence attempt to provide fact finders with reliable relevant facts and exclude all else.

- **Sample Primary Issue Statements:**

  - In order for evidence to be admitted, it must be relevant, i.e., tend to prove or disprove a material issue in dispute. Although relevant, the court has discretion to exclude the evidence if it finds that the probative value is outweighed by its danger for unfair prejudice, confusion, or undue delay.

  - Relevant evidence is generally inadmissible if it is barred by the hearsay rule and no exception to the hearsay rule applies.

  - Subsequent remedial measures are inadmissible to show negligence, culpable conduct, or defective product.

  - Settlement negotiations including criminal plea bargaining are inadmissible. However, an offer to compensate a criminal witness may be admissible in a criminal case as settlement negotiations are not protected.

  - The spousal privilege assumes that communications between a validly married husband and wife are confidential even if the couple later divorces.

  - The physician-patient privilege protects communications intended to be confidential including details contained in the patient's medical records.

- All physical evidence to be introduced must be able to show a prior chain of custody and all non-testimonial evidence must be authenticated.

- For a person to testify as a witness, she must be competent. This requires: 1) personal knowledge, 2) present recollection, and 3) ability to communicate. Any document can be used to refresh a witness's memory.

- Past criminal records of the D are not admissible to prove the character or propensity of a person in order to show action in conformity therewith. However, it may be admissible for other purposes such as motive, opportunity, intent, preparation, plan, knowledge, identity, or absence of mistake or accident.

- Under the Best Evidence Rule, if a party wishes to prove the content of a writing, photo, or drawing, they must submit the original or a duplicate at trial.

- An expert witness must be qualified by knowledge, skill, experience, training, or education and their opinion must be helpful to the trier of fact.

- Hearsay is an out-of-court statement of fact offered to prove the truth of the matter asserted. Many statements are not hearsay such as prior inconsistent statements and admissions of a party opponent.

Essay Questions

Question Number 1

Trooper Todd pulled over a car driven by Doug. When Doug rolled down his window, the Trooper noticed that Doug's eyelids were abnormally droopy, and the eyes themselves were bloodshot. After Doug gave consent to a search of his car, the Trooper found an empty plastic bag that smelled like marijuana and had the words "Capitol Hill Chronic" written on it. Doug was arrested and subsequently charged with driving under the influence of marijuana.

During Doug's trial by jury, the prosecution called the Trooper as its first witness. The Trooper testified that he stopped Doug's car because he observed Doug driving erratically. On cross-examination, Doug's attorney sought to introduce an uncertified copy of the police report, in which the Trooper wrote, "I stopped the car after noticing an offensive bumper sticker that read, 'Need a cop? Call the donut shop.'" The prosecution objected to the introduction of the police report.

Jerry was the second witness. The prosecution tendered Jerry as an expert witness who would testify that, based on his experience as a former drug dealer with two convictions, he understood the phrase "Capitol Hill Chronic" to be the name of a potent marijuana strain grown in the Seattle area. Doug's attorney objected to the proffered expert testimony.

The sole witness for the defense was Doug's friend Tom, who testified that he had been fishing with Doug earlier in the day and that Doug "seemed to be sober." The prosecution moved to strike Tom's comment about Doug's sobriety.

1. Should the court have sustained the objection to the police report? Explain.

2. Should the court have sustained the objection to Jerry's expert testimony? Explain.

3. Should the court have granted the motion to strike part of Tom's testimony? Explain.

Question Number 2

Debbie was a passenger in a Neptune automobile being used as a taxi. Another car rear-ended the taxi while it was stopped at a red light. The taxi burst into flames, causing Debbie to suffer severe burns.

After the fatal accident, Neptune Motors redesigned its fuel tanks to include a protective shield around the tank. Debbie filed a lawsuit against Neptune Motors that alleged a defective fuel tank design.

At a pre-trial hearing, the court is considering both parties' motions in limine to prohibit the introduction of certain evidence at trial.

1. Debbie has moved to exclude a repair log, prepared by the taxi company, indicating that the taxi in which she was riding had been involved in a previous accident that may have compromised the tank's structural integrity. Should the court exclude this evidence? Explain.

2. Debbie has moved to exclude evidence that the driver of the other car admitted to the police that he was speeding when he struck the taxi. The other driver died a month ago due to a heart attack. Should the court exclude this evidence? Explain.

3. Neptune Motors has moved to exclude evidence of the fuel tank redesign. Should the court exclude this evidence? Explain.

4. Neptune Motors has moved to exclude evidence indicating that after Debbie's lawyer sent a demand letter to Neptune, the company offered to pay 100% of her medical bills stemming from the accident in exchange for a mutual release of claims. Should the court exclude this evidence? Explain.

Question Number 3

Pedestrian filed a complaint for negligence against Driver. The complaint alleged that Driver was distracted by talking on her cell phone, failed to stop at a crosswalk where Pedestrian was crossing the street, and hit Pedestrian with her car. In her answer, Driver denied that she was using her cell phone at the time of the accident and also claimed that the stop sign was obscured by a tree and almost impossible to see.

At a jury trial, Pedestrian's lawyer called the first witness, Able, who was expected to testify that the stop sign was easily visible. However, the judge commented that she drove through the same intersection every morning on her way to the courthouse and that the sign had been obscured for several years by the branches of a nearby tree. The judge took judicial notice of the sign's lack of visibility and instructed the jury of the same.

Pedestrian's attorney asked the second witness, Baker, whether Driver was talking on a cell phone at the time of the accident. Baker testified, "Well, although I didn't see any phone, I did see Driver's mouth moving right before he hit Pedestrian, and there wasn't anyone else in the car. So I think he must have been talking on the phone with one of those hands-free kits."

The third witness, Charlie, was Driver's husband at the time of the accident, but the couple had divorced by the time of the trial. Pedestrian's attorney called Charlie as the third witness and asked him, "What did Driver say to you about the accident?" Charlie responded, "She told me that she shouldn't have been talking on the phone while driving and that the accident was her fault."

Assuming that Driver's lawyer made all appropriate objections, did the court err in:

1. Taking judicial notice of the stop sign being obscured and instructing the jury accordingly? Explain.

2. Admitting Baker's testimony? Explain?

3. Admitting Charlie's testimony? Explain.

Question Number 4

At the trial of O.K. Sampson, a famous athlete who has been charged with murder, the prosecution seeks to introduce, among other things, the following testimony and other evidence during its case in chief:

1. A blood sample collected at the crime scene that allegedly contains Sampson's DNA.

2. Evidence that Sampson had pled no contest to an assault charge four years ago.

3. Testimony by a business associate of Sampson's, offered for the purpose of identifying Sampson's handwriting on a suicide letter allegedly written by Sampson shortly after the police issued a warrant for Sampson's arrest due to the murder charge.

4. Handwritten notes of a private investigator, originally hired by the victim's family, that were written when the investigator viewed the crime scene. The investigator will testify at trial, but because of a subsequent head injury, she is unable to recall what she observed during her investigation, even after re-reading her notes.

Sampson's defense counsel team has made two strategic decisions. The first is not to have Sampson testify in his own defense. The second is to file a pre-trial motion in limine to exclude the four items above from evidence at trial.

1. Should the court exclude the DNA sample on grounds that it is unfairly prejudicial? Explain.

2. Should the court exclude the evidence of Sampson's no-contest plea to assault? Explain.

3. Should the court exclude the testimony of Sampson's business associate on grounds that he lacks the required expertise to authenticate handwriting? Explain.

4. Should the court exclude the private investigator's notes? Explain.

Question Number 5

Church filed a lawsuit against Minister, a former employee who allegedly embezzled money from Church's bank account, in order to recover the funds. The following are excerpts from the trial transcript:

DIRECT EXAMINATION OF MINISTER
* * *

Q: Now Reverend, you are an ordained minister, correct?
A: That's right.
(1) Q: Does your religion forbid lying?
A: Yes, absolutely.

* * *

Q: Did mail addressed to Church, but not you personally, ever cross your desk?
A: On occasion. Sometimes we'd be short-staffed, and I'd help out as needed. That often included opening and sorting the mail.
Q: When you were helping with the mail, did you ever open envelopes containing checks?
A: Yes.
Q: What would you do when you opened a piece of mail that contained a check?
(2) A: I'd immediately place it in the staff mailbox of Church's treasurer. No exceptions. That's how I always handled it.

* * *

Q: Do you recall a meeting with the treasurer on June 19, 2006, to discuss discrepancies between Church's financial records and its bank statements?
A: Not specifically, no. I attended many, many meetings during my time at Church, and most of them are a blur.
Q: I hand you what's been marked for identification as Plaintiff's Exhibit "M." Can you identify this document?
A: Yes, this appears to be some notes I wrote during a meeting with the treasurer on June 19th.
(3) Q: Does this document refresh your memory as to that meeting?
A: Yes, it does.
(4) Q: Would you please read it into the record for us?

* * *

DIRECT EXAMINATION OF JOE DOAKES, CPA

Q: Mr. Doakes, did you render professional services to Church?
A: Yes, they hired me to perform a forensic accounting of Church's finances.
Q: Did you find anything out of the ordinary?
(5) A: Yes. I concluded that Minister had stolen money from Church.

* * *

At each of the numbered points, could a valid objection or motion to strike be made? Explain.

Essay Answers

Answer Number 1

Summary

Hearsay [HS] is a generally inadmissible out-of-court statement offered to prove the truth of what it asserts. An uncertified copy of a police report could be HS, unless it is offered only to impeach T (attack his credibility), in which case a limiting instruction to the jury may have been appropriate. An expert witness with scientific, technical, or other specialized knowledge (but not necessarily a formal education – as J, here) may offer opinion testimony that will help the trier of fact understand the evidence or determine a fact at issue. The court may admit non-expert witness opinion testimony that is rationally based upon the witness' personal knowledge, and would be helpful for the determination of a fact in issue. Here, T's opinion is based upon personal knowledge, and is also helpful to determining a fact at issue.

Issues Raised

(1) Hearsay
  (a) Generally Inadmissible
  (b) An Out of Court Statement Offered to Prove the Truth of the Matter Asserted
  (c) Impeachment Exception
(2) Testimony by Experts: Qualification of Experts
  (a) Witnesses with scientific, technical, or other specialized knowledge
  (b) Experts may offer testimony in the form of an opinion if
    (i) testimony would help the trier of fact understand the evidence, or
    (ii) determine a fact at issue.
  (c) No formal education required if qualified by knowledge, skill, experience, or training
(3) Opinion Testimony by Lay (Non-Expert) Witnesses
  (a) Admissible by judges' discretion
  (b) Opinion testimony must be
    (i) rationally based on the witness' perception (i.e., personal knowledge)
    (ii) helpful to a clear understanding of testimony or determination of a fact in issue
    (iii) not based upon scientific, technical, or other specialized knowledge

Sample Answer

(1)   Hearsay. Hearsay, which is generally inadmissible, is an out-of-court statement offered to prove the truth of what it asserts.

(a) Truth of the Matter Asserted. While an uncertified copy of a police report could be hearsay, in this case, Doug's attorney can fairly characterize the evidence as being offered not to prove what it asserts (i.e., that Trooper stopped Doug's car after seeing an "offensive" bumper sticker), but rather for the purpose of impeaching Trooper.

(b) Impeachment. Impeachment is introducing evidence for the purpose of attacking the credibility of a witness. Here, Trooper has testified that he stopped Doug's car due to erratic driving, but Trooper's earlier statement in the police report suggests that he may have done so because he took offense to the message displayed on the car. The two statements could be construed as inconsistent, which calls into question whether Trooper's testimony is truthful. Thus, the court should not have sustained the objection, although a limiting instruction to the jury may have been appropriate.

(2) Testimony by Experts: Qualification of Experts. An expert witness with scientific, technical, or other specialized knowledge may offer testimony in the form of an opinion if such testimony would help the trier of fact understand the evidence or determine a fact at issue. Formal education is not required, as the expert may be qualified by knowledge, skill, experience, training, or education. Here, Jerry's experience as a drug dealer – and the knowledge he acquired while dealing drugs – strongly suggests that he has specialized knowledge of drug-related slang. This would be helpful to a jury that otherwise probably would not understand the meaning or significance of "Capitol Hill Chronic." In this case, a critical fact at issue is whether Doug was under the influence of marijuana while he was driving, and the fact that Doug had a plastic bag labeled with a marijuana reference makes it more likely that he was, in fact, intoxicated. Accordingly, the court should have overruled the objection to Jerry's testimony.

(3) Opinion Testimony by Lay Witness. The judge has discretion to admit non-expert witness opinion testimony if: a) the opinion is rationally based on the witness' perception (i.e., the witness has personal knowledge); b) the opinion would be helpful to a clear understanding of the testimony or determination of a fact at issue; and c) the opinion is not based upon scientific, technical, or other specialized knowledge. Here, Tom's opinion about Doug is based upon Tom's personal knowledge, as the two had been fishing together when Doug "seemed to be sober."

Tom's opinion is also quite helpful to determining a fact at issue; Doug was charged with driving under the influence of a drug, and as noted above, a key element of the crime is being *not* sober while behind the wheel. To be sure, Tom's opinion is not conclusive, since Doug could have smoked marijuana after the fishing trip, but before the traffic stop. Still, if Doug was seen in a sober condition earlier in the day, it is less probable that he was under the influence later the same day.

Finally, an observation that a person "seemed to be sober" does not need specialized, expert knowledge. In light of this and the other two factors discussed above, the judge should not have struck Tom's testimony.

Answer Number 2

Summary

Hearsay [HS] is a generally inadmissible out-of-court statement offered to prove the truth of what it asserts, as the taxi company's repair log would be here, if not for the "business records exception." The repair log is a record of a regularly-conducted activity, created in the regular course of business, near in time to the event described, based upon personal knowledge, kept with the regular practice of the business, reliable, and certified by a knowledgeable witness. Here, the log should satisfy all the required elements. Statements against interest (that expose the speaker to criminal or civil liability) are another HS exception if the declarant is unavailable to testify (as the dead driver is, here). Evidence of remedial or corrective measures and settlement offers are not admissible to prove negligence or culpable conduct (as D is improperly attempting to do here), but may be offered to prove ownership or impeach.

Issues Raised

(1)   Hearsay:
    (a) Generally Inadmissible
    (b) An Out of Court Statement Offered to Prove the Truth of the Matter Asserted
    (c) Business Records Exception
        (i) Regularly-conducted activity
        (ii) Created in the regular course of business
        (iii) Near in time to the event described
        (iv) Based upon the personal knowledge of the person who created the record
        (v) Made in keeping with a regular practice of the business
        (vi) Reliable
        (vii) Certified
(2)   Declarant Unavailable: Statement Against Interest
(3)   Subsequent Remedial Measures
(4)   Offers of Compromise: Civil Proceeding

Sample Answer

(1)   Hearsay: Business Records Exception.   Hearsay, a statement made outside the particular proceeding in question and offered into evidence to prove what it asserts, is generally not admissible. The taxi company's repair log is apparently hearsay, as Neptune apparently wants to prove that the automobile had been damaged previously in order to suggest that the fire was due to the prior accident, and not culpable conduct by Neptune.

However, one of the most common exceptions to the general rule of non-admissibility is the "business records exception." For hearsay to be admissible as a business record, the record must be of regularly-conducted activity, created in the regular course of business near in time to the event described in the record, based upon the personal knowledge a person in the business who created the record, made in keeping with a regular practice of the business, and reliable. Further, it must be certified by a witness with knowledge of whether the record satisfies all of these elements. Assuming that Neptune can obtain the required certification by an employee of the taxi company, the court should admit the repair log. Nothing in the facts suggests that the log does not satisfy any of the elements set forth above.

(2)   Hearsay: Declarant Unavailable: Statement Against Interest.   Another hearsay exception applies to a "statement against interest"; i.e., one that could subject the speaker to civil or criminal liability, or render a claim of his invalid. This exception is only available when the declarant is "unavailable." Death before trial is sufficient for the witness to be deemed unavailable, and the statement made to the police could have subjected him to both criminal liability for breaking the speed limit and civil liability for Debbie's injuries. The court should admit the statement made by the driver of the other car.

(3)   Subsequent Remedial Measures. Evidence of remedial or corrective measures taken after an accident is not admissible to prove negligence or culpable conduct in connection with the accident. This rule is based upon a policy of not discouraging parties to take such steps when they are appropriate. While this rule does not apply when the evidence is offered for another purposes, such as proving ownership or impeachment, here it seems that Debbie wishes to introduce evidence of the fuel tank redesign to support her claim that the original design is defective. Accordingly, the evidence is not admissible, and the court should exclude it.

(4)   Offers of Compromise: Civil Proceeding. Similarly, the law intends to encourage out-of-court settlements. For that reason, evidence of settlement offers is inadmissible to prove validity of the claim. While a purely gratuitous offer to pay someone's medical expenses is admissible, this exception does not apply because the offer was conditioned upon Debbie releasing her claim against Neptune. The offer was thus a settlement offer, and the court should exclude it.

Answer Number 3

Summary

A court may take judicial notice only of facts that are generally known or are readily determinable via an unquestionably reliable source. Thus, a judicial determination that the stop sign was obscured was improper here. A witness is presumed to be competent to testify, but may be disqualified for inability to understand the concept of truthful testimony, a lack of personal knowledge (as B lacked here as to the phone use, but not the accident scene), a lack of memory, or an inability to communicate. B's equivocation goes to weight, not admissibility, and so was properly allowed. Hearsay is a generally inadmissible out-of-court statement offered to prove the truth of the matter asserted. Hearsay may be admitted if an exception applies, e.g., admission by a party-opponent, as C's testimony about D's statement, here. However, C's statement was a confidential communication between spouses, and so is barred by the marital communication privilege unless waived by D, despite their subsequent divorce. Since D did not waive the privilege, the statement is inadmissible.

Issues Raised

(1)   Judicial Notice
        (a) Generally Known
        (b) Capable of Accurate and Ready Determination
(2)   Witness Competency: Personal Knowledge
(3)   Hearsay
        (a) Rule of Exclusion
        (b) Admission by Party-Opponent
(4)   Marital Communication Privilege

Sample Answer

(1)   Judicial Notice. The doctrine of judicial notice allows a court, in limited circumstances, to establish a fact conclusively (in a civil case) or satisfy the prosecution's burden of production (in a criminal case) without hearing testimony or requiring a party to submit evidence. A court may (and in some cases, must) take judicial notice of facts that are: a) generally known; or b) capable of accurate and ready determination by consulting a source whose accuracy cannot reasonably be questioned. An example of the former would be taking judicial notice of the fact that the city of Seattle is located in the state of Washington. As for the latter, an example would be a court consulting a calendar and then taking judicial notice that January 1, 2008, was a Tuesday. However, the judge's personal observations at the accident scene fall into neither category, and it was an error for the court to take judicial notice of the stop sign being obscured by trees.

(2)   Witness Competency: Personal Knowledge. While a witness is presumed to be competent to testify, a witness may be disqualified for inability to understand the concept of truthful testimony, a lack of personal knowledge, a lack of memory, or an inability to communicate.   In this case, Driver's attorney might object that Baker lacked personal knowledge of whether Driver had been talking on a cell phone or using a hands-free cell phone kit. However, Baker was a witness at the accident scene, and the requirement of personal knowledge does not prohibit testimony where the witness qualifies his statement with a phrase such as, "I think . . . ." (the case here). Usually this type of equivocation goes to the weight, not admissibility of testimony, and accordingly, the court probably did not err in admitting Baker's testimony.

(3)   Hearsay: Admission by Party-Opponent. Hearsay is a statement, made by the declarant outside of the particular proceeding, offered to prove the truth of the matter asserted in the statement.

(a) Rule of Exclusion. Hearsay is generally not admissible. However, a statement that would otherwise be inadmissible hearsay may be admitted if the statement falls into a hearsay exception or a "non-hearsay" category established by the evidence rules.

(b) Admission by Party-Opponent. One example of "non-hearsay" under the rules is an admission by a party-opponent. The term "admission" is something of a misnomer, since any statement or assertive conduct may qualify. For a statement to be deemed a party-opponent admission, it must be made (or adopted) by a party and offered against that party. Here, Charlie's testimony about what Driver said after the accident, which was offered by Pedestrian's attorney, is a party-opponent admission and is not barred by the hearsay rule.

(4)   Marital Communication Privilege. However, the statement is barred by the marital communication privilege unless waived by the non-testifying spouse (here, Driver). Confidential communications made between spouses during marriage are privileged, even if the spouses subsequently divorce, which occurred here. (The marital communications privilege should be distinguished from the quasi-privilege rule of spousal incompetency, which prohibits compelling a person to testify against his or her spouse, but expires if the marriage is terminated.) Since the facts do not indicate a waiver of the privilege by Driver, the court erred when it admitted Charlie's testimony.

Answer Number 4

Summary

The court may exclude otherwise-relevant evidence if there is a danger of unfair prejudice. The DNA evidence here may be prejudicial, but not unfairly so: it is factual, and it is not an emotional plea. Evidence of the assault plea is inadmissible to demonstrate S's propensity for violent acts or criminal behavior. Evidence of a prior conviction may be used to impeach the accused if: (a) the crime is a felony or one involving dishonesty; and (b) the probative value outweighs the prejudicial effect. But since S did not testify, he cannot be impeached. Documentary evidence, such as the suicide letter, must be authenticated by testimony, unless the document is "self-authenticating." Non-experts may testify as to the genuineness of familiar handwriting, as the business associate likely had here. Hearsay is an out-of-court statement offered to prove the truth of what it asserts. If the investigator's notes are offered to prove the statements therein, they are hearsay. Though hearsay is generally inadmissible, an exception applies to a "recorded recollection," if a witness cannot now recollect fully, but made (or adopted) a record while the matter was still fresh his memory, that record may be introduced. Here, the investigator made notes at the crime scene, so if the notes are accurate, the account in the notes may be read into the record.

Issues Raised

(1)   Relevance: Balancing Against Prejudice
         (a) Danger of unfair prejudice
(2)   Character Evidence: Other Crimes, Wrongs, or Acts
(3)   Impeachment by Evidence of Conviction of Witness
(4)   Document Authentication and Identification: Non-Expert Opinion on Handwriting
(5)   Hearsay
         (a) Rule of Exclusion
         (b) Recorded Recollection

Sample Answer

(1)   Relevance: Balancing Against Prejudice. The court should not exclude the DNA sample. Rule 403 allows the court to exclude otherwise-relevant evidence for a variety of reasons. One of those reasons is a danger of unfair prejudice. However, evidence is not unfairly prejudicial simply because it is unfavorable to the party against whom it is being introduced, even if the evidence is extremely damaging (such as the defendant's DNA being found at the crime scene). Excluding evidence on grounds of unfair prejudice is usually reserved for situations where the evidence may inflame the jury into making a decision on the basis of emotion instead of fact; one example would be a gruesome photo of the victim's dead body. The evidentiary power of the DNA sample, by contrast, is factual, not emotional, and the court should not exclude it.

(2)   Character Evidence: Other Crimes, Wrongs, or Acts. The court should exclude evidence of Sampson's no-contest plea *unless* the prosecution gives notice that it wishes to introduce the evidence for a permissible purpose, such as rebutting a claim of accident, showing a common plan, or proving identity. The prosecution cannot, however, introduce evidence of the assault plea to demonstrate Sampson's propensity for violent acts or criminal behavior. The facts do not suggest that the prosecution has any basis for introducing evidence of the plea other than to show propensity, so the court should exclude it.

(3)   Impeachment by Evidence of Conviction of Witness. Sampson's no-contest plea might, in theory, be admissible against him for the limited purpose of impeaching him. Evidence of a prior conviction may be used to impeach the accused if: (a) the crime is a felony or one involving dishonesty; and (b) the probative value outweighs the prejudicial effect. Here it is unclear whether the assault was a felony. But moreover, since Sampson will not give testimony and will not be a witness, there will be nothing to impeach, and therefore this exception does not apply.

(4)   Document Authentication and Identification: Non-Expert Opinion on Handwriting. The court should admit the testimony of Sampson's business associate. Documentary evidence, such as the suicide letter, must be authenticated. While some documents are self-authenticating, others must be authenticated by testimony. Non-experts may testify as to the genuineness of handwriting if they have familiarity with the alleged author's handwriting. Assuming that the business associate became familiar with Sampson's handwriting in the course of their dealings, the court should admit the associate's opinion on who wrote the suicide letter.

(5)   Hearsay. Hearsay is an out-of-court statement offered into evidence to prove the truth of what it asserts. Assuming that the prosecution wants to introduce the investigator's notes for the purpose of proving statements contained in the notes, they are hearsay.

(a) Rule of Exclusion. As a general rule, hearsay is inadmissible.

(b) Recorded Recollection. However, one exception to the rule against admitting hearsay applies to a "recorded recollection." When a knowledgeable witness has insufficient memory to testify fully and accurately, but made (or adopted) a factually correct record while the matter was still fresh in the witness' memory, the record may be read into evidence. (It may not itself be received as an exhibit unless offered by an adverse party.) Here, the investigator cannot now recall much of what she saw, but she made notes of her observations while she was looking at the crime scene. Assuming that the notes are accurate, the prosecution may use this exception to have the investigator's notes read into the record.

Answer Number 5

Summary

Religious beliefs are not admissible in regard to a witness' credibility, so whether M's religion forbids lying is inadmissible. Evidence of a habit (automatic behavior without premeditation) is generally admissible to show conformity therewith; M's testimony of his routine relating to checks likely qualifies. A writing may be used to help refresh a friendly witness' memory, as M's was, here. However, the witness may not actually read aloud from the writing, but must instead testify from his (refreshed) memory. A witness may not provide a legal conclusion, but may offer an opinion about the ultimate issue. The witness' words must be understandable by a jury of lay persons, and not a confusing legal term of art. Here, testimony that M had "stolen" money is admissible, whereas testimony that he had "committed the tort of conversion" is not.

Issues Raised

(1)   Religious Beliefs
(2)   Habit and Routine Practice
(3)   Writing Used to Refresh Memory
    (a) General Rule
    (b) Oral Testimony
(4)   Opinion on the Ultimate Issue of Fact: Legal Conclusion

Sample Answer

(1)   Religious Beliefs.   At point 1, counsel should object.   Religious beliefs are not admissible to bolster or attack a witness' credibility. While they may be admissible for another purpose, such as bias, the question about whether Minister's religion forbids lying seems to have no purpose other than trying to establish Minister's credibility.

(2)   Habit and Routine Practice.   The answer at point 2 probably does not warrant a motion to strike. Evidence of a person's habit is generally admissible, whether corroborated or not, and regardless of the presence of eyewitnesses, to show conformity therewith. A "habit" is automatic behavior without premeditation. Minister testified that he'd place any mail with checks in the treasurer's mailbox "immediately" and with "[n]o exceptions." The behavior described by Minister likely qualifies as a habit.

(3)   Writing Used to Refresh Memory.   Point 3 does not warrant an objection, but counsel should object at point 4.

    (a) General Rule.   If a friendly witness cannot recall factual details, a writing — or anything else — may be used to help refresh the witness' memory. Thus, it was not improper for counsel to refresh Minister's memory with the notes, and no objection should be made at point 3.

    (b) Oral Testimony.   However, the witness may not actually read aloud from the writing. He must instead testify from his (refreshed) memory. Opposing counsel has the right to inspect the writing and can even introduce it into evidence (assuming it otherwise complies with the requirements for admissibility), but having the witness read the document into the record is improper. Counsel should object at point 4.

(4)   Opinion on the Ultimate Issue of Fact: Legal Conclusion.   The testimony at point 5 probably does not justify a motion to strike the CPA's answer. While a witness may not provide a legal conclusion, a witness may provide an opinion that embraces the ultimate issue to be decided by the trier of fact. The test for determining admissibility is usually whether the words used by the witness would be understandable by a jury of lay persons, as opposed to a legal term of art that the jury might not understand. Saying that Minister had "stolen" money is an example of the former and is not objectionable. By contrast, if the CPA opined instead that Minister had "committed the tort of conversion," a motion to strike the answer as an impermissible legal conclusion would have been warranted.

CHAPTER 13

CONSTITUTIONAL

LAW

RIGOS BAR REVIEW SERIES

UNIFORM MULTISTATE ESSAY EXAM (MEE) REVIEW

CHAPTER 13

CONSTITUTIONAL LAW

Table of Contents

A.	**Sub-Topic Exam Issue Distribution**		13-577
B.	**MEE Subject Coverage**		13-579
	I.	**Opening Argument**	13-579
	2.	**Primary Issue Statements**	13-579
	3.	**Text**	MBE Volume 2
	4.	**Magic Memory Outlines®**	MBE Volume 2
E.	**Constitutional Law Essay Questions**		13-581
F.	**Constitutional Law Essay Answers**		13-585
G.	**Acronyms**		15-641

RIGOS BAR REVIEW SERIES
MEE SUB-TOPIC FREQUENCY DISTRIBUTION

CONSTITUTIONAL LAW

Beginning in 2010 we have distributed all NCBE Constitutional Law essay questions released since they began testing the subject.

	2/09	7/08	2/08	7/07
Opening Argument				
FEDERAL COURTS' AUTHORITY – JUDICIAL REVIEW				
Original Jurisdiction & Appellate Jurisdiction				
Judicial Restraint				
Justiciability: Ripeness; Finality; Mootness; Standing: Injury; Causation; Redressability				
11th Am. Ban on Suing a State; Exceptions				
SEPARATION OF POWERS – Federal Congressional Powers				
Commerce Power				
10th Am. Limits: Congress may not regulate states directly				
Tax & Spend Power; Bankruptcy; Postal Power				
Citizenship & Rules of Immigration				
Property & Takings / Eminent Domain				
Delegation of Legislative Power				
FOURTEENTH AM. (§5): Laws to enforce civil rights guaranteed				
SEPARATION OF POWERS – FED EXECUTIVE POWER				
FEDERALISM – IMMUNITIES & TAXATION				
SUPREMACY CLAUSE - Fed Law Controls; Preemption				
FEDERALISM - DORMANT COMMERCE CLAUSE				
INDIVIDUAL RIGHTS – EQUAL PROTECTION CLAUSE				
Classifications: Suspect Class; Quasi-Suspect Class; Non-Suspect Class				
Level of Scrutiny: Strict Scrutiny; Intermediate Scrutiny; Rational Basis Test				
INDIVIDUAL RIGHTS – DUE PROCESS	/			
Notice & Oppty. to be Heard if State Deprives Life, Liberty, or Property Interest	/			
Timing of Due Process: Pre-or-Post Deprivation—Mathews v. Eldridge		/		

	2/09	7/08	2/08	7/07
Substantive Due Process: "May the government infringe on this individual right?"				
Fundamental Rights – Strict Scrutiny Test: Compelling Interest, No Less Intrusive Means				
1st Am: Voting, Interstate Travel Right to Refuse Medical Treatment				
Privacy: Contraception; Abortion; Marriage; Procreation; Education; Relations	/			
INDIVIDUAL RIGHTS: 14TH AM.— Privileges or Immunities: Gov. infringement on fed rights				
Contracts Clause (Art. I, §10): State impairment of contracts without significant public need				
Ex Post Facto Law: Conduct criminalized retroactively				
Bills of Attainder: Punishing without a judicial trial				
FIRST AMENDMENT RIGHTS – FREEDOM OF RELIGION				
Free Exercise Clause: Beliefs; Conduct: Education; Controlled Substances; Polygamy				
Establishment Clause: Gov. may not prefer one religion or over another religion or over non-				
Lemon Test: Primary purpose secular; Primary effect neither advances nor inhibits; no excessive entanglement				
FIRST AMENDMENT RIGHTS – FREEDOM OF SPEECH		/		
Content-Neutral vs. Content-Specific		/		
Public or Private Forum		/		
Protected or Unprotected Speech		/		
Law Unconstitutional on its Face vs. as Applied.				
Vague or Overbroad				
Content Neutral Speech: regulated for time, place, & manner				
Content Specific: Unprotected Speech		/		
Defamation: Public vs. Private Figure: NY Times v. Sullivan – "Actual Malice"		/		
Fighting Words				
Illegal Commercial Speech				
Obscenity & Child Pornography				
Incite Unlawfulness				
Protected Speech: Political; Legal Commercial; Non-Obscene/ Sexually Explicit		/		
Freedom of the Press		/		
Loyalty Oaths as a Precondition to Public Employment				
Freedom of Association : Group Membership				

OPENING ARGUMENT AND PRIMARY ISSUES

CONSTITUTIONAL LAW

The following material is a brief overview of some, but not all, of the key issues in Constitutional Law. Candidates in jurisdictions that administer MEE essays on the six MBE subjects should consult the two-volume *Rigos Bar Review Series – MBE* Volume 2 at page 5-169 for complctc tcxtual coverage and Magic Memory Outlines® software. These books and other Rigos Bar Review Series publications are sold at law school bookstores throughout the nation and online at http://lawschool.aspenpublishers.com.

There are a few thoughts that should usually be stated at the beginning of every answer. These will score you easy points and let the grader know you are in the right topic area.

Most essays should have an "opening argument": a brief, broad statement that shows you understand the broad significance of a legal topic. The opening argument also suggests to the grader that she is about to read a thoughtful and well-organized essay.

Many subjects also have "primary issues" that can be discussed up front or integrated into the essay answer. IMPORTANT: Do not merely regurgitate these statements on the exam without addressing the issues actually raised by the facts, or you will not pass.

- **Constitutional Law Opening Argument:** The state and federal government may act as long as the regulation is rationally related to a legitimate government interest and the act is not proscribed by the Constitution.

- **Sample Primary Issue Statements:**

  - A regulation that infringes a person's right to life, liberty, or property must meet the test of the Substantive and Procedural Due Process clauses under the 5th Amendment.

  - The court will apply strict scrutiny if the regulation hinders a fundamental right such as 1st Amendment rights, voting, interstate travel, privacy, and refusal of medical treatment. The government must show that its act was necessary to promote a compelling government interest and no less restrictive means were available.

  - Procedural Due Process requires that the person be given notice and an opportunity to be heard by an unbiased tribunal.

  - Under the 5th Amendment, regulations must apply equally to all individuals. If the law is not discriminatory on its face, then the class must show a disproportionate impact in its application and a discriminatory intent.

- A law that discriminates on the basis of race, alienage, or national origin is subject to strict scrutiny and must be necessary to promote a compelling governmental interest.

- A court applies the *Lemon* test to determine whether a law violates the Establishment Clause. The test requires that the primary purpose of the law be secular, that the law neither advances nor inhibits religion, and that law does not foster excessive government entanglement or require close government monitoring.

- Obscene material is not protected by the First Amendment. For material to be deemed obscene, it must appeal to the prurient interest in sex, be patently offensive, and have no serious literary, artistic, political, or scientific value. The issues of prurient interest and patent offensiveness involve the application of contemporary local standards.

- Prior restraints on speech are presumptively unconstitutional; the preference is to allow the speech and then punish it if necessary.

Essay Questions

Question Number 1

Due to a sharp increase in the amount of crime committed by out-of-state visitors, the State of Harrison enacted a statute requiring non-residents to apply for and receive a "Harrison Visitor Card" before entering the state. The Harrison Visitor Card application form, which is available only in English, requires a prospective visitor to provide information that is used to run a background check on the applicant.

Juan Jaramillo, a resident of Ecuador, was unable to complete the application form because he does not understand English. While visiting the United States, a police officer turned Juan away at the Harrison state line because Jaramillo did not have a Harrison Visitor Card.

Jaramillo has retained counsel to file a federal lawsuit challenging the Harrison Visitor Card statute and its implementation. An expert witness hired by Jaramillo's lawyer will testify that, in her opinion, about 1 in 10 people who wish to visit Harrison will be unable to obtain a Harrison Visitor Card because of the language barrier posed by the English-only application form. The expert will further opine that the state's refusal to provide foreign translations of the application disproportionately impacts non-U.S. citizens.

1. If Jaramillo asserts an Equal Protection claim, will he prevail? Explain.

2. If Jaramillo asserts a Due Process claim, will he prevail? Explain.

Question Number 2

In response to a case of Mad Cow Disease discovered in another state, the East Dakota legislature enacted the "Mad Cow Disease Protection Law" (MCDPL), which bans the sale of beef food products unless the animal is raised within 50 miles of the place where the final product is sold. The MCDPL has effectively banned the sale of beef from cattle raised outside of East Dakota, and the state's cattle ranchers have enjoyed record sales and profits as a result.

The West Dakota Livestock Association (WDLA), a trade organization comprised of cattle ranchers in that state, filed a federal lawsuit challenging the East Dakota MCDPL. After a hearing, the court issued a preliminary injunction barring enforcement of the MCDPL pending a final decision on the merits.

To fund increased cattle health inspections while the WDLA lawsuit was awaiting trial, the East Dakota legislature passed another statute creating a "Mad Cow Tax." The tax is a $1-per-animal charge on all cattle raised in the state, brought into the state, or transported through the state. The WDLA wants to challenge the Mad Cow Tax as well.

1. East Dakota has moved to dismiss the lawsuit and dissolve the injunction on the grounds that the WDLA itself does not export cattle and therefore lacks standing to challenge the MCDPL. Should the court grant this motion? Explain.

2. If the court denies the motion to dismiss, should the court enter a declaratory judgment striking down the MCDPL? Explain.

3. If the court allows the WDLA to amend its complaint in order to challenge the Mad Cow Tax, should it strike down the tax on constitutional grounds? Explain.

Question Number 3

Congress recently passed the "Patriotic Citizen Act," which reads:

(a) Terrorists and terrorism pose a grave threat to the safety and well-being of the United States and the American people.

(b) Except as provided in subsection (c), no person or entity may speak, write, publish, or otherwise express criticism of the United States' efforts to fight terrorists or terrorism.

(c) A person or entity may speak, write, publish, or otherwise express criticism of the United States' efforts to fight terrorists or terrorism if: (1) the person or entity first submits a printed copy of the criticism to the Secretary of Homeland Security; and (2) the Secretary or his designee determines, in the exercise of his sole discretion, that the criticism will not hinder, impede, or obstruct the United States' efforts to fight terrorists or terrorism.

Paula Protestor was charged with violating the Patriotic Citizen Act after she printed and distributed flyers criticizing the federal government's practice of detaining suspected terrorists in prisons located outside of the United States. She did not seek or obtain the approval required by subsection (c) before doing so.

What constitutional arguments could Paula assert in challenging her prosecution? Explain.

Question Number 4

The Holy Order of Brother Juniper (HOBJ) is a religious organization in the state of Minnetucky. In order to establish a private high school, HOBJ successfully lobbied its congressional delegation to introduce legislation granting all high schools in Minnetucky a $1 million grant of federal funds from the Department of Education to be used as each school saw fit. Congress passed the legislation, and the president signed it into law.

Andy Atheist filed a federal lawsuit seeking an injunction against the grant of federal money to HOBJ. In his complaint, Andy challenged the grant as being in violation of the Establishment Clause of the U.S. Constitution. The complaint also stated that Andy was "a taxpaying citizen who will be injured by the unconstitutional expenditure of his mandatory contributions to the United States Treasury."

While Andy's lawsuit was pending, he was elected to the Minnetucky Legislature. His first official act was introducing state legislation that would automatically revoke the teaching license "held by any individual employed by the Holy Order of Brother Juniper." The legislation includes a finding that license revocation is needed "as a punitive measure against an organization that promotes a religion with no scientific merit."

1. Does Andy have standing to challenge the federal grant of funds to HOBJ? Explain.

2. Irrespective of standing, does the federal grant actually violate the Establishment Clause? Explain.

3. If Andy's state legislation is enacted into law, what arguments could HOBJ and its teachers make in a judicial challenge to the statute? Explain.

Question Number 5

In the 2008 Congressional elections, the Republicrat party took control of the House of Representatives. The centerpiece of the Republicrats' campaign platform was the five-point "Compact with the Country." The Compact promised that if the Republicrats became the majority party in the House, they would introduce and vote upon the following proposed legislation during the 111th Congress:

1. A bill to create a new United States Court of Appeals for the Twelfth Circuit, created by carving the states of Washington, Oregon, Idaho, and Montana out of the Ninth Circuit. The bill is premised upon a finding that the Ninth Circuit contains too many "activist liberal judges."

2. A bill to abolish the national United States Postal Service and replace it with a network of state postal systems. The bill is premised upon a finding that the U.S. Postal Service operates in an inefficient and wasteful manner.

3. A bill establishing a new federal minimum drinking age of 25. The bill is premised upon a finding that too many young adults between the ages of 21 and 24 are drinking and driving.

4. A bill criminalizing the possession of any "obscene" material that has been transported across state lines. Under the bill, material is obscene if: (1) it appeals to the prurient interest in sex, as measured by current community standards; (2) the material is patently offensive, as measured by current community standards; and (3) taken as a whole, the material lacks serious literary, artistic, political, or scientific value. The bill is premised upon a finding that obscene material is not protected speech under the First Amendment.

5. A bill delegating complete authority to the Internal Revenue Service to create a new tax code. The bill is premised upon a finding that the current tax laws are too complex.

Is the legislation proposed by the Compact constitutional? Explain.

     Course 5328. Copyright by Rigos Bar Review Series – MEE.

Essay Answers

Answer Number 1

Summary

Equal Protection analysis applies when the state treats similarly-situated people differently. The burden of proof depends upon the petitioner's class. Race, alienage and national origin are suspect classes, and the law must survive "strict scrutiny" (be narrowly tailored to promote a compelling governmental interest). J is in this class due to alienage (citizenship) and national origin. If the law does not discriminate on its face, J must be able to show both a highly disproportionate impact and a discriminatory intent. Aside from gender and illegitimacy, which are "quasi-suspect" classes, all other classes are non-suspect, requiring only rational relation to a legitimate governmental interest, which is satisfied here. Substantive Due Process analysis applies when the government infringes upon a life, liberty, or property right. "Fundamental" rights, like traveling freely from state to state triggers strict scrutiny analysis: the restriction must advance a compelling government interest (the law here satisfies this), and there may be no less intrusive means available (the law here fails this, as it is overbroad).

Issues Raised

(1) Equal Protection
   (a) Suspect Class: Strict Scrutiny
      (i) Race
      (ii) Alienage (citizenship)
      (iii) National Origin
   (b) Non-Suspect Class: Rational Basis Review
      (i) Rationally Related to a Legitimate Governmental Interest
      (ii) Moving Party has Burden of Proof
(2) Substantive Due Process
   (a) Fundamental Right: Interstate Travel
   (b) Strict Scrutiny
      (i) Restriction Advances a Compelling Government Interest
      (ii) No Less Intrusive Means Available
      (iii) Government has Burden of Proof

Sample Answer

(1) Equal Protection. Jaramillo's Equal Protection claim will probably fail. Equal Protection analysis applies when the state treats similarly-situated people differently. The burden of proof (and likelihood of success) depends upon whether the person asserting the claim is a member of a suspect class or a non-suspect class. Here, Jaramillo could characterize himself as belonging to four classes.

(a) Suspect Class: Strict Scrutiny. Race, alienage (citizenship), and national origin are suspect classes. When the class is suspect, the law must be narrowly tailored to promote a compelling governmental interest. This is a high hurdle for the government, which has the burden of proof under strict scrutiny. Jaramillo is a member of the suspect classes of both non-citizens and individuals born outside the U.S. (Obviously, these two classes will overlap considerably.)

However, where the law in question does not discriminate on its face, the plaintiff must be able to show both a highly disproportionate impact and a discriminatory intent. This analysis applies here because the English-only application policy does not expressly bar citizens of other countries or people not born in the U.S. from visiting the State of Harrison. (Indeed, there will be no language problem for most people from other English-speaking countries.) While the expert testimony may establish disproportionate impact, here there is little, if any, evidence that the state intends to discriminate against the two classes. Thus, Jaramillo will be unable to proceed under a strict scrutiny analysis.

(b) Non-Suspect Class: Rational Basis Review. Aside from the "quasi-suspect" classes of gender and illegitimate birth, all other classes are non-suspect. While the Harrison Visitor Card program may disproportionately impact people who do not speak English, such as Jaramillo, those individuals comprise a non-suspect class.

Even if Jaramillo can establish a discriminatory intent (see above) in the state's practice of using only English application forms, rational basis review requires the state to show merely that the policy is "rationally related to a legitimate governmental interest," and Jaramillo has the burden of proof. The government has a legitimate interest in promoting efficiency, and using one standard form has a rational nexus to that interest. Jaramillo will probably be unable to meet his burden of proving otherwise.

Similarly, the class of people who are not residents of Harrison, including U.S. citizens from every other state, is not suspect. If the entire statute is challenged as intentional discrimination against non-residents, the government can simply point to the increase in crime committed by non-residents as a rational basis for restricting out-of-state visitors.

(2)   Substantive Due Process. By contrast, Jaramillo will likely prevail on his Due Process claim. Substantive Due Process analysis applies when the government infringes upon a life, liberty, or property right.

(a) Fundamental Right: Interstate Travel. Some life, liberty, and property rights are deemed "fundamental." One of those rights is traveling freely from state to state. Here, the Harrison Visitor Card law substantially impairs the rights of all non-residents, including Jaramillo, to travel freely to Harrison from another state.

(b) Strict Scrutiny. When the right being infringed upon is fundamental, the government has the burden of showing that the restriction advances a compelling government interest, and there are no less intrusive means available. This is a very difficult showing to make.

While preventing crime is probably a "compelling" interest, the Harrison Visitor Card law is hardly the least intrusive means available to combat the problem. The Harrison Visitor Card requirement imposes a significant burden on all non-residents, criminal or not, who wish to enter the state. Accordingly, the overbreadth of the statute will probably prevent it from withstanding a Substantive Due Process challenge.

Answer Number 2

Summary

Standing requires the plaintiff to show a personal stake in the outcome of the case. Third-party standing for associations like the WDLA exists if the right being asserted is related to the association's purpose. Here, WDLA's exists to promote cattle ranching and wishes to assert rights of West Dakota cattle ranchers impacted by the MCDPL, so it has standing. Under the Dormant Commerce Clause, states may not intentionally discriminate in favor of local interests or unduly burden interstate commerce. States generally may tax commerce if the tax is not protectionist and there is a substantial nexus between the state interest and the activity that is taxed. The Mad Cow Tax unconstitutionally taxes goods still in the stream of interstate commerce, rather than at the beginning, end, or a break in transit.

Issues Raised

(1)   Standing
       (a) Third-Party Standing
       (b) Close Relationship: Association
(2)   Dormant Commerce Clause
       (a) State May Not Unduly Burden Interstate Commerce
       (b) State May Not Intentionally Discriminate in Favor of Local Business
(3)   Taxation by the State
       (a) Not Protectionist
       (b) Substantial Nexus
       (c) Not Taxed in the Midst of the Commerce Stream

Sample Answer

(1)   Standing. The court should deny the motion to dismiss for lack of standing. In general, the doctrine of standing requires the plaintiff to show a personal stake in the outcome of the case.

(a) Third-Party Standing. Put another way, a plaintiff usually must assert his own rights, and not the rights of others. Here, the WDLA apparently wants to assert the rights of its members, since it is a trade organization and presumably not a cattle-ranching entity itself.

(b) Close Relationship: Association. A major exception to the prohibition on "third-party standing" is a close relationship between the plaintiff and the injured party. Associations, such as the WDLA, have standing to assert the rights of its members if the right(s) being asserted is related to the association's purpose. In this case, the WDLA exists to promote cattle ranching and wishes to assert rights of West Dakota cattle ranchers impacted by the MCDPL. The court should accordingly decline to dismiss on standing grounds.

(2)   Dormant Commerce Clause. The federal government's power to regulate interstate commerce has been interpreted to prohibit states from intentionally discriminating in favor of local interests (i.e., intentional economic protectionism) or unduly burdening interstate commerce. Here, nothing suggests that East Dakota is trying to further the economic interests of in-state cattle-ranchers. The MCDPL is a safety measure.

However, the MCDPL is probably an undue burden on interstate commerce. The appropriate analysis involves weighing the state interest and alleged benefit against the impact on interstate commerce. Here, East Dakota has a very legitimate interest in ensuring the safety of its food, but the MCDPL has a crippling effect on interstate commerce, as it effectively locks out-of-state cattle ranchers out of the East Dakota market. Further, the benefit of the MCDPL is questionable, especially without a showing that East Dakota cattle are somehow less likely to have Mad Cow Disease. Because of the undue burden, the court should enter a declaratory judgment striking down the MCDPL as unconstitutional.

(3)   State Commerce Taxation. The court should also strike down the Mad Cow Tax. States generally may tax commerce if the tax is not protectionist and there is a substantial nexus between the state interest and the activity that is taxed. The Mad Cow Tax applies equally to in-state and out-of-state cattle ranchers, and there is a meaningful connection between ensuring the sale of safe beef and taxing cattle.

However, the Mad Cow Tax is unconstitutional because it taxes cattle that merely pass through the state. While states may tax goods at the beginning, end, or any break in transit, they cannot tax goods that are merely in the stream of interstate commerce. For that reason, the Mad Cow Tax is unconstitutional.

Answers 13-588   Course 5328. Copyright by Rigos Bar Review Series – MEE.

Answer Number 3

Summary

Under the First Amendment right to Freedom of Speech, laws regulating speech are either content-neutral or content specific (as here). Outright, restrictions on protected speech (including political speech) must be necessary to promote a compelling governmental interest. Here, the Act unconstitutionally goes far beyond what is necessary to protect the country from terrorism. Laws restricting speech may attacked as facially invalid: overbroad, vague, or giving unfettered discretion (as here). Prior restraint prohibits speech instead of allowing for after-the-fact punishment of speech, and is presumptively unconstitutional. Here, the Act unconstitutionally requires an advance copy of the proposed speech be approved by the Secretary of Homeland Security.

Issues Raised

(1)   First Amendment: Freedom of Speech
(2)   Content-Specific Speech
(3)   Protected Speech: Political Speech
(4)   Facial Attack: Unfettered Discretion
        (a) Facially Invalid
            (i) Overbreadth
            (ii) Vagueness
            (iii) Unfettered Discretion
        (b) Unconstitutional as Applied
(5)   Prior Restraint

Sample Answer

(1)   First Amendment: Freedom of Speech. Paula (P) may challenge her prosecution with multiple arguments rooted in the First Amendment right to Freedom of Speech.

(2)   Content-Specific Speech.   Laws that regulate speech are either content-neutral or content specific. Here, because the Patriotic Citizen Act singles out speech on a particular topic — the federal government's anti-terrorism efforts — the Act is content-specific.

(3)   Protected Speech: Political Speech. While the government may ban unprotected speech (e.g., obscenity or defamation) outright, restrictions on protected speech must be necessary to promote a compelling governmental interest. Political speech, such as P's flyers on the government's detainment of suspected terrorists, is protected speech.

Protecting the United States from terrorists and terrorism is almost certainly a compelling governmental interest, especially in light of the 9/11 terrorist attacks that killed thousands of innocent people, destroyed property worth billions of dollars, and significantly harmed the national economy. However, by generally prohibiting any speech that is critical of anti-terrorist efforts, the Act goes far beyond what is necessary to protect the country from terrorism. The Act is therefore unconstitutional.

(4) Facial Attack: Unfettered Discretion. Laws restricting speech may attacked as facially invalid or unconstitutional as applied. A facial attack allows one to challenge the constitutionality of a law without having to consider the context of the speech in question. Grounds for facial attacks include vagueness, overbreadth, and unfettered discretion. The latter of the three applies to this case. The Act allows the Secretary of Homeland Security (or his designee) to "exercise . . . his sole discretion" in determining whether to permit speech that is critical of anti-terrorism efforts. It is hard to imagine a more blatant case of unfettered discretion.

(5) Prior Restraint. The term "prior restraint" refers to a law that prohibits speech instead of allowing for after-the-fact punishment of speech. Prior restraints are presumed to be unconstitutional. An example would be a law that requires a speaker to obtain a permit before speaking. Such a permit requirement is analogous to the Act's provision that requires the speaker to submit a printed copy of the proposed speech to the Secretary of Homeland Security for approval. Thus, the Act is an unconstitutional prior restraint on speech. While an important government interest such as national security may overcome the presumption of unconstitutionality, the excessive scope of the Act (see above) would likely prevent the government from invoking this exception to justify the Act.

Answer Number 4

Summary

Standing to seek judicial relief requires an injury, causation, and redressability. Paying federal taxes does not impart standing to challenge federal policy, unless a taxpayer challenges a tax-and-spend based expenditure on grounds of the Establishment Clause. A has challenged on this basis, so he has standing as a taxpayer. The government may fund all schools, but religious schools may not use federal money for religious purposes without violating the Establishment Clause. The statute is also an unconstitutional bill of attainder, as the government is using the legislative process to punish a person or group (here the teachers, by taking their licenses) without a judicial trial. The Free Exercise Clause restricts the government's ability interfere with the "free exercise" of religion by subjecting such action to strict scrutiny (no less restrictive means available to achieve a compelling secular end). Procedural due process requires notice and a meaningful opportunity to be heard when there is a deprivation of life, liberty, or property interest (as here, professional licenses are property). *Mathews v. Eldridge* holds that some liberty and property rights (and all lives) cannot be taken away without a pre-deprivation due process proceeding, and uses a balancing test to determine the required timing.

Issues Raised

(1) Standing
    (a) Injury
    (b) Causation
    (c) Redressability
(2) Limited Taxpayer Standing
    (a) No Standing to Challenge Federal Spending
    (b) Exception for Claims Under Establishment Clause
(3) Establishment Clause: Financial Aid
(4) Bills of Attainder
(5) Free Exercise Clause
    (a) Intent to Interfere With, Restrict, Prohibit, or Regulate Religious Conduct
    (b) Subject to Strict Scrutiny.
        (i) No Less Restrictive Means Available
        (ii) Compelling Secular End
        (iii) Government Has Burden of Proof
(6) Procedural Due Process: Timing
    (a) Pre-Deprivation Due Process Proceeding Required for Deprivation of:
        (i) Life (all)
        (ii) Liberty (most)
        (iii) Property Rights (some)
    (b) *Mathews v. Eldridge* Test
        (i) Individual Interest and Risk of Erroneous Deprivation
        (ii) Cost to the Government of Pre-Deprivation Proceedings
        (iii) Availability and Administrative Burden of Additional Safeguards

Sample Answer

(1) Standing. A plaintiff must have "standing" in order to seek judicial relief. Standing requires that the plaintiff establish an injury (such as economic harm), causation (i.e., the injury can be traced to the defendant's conduct), and redressability (i.e., the relief sought must eliminate the harm).

(2) Limited Taxpayer Standing. In most cases, merely being a federal taxpayer is insufficient to create standing to challenge the spending of federal money. An exception exists, however, when a taxpayer seeks to make an Establishment Clause challenge to an expenditure enacted under Congress' tax and spending powers. That is the challenge Andy has asserted in his lawsuit, and accordingly, he has standing to bring it.

(3) Establishment Clause: Financial Aid. The grant of federal money to Minnetucky schools violates the Establishment Clause. The government may provide financial aid to all schools, religious and secular, on the same terms, but religious schools may not use that money for religious purposes. In this case, each school has complete discretion on how to spend the federal grant, which could include using the money for impermissible religious purposes.

(4)   Bills of Attainder.   HOBJ and the teachers could challenge the Minnetucky legislation as an unconstitutional bill of attainder. Both the federal and state governments may not use the legislative process to punish a named individual or group without a judicial trial. The prohibition on bills of attainder includes both criminal and civil punishment. Here, legislatively stripping HOBJ teachers of their professional licenses is precisely the type of legislative punishment that the Constitution forbids.

(5)   Free Exercise Clause.   The First Amendment restricts the government's ability to interfere with the "free exercise" of religion. Where there is evidence of government intent to interfere with, restrict, prohibit, or regulate religious conduct, the law will be subject to strict scrutiny. The government must show that there are no less restrictive means available to achieve a compelling secular end. Here, the statute expressly interferes with religious conduct, and it is questionable whether a secular end even exists. Even if discouraging beliefs "with no scientific merit" is a meaningful secular purpose, stripping all HOBJ teachers of their professional licenses without any pre-deprivation due process (see below) goes well beyond the least restrictive means available to accomplish that end. HOBJ and its teachers should challenge the Minnetucky legislation on Free Exercise grounds.

(6)   Procedural Due Process: Timing.   Finally, the Minnetucky legislation poses a procedural due process problem. Deprivation of a life, liberty, or property interest requires both notice and a meaningful opportunity to be heard, and a professional license is a property interest. Even though the teachers could file suit after their licenses are revoked, under *Mathews v. Eldridge*, some liberty and property rights (and all lives) cannot be taken away without a pre-deprivation due process proceeding. To determine whether the proceeding must take place before or after deprivation, the court will balance the importance of: (a) the individual interest and the risk of erroneous deprivation; against (b) the cost to the government of pre-deprivation proceedings and the availability and administrative burden of additional safeguards. Here, the individual interest — the ability to earn a living in one's profession — is quite important, and there seems to be a significant risk of erroneous deprivation, since the Minnetucky statute is clearly unconstitutional (see above). By contrast, the facts suggest nothing unusual with respect to availability and administrative burden of additional safeguards, and the cost of pre-deprivation proceedings should not be excessive, given that the bill applies only to a small group of individuals. Further, nothing indicates that the pre-deprivation hearings would be unusually expensive, at least as compared to any other hearing. The *Mathews v. Eldridge* test suggests that even if Minnetucky had a valid basis for stripping the HOBJ teachers' licenses, the state would first have to provide the teachers with hearings before it could revoke the licenses.

Answer Number 5

Summary

Art. III of the Constitution requires only one Supreme Court, so Congress may establish or abolish lower courts. Federal congressional power is limited to powers enumerated in the Constitution, including federal postal power. The bill establishing a federal drinking age of 25 invades the powers reserved to the states under the 10th Amendment—specifically states' "police power," here. The bill criminalizing the possession of obscene material violates the First Amendment. Although obscene speech is not protected, possession of obscene material (other than child pornography) in one's own home is a protected privacy right. The statute addresses only obscene material transported across state lines, which falls under Congress' purview by its power to regulate interstate commerce. Congress may delegate legislative power to an agency, committee, the executive branch, or the judiciary, including allowing the IRS to create a new tax code.

Issues Raised

(1) Article III Courts
(2) Congressional Enumerated Powers: Postal Power
(3) Federalism: Federal Congressional Powers
(4) Congressional Enumerated Powers: Tax and Spend Power
(5) First Amendment: Unprotected Speech
    (a) Obscenity
    (b) Child Pornography
(6) Congressional Enumerated Powers: Commerce Power
(7) Delegation of Legislative Powers

Sample Answer

(1) Article III Courts. The bill to create a new 12th Circuit Court of Appeals for certain states currently in the 9th Circuit is constitutional. Article III of the Constitution requires only that there be one Supreme Court. Congress has the power to establish or abolish lower Article III courts, such as the Courts of Appeal.

(2) Congressional Enumerated Powers: Postal Power. The bill to abolish the national postal service and replace it with a system of state postal services is unconstitutional. Federal congressional power is limited to the powers enumerated in the Constitution, but the postal power is one of the enumerated powers. Further, the postal power is exclusive to the federal government, and the creation of state postal systems would violate this exclusivity.

(3) Federalism: Federal Congressional Powers. The bill establishing a federal drinking age of 25 is, as described, unconstitutional. Again, federal congressional power is limited to the enumerated powers; other powers are reserved to the states under the 10th Amendment. Only the states, and not the federal government, have the general "police power" to legislate for health, safety, and welfare.

(4)   Congressional Enumerated Powers: Tax and Spend Power. While Congress could pressure the states to raise the drinking age by withholding federal money from states that refuse to comply (and has done so in the past), a simple federal decree establishing a drinking age is not constitutional.

(5)   First Amendment: Unprotected Speech. The bill criminalizing the possession of obscene material is unconstitutional.

    (a) Obscenity. While it is true that obscene speech is not protected under the First Amendment, and the definition of obscenity in the bill is the same obscenity test established by the Supreme Court, private possession of obscene material in one's own home is protected as a privacy matter.

    (b) Child Pornography. Despite the general rule above, mere possession of child pornography may be prosecuted.

(6)   Congressional Enumerated Powers: Commerce Power. The proposed obscenity statute, if constitutional, would apply only to obscene material transported across state lines. This type of limitation allows Congress to regulate matters otherwise reserved to the states under the Tenth Amendment because Congress has the power to regulate interstate commerce. Nonetheless, the statute is unconstitutional for the First Amendment reason discussed above.

(7)   Delegation of Legislative Powers. The bill allowing the IRS to create a new tax code is constitutional. For the most part, Congress may delegate legislative power to an agency, committee, the executive branch, or the judiciary. The major restrictions on this ability to delegate are: (a) Congress may not reserve veto power over the actions of a delegatee; and (b) Congress may not delegate the powers to impeach or declare war. Other delegations, including the proposal for a new IRS-created tax code, are constitutional.

CHAPTER 14

CRIMINAL LAW

AND

PROCEDURE

RIGOS BAR REVIEW SERIES

UNIFORM MULTISTATE ESSAY EXAM (MEE) REVIEW

CHAPTER 14

CRIMINAL LAW AND PROCEDURE

Table of Contents

A.		Sub-Topic Exam Issue Distribution	14-599
B.		MEE Subject Coverage	14-603
	I.	Opening Argument	14-603
	2.	Primary Issue Statements	14-603
	3.	Text	MBE Volume 2
	4.	Magic Memory Outlines®	MBE Volume 2
C.		Criminal Law and Procedure Essay Questions	14-605
D.		Criminal Law and Procedure Essay Answers	14-611
E.		Acronyms	15-641

RIGOS BAR REVIEW SERIES
MEE SUB-TOPIC FREQUENCY DISTRIBUTION

CRIMINAL LAW & CRIMINAL PROCEDURE

Beginning in 2010 we have distributed all NCBE Criminal Law and Procedure essay questions released since they began testing the subject.

	2/09	7/08	2/08	7/07
CRIMINAL LAW— Opening Statement				
Requirements for Criminal Liability				
Actus Reus: Omission/Failure to Act & Legal Duty to Act				
Mens Rea: Intent; Malice; Recklessness; Criminal Negligence; Strict Liability				
Knowledge of the Law & Mistake of Law				
Transferred Intent: Between Victims & Between Crimes				
Causation: "But For" Test & Substantial Factor Test; Proximate Cause				
Accomplice Liability				
DEFENSES				
Insanity— M'Naghten Test; Irresistible Impulse; MPC Substantial Capacity; Durham Test				
Competence to Stand Trial: Intoxication; Infancy				
Duress & Entrapment				
Defense of Self: Reasonable Force; Imminent Harm				
Defense of Others & Defense of Property				
INCHOATE OFFENSES				
Solicitation				
Conspiracy				
Attempt				
HOMICIDE				
Murder—Malice Aforethought; Causation				
First Degree: Premeditation				
Felony Murder; BARRK Felonies: Burglary, Arson, Robbery, Rape, Kidnapping				
Second Degree				
Manslaughter—Involuntary & Voluntary				
Negligent Homicide				

	2/09	7/08	2/08	7/07
THEFT				
Larceny				
Receiving Stolen Goods				
Robbery				
Burglary – BEDIN: Breaking; Entering; Dwelling; With Intent; Night				
BATTERY				
ASSAULT				
RAPE—Consent; Statutory Rape				
KIDNAPPING/ FALSE IMPRISONMENT				
ARSON				
BLACKMAIL & EXTORTION				
CRIMINAL PROCEDURE—Opening Statement			/	
Applicable Law: Federal Constitution			/	
Due Process Clause of the 14th Am applies 4th, 5th, & 6th Ams to states			/	
FOURTH AMENDMENT— SEARCH & SEIZURE			//	
Legitimate Expectation of Privacy & "Plain View" Doctrine			/	
Arrest: Probable Cause			/	
Warrant			/	
Effect of Unlawful Arrest				
Detention & Seizure of Persons—"In Custody"			//	
Probable Cause to Search				
Warrant Search; Scope of Warrant; Exceptions to a Warrant				
Search Incident to Arrest & Inventory of Impounded Property				
Protective Sweep				
Automobiles: Stop; Search; Locked Places; Impound				
Stop and Frisk—Terry Stops: "articulable and reasonable suspicion" of criminal activity				
Consent to Search				
Exigent Circumstances: In Hot Pursuit; Emergencies; Evanescent (Disappearing) Evidence				
Wiretapping/Eavesdropping				
FIFTH AMENDMENT—CONFESSION & INTERROGATION			/	

	2/09	7/08	2/08	7/07
Coercion *vs.* Voluntary			//	
Miranda—Four Warnings; "Custodial Interrogation"			/	
Waiver of Miranda			/	
Effect of Assertion of Miranda Rights			/	
Invoking Right to Silence and/or Right to Counsel			/	
Subsequent Waiver or Assertion of Rights			/	
Impeachment Use				
Held to answer for crime without grand jury indictment				
Double Jeopardy				
Lesser Included Offenses				
Compelled to be a witness against self				
SIXTH AMENDMENT—PRE-TRIAL & TRIAL PROCEEDINGS				
Speedy and public trial				
Impartial jury where crime committed				
Right to Counsel				
Waiver of Right to Counsel				
Identification Procedures				
Indictment or Information & Preliminary Hearings				
Guilty Pleas				
Right to a Speedy and Public Trial by Jury				
Right to a Separate Trial				
Right to be Present at Trial				
Rights Provided by the Confrontation Clause				
Remedies for Violations of Constitutional PROTECTIONS				
Exclusionary Rule			//	
Fruits of the Poisonous Tree: Wong Sun v. United States			/	
Harmless Error			//	

OPENING ARGUMENT AND PRIMARY ISSUES

CRIMINAL LAW AND PROCEDURE

The following material is a brief overview of some, but not all, of the key issues in Criminal Law and Procedure. Candidates in jurisdictions that administer MEE essays on the six MBE subjects should consult the two-volume *Rigos Bar Review Series – MBE* Volume 2 at page 6-305 for complete textual coverage and Magic Memory Outlines® software. These books and other Rigos Bar Review Series publications are sold at law school bookstores throughout the nation and online at http://lawschool.aspenpublishers.com.

There are a few thoughts that should usually be stated at the beginning of every answer. These will score you easy points and let the grader know you are in the right topic area.

Most essays should have an "opening argument": a brief, broad statement that shows you understand the broad significance of a legal topic. The opening argument also suggests to the grader that she is about to read a thoughtful and well-organized essay.

Many subjects also have "primary issues" that can be discussed up front or integrated into the essay answer. IMPORTANT: Do not merely regurgitate these statements on the exam without addressing the issues actually raised by the facts, or you will not pass.

- **Criminal Law Opening Argument:** Criminal law protects the peace and dignity of the state.

- **Sample Primary Issue Statements:**

  - A crime requires both a culpable act or failure to act (actus reus) and a culpable mental state (mens rea) of intent, knowledge, recklessness, or criminal negligence.

  - The criminal degree of proof is "beyond a reasonable doubt."

  - A criminal attempt to commit a crime applies if the D does an act constituting a substantial step toward commission of the crime.

  - Criminal solicitation applies if D offers anything of value to another to engage in specific criminal conduct.

  - Criminal conspiracy applies when two or more people agree to commit a crime and any one of them takes a substantial step in furtherance of their agreement.

  - Homicide is the killing of a human being by the act, procurement, or omission of another.

- First degree murder requires premeditated intent to cause death, extreme indifference to human life, or felony murder.

- Felony murder is the death of a third party non-participant that occurred during the attempt, the act, or flight from a dangerous felony including burglary, arson, rape, robbery, or kidnapping.

- **Criminal Procedure Opening Argument:** Proper criminal procedure protects the rights of the accused and attempts to ensure a fair legal process.

- **Sample Primary Issue Statements:**

  - The court will find a 4th Amendment improper search violation if there is state action, a reasonable expectation of privacy, and the state lacked probable cause (PC) to act.

  - Under the 4th Amendment, a person can be arrested only pursuant to a warrant issued by a neutral magistrate who has made a determination of probable cause (a crime was committed and the person sought did it). Arrest without a warrant is allowed if made pursuant to probable cause and some exception (felony suspect in a public place, exigent circumstances).

  - Miranda warnings are required if the person is under custodial interrogation (right to remain silent, anything said can be used against you in a court of law, right to an attorney, if you cannot afford an attorney, court will appoint one). A search and seizure of the person or place under the 4th must be accompanied by PC and a warrant unless a warrant exception applies. Evidence obtained in violation of such will be excluded under the exclusionary rule as the fruits of the poisonous tree.

  - If the police have acted without a proper warrant, the state can still prove probable cause at a Gerstein hearing within 48 hours of the arrest.

  - Arraignment must occur within 14 days of the arrest in most states.

RIGOS BAR REVIEW SERIES

UNIFORM MULTISTATE ESSAY EXAM (MEE) REVIEW

CHAPTER 14

CRIMINAL LAW AND PROCEDURE

Essay Questions

Question Number 1

Sharky, an inexperienced and somewhat incompetent criminal, lives in the state of East Dakota. One night, he decided to pay a visit to the Shop-'n'-Spend convenience store. After arriving at the store, he got down on his hands and knees in the parking lot. Sharky crawled through the front doors, which had been propped open to let fresh air inside. He then moved slowly across the floor toward the cash register and jumped up. With a loaded pistol in his hand, he shouted, "Give me the money and nobody gets hurt!" But to Sharky's surprise, nobody was behind the counter. A sign taped to the register read, "Back in 2 minutes." Disappointed, Sharky decided to help himself to a snack. He grabbed a can of soda and a candy bar, and then left the store.

On his way home, Sharky drove by the Pump-'n'-Pay gas station. Thinking that he might have better luck there, he pulled into the parking lot and got out of his car. With his pistol in one hand, he tried to open the door to the building where the cashier was located. But the door was locked. A sign indicated that the gas station had already closed for the night, and the lights were off.

By this point, Sharky was frustrated and angry. He took a half-empty bottle of motor oil sitting by a trash can, poured the contents on the side of the building, and put a lit match to the oil. The resulting fire destroyed the building and killed a homeless man who — unbeknownst to Sharky — was sleeping behind the gas station.

An East Dakota statute provides in part, "Arson is the malicious burning of any building." Also, East Dakota has adopted the Model Penal Code for its statutes regarding inchoate offenses.

1. Can Sharky be convicted of robbery? Explain.

2. Can Sharky be convicted of attempted robbery? Explain.

3. Can Sharky be convicted of murder? Explain.

Question Number 2

After a long night of consuming many beers at the Tap-a-Keg Tavern, Billy Bob stumbled out of the bar and began walking home. Due to his level of intoxication, he was unable to distinguish his house from other similar tract homes in his suburban neighborhood. At approximately 3 a.m., while believing that he was standing on his own porch, Billy Bob opened the unlocked front door of Ned's house. Billy Bob went inside and passed out on the living room sofa.

A few hours later, after the sun had risen, Ned woke up and went from his bedroom to the kitchen to cook breakfast. When Ned saw Billy Bob on the sofa, Ned panicked and called 911. When the operator asked him what the emergency was, Ned exclaimed, "There's a burglar sleeping in my living room!"

The police came to Ned's house and arrested Billy Bob. At the county jail, Billy Bob was released on his own recognizance after he had sobered up. Billy Bob returned to Ned's house and stood outside on the sidewalk. When Ned stepped outside of his house to retrieve his mail, Billy Bob pulled a knife out of his pocket and told Ned, "If you're smart, you won't make a move." After a minute of holding the knife at Ned's throat, Billy Bob said, "I'm going to give you a break. Now get out of here before I change my mind. Ned ran back into the house and called 911. The police responded and arrested Ned once again.

1. Can Billy be charged with common law burglary? Explain.

2. What crime(s) could Billy Bob be charged with as a result of the incident on the sidewalk? Explain.

Question Number 3

Despite two prior convictions for the same offense, Sam was arrested by the Anytown Police Department (APD) and charged once again with burglary. To avoid a harsh sentence under the Anystate "three strikes law," Sam entered into a plea bargain that required him to cooperate as a confidential informant for the APD, which was investigating a rash of burglaries in Anytown.

Detective Dave asked Sam, who had already provided the APD with several accurate tips if he could help with an investigation of Bob, the suspected leader of a local burglary ring. Sam said, "Sure. Bob and his boys break into people's houses, steal stuff, and then resell it on those Internet auction sites. They're smart, though. They stash the goods for maybe six months to a year in Bob's basement before selling them. Bob told me all about this when he asked if I wanted to work with him. He even showed me a bunch of big-screen TVs he'd ripped off and said I could have one if I'd join his crew. Just go to 491 Birch Tree Lane."

After this interview, Detective Dave prepared and signed an affidavit that set forth in detail Sam's history as a confidential informant for the APD and the allegations Sam had made about Bob. While reviewing the affidavit and application for a warrant, Magistrate Marvin commented, "491 Birch Tree? That's two blocks from where I live. I'll bet this is the guy who broke into my house and stole my DVD player. And even if it isn't, your informant's tip looks pretty solid." Magistrate Marvin then signed a warrant authorizing the requested search.

APD officers lawfully executed the warrant, seized several televisions, stereos, computers, and DVD players found in Bob's basement, and arrested Bob. After booking and processing Bob, the APD placed him in a jail cell with an undercover officer posing as a fellow inmate. The "cellmate" asked, "So what are you in for?" Bob replied, "Some pretty serious theft, man. They found all sorts of stuff we ripped off." The county prosecutor subsequently charged Bob with larceny.

1. Can Bob successfully challenge the legality of the search and suppress the evidence found in his basement? Explain.

2. Can Bob successfully move to suppress the statement he made to the undercover officer in the jail cell? Explain.

Question Number 4

The Ocean City Police received a call reporting that a misdemeanor fistfight had occurred at the local beach. The caller described one of the participants as a Caucasian female sporting hair that had been dyed purple and wearing a neon green swimsuit.

Officer Olivia responded to the telephone call and drove to the scene of the crime. When she arrived, she immediately spotted a woman matching the description provided by the caller. Officer Olivia approached the suspect and said, "Ma'am, we received a report of a person who looks like you getting into a physical altercation. I need you to stay here for a moment while I investigate. But first, I have to check you for weapons."

Officer Olivia observed no unusual bulges under the woman's skin-tight swimsuit, but proceeded to perform a quick pat-down search. At one point, she felt a small, soft item underneath the swimsuit. She reached inside and pulled out a small packet filled with a white powder. Officer Olivia proceeded to arrest the suspect and transported her to jail. A laboratory test determined that the white powder was crushed alprazolam, a Schedule IV controlled substance that is commonly prescribed by physicians. The suspect was then charged with unlawful possession of a controlled substance.

At her trial, the defendant elected to take the stand in her own defense. During cross-examination, the prosecutor asked her, "Has a doctor ever written you a prescription for alprazolam?" The defendant responded, "I decline to answer that question on the grounds that the answer may incriminate me." The judge held the defendant in contempt for refusal to answer.

1. Would a motion to suppress the alprazolam be granted? Explain.

2. Did the court err in holding the defendant in contempt? Explain.

　　　　　　Course 5328. Copyright by Rigos Bar Review Series – MEE.

Question Number 5

Adam is the owner of a relatively unsuccessful debt collection agency. Worried about being unable to pay his own bills, Adam began moonlighting as a bookie and using his employees to collect from losing bettors. In order to conceal the illegal nature of the scheme from his staff, Adam enlisted the help of his trusted assistant Bill. Adam explained to Bill what he was doing and asked Bill to enter the "debts" into the agency's database with a lawful sports betting parlor listed as the creditor. Bill complied.

Charlie, one of the telephone collectors employed by Adam, queried the database for a random debt and saw the following appear on his computer screen:

Debtor: Willy Wager
Address: 317 Meridian Street
Telephone: 555-6170
Creditor: Pro-Action Sportsbook
Amount: $500.00
Notes: Losing bet on Brighton Blue Sox baseball game, 07/22

Unaware of what Adam and Bill had done, Charlie picked up the phone and called Willy. When Willy answered, he invited Charlie to "take a long walk off a short pier" and hung up.

Company policy prohibited the employees from trying to collect debts in person. Nonetheless, an angry Charlie decided to pay Willy a visit after work. When Willy answered the door, Charlie punched him in the face and exclaimed, "That'll teach you to mouth off to someone who knows where you live, deadbeat!"

As Charlie drove away, Willy wrote down the license plate number and called the police, who promptly arrested Charlie. After Charlie was booked and properly read his *Miranda* rights, he told the police, "I don't want to talk. I do want a lawyer. I have nothing more to say."

After Charlie was formally charged, the police asked Willy to come down to the station for an interview. Without Charlie's attorney being present, the officer who met with Willy showed him all "mug shots" taken during the week of Charlie's arrest and asked Willy if he recognized any of the arrestees. Willy flipped through the pictures, pointed to one, and said, "That's the man."

1. Can Andy, Bill, and/or Charlie be charged with conspiracy to commit battery? Explain.

2. If Charlie is charged with battery, can he successfully move to exclude Willy's statement identifying Charlie as the perpetrator? Explain.

Question Number 6

While sweeping the floor, Jake, the night janitor at the Last National Bank, noticed that the vault door had been left slightly open. He opened the door, entered the vault, and looked in awe at the vast amounts of cash inside. After a few minutes, he said out loud to himself, "Looks as if I'll finally be able to buy that fancy SUV I've been wanting." Jake took a bundle of $100 bills, stuck them in his pocket, and walked out of the vault.

Immediately after he exited the vault, Jake began feeling guilty. He thought for a moment and said to himself, again out loud, "It just wouldn't be right. I can't do this." Jake returned to the vault, put the money back where it had been, left the vault, and locked the vault door. He then wrote the following in his incident log: "Found vault door ajar. No sign of forced entry or anything missing. Closed and secured the door."

The bank's head of security reviewed the report the next morning and decided to look at the security camera tapes from the previous day. Clear video and audio evidence of Jake's actions had been recorded. When Jake reported to work that evening, he was greeted by the police, who arrested him.

After Jake was booked, Detective interviewed him. Detective properly read Jake his *Miranda* rights and asked if he understood them. Jake replied that he did. Detective then asked Jake if he was still willing to talk. Jake replied that he was.

Once Jake had answered some basic background questions, Detective asked, "So, can you tell me what you did last night?" Jake responded, "You said I could have a lawyer, right? Detective replied, "That's correct. It's your decision." Jake thought for a moment and said, "Well, since you've got the tape, I don't see how it would make a difference." He then confessed to his actions.

1. If Jake is charged with a crime and later moves to suppress his confession, will the court grant his motion? Explain.

2. Can Jake be convicted of embezzlement? Explain.

3. Can Jake be convicted of larceny? Explain.

Essay Answers

Answer Number 1

Summary

A robbery conviction requires larceny, and also the property must be taken (1) from the owner's person or presence, and (2) through intimidation or force. Larceny requires (1) a trespassory taking, and (2) carrying away, of (3) tangible personal property, (4) in the possession of another, with intent to deprive permanently. S's acts satisfy all larceny elements, but he did not satisfy either of the two elements of robbery—although he attempted to do so. The MPC defines the crime of attempt as (1) specific intent to commit the underlying crime, and (2) taking a "substantial step" in furtherance of the crime. S intended to intimidate the clerk to take and carry away the cash, and he took a substantial step when he snuck in with a gun. He attempted the same crime at the gas station. He took a substantial step by attempting to enter while armed and dangerous, and his intent to permanently deprive them may be inferred. S may not defend by claiming that he abandoned the attempt, as he stopped only because the crime had become too difficult. S may also be convicted of felony murder (a foreseeable death occurs during the course of a "dangerous" felony, even with no intent to cause a death). Here, arson is a dangerous felony, and S set fire to a non-abandoned building with malice. It was foreseeable that his action could cause injury or death, so S committed felony murder.

Issues Raised

(1) Robbery
    (a) Property Must Taken from the Owner's Person or Presence
    (b) Taking Through Intimidation or Force
(2) Larceny
    (a) Trespassory Taking
    (b) Carrying Away
    (c) Tangible Personal Property
    (d) In the Possession of Another
    (e) With Intent to Deprive Permanently
(3) Attempt
(4) Abandonment of Attempt
(5) Felony Murder
    (a) Death During the Course of a Dangerous Felony
    (b) Death was Foreseeable
(6) Arson
    (a) Malice
    (b) Foreseeability

<h1 align="center">Sample Answer</h1>

(1) Robbery. Sharky cannot be convicted of robbery. A robbery conviction requires all elements of larceny, as well as: 1) the property must be taken from the owner's person or presence; and 2) the taking must be accomplished through intimidation or force.

(2) Larceny. In turn, a larceny conviction requires: 1) a trespassory taking; 2) and carrying away; 3) of tangible personal property; 4) in the possession of another; 5) with intent to deprive permanently that person of the property. Here, Sharky's acts in the convenience store satisfy all elements of larceny. He took and carried away from the store a can of soda and candy bar that he neither owned nor purchased, and since he was going to eat and drink the goods, he presumably intended to deprive the store of them permanently.

However, neither of the two additional elements of robbery were satisfied. Sharky took the goods in the presence of nobody, and he used no intimidation or force when he did so. Therefore, Sharky did not commit robbery.

(3) Attempt. Sharky did, though, commit the crime of attempted robbery. Under the Model Penal Code (MPC), the inchoate crime of attempt involves: 1) specific intent to commit the underlying crime; and 2) taking a "substantial step" in furtherance of the crime. Sharky intended to intimidate (and possibly shoot) the convenience store clerk to take and carry away the cash in the clerk's possession. He took a substantial step toward that crime when he snuck into the store with a loaded gun. When that failed, he intended to commit the same crime at the gas station. His substantial step there was trying to open the door and enter while armed and dangerous. Nothing suggests that he planned on returning the money from either target, and given the circumstances, it is fair to infer that he intended to deprive them permanently of that money.

(4) Abandonment of Attempt. While it is generally an affirmative defense under the MPC if the actor abandons the attempt before actually committing the crime, the defense is not available if the abandonment is solely because the crime has become impossible or too difficult, which is what occurred here. Thus, Sharky may be convicted of attempted robbery for his acts at both the convenience store and the gas station.

(5) Felony Murder. Sharky may also be convicted of murder; specifically, <u>felony murder</u>. If a death occurs during the course of a "dangerous" felony, and that death was foreseeable, the actor may be charged with felony murder even if he had no intent to cause a death.

(6) Arson. Here, Sharky committed the dangerous felony of arson, as defined by East Dakota law, when he maliciously torched and burned down the gas station. (Note that the East Dakota statute differs from the common law of arson, which required that the building be a dwelling.) "Malice" involves evil intent; here, Sharky acted intentionally, and the reason for his act (apparently to demonstrate his anger) was evil. Further, it is foreseeable that setting fire to a non-abandoned building may cause harm or death to a person inside or nearby. His killing of the homeless person, unintentional as it may have been, was felony murder.

Answer Number 2

Summary

Burglary is the intentional breaking and entering into the dwelling of another at night with the specific intent to commit larceny or a felony inside. During Billy Bob's (BB) first visit to Ned's (N) house, the breaking requirement is satisfied, but BB lacked any specific intent to commit larceny or a felony inside N's house (which he thought was his own). BB's drunken state presents the defense of voluntary intoxication as a defense (which may eliminate his ability to form the requisite intent). Assault is either attempted battery or intentionally placing another person in reasonable apprehension of immediate bodily harm (as BB did with his knife). Criminal false imprisonment is the intentional and unlawful confinement of another person. A threat of immediate physical force, such as BB putting a knife to N's throat and warning him not to move, qualifies as confinement. Any time period of confinement is sufficient, even one minute, as here.

Issues Raised

(1) Burglary
   (a) Breaking
   (b) Specific Intent to Commit Larceny or a Felony
(2) Voluntary Intoxication
(3) Assault: Apprehension of Immediate Bodily Harm
(4) False Imprisonment
   (a) Intentional Confinement
   (b) Threat of Immediate Physical Force Qualifies
   (c) No Minimum Time Period
   (d) Confined Party Must be Aware
   (e) No Reasonable Means of Escape

Sample Answer

(1)   Burglary. At common law, burglary is the intentional breaking and entering into the dwelling of another at night with the specific intent to commit larceny or a felony inside. The facts clearly indicate that the "entering," "dwelling of another," and "night" elements were satisfied during Billy Bob's (BB) first visit to Ned's (N) house.

(a) Breaking. The breaking requirement is satisfied by physical or constructive opening, for the purpose of entering the dwelling, of anything closed. No force, violence, or damage is required; even opening an unlocked door, which occurred here, is sufficient.

(b) Specific Intent to Commit Larceny or a Felony. However, the facts indicate that BB lacked any specific intent to commit larceny or a felony inside N's house. BB believed N's house to be his own and merely went to sleep. Because this element was not satisfied, BB cannot be charged with common law burglary.

(2)   Voluntary Intoxication. Also, BB's drunken state when he entered N's house raises the issue of voluntary intoxication as a defense. Usually, a defendant's (D) voluntary intoxication (such as BB's consuming multiple beers at the tavern) will not excuse a criminal act. However, if the crime requires specific intent, such as the larceny/felony component of burglary, it may be a defense that the D was too intoxicated to form the required specific intent.

(3)   Assault: Apprehension of Immediate Bodily Harm. BB may be charged for the crime of assault, which is either attempted battery or intentionally placing another person in reasonable apprehension of immediate bodily harm. BB committed the latter form of criminal assault when he pulled a knife on N and held it to N's throat.

(4)   False Imprisonment. Criminal false imprisonment is the intentional and unlawful confinement of another person. A threat of immediate physical force, such as BB putting a knife to N's throat and warning him not to move, qualifies as confinement. Further, any measurable time period of confinement, such as the one minute in this case is sufficient. BB may therefore be charged with falsely imprisoning N.

Answer Number 3

Summary

Under the 4th Amendment, B will likely be able to challenge the search and suppress evidence of the electronics found in his basement. A valid search requires probable cause (PC) and either a proper warrant or a recognized exception to the warrant requirement. Here, PC was established by a confidential informant's tip, provided that a magistrate determined that the information was reliable and the informant was reliable, as here. But the warrant issued by MM was defective, as he was not "neutral and detached," so the search was unlawful, and evidence seized will be suppressed. Prior to charging, B has a right not to incriminate himself under the 5th Amendment if he was detained and the custodial interrogation is conducted by someone whom he understands to be a police officer (unlike the undercover "cellmate"). _Miranda_ rights are intended to guard against police coercion, and that was not present here. After charging, B's 6th Amendment right to counsel would have prohibited the police from questioning B through a "cellmate" without B's lawyer, though voluntary statements are admissible. Since B had not yet been charged, his 6th Amendment rights had not yet attached.

Issues Raised

(1)   Search
    (a) Probable Cause: Informant Tips
    (b) Warrant: Neutral and Detached Magistrate
(2)   Custodial Interrogation
    (a) Fifth Amendment: _Miranda_
    (b) Sixth Amendment: Right to Counsel

Sample Answer

(1)   Search. Bob will likely be able to challenge the legality of the search and suppress evidence of the electronics found in his basement. Under the Fourth Amendment, a valid search requires probable cause and either: 1) a warrant issued by a "neutral and detached" judge or magistrate; or 2) a recognized exception to the general requirement of a warrant.

(a) Probable Cause: Informant Tips. Here, there was probable cause established by Sam's tip. When probable cause is based upon a confidential informant's (CI) tip, factors considered by the magistrate include whether the information is reliable and whether the informant is reliable. In this case, the reliability of the tip is demonstrated by its plausibility (i.e., it is not obviously false or illogical) and the fact that it is predicated upon the CI's personal, firsthand knowledge. Sam's reliability as a CI is demonstrated by his history of providing reliable tips to the police and, perhaps somewhat perversely, Sam's own experience with the same kind of crime at issue.

(b) Warrant: Neutral and Detached Magistrate. However, the warrant issued by Magistrate Marvin was defective, and the facts do not suggest that an exception applied. Marvin was not "neutral and detached"; he believed himself to be a victim and neighbor of the warrant's target. Without a valid warrant or warrant exception, the search was unlawful, and as a general rule, evidence seized during an illegal search will be suppressed.

(2) Custodial Interrogation. By contrast, though, Bob's statement to the undercover "cellmate" is admissible and will not be suppressed.

(a) Fifth Amendment: *Miranda*. Prior to charging, Bob's right not to incriminate himself is based upon the Fifth Amendment. That right applies only when: 1) the suspect is detained for custodial interrogation; and 2) the interrogation is being conducted by someone whom the suspect understands to be a police officer. Here, Bob did not know that his cellmate was a police officer. Fifth Amendment interrogation and <u>Miranda</u> rights are intended to guard against the coercive atmosphere that exists when one is questioned by the police. That coercion is not present when the suspect is responding to a question asked by someone he believes to be a cellmate.

(b) Sixth Amendment: Right to Counsel. Had the interrogation taken place after Bob was charged, his <u>Sixth</u> Amendment right to counsel would have prohibited the police from questioning Bob through a "cellmate" in the absence of Bob's lawyer. (By contrast, if the undercover "cellmate" merely listened to voluntary statements by Bob, those statements could be introduced without violating the Sixth Amendment.) However, because Bob had not yet been charged, his Sixth Amendment rights had not yet attached when the "cellmate" asked Bob what he was "in for."

Answer Number 4

Summary

Probable cause (PC) for arrest requires the police to reasonably believe that it is likely that a criminal violation has occurred and that the suspect was the person who committed the crime. Even with PC, a warrant is required unless the person is a felony suspect in a public place or exigent circumstances exist. This was a misdemeanor and there were no exigent circumstances, so arrest was improper. Without PC and/or a warrant, an officer might detain a suspect in a <u>Terry</u> stop if there exists an "articulable and reasonable suspicion" of the suspect's involvement in criminal activity. Here, the woman matched a detailed description, so O had sufficient grounds to detain the woman. A valid <u>Terry</u> stop allows the O to perform a limited pat-down of the suspect's outer clothing for concealed weapons to ensure officer safety. Here, the crime was a fistfight, and a visual inspection revealed no concealed weapons. Thus, the frisk violated the suspect's 4th Amendment rights, and the evidence thus obtained is inadmissible. Under the 5th Amendment, a person may not be compelled to incriminate herself via her own testimony. However, if a criminal D chooses to testify (as here), she completely waives her right against self-incrimination and cannot invoke it later. It was thus improper for D not to answer the question, and the court was justified in holding her in contempt.

(1)   Arrest
    (a) Probable Cause
        (i) likely that a criminal violation has occurred
        (ii) suspect was the person who committed the crime
    (b) Felony Suspect in Public
    (c) Exigent Circumstances
(2)   *Terry* Stop
    (a) Articulable and Reasonable Suspicion
    (b) Frisk
(3)   Exclusionary Rule
(4)   Right to Remain Silent: Trial

Sample Answer

(1)   Arrest. For a police officer to have probable cause to arrest a person, it must be likely that a criminal violation has occurred and that the suspect was the person who committed the crime. Further, even if probable cause exists, a warrant is required unless the person is a felony suspect in a public place or exigent circumstances (e.g., disappearing evidence) exist. Because the reported crime was a misdemeanor and the facts suggest no exigent circumstances, Officer Olivia could not have arrested the suspect.

(2)   *Terry* Stop. Despite the lack of probable cause and/or a warrant, an officer may, in some circumstances, detain a suspect. This is known as a <u>Terry</u> stop.

(a) Articulable and Reasonable Suspicion. A <u>Terry</u> stop requires "articulable and reasonable suspicion" of criminal activity and the suspect's involvement in that activity. A mere "hunch" is insufficient. However, because the woman on the beach matched a detailed description of one of the people involved in the fight (including a distinctive and unusual hair color), the officer had sufficient grounds to detain the woman.

(b) Frisk.   During a valid <u>Terry</u> stop, if the officer has reasonable and articulable suspicion that the person detained is armed and dangerous, the officer may perform a limited pat-down of the suspect's outer clothing for concealed weapons. The basis for the frisk is to ensure officer safety. In this case, the officer did not have grounds to conduct a pat-down. The crime was described as a fistfight, and moreover, a visual inspection of the woman's form-fitting swimsuit should have made it clear that she had no concealed weapons. The frisk and subsequent seizure of the alprazolam violated the suspect's Fourth Amendment rights.

(3)   Exclusionary Rule. In most cases, evidence obtained by violating the defendant's (D) constitutional rights may not be introduced by the prosecution at D's criminal trial in order to provide direct proof of the D's guilt. The exclusionary rule is enforced by the court granting a motion to suppress the illegally-obtained evidence. Because the alprazolam was obtained by violating the D's Fourth Amendment rights, the court should grant a motion to suppress it.

(4)   Right to Remain Silent: Trial. The Fifth Amendment provides, in relevant part, that a person may not be compelled to incriminate herself via her own testimony.   In most circumstances, a witness must take the stand if called and may assert this right only in response to a specific question. By contrast, a criminal D may elect not to take the stand at all, and her refusal to do may not be considered evidence of guilt. However, if a criminal D chooses to testify, she completely waives her right against self-incrimination and cannot invoke it later. Because the D in this case chose to testify, it was improper for her not to answer the question, and the court was justified in holding her in contempt.

Answer Number 5

Summary

C criminally battered W (intentional or reckless unlawful application of force, directly or indirectly, to another person, thereby resulting in a harmful or offensive touching— here accomplished by punching), but A, B, and C did not conspire to commit battery. Conspiracy is a spoken or unspoken agreement to commit a criminal act, with at least one of the conspirators taking an actual, overt step in furtherance of the agreement. C never agreed to commit an unlawful act, and was an unknowing participant in A and B's scheme, despite the fact that he battered W on his own initiative. A and B may have criminally conspired in their illegal gambling and "collection" schemes, but not to commit battery. In states that follow the <u>Pinkerton</u> rule, conspiracy liability is limited to crimes that were foreseeable, unlike here. When C was formally charged, his 6th Amendment right to counsel attached for all "critical stages" of the proceedings. In-person confrontations (including "line-ups" and "show-ups") are critical, but a photo identification is not; so C had no right to counsel when W identified him.

Issues Raised

(1) Battery
    (a) Intentional or Reckless Direct or Indirect Force Upon Another Person
    (b) Resulting in a Harmful or Offensive Touching
(2) Conspiracy
    (a) Agreement
    (b) Foreseeable
(3) Sixth Amendment: Right to Counsel: Photo Identifications

Sample Answer

(1) Battery. Even though Charlie committed the crime of battery against Willy, neither Adam nor Bill nor Clyde are liable for the inchoate offense of conspiracy to commit battery. Criminal battery is the intentional or reckless unlawful application of force, directly or indirectly, to another person, thereby resulting in a harmful or offensive touching. When Charlie punched Willy, Charlie applied force directly to Willy's face that was offensive at a minimum and possibly harmful. Charlie's intent was demonstrated by both his trip "to pay Willy a visit" after Willy insulted Charlie and Charlie's comment ("That'll teach you . . . !") immediately after punching Willy. Further, touching or using force against another person is generally presumed to be unlawful absent consent by the victim or a privilege (e.g., self-defense), neither of which were present here.

(2) Conspiracy. Nonetheless, Charlie's battery created no conspiracy liability. Conspiracy is a spoken or unspoken agreement between two or more persons to commit a criminal act, with at least one of the conspirators taking an actual, overt step in furtherance of the agreement.

(a) Agreement. Charlie never agreed with anybody to commit an unlawful act. He was duped by Adam and Bill into being an unknowing participant in their scheme, and he battered Willy on his own initiative. He thus cannot be charged with conspiracy. While Adam and Bill may have some sort of liability for conspiracy as a result of their illegal gambling and "collection" scheme, they cannot be charged with conspiracy to commit battery. As discussed above, the battery was committed by Charlie, who was not a conspirator.

(b) Foreseeable. Further, in states that follow the Pinkerton rule (including those that have adopted the Model Penal Code), conspiracy liability is limited to crimes that were foreseeable. It was likely not foreseeable to Adam and Bill that their telephone collector would have visited a "debtor" in person, especially given that doing so was a violation of company policy.

(3) Sixth Amendment: Right to Counsel: Photo Identifications. If Charlie is charged with battery, Willy's statement that identified Charlie will not be excluded. When Charlie was formally charged, his Sixth Amendment right to counsel attached, and he had a right to counsel at all "critical stages" of the proceedings. However, while in-person confrontations (including "line-ups" and "show-ups") are deemed critical, a photo identification is not a critical stage, and thus Charlie had no right to counsel when Willy identified him.

Answer Number 6

Summary

Under the 5th Amendment and <u>Miranda</u>, if a suspect is in custody and being questioned by the police, his confession is inadmissible if he has not been given the <u>Miranda</u> warnings. A suspect's waiver of his <u>Miranda</u> rights is effective only if it is made knowingly, intelligently, and affirmatively, as J's waiver was here. A suspect who originally waived his <u>Miranda</u> rights may later assert them, but only if he does so clearly and unequivocally, as J failed to do. Embezzlement is taking control over property due to a fiduciary relationship with another person with the intent to deprive the owner of it permanently. J is not a fiduciary, however he has committed larceny: the trespassory taking (i.e., without permission) and carrying away of tangible personal property possessed by another, done with the intent to permanently deprive the other person of the property. J's later decision to return the property does not negate the earlier intent to permanently deprive. By putting the cash in his pocket and exiting the vault, J satisfied the "carrying away" requirement.

Issues Raised

(1)   Confession and Interrogation: *Miranda*
    (a) Waiver
    (b) Subsequent Assertion of Rights
(2)   Embezzlement
(3)   Larceny
    (a) Trespassory
    (b) Intent to Deprive Permanently
    (c) Carrying Away

Sample Answer

(1)   Confession and Interrogation: *Miranda*. Under the Fifth Amendment and <u>Miranda</u>, if a suspect is in custody and being questioned by the police, his confession is inadmissible unless he has been given the <u>Miranda</u> warnings (you have the right to remain silent; anything you say can be used against you; you have the right to an attorney; if you cannot afford an attorney, one will be appointed for you).

    (a) Waiver. A suspect's waiver of his <u>Miranda</u> rights is effective only if it is made knowingly, intelligently, and affirmatively. The facts indicate that Jake initially waived his rights.

    (b) Subsequent Assertion of Rights. A suspect who originally waived his <u>Miranda</u> rights may later assert them. However, assertion of the right to counsel must be clear and unequivocal. Jake's question about whether he had the right to an attorney falls far short of this standard, and accordingly, the court will not suppress his confession.

(2)   Embezzlement. Embezzlement is when a defendant (D) has control over property due to a fiduciary relationship with another person, and the D takes that property with the intent to deprive the owner of it permanently. A bank's janitor does not have control over the bank's cash on hand, and therefore Jake cannot be convicted of embezzlement.

(3) **Larceny.** By contrast, larceny is the trespassory taking and carrying away of tangible personal property (such as money) possessed by another, done with the intent to permanently deprive that other person of the property.

(a) Trespassory. A taking is trespassory if the D lacked express or implied permission to take the property. A bank's janitor almost certainly lacks permission to take money in the bank's vault.

(b) Intent to Deprive Permanently. The requisite intent is assessed at the time of the taking. When Jake took the money, he intended to spend it on an SUV, and he therefore intended to deprive the bank of the cash permanently. A later decision to return the property, which occurred here, does not negate the earlier intent.

(c) Carrying Away. The "carrying away" requirement is satisfied by even the slightest movement of the property. Jake's taking the cash it into his hands, putting it in his pocket, and exiting the vault is more than sufficient to satisfy this requirement. When Jake did this, the crime of larceny was completed, and he may be convicted for it.

CHAPTER 15

ACRONYMS

AND

MNEMONICS

Chapter 1: Business Associations

General

Filing Information Requirements for Business Associations: **NAB**

Names
Addresses
Business Activity

Agency

General Fiduciary Duty of Agent: **HOLT**

Honest Dealings
Obedience
Loyalty
Trust

Involuntary Agency Termination: **ISIS**

Incapacity / Death of Principal
Source of Agency Supply Destroyed
Illegality of Agency Agreement
Subject Matter of Agency Destroyed

Partnerships

Partners' Fiduciary Loyalty: **CAP**

Competition is Prohibited
Adverse Interests Create Conflicts
Partnership Benefits and Property must be Accounted For

Partnership Liquidation Priority: **CPU**

Creditors, including Partner Creditors
Partners Capital Account and Contributions
Undistributed Profits

Corporations

Articles of Incorporation Minimum Required Information: **RINS**

Registered Office and Agent
Incorporator(s)
Name of Corporation
Stock Information

Non-Indemnification Reasons: **FICE**

Fiduciary Duty Breach
Intentional Wrongdoing
Criminal Act, or
Excess Distribution to Shareholders

Corporate Board Conflicts of Interest Violations: **CUT**

Competing with Corporation
Usurping Corporate Opportunity
Trade Secret Appropriation

Business Judgment Rule: **RIS**

Reasonable Decision at the Time
Made **I**n Good Faith
Supported by Rational Basis after Investigation

Shareholder Suit Seeking Dissolution Reasons: **FOWD**

Fraud
Oppression
Waste of Assets
Deadlock

LLCs

Filed LLC Articles Must Contain: **NOMAD**

Name
Organization
Manager-Managed
Address and Registered Agent
Date of Dissolution

LLC Dissociation Events: **WIDE**

Withdrawal
Insolvency
Death or Incapacity
Expulsion

Chapter 2: Conflict of Laws

Escape Devices from the Restatement's jurisdiction Vested Rights Approach: **RADS**

R*envoi* to apply own law
Area of Substantive Law changed
D*épecage* so law applied issue-by-issue
Substance Versus Procedure rule applied

"Interest Analysis" Policy Approach: **CUT**

Contact with the Case
Unprovided-For or No-Interest Cases
True Conflict

Chapter 3: Family Law

Requirements for Registered Domestic Partnerships: **SURE**

Share household
Unmarried to other person
Registered
Eighteen or Older

Valid Marriage Requirements: **CALF SAW**

Consanguinity
(Not) **A**lready Married
License
Filing

Solemnization
Age of Majority
Witnesses

Grounds for Declaration of Marriage Invalidity: **DAFT LUV**

Duress
Already Married
Fraud
Too Closely Related

Lacked Capacity
Underage
Void Out-of-State Marriage

Factors Affecting a "Just and Equitable" Distribution: **DEP**

Duration of Marriage
Economic Circumstances
Property Amount

Child Support Law: **SODA THIEF**

Standard Calculation
Other Expenses
Deviations
Adjustments and Modifications

Long-Distance **T**ransportation
Health Care
Life **I**nsurance
Educational Support
Federal Tax Exemptions

Chapter 4: Federal Civil Procedure

Required Complaint Contents: **JARR**

Jurisdiction
Allegation of Facts
Right to Relief
Relief Requested

Class Action Lawsuit Requirements: **CULP**

Common Questions
Usual Claim
Large Membership
Protection

Methods of Discovery: **PRIDE**

Production of Documents
Requests for Admission
Interrogatories
Depositions
Examinations (Physical and Mental)

Remedies for Discovery Abuse: **POSE**

Protective Orders,
Orders Compelling Discovery,
Sanctions for Violation of Order,
Exclusion of Witness

Factors for Granting Equitable Relief / Injunction: **ROMP**

Risk of Irreparable Harm
P's Harm **O**utweighs Herm to D
Likelihood of Success of the **M**erits
Public Interest

Basis for Challenges for Cause: **LIB**

Lack of Qualifications
Incapacity
Bias (Actual or Implied)

Grounds for a New Trial: **JET**:

Juror Misconduct
Errors of Law
Timeliness

Chapter 5: Trusts, Wills and Estates

Required Trust Elements: **SIT with PA**

Settlor / Donor / Grantor / Trustor
Intent to Properly Create a Trust
Trustee

Property / *Res*
Ascertainable Beneficiaries

Trustee's Responsibilities and Liability: **PIN CALL**

Properly Administer
Inform Beneficiaries
Not Delegate Duties

Commingling of Assets Not Allowed
Account to Beneficiaries
Litigate on Behalf of Trust
Loyalty to Trust

Loyalty to Trust Violation: **SOB**

Self-Dealings
Opportunity of the Trust
Borrowing from the Trust

Formal Will Requirements: **SIT with MA**

Signed
Intent
Testamentary Age

Mental Capacity
Attested to

Testor Mental Capacity Requires Understanding of: **POT**

Property: Nature and Extent of One's Property
Objects: Natural Objects of One's Bounty
Testamentary Effect of Executing the Devise

Undue Influence Factors: **LOAF**

Large unnatural Devise
Opportunity to exert undue influence
Active Participation if Drafting
Fiduciary Relationship

Chapter 6 : UCC Article 3 – Commercial Paper

Negotiable Instruments Requirements: **NUTSS**

Negotiable Words
Unconditional Promise to Pay
Time Certain
Sum certain in Money
Signed by Maker / Drawer

Holder in Due Course: **FINNS**

For Value
In Good Faith
No Notice
Negotiation
Shelter Rule

Personal Defenses: **MUUFFO**

Mutual Mistake
Unauthorized Completion
Uncompletion of a Condition Precedent
Fraud in the Inducement
Other Claims

Real Defenses: **FIDDLS FUM**

Fraud in Execution
Illegality
Discharge in Bankruptcy
Duress
Lack of Capacity
Statute of Limitations

Forgery
Unauthorized Signature
Material Alteration

Transfer Parties' Warranties: **GANDS**

Good Title
Alterations Not Present
No Knowledge of Insolvency
Defenses Not Present
Signatures are Genuine and Authorized

Presentment Parties' Warranties: **GAD**

Good Title
Alterations Not Present
Drawer's Signature

Chapter 7:   UCC Article 9 – Secured Transactions

Super-Creditor Status: **PMSI**

Purchase
Money
Security
Interest

Attachment Requirements: **A Recreational Vehicle – ARV**

Security **A**greement
Rights in Collateral
Value Given by Creditor

Ways to Perfect: **Perfection Calls for Many Things – PCFMT**

Possession
Control
Filing a Financing Statement
Mere Attachment
Notations of Certificates of **T**itle

Chapter 8: ABA Professional Responsibility Rules

Client's Decisions: **AJET**

Accept or reject a settlement offer; or in a criminal case
Jury trial waiver
Entering a plea
Testifying at trial

Factors in Determining the Reasonableness of a Fee (case-related): **SANTA**

Skill Required in matter
Amount Involved
Novelty and Difficulty
Time Involved / Opportunities Foregone
Average Customary Fee

Factors in Determining the Reasonableness of a Lawyer's Fee: **REBER**

Relationship with C
Expertise of L
Basis of Fee
Experience / Reputation of L
Result of Matter

No Lawyer-Client Business Dealings Unless: **TICC**

Terms of Transaction Are Fair
Independent Counsel Advice
Client **C**onsent in Writing

Lawyer **must** Terminate / Withdraw from Representation if **VID**

Violate MRPCs
Impaired Ability to Represent
Discharged by Client

Lawyer **may** Terminate / Withdraw from Representation if: **CURBSO**

Client Pursuing **C**riminal Action
Used Lawyer to Commit Crime
Repugnant Objective
Burden on Lawyer Unreasonable
Serious Client Failure
Other Good Cause for Withdrawal Exists

Prohibited Lawyer Criminal Case Statements: **TOPIC**

Test Results
Opinion or Future Witness Testimony
Plea or Confession
Inadmissible Evidence
Character

A Lawyer may be a witness if any of the following reasons apply: **HULA**

Hardship on Client
Uncontested or Formality
Legal Services Rendered Value
Another Firm Lawyer Witness

Fee sharing with non-lawyers is permitted if involving: **PEND**

Purchase of Practice
Employee Payment Plans
Nonprofit Organization
Death or Disability of Lawyer

Lawyer oral solicitation seeking future representation is prohibited other than from: **ROFF**

Relatives
Other lawyers
Former clients
Friends

Three situations where Lawyer is not required to report misconduct: **CAD**

Confidential information of C
Assistance program source
Defense attorney retained

Chapter 9: Common Law Contracts and UCC Sales Article 2

Your overall memory ladder acronym for contract law: **OAC LLS VIPR TAD**

Offer by offeror with definite terms expressing intent to be bound that is not yet revoked or rejected creating the power of acceptance in a particular offeree
Acceptance by offeree through a return promise or performance
Consideration – benefit received by promisor or detriment incurred by promisee

Offer – **DIPP**

Definite Terms with
Intention to create a present
Power of Acceptance in a
Particular Offeree

Remember the formation **OAC** trilogy of **o**n **a**pproved **c**redit

Legal capacity of contracting parties – not **i**nfant, **i**nsane, or **i**ntoxicated (3Is)
Legal subject matter and not against public policy
Statute of frauds (SOF) compliance – writing signed by D – if a **MOULS** contract

Void or voidable circumstances – **MUFFED**
Interpretation of contract – **II PACC**
Performance and breach
Remedies – **MRS DAISI**

Third party beneficiary – creditor or done
Assignment of Rights by promisee to assignee
Delegation of Duties by obligor to delegatee

Common Law Contract Subjects: **SIR**

Services include personal (employee's labor), professional (attorney's advice), and construction (builder's construction).
Intangibles include software, patents, trademarks, copyrights, accounts receivable, legal claims, and money.
Real estate includes contracts for the sale, purchase, or encumbrance of land.

UCC Order of Imposing Gap-Filling Terms: **CPU**

Course of performance
Past course of dealings
Usage of trade

Acceptance Changes that Materially Alter Bargain: **MOP**

Materially change the essence of the bargain
Objected to by the offeror, or such additional terms were
Precluded in the offer

Incapacity Defenses: **3 Is**

Infants
Insanity
Intoxication

Reasonable Terms Required for Non-Compete Agreements: **SAT**

Subject
Area
Time

Statute of Frauds Requiring a Writing and D's Signature: **MOULS**

Marriage Including Property Transfer
Over One Year to Performance
UCC If $500 US or More – PAWS Exceptions
Land Sale or Lease
Suretyship Promises

UCC If $500 US or More: **PAWS** Exceptions: to SOF

Part Performance
Admission by D
Written Merchant-to-Merchant Confirmations

Void or Voidable Circumstances: **MUFFED**

Mistakes
Unconscionability
Fraud
Fiduciary's Undue Influence
Estoppel Defenses
Duress

Fraud In the Inducement: **FIRD**

False Statement of a Material Fact
Intention to Deceive
Reliance on the False Statement
Damages

Interpretation of Contract: **II PACC**

Intentions of Parties Control
Incorporation by Reference
Parol Evidence Rule – DUCAS Exceptions
Ambiguity
Controlling Statute
Conflict of Laws

Parol Evidence Rule: **DUCAS** Exception

Defect in Formation
UCC Trade and Dealings
Condition Precedent
Ambiguity Interpretation
Subsequent Modifications

Free **o**n **B**oard (**FOB**)

Free **A**longside (**FAS**)

Cost, **I**nsurance, and **F**reight (**CIF**)

Letter **o**f **C**redit (**LOC**)

Cash **o**n **D**elivery (**COD**)

Warranty Exclusions and Disclaimers Require: **5 Cs Test**:

Clear
Conspicuous
Conscionable
Consistent
Consumer Purchaser

Excusable Nonperformance: **CIISSU**

Cooperation Lacking or Hindrance
Illegality After Formation
Incapacity of Personal Service Contractor
Source of Supply Impassible
Subject Matter Destroyed
UCC Failure of a Presupposed Condition

REMEDIES: **MRS DAISI**

Money Damages
Rescission / Reformation / Replevin / Restitution – 4 Rs
Specific Performance

Declaratory Judgment
Accounting
Injunctions
Statute of Limitations
In Quasi-Contract

Rescission / Reformation / Replevin / Restitution: **4 Rs**

Rescission or a Complete Undoing
Reformation or Changing the Contract
Restitution – value added or compensate victim
Replevin of Stolen Goods

Chapter 10: Torts

Parent – Child Liability: **SAD**

Supervision Failure
Agency for Family
Dangerous Instrumentality

Proof Not Required: **BAFTD**

Battery
Assault
False imprisonment
Trespass to land
Defamation

SOP

Defense of **S**elf
Defense of **O**thers
Defense of **P**roperty

Negligence: **ABCD**

A D's duty to P
Breach of Duty
Causes Harm
Damages to P

Fraud Element: **FIRD**

False Statement of Fact
Intention / Scienter
Reliance
Damages

Product Defense Balancing Test: **RAD**

Reasonable
Alternative
Design

Product Liability Defenses: **SCAAM**

State of the Art
Comparative Fault
Assumption of the Risk
Alteration
Misuse or Overuse

Defamation Definition: **FPID**

False statement of fact concerning P
Publicized to a third person (in understandable language) with a wrongful
Intention or at least negligence in exposing the P to hatred, contempt, ridicule, or disgrace that
      creates
Damages to P's reputation and good name

Per Se Defamation Damage Categories: **LUNI**

Loathsome Disease
Unchastity or Other Serious Sexual Misconduct
Notorious Criminal Allegation
Injury in Trade, Business, or Profession

Defamation Defenses: **TEMPR**

Truth
Express or Implied Consent
Mere Subjective Opinion
Privilege
Retraction

Chapter 11: Real Property and Future Interests

Joint Tenancy Four Unities Required: **PITS**

Possession
Interest
Time
Source of Title

Rights and Liabilities of Co-Ownership: **PADS**

Possession
Accountability
Duty Fair Dealing
Share Contribution

Easement Methods: **PINE**

Prescription (Similar to Adverse Possession)
Implication
Necessity
Express

An Easement by Prescription requires: **CHO**

Continual Possession for Statutory Period
Hostile to True Owner's Interest
Open and Notorious

An Easement by Implication: **CRAN**
Continuous or Permanent
Reasonably Necessary
Apparent upon Inspection
No Practical Alternative Route

Easement Termination is caused by: **L RAMPS**

Lack of Necessity
Release or Estoppel
Abandonment
Merger
Physical Blockage
Severance

License to Use or Come on Land: **NNAPP**
Non-exclusive
Non-**A**ssignable
Personal
Permissive right to use or come onto the property of another

Requirements for the Benefit / Burden of Covenants to Run: **SPIT**

SOF Writing Required
Privity of Estate (Horizontal and Vertical)
Intent to Bind Successors in Interest
Touch and Concern the Land

Requirements for Equitable Servitudes to Run: **SITS**

SOF Requirement
Intent
Touch and Concern the Land
Successor Notice

Property Listing Agreements: **DEWD**

Duration
"**E**arned" Conditions
Writing
Description of Property

Land Sale Contracts – Marketable Title: **LIPP**

Legal Description
Identification of Closing Entity
Price
Parties

Deed Requirements: **SADD**

SOF Requirements
Acknowledgement
Description of Property
Delivery of Deed

Part Performance Exceptions: **PIP**

Possession Delivered
Improvements Made
Payment by Buyer

Statutory (Warranty) Deed: **TAFED**

Title of Seisin
Authority and Right to Convey
Free of Encumbrances – Marketable Title
Enjoyment Quiet
Defend Buyer's Interest

Bona Fide Purchaser: **FINS**

For Value
In Good Faith
No Record or Inquiry Notice
Shelter Rule

Adverse Possession: **ECHO**

Exclusive
Continuous
Hostile to True Owner
Open and Notorious

Instrument and Recording Requirements: **SADD**

SOF Compliance
Acknowledgment by Notary
Description of Land
Delivery and Acceptance

Rule Against Perpetuities **(RAP)** includes **CEO** (**C**hief **E**xecutive **O**fficer)

Contingent Remainders
Executory Interests
Open Class Remainders

Chapter 12: Evidence

"Daubert" Reliable Methods: **SRA**

Sufficient Facts
Reliable Principles and Techniques
Applied Reliably

Evidence Foundation: **PIFA**

Pertinent
Insufficient Present Recollection
Fresh When Adopted
Accurate

Chapter 13: Constitutional Law

Suspect Class: **RAN**

Race
Alienage (or citizenship)
National Origin

Privacy Rights: **CAMPER**

Contraception
Abortion
Marriage
Procreation
Education
Relations

Not Absolute: **CUL**

Compelling State Interest
Unrelated to the Suppression of Ideas
Least Restrictive Means of protecting the interest involved

Chapter 14: Criminal Law and Procedure

Felonies: **BARRK**

Burglary
Arson
Robbery
Rape
Kidnapping

Burglary: **BEDIN**

Breaking
Entering
Dwelling House of Another
Intent to Commit a Felony or Larceny
Night

State Intrusion on a Legitimate Expectation of Privacy: **SIP**

State action,
Intrusion on private citizens who have a
Privacy expectation

Four Protected Miranda Warnings: **RARI**

Right to remain silent
Anything you say can be used against you
Right to the presence of an attorney
If you cannot afford an attorney, one will be appointed

Right to a Speedy Trial Factors: **LEAP**

Length of Delay
Explanation
Assertion Time
Prejudice

General MEE Information

Analysis I-15
Answer Analysis I-17
Answer Sequence I-15
Call of the Question........................ I-16
Combination Questions I-5
Computer Type or Handwrite I-7
Course Evaluation Form.................... 659
Essay Writing Strategies I-9
Exam Site Tips I-9
Exam Structure................................. I-3
Grading Process................................. I-5
Issue Spotting I-7, 16
Magic Memory Outlines® I-6
MBE Topic Essays I-4
Opening Argument........................... I-15
Organization I-6, 14, 17
Paragraph Structure I-18, 19
Positive Mental Attitude.................... I-3
Practice Essays I-3, 7
Preparation Time Commitment.......... I-7
Requirement Format.......................... I-5
Schedule for Preparation I-23
Scoring I-5
Study Tips I-8
Subjects Tested.................................. I-4
Subject Distribution History............. I-22
Time Management....................... I-9, 13
Time Per Question....................... I-4, 13
Topics I-4
Typing I-7
Uniform National Exam I-3
Writing Tips I-9

Agency

Actual Customer Notice .... T 1-42
Agent's Breach of Warranty
   of Authority .... T 1-41
Agency Coupled with an
   Interest...................................... T 1-42
Agency Termination.................... T 1-41
Agent Liability .... T 1-39

Agent's Duties .... T 1-40
Apparent Authority................. T 1-37, 42
Assumption of Risk .... T 1-41
At Will Contract .... T 1-36
At-Will Employee .... T 1-42
Breach of Fiduciary Duty .... T 1-40
Business Entities.......................... T 1-38
Business Manager........................ T 1-37
Capacity .... T 1-38
Compensation .... T 1-41
Conflict of Interest...................... T 1-40
Constructive Notice .... T 1-42
Contract Liability......................... T 1-38
Creation of Agency...................... T 1-36
Criminal Liability .... T 1-40
Dangerous Activity Delegation .... T 1-39
Death of Principal........................ T 1-42
Definition.................................... T 1-35
Del Credere Agent....................... T 1-36
Delegation of Duties.................... T 1-40
Deliveryperson .... T 1-37
Disclosed Principal...................... T 1-39
Employment Nexus .... T 1-39
Estoppel Authority....................... T 1-37
Exceeding Express Authority .... T 1-41
Express Authority .... T 1-36
Express Authority Limitations ..... T 1-36
Factor.. T 1-36
Fellow Servant Rule .... T 1-41
Fiduciary Duties .... T 1-40
Frolic and Detour......................... T 1-39
Full Disclosure............................ T 1-40
General Agency .... T 1-36
Gratuitous Agent .... T 1-40
Illegality of Agency..................... T 1-42
Implied Authority .... T 1-37
Implied Authority Lacking .... T 1-37
Incapacity of Agent .... T 1-38
Incapacity of Principal................. T 1-42
Indemnification............................ T 1-41
Independent Contractors............... T 1-39
Infant Agent................................ T 1-38
Infant Principal .... T 1-38
Inform Principal.......................... T 1-40
Inherent Authority .... T 1-37

Involuntary Termination ....T 1-42
Land or Related ....T 1-36
Liability of the Agent ....T 1-40
Liability of the Principal ....T 1-38, 39
Liability to Third Parties ....T 1-38
Necessity ....T 1-38
Negligent Selection or
    Appointment ....T 1-40
Non-Delegable Activities ....T 1-39
Nondisclosure of Principal's
    Incapacity ....T 1-38
Notice to Creditors or
    Customers ....T 1-42
Oral Appointment ....T 1-36
Ostensible Authority ....T 1-37
Partially Disclosed Principal ....T 1-39
Past Customers ....T 1-42
Principal's Duties ....T 1-41
Prior Issue Distribution ....T 1-13
Purchase Agent ....T 1-37
Ratification ....T 1-37
Real Estate ....T 1-36
Registration Alteration ....T 1-35
Registration Cancellation ....T 1-35
Registration Requirements ....T 1-35
Registration Status ....T 1-35
Reimbursement ....T 1-41
Renunciation of Agency ....T 1-41
Revocation ....T 1-41
Safe Work Place ....T 1-41
Sales Representative ....T 1-36
Salesperson ....T 1-37
Shop Rights Doctrine ....T 1-41
Source of Agency Supply
    Destroyed ....T 1-42
Special Agency ....T 1-36
Standard of Care ....T 1-40
Statute of Frauds ....T 1-36
Subject Matter of Agency
    Destroyed ....T 1-42
Termination ....T 1-41
Tort Liability ....T 1-39
Undisclosed Principal ....T 1-39
Voluntary Termination ....T 1-41
Work Place Safety ....T 1-41

Partnership

Action Against Partner ....T 1-61
Action Against Partnership ....T 1-61
Adverse Interests ....T 1-60

Agency ....T 1-62
Books and Records ....T 1-61
Capacity ....T 1-58
Capital Accounts ....T 1-58
Capital and Profit ....T 1-57
Charging Orders ....T 1-59
Co-Owner Requirement ....T 1-57
Common Property ....T 1-57
Competition with Partnership ....T 1-60
Contract Liability ....T 1-62
Contribution Right ....T 1-65
Conversions ....T 1-65
Conveyance of Partnership
    Interest ....T 1-59
Conveyance of Partnership
    Property ....T 1-62
Contributions ....T 1-58
Death of Partner ....T 1-63
Default Provisions ....T 1-57
Definitions ....T 1-57
Dissociation ....T 1-63
Dissolution ....T 1-64
Duty of Loyalty ....T 1-60
Entity Organization ....T 1-58
Express Partnership ....T 1-58
Expulsion ....T 1-63
Fair Dealing ....T 1-60
Fictitious Name ....T 1-58
Fiduciary Duties ....T 1-60
Formation Methods ....T 1-58
General Partner ....T 1-66
Good Faith ....T 1-60
Illegality ....T 1-64
Implied Partnership ....T 1-58
Information ....T 1-61
Insolvency ....T 1-63
Joint and Several Liability ......T 1-58, 62
Joint Property ....T 1-57
Joint Tenancy ....T 1-57
Joint Venture ....T 1-57
Judicial Dissolution ....T 1-64
Judicial Expulsion ....T 1-63
Liability to Partnership ....T 1-61
Liability to Third Parties ....T 1-61
Limited Liability Partnership ....T 1-68
Limited Partner ....T 1-67
Limited Partnerships ....T 1-65
Loyalty ....T 1-60
Management ....T 1-61
Mergers ....T 1-65
Non-Waivable Provisions ......T 1-57, 58
Outside Ordinary Course ....T 1-61

Partner by Estoppel .... T 1-58
Partner's Creditors....................... T 1-67
Partners' Ownership Interest .... T 1-59
Partnership at Will...................... T 1-57
Partnership Creditors................... T 1-59
Partnership Dissolution .... T 1-64
Partnership for a Definite Term ... T 1-57
Partnership for a Particular
    Undertaking .... T 1-57
Prior Issue Distribution .... T 1-53
Professional Practice .... T 1-68
Profit and Loss .... T 1-57, 60
Property Rights .... T 1-59
Purchase of Dissociated Interest .. T 1-63
Real Property Transfer .... T 1-62
Records .... T 1-61
Relations of Partners to
    One Another .... T 1-60
Revised Uniform Partnership
    Act (RUPA) .... T 1-57
Right to Books and Records .... T 1-61
Rights of Partners .... T 1-72
Share of Profits .... T 1-57
Sharing Profits .... T 1-58
Statement of Denial .... T 1-58
Statement of Dissolution .... T 1-65
Statement of Partnership
    Authority .... T 1-57
Statute of Frauds........................ T 1-58
Tenancy by the Entireties .... T 1-57
Tenancy in Common .... T 1-57
Tenancy in Partnership .... T 1-58
Tort Liability .... T 1-62
Transactions with Partnership ...... T 1-60
Types of Partnerships .... T 1-57
Withdrawal from Partnership .... T 1-63
Windup .... T 1-64
Wrongful Dissociation .... T 1-63

Corporations and LLCs

Action Without Meeting............... T 1-93
Administrative Dissolution .... T 1-98
Adoption of Pre-Incorporation
    Contracts................................. T 1-85
Alter Ego .... T 1-96
Annual Meeting.......................... T 1-93
Annual Report .... T 1-87
Appointment of Directors............. T 1-89
Appraisal Rights .... T 1-95
Article Amendments .... T 1-86

Articles of Incorporation .... T 1-86
Attributes of Business Entities ... T 1-104
Authorized Shares .... T 1-92
Balance Sheet Test .... T 1-96
Board Meetings .... T 1-89
Board of Directors .... T 1-89
Business Judgment Rule .... T 1-91, 94
Bylaws .... T 1-87
Canceled Shares.......................... T 1-92
Close Corporations ..... T 1-87, 90, 92, 98
Competing with Corporation........ T 1-90
Concurrent Affiliates .... T 1-96
Conflicts of Interest .... T 1-90
Conglomerate Combinations .... T 1-97
Consolidations .... T 1-97
Corporate Liability .... T 1-88
Corporate Records .... T 1-94
Corporation by Estoppel............... T 1-87
Court Ordered Indemnification .... T 1-91
Creditor Proceeding..................... T 1-99
Cumulative Voting .... T 1-89
De Facto Corporations.................. T 1-86
De Jure Corporations.................... T 1-86
Deadlock................................... T 1-99
Default Provisions .... T 1-86
Derivative Action .... T 1-94
Direct Action .... T 1-94
Directors .... T 1-89
Director Elections .... T 1-89
Dismissal of Officers................... T 1-91
Dissenter Rights.......................... T 1-95
Dissolution................................ T 1-98
Dividends............................ T 1-89, 95
Domestic Corporations................. T 1-87
Election of Directors.................... T 1-89
Electronic Transmissions.............. T 1-90
Equitable Insolvency .... T 1-95
Equitable Liability .... T 1-97
Estoppel Status .... T 1-87, 96
Failure to Separate .... T 1-96
Fiduciary Duties .... T 1-90, 91
Financial Statements.................... T 1-94
Foreign Corporations................... T 1-87
Formation .... T 1-85
Fraud.............................. T 1-91, 96, 99
Frequency of Testing.................... T 1-85
Fundamental Changes .... T 1-97
Hierarchy of Authority .... T 1-87
Holding Companies .... T 1-97
Horizontal Combinations.............. T 1-97
Hostile Takeover Protection .... T 1-97
Incorporator .... T 1-85, 86

Indemnification Agreements..........T 1-91
Initial Report ....T 1-87
Inspection of Books and
    Records...................................T 1-94
Interested Transactions ....T 1-85, 90
Judicial Dissolution......................T 1-98
Limited Liability Companies
    (LLC)....................................T 1-100
    All Members Manage ....T 1-101
    Dissociation of Member ....T 1-103
    Dissolution............................T 1-103
    Fiduciary Duties ....T 1-101
    Filing Articles ....T 1-100
    Management Authority...........T 1-101
    Managing Member ....T 1-101
    Manager Liability ....T 1-101
    Member Rights ....T 1-101
    Name Restrictions..................T 1-100
    Operating Agreement ....T 1-101
    Pierce LLC Veil.....................T 1-102
    Third Party Liability ....T 1-102
Long-Arm Statutes........................T 1-88
Meetings.....................................T 1-93
Mere Sham ....T 1-96
Mergers ....T 1-97
Minority Shareholders Relief........T 1-95
Name ....T 1-86
Name Reservation ....T 1-86
Negotiable Securities ....T 1-92
Notice of Meetings........................T 1-93
Officers...................................T 1-89, 91
Oppression ....T 1-90, 99
Ordinary Decisions ....T 1-94
Organizational Meeting.................T 1-87
Outstanding Shares ....T 1-92
Payment for Shares ....T 1-92
Permissive Indemnification...........T 1-91
Piercing the Corporate Veil...........T 1-96
Powers..T 1-88
Preferred Shares ....T 1-92
Preemptive Rights ....T 1-92
Prior Issue Distribution ....T 1-79
Professional Service
    Corporations ....T 1-99
    Death of Shareholder..............T 1-100
    Prohibited Activities................T 1-99
    Requirements ....T 1-99
    Shareholder Personal
        Liability ....T 1-99, 100
    Trade Name Restrictions ....T 1-99
Promoter......................................T 1-85
Purpose.......................................T 1-88

Quorum Requirements .... T 1-93
Ratification of
    Pre-Incorporation Contracts ...... T 1-85
Receivership .... T 1-99
Records and Financial
    Statements .... T 1-94
Redeemed Shares .... T 1-92
Registered Agent .... T 1-86, 88
Registered Office......................... T 1-86
Regular Board Meetings............... T 1-89
Removal of Directors .... T 1-89
Revised Model Business
    Corporation Act (RMBCA)....... T 1-85
Shareholder Decision Control ...... T 1-95
Shareholder Dissolution Action ... T 1-98
Shareholder Liability.................... T 1-95
Shareholder Meetings................... T 1-93
Shareholder Resolutions............... T 1-93
Shareholder Rights .... T 1-93
Shareholder Voting .... T 1-93
Shareholder's Derivative
    Action .... T 1-94
Special Meetings .... T 1-89
State Nexus................................. T 1-88
Stock Fair Value.......................... T 1-95
Stock Information......................... T 1-92
Stock Option............................... T 1-92
Stock Right................................. T 1-92
Stock Shares .... T 1-92
Stock Subscriptions .... T 1-92
Stock Warrant............................. T 1-92
Subsidiaries .... T 1-97
Successor Affiliates..................... T 1-96
Synergetic Factors .... T 1-98
Trade Secret Appropriation .... T 1-90
Transacting Business.................... T 1-88
Treasury Shares .... T 1-92
Ultra Vires .... T 1-89
Undisclosed Principal................... T 1-85
Usurp Corporate Opportunity....... T 1-90
Veil Piercing............................... T 1-96
Vertical Combinations.................. T 1-97
Voluntary Dissolution .... T 1-98
Voting Proxy .... T 1-90, 93
Voting Trusts and Agreements..... T 1-94
Waste of Assets .... T 1-99

Conflict of Laws

Abducted Child .... T 2-142
Annulment................................... T 2-138

Choice of Forum by
    Agreement .... T 2-134
Child Custody Judgments............ T 2-141
Child Support Judgments .... T 2-142
Choice of Law .... T 2-135, 138
Choice of Law by Agreement .... T 2-139
Civil Fines .... T 2-139
Claim Preclusion .... T 2-141
Collateral Estoppel .... T 2-141
Connecting Factors............. T 2-137, 138
Constitutional Limitations.......... T 2-140
Contracts........................... T 2-135, 138
Corporations .... T 2-135, 138
Criminal Laws .... T 2-139
Dépeçage Doctrine .... T 2-136
Divisible Divorce .... T 2-134, 141
Divorce .... T 2-134, 138, 141
Domicile .... T 2-133
Due Process .... T 2-140
Erie Doctrine .... T 2-140
Escape Devices........................... T 2-135
False Conflict .... T 2-137
Family Law .... T 2-138
Federal-State Conflicts............... T 2-140
Federal Supremacy .... T 2-140
First Restatement........................ T 2-135
"Foreign" .... T 2-133
Foreign Law .... T 2-139
Foreign Nations .... T 2-139
"Forum".................................... T 2-133
Forum Non Conveniens .... T 2-135
Full Faith and Credit .... T 2-140
General Factors .... T 2-137
Inconsistent Judgments .... T 2-141
Intent to Remain .... T 2-133
Interest Analysis........................ T 2-136
International Judgments .... T 2-141
Intestate Succession.................... T 2-138
Issue Preclusion......................... T 2-141
Jurisdiction of Courts .... T 2-134
Klaxon Doctrine .... T 2-140
Marriage .... T 2-138
Modern Approach .... T 2-137
Most Significant Relationship.... T 2-137
No-Interest Case......................... T 2-134
Parental Kidnapping Protection
    Act (PKPA) .... T 2-141
Penal Laws .... T 2-139
Penal Judgments......................... T 2-141
Personal Jurisdiction .... T 2-134
Physical Presence .... T 2-133
Proof of Foreign Law .... T 2-139

Public Policy....................... T 2-139, 141
Punitive Damages...................... T 2-139
Real Property .... T 2-135, 138
Renvoi Doctrine .... T 2-135, 139
Res Judicata .... T 2-141
Residence................................... T 2-134
Restatement (First) .... T 2-135
Restatement (Second)................. T 2-137
Revenue Laws .... T 2-140
Same-Sex Marriage .... T 2-138
Second Restatement.................... T 2-137
Separation .... T 2-138
Statutes of Limitations............... T 2-138
Statutory Full Faith and Credit ... T 2-141
Substance Versus
    Procedure .... T 2-136, 137, 138
Torts.............................. T 2-135, 137
True Conflict .... T 2-137
Uniform Child Custody Jurisdiction
    Act (UCCJA) .... T 2-141
Uniform Child Custody Jurisdiction
    and Enforcement Act
    (UCCJEA) .... T 2-141
Uniform Conflict of Laws
    Limitations Act....................... T 2-138
Uniform Interstate Family Support
    Act (UIFSA) .... T 2-142
Unprovided-For Case .... T 2-136
Validity of Marriage .... T 2-138
"Vested Rights" Approach .... T 2-135

Family Law

Actions Prior to Dissolution .... T 3-172
Adoption .... T 3-180
Annulment .... T 3-173
Best Interests of the Child .. T 3-172, 176
Child Support............................. T 3-178
Children .... T 3-172, 177
Committed Intimate
    Relationship............................ T 3-176
Common Law Marriages............ T 3-172
Custodial Interference .... T 3-178
Decision Making .... T 3-177
Declarations Regarding
    Validity .... T 3-173
Determination of Paternity .... T 3-179
Dispute Resolution .... T 3-177
Dissolution........................ T 3-173, 174
Domestic Violence .... T 3-172
Educational Support .... T 3-179

Federal Tax Exemptions ....T 3-179
Genetic Testing ....T 3-179
Goodwill.....................................T 3-175
Grounds for Invalidity................T 3-173
Grounds for Dissolution.............T 3-174
Guardian Ad Litem ....T 3-180
"Hidden" Joint Property.............T 3-176
Invalidity ....T 3-173
Joint Property ....T 3-175
Jurisdiction ....T 3-173, 174
"Just and Equitable" Distribution
   of Property..............................T 3-175
Legal Separation ....T 3-173
Life Insurance ....T 3-179
Maintenance...............................T 3-176
Marriage ....T 3-171
Meretricious Relationship...........T 3-176
Modification of Parenting
   Plan.......................................T 3-178
Non-Marital Dissolution ....T 3-176
Non-Parent Visitation ....T 3-177
Parenting Plans...................T 3-172, 177
Paternity ....T 3-179
Permanent Parenting Plans.........T 3-177
Personal Jurisdiction ....T 3-174
Post-Secondary Educational
   Support ....T 3-179
Presumption of Paternity............T 3-179
Primary Residential
   Placement...............................T 3-177
Property Division ....T 3-175
Protection Orders ....T 3-172
Reconciliation ....T 3-173
Registered Domestic
   Partnerships...........................T 3-172
Relocation of Child....................T 3-178
Residential Schedule ....T 3-177
Responsibility for Children.........T 3-176
Separate Property ....T 3-175
Separation..................................T 3-173
Spousal Maintenance ....T 3-176
Surrogate Parentage ....T 3-180
Tax Exemptions ....T 3-179
Temporary Child Support
   Orders...................................T 3-172
Temporary Parenting Plan..........T 3-172
Temporary Restraining Orders....T 3-172
Uniform Parentage Act ....T 3-179
Validity Requirements ....T 3-171

Federal Civil Procedure

Abode Service .... T 4-210
Actions Against
   Corporations .... T 4-211, 215
Addition of Parties .... T 4-221
Amended Pleadings.................... T 4-218
Answer .... T 4-215, 216
Appeals...................................... T 4-236
Attorney-Client Privilege .... T 4-224
Attorney Fees .... T 4-235
Attorney's Thought Processes.... T 4-224
Bench Trial...................... T 4-231, 234
Burden of Proof......................... T 4-230
Capacity..................................... T 4-220
Challenge for Cause .... T 4-231
Challenges to Jurisdiction .... T 4-213
Challenges to the Pleadings........ T 4-217
Change of Venue........................ T 4-215
Claim Preclusion .... T 4-237
Claim Splitting .... T 4-216
Class Actions............................. T 4-221
Closing Argument .... T 4-232
Collateral Estoppel .... T 4-238
Commencement of Action .... T 4-209
Commission of Tort .... T 4-211
Community Property
   Considerations.......................... T 4-210
Compelling Discovery................. T 4-227
Complaint .... T 4-215
Compulsory Counterclaims........ T 4-218
Compulsory Joinder .... T 4-220
Confer Requirement .... T 4-223
Consent to Jurisdiction .... T 4-211
Consolidation of Defenses . T 4-213, 217
Consulting Experts .... T 4-224
Costs .... T 4-235
Counterclaims............................ T 4-218
Court of Appeals .... T 4-237
Crossclaim .... T 4-218
Default....................................... T 4-219
Depositions................................ T 4-225
Discovery .... T 4-223
Discovery Abuse .... T 4-226
Discovery Sanctions................... T 4-226
Discretionary Review .... T 4-236
Dismissals.................................. T 4-228
Diversity Jurisdiction .... T 4-214
Domicile .... T 4-211
Electronically Stored
   Documents.......................... T 4-227
Entry of Judgment .... T 4-234

Equitable Relief........................ T 4-227
Ex Parte Contacts .... T 4-223
"Exception" to Proposed Jury
    Instructions .... T 4-232
Exclusion of Witness................. T 4-227
Expert Witnesses .... T 4-224
Extraordinary Writs................... T 4-236
Fact Witness .... T 4-225
Failure to Appear....................... T 4-220
Failure to Join Indispensable
    Party .... T 4-220
Failure to State a Claim............. T 4-217
Federal Question .... T 4-214
Federal Tort Claims................... T 4-209
Filing .... T 4-209
Forum Non Conveniens.............. T 4-215
Freedom of Information Act ...... T 4-224
Impleader.................................. T 4-221
Improper Venue................. T 4-215, 217
In Rem Jurisdiction .... T 4-214
Indispensable Parties................. T 4-220
Initial Disclosures..................... T 4-225
Insurance Agreement
    Production .... T 4-224
Insurer as Party......................... T 4-221
Insuring Risk .... T 4-212
Internet Transactions .... T 4-212
Interrogatories .... T 4-225
Involuntary Dismissal .... T 4-228
Issue Preclusion........................ T 4-238
Joinder of Claims .... T 4-215
Joinder of Indispensable
    Parties .... T 4-220
Joinder of Parties....................... T 4-221
Judgment as a Matter of Law ..... T 4-233
Juror Bias........................ T 4-231, 233
Juror Misconduct....................... T 4-233
Juror Qualifications .... T 4-231
Jury Deliberations .... T 4-232
Jury Instructions .... T 4-232
Jury Selection .... T 4-231
Jury Size .... T 4-231
Jury Trials......................... T 4-231, 234
Jury Verdict.............................. T 4-232
Lack of Personal Jurisdiction ..... T 4-217
Lack of Subject Matter
    Jurisdiction .... T 4-217
Legal Malpractice...................... T 4-224
Litigation Costs .... T 4-235
Long-Arm Statute...................... T 4-211
Members of Military .... T 4-219
Mental Examinations.................. T 4-226

Minimum Contacts .... T 4-211
Mistrials................................... T 4-231
Motion for New Trial .... T 4-235
Motions in Limine .... T 4-230
Motion to Dismiss .... T 4-217
Motion to Strike Testimony........ T 4-230
Motion to Vacate Default
    Judgment............................... T 4-219
Motion to Vacate Judgment........ T 4-235
Negative Inference..................... T 4-227
Notice Pleading .... T 4-216
Objections.......................... T 4-230, 232
Occurrence Witness.................... T 4-224
Opening Statement .... T 4-230
Orders Compelling Discovery .... T 4-227
Ownership of Property .... T 4-212
Parties .... T 4-220
Peremptory Challenge .... T 4-231
Permissive Counterclaims .... T 4-218
Permissive Joinder of Parties...... T 4-221
Personal Jurisdiction.................. T 4-209
Personal Service on
    Individuals .... T 4-210
Physical Examinations................ T 4-226
Pleading Special Matters .... T 4-216
Pleadings.................................. T 4-215
Polling the Jury......................... T 4-232
Post-Trial Motions..................... T 4-235
Pre-Answer Motion to Dismiss .. T 4-216
Pre-Filing Notice
    Requirements .... T 4-209
Pre-Trial Conference .... T 4-230
Pre-Trial Order .... T 4-230
Pre-Trial Proceedings .... T 4-228
Preclusion .... T 4-237
Preliminary Equitable Relief...... T 4-228
Preliminary Injunction............... T 4-228
Privileges .... T 4-223
Process Server .... T 4-210
Production of Documents .... T 4-226
Products Liability .... T 4-212
Protective Orders .... T 4-223, 226
Real Party in Interest .... T 4-220
Relating Back .... T 4-218
Removal Jurisdiction.................. T 4-214
Requests for Admission.............. T 4-226
Res Judicata .... T 4-237
Rule 11..................................... T 4-216
Rulings on Evidence.................. T 4-230
Sanctions............................ T 4-216, 227
Scope of Discovery.................... T 4-223
Separate Trials.......................... T 4-221

Service After Initial Service of
Process ....T 4-211
Service by Publication ....T 4-210
Service of Process ....T 4-210
Service on Corporations and
Business Associations ....T 4-211
Service on the Federal
Government...............................T 4-211
Setting Aside the Verdict ....T 4-233
Signing of Pleadings ....T 4-216
Spoliation ....T 4-227
Standard of Review ....T 4-236
Subject Matter Jurisdiction ....T 4-214
Subpoena....................................T 4-225
Substitution of Parties ....T 4-221
Sufficiency of Evidence ....T 4-234
Summary Judgment.....................T 4-229
Supplemental Jurisdiction ....T 4-214
Supplementation of Discovery
Responses.................................T 4-226
Supreme Court ....T 4-237
Temporary Restraining Order
(TRO).......................................T 4-228
Third Party Practice....................T 4-221
Timeliness of Defenses ....T 4-213
Timeliness of Objection or
Motion to Strike ....T 4-230
Trials ....T 4-230
Ultimate Sanctions ....T 4-227
Unanimous Verdict ....T 4-232
United States Supreme Court......T 4-237
Venue ....T 4-215
Verdict..T 4-232
Voir Dire ....T 4-231
Voluntary Dismissal....................T 4-228
Waiver of Defenses.....................T 4-217
Waiver of Jurisdiction................T 4-211
Waiver of Privilege ....T 4-224
Waiver of Service........................T 4-210
Work-Product.............................T 4-223
Writ of Mandamus ....T 4-236
Writ of Prohibition......................T 4-236

Trusts, Wills, and Estates

Trusts and Future Interests

Acceptance Not Required ....T 5-278
Account to Beneficiaries.............T 5-282
Accounting Designations ....T 5-275
Accretions ....T 5-290
Administration of Trust..............T 5-281
Agent of Trustee.........................T 5-282
Animal Beneficiaries...................T 5-278
Appointment...............................T 5-277
Ascertainable Beneficiaries........T 5-278
Attachment for Taxes ....T 5-284
Avoiding Probate........................T 5-276
Beneficiaries' Rights ....T 5-283
Beneficiary Accounting
Designation Conflict ....T 5-275
Borrowing from Trust ....T 5-283
Capacity......................................T 5-277
Charging Order...........................T 5-284
Charitable Trusts ....T 5-285
Claim Against Trust ....T 5-285
Claim Against Trustee................T 5-285
Class Beneficiaries ....T 5-278
Class Gifts ....T 5-280
Commingling of Assets..............T 5-282
Consolidation ....T 5-286
Constructive Trust......................T 5-276
Contingent Remainder................T 5-280
Contrary Will Devise ....T 5-279
Corpus Invasion.........................T 5-276
Creditors' Rights ....T 5-283
Custodian for Minor ....T 5-279
"Cy Pres" Doctrine.....................T 5-285
Defense of Trustee ....T 5-283
Defined Selection of
Beneficiaries............................T 5-278
Delegating Duties ....T 5-282
Disabling Restraint on
Alienation ....T 5-284
Discretionary Trust.....................T 5-284
Distribution Decisions................T 5-275
Distribution Discretion...............T 5-275
Diversification of Assets ....T 5-281
Donor..T 5-277
Donor Termination ....T 5-286
Estate Taxes...............................T 5-276
Executory Interest ....T 5-280
Expiration of Term.....................T 5-286
Express Trusts ....T 5-275
Family Support...........................T 5-284
Fertile Septuagenarians ....T 5-281
Forfeiture Restraint on
Alienation ....T 5-284
Fraudulent Transfers ....T 5-284
Future Family Beneficiaries.......T 5-278
Future Interests..................T 5-278, 280
Gifts to Charities ....T 5-280
Grantor ....T 5-277

Highly Speculative Investments . T 5-281
Illegality .... T 5-277, 286
Impermissible Purpose .... T 5-277
Implied Trusts .... T 5-276
Impossibility................................ T 5-286
Income Interest Terminates .... T 5-286
Income Interests .... T 5-275
Incorporation by Reference .... T 5-288
Indefinite Class.......................... T 5-278
Inform Beneficiaries................... T 5-282
Instrument Exculpatory
    Provisions .... T 5-283
Instrument Alienation
    Restrictions............................ T 5-284
Intent to Properly Create .... T 5-277
Inter Vivos Trust .... T 5-279
Joint and Several Liability of
    Co-Trustees .... T 5-283
Judicial Review Petition............. T 5-279
Laches.. T 5-283
Liability of Trustee.................... T 5-283
Life Insurance............................ T 5-278
Litigate on Behalf of Trust .... T 5-282
Living Trust................................ T 5-276
Loyalty to Trust......................... T 5-282
Mere Desire .... T 5-277
Merger .... T 5-277, 286
Modification of Trusts................ T 5-279
Multiple Trustees........................ T 5-281
Natural Objects of Bounty.......... T 5-288
Non-Judicial Resolution of
    Dispute .... T 5-279
Not Delegate Decisions.............. T 5-282
Objective Manifestation of
    Intent..................................... T 5-277
Opportunity of Trust................... T 5-283
Petition to Terminate.................. T 5-286
Pour-Over Provision........... T 5-279, 286
Power of Appointment .... T 5-290
Power to Consume .... T 5-276
Principal Interests...................... T 5-275
Probate.. T 5-276
Productivity of Property .... T 5-281
Promise to Create .... T 5-278
Property Administer .... T 5-281
Protecting Assets .... T 5-276
Prudent Business Person
    Investment Standard................ T 5-281
Purpose Accomplished, Illegal,
    or Impossible .... T 5-286
Reduce Estate Taxes................... T 5-276
Remainder Class......................... T 5-278

Required Trust Elements .... T 5-276
Remainders .... T 5-280
Res .... T 5-277
Resolution of Dispute .... T 5-279
Restraints on Alienation .... T 5-284
Resulting Trust .... T 5-276
Reversion .... T 5-280
Revocation of Trusts................... T 5-279
Rule Against Perpetuities ... T 5-280, 281
Rule in Shelley's Case................ T 5-289
Secret Trust................................ T 5-276
Self-Dealings .... T 5-282
Self-Serving Trusts..................... T 5-284
Settlor .... T 5-277
Significant Non-Routine
    Transactions............................ T 5-281
Spendthrift Trust................ T 5-284, 287
Split Interests .... T 5-275
Statute of Limitations .... T 5-283
Support Trust .... T 5-284
"Surviving Heirs" .... T 5-278, 290
Termination of Custodian for
    Minor .... T 5-279
Tax Attachments......................... T 5-284
Term Expires .... T 5-286
Termination .... T 5-286
Testamentary Trust..................... T 5-279
Third Party Liability .... T 5-285, 286
Total Asset Management
    Standard.................................. T 5-281
Totten Trust .... T 5-298
Transfer Rights .... T 5-284
Trust Elements........................... T 5-276
Trust Organization Formation .... T 5-278
Trust Property .... T 5-277
Trustee .... T 5-277
Trustee Removal......................... T 5-283
Trustee's Allocation Liability..... T 5-282
Trustee's Defenses..................... T 5-283
Trustee's Responsibilities and
    Liability .... T 5-281
Types of Trusts .... T 5-275
Uniform Transfers to Minors
    Act .... T 5-279
Use Restriction .... T 5-284
Utility of Entity......................... T 5-276
Vested Remainder .... T 5-278
Vested Remainder Subject to
    Open .... T 5-280
"Wait and See" Rule................... T 5-280
Wrongdoing Remedy.................. T 5-276

Wills and Decedents' Estates

Abatement ....T 5-300
Accessions.............................T 5-290
Accretions ....T 5-290
Acknowledged ....T 5-288
Ademption...............................T 5-290
Adjudication of Testacy or
   Intestacy ....T 5-297
Administration Functions............T 5-300
Admission to Probate ....T 5-299
Adopted Children.......................T 5-289
Advancement ....T 5-294
Affidavit Attestation ....T 5-288
After-Acquired Property ....T 5-289
After-born Children......................T 5-289
Alternatives to Probate.................T 5-297
Ancillary Administration ....T 5-297
Anti-lapse Statute ....T 5-290
Attestation Requirement ....T 5-288
Beneficiary Accounting
   Designation Conflict ....T 5-275
Born Out of Wedlock...................T 5-289
Capacity Absent ....T 5-293
Cash Legacies ....T 5-300
Child Support ....T 5-292, 300
Claim Approval and Rejection....T 5-299
Claim Time Limit.......................T 5-299
Class Beneficiaries ....T 5-290
Codicils ....T 5-291
Collateral Relatives ....T 5-296
Collect Estate Assets ....T 5-299
Community Property....................T 5-295
Community Property
   Agreement................................T 5-298
Competent Attestation.................T 5-288
Components of Will ....T 5-288
Conditional Wills ....T 5-292
Contract to Make a Will or
   Devise......................................T 5-292
Corpus Management ....T 5-297
Costs of Administration ....T 5-300
Court's Equitable Power ....T 5-288
Creditors....................................T 5-299
Cy Pres Doctrine ....T 5-289
Dead Man's Statute ....T 5-294
Defined Selection.......................T 5-290
Demonstrative Legacy ....T 5-300
Dependent Relative
   Revocation ....T 5-291
Destroyed Wills..........................T 5-299

Determining Shares for
   "Issue"......................................T 5-290
Devise to "Issue" ....T 5-290
Directive to Physician ....T 5-297
Disclaimer ....T 5-290
Disinheritance............................T 5-289
Distribute to Beneficiaries..........T 5-300
Divorce......................................T 5-289
Doctrine of Worthier Title..........T 5-289
Equitable Power ....T 5-288
Escheatment ....T 5-300
Estate Taxes...............................T 5-300
Estates of Absentees...................T 5-297
Exoneration ....T 5-291
Extrinsic Evidence......................T 5-288
Failure to Adhere to Statutory
   Formalities................................T 5-293
Family Allowance ....T 5-300
Family Maintenance...................T 5-300
Federal Estate Taxes...................T 5-300
Fiduciary.......................... T 5-294, 298
Formal Wills..............................T 5-287
Former Spouse............................T 5-289
Fraud in the Execution ....T 5-293
Fraud in the Inducement.............T 5-293
Funeral Expenses........................T 5-300
General Legacies ....T 5-300
Grounds to Contest Will.............T 5-293
Half-Blood Children...................T 5-289
Health Care Directive.................T 5-297
Holographic Wills or Codicils....T 5-292
Homestead Interest.....................T 5-292
Identification of Beneficiaries....T 5-288
"In Terrorem" Clauses ....T 5-294
Incorporation by Reference........T 5-288
Independent Significance ....T 5-288
Insolvent Estate Priority.............T 5-300
Insurance Proceeds.....................T 5-298
Integration ....T 5-288
Intent Requirement.....................T 5-287
Interested Witnesses...................T 5-288
Interpretation Issues ....T 5-288
Intestate Succession....................T 5-294
Joint Bank Account ....T 5-298
Joint Tenancy ....T 5-298
Joint Wills ....T 5-292
Judgment Debts ....T 5-300
Lapsed Devise ....T 5-290
Last Illness Expenses ....T 5-300
Living Will ....T 5-297
Lost Wills ....T 5-299
Marital Property ....T 5-295

Medical Powers .... T 5-297
Mental Capacity .... T 5-288
Mutual Wills............................... T 5-292
Non-Intervention Powers .... T 5-299
Non-Monetary Gifts .... T 5-300
Non-Probate Asset Liability....... T 5-297
Non-Probate Assets .... T 5-297
Notice to Creditors .... T 5-299
Nuncupative (Oral) Wills .... T 5-292
Omitted Later Spouse................. T 5-289
Omitted Surviving Children .... T 5-289
Open Class.................................. T 5-290
Oral Wills .... T 5-292
Order of Distribution When
    Assets Insufficient .... T 5-300
Organ Donation Directives......... T 5-297
Out of Wedlock Children .... T 5-289
Partial Revocation .... T 5-291
Past obligations .... T 5-293
Pay-on-Death Accounts.............. T 5-298
Pension Plan .... T 5-298
Per Capita .... T 5-295
Per Capita at Each
    Generation .... T 5-295
Per Capita with
    Representation......................... T 5-295
Per Stirpes .... T 5-295
Personal Representative .... T 5-298
Personal Liability of
    Personal Representative .... T 5-299
"Pour-Over Wills"...................... T 5-298
Power of Appointment .... T 5-290
Power of Attorney .... T 5-296
Pretermitted Surviving
    Children.................................. T 5-289
Previous Will Revived .... T 5-294
Probate Jurisdiction .... T 5-297
Probate Proceedings .... T 5-297
Probate Venue .... T 5-297
Property Problems .... T 5-290
Related Documents .... T 5-296
Requirements for Wills .... T 5-287
Republish by Reference .... T 5-291
Residuary Gifts.......................... T 5-300
Restrictions on Disposition .... T 5-292
Revocation.................................. T 5-291
Rule in Shelley's Case................ T 5-289
Satisfaction .... T 5-291
Separate Property .... T 5-295
Shares for "Issue"....................... T 5-295
Signature Requirement................ T 5-287
Slayer and Abusers .... T 5-290

Specific Gifts .... T 5-300
Spouse Forced Share .... T 5-292
State Taxes.................................. T 5-300
Subsequent Divorce.................... T 5-289
"Surviving Heirs"....................... T 5-290
Survivorship Property................. T 5-295
Taker Problems........................... T 5-289
Taxation...................................... T 5-300
Tax Allocation .... T 5-300
Testamentary Age....................... T 5-287
Testamentary Intent .... T 5-287
Testimony Regarding
    Attestation.............................. T 5-288
Totten Trust .... T 5-298
Traditional Wills........................ T 5-287
Trust Res.................................... T 5-298
Undue Influence .... T 5-293
Uniform Simultaneous Death
    Act .... T 5-294
Uniform Wills and
    Probate Code (UPC) .... T 5-287
Unsecured Debts......................... T 5-300
Will Challenges .... T 5-293, 299
Will Components......................... T 5-288
Will Requirements...................... T 5-287

UCC – Commercial Paper

Acceleration Clause.................... T 6-333
Acceptable Signatures .... T 6-334
Accommodation Indorser .... T 6-341
Advantages Over Ordinary
    Contracts................................ T 6-331
Agent Liability........................... T 6-334
Alterations Not Present............... T 6-342
Amount Contradiction .... T 6-332
Article 3 .... T 6-331
Article 4 .... T 6-331, 344
Bank Certification .... T 6-346
Bank Deposits and Collections... T 6-344
Bank Liability and Recovery for
    Forged Signature .... T 6-343
Bank Sequencing .... T 6-345
Bankruptcy .... T 6-338
Bearer Paper .... T 6-332, 336
Blank Indorsement...................... T 6-340
Capacity .... T 6-339
Certificate of Deposit .... T 6-332
Certification................................ T 6-345
Check.. T 6-331
Check Hold................................. T 6-345

Chronological Liability ....T 6-340
Collection Guaranteed
    Indorsement.............................T 6-341
Comparative Negligence.............T 6-339
Contradictory Terms ....T 6-332
Conversion ....T 6-344
Currency of Any Country ....T 6-334
Dates...T 6-333
Defenses ....T 6-337
Defenses Not Present ....T 6-342
Destroyed Instrument...................T 6-344
Discharge in Bankruptcy.............T 6-338
Dishonored Checks ....T 6-340
Draft ....T 6-332
Drawee's Responsibilities............T 6-344
Drawer's Negligence....................T 6-346
Drawer's Signature Authorized ..T 6-342
Dummy Vendor............................T 6-337
Duress...T 6-338
Exceptions to Negotiation
    Requirement ....T 6-337
Expedited Funds Availability
    Act..T 6-345
Extension Provision ....T 6-333
Failure of Consideration..............T 6-338
Federal Trade Commission ....T 6-338
Fictitious Payee ....T 6-337
For Value.....................................T 6-335
Forged Instrument Liability ....T 6-346
Forgery ....T 6-339, 344
Fraud in Execution ....T 6-338
Fraud in the Inducement..............T 6-338
Future Contract ....T 6-333
Future Performance......................T 6-335
General Real Defenses.................T 6-338
Good Faith...................................T 6-335
Good Title ....T 6-342
Gift Donee...................................T 6-335
Handwritten Terms ....T 6-332
Holder in Due Course (HDC) .....T 6-335
Illegality ....T 6-338
Impostor ....T 6-337
Improper Negotiation...................T 6-343
Improperly Completed ....T 6-335
Incomplete Instruments................T 6-335
Indorsement.................................T 6-340
Indorsement Without Recourse...T 6-341
Indorser Liability.........................T 6-340
Indorser's Signature Forged........T 6-344
Issue Requirement........................T 6-334
Knowledge of Insolvency ....T 6-342
Lack of Capacity ....T 6-339

Legal Right Retention Clause .... T 6-333
Liability of Parties...................... T 6-339
Lost Instrument .... T 6-344
Material Alteration .... T 6-339
Midnight Deadline...................... T 6-340
Multiple Payees .... T 6-345
Mutual Mistake .... T 6-338
Negligence.................. T 6-339, 343, 346
Negligent Supervision .... T 6-339
Negotiable Instrument................. T 6-332
Negotiable Words........................ T 6-332
Negotiation .... T 6-336
No Knowledge of Insolvency..... T 6-342
Non-Violating Conditions .... T 6-333
Notice of Claim or Defense........ T 6-336
Notice of Dishonor .... T 6-340
Occurrence Time Uncertain .... T 6-334
Open Sum.................................... T 6-334
Order Paper .... T 6-332, 336
Other's Claims............................ T 6-338
Overdraft Check .... T 6-345
Overdue Check .... T 6-345
Owner's Negligence.................... T 6-343
Partial HDC .... T 6-335
Payable on Demand..................... T 6-331
Payable on Sight......................... T 6-331
Payee Designation Incomplete ... T 6-344
Payee Incomplete .... T 6-335
Payment Guaranteed
    Indorsement............................ T 6-341
Payment in Full Indorsement ..... T 6-341
Personal Defenses .... T 6-338
Phantom Employee .... T 6-337
Postdated Check .... T 6-345
Prepayment Options .... T 6-333
Presentment Party Warranties .... T 6-342
Primary Liability .... T 6-340
Printed Terms .... T 6-332
Prohibited Negotiation .... T 6-336
Promise to Pay Only................... T 6-333
Qualified Indorsement................ T 6-341
Real Defenses............................. T 6-338
Representative Liability .... T 6-334
Restrictive Indorsement.............. T 6-341
Secondary Liability .... T 6-340
Shelter Rule .... T 6-336
Signature Forged .... T 6-342
Signature Form........................... T 6-334
Signatures Genuine and
    Authorized.............................. T 6-342
Signed by Maker/Drawer .... T 6-334
Special Indorsement .... T 6-341

Stale Check.................................. T 6-344
Statute of Limitations .... T 6-339
Stolen Instrument .... T 6-344
Stop Payment Order .... T 6-345
Subrogation Rights..................... T 6-346
Sum Certain in Money .... T 6-334
Three-Party Paper....................... T 6-331
Time Certain............................... T 6-333
Time Uncertain........................... T 6-334
Transfer Parties Warranties........ T 6-342
Two-Party Paper......................... T 6-331
Typed Terms .... T 6-332
Unauthorized Alteration............. T 6-345
Unauthorized Completion .... T 6-338
Unauthorized Signature...... T 6-339, 345
Uncompletion of Condition
    Precedent .... T 6-338
Unconditional Promise to Pay.... T 6-333
Underlying Obligation................ T 6-343
Unqualified Indorsement............ T 6-340
Warranty Disclaimer .... T 6-343
Warranty Liability .... T 6-342
Warranty Liability Exception..... T 6-343
Wrongful Dishonor .... T 6-345
Wrongful Honor .... T 6-344

UCC – Secured Transactions

20-Day Grace Period.......... T 7-382, 387
Account .... T 7-380
Adding Value to Collateral .... T 7-393
Agreement Not to Assert
    Defenses .... T 7-384
After-Acquired Property .... T 7-384
Asset Bargain Sale .... T 7-394
Attachment .... T 7-385
Attorney Fees .... T 7-384
Automobile Dealers.................... T 7-389
Bankruptcy Preferences.............. T 7-394
Bankruptcy Stay .... T 7-390
Bankruptcy Trustee .... T 7-392
Bona Fide Consumer
    Transferee............................... T 7-389
Buyer in the Ordinary Course of
    Business................................... T 7-392
Carrier Lien .... T 7-395
Chattel Liens .... T 7-393
Chattel Paper .... T 7-380
Collateral Categories.................. T 7-379
Collateral
    Description ...... T 7-381, 383, 385, 387

Collateral Sale .... T 7-381
Commercial Tort Claims .... T 7-380
Competing Perfected Interests.... T 7-392
Consignment............................... T 7-388
Consumer Credit Contract.......... T 7-384
Consumer Goods .... T 7-379
Consumer Transferee.................. T 7-389
Continuation of Perfection .... T 7-386
Control....................................... T 7-386
Costs and Attorney Fees............. T 7-384
Creditors .... T 7-381
Creditors' Remedies .... T 7-384
Debtor Duties............................. T 7-384
Debtor Movement....................... T 7-388
Debtor's Name Change or
    Error....................................... T 7-387
Default .... T 7-384
Deficiency Judgment.................. T 7-391
Deposit Account .... T 7-380, 386
Description of
    Collateral .... T 7-381, 383, 385, 387
Disposition Proceeds
    Application .... T 7-390
Disposition Sale......................... T 7-390
Document of Title....................... T 7-380
Documentary Collateral.............. T 7-380
Equipment.................................. T 7-379
Equipment Transferee .... T 7-389
Electronic Chattel Paper .... T 7-386
Entrusting to Merchant .... T 7-393
Exceptions to Priorities.............. T 7-392
Farming Products................ T 7-380, 393
Filing of Financing Statement .... T 7-386
Filing of Lien............................. T 7-393
Filing Place................................ T 7-387
Financing Statement .... T 7-387
Floating Lien .... T 7-383
Future Advances......................... T 7-383
General Intangibles..................... T 7-381
Good Faith Required .... T 7-384
Household Goods .... T 7-382
Instrument.................................. T 7-380
Insurance Policy .... T 7-381
Intangible Collateral .... T 7-380
Inventory.................................... T 7-379
Inventory PMSI .... T 7-392
Inventory Transferee .... T 7-389
Investment Property............ T 7-380, 386
Judgment Creditor .... T 7-392
Junior Interests........................... T 7-391
Laborer's Lien .... T 7-393
Lien Filing .... T 7-393

Lien Priority ....T 7-393
Letter of Credit Rights ....T 7-381, 386
Loan for Specific Collateral........T 7-382
Materials Lien ....T 7-393
Mere Attachment
    Perfection ....T 7-382, 389
Multi-State Transactions ....T 7-388
Perfection ....T 7-385
Policy of Insurance......................T 7-381
Possession ....T 7-386
Primary Use Controls...................T 7-380
Priority Exceptions......................T 7-392
Priority Rules ....T 7-391
Preferential Bankruptcy
    Interests Avoided ....T 7-394
Proceeds ....T 7-381, 383, 388
Prohibition on Assignment of
    Security Interest ....T 7-384
Purchase Money Security
    Interest (PMSI)........................T 7-381
Real Property Liens.....................T 7-393
Recoupment Rights ....T 7-384
Remedies ....T 7-384
Repossession Right ....T 7-389
Retail Inventory..........................T 7-382
Retention of Collateral ....T 7-390
Rights in Collateral ....T 7-385
Security Agreements ....T 7-382, 385
Senior Interests...........................T 7-391
Set-Off Rights ....T 7-384
Super Priority on Inventory.........T 7-382
Tangible Goods ....T 7-379
Termination Statement.................T 7-388
Title Certificate ....T 7-389
Title Transferee..........................T 7-389
Unauthorized Sale, Removal,
    or Conversion by Debtor..........T 7-391
Value Given ....T 7-385
Vehicle Dealers ....T 7-389
Warehouse Lien ....T 7-394
Working Capital Loan..................T 7-382
Writing Required........................T 7-385

ABA Rules of Professional Conduct

Accepting Appointments.................T 8-454
Admission Truthfulness ....T 8-458
Adverse Authority Disclosure........T 8-445
Advertising....................................T 8-456
Advisor Role ....T 8-443
Advocate Role ....T 8-444, 450

Aggregate Settlements....................T 8-434
Assist Judge in Violation................T 8-460
Attorney-Client Privilege ....T 8-428
Bar Admission Matters...................T 8-458
Business Organization Internal
    Reporting....................................T 8-438
Business Transaction with Client.. T 8-432
Candid and Honest Advice..............T 8-440
Candor Towards Tribunal ....T 8-445
    Ex Parte Proceeding ....T 8-446
    False Statement ....T 8-445
    Later Falsity Discover ....T 8-445
Certification Designation ....T 8-457
Choice of Disciplinary Authority.. T 8-460
Client Urging MRPC Violation.....T 8-440
Client Communications.................T 8-423
Communication with
    Represented Persons...................T 8-451
Compensation for
    Recommendations ....T 8-456
Competence..................................T 8-421
Confidentiality Restraints..............T 8-427
    Exceptions ....T 8-428
Conflict of Interest ....T 8-430
    Direct Adversely ....T 8-430
    Fundamentally Antagonistic ......T 8-431
    Informed Consent ....T 8-430
    Materially Limited......................T 8-430
    No Harm to Relationship............T 8-430
    Organizational Clients.................T 8-431
    Prior Client ....T 8-429
Contingency Fee Agreement.........T 8-426
    Prohibited Matters ....T 8-426
    Writing Requirement ....T 8-426
Corporate Client ....T 8-438
Counsel a Crime or Fraud ....T 8-422
Court Appointment........................T 8-429
Criminal Act by Lawyer...............T 8-459
Diligence ....T 8-423
Decisions – Client and Lawyer .....T 8-422
Decorum of Tribunal....................T 8-447
Depositions of Third Parties..........T 8-451
Diminished Capacity ....T 8-438
Direct Solicitation ....T 8-456
Directing Lawyer's Judgment ....T 8-433
Disciplinary Matters.....................T 8-458
Disclosing Confidences................T 8-428
Discovery of Lawyer....................T 8-449
Dishonesty or Fraud ....T 8-460
Disqualification ....T 8-436
Double Billing..............................T 8-425
Emergency Situation ....T 8-421

Escrow Funds .... T 8-439
Evaluation for Third Party............. T 8-444
Ex Parte Proceedings..................... T 8-446
Expediting Litigation..................... T 8-445
External Fee Splits .... T 8-427
Exculpatory Evidence Disclosure . T 8-449
False Statement by Lawyer .... T 8-450
False Statements About Judges ..... T 8-458
Fair Warning to Prospective
    Clients...................................... T 8-442
Fairness to Opposing Party .... T 8-446
    Discovery Standards................... T 8-446
    Interference with Evidence........ T 8-446
    Falsify Evidence .... T 8-446
    Trial Abuses .... T 8-446, 447
    Witness Inducement .... T 8-446
Fees... T 8-424
    Agreement Required .... T 8-423
    Contingencies............................. T 8-426
    Cost Treatment .... T 8-426
    Divisions of Fees .... T 8-427
    Locality Average .... T 8-424
    Reasonable Factors..................... T 8-424
    Referral Services .... T 8-456
    Share with Non-Lawyer .... T 8-452
Fields of Practice Communication T 8-457
Financial Assistance to Clients ..... T 8-433
Firm Names and Letterheads......... T 8-457
Former Client Conflicts................. T 8-435
Former Judge or Neutral .... T 8-437
Frivolous Position .... T 8-444
Future Death Disclosure................ T 8-428
Gifts from Clients......................... T 8-432
Good Faith Argument.................... T 8-444
Government to Private Practice..... T 8-437
Governmental Organization Client T 8-438
Holding Public Office .... T 8-457
Human Future Death .... T 8-428
Improper Government Influence... T 8-460
Improper Judicial Influence .... T 8-447
Improper Political Contributions... T 8-458
Imputed Disqualifications .... T 8-436
Inadvertently Sent Documents ...... T 8-451
Independence of Lawyer .... T 8-443, 452
Information About Legal Services T 8-455
    Advertising................................ T 8-455
    Comparisons............................... T 8-455
    Unjustified Expectations .... T 8-455
Informed Consent .... T 8-430
Insurance Company Fee Payments T 8-433
Intermediary Role......................... T 8-443
IRS Form 8300 .... T 8-429

Law Firm and Associations.......... T 8-451
    Associate Responsibility .... T 8-452
    Non-Lawyer Assistants .... T 8-452
    Partner Responsibilities.............. T 8-451
    Supervisor's Responsibilities ..... T 8-452
Law Reform Activities .... T 8-455
Law-Related Services.................... T 8-454
Lawyer Board Member.................. T 8-431
Lawyer Defendant .... T 8-428
Lawyer Outside State .... T 8-460
Legal Malpractice......................... T 8-422
Legal Services Organization.......... T 8-455
Limiting Liability – Prospective.... T 8-434
Literary and Media Rights............. T 8-432
Malpractice Settlement.................. T 8-434
Mediation.................................... T 8-444
Meritorious Claims .... T 8-444
Misconduct .... T 8-459
Multi-Jurisdiction Practice .... T 8-453
Multiple Law Offices .... T 8-457
Neutral Role................................ T 8-444
No Further Representation Clause. T 8-454
Noisy Withdrawal......................... T 8-441
Non-Adjudicative Proceedings...... T 8-450
Non-Compete Agreements .... T 8-454
Non-Profit Limited Representation T 8-455
Office Sharing .... T 8-434, 455
Opinion Letters............................ T 8-444
Opinion Withdrawal .... T 8-444
Organizational Clients........... T 8-431, 438
Partnership with Non-Lawyer .... T 8-452
Personal Opinion During Trial ...... T 8-447
Political Contributions.................. T 8-458
Post-Conviction Duty .... T 8-450
Practice with Non-Lawyer............. T 8-453
Pro Bono Service .... T 8-454
Prohibited Client Transactions ...... T 8-432
Prohibited Trial Publicity .... T 8-447
Professional Misconduct .... T 8-458
Proficiency Required..................... T 8-421
Property of Client .... T 8-439
Proprietary Interest in Claim .... T 8-434
Prosecutor's Responsibilities......... T 8-449
Prospective Clients .... T 8-439, 442
Public Office........................... T 8-457, 460
Public Organization Client .... T 8-455
Public Service.............................. T 8-454
Recommendation for
    Compensation .... T 8-456
Related Attorneys .... T 8-431
Reporting Misconduct .... T 8-458, 459
Reporting up in Organization T 8-431, 438

Representation Withdrawal............T 8-429
Represented Person.........................T 8-450
Reservation of Rights Clause.........T 8-433
Retainers and Advances.................T 8-439
Safeguarding Property....................T 8-438
Safety Information ....T 8-448
Sarbanes-Oxley Act ....T 8-429, 441
Sale of Law Practice......................T 8-442
Screening................................T 8-436, 437
Scope of Representation.................T 8-422
Sexual Relations with Clients ....T 8-435
Solicitations of Prospective ClientsT 8-456
Subsequent Discovery of Falsity....T 8-445
Termination of Representation.......T 8-440
Third Party Claims to Funds ....T 8-439
Third Party Fee Payors..................T 8-433
Third Party Neutral ....T 8-444
Third Party Rights ....T 8-451
Trade Names for Law Firms ....T 8-457
Trial Publicity Prohibited...............T 8-447
Trust Accounts ....T 8-439
Truthfulness in Statements.............T 8-450
Unauthorized Practice of Law........T 8-453
Unlicensed Practice Practicality.....T 8-460
Unauthorized Practice ....T 8-453
Unrepresented Person.....................T 8-451
Using Information Disadvantaging
    the Client ....T 8-432
Whistleblowing ....T 8-427, 438
Withdrawals ....T 8-440
Witness-Lawyer Conflict ....T 8-448
Written Solicitation ....T 8-457

RIGOS BAR REVIEW SERIES MEE REVIEW

COURSE EVALUATION FORM

Once again, thank you for choosing **Rigos Bar Review Series!** We hope you feel that these materials have given you the tools and confidence to tackle the Multistate Essay Exam!

We are constantly striving to provide the best possible study materials available. We want to hear from you! If you would kindly take a few minutes to fill out the form below and mail it back to us at 230 Skinner Building, 1326 Fifth Avenue, Seattle WA 98101, or fax it to us at (206) 624-0731. Let your voice be heard in the effort to improve the **Rigos Bar Review Series MEE Review.** THANK YOU!

****

For each of the categories listed below, please rate **Rigos Bar Review Series MEE Review** on a scale of 1 to 5.

| 5 = Excellent | 4 = Very Good | 3 = Good | 2 = Fair | 1 = Poor |

How do you rate the overall presentation of Rigos Bar Review Series?

Arrangement of Materials	5	4	3	2	1
Colors / Typography	5	4	3	2	1
Convenient Binder Format	5	4	3	2	1
Ease of Use	5	4	3	2	1
Professionalism	5	4	3	2	1

How do you rate the Rigos Bar Review Series materials in terms of accuracy (typographical, legal, etc.)?

Preface	5	4	3	2	1
Chapter Texts	5	4	3	2	1
MEE Tips	5	4	3	2	1
Questions / Answers	5	4	3	2	1
Magic Memory Outlines®	5	4	3	2	1

How do you rate the helpfulness of each component of Rigos Bar Review Series?

Preface	5	4	3	2	1
Chapter Texts	5	4	3	2	1
MEE Tips	5	4	3	2	1
Questions / Answers	5	4	3	2	1
Magic Memory Outlines®	5	4	3	2	1

How well has Rigos Bar Review Series prepared you for each of the following aspects of the MEE?

Substantive Knowledge	5	4	3	2	1
MEE Essay Format	5	4	3	2	1
Time Management	5	4	3	2	1
MEE Helpful Tips	5	4	3	2	1
Confidence Level	5	4	3	2	1

Continued on back of page

If you felt that some chapters of the Rigos Bar Review Series MEE Review were better than others, rate them individually below:

Business Associations	5	4	3	2	1
Conflict of Laws	5	4	3	2	1
Family Law	5	4	3	2	1
Federal Civil Procedure	5	4	3	2	1
UCC – Commercial Paper	5	4	3	2	1
UCC – Secured Transactions	5	4	3	2	1
Trusts, Wills and Estates	5	4	3	2	1
MBE Topic Essays	5	4	3	2	1

Did you prepare a Magic Memory Outline® for all MEE subjects?
Yes _____ No _____

Did you pass the MEE?
Yes _____ No _____ Don't know yet _____

If you have any additional comments, critiques or suggestions for improvements of any part of the **Rigos Bar Review Series MEE Review**, please tell us about them below. Did you create any new acronyms – mnemonics? Please feel free to attach additional pages.

_____

_____

_____

If you wish to, please give us the information below. It will allow us to attribute your comments and to follow up on your concerns.

PHONE: _____   EMAIL: _____

ADDRESS: _____

NAME: _____

LAW SCHOOL: _____

GRAD DATE: _____

What is the likelihood that you would do each of the following?

Recommend **Rigos Bar Review Series** to others	5	4	3	2	1
Keep **Rigos Bar Review Series** for future reference	5	4	3	2	1
Buy other products from this company in the future	5	4	3	2	1

Did you study all of the text?
Yes _____ No _____

Did you work all of the MEE practice questions?
Yes _____ No _____